Health Psychology

Theory, Research and Practice

Second edition

David F. Marks, Michael Murray,
Brian Evans, Carla Willig,
Cailine Woodall and Catherine M. Sykes

SAGE Publications
London ● Thousand Oaks ● New Delhi

Second edition first published 2005

First edition published 2000, reprinted 2001, 2002, 2004

Reprinted 2006

SAGE Publications Ltd
1 Oliver's Yard
55 City Road
London EC1Y 1SP

SAGE Publications Inc.
2455 Teller Road
Thousand Oaks, California 91320

SAGE Publications India Pvt Ltd
B-42, Panchsheel Enclave
Post Box 4109
New Delhi 110 017

British Library Cataloguing in Publication data

A catalogue record for this book is available
from the British Library

ISBN 1-4129-0336-X
ISBN 1-4129-0337-8 (pbk)

Library of Congress Control Number available

Typeset by C&M Digitals (P) Ltd., Chennai, India
Printed in Great Britain by TJ International, Padstow, Cornwall

Contents

Author Biographies

DAVID F. MARKS is Head of the Department of Psychology and Professor of Psychology at City University, London, UK. Previously he has held positions at the University of Sheffield, UK, the University of Otago in New Zealand, and Middlesex University, UK. His other books include *The Psychology of the Psychic* (1980, with R. Kammann), *Theories of Image Formation* (1986), *Imagery: Current Developments* (1990, with J.T.E. Richardson and P. Hampson), *The Quit For Life Programme: An Easier Way to Stop Smoking and Not Start Again* (1993), *Improving the Health of the Nation* (1996, with C. Francome), *Dealing With Dementia: Recent European Research* (2000, with C.M. Sykes), *The Psychology of the Psychic* (Revised Edition) (2000), *The Health Psychology Reader* (2002), *Research Methods for Clinical and Health Psychology* (2004, with L. Yardley), and *Overcoming Your Smoking Habit* (2005). He was Chair of the Special Group in Health Psychology of the British Psychological Society, Convenor of the Task Force on Health Psychology of the European Federation of Professional Psychologists' Associations, Chair of the Standing Conference on Public Health, and a member of the Department of Health's Scientific Committee on Tobacco and Health. He is Founder and Editor of the *Journal of Health Psychology*.

MICHAEL MURRAY is Professor of Social and Health Psychology in the Division of Community Health, Memorial University of Newfoundland, Canada. Previously he has held positions at St Thomas' Hospital Medical School, London, UK and at the University of Ulster, Ireland. He is a Visiting Professor of Psychology at City University, London, UK. His previous books include *Smoking Among Young Adults* (1988, with L. Jarrett, A.V. Swan and R. Rumen) and *Qualitative Health Psychology: Theories and Methods* (1999, with K. Chamberlain). He served as Chair of the Health Psychology Section of the Canadian Psychological Association and was founding editor of the *Canadian Health Psychologist*. He is an Associate Editor of the *Journal of Health Psychology*.

BRIAN EVANS teaches psychology at Middlesex and City Universities, London, UK. At Middlesex University he is programme leader of the MSc degree in Psychology and Health. Previously he has held positions at the University of Sussex, UK, and at Concordia University, Montreal, Canada. He is interested in the analysis of psychological research and theory in its socio-political context and his previous publications include *IQ and Mental Testing: An Unnatural Science and Its Social History* (1981, with B. Waites).

CARLA WILLIG teaches psychology at City University, London, UK. Previously she has held positions at Plymouth and Middlesex Universities. Her research is primarily concerned with the relationship between discourse and practice, particularly in relation to risk taking. She has published journal articles and book chapters on the discursive construction of trust and sexual safety, and she has contributed to theoretical and epistemological debates concerning social constructionist psychology. She edited *Applied Discourse Analysis: Social and Psychological Interventions* (1999) and is a member of the Editorial Board of the *Journal of Health Psychology*.

CAILINE WOODALL became chronically ill in her thirties and, after several years of being severely disabled, became interested in the psychological aspects of illness. She has completed an MSc in Health Psychology at City University, London, UK. Her research focused on the social construction of illness through discourse. Her main interests relate to chronic illness and disability.

CATHERINE M. SYKES teaches health psychology at City University, London, UK where she is Director of the Doctor of Psychology and Stage 2 Health Psychology Training Programme. She has held previous posts at Middlesex University Health Research Centre and King's College Hospital, London. Her current research is concerned with the experience of coronary interventions. She has publications in the field of smoking cessation, health promotion evaluation and informal carers of people with Alzheimer's Disease and Related Disorders. She is a member of the editorial board of the *Journal of Health Psychology*.

Copyright Acknowledgements

Preface and Acknowledgements

The aims of this book

This textbook provides an in-depth introduction to the field of health psychology with special relevance to health promotion, disease prevention and health care. It is suitable for advanced undergraduate and postgraduate courses in psychology, medicine, nursing and health care. The authors aim to present an eclectic but critical view of the field, its theories, research and applications. We aim to dig below the surface to expose the underlying theoretical assumptions and to critically analyse methods, evidence and conclusions.

The importance of psychological processes in the experience of health and illness is being increasingly recognized. Evidence for the role of behaviour and emotion in current trends of morbidity and mortality is accumulating; much research has also been conducted on the effects of stress and psychological characteristics on the onset, course and management of physical illness.

Health psychology is growing rapidly and health psychologists are in increasing demand in health care and medical settings. In the USA, the single largest area of placement of psychologists in recent years has been in medical centres. Psychologists have become vital members of multidisciplinary clinical and research teams in rehabilitation, cardiology, paediatrics, oncology, anaesthesiology, family practice, dentistry, and other medical fields. In Europe, health psychology is also becoming established as a new sub-profession of psychology alongside clinical and counselling psychology. Theory and policy are being put into practice through improvements in training (Marks et al., 1998).

In the first 25 years the focus of health psychology was primarily clinical in nature. This fact is reflected by the largest part of this book (Part 3) on illness experience and health care. In the next decades, it is expected that more effort will be directed towards creating effective interventions for disease prevention and health promotion, especially with reference to the risk factors of unsafe sexual behaviour, smoking, alcohol, diet, inactivity and stress.

Against the view that health behaviours are an individual responsibility, governed by freely taken choices, a large amount of the burden of disease is the product of a toxic environment that pushes people towards health-aversive behavioural choices. Interventions must be multi-levelled, not purely behavioural or educational in kind, as the evidence suggests that such approaches alone are ineffectual and too small in scale (Marks, 1996, 2002a, 2000b).

In addition to working in clinical environments, health psychologists have a contribution to make in developing and evaluating health promotion interventions. Psychologists carry out these activities in close collaboration with communities, other health care practitioners and policymakers. Changes in policy and practice are urgently needed to increase equity and enhance the well-being of the most vulnerable members of society. This book adopts a preventive perspective with a focus on positive health enhancement through the use of multi-level strategies taking into account the whole context of health-related experience and behaviour.

Health psychology is a richly interdisciplinary field requiring an understanding of the cultural, socio-political and economic roots of behaviour and experience. The authors of this textbook apply an international, cross-cultural and interdisciplinary perspective. We suggest that social, economic and political changes have not kept pace with industrial, scientific and medical achievements. As the gaps between the 'haves' and the 'have-nots' widen, and the population is ageing, the impacts of learned helplessness, poverty and social isolation are increasingly salient features of society. The contemporary emphasis on improving health care – a significant and worthy task – is little more than tinkering in a way that is reminiscent of Nero fiddling while Rome burns.

In preparing to deal with these issues, all those concerned with health promotion and disease prevention require in-depth understanding, not only of the complexities of human behaviour in its social context, but of the lived experience of health, illness and health care. By integrating quantitative and qualitative approaches, this book is intended to be a step in that direction.

What the book covers

This book places health psychology within its global, social and political context. This requires a glimpse of the 'bigger picture' using a wide-angle lens as well as giving detailed analyses of the 'nitty-gritty' of theory, research and practice. The book has been restructured into four parts instead of three and five new chapters expand the scope to reflect the widening interest in the field. The book has been updated, with one quarter of the 1000 plus references from the years 2000–2005.

Part 1 introduces the *broader demographic, social, economic and political context of health psychology.* The first three chapters introduce the field and place the study of health psychology within its global social and political context. A new Chapter 3 discusses social inequalities and social justice as health issues. Chapter 4 gives an introductory analysis of culture and health. This cross-cultural perspective is maintained throughout the rest of the book. Chapter 5 is concerned with research methods and is designed as an introduction to methods described in more detail in a companion volume by Marks and Yardley (2004).

Part 2 covers the principal areas of health experience and behaviour of interest to health psychologists. The topics covered have all been researched and theorized from the perspective of *how health is influenced by the way people think, feel and behave.* These experiences and behaviours are seen as the major psychological determinants of the long-term health and quality of life of the 6.4 billion humans alive today. We examine food and eating (Chapter 6), alcohol and drinking (Chapter 7), tobacco and smoking (Chapter 8), sexual behaviour and experience (Chapter 9), and exercise and activity (Chapter 10).

Part 3 covers *applications of health psychology to illness experience and health care.* We explore many of the principal areas for the improvement of health care through psychological understanding: illness beliefs and explanations (Chapter 11), illness and personality (Chapter 12), stress and coping (Chapter 13), communication, messages and meanings (Chapter 14), treatment adherence and patient empowerment (Chapter 15), preventing and controlling pain (Chapter 16), and cancer and chronic illnesses (Chapter 17).

Part 4 covers *health promotion and disease prevention.* We discuss immunization and screening (Chapter 18), work and health (Chapter 19), and health promotion (Chapter 20).

Making the best use of this book

The reader can select chapters relevant to the main approaches to health psychology: clinical, community, public health or critical health psychology (see Figure P.1). Part 1 is core reading of relevance to all students of health psychology.

Chapters can be read in any order according to your personal interests and preferences. In most cases chapters are free-standing and assume no prior reading of other chapters.

Clinical health psychology Chapters 1, 5, 6–18	Public health psychology Chapters 1–5, 8–14, 18–20
Community health psychology Chapters 1–10, 18–20	Critical health psychology Entire book

Figure P.1   Relevance of the different chapters to the four main approaches to health psychology

Key terms are identified by **bold** with the icon KT in the margin and defined in the **Glossary** at the end of the book.

A useful companion to this textbook is *The Health Psychology Reader* (Marks, 2002a), which reprints and discusses 25 key articles accompanied by introductions to the main themes. [We will refer to articles in the *Reader* using square brackets like the ones around this sentence.]

The companion website

A companion website also has been developed to complement *Health Psychology: Theory, Research and Practice* (Second Edition). Additional material is arranged chapter by chapter to enable you to deepen and extend your understanding of the topics dealt with in the textbook. The URL is: **www.sagepub.co.uk/marks**.

The website contains the following features:

- Chapter summaries
- Video clips of the authors and key researchers discussing 'hot topics'
- Links to downloadable PDF files of relevant new articles from SAGE journals including the *Journal of Health Psychology*
- Links to websites relevant to each topic
- PowerPoint slides for lecturers

Acknowledgements

DFM: Thanks to my family for continuing support and to my co-authors, Michael, Carla, Brian, Cailine, Catherine and Anna. 'Salamat' to Emee Vida G. Estacio for reliable, efficient and well-organized assistance. Emee also designed the companion website. A big 'Thank you' also goes to Ewan McDougall for his painting on the cover.

MM: As always, I acknowledge the continuing support of my family.

BE: Thanks to Nick Heather.

CW: Thanks to Geoff Mercer, Vic Finkelstein, Sally French, Mike Bury and Carol Thomas.

CMS: Thanks to Stephen Jenkins and Glain Jones for your guidance and faith in me during my time at King's College Hospital and to Ahmad for his continuous support.

<table>
<tr><td>**Part One**</td><td>**Health Psychology in Context**</td></tr>
</table>

This book provides an overview of the field of health psychology studied as both natural and human science. In Part 1 we are concerned with the social, cultural and psychological context of the health and illness experience. Chapter 1 introduces and discusses the concept of health and reviews the development of health psychology as a new field of inquiry. Two contrasting approaches from natural and human science are contrasted and compared. The value of an interdisciplinary approach and links with other disciplines and professions is emphasized. The role of frameworks, theories and models is discussed. The nature of the biopsychosocial model is examined and disability and ageing are discussed as core issues in the field. Four contrasting but complementary approaches to health psychology are defined: clinical, public health, community and critical health psychology.

Chapter 2 discusses the contextual factors of the macro-social environment; the demographic, economic and societal factors which operate globally to structure the health experience of populations, communities and individuals. The chapter uses a wide-angle lens to explore the bigger picture of the global context for human health and suffering. The focus is on human health variations across societies and the chapter considers population growth, poverty and increasing longevity as determinants of health status. Research on gender, ethnicity and disability suggest that *inequality* is a persistent characteristic of our health-care systems.

Chapter 3 examines the influence of social inequalities and social injustice in health outcomes. The universal existence of health gradients in developing and industrialized societies shows how much of health experience is determined by social, cultural and economic circumstances and how little by health-care systems. Measures to tackle social injustice are required at a political/policy level and health psychologists can play a role as agents of change. There is substantial evidence linking poor social conditions with ill-health. The explanations for this include material, behavioural and psychosocial factors. The explanation of health inequalities creates many important challenges for theory and research in health psychology.

Chapter 4 examines the ways in which health and illness have been construed across time and place. Western biomedical procedures often tend to be viewed as 'scientific' and 'evidence based' while the medical systems of other cultures and 'complementary' therapies are seen as 'unscientific' or 'magical'. These assumptions need to be evaluated in the light of studies conducted with participants from different cultures and ethnic groups who make their own accounts of health and illness and act upon them in positive and functional ways. Anthropological and sociological studies of health and medicine have generated a range of theories and concepts that enhance the understanding of health and illness.

Chapter 5 describes the most useful methods for carrying out research in health psychology. The three categories considered are quantitative, qualitative and action research methods. These types of methods all have a significant role to play in contributing towards the goal of assessing, understanding and improving health, illness and health care outcomes. Research designs that are quantitative in nature place emphasis on reliable and valid measurement in controlled experiments, trials, and surveys. Qualitative methods use interviews, focus groups, narratives or texts to explore health and illness concepts and experience. Multiple sources of evidence are synthesized in systematic reviews and meta-analyses. Action research enables change processes to feed back into plans for improvement, empowerment and emancipation.

1 Health Psychology as a New Field of Inquiry

The desire for the prolongation of life ... we may take to be one of the most universal of all human motives. (Kenneth Arrow, 1963: 75)

Outline

This chapter introduces health psychology as a new field of inquiry. We discuss the concept of health from a cross-cultural perspective and explore the nature of health psychology in its social context. Next we compare and contrast two epistemological approaches and examine the nature of theories, frameworks and models. We describe a framework consisting of a core and influences at four levels. We examine the nature of the biopsychosocial model and discuss disability and ageing as core issues in the field. Finally, we describe four complementary approaches to health psychology which focus on clinical, community, public health and critical concerns.

What is Health?

The attainment and preservation of health reaches to the very core of human existence. In its broadest sense, **well-being** is an overarching concern for every human being, group and society. Health is described and explained in various discourses that are socially constructed. The concepts of 'health', 'mind' and 'body' vary across time and place, but for all cultures and cosmologies they play a fundamental role in the experience of being human.

The word 'health' is derived from Old High German and Anglo-Saxon words meaning 'whole', 'hale' and 'holy'. Historically and culturally there are strong associations with concepts such as wholeness, goodness, holiness, hygiene, cleanliness, sanitariness, sanity, saintliness and godliness. There are equally strong associations between the concepts of disease, disorder, disintegration, uncleanness, unsanitariness, insanity, badness, evil, evil spirits and satan. An emphasis on health as wholeness and naturalness was present in ancient China and classical Greece where health was seen as a state of 'harmony', 'balance' or 'equilibrium' with nature. These beliefs are found in many healing systems to the present day.

KT

Galen (BC 200–129), the early Greek physician, followed the Hippocratic tradition in believing that *hygieia* (health) or *euexia* (soundness) occur when there is a balance between the hot, cold, dry and wet components of the body. The four bodily humours were believed to be blood, phlegm, yellow bile and black bile that were hot and wet, cold and wet, hot and dry, and cold and dry respectively. Diseases were thought to be caused by external 'pathogens' that disturbed the balance of the body's four elements: hot, cold, dry and wet. Galen believed that the body's 'constitution', 'temperament' or 'state' could be put out of equilibrium by excessive heat, cold, dryness or wetness. Such imbalances might be caused by fatigue, insomnia, distress, anxiety, or by the residues of food resulting from the wrong quantity or quality.

Concepts of health and illness are embodied in the everyday talk and thought of people of all languages, cultures and religions. It is difficult, if not impossible, to establish a 'lingua franca', a single universal account. The World Health Organization (WHO) published a definition in 1946 that was intended to have universal application. This definition stated that health is: 'the state of complete physical, social and spiritual well-being, not simply the absence of illness'. This perfect state of 'complete physical, social and spiritual well-being' can never be reached, but sets an aspirational target in the form of a 'health heaven'. Sadly, the opposite state of a 'health hell' is more available to many.

The WHO definition overlooked some key elements of well-being. Social factors are embedded within cultures and this should not be left purely implicit. Economic forces also cannot be ignored, as we shall see in the next chapter. The important *psychological* aspects to well-being also cannot be neglected in any meaningful definition of health. Psychological processes are embedded in a social world, a world of interaction with others. It is therefore helpful in certain contexts to describe and think of psychological processes as 'psychosocial' in nature, highlighting the social embeddedness of all things psychological. This is especially the case in the context of health, illness and health care.

We have amended the WHO definition of health to take account of these missing elements (see Box 1.1).

BOX 1.1

A DEFINITION OF HEALTH

Health is a state of well-being with physical, cultural, psychosocial, economic and spiritual attributes, not simply the absence of illness.

How we define health has implications for theory, practice, policy and health promotion. The term 'health promotion' was first coined in 1974 by the Canadian Minister of National Health and Welfare, Marc Lalonde (1974), who argued that health and illness are not dependent only on medical conditions but also on the environment and living conditions. The World Health Organization (1986) defined health promotion as: 'the process of enabling people to increase control over, and to improve their health. To reach a state of complete physical, mental and social well-being an individual or group must be able to identify and to realise aspirations, to satisfy needs, to change or cope with the environment ...' (p. i).

The 'health promotion approach' provides a unifying concept for those who emphasize *the need to make changes in ways and conditions of living in order to improve health*. Health-care practitioners are more than providers of services, they are *agents of change*, facilitating the empowerment of individuals and communities to increase their control over and to improve their health (D.F. Marks, 1999). The theories and research in health psychology have as yet been only partially applied to the practice of health promotion (Bennett and Murphy, 1997). However, as we shall see, health psychology has much to offer to a multidisciplinary approach that considers both the environmental context and behaviour as key determinants of health.

Health psychologists can take on different roles in: carrying out research; providing and improving health services in hospitals and clinics; carrying out health promotion in communities; or working actively on policy and social change to help improve living conditions so that people are enabled to act on their own terms.

In working towards the reduction of inequalities, whether in the context of disability, poverty or ethnicity, people's rights to health and freedom from illness are a life and death matter that is the responsibility of all (Marks, 2004). Health psychology needs to consider these facts at their most fundamental theoretical level.

Epistemologies for Studying Experience and Behaviour

Traditionally, there have been two primary theories of knowledge, or epistemologies, for studying and trying to understand human behaviour and experience. The first is the natural science approach that analyses behaviour and experience in a manner similar to the way in which physicists, chemists or biologists conduct investigations in the form of experiments to search for a single, 'true' account of reality. The second is the human science approach that explores behaviour and experience with the objective of discovering underlying meaning or understandings. The field of health psychology finds both traditions useful. Table 1.1 presents some contrasting features of the two approaches.

The two approaches have different objectives but, from a pragmatic point of view, are not necessarily mutually exclusive. The natural science approach aims to identify causal relationships between variables. It asks 'does x cause y?' and attempts to generate accurate predictive models. By contrast, the human science approach aims to analyse meanings and reasons. It asks 'how does y feel about x?' or 'what does y mean to x?' and produces detailed accounts of human action.

The natural science tradition is represented by the **medical model** and by its offshoot, the **biopsychosocial model**. In the medical model all health and illness are understood to be physical in nature and the mind is seen purely as activity of the brain and nervous system. Engel's (1977) biopsychosocial model challenged the medical model with the proposal that health and illness are a consequence of physical, psychological and cultural variables. The three Ps of the biopsychosocial model – people,

KT

Table 1.1   *Contrasting the natural science and human science approaches to health psychology*

Aspect	Natural science	Human science
Objective	Identifying causes: Does X cause Y?	Identifying meanings: What does X mean to Y?
Epistemology	Realism: only one true description of nature (reality)	Social constructivism: multiple true descriptions (plurality)
Ontology	Everything has a physical structure (mind = body)	Psychological experiences (subjectivity, consciousness, etc.) are not reducible to physics (mind ≠ body)
Model	Naturalistic/medical model (3 Ds: diagnosis, disease, drugs)	Biopsychosocial model (3 Ps: people, prevention, psychology)
Research methods	Quantitative – e.g. observation, experiments, controlled trials	Qualitative – e.g. discourse analysis, grounded theory, interpretative phenomenological analysis
Interventions	Physical/pharmacological/ behavioural	Social/psychological/ cognitive/phenomenological

prevention, psychology – can be contrasted with the three Ds of the medical model – diagnosis, disease, drugs.

Critics have suggested that the biopsychosocial model remains essentially biomedical and that its theoretical basis has yet to be properly worked out (e.g. Armstrong, 1987). However, while the precise causal pathways appear to be complicated and remain somewhat elusive, new psychological theories and approaches see non-physical events as having great significance in health, illness and health care. Whatever one's epistemological predilections, the study of health psychology is concerned with developing a better understanding of the mind and the body and the relationship between the two.

The second epistemology is the human science tradition as represented by research on **discourse**, **narrative** and **social representations**. People's accounts of health and illness are an illuminating topic of study in its own right. Much of the research on health and illness narratives has been influenced by **social constructionism** (Stainton-Rogers, 1991). From this perspective, there is no single, fixed 'reality' but a multiplicity of descriptions or 'drafts', each with its own unique pattern of meanings. Mulkay (1991: 27–8) suggests the existence of 'many potential worlds of meaning that can be imaginatively entered and celebrated, in ways that are constantly changing to give richness and value to human experience'. One of the popular ways of studying 'worlds of meaning' has been to analyse the social psychological functions of different accounts using a 'discursive approach' (Potter and Wetherell, 1987). Discursive psychology was influenced by Berger and Luckmann (1966), who argued that there is no single, true 'reality', and that people's concept of 'reality' is a purely social construction. Earlier intellectual forbears were Pascal, Marx and Nietzsche, who all believed that conscious thinking is constructed within a particular socio-historical context.

However, social constructionists continue to engage in a lively debate regarding the extent to which social constructions are grounded in material reality (see Parker, 1998). Some are relativists, in which there is no single reality at all, while others are critical realists in which there is one reality which has different descriptions or perspectives. Relativist social constructionists, inspired by Nietzsche, emphasize the flexibility of discourse and the sense in which language can be said to construct reality. Critical realist social constructionists, inspired by Marx, acknowledge that discourses construct different versions of reality, but they argue that the material world cannot accommodate all constructions equally well.

In addition to wide variations in health beliefs between cultures, there is significant within-culture diversity. Folk beliefs, knowledge and practices among individuals from different communities and social groups rub shoulders with each other and with the health-care professionals in a virtual Tower of Babel. These diverse beliefs meld with practices and lifestyles in accord with people's worldviews and values. Wide discrepancies frequently occur between patients' and the scientifically-schooled beliefs of the health-care professionals (see Chapters 4 and 11). Such differences help to explain some of the communication and concordance difficulties that are frequently evident between health-care professionals and patients (see Chapters 14 and 15).

A Cross-Cultural Perspective

Theories in health psychology provide accounts of how psychological processes affect individual health experience. In evaluating these theories it must be acknowledged that they are cultural products of the predominantly English-speaking world of the USA, Europe and British Commonwealth. More specifically, many of health psychology's theories are extensions and adaptations of US/European cognitive and social psychology from 1950 to 1990. During this time there was a resurgence of research in artificial, laboratory environments using structured psychometric instruments, questionnaires and performance tests designed to reveal the mechanisms underlying human behaviour. Although these methods were popular and influential, it has been argued that they often lacked 'ecological validity', or, in other words, that the findings could not be generalized to the world that lies outside the laboratory. Critics have suggested that the laboratory experiment and the questionnaire are subject to more bias than their proponents are willing to admit (Harré, 1979).

North American/European psychological theory can be viewed as part and parcel of an **indigenous** psychology that may be inapplicable to cultures outside (Heelas and Lock, 1981). This view was supported by Lillard (1998), who catalogues evidence that 'European American' folk psychology shows major differences from the folk psychologies of other cultures. One example of a cultural value that is embedded in US/European societies is **individualism**, which dictates that individuals are responsible for their own health (Brownell, 1991). Over-concern with personal responsibility for health can lead to victim blaming. Brownell warned that the 'tendency to overstate

KT

KT

the impact of personal behaviour on health' could feed the victim-blaming ethos that is already strong in western societies (Brownell, 1991: 303).

Cross-cultural psychology emphasizes cultural diversity and casts a sceptical eye over the **ethnocentrism** of contemporary psychology. It considers national or large group samples as the unit of analysis rather than individuals. Research has focused primarily on mental health (e.g. Dasen et al., 1988) and relatively little attention has been paid to physical health. A truly cross-cultural approach to health psychology is at a relatively early stage of development. However, it is clear that more understanding of cross-cultural differences in methods for preserving well-being and healing the sick will facilitate both theory and practice.

What is Health Psychology?

BOX 1.2

HEALTH PSYCHOLOGY: A NEW DEFINITION

Health psychology is an interdisciplinary field concerned with the application of psychological knowledge and techniques to health, illness and health care.

Box 1.2 provides a working definition. In discussing this definition, we can say that the objective of health psychology is to promote and maintain the well-being of individuals, communities and populations. The primary focus is *physical* rather than *mental* health although, like two sides of a coin, these are not easy to separate. Health psychology is concerned with understanding the relationships between mind and body as these affect the overall state of an individual's well-being. At a practical level, it is concerned with the behavioural and experiential interfaces between the individual, the health-care system, and society. This is why an interdisciplinary approach is needed.

A more comprehensive but complicated definition was proposed by Joseph Matarazzo in 1982 (see Box 1.3).

BOX 1.3

HEALTH PSYCHOLOGY: MATARAZZO'S (1982) DEFINITION

Health psychology is the aggregate of the specific educational, scientific, and professional contributions of the discipline of psychology to the promotion and maintenance of health, the prevention and treatment of illness, the identification of aetiologic and diagnostic correlates of health, illness, and related dysfunction and to the analysis and improvement of the health care system and health policy formation. (Matarazzo, 1982: 4)

Table 1.2 *Leading causes of mortality among adults worldwide, 2002*
(http://www.who.int/whr/2003/en/Facts_and_Figures-en.pdf)

Rank	Cause	Deaths (000)
Mortality: adults aged 15–59		
1	HIV/AIDS	2,279
2	Ischaemic heart disease	1,332
3	Tuberculosis	1,036
4	Road traffic injuries	814
5	Cerebrovascular disease	783
6	Self-inflicted injuries	672
7	Violence	473
8	Cirrhosis of the liver	382
9	Lower respiratory infections	352
10	Chronic obstructive pulmonary disease	343
Mortality: adults aged 60 and over		
1	Ischaemic heart disease	5,825
2	Cerebrovascular disease	4,689
3	Chronic obstructive pulmonary disease	2,399
4	Lower respiratory infections	1,396
5	Trachea, bronchus, lung cancers	928
6	Diabetes mellitus	754
7	Hypertensive heart disease	735
8	Stomach cancer	605
9	Tuberculosis	495
10	Colon and rectum cancers	477

This definition has been adopted by the American Psychological Association (APA), the British Psychological Society and other organizations. It serves as health psychology's 'official' definition. [More detailed discussion of Matarazzo's (1982) definition, including ideas for a redefinition by McDermott (2001), is available in *The Health Psychology Reader* (Marks, 2002a).] Recently, the social context of health has received more recognition and health psychologists have been increasingly working with families, workplaces, organizations and communities. The already broad scope of health psychology is becoming even broader. Notice that Matarazzo's definition includes *'the analysis and improvement of the health care system and health policy formation'*.

Health psychology grew rapidly during the 1980s and 1990s. By 2005 more than 3,000 psychologists had become members of the APA's Health Psychology Division 38, the largest in the association, and the BPS Division of Health Psychology had 1,000 members. Similar organizations are rapidly growing across the world.

Health psychology's fast growth can be attributed to three factors. First, in the 1970s and 1980s there was increasing awareness of the vast amounts of illness and mortality that are determined by behaviour. Epidemiological research suggests that *all* of the leading causes of death in western societies are *behavioural*. This means that many deaths are potentially preventable if effective interventions can be found. Table 1.2 lists the major causes of global mortality.

Traditionally mortality has been a principal statistical benchmark for quantifying ill-health. The mortality rates for different conditions in younger and older people are shown in Table 1.2. Recently there has been increasing interest in computing measures

Table 1.3 *Rank order of DALYs for the ten leading causes of disability, World 1990–2020 (Murray and Lopez, 1997)*

Rank position	1990 Diseases or Injury	2020 Diseases or Injury
1	Lower respiratory infections	Ischaemic heart disease
2	Diarrhoeal diseases	Unipolar major depression
3	Conditions arising during the perinatal period	Road traffic accidents
4	Unipolar major depression	Cerebrovascular disease
5	Ischaemic heart disease	Chronic obstructive pulmonary disease
6	Cerebrovascular disease	Lower respiratory infections
7	Tuberculosis	Tuberculosis
8	Measles	War injuries
9	Road traffic accidents	Diarrhoeal diseases
10	Congenital anomalies	HIV/AIDS

KT

of **disability**. The **Global Burden of Disease (GBD)** study projected mortality and disability over 25 years (Murray and Lopez, 1997). The trends gleaned from the GBD study suggest that health trends will be determined mainly by ageing, the spread of HIV, the increase in tobacco-related mortality and disability, psychiatric and neurological conditions and the decline in mortality from communicable, maternal, perinatal and nutritional disorders (Murray and Lopez, 1997).

KT

The GBD uses the **disability-adjusted life year (DALY)** as a quantitative indicator of burden of disease that reflects the total amount of healthy life lost, to all causes, whether from premature mortality or from some degree of disability during a period of time. The DALY is the sum of years of life lost from premature mortality plus years of life with disability, adjusted for severity of disability from all causes, both physical and mental (Murray and Lopez, 1997). The GBD study prepared figures by age, sex and region for 1990 and 2020. The overall positions of each cause for 1990 and 2020 are shown in Table 1.3.

Notice that while various cancers feature highly in the list of causes of mortality (Table 1.2), they do not appear in the top ten causes of disability (Table 1.3). However, diseases of the cardiovascular system cause many deaths and also cause a large proportion of disability. The contribution of communicable maternal, perinatal and nutritional disorders to the GBD is expected to decline from 44% in 1990 to 20% in 2020. Meanwhile the contribution from non-communicable diseases is expected to rise from 41% in 1990 to 60% in 2020.

Many of the leading risk factors for disability and mortality are psychologically or behaviourally mediated (see Table 1.4).

The data in Table 1.4 indicate that nearly 30% of the total global burden of disease is attributable to five risk factors. The largest risk factor (underweight) is associated with **poverty**, which is discussed in Chapters 2 and 3. The remaining four risk factors

KT

are discussed in Part 2 (see especially Chapters 6–10). Health psychology can contribute expertise to policy and programme developments designed to modify risks and prevent disability and mortality.

A second factor in health psychology's recent growth has been the ideology that *individuals are responsible for their own health*. Individualism places the primary responsibility for good health on the individual and individuals must therefore become

Table 1.4   *Leading five risk factors for global disease burden computed in*
DALYs (Ezzati et al., 2002)

Risk factor	Number of DALYs (millions)	Percentage of DALYs
Childhood and maternal underweight	138	9.5
Unsafe sex	92	6.3
High blood pressure	64	4.4
Tobacco	59	4.1
Alcohol	58	4.0
Totals	411	28.3

experts on their own health and lifestyles. Several industries cater to the needs of consumers who are exhorted to live 'healthier lifestyle'. Fitness, dieting, designer sports-
wear, Atkins diets, light alcohol drinks, low tar and even non-combustible cigarettes
cater for our every health wish and fear. At the same time, the perceived political correctness of health advocacy has led to a backlash in the form of accusations of 'health
fascism' by organizations appealing to ideas of human liberty and choice in suggesting that adult consumers should be free to smoke, drink, and eat as much as they like
if and when they choose to do so.

Individualism sees each individual person as a self-contained unit, requiring minimum levels of sharing, caring and interdependency. This value is particularly strong
in regions where health psychology developed the fastest – the USA, Canada, northern
Europe, Australia, New Zealand. This view suggests in its extreme form that there is
really no such thing as 'society' or 'community', that people primarily should only look
after themselves and their families. However, an alternative view sees the need for
policy interventions designed to support and promote health at societal and community levels. The individual alone may be unable to make improvements in health-
related behaviour as a consequence of economic or political factors.

A third trend that has fostered an interest in health psychology has been a disenchantment with biomedical health care among both patients and practitioners. This
has led to a search for alternative perspectives which value the experience of patients
and attempt to improve services in light of an understanding of the psychosocial
aspects of health care. In spite of their very high costs (Figure 1.1), health-care systems
are perceived by some to be inefficient, ineffective and producing low levels of satisfaction. The poor quality of communication experienced by patients with health-care
professionals has been a particularly strong focus of complaints and criticism. The
dominance of the medical model has been heavily criticized since the 1970s (Illich,
1976) and the decline of disease in the twentieth century, attributed by doctors to the
efficacy of modern medicine, has been attributed by some to be due mainly to better
hygiene and reduced poverty (McKeown, 1979).

Disenchantment with the medical model and a growing awareness of the importance of psychological and social influences on health and illness have led social
scientists and others to propose new ways of conceptualizing health and illness.
Psychosocial factors have been claimed to be as important or more important than the
purely biological causes of well-being. This position led to the development of the
biopsychosocial model (Engel, 1977). This new model has been a major influence in
the evolution of health psychology as a new field of study.

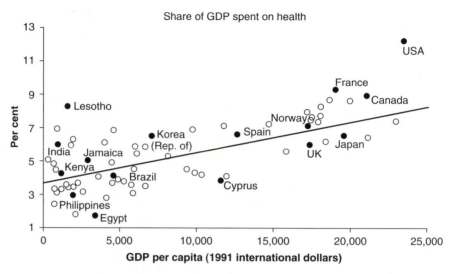

Figure 1.1 Income and health spending in 70 countries (World Bank, 1993: 110, Fig. 5.1; reproduced with permission)

For many reasons, therefore, health psychology has become an exciting, dynamic and popular field. Many new books and journals have appeared and there is considerable attention from the media. Health promotion programmes are increasingly employing psychological knowledge and approaches in a variety of interventions. Primary health care physicians are employing more clinical, counselling and health psychology expertise, while surgeons, anaesthetists and many other clinicians are to an increasing extent applying health psychology research and practice in their clinical work.

A primary role of the health psychologist is to improve the psychosocial conditions for the promotion and maintenance of health. The study and enhancement of the psychosocial resources available to individuals and groups are a primary focus for the field. However, the gap between theory and practice is large and could be narrowed. There are constraints on the ability of health-care systems to influence health outcomes at a population level because of the significant social and economic determinants that structure the health of individuals and communities. In order to help make genuine improvements to the health-care system and health policy formation, psychologists need to be fully aware of the social and economic context in which they, the other professionals and communities live and work.

Theory in Health Psychology

Theory in health psychology consists of three broad types that vary according to their level of generality: these are *frameworks, theories* and *models*. Frameworks have some of the characteristics of paradigms as described by Kuhn (1970) as they refer to a complete system of thinking about a field of inquiry. However, unlike paradigms that include

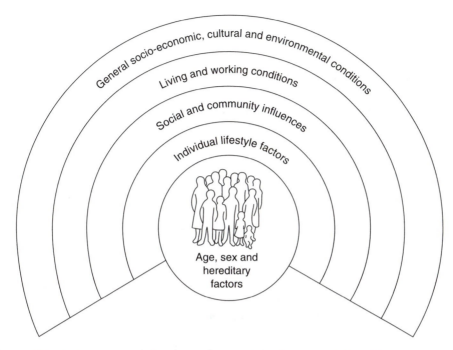

Figure 1.2   A framework for the determinants of health (adapted from Dahlgren and Whitehead, 1991: Figure 1; reproduced with permission)

explicitly stated assumptions, laws and methods, frameworks are looser and less developed in nature, but are intended to be of general application.

Examples of frameworks in the fields of health and health care would be the so-called medical model and the more recent biopsychosocial model. However, these have been consistently referred to as **models** in the literature and, to avoid confusion, we will do the same here. It is necessary to consider theory building at its most general level and for this we reserve the term 'framework'.

An example of a **framework** for considering the general determinants of health is presented in Figure 1.2 (Dahlgren and Whitehead, 1991). This framework is useful in conceptualizing the main influences on health. It has influenced the structure of this book. It also corresponds with the different sub-fields of health psychology.

This framework has a multi-layered, onion-like structure that places the individual, endowed with fixed factors of age, sex and genetic make-up, at the core (over which we have little or no control) but surrounded by four layers of influence. From this perspective, health psychology can be structured as follows.

Core: age, sex and hereditary factors (covered throughout this book).
Level 1: individual lifestyle (covered by Part 2 of this book).
Level 2: social and community influences (covered throughout this book).
Level 3: living and working conditions (covered by Part 3 of this book).
Level 4: general socio-economic, cultural and environmental conditions (covered by Part 1 of this book).

This framework has six characteristics:

1 It is concerned with all of the determinants of health, not simply with the course of events during the treatment of illness.
2 It places the individual at the core but acknowledges the primary determining influence of society through the community, living and working conditions, and the surrounding socio-economic, cultural and environmental conditions.
3 It places each layer in the context of its neighbours, reflecting the whole situation, including possible structural constraints upon change.
4 It has a true interdisciplinary flavour and is not purely a medical or quasi-medical model of health.
5 It is even-handed and makes no claims for any one discipline as being more important than others.
6 It acknowledges the complex nature of health determinants.

Different theories and models are needed that vary in level of specificity for differing settings and contexts. However, ideally, there is a need for a general paradigm for understanding the health of the individual within which more specific theories and models can be nested. Such a paradigm should attempt to represent in an explicit, detailed and meaningful way the constraints upon and links between individual well-being, the surrounding community and the health-care system (Marks, 1996). As yet, no such general paradigm exists. However, perhaps the diversity of perspectives, issues and questions, which are of interest to scholars in the field, makes health psychology non-amenable to any single paradigm.

KT The next level of generality in theory building is the **theory**. The status of health psychology as a scientific endeavour rests upon its ability to provide explanatory accounts or theories of health experience and behaviour. Much current theory is intended to meet scientific criteria of accurate prediction and verifiability. Examples of theories in health psychology are those that are primarily concerned with the psychological resources needed to cope effectively with changing circumstances brought about by major life events including illness. Such resources may be classified into five main categories: economic, psychological, biological, social and spiritual. Processes that fall into these categories are: socio-economic status, resilience, immunocompetence, social support and beliefs, respectively. Theories in each of these areas will be presented in this text.

KT Many so-called 'theories' in health psychology have consisted of little more than **flowchart models**. Such models use a 'black-box' approach that focuses upon informational processes in the heads of individuals as these influence, and are influenced by, social and physiological processes directly or indirectly related to health or illness. An example of a flowchart model is provided in Figure 1.3. This provides a hypothetical model of processes that are claimed to be related to hypertension (Spicer and Chamberlain, 1996).

The model proposes that hypertension is *influenced* by anger suppression, social support, alcohol consumption and socio-economic status. The level of influence may be either *causal*, at the strongest level of association, or *correlational*, at a weaker level of association. The model also suggests that social support is influenced by anger suppression and alcohol consumption and that social support moderates the relationship between anger suppression and hypertension.

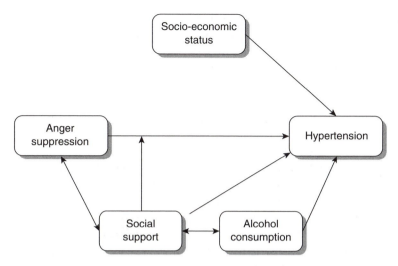

Figure 1.3 A flowchart representing a hypothetical model of hypertension (Spicer and Chamberlain, 1996: 163; reproduced with permission)

Flowchart models can be analysed on three distinct levels: the theoretical level consisting of the constructs and causal relations; the measurement level containing the variables that map onto the constructs; and the statistical level that maps the statistical relationships between variables onto the theoretical relationships. The statistical analysis of flowcharts is becoming an ever more technical discipline in its own right and there are sophisticated computer programs designed especially for this purpose (Bentler, 1989; Byrne, 1994).

At the theoretical level, flowcharts often contain a mix of constructs from ontologically distinct domains that are nevertheless believed to be causally connected. Causal connectedness between these constructs is indicated by the lines and arrows that are drawn between boxes. These lines and arrows attempt to give a form of explanatory coherence and scientific meaning to the model. Thus, the flowchart model has a significance that appears to place it within a natural science epistemology of knowledge and understanding.

In fact, the hypertension model in Figure 1.3 is a complex network of constructs selected from five domains or levels:

1 Hypertension is a *physiological* construct.
2 Anger suppression is a *psychological* construct.
3 Alcohol consumption is a *behavioural* construct.
4 Social support is a *social* construct.
5 Socio-economic status is a *sociological* construct.

This analysis suggests that there are, embedded in this flowchart, some deep, unanswered philosophical questions about the mechanisms for translating between the different levels of the system. For example, how does anger suppression (a psychological process) *cause* hypertension (a physiological process)? Normally, health psychologists do not attempt to answer (or even ask!) such questions at a philosophical level, but they remain significant questions nevertheless. The health psychologist attempts to collect as much empirical evidence as possible to confirm or disconfirm the anger suppression hypothesis by measuring hypertension directly and anger suppression via questionnaires, interviews or observation in the same group of participants. It is then possible to investigate statistically whether there is a link, causal or otherwise, between anger suppression and hypertension.

One alternative way of interpreting a flowchart is to see it as an essentially narrative device in the form of a diagram that can be given a particular scientific meaning. This kind of analysis is more in tune with the human science approach. Following extensive elaboration carried out by unpacking of the flowchart boxes and more detailed explication of how the contents of each box affects the others, a 'story' is being told by the model that can be allowed gradually to unfold.

To give the hypertension model a truly *causal* interpretation, the five constructs need to be connected and compatible so that the links become genuinely causal. One solution to the 'arrow problem' is to see that biopsychosocial constructs can actually operate on multiple levels. One example of a multi-level construct is that of 'emotion'. Emotion is said to operate simultaneously on at least three different levels – sociological, psychological and physiological (Lazarus et al., 1980).

Thus, 'anger suppression' in the hypertension model operates on all three of these levels. However, it is at the physiological level that anger suppression can causally influence hypertension. A similar explanatory exercise needs to be performed with each of the interconnecting arrows in the model. This exercise may have a complexity that is belied by the bold simplicity of the arrows and the surface definition of the connected constructs. However, the flowchart model is an important conceptual device in the construction of scientific accounts of health and illness.

Health psychology draws much of its appeal from its claim that, by including the psychosocial, there is the possibility of providing a more meaningful, 'human' account of health, illness and health-care issues. New theories are created by employing psychological constructs to weave an account that provides fresh understanding. However, if a theory is to have any scientific value, its assumptions and contents have to be stated in a fully explicit and precise manner. The existence of unexplained assumptions has been a stumbling block for acceptance of the biopsychosocial model as an improvement upon the medical model.

Although the rhetoric of creating a challenge to the medical model attracted attention to the biopsychosocial model, this challenge in the name of psychology and the social sciences is not seen by everybody to be sufficiently radical or persuasive (e.g. Ogden, 1997). This means that a stronger case must be made on behalf of psychosocial models if the traditional medical model is to lose pole position in western thinking about health, illness and health care.

The Biopsychosocial Model

Health psychologists work in a variety of settings including health promotion units, primary health care, general hospitals, companies and organizations, academic departments and research units. Some of the more traditional settings are clinical environments with medical agendas and practices. Although health psychologists frequently argue against the medical model and in favour of the biopsychosocial model (e.g. Broome and Llewellyn, 1995), the majority of health psychology practice still occurs in the context of clinical medicine.

The biopsychosocial model (or BPSM) has been vigorously advocated by psychologists and others concerned with the health of the individual considered as a totality. The biopsychosocial model claims that health and illness are: the product of a combination of factors including biological characteristics (e.g. genetic predisposition), behavioural factors (e.g. lifestyle, stress, health beliefs), and social conditions (e.g. cultural influences, family relationships, social support). In spite of its widespread acceptance, however, there is a problem with the BPSM. It can be argued that the BPSM is not really a model in the formal sense but more a way of thinking about health and illness which has a heuristic function in justifying and legitimating research (Marks, 2002a, 2002b). The BPSM is seen by many clinical health psychologists as a challenge to the biomedical model, a rhetorical weapon with which to knock down that version of reality which says that all health and illness are the product of physical processes and reactions inside the body (Ogden, 1997).

Psychiatrist George Engel (1977; Marks, 2002a) proposed the BPSM in response to what was perceived to be a 'crisis' for psychiatry with too many disparate theories and methods to be considered 'neat and tidy' like the rest of medicine. Engel discusses some problems with the biomedical model, in particular its reductionistic, dualistic, pathogenic assumptions. Engel argued that:

> a medical model must also take into account the patient, the social context in which he lives, and the complementary system devised by society to deal with the disruptive effects of the illness, that is, the physician role and the health care system. This requires the biopsychosocial model. (1977: 130)

In making a plea for medical practice to become more caring, considerate and patient-orientated, Engel had a valid point. But Engel left much unsaid. By some oversight, he never actually defined the BPSM, leaving it open for people to interpret it in different ways, like a projective ink-blot. The American Psychological Association's Division 38 webpages describe the BPSM as 'a combination of factors' that produce health and illness, as quoted above. But a combination of factors does not make a model. The BPSM is really a set of beliefs and values about health, illness, psychology and culture that the health psychology discipline has signed up to along with its 'official' definition.

The existence of the BPSM owes little to any particular model or scientific theory, but it has symbolic value in seeing psychosocial factors to be as important in understanding health and illness as DNA, cells and biology. Armstrong (1987) argues that Engel's 'new model' is 'nothing of the kind. It is simply the old one with a gloss.' One might therefore call it 'old wine in new bottles'. The BPSM has given service as a cover-term for beliefs and values, but, as a Trojan horse to reform biomedicine, the BPSM needs a much stronger construction. Something much more solid and concrete is needed, theories which give coherent accounts of *how* it is exactly that psychosocial processes influence health and illness.

In spite of the fast growth of health psychology, there has been no significant paradigm shift in clinical medicine and the biopsychosocial model has not replaced the medical model in hospitals and clinics, nor is this likely to happen. The nature of medicine is perhaps being reintepreted, renegotiated and reconstructed. Health-care services, for the most part, remain principally medical rather than psychosocial concerns, but the psychosocial component is today receiving more attention. [For further discussion of the BPSM, see Marks (2002a), in which the original sources of Engel (1977), Armstrong (1987) and Ogden (1997) are reprinted.]

Until now there has been precious little critical analysis of health psychology in its socio-political context. Equally, there has been hardly any discussion of the implications of the individualistic nature of western culture, psychology and health-care systems for the current development of the field. Health psychology to the present day should perhaps be more aptly termed 'illness psychology' as its main focus is illness behaviour and illness management (Marks, 1996). There is a need for an explicitly social orientation as represented by the framework in Figure 1.2.

From this perspective, health psychology is viewed as an interdisciplinary field having many links with other human sciences and also with the humanities and literature. In attempting to address issues shared with other disciplines, health psychology is inevitably a highly social and practical field of inquiry. In the next two sections we introduce two of the core aspects of health – disability and ageing.

Disability

One important aspect of the social context of health is disability. We use D. Marks' (1999) definition of disability: 'the complex relationship between the environment, body and psyche, which serves to exclude certain people from becoming full participants in interpersonal, social, cultural, economic and political affairs' (p. 611). This definition avoids the individual versus social dichotomy and reflects the importance of both as independent, interacting dimensions of disability. Disability constitutes a major factor in the overall health status of any population (Murray and Lopez, 1997). Yet disability has rarely been a focus for investigation within health psychology. For the most part, disability has been an add-on to lists of other forms of social oppression (race, gender, class, sexuality), without receiving the same level of discussion as these other factors. When it has been looked at within psychology the focus has mainly been on 'adjustment' (Johnston, 1995), although more recently, it can be found within the burgeoning qualitative work on chronic illness.

The historical reasons for the omission of disability research from newer disciplines like psychology are detailed in D. Marks (1999a) as follows:

- restriction to the private sphere;
- need to establish scientific credibility generating a research bias towards the general (i.e. non-disabled) population;
- absence of disabled people from academia;
- disability studies developing as an academic specialism.

The growth of the disability movement and disability studies may have encouraged a reluctance to cross over an imputed academic boundary. A popular slogan used by disabled activists, 'nothing about us without us', encapsulates a powerful imperative for treating disability as a specialism that may have increased such reluctance. Similarly, although the boundaries between illness and disability are often ill-defined, there has been some reticence to explore illness-specific issues within disability studies, probably to resist diluting its commitment to the 'social model' of disability (e.g. Oliver, 1990). This locates disability within social and institutional structures and practices rather than within the biologically determined reality of individual impairment and sees the environment as the source of disablement. Disability represents 'a central and powerful organising principle within contemporary subjectivity and social relations' (D. Marks, 1999b: 11) and as such should be viewed as not just interdisciplinary but omnidisciplinary.

While the social perspective views disability as the end-result of social and physical barriers, disability is also intimately related to issues of identity, relationships and health/illness status. It can affect anyone at anytime and everybody is likely to experience some disability at some point in their lives, especially given our increasing longevity. While accepting disability as a socially constructed source of oppression, it is vital not to deny its personal dimensions. As Morris (1991: 16) stated, 'we can insist that society disables us by its prejudice and by its failure to meet the needs created by disability, but to deny the personal experience of disability is, in the end, to collude in our oppression'.

Dejong and Basnett (2001) identify eight ways in which the health-care needs of disabled people may differ from those of the non-disabled population:

1 thinner margins of health as functional limitations increase vulnerability;
2 less opportunity for health maintenance and preventive health care;
3 disability from young age associated with earlier chronic health problems;
4 secondary conditions resulting in additional functional losses;
5 longer and more complicated treatment and recovery processes;
6 continuous pharmacological support, particularly regarding mental illness and pain management;
7 need for special equipment and technologies;
8 need for long-term services like personal assistance.

Disability, therefore, should be a significant concern within health psychology and to this end, links must be forged with disability studies and interdisciplinary projects promoted. In this textbook, we start to make these links.

Ageing

Current demographic trends (see Chapter 2) show that in the industrialized world, birth rates are falling and people are living longer. In 2005, 60 years after the end of the Second World War, postwar baby-boomers are entering retirement and starting to draw on government pensions and health systems. Abbott (2004) refers to Thomas

More's *Utopia* (1516) that dreams about an egalitarian paradise with no poverty or greed. Old age 'which … is a disease of itself' had not been eliminated from More's Utopia. Living a long and healthy life may well be part of a utopian vision, but is it ever going to be a genuine possibility? Are weakness and deterioration not essential components of becoming older?

Life expectancy in the developed world is rising, and it is showing little sign of levelling off. With falling birth rates, and fewer people entering the workplace, paying for the care of older people is a major concern. Abbott (2004) points out that there is an economic incentive, as well as a humanitarian one, for breaking the association between old age and ill health. Compulsory retirement from work is becoming illegal as an ageist policy that is removing many competent people from the active work-force. More research is needed to investigate the genetic and environmental factors that allow people to remain healthy and active right through their sixties, seventies and eighties.

The European Commission (EC) is launching 'The Genetics of Healthy Ageing' (GEHA) study to collect data on the genetic make-up, health and lifestyle of 2,800 pairs of siblings who are over 90 years old. The group will be compared with the same number of younger controls. The GEHA study will investigate which genes the elderly brothers and sisters have in common, and which occur more frequently than in the general population. The GEHA study will cost €9 million.

Studies on twins indicate that only 25% of the variation in life span (Skytthe et al., 2003) and half of the variation in cognitive function late in life (McGue and Christensen, 2002) can be attributed to genetic differences. The rest of the variation is caused by environmental and behavioural influences. These researches suggest that around 75% of the variation in our lifespan is determined by our behaviour and environment.

Professor Claudio Franceschi, of the Italian National Research Centre on Ageing, and his partners will analyse the genetic make-up of brothers and sisters. They hope to develop medicines to help people stay healthy for longer. Previous studies, using model organisms and animals, have demonstrated a genetic component in longevity. The EC study will also consider the effect of lifestyle – environmental and behavioural influences – on the age that people reach. This includes whether people smoke, drink alcohol and eat fatty foods (European Research Information Centre, 2004).

Many of these influences are discussed in detail in Part 2 of this book. Not smoking, reducing intake of saturated fats and alcohol, and increasing activity to higher levels are four key issues for healthy ageing. More systematic research on the genetic and environmental interactions that influence longevity is needed.

Four Approaches to Health Psychology

Four complementary approaches to health psychology are evolving (Marks, 2002a, 2002b). Each approach offers theory, research and recommendations for practice. Although there are differences in interests and ways of working, the approaches blend into each other (see Figure 1.4). The approaches map perfectly onto the four main influences

Clinical health psychology	Public health psychology
Core: age, sex and hereditary factors + **Level 1**: individual lifestyle – treatment; secondary and tertiary prevention	**Level 3**: living and working conditions – health education; health promotion and primary prevention
Community health psychology	Critical health psychology
Level 2: social and community influences – community action and research	**Level 4**: general socio-economic, cultural and environmental conditions – critique and design of policies and structures

Figure 1.4 Four approaches to health psychology (Marks, 2002a, 2002b)

on health that we describe above (see Figure 1.2). We introduce each approach below and indicate which chapters in this book cover the most relevant topics.

Clinical health psychology

Clinical health psychology seeks to relate psychological variables to biomedical conditions in order to understand health outcomes and quality of life. Methods include experimental psychophysiology, quantitative assessment of coping, beliefs and quality of life associated with illness and interventions, randomized controlled trials, meta-analysis, interpretative and case studies of experience of illness and health care (see Chapter 5 for more details of relevant methodology).

The approach overlaps with clinical psychology. **Clinical health psychology** is research-based and develops health services designed to improve the care of patients. It is the best established of the four approaches. The principal characteristics of clinical health psychology are summarized in Table 1.5 (column 2). Clinical health psychology is at the 'sharp end' of health care and is undoubtedly making an impact in clinical care (see Chapters 15, 16, 17 and 18). As members of a relatively new health-care profession, clinical health psychologists are establishing the evidence base, demonstrating to health service planners and policymakers that clinical health psychology is safe, cost-effective, and a service that is well-received by patients.

KT

Public health psychology

The approach of **public health psychology** is allied to epidemiology and health promotion. It is broadly realist but also interpretative, seeking to identify and manipulate psychological variables predicting health and healthy behaviour in the general population.

KT

Table 1.5   The characteristics of clinical, public, community and critical health psychology (adapted from Marks, 2002b)

Characteristic (1)	Clinical health psychology (2)	Public health psychology (3)	Community psychology (4)	Critical psychology (5)
Definition	'The aggregate of the specific educational, scientific, and professional contributions of the discipline of psychology to the promotion and maintenance of health, the prevention and treatment of illness, the identification of aetiologic and diagnostic correlates of health, illness and related dysfunction and to the analysis and improvement of the health care system and health policy.' (Matarazzo, 1982: 4)	The application of psychological theory, research and technologies towards the improvement of the health of the population.	'Advancing theory, research and social action to promote positive well-being, increase empowerment, and prevent the development of problems of communities, groups and individuals.' (Society for Community Research and Action, 2005)	The analysis of how power, economics and macro-social processes influence health, health care, and social issues, and the study of the implications for the theory and praxis of health work.
Theory/philosophy	Biopsychosocial model: health and illness are: 'the product of a combination of factors including biological characteristics (e.g. genetic predisposition), behavioural factors (e.g. lifestyle, stress, health beliefs), and social conditions (e.g. cultural influences, family relationships, social support).' (APA, 2005)	Social and economic model: No single theory and philosophy; supportive role in public health promotion which uses legal and fiscal instruments combined with preventive measures to bring about health improvements. Working towards general theories, e.g. health literacy improves health.	'Change strategies are needed at both the individual and systems levels for effective competence promotion and problem prevention.' (Society for Community Research and Action, 2001). Acknowledges the interdependence of individuals and communities. Shares some of the aims of public health psychology, e.g. improving health literacy.	Critical psychology: analysis of society and the values, assumptions and practices of psychologists, health-care professionals, and of all those whom they aim to serve. Shares some of the aims of community health psychology, but with universal rather than local constituency.

Table 1.5 (Continued)

Characteristic (1)	Clinical health psychology (2)	Public health psychology (3)	Community psychology (4)	Critical psychology (5)
Values	Increasing or maintaining the autonomy of the individual through ethical intervention.	Mapping accurately the health of the public as a basis for policy and health promotion, communication and interventions.	Creating or increasing autonomy of disadvantaged and oppressed people through social action.	Understanding the political nature of all human existence; freedom of thought; compassion for others.
Context	Patients in the health-care system, i.e. hospitals, clinics, health centres.	Schools, work sites, the media.	Families, communities and populations within their social, cultural and historical context.	Social structures, economics, government, and commerce.
Focus	Physical illness and dysfunction.	Health promotion and disease prevention.	Physical and mental health promotion.	Power.
Target groups	Patients with specific disorders.	Population groups who are most vulnerable to health problems.	Healthy but vulnerable or exploited persons and groups.	Varies according to the context: from the entire global population to the health of an individual.
Objective	To enhance the effectiveness of treatments.	To improve the health of the entire population: reducing morbidity, disability, and avoidable mortality.	Empowerment and social change.	Equality of opportunities and resources for health.
Orientation	Health service delivery.	Communication and intervention.	Bottom up, working with or alongside.	Analysis, argument, critique.
Skills	Assessment, therapy, consultancy and research.	Statistical evaluation; knowledge of health policy; epidemiological methods.	Participatory and facilitative; working with communities; community development.	Theoretical analysis; critical thinking; social and political action; advocacy; leadership.
Research methodology	Efficacy and effectiveness trials; quantitative and quasi-experimental methods.	Epidemiological methods; large-scale trials; multivariate statistics; evaluation.	Participant action research; coalitions between researchers, practitioners and communities; multiple methodologies.	Critical analysis combined with any of the methods used in the other three approaches.

Typical methods include large-scale surveys, interpretative and quantitative analyses of beliefs influencing behaviour, evaluation of impact of health promotion on attitudes and behaviour (see Chapters 5, 18, 19 and 20). Individual health is seen as more an outcome of social, economic and political determinants than a simple consequence of individual behaviour and lifestyle. It is an activity involving epidemiological studies, public health interventions and evaluation. Public health psychology is a multidisciplinary activity seeking to integrate epidemiological studies, public health interventions and evaluation. A summary of the characteristics of public health psychology is given in Table 1.5 (column 3).

Community health psychology

KT

Community health psychology seeks to empower lay communities to take greater control over health and health care. Typical methods include case studies and action research (see Chapter 5). This approach focuses on community development both in research and action. Community psychology involves working in coalition with members of vulnerable communities and groups and aims at their 'empowerment' more generally, forms of social change that tackle the conditions that make them vulnerable (such as social exclusion and poverty) and that enable them to flourish in adversity (see Chapters 2, 3 and 20). Community health psychology is summarized in Table 1.5 (column 4).

Critical health psychology

The critical approach to health psychology is allied to critical theory and other social sciences. It tends to be constructivist, seeking to analyse and critique assumptions and discourse associated with health and illness, including that of health professionals and researchers, in order to promote awareness of socio-political functions and consequences of these. Research methods include theoretical and policy analysis, discourse analysis, and ethnography (see Chapter 5).

KT

  Critical health psychology aims to analyse how power, economics and macro-social processes influence or structure health, health care, health psychology and society at large (see Table 1.5, column 5). It is concerned with the political nature of all human existence, admits compassion in theory and practice, values freedom of thought and is aware of the social interdependence of human beings as actors. The context for study is the whole of society, government and commerce. In particular it is concerned with the impact of power structures as facilitators or barriers to achieving health. The critical psychologist attempts to apply critical analysis, and evidence obtained by the other three approaches. Rhetorical argumentation is used to persuade others of the political nature of human activity, pulling open the blinds to glimpse the 'bigger picture'.

  Critical health psychology cuts across the other three perspectives such that we can have critical approaches within clinical, public and community health psychology. A unifying feature is an awareness of issues of power in shaping health and illness and the very character of health psychology itself. It explores the assumptions underlying our everyday lives and critiques the methods and theories historically used by psychology. It is concerned with developing knowledge and strategies to help build a healthier world (Murray and Campbell, 2003). [Further discussion of critical health psychology can be found in Marks (2002a) and Murray (2004b)]. A critical approach is applied throughout this text.

Future Research

1 Research is needed at a basic conceptual and theoretical level to unravel the biopsychosocial model and to specify more clearly the differences between it and the medical model.
2 Transcultural studies of health, illness and health care are needed to facilitate communication and understanding of systems of healing among different cultural, ethnic and religious groups.
3 Studies focusing on disability and its impact upon and interaction with health status and social context are needed.
4 More systematic research on the genetic and environmental interactions that influence longevity is needed to improve our understanding of ageing.

Summary

1 Health is a positive state of being with physical, cultural, psychosocial, economic and spiritual attributes, not simply the absence of illness.
2 Health psychology is concerned with the application of psychological knowledge and techniques to health, illness and health care. Its primary objective is to understand and to help improve the well-being of individuals and communities.
3 Health psychology grew rapidly during the last quarter of the twentieth century due to: (a) increasing evidence that much of the illness and mortality is caused by lifestyles and health-damaging behaviour; (b) a strengthening of the philosophy in industrialized countries that individuals are responsible for their own health; (c) increasing disenchantment with the medical model and its dominance of health care.
4 Levels of analysis in health care can be structured in terms of core issues affecting individual health status such as age, sex and hereditary factors, then four levels of influence consisting of individual lifestyle (level 1), social and community influences (level 2), living and working conditions (level 3), and general socio-economic, cultural and environmental conditions (level 4).
5 Two epistemological approaches within health psychology analyse health and illness in different ways: from the perspective of natural science (realism) and from the perspective of human science (constructivism).
6 The biopsychosocial model suggests that health is created by psychosocial as well as biological determinants. However, more radical revision may be necessary before the medical model is replaced.
7 Theory building in health psychology occurs at three levels of generality: (a) frameworks; (b) theories; (c) models.

8   A social orientation is necessary if we are to understand health behaviour and experience in its context of society and culture. Such an orientation focuses upon health as much as illness, preventive care as much as cure, and considers families, groups and communities as much as individuals. Disability and ageing are considered as core topics of the field.

9   Four complementary approaches are evolving which focus upon clinical, community, public health and critical issues.

10   Health psychology has the potential to become a socially relevant, non-ethnocentric and immensely practical application of knowledge about human nature in both health and illness.

 Key Terms

biopsychosocial model	indigenous
clinical health psychology	individualism
community health psychology	medical model
critical health psychology	models
disability	narrative
disability-adjusted life year (DALY)	poverty
discourse	public health psychology
ethnocentrism	social constructionism
flowchart model	social representations
framework	theory
global burden of disease (GBD)	well-being

2

The Macro-Social Environment and Health

As in earlier times, advances in the 21st century will be won by human struggle against divisive values – and against the opposition of entrenched economic and political interests. (Human Development Report, 2000: 6)

Outline

This chapter introduces the demographic, economic and societal context for health on a global scale. Our focus is on human health variations across societies. We use a wide-angle lens to explore the bigger picture of the global context for human health and suffering. The evidence of universal health gradients relating health experience to economic wealth is described. The significance of gender, ethnicity and disability is discussed. The reduction of inequalities is a major priority for policymakers and service planners.

Global Health Trends

This chapter reviews the most significant demographic and socio-economic parameters affecting human health. The statistical information that is discussed is not for the faint hearted. The health of a nation is dependent in major ways on its economic power and on any shifts in power balance relative to others. The health of individuals is dependent upon the families and communities to which they belong. All are influenced by powerful demographic, social and economic forces that are difficult but not impossible for individuals or societies to influence and control. Economic and environmental policies are created by governments which are, in the rich North, democratically elected institutions. In this sense a rich society gets the health that its population chooses at the ballot box. Poor countries, on the other hand, have less room to manoeuvre. They fall victim to the massive inequalities that divide them from the fortunate few.

On a global scale, human health is affected by a host of factors, the most significant being poverty, droughts, famines, epidemics and wars. In recent years we have witnessed all of these health scourges, and the impact that they can have on human health, illness and suffering. Curiously, none receives any real attention in mainstream health psychology. Yet all have enormous psychological implications and impacts on the health of the affected populations. The focus of attention for health psychology has been social

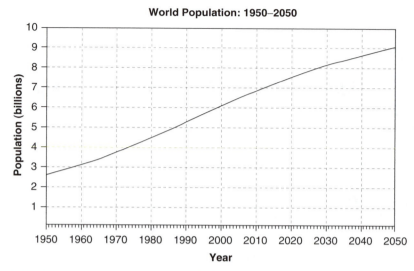

Figure 2.1 World population 1950–2050 (US Census Bureau, 2005; reproduced with permission)

Source: US Census Bureau, International Data Base, April 2004 version

cognitive processes concerned with health beliefs and behaviours at the level of individuals (Marks, 1996). In seeking to place health psychology in a broader international context, however, we address, among other issues, health variations and one of their root causes, poverty. Of necessity, our discussion will skate over the surface of an iceberg of mammoth proportions. However, to ignore the issue of poverty in a textbook on health psychology is, in the authors' view, tantamount to denying a Titanic disaster for the whole of civilization.

Exploding population

The world population is said to be 'exploding' (see Figure 2.1). From 500,000 years ago to around 10,000 BC the global population is thought to have remained below 10 million (Borrini-Feyerabend, 1995). At this stage human beings (*homo sapiens*) lived as hunter-gatherers (see Chapter 6). A large increase occurred with the development of agriculture and 2,000 years ago the world population was about 300 million and doubling every 1,240 years. Then a massive acceleration occurred from around 1 billion in 1800 to 6.3 billion in 2004 and is predicted to reach 9 billion in 2050 and plateau at around 11 billion in 2100. It has been speculated that about 5.8% of all people ever born are alive today (Haub, 2002).

The US Census Bureau (2005) publishes an estimate of the world's population on its website daily (www.census.gov/cgi-bin/ipc/popclockw). Over the one-year period, 1 July 2004–1 July 2005, the world population was predicted to increase from 6,372,797,742 to 6,446,131,400, an increase of 73.5 million. *This is a daily increase of around 200,000 people, equivalent to the population of the English city of Southampton sufficient to replace all those killed by the Asian Tsunami in December 2004.*

While population numbers have been increasing, life expectancy has also been increasing almost everywhere and there has been a dramatic decrease in both infant and adult mortality. These improvements have resulted largely from a decline in the occurrence of fatal infectious diseases. Several implications arise from the increasing life expectancy and increasing population. Life expectancy in Britain is currently around 75 years for men and 80 years for women. The retirement age is 65 years for men and 60 for women. A working man can expect 10 years of pensioned retirement on average and a working woman about 20 years. Recent research suggests that life expectancy will increase considerably in the twenty-first century and that it could be as high as 100 years. Research carried out by Oeppen and Vaupel (2002) suggests that life expectancy increases of three months every year are occurring in developed countries (see Figure 2.2).

If this reliable linear trend continues, life expectancy will approach 100 years by about 2060. There is no obvious end to these reliable increases in the developed world. A baby girl born today in France or Japan has a 50% chance of living to the age of 100 years. If life expectancy increases in the twenty-first century to 85, 90 or even 100, this will place our social security, health and pensions systems in a perilous position.

Further reasons to be concerned about social and health care over the next few decades come from demographic studies of the changing age profile of our population.

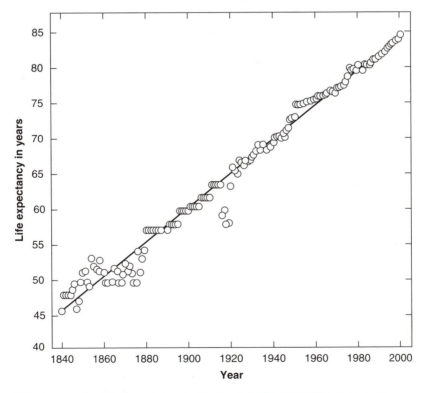

Figure 2.2 Increasing life expectancy in England, 1840–2000 (Oeppen and Vaupel, 2002)

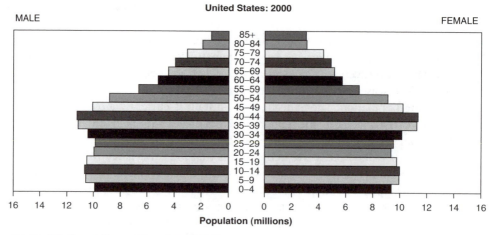

Source: U.S. Census Bureau, International Data Base.

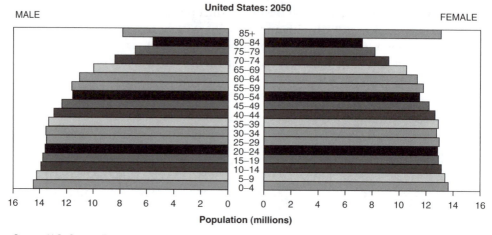

Source: U.S. Census Bureau, International Data Base.

Figure 2.3 A population pyramid for the US population for the years 2000 (upper figure) and 2050 (lower figure) (US Census Bureau. Reproduced with permission.)

This can be represented as a 'population pyramid'. For example, consider the United States, where the number of people older than 85 is predicted to increase dramatically by 2050 (see Figure 2.3).

Poverty

Of the 6.4 billion people living in 2005, approximately 5 billion (81%) are living in developing countries. World **poverty** is on a massive scale. One billion people are living on less than one dollar per day – that is, one in every six people worldwide. For them, health services and modern medicines are out of reach. Many initiatives that have attempted to improve the health of people in extreme poverty have failed (World Bank, 2004).

The United Nations Development Programme defines poverty as 'a level of income below that people cannot afford a minimum, nutritionally adequate diet and essential non-food requirements' (United Nations Development Programme, 1995). Half of the world's population lacks regular access to treatment of common diseases and most essential drugs. In the mid-1990s there were approximately 15 million refugees and 15 million internally displaced persons.

Poverty is the greatest cause of ill-health and early mortality. The health effects of poverty are tangible everywhere and the biological and socio-economic mechanisms are everywhere the same. The major impacts of poverty on health are caused by the absence of:

- safe water;
- environmental sanitation;
- adequate diet;
- secure housing;
- basic education;
- income generating opportunities;
- access to health care.

The most common health outcomes are infectious diseases, malnutrition and reproductive hazards (Anand and Chen, 1996). A major killer disease is acquired immune deficiency syndrome (AIDS) (Figure 2.4). In 2004, 6 million people living with HIV/AIDS in developing countries urgently needed access to antiretroviral treatment (ART). The World Health Organization (WHO) began the '3 by 5 Initiative' because in 2004 less than 10% of sufferers had access to ART. WHO set a target of 3 by 5 – providing access

Figure 2.4 Frank, AIDS orphan, and grandma Suzan (WHO/Dieter Telemans. from the 'River of life' photo gallery; reproduced with permission)

to ART to 3 million people living with HIV/AIDS in developing countries by the end of 2005. Inevitably such a programme will lead to controversy. What criteria are to be used in deciding which 3 million people receive this expensive medicine? In July 2004 WHO stated that it hoped to extend its free drugs programme beyond 2005 to reach the 3 million other AIDS victims who also need help. Further discussion of HIV/AIDS can be found in Chapters 9 and 17.

Inequity and Growth

Economic growth is the rate of increase in the total production of goods and services within an economy. Such growth increases the capacity of an economy to produce new goods and services allowing more needs and wants to be satisfied. A growing economy increases employment, stimulates business enterprise and innovation. Sustained growth is fundamental to the raising of living standards and to providing greater quality of life. **Gross national income (GNI)** is defined as the monetary value of all goods and services produced in a country over a year. GNI is a useful indicator for measuring growth.

KT

It might be expected that economic growth should lead to increasing prosperity for all and even to a reduction of **inequalities**. A World Bank study of 21 developing countries over the period 1950–85 by Lal and Myint (1996) made a distinction between 'mass structural poverty', 'destitution' and 'conjunctural poverty'. Lal and Myint found that in all countries studied, growth in income per capita led to the alleviation of mass poverty. They found that growth does 'trickle down', and that when growth collapses there is increasing poverty. However, Lal and Myint found no clear connection between changes in inequality and growth performance.

This economic research means that, while the level of mass poverty tends to be reduced by economic growth, *disparities in wealth across a society are not reduced by growth*. World Bank data even suggest that, over two decades, growth-orientated structural adjustment programmes have worsened inequality in many cases (Shakow and Irwin, 1999). This is a hard fact of life that can be difficult to accept from a social justice perspective (see Chapter 3) and it has many knock-on effects for human health.

KT

GNI and **income distribution**, therefore, appear to operate independently of each other. It has been established for many years that health and GNI are highly related. Recently some interest was generated by the hypothesis that income distribution also played a role in the health of a society (Wilkinson, 1996). Income distribution can be measured by computing the percentage share of income or consumption taken by the lowest and highest income groups in a society. For example, in one of the poorest countries, Tanzania, in 1991 the best off 20% of households controlled 62.7% of the country's income while the worst off 20% controlled only 2.4% of income (World Bank, 1993). In one of the richest nations, the USA, income inequality is not only huge but continues to grow. According to US Census Bureau (2005) data, in 1967 the lowest 20% of the population had 4% of aggregate income while the top 20% had 43.8%. By 2001 the lowest 20% share had dropped to 3.5% and the share of the richest 20% had grown to 50.1%. Further, the top 5% households had 17.5% of income in 1967 and 22.4% in 2001.

It was argued by Wilkinson (1996) that the average life expectancy is higher when income differences are relatively small and societies are more socially cohesive. It has also been suggested that the same basic principles determine the health of populations in both rich and poor countries (Rodgers, 1979). Recent analyses suggest that Wilkinson's findings and also Rodgers' are unreliable for a variety of methodological and statistical reasons (Deaton, 2001). [For a discussion of income distribution effects on health, see Carroll, Davey Smith and Bennett (1996), Reading 10 in Marks (2002a).] However, this is still an area for research. Recent evidence suggests that such a relationship does exist for infant mortality in many wealthy countries (Lynch et al., 2000) and for all mortality in the USA (Ross et al., 2000). Further, the focus on income inequality in research may have led to a lack of emphasis on other measures of social inequality. As Lynch and Davey Smith stress: 'social inequality is multidimensional – it is not limited to income differences – and is expressed in education, occupation, housing, access to services, and discrimination according to ethnicity, gender and age' (2002: 550). There is a need for health psychology to explore further the psychosocial dimensions of health inequality (see also Chapter 3).

Poverty is linked to debt and trade justice

If poverty levels are to be significantly reduced it is necessary for wealthier countries to allocate more resources to the development of their poorer neighbours. However, if such development is to be really significant, further loans may not be the best way forward. It is also necessary for the richer countries of the North to practise trade justice.

If the WHO's Health For All strategy is going to have any chance of success, health must be given a higher priority in global development policies. International debt is a significant factor in poverty. Sub-Saharan Africa contains 34 of the 41 most indebted countries, and the proportion of people living in absolute poverty (on under one dollar per day) is growing. The health of sub-Saharan Africans is among the worst in the world. Consider the following indicators:

- Two-thirds of Africans live in absolute poverty.
- More than half lack safe water.
- Seventy per cent are without proper sanitation.
- Forty million children are not in primary school.
- Infant mortality is 55% higher than in other low-income countries.
- Average life expectancy at 51.
- The incidence of malaria and tuberculosis is increasing.

A large part of the cause of these problems is sub-Saharan Africa's large international debts. It spends at least four times more on servicing debt repayments than on health care. The worst case is Mozambique, which in 1998 owed nearly five times more than its annual national income. UNICEF estimated that 500,000 children were dying every week because of the debt crisis (Logie and Benatar, 1997). In 1995 the Jubilee 2000 campaign was started in the UK with the aim of getting the unpayable debt of 50 of the world's poorest nations written off by the end of the year 2000. This would cost no more than US$100 billion, about the same as the amount that in 1997 the International Monetary Fund (IMF) promised to loan one country, South Korea, because its economic collapse threatened the value of stocks on financial markets in New York, London and Tokyo.

The World Bank's (1993) *World Development Report 1993: Investing in Health* contains evidence that the post-1950 decline in mortality in developing countries can be attributed to policies that:

- make investments to reduce poverty;
- make health expenditure more cost effective;
- increase the effectiveness of public health measures;
- improve essential clinical services;
- improve schooling, particularly for girls;
- improve the rights and status of women.

At the United Nations in 2000, 189 countries adopted the 'Millennium Development Goals', including halving poverty rates by 2015, reducing child mortality, decelerating the growth of AIDS and educating all children. A statement in April 2004, by the policy-making development committee of the World Bank and International Monetary Fund, declared that most of the Millennium Development Goals would not be met by most developing countries, particularly in sub-Saharan Africa. A World Bank study found the proportion of people living in dire poverty was nearly halved in the two decades to 2001 but progress was uneven, with millions in Africa and Latin America remaining poor but with good progress in Asia.

The greatest progress has been made in China and India. It is expected that the world poverty rate in 1990 of 28% will be reduced by half by 2015. However, poverty in the 20-year period worsened in sub-Saharan Africa. The number of people living on less than one US dollar per day increased from 164 million – 42% of the population – to 314 million, or 47%. In Latin America and the Caribbean, the proportion of poor in 2001 was about the same as in 1981, at around 10%.

The evidence suggests that, in addition to new biomedical discoveries and technologies, some dramatic economic changes are needed if we are to experience further health improvements during the twenty-first century. Among these changes, the cancellation of unpaid debts of the poorest countries and trade justice would have the potential to bring health improvements to match those of the last 50 years. Yet it may be the case that health improvements are a pre-condition of economic growth, as suggested by the evidence collected by the WHO Commission on Macroeconomics and Health. The Commission Report stated that: 'in countries where people have poor health and the level of education is low it is more difficult to achieve sustainable economic growth' (WHO, CMH Support Unit, 2002). Sadly, therefore, if current trends continue, the health of many national populations in sub-Saharan Africa may worsen (see below).

Inequalities in Poor Countries

Many of the determinants of ill-health among developing countries in the twenty-first century were originally identified by Chadwick in Victorian England: poverty, housing, water, sewerage, the environment, safety and food. So what's new? In addition, there are illiteracy, tobacco, AIDS/HIV, and lack of access to immunization, medication and health care.

The universality of **health gradients** across human societies is evidenced by information from the Demographic and Health Surveys (DHS) programme of the World Bank (2002) (Marks, 2004). The DHS collect data on a large number of health, nutrition, population and health service utilization measures, as well as on the respondents' demographic, social and economic characteristics. The DHS are large-scale household sample surveys carried out periodically in 44 countries across Asia, Africa, the Middle East, Latin America and the former Soviet Union. The DHS use a standard set of questionnaires to collect individual, household and community level data. Socio-economic status is evaluated in terms of data concerning assets gathered through the DHS questionnaire that is typically answered by the head of each household. The asset score is generated from the household's ownership of a number of consumer items ranging from a fan to a television and car; dwelling characteristics such as flooring material; type of drinking water source and toilet facilities used; and other characteristics that are related to wealth status.

Each household asset is assigned a weight or factor score generated through principal components analysis. The resulting asset scores are standardized and then used to define wealth quintiles. Each household is assigned a standardized score for each asset, where the score differed depending on whether or not the household owned that asset (or, in the case of sleeping arrangements, the number of people per room). These scores are summed for each household, and individuals are ranked according to the total score of the household in which they reside. The sample is then divided into population asset wealth quintiles – five groups with the same number of individuals in each.

The under-5 mortality rates (U5MRs) for the five asset quintiles for 22 countries in sub-Saharan Africa are shown in Figure 2.5. The U5MR indicator is defined as the number of deaths to children under 5 years of age per 1,000 live births. This figure shows death gradients in all countries in this region. A wide gap in health outcomes

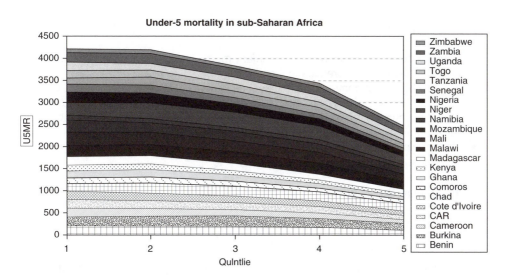

Figure 2.5 Under-5 mortality rates in 22 countries in sub-Saharan Africa across wealth quintiles (1 = richest; 5 = poorest) (Marks, 2004)

exists between the rich and the poor even within these very poor countries. Similar gradients exist throughout the 44 countries included in the DHS.

Marks (2004) found that the U5MRs in the 44 countries in the DHS were positively correlated with female illiteracy rates (0.69, $p < .0001$) and the proportion of households using bush, field or traditional pit latrines (0.60, $p < .0001$) and negatively correlated with the proportion of households having piped domestic water (–0.65, $p < .0001$), national health service expenditure (–0.33, $p < .01$), the number of doctors per 100,000 people (–0.51, $p < .0001$), the number of nurses per 100,000 people (–0.35, $p < .01$), and immunization rates (–0.27, $p < .05$).

This study suggests that the most significant predictors of infant survival are educational and environmental. Having high literacy among the female population and widespread access to domestic water supplies and toilets are both highly associated with low infant mortality. Health service variables such as high numbers of doctors and nurses, immunization rates and health service expenditure are associated with lower mortality rates, but to a lesser degree than high literacy and access to domestic water and sanitation.

Ill-health and poverty as a vicious circle, conflict and climate change

Soucat and Yazbeck (2002) have suggested that poverty and ill-health are a vicious circle: ill-health causes poverty and poverty causes ill-health. This scenario is represented in Box 2.1.

BOX 2.1

ILL-HEALTH AND POVERTY ARE IN A VICIOUS CIRCLE (SOUCAT AND YAZBECK, 2002)

Poverty leads to ill-health:

- Seventy per cent of the variance in infant mortality can be attributed to across and within country differences in income.
- Half the burden of communicable diseases is concentrated in the poorest 20%.
- Globally the poorest 20% experience three and a half times the mortality and four times the number of DALYs (Disability Adjusted Life Years) loss of the richest 20%, an equivalent to excess mortality of nearly 10 million deaths a year.
- Communicable diseases are responsible for 60% both of deaths and DALYs loss in the poorest groups.

Ill-health leads to poverty:

- Africa's income growth per capita is being reduced by about 0.7% per year because of HIV/AIDS.
- A 20% loss of GNP in sub-Saharan Africa may be attributed to malaria.
- Studies in East Africa show that 50% of financial crises in poor families are triggered by illnesses such as TB, HIV and severe malaria.

One major consequence of inequality is conflict, including full-scale war and terrorism. Different social groups are divided by wealth, geography, class, culture and/or religion. When the exercise of political and economic power by one group over another becomes intolerable, the offended group may seek redress through violent means and civil war (Cohen, 1974). Stewart (2002) describes four causes of within-state wars: group motivation, private motivation, failure of the social contract and environmental, or green, war. The first concerns the motives, resentments and ambitions of groups in competing for resources (Horowitz, 1985; Stewart, 2001). Inequality between groups is a reliable feature of civil unrest with consistent evidence of horizontal inequalities of power, wealth and influence between warring groups (Nafziger et al., 2000).

Stewart concludes:

> Reducing large horizontal inequalities is essential to eliminate a major source of conflict. Policies that diminish private incentives to fight, especially once conflict is under way, are also needed. Above all, there is a need to secure inclusive government from political, economic, and social perspectives and a flourishing economy so that all major groups and most individuals gain from participation in the normal economy. (2002: 345)

Stewart suggests that the same argument applies to the international situation including the sharp economic and social differences that exist between rich and poor societies.

In the future, the incidence of infectious diseases and shortages of food and water may be exacerbated by global warming. Gastrointestinal infections by a range of organisms, including bacteria that cause typhoid and cholera, are more common in hotter weather. Many infectious diseases are caused by parasites or viruses transmitted by carriers, for example, insects transmit conditions such as malaria, dengue, and yellow fever. Many of these carriers are sensitive to heat and humidity, so an increase in one or both will put a larger proportion of the population at risk. Computer models predict the proportion of the world's population potentially at risk from malaria will increase from 45% to 60% later this century (Hartog, 2001). The impact on countries that could not afford counter-measures could be devastating as currently some 300 to 500 million people are infected with malaria from which 2 million (mainly young children) die each year (Martens et al., 1995).

Mooney (2004) has described the resistance and complacency with which global warming is treated by the public at large and the majority of politicians. The concept of human-caused, or anthropogenic, global warming has been poorly communicated to and understood by the public at large. The 'greenhouse effect' in which atmospheric gases like carbon dioxide trap the earth's heat and prevent it from escaping is a well-established phenomenon. Atmospheric carbon dioxide levels have been steadily rising as a consequence of fossil fuel emissions, and in 2004 stand at 380 parts per million (ppm) and there has been an associated one degree Fahrenheit rise in global temperatures between the early 1800s and the present, with most of the change occurring in the past decade. Carbon dioxide levels have not exceeded 300 ppm for the last 400,000 years. By 2040 or 2060, it is projected that the figure will reach 500 ppm (Mooney, 2004).

Climate change is predicted to increase food production at high and mid-latitudes but decrease it at lower latitudes. Food production will be reduced in the tropics, where there are regions that are currently barely able to feed their populations due to high temperature, pests and lack of water. One climate change scenario in Africa has predicted that that there will be an additional 55 to 65 million people at risk of hunger by the 2080s (Parry and Rosenzweig, 1999). The number of people affected by water shortages, currently about 1.7 billion, is also expected to rise sharply (Hartog, 2001).

Against these gloomy prospects, the World Bank (2002) has set ambitious goals for the 25 year period, 1990–2015:

> We know what needs to be done to reduce infant and child deaths. Malnutrition, unsafe water, war and civil conflict, and the spread of HIV/AIDS all contribute to the annual toll. And immunization, disease prevention, and campaigns to teach treatment of diarrhea can all help to reduce deaths.
>
> There are large and persistent differences in mortality rates between regions and progress has been too slow to achieve a two-thirds reduction by 2015. Mortality rates in Africa, which had been falling, are now higher on average than in 1990. (World Bank, 2002: 1)

It is difficult to imagine how these targets will be met unless the richest countries have the political will to help to make them happen.

Reallocation of military expenditure as a solution to world poverty?

If ill-health and poverty really are a vicious circle, how can that circle be broken? Of the greatest importance is the redistribution of wealth between the rich and the poor countries to reduce poverty. The rich countries may claim that they are already giving enough funds in the form of official development assistance (ODA). However, in 2001, members of the Development Assistance Committee of the Organization for Economic Cooperation and Development (OECD), consisting of 23 of the richest countries, gave an average of 0.22% of gross national income (Human Development Report, 2003). The country giving the lowest percentage was the USA (0.11%). The amount of ODA as a percentage of GNI is rising slightly over time (World Development Report, 2000/2001). In comparison, the high-income OECD countries are allocating an average of 1.7% of their GNI on military expenditure. In absolute terms that is $404.41 billion per annum on military expenditure and only $52.336 billion on aid. These priorities need to be re-evaluated.

One of the most significant causes of ill-health in the poor world is lack of clean drinking water. In discussing the world water shortage Daudpota (2000) points out that only 2.5% of the water on this planet is freshwater, two-thirds being locked in glaciers and icecaps. Less than one-hundredth of one per cent is drinkable and renewed each year through precipitation. As the global population climbs from 6 billion to 9 billion by 2050 the amount of drinkable water available per person will fall by 33%. The increased shortage will affect mainly the poor where the water shortage is already most acute. More than a billion people lack potable water, and nearly 3 billion lack even minimal sanitation. As stated above, under-5 mortality rates are significantly related to the proportion of households using bush, field or traditional pit latrines and negatively with the proportion of households having piped domestic water. The WHO estimates that 250 million cases of water-related diseases such as typhoid and cholera arise annually, resulting in 2–5 million deaths. It is estimated that 34–76 million people could die from these causes over the next 20 years. Intestinal worms infect some 1.5 billion people, killing nearly 100,000 a year. Tens of millions of farming families in poor countries cannot afford to irrigate their land, lowering their crop production and leaving them vulnerable to drought. More than doubling annual investment in water supply to $180 billion (Parliamentary Office of Science and Technology, 2002) is necessary, with the focus on sustainable use of water.

If the expenditure of the rich countries on defence were cut by 50%, that would release $200 billion per year for other uses. That would be sufficient capital to give every person on this planet a water supply, and leave $20 billion over for improved health and education. However, the priority being given by the USA and Britain to the 'War Against Terrorism' suggests that such a transformation of foreign policy would be little short of a miracle.

Gender

In this and the next two sections we discuss gender, ethnicity and disability. The vast majority of psychological research on these topics has occurred in the developed world. Major differences occur across place and time in the health prospects of men and women. Recent research has focused on the political, psychosocial and economic implications of gender. A medical textbook from the nineteenth century stated: 'childbearing is essentially necessary to the physical health and long life, the mental happiness, the development of the affections and whole character of women. Woman exists for the sake of the womb' (Holbrook, 1871, pp. 13–14; cited in Gallant et al., 1997). Attitudes have changed and, supported by policy and legislation, women's health is towards the top of the health researcher's agenda. These changes have been supported in the USA by the foundation of the Office of Research on Women's Health (ORWH) by the National Institutes of Health in 1990, leading to special research projects, reports and symposia across many health disciplines including psychology.

In industrialized societies today men die earlier than women but women have poorer health than men (Macintyre and Hunt, 1997). In 1996 in the UK boys had a life expectancy of 74.4 years compared with 79.7 years for girls. This excess mortality of 5.3 years in males in 1996 increased over the course of the twentieth century from only 3.9 years in 1900–1910. However, the evidence suggests that from the paleolithic period to the industrial revolution men lived longer than women, 40 years as compared to 35. Also, in less developed countries (e.g. India, Bangladesh, Nepal and Afghanistan) men still live longer than women (WHO, 1989). Thus, there are significant historical and regional differences in gender-related health. To complicate the picture further, the socio-economic status (SES)–mortality gradient appears to be steeper for men than for women while illness rates, treatment rates, absenteeism and prescription drug use are generally higher for women (Macintyre and Hunt, 1997).

Women have higher morbidity rates but lower mortality rates. Women suffer more non-fatal chronic illnesses and more acute illnesses. They also make more visits to their family physicians and spend more time in hospital. Women suffer more from hypertension, kidney disease and autoimmune diseases such as rheumatoid arthritis and lupus (Litt, 1993). They also suffer twice the rate of depression. Men, on the other hand, have a shorter life expectancy, suffer more injuries, suicides, homicides and heart disease.

In addition to biological factors, the political and economic causes of gender-related health differences are complex and multi-faceted. These differences need to be considered in their full context, including policy issues, SES, psychosocial factors, lifestyle differences, life cycle changes and violence. Chronic conditions such as cancer, depression and anxiety also show gender-related differences that merit theoretical analysis.

Psychosocial and lifestyle differences are likely to play a major role in mediating gender-related health differences. In industrialized societies women suffer more from poverty, stress from relationships, childbirth, rape, domestic violence, sexual discrimination, lower status work, concern about weight and the strain of dividing attention between competing roles of parent and worker. Financial barriers may prevent women, more than men, from engaging in healthier lifestyles and desirable behaviour change (O'Leary and Helgeson, 1997).

Social support derived from friendships, intimate relationships and marriage, although significant, appears to be of less positive value to women than to men. Although physical and mental well-being generally benefit from social support, women often provide more emotional support to their families than they receive. Thus, the loss of a spouse has a longer and more devastating effect on the health of men than on that of women (Stroebe and Stroebe, 1983). The burden of caring for an elderly, infirm or dementing family member also tends to be greater for females in the family than for males, especially daughters (Grafstrom, 1994). Gallant et al. (1997) have made a useful review of the literature on the psychological, social and behavioural influences on health and health care in women. While the health of women is a focus for renewed efforts in health care, the health of men cannot be taken for granted. Men are more likely to suffer diseases of the cardiovascular system, more often suffer a violent death and die younger. More research is needed on the health of men, why they suffer more from alcoholism and drug dependency, and why they are so reluctant to seek health from professionals.

Ethnicity

Empirical evidence suggests that the health of minority ethnic groups is generally poorer than that of the majority of the population. This pattern has been consistently observed in the USA between African-Americans (or blacks) and whites for at least 150 years (Krieger, 1987). There has been an increase in income inequality in the USA that has been associated with a levelling off or even a decline in the economic status of African-Americans. The gap in life expectancy between blacks and whites widened between 1980 and 1991 from 6.9 years to 8.3 years for males and from 5.6 years to 5.8 years for females (National Center for Health Statistics, 1994). Under the age of 70, cardiovascular disease, cancer and problems resulting in infant mortality account for 50% of the excess deaths for black males and 63% of the excess deaths for black females (Williams and Collins, 1995). Similar findings exist in other countries. Analyses of three censuses from 1971 to 1991 have shown that people born in South Asia are more likely to die from ischaemic heart disease than the majority of the UK population (Balarajan and Soni Raleigh, 1993).

There are many possible explanations for these persistent health differences between people of different races who live in the same country and are served by the same educational, social, welfare and health-care systems (Williams and Collins, 1995; Williams et al., 1997). First, the social practice of **racism** means that minority ethnic groups are the subject of discrimination at a number of different levels. Such discrimination could lead directly or indirectly to health problems additional to any effects related to SES, poverty, unemployment and education. Discrimination in the health-care system exacerbates the impacts of social discrimination through reduced access to the system and poorer levels of communication resulting from language differences.

Second, ethnocentrism in health services and health promotion favours the needs of majority over minority groups. The health needs of members of minority ethnic groups are less likely to be appropriately addressed in health promotion that in turn leads to lower adherence and response rates in comparison to the majority population. These problems are compounded by cultural, lifestyle and language differences. For example, if interpreters are unavailable, the treatment process is likely to be improperly understood or even impaired and patient anxiety levels will be raised. The lack of permanent addresses for minority ethnic group families created by their high mobility makes communication difficult so that screening invitations and appointment letters are unlikely to be received.

Third, health status differences related to race and **culture** are to a large extent mediated by differences in SES. Studies of race and health generally control for SES and race-related differences frequently disappear after adjustment for SES. Race is strongly correlated with SES and is even sometimes used as an indicator of SES (Williams and Collins, 1995; Modood et al., 1997).

Fourth, differences in health-protective behaviour may occur because of different cultural or social norms and expectations. Fifth, differences in readiness to recognize symptoms may occur also as a result of different cultural norms and expectations. Sixth, differences could occur in access to services. There is evidence that differential access to optimal treatment may cause poorer survival outcomes in African-Americans who have cancer in comparison to other ethnic groups (Meyerowitz et al., 1998; see Box 2.2). Seventh, members of minority ethnic groups are more likely to inhabit and work in unhealthy environments because of their lower SES. Eighth, there could be genetic differences between groups that lead to differing incidence of disease and some diseases are inherited. There are several well-recognized examples, including sickle cell disorder affecting people of African-Caribbean descent, thalassaemia, another blood disorder that affects people of the Mediterranean, Middle Eastern and Asian descent, and Tay-Sachs disease that affects Jewish people.

Other possible mechanisms underlying **ethnicity** differences in health are differences in personality, early life conditions, power and control, and stress (Williams and Collins, 1995; Taylor et al., 1997). Research is needed with large community samples so that the influence of the above variables and the possible interactions between them can be determined. Further research is needed to explore the barriers to access to health care that exist for people from different groups (see Box 2.2).

BOX 2.2

A BEHAVIOURAL MODEL OF ACCESS TO HEALTH CARE

Andersen and Newman (1973) developed a behavioural model of health services use and suggested that access to care was determined by different characteristics of people including predisposing factors (e.g. age, gender, education, ethnicity, health beliefs), enabling factors (e.g. having a regular source of medical care and health insurance) and need (e.g. their perceptions of their health and physician's judgements about their need for care).

The model evolved from using a simple measure of access (e.g. whether or not people see a physician or are admitted to a hospital) to one stressing whether access is effective (e.g. improves people's health) and efficient (can be effective and still contain costs). Andersen focused on access for vulnerable population groups (e.g. homeless persons and people with HIV) and understanding how community and organizational factors (as well as personal characteristics) influence access to care and why there are such large ethnic differences in health and access to care.

Disability

Current estimates suggest that the global population of people with disabilities is between 235 million and 549 million individuals (Metts, 2000). However, its accurate measurement is beset with problems. The theoretical and methodological issues surrounding the measurement of disability are covered in depth within the disability literature (e.g. Albrecht et al., 2001; D. Marks, 1999a, b) but they include: variations in definitions and measurement systems (e.g. functional limitation versus disease/impairment presence); lack of data and inadequate analyses of available data; blurring of the concepts of illness and disability; and an over-reliance on self-report measures leading to under-reporting (e.g. chronic conditions individuals have adapted to or perceive as concomitants of old age and mental health conditions tend not be reported as disabilities). Despite these and many other issues relating to the availability of data on disability and health, it is generally thought that people with disabilities make up around 10% of the population.

The experiences of disabled people are in many ways similar to the experiences of other disadvantaged groups. As with racism experienced by ethnic minorities and gender discrimination experienced by women, the social practice of 'disablism' results in discrimination against people with disabilities at many levels.

In an influential paper Verbrugge and Jette (1994) discuss the 'disablement process' that (1) describes how chronic and acute conditions affect functioning in specific body systems, generic physical and mental actions, and activities of daily life, and (2) describes the personal and environmental factors that speed or slow disablement, namely, risk factors, interventions and 'exacerbators'. Disability is defined as 'difficulty doing activities in any domain of life (from hygiene to hobbies, errands to sleep) due to a health or physical problem' (p. 1). Verbrugge and Jette distinguish between 'intrinsic disability' (without personal or equipment assistance) and 'actual disability' (with such assistance). Disability should therefore not be viewed as a personal characteristic, but as *a gap between personal capability and environmental demand*. Researchers and clinicians previously tended to overlook the efforts people make to reduce demand by activity accommodations, environmental modifications, psychological coping and external supports. Verbrugge and Jette compared the disablement experiences of people who acquire chronic conditions early in life (lifelong disability) and those who acquire them in mid- or late life (late-life disability).

The psychological effects of discrimination, prejudice and physical and social exclusion affect health outcomes negatively, over and above the effects of the disability itself or SES and poverty-related factors. The link between disability and SES factors is well established. People with disabilities are two to three times more likely to be unemployed and to stay unemployed for longer than non-disabled people. They are more likely to suffer poverty, debt, exclusion from or restriction to lower status work and poorer education (e.g. Metts, 2000).

As described earlier, these factors are consistently associated with poorer health outcomes, although these relationships are not unidirectional. The link between disability and poverty appears to be two-way: people with disabilities are at increased risk of poverty (mediated by employment status) but poverty also increases the risk of disability (mediated by factors such as diet, housing quality etc.). Marginalization and exclusion from services, and from social and community activities, can also make people with disabilities and their families worse off. Many people with disabilities also incur additional costs related to their disability (e.g. medicines, equipment, travel, services and care costs).

The consequences of disability do not affect people with disabilities alone; it also impacts upon their families economically, socially, psychologically and health-wise. The UK 1995 General Household survey reported there were 5.7 million carers (of which they estimated as many as 50,000 were young carers). The risks relating to the caring role include loss of employment and earnings and the associated reductions in living standards and increased poverty, as well as health problems. The National Carers Association has stated that 52% of carers (about 3 million) were treated for stress-related illnesses in 1998. Grant (1995) found that carers often neglected their own needs for food, warmth and social contact while striving to meet the needs of a person suffering from disability.

The process of accessing welfare benefits is another important issue for many people with disabilities. While benefits may help to alleviate the effects of poverty experienced by people with disabilities and their families, there is substantial evidence that, where available, disability benefit programmes have a poor take-up rate. In the UK, it is estimated that some 50% of people with disabilities are not receiving benefits to which they are entitled, equating to some £6 billion in disability living allowance alone. Similarly, an estimated £660 million in carers' allowance goes unclaimed each year (Carers Online, 2003). Apart from literature on the link between poverty and disability, there is a dearth of mainstream literature on the psychological and health-related aspects of (frequent and repetitive) engagement with welfare benefit systems for people with disabilities and their carers. However, there is considerable reference to these issues in experiential studies, the grey literature and the disability arts arena (e.g. Maynard Campbell and Maynard Lupton, 2000). There is an opportunity for health psychology to address this gap in the academic literature.

Disability may not be the only source of disadvantage negatively impacting on the health of a person with a disability. In a recent publication, Berthoud (2003) argues that there are six sources of disadvantage relating directly to employment – family structure, skill level, impairment, age, labour-demand and ethnic group – and that they have additive effects. These sources of disadvantage also relate directly to disability, and gender is a seventh interacting factor. The impact of multiple illness/disability conditions must also be considered (e.g. Berthoud (2003) reports the greater the number of impairments the higher the risk of unemployment). Currently data is lacking concerning disability and the effects of multiple disadvantages and secondary conditions, how they interact with each other and how they independently and cumulatively impact on health.

Implications for Health Psychology

This chapter has introduced some of the principal global demographic, economic and social factors that are impacting upon health behaviour and experience. We have discussed inequalities of health experience as a consequence of poverty, gender, ethnicity, and disability. In comparison to many of the areas discussed later in this volume, the topics of this chapter are relatively neglected within health psychology. We saw in Chapter 1 that the widely adopted definition of health psychology by Matarazzo (1982) includes 'the analysis and improvement of the health care system and health policy formation'. We also discussed in Chapter 1 the four layers of influence in Dahlgren and Whitehead's (1991) framework consisting of:

Level 1: individual lifestyle;
Level 2: social and community influences;
Level 3: living and working conditions;
Level 4: general socio-economic, cultural and environmental conditions.

This chapter has been concerned with Level 4 and the improvements to health policy that are necessary to improve the health experience of 5 billion people who live in the developing countries of the South. The countries and institutions of the North have no special insulation against the demographic and economic factors outlined here. Profound changes in how global health and social systems can operate to protect the health of citizens must occur. Fifty years, or two generations, is a thin slice of time in which to see a 50% expansion of the world population. The large proportion of this expansion to around 9 billion will be among the poor countries of the developing South. And while this is happening, life expectancy will be increasing almost everywhere. Western populations may well see life expectancy reaching 100 or more in 2050 or 2060. Yet diseases like AIDS/HIV are not abating in the developing world, and so life expectancy could be in decline in sub-Saharan Africa.

The leaders of international organizations are critical of political leaders who promise much but deliver little when it comes to the prevention of HIV infection and AIDS. While the war against terrorism is receiving huge sums of money, the 'war' against AIDS is receiving relatively little from Washington (see Box 2.3).

BOX 2.3

ANNAN URGES USA TO FIGHT AIDS (BBC NEWS, UK EDITION, 13 JULY 2004 HTTP://NEWS.BBC.CO.UK)

UN Secretary General Kofi Annan called on the United States to show the same commitment to the fight against HIV/Aids as to the war on terror. Terrorism could kill thousands but 'here we have an epidemic that is killing millions', he said in an interview with the BBC. Mr Annan appealed to the US to devote more money to tackling HIV/Aids.

Mr Annan, at the International Aids Conference in Bangkok, singled out Washington for being slow to deliver on its promises. He expressed disappointment that some of the $15 billion earmarked by President George W. Bush to tackle HIV/Aids was not yet going to the global fund – the body set up to raise money for Aids programmes.

'At a time when millions of dollars are being put into the fight against international terrorism, where is the "international solidarity" on Aids?' Mr Annan asked. The BBC reported Mr Annan as saying that the priority now was to move forward, commit more funds, and show leadership – from politicians, private business and the wider community.

On the issues discussed at the Aids conference in Bangkok, Mr Annan said he was distraught about what he called the 'false debate' on whether abstinence or condom use was the best way to prevent the spread of the disease. He said both sides of the argument shared the same objective – to get infection rates down – and it was skewing the issue.

Anita Tiessen, deputy director of Unicef, stated: 'There has not been enough money, but more importantly there hasn't been enough political leadership. It is a complicated disease, and it is complicated to prevent it because it is about sexual behaviour … One of the most critical issues is that children are really being affected. We expect that by the end of the decade there will be 25 million children who are orphans because their parents have died of Aids … These are children who are then not getting an education, possibly having to raise their younger siblings, and very, very much at risk of exploitation by prostitution or trafficking.'

Changes in priorities are necessary if the war against AIDS is to be given as high a priority as the war against terrorism. All those working in health care have good reason to reflect on this issue. Health is a political issue. It incorporates both scientific and moral work, and needs both. Poor health anywhere must be addressed everywhere.

So what are the implications for the future of psychology, and for that of health psychology in particular? If one can be permitted to speculate, much of the research that fills the psychology textbooks of today will be seen as irrelevant to the eras of 2050 and 2100. Some might argue that it is mostly irrelevant already. Current theory and research are dictated by the experience and behaviour of a sub-section of the one in six of the world population, those born on the 'right side of the railway tracks', a mainstream psychology for people who see themselves as living in the 'mainstream'.

For the Brave New Worlds of 2050 and 2100, will these priorities have changed beyond recognition, at least, in the minds of the community of critical workers and scholars? Will global warming, population increases, poverty, longevity, and ideologies of oppression, survival and suffering be major issues on the agenda? Will concepts in vogue today such as 'stress', 'coping', 'resilience', 'hardiness' and 'change' be given wider psychosocial interpretation and meaning? Will theories and research concerned with sustainability, empowerment, altruism, sharing, cooperation, communitarianism, and cultural and religious understanding have come to the fore? Will new concepts, theories and methods have been created to deal with the many significant social and psychological problems of the day? The answer to all of these questions must be 'Yes!' – but it depends on you.

Future Research

1   The causes of poverty and interventions to ameliorate poverty should be *the* priority for economic and social research by international organizations and academic institutions interested in protecting and preserving health.
2   Studies in psychology and sociology must be designed to understand humanitarian values, altruism, oppression, fear, aggression and cross-cultural issues.
3   Possible mechanisms underlying ethnicity differences in health, such as differences in personality, early life conditions, power and control, and stress (Williams and Collins, 1995; Taylor et al., 1997), must be explored. Research is needed with large community samples so that the influence of the above variables and their possible interactions can be determined.
4   Currently data are lacking on disability and the effects of multiple disadvantages and secondary conditions, how they interact with each other and how they independently and cumulatively impact on health.

Summary

1   The world population is exploding. From about 1 billion in 1800 it is predicted to reach 9 billion in 2050 and 11 billion in 2100. Of 6.4 billion people alive in 2005, approximately 5 billion (81%) live in developing countries.
2   As the global population climbs from 6 to 9 billion by 2050 the amount of drinkable water available per person will fall by 33%. The increased shortage will affect mainly the poor where the water shortage is already most chronic. More than a billion people already lack potable water, and nearly 3 billion lack even minimal sanitation.
3   The greatest influence on health for the majority of people is poverty. Half of the world's population lacks regular access to treatment of common diseases and most essential drugs. Globally, the burden of death and disease is much heavier for the poor than for the wealthy.
4   In developed countries life expectancy is increasing by three months every year. If this trend continues, life expectancy will approach 100 years by about 2060. If life expectancy increases in the twenty-first century to 85, 90 or even 100, this will place our social security, health and pensions systems in a perilous position.
5   Economic research suggests that, while the level of mass poverty tends to be reduced by economic growth, disparities in wealth across a society are not reduced by growth.

6 Inequalities in the form of health gradients are a universal feature of the health of populations in both rich, developed and poor, developing countries.

7 If development is to proceed at the kind of pace set by the UN Millennium Development Goals, it will be necessary for wealthier countries to allocate more resources to development of poorer countries. Following the aims of the post-Jubilee 2000 movement, the international debts of the poorest countries ideally should be cancelled so that they can afford to spend more on health care and education.

8 Gender differences in health, illness and mortality are significant and show striking interactions with culture, history and SES.

9 The health of minority ethnic groups is generally poorer than that of the majority of the population. Possible explanations include racial discrimination, ethnocentrism, SES differences, behavioural and personality differences, cultural differences and other factors. Discrimination in the health-care system could exacerbate the impacts of social discrimination by virtue of reduced access to the system, poorer levels of communication and poorer compliance.

10 Ethnocentrism in health services and health promotion marginalizes minority groups leading to lower adherence and response rates in comparison to the majority population. Differences in culture, language, lifestyle, health-protective and health-seeking behaviours are likely to compound the problems of racism and ethnocentrism. Health status differences related to race and culture appear to be partly mediated by differences in SES.

11 The explanation of health variations creates many interesting challenges for future research in health psychology and related disciplines. The reduction of inequalities is a priority for policymakers and service planners. A critical health psychology perspective argues for a transformation of health psychology to encompass an agenda that is relevant to the social struggles of yesterday, today and tomorrow.

Key Terms

KT

culture

ethnicity

gross national income (GNI)

health gradient

income distribution

inequalities

racism

<table>
<tr><td>**3**</td><td># Social Inequalities, Social Justice and Health</td></tr>
</table>

If you tremble with indignation at every injustice then you are a comrade of mine.
(Ernesto 'Che' Guevara)

Outline

There is substantial evidence linking poor social conditions with ill-health. The explanations for this include material, behavioural and psychosocial factors. This chapter considers the extent of social inequalities in health within developed countries, the competing explanations and the role of health psychology in creating a healthier society. The explanation of health inequalities creates many important challenges for theory and research in health psychology. This chapter also considers the concept of disability.

Social Conditions and Health

Early evidence

One of the earliest reports on the relationship between health and social conditions was by the French physician Villerme (1782–1863) who in the 1820s examined the health of residents in different neighbourhoods of Paris. From a careful review of the data he concluded that there was a relationship between the wealth of the neighbourhood and the health of its residents. Those living in the poorer neighbourhoods had a higher death rate and military conscripts from those neighbourhoods were smaller, had more illnesses and disabilities (Krieger and Davey Smith, 2004).

Shortly afterwards Frederich Engels published his classic *The Condition of the Working Class in England in 1844* (Engels, 1845). This book provided a detailed description of the appalling living and working conditions and the limited health care of working-class residents of Manchester. He wrote:

All of these adverse factors combine to undermine the health of the workers. Very few strong, well-built, healthy people are to be found among them ... Their weakened bodies are in no condition to withstand illness and whenever infection is abroad they fall victims to it. This is proved by the available statistics of death rates. (1845/1958: 118–19)

When Engels compared the death rates within the city he found that they were much higher in the poorer districts. Further, he realized the importance of early development and noted: 'common observation shows how the sufferings of childhood are indelibly stamped on the adults' (p. 115).

Although these early researchers realized the importance of the impact of adverse social conditions, interest in the social aspects of health was marginalized with the rise of germ theory and the growth of Social Darwinism (Krieger and Davey Smith, 2004). The former theory focused on controlling specific pathogens rather than social reform whereas the second argued that innate inferiority, not social injustice, was the cause of ill-health. However, the growth of social movements in the 1960s rekindled interest in this field.

Black Report

In 1977 the UK government established a working group to investigate social inequalities in health further. The subsequent **Black Report** (Townsend and Davidson, 1982), named after Sir Douglas Black, the working group chair, summarized the evidence on the relationship between occupation and health. It showed that those classified as unskilled manual workers (Social class V) consistently had poorer health status compared with those classified as professionals (Social class I). Further, the report graphically portrayed a social gradient in health status. It concluded:

KT

> present social inequalities in health in a country with substantial resources like Britain are unacceptable and deserve to be so declared by every section of public opinion ... we have no doubt that greater equality of health must remain one of our foremost national objectives and that in the last two decades of the twentieth century a new attack upon the forces of inequality has regrettably become necessary. (Townsend and Davidson, 1982: 79)

The report not only clearly documented the link between social position and health but detailed four possible explanations:

- Artefact explanations: the relationships between social position are an artefact of the method of measurement.
- Natural and social selection: the social gradient in health is due to those who are already unhealthy falling downwards while those who are healthy rise upwards.
- Materialist and structuralist explanations: these explanations emphasize the important role of economic and associated socio-structural factors.
- Cultural/behavioural explanations: these explanations 'often focus on the individual as the unit of analysis emphasizing unthinking, reckless or irresponsible behaviour or incautious lifestyle as the moving determinant' (p. 23).

While accepting that each explanation may contribute something, the report emphasized the importance of the materialist explanations and developed a range of policy options that could address the inequalities.

Social Inequality and Health

Extent of social inequality

KT

Over the past 20 years there has been a steady increase in **social inequality** in many western societies. In the UK the proportion of individuals living in poverty increased from 15% in 1981 to 24% in 1993/94. There was a slight decline to 22% in 2002/03 but this still represented 12.4 million people (Paxton and Dixon, 2004). Other indicators of social inequality in the UK include:

- The richest people have increased their share of total income. The richest 1% increased their share of income from 6% in 1980 to 13% in 1999.
- The unequal distribution of wealth continues to increase. The percentage of wealth held by the richest 10% of the population increased from 47% in 1990 to 56% in 2001.

In the US there is also evidence of a continuing increase in social inequality. Using a more restrictive definition of poverty, the US Census Bureau estimated that the proportion of Americans living in poverty increased from 11.3% in 2000 to 12.5% in 2003. In households of single mothers, poverty increased from 25.4% in 2000 to 28% in 2003. The inequality in income between the richest and poorest households increased by 3.6% between 2002 and 2003, the largest increase since figures started to be recorded in the 1960s.

There is now a substantial amount of research evidence from dozens of countries linking social inequalities with health. These studies have consistently shown that the life expectancy of those in the lower social classes is lower than those in the higher social classes. There is also evidence that there is a social gradient in morbidity and mortality such that those one step down the social ladder are more unhealthy than those at the top and so on.

This persistent gradient is often referred to as a health gradient. When mortality is the measure, a more apposite term would be 'mortality' or 'death gradient'. 'Death gradients' have been observed in all human societies in both rich/developed countries and in poor/developing countries (Marks, 2004). Such gradients are normally continuous throughout the range of economic variation. If the gradient were stepped, or flat at one end of the range and steep at the other, it could be inferred that the causative mechanism(s) had a threshold value before any of the 'ill-effects' could appear. However there is no evidence of any such thresholds. For the vast majority of data, the gradient is a continuous one. In reviewing health inequalities in 14 countries, Benzeval and colleagues (1995) concluded:

> People who live in disadvantaged circumstances have more illnesses, greater distress, more disability and shorter lives than those who are more affluent. Such injustice could be prevented, but this requires political will. ... Health inequalities are endemic characteristics of all modern industrial societies, but the size of the differential varies between countries and over time, indicating that there is nothing fixed or inevitable about having such a health divide. (1995: xvii)

Socio-economic status

KT

The health variations reflect the social and economic circumstances of individuals. In rich countries one of the most significant factors is **socio-economic status (SES)**. SES

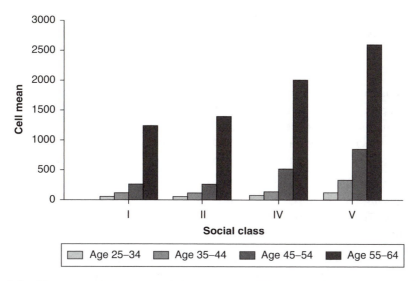

Figure 3.1 Mean annual death rates (all causes) per 100,000 men by age and social class, 1991–93, for England and Wales (computed from Blane et al., 1997: Table 1)

is normally defined in terms of occupation, education or income, but it is a complex and multidimensional construct that defies simple definition.

Data from many quantitative studies show that SES is strongly correlated with illness and mortality. The health gradient such as that shown in Figure 3.1 shows continuously increasing poor health as SES changes from high to low. Figure 3.1 shows male all-cause mortality plotted against social class for England and Wales for 1991–93. Similar gradients exist in the USA and throughout industrialized countries.

The mediators of SES effects on health experience are likely to be behavioural and psychosocial. The behavioural factors include diet, exercise and smoking while the psychosocial factors include such processes as self-efficacy, self-esteem and perceived control (Siegrist and Marmot, 2004).

One of the largest studies exploring the relationship between health and occupation has been the Whitehall Studies. The original Whitehall Study was designed to examine risk factors for coronary heart disease. The Whitehall II Study had as its explicit objective the investigation of this social gradient in health status. It collected data on over 10,000 civil servants and related their health to their position in the civil service. Once again it confirmed the social gradient.

Earlier we mentioned the four primary explanations of the social gradient in health that were outlined in the Black Report. The European Science Foundation (2000) has organized research collaboration into three main clusters:

- Life course influences: this explanation focuses on early life influences. There is increasing evidence on the importance of foetal and early childhood environment on subsequent health status. The deprived social conditions some children experience in their early years have a long-term impact on their later health and social well-being.
- Midlife behaviours and emotions: this explanation focuses on everyday life experiences and working conditions. This dimension considers both material and psychosocial

environment. One particular focus has been on the experiences of stress and perceived control over adverse life events.

- Macro-social factors: this explanation focuses on inequalities in income, community characteristics and other large-scale social processes (Wilkinson, 1996).

It is obvious that no single explanation is sufficient but that a multitude of material, social, and psychological factors contribute to explaining the impact of SES on health.

Health inequalities can be considered from an **ecological approach** or **systems theory approach**. Bronfenbrenner's (1979) ecological approach conceptualized developmental influences in terms of four nested systems:

- *microsystems*: families, schools, neighbourhoods;
- *mesosystems*: peer groups;
- *exosystems*: parental support systems, parental workplaces;
- *macrosystems*: political philosophy, social policy.

These systems form a nested set, like a set of Russian dolls, microsystems within mesosystems, mesosystems within exosystems and exosystems within macrosystems (Figure 3.2).

Ecological theory assumes that human development can only be understood in reference to the structural ecosystems. We described a general systems framework for understanding the determinants of health and illness in Chapter 1 (Figure 1.2). Of key importance is the principle that it is the *perceived environment* and not the so-called 'objective' environment that affects human behaviour and experience.

In Box 3.1 we list some of the characteristics of low SES using Bronfenbrenner's systems approach. The box shows how many different disadvantages there can be across all four systems of the social, physical and economic environment. In addition to these factors, we can add the high levels of perceived injustice that many people with low SES may well feel.

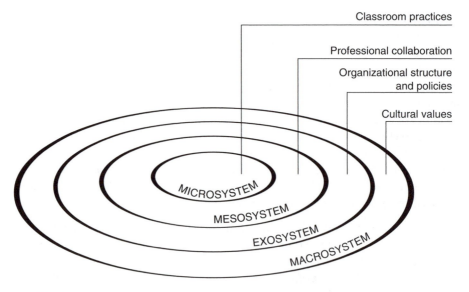

Figure 3.2 Bronfenbrenner's ecological systems model (Odom et al., 1996: 18–30; reproduced with permission)

KT

BOX 3.1

BEHAVIOURS AND EXPERIENCES ASSOCIATED WITH LOW SES

Microsystems: families, schools, neighbourhoods

- low birth weight
- family instability
- poor diet/nutrition
- parental smoking and drinking
- overcrowding
- poor schools and educational outcomes
- poor neighbourhoods

Mesosystems: peer groups

- bullying, gangs and violence
- smoking
- drinking
- drugs
- unprotected sex

Exosystems: parental support systems, parental workplaces

- low personal control
- less social support
- unemployment or unstable employment
- high stress levels
- low self-esteem
- poorer physical and mental health

Macrosystems: political philosophy, social policy

- poverty
- poor housing
- environmental pollution
- unemployment or unstable employment
- occupational hazards
- poorer access to health services
- inadequate social services

Any explanation of the SES–health gradient needs to consider psychosocial systems that structure inequalities across a broad range of life opportunities and outcomes, health, social and educational. As illustrated in Box 3.1, in comparison to someone at the high end of the SES scale, the profile of a low SES person is one of multiple disadvantage. The disadvantages of low SES accumulate across all four ecosystems.

It is this kind of *accumulation* and *clustering* of adverse physical, material, social and psychological effects that could explain the health gradient. While each factor alone can be expected to produce a relatively modest impact on mortality, the combination and interaction of many kinds of ecosystem disadvantage are likely to be sufficiently large to generate the observed gradient.

Studies in many countries have shown that people with lower SES have a higher behavioural risk profile. A study analysed the gradients in behavioural risk factors in 11 European countries using data from the Eurobarometer survey. Inequities between high and low education groups in each country were investigated. A north–south difference in behavioural risk inequalities occurred for heavy smoking and infrequent vegetable consumption in men, with larger inequalities in northern European countries than in southern European countries. This pattern matches the gradients for ischaemic heart disease in men, which also show larger gradients in the north and smaller gradients in the south. The evidence suggests that the behavioural factors of smoking and diet contribute to the SES-related health gradient.

Explanations for Social Inequalities in Health

Much recent work has focused on the relationship between the extent of social inequality in a particular society and the extent of ill-health. This research was particularly developed by Wilkinson (1996) who argued that health was poorer in the more unequal societies. This research has attracted substantial critique and it would seem that the relationship is not so straightforward as was initially conjectured (Lynch et al., 2004). However, as Lynch and Davey Smith (2003) warn, we should be careful not to throw the 'social inequality baby' out with the 'income inequality bathwater'. Rather there is much more to social inequality than inequality of income.

Scientific explanations

Contemporary research into explanations for social inequalities in health has been reviewed by Macinko et al. (2003). Their classification extends the fourfold explanation developed in the Black Report and is summarized in Table 3.1.

KT

The **psychosocial explanations** are considered at the more individual (micro) and the more social (macro) level. At the micro level it is argued that 'cognitive processes of comparison', in particular perceived relative deprivation, contribute to heightened levels of stress and subsequent ill-health. At the macro level psychosocial explanations focus on impairment of social bonds and limited civic participation, so-called social capital (see below), that flows from income inequality. These explanations are particularly favoured by Wilkinson (1996) to explain the social gradient in health.

The neo-material explanations have drawn increased support recently in critiques of the psychosocial approaches (see Macleod and Davey Smith, 2003). They focus on the importance of income and living conditions. At the micro level it is argued that in more unequal societies those worse off have fewer economic resources, leading to increased vulnerability to various health threats. At the macro level high income inequality contributes to less investment in the social and physical environment. Those who favour the neo-material explanations argue that the psychosocial explanations

Table 3.1 *Explanations for the relationship between income inequality and health (Macinko et al., 2003)*

Explanation	Synopsis of the argument
Psychosocial (micro): Social status	Income inequality results in 'invidious processes of social comparison' that enforce social hierarchies causing chronic stress leading to poorer health outcomes for those at the bottom.
Psychosocial (macro): Social cohesion	Income inequality erodes social bonds that allow people to work together, decreases social resources, and results in low trust and civic participation, greater crime, and other unhealthy conditions.
Neo-material (micro): Individual income	Income inequality means fewer economic resources among the poorest, resulting in lessened ability to avoid risks, cure injury or disease, and/or prevent illness.
Neo-material (macro): Social disinvestment	Income inequality results in less investment in social and environmental conditions (safe housing, good schools, etc.) necessary for promoting health among the poorest.
Statistical artefact	The poorest in any society are usually the sickest. A society with high levels of income inequality has high numbers of poor and consequently will have more people who are sick.
Health selection	People are not sick because they are poor. Rather, poor health lowers one's income and limits one's earning potential.

ignore the broad political context within which social and health inequalities are nested.

There are also the artefact and selection explanations of the social inequalities in health. Although these initially attracted attention, there is less support for these arguments today.

Lay explanations

Recently there has been increasing interest in what ordinary people have to say about social inequalities in health. This literature connects with the broader literature on popular health beliefs (Chapter 4). In an early qualitative study of a sample of women in England, Calnan (1987) found that working-class women were reluctant to accept that they were less healthy than middle-class people. As one working-class woman said: 'I think as long as they eat the right foods and do have a proper balanced diet, I mean, even the poorest of people can be just as healthy as the others' (p. 76). Those who did accept that wealthy people had better health attributed it to differential access to health care. Conversely, professional women were more likely to accept the existence of a health gradient and attributed the poorer health of working-class people to low job satisfaction, low wages, poor diet and the hazards of the working environment.

The reluctance of working-class people to attribute the cause of social variation in ill-health to structural factors was explored by Blaxter (1997). Her secondary analysis of a large survey of British health and lifestyle found limited evidence of popular discussion about health inequalities. This was especially the case among people from poorer backgrounds.

Chamberlain (1997) reviewed evidence from qualitative research concerning how people from upper and lower SES positions understand health and illness. These studies interviewed small groups of middle-class and working-class women and men classified on the basis of their occupations. Several differences are evident between these two groups.

Working-class people tend to use more physicalistic terminology in their accounts of health and illness while middle-class people are more mentalistic and person-centred. Contact and communication with professionals can be affected by their class relationship with patients so, not surprisingly, surgeons and doctors are often perceived as 'upper' class by working-class patients, while nurses are seen as more 'down to earth'.

Meanings of health show class-related differences. Working-class men and women see health in a more utilitarian way concerned with an absence of disease, being able to work and get through the day without feeling ill. Middle-class people see health as a value concerned with feeling good and having energy to indulge in leisure activities.

Chamberlain (1997), however, suggests a more complex picture with four differing views of health. The *solitary* view, presented by lower SES participants, sees health as involving only physical components of energy, lack of symptoms and a good diet. The *dualistic* view, held by some lower and higher SES people, sees health as having both physical and mental aspects, which act in parallel and independently of each other. The *complementary* view, presented mainly by upper SES people, sees physical and mental elements as integrated together in an alliance. The *multiple* view, held by higher SES people, sees multiple aspects to health – physical, mental, emotional, social, spiritual – as interdependent, interconnected, in balance in health and out of balance in illness.

Lay explanations about social inequalities in health are apparent from an early age. A study in Scotland (Backett-Milburn et al., 2003) found that children identified social relationships and social life as important as material concerns in explaining health inequalities. This indicated that their direct experiences of relationships and unfairness were important for them in making sense of health inequalities. Further studies are needed to explore the relationship between social positioning and health experience.

Class, race and gender and health inequities

Much of the research on social inequalities in health has focused on differences in income or wealth. As such it has ignored issues of power and politics. A more inclusive approach has been developed by Hofrichter (2003) who considers inequalities in terms of class, gender and race. These three social groupings are linked by issues of social and material exploitation. This approach enables the development of a more expansive approach to explaining health inequities in terms not only of income inequality and poverty but also in terms of institutional racism, gender discrimination, corporate globalization, degradation of the environment, destruction of the public sector, dangerous workplace conditions, and neighbourhood characteristics.

An important factor in explaining these processes is the weakening of working-class power and the strengthening of capital over the past generation. It has been found that greater working-class power and political participation is associated with improved community health (Muntaner et al., 2002). Examples of the negative impact of increased corporate power itemized by Hofrichter include:

economic disinvestment in poor communities, extensive layoffs, mass firings and restructuring, gentrification, targeting of industrial and toxic waste facilities in communities of colour, elimination of protective regulatory structures, profiteering by drug companies seeking to maintain control of patents, financial speculation, use of dangerous technologies, restricting competition, shifting the tax burden to the less fortunate, tax subsidies to wealthy corporations, and failure to improve living conditions for farm workers. (2003: 23)

It is these factors that in turn threaten already weakened communities, leading to further stress and ill-health.

An integrative model has been developed by Coburn (2004). In this class/welfare model issues of income inequality and social cohesion are nested within a broader causal chain. This model argues that over the past 20 years the power of business has increased while that of the working class has declined. This has been achieved through the introduction of neo-liberal policies by the ruling class that have increased income inequality and led to poverty and reduced access to services. In those countries with more social democratic rather than neo-liberal governments the power of capital has been resisted and the impact on health has been less. They have achieved this through a combination of both material and psychosocial advantages.

Health and Place

Although the evidence linking ill-health and poverty is clearly established there is also evidence of regional or area variations. This has given rise to a growing programme of research on health and place that has explored how major structural changes, such as those itemized above, lead to ill-health.

Taylor et al. (1997) have described the features of 'healthy' and 'unhealthy' environments:

> Across multiple environments, unhealthy environments are those that threaten safety, that undermine the creation of social ties, and that are conflictual, abusive or violent. A healthy environment, in contrast, provides safety, opportunities for social integration, and the ability to predict and/or control aspects of that environment. (Taylor et al., 1997: 411)

Unhealthy environments are associated with chronic stress and 'the lower one is on the SES continuum, the greater the amount of hassle and time needed to address basic tasks of living' (Taylor et al., 1997: 419). Diez Roux et al. (2001) investigated how a person's local neighbourhood can act as an independent predictor of health using data from the Atherosclerosis Risk in Communities Study (ARIC Investigators, 1989). Diez Roux investigated the relationship between neighbourhood characteristics and the incidence of coronary heart disease among residents of four localities in the USA. A summary score for the socio-economic environment of each neighbourhood included information about wealth and income, education, and occupation.

During a median of 9.1 years of follow-up, 615 coronary events occurred in 13,009 participants. Residents of disadvantaged neighbourhoods (those with lower summary scores) had a higher risk of disease than residents of advantaged neighbourhoods, even after controlling for personal income, education, and occupation. These findings show that, even after controlling for personal income, education and occupation, living in a disadvantaged neighborhood is associated with an increased incidence of coronary heart disease.

In an accompanying editorial, Marmot (2001) states:

Walk the slums of Dhaka, in Bangladesh, or Accra, in Ghana, and it is not difficult to see how the urban environment of poor countries could be responsible for bad health. Walk north from Manhattan's museum district to Harlem, or east from London's financial district to its old East End, and you will be struck by the contrast between rich and poor, existing cheek by jowl. It is less immediately obvious why there should be health differences between rich and poor areas of the same city. It is even less obvious, from casual inspection of the physical environment, why life expectancy for young black men in Harlem should be less than in Bangladesh. (p. 183)

Ethnic variations in health within rich countries are very large. For example, white men in the 10 'healthiest' counties in the US have a life expectancy above 76.4 years while black men in the 10 least healthy counties have a life expectancy of 61 years in Philadelphia, 60 in Baltimore and New York, and 57.9 in the District of Columbia. The main determinants of the excess deaths among Harlem men are circulatory disease, homicide and HIV infection. However the study by Diez Roux et al. (2001) suggests that socio-economic characteristics of communities, in addition to individual characteristics such as income, education and occupation, are related to the incidence of coronary events.

We have to explain not only why the poorest members of rich societies have higher rates of disease, but also why health follows a social gradient. As indicated above, the usual explanation for inequalities in health is lifestyle. There are clear socio-economic differences in smoking and other unhealthy types of behaviour that are risk factors for coronary artery disease. Yet controlling for these factors had little effect on the socio-economic differences in coronary heart disease in the study by Diez Roux et al. Something in addition to smoking, physical activity, hypertension, diabetes, low-density lipoprotein cholesterol, high-density lipoprotein cholesterol, and body-mass index must be responsible for the differences in the incidence of heart disease

Marmot (2001) states: 'the mind is a crucial gateway through which social influences affect physiology to cause disease. The mind may work through effects on health-related behavior, such as smoking, eating, drinking, physical activity, or risk taking, or it may act through effects on neuroendocrine or immune mechanisms' (p. 203). The Whitehall II Study showed that level of control over one's work was an important predictor of the risk of cardiovascular disease and that it had an important role in accounting for the social gradient in coronary heart disease and depression (Marmot et al., 2001). People who report feeling low control at home and over life circumstances have an increased risk of depression, especially among women in low-status jobs. The findings of Diez Roux et al. (2001) suggest an important target for intervention: the neighbourhood. This finding is exactly what would be expected from a community perspective to health psychology. The studies reviewed above suggest that behavioural, material and local circumstances vary with SES. It is impossible to decide with the presently available information how much each of these causes is contributing to the gradients in illnesses and deaths. Understanding the material, behavioural and locality-based causes and the interactions between the three is a priority for further research.

Three theoretical approaches to the study of health and place have been identified (Curtis and Rees Jones, 1998):

- Hazard exposure: physical and biological risk factors are spatially distributed. This approach posits a direct pathway between hazard exposure and health risk.
- Social relationships: space and place shapes the character of social relationships and in turn psychosocial and behavioural risk factors.
- Sense of place and subjective meanings: this approach considers the shared social meanings people have of their community.

The second explanation connects with the growing literature on social capital while the third is connected with the literature on community identity and community narratives.

Social capital

There is increasing interest in **social capital** as an aid to explaining social variations in health. The concept has been especially promoted by Robert Putnam who used it to characterize civic life in Italy (Putnam et al., 1993). He argued that certain communities had higher degrees of civic engagement, levels of interpersonal trust and norms of reciprocity. Together, these characteristics contributed to a region's degree of social capital. Putnam (2000) subsequently explored the extent of social capital in the USA and argued that over the past generation there has been a steady decline in participation in social organizations and thus a steady decline in social capital.

There have been a series of studies investigating social variations in social capital and its connection with health. States with a low degree of income inequality also have low social capital as measured by group membership and social trust. Further, those states with high rates of social mistrust and low rates of membership of voluntary organizations have higher mortality rates.

A qualitative study by Campbell, Wood and Kelly (1999) compared the **sense of community** engagement in two communities near London. They reported evidence that two aspects of social capital (trust and civic engagement and perceived citizen power) were higher in the 'high health' community while two aspects (local identity and local community facilities) were higher in the 'low health' community. They suggested that certain aspects of social capital, in particular perceived trust and civic engagement, are more health enhancing than others. Whereas Putnam emphasized the importance of voluntary associations, Campbell et al. found that these were rare in both communities. However, whereas the 'low health' community made almost no reference to community-level networks in their community, these phenomena (e.g. residents' association) were important in the 'high health' community.

An important distinction that Putnam (2000) makes is that between bridging and bonding social capital. The former refers to inward looking social ties that bond the community together. Bridging social capital refers to links with diverse groups and provides an opportunity for community members to access power and resources outside their community. Campbell (2004) stresses that both forms of social capital are essential in building healthy communities.

There has been a wide range of criticisms of social capital as an explanatory concept (e.g. Lynch et al., 2000). These include confusion over what exactly the term implies, debates over ways of measuring it, and ignorance of the broader political context.

KT

KT

However, an interest in social relations does not preclude acceptance of the importance of political and material factors. However, Baum (2000) emphasizes caution in the use of the concept in that 'there are dangers that the promotion of social capital may be seen as a substitute for economic investment in poor communities particularly by those governments who wish to reduce government spending' (p. 410).

Community identity

KT

An alternative to the rather behaviourist asssumptions underlying much of the work on social capital is to consider the character of the **sense of community** meaning. The most comprehensive investigation of these processes is the work by Popay and colleagues (Popay et al., 2003). They conducted a detailed ethnographic study of four neighbourhoods in North West England. They found that residents of the more disadvantaged neighbourhoods identified place as the major explanation for health inequalities whereas those in relatively advantaged areas preferred individualistic explanations. However, the residents often suggested a complex interaction of macro-structural, place and lifestyle factors. For example, the residents of the more disadvantaged areas described how macro-structural factors interacted with place-based factors shaping particular lifestyle patterns. The mediating factor linking these factors was often seen as stress.

The way the residents described their communities was categorized into three normative guidelines:

- Relationships: this guideline emphasized the importance of supportive social relationships with neighbours, trust and respect between people, and respect for property.
- Physical dimensions: this guideline referred to aspects of safety, appropriateness, convenience and cleanliness.
- Ontological identity: this guideline is concerned with the relationship between one's sense of identity and place.

These guidelines helped to distinguish between 'good' and 'bad' neighbourhoods. It was not simply the material disadvantage of the neighbourhood but rather the community dynamics and the extent to which the residents could identify with it. The residents of more disadvantaged areas reported more problems with their neighbours and less safety. These residents were also less likely to identify with their neighbourhood.

An important component of this research is the emphasis on the importance of community narratives (Williams, 2003). Attention to these narratives enables the researcher to understand the lived experience of people's lives, of the connections between social and political change and everyday life.

Reducing Inequalities

If inequalities can be reduced at all, the evidence suggests that this will only happen by adopting a thoroughly multi-layered approach. Dahlgren and Whitehead (1991) identified four different levels for tackling health inequalities:

1 Strengthening individuals.
2 Strengthening communities.
3 Improving access to essential facilities and services.
4 Encouraging macroeconomic and cultural change.

These four levels correspond to the four layers of influence in Whitehead's 'onion model' of the determinants of health outlined in Chapter 1 (see Figure 1.2). Extra microsystem and mesosystem levels as in Bronfenbrenner's model could perhaps be added to Whitehead's list. Psychologists do not usually talk quite so simplistically about 'strengthening' individuals; we analyse the personal characteristics and skills associated with positive health (e.g. self-efficacy, hardiness, sense of coherence, social skills). Developing interventions aimed at individual health beliefs and behaviours is a core feature of psychological theory, research and practice.

Interventions aimed at tackling inequalities at an individual level have shown mixed results. There are four possible reasons. First, people living and working in disadvantaged circumstances have fewer resources (time, space, money) with which to manage the process of change. Second, health-threatening behaviours such as smoking tend to increase in difficult or stressful circumstances as they provide a means of coping. Third, there may have been a lack of sensitivity to the difficult circumstances in which people work and live that constrain the competence to change. Fourth, there has been a tendency to blame the victim. For example, cancer sufferers may be blamed for the disease if they are smokers on the grounds that they are responsible for the habit that caused it.

Overall, efforts directed at the individual level have been inconclusive and small scale. Because many health determinants are beyond the control of the individual, psychological interventions aimed at individuals are likely to have limited impact on public health problems when considered on a wider scale. This suggests that there is a need for psychologists to work beyond the individual level, with families, communities, work sites and community groups.

Benzeval et al. (1995) suggested that efforts to tackle inequalities typically have two shortcomings. First, excessive attention is given to the health experiences of white males of working age as compared to women, older people, people with disabilities and minority ethnic groups. More attention must be given to the health concerns of these under-served groups. Second, the policy areas dealt with in detail – housing, income maintenance, smoking and access to health care – are insufficiently comprehensive as an agenda for tackling inequalities. Tackling health inequalities at the level of services to individuals is insufficient. The correction of inequalities in health demands 'a wide-ranging and radical reshaping of economic and social policies' (Benzeval et al., 1995: 140). In other words, policy change at Levels 3 and 4 is required to bring about economic and cultural change.

Stigma

Humans have an innate tendency to categorize and stereotype individuals on the basis of differences between them. This process provides a kind of shorthand for what to expect from another person and how to react towards them. However, categories have a tendency to coalesce into dichotomies, so that people are labelled as male or female, black or white, gay or straight, young or old, healthy or ill, able or disabled (Gordon and Rosenblum, 2001). Such dichotomization implicitly involves judgements about which differences are socially valued, desired and accepted and which are devalued, feared and objectionable and therefore stigmatized.

Stigma refers to unfavourable reactions towards people when they are perceived to possess attributes that are denigrated. Stigmatization is universal, found in all cultures throughout history. The majority of people will experience it at some time, as both the young and the elderly are stigmatized groups. In addition people can be multiply stig-matized, as in the case of HIV/AIDS, which is associated with certain highly stigmatized groups (e.g. homosexuals, sex workers, intravenous drug users) and adds a further source of stigma as well as intensifying existing stigma(s). Stigma involves a pattern of discrediting, discounting, degradation and discrimination, directed at stigmatized people and extending to their significant others, close associates and social groups.

Stigmatization devalues the whole person, ascribing them a negative identity that persists (Miles, 1981), even when the basis of the stigma disappears (e.g. when some-one recovers from mental illness they remain characterized forever as a person who had mental health problems). It is a form of social oppression and operates to disqualify and marginalize stigmatized individuals from full social acceptance and participation. Health-care professionals are as likely to stigmatize as any other group, influencing their behaviour and decision-making in the provision of health care. The consequences of stigma include physical and psychological abuse, denial of economic and employ-ment opportunities, non-seeking or restricted access to services and social ostracism. It is not surprising then that individuals frequently expend considerable effort to combat stigmatization and manage their identities, including passing (acting as if they do not have the stigmatized attribute), covering (de-emphasizing difference), resistance (e.g. speaking out against discrimination) and withdrawal. They may also internalize the stigmatization, feeling considerable guilt and shame and devaluing themselves.

The pervasive western idealization of physical perfection, independence and beauty may play an important role in the constant devaluation of disabled people and people who are ill. Particular characteristics of illness or disability increase stigmatization including perceptions that the condition is the person's own fault (e.g. obesity), incur-able and/or degenerative (e.g. Alzheimer's disease), intrusive, compromises mobility, contagious (e.g. HIV/AIDS) and highly visible. Goffman (1963) distinguished between discredited and discreditable categories of stigma. Discredited refers to conditions that are self-evident, in which the stigma is visible. Discreditable conditions relate to con-ditions where the stigma is not visible but may be discovered, at which point they would become stigmatized. Stigma is also increased when it is perceived to be threat-ening or disruptive (Neuberg et al., 2000), which may account for the high level of stigma associated with mental illness, intellectual disabilities and HIV/AIDS.

The lower value placed on the lives of disabled people can be seen in the way dis-abled people are segregated from the general population including education, hous-ing, employment and transportation. It is also apparent in the way crimes against disabled people are minimized (e.g. discourses of abuse rather than theft/fraud/rape, acquittals and light sentences in cases of 'acceptable' euthanasia). For both disabled people and those with severe or terminal illness, stigma may be central to debates around suicide/euthanasia and abortion (see below). Stigma is a powerful determinant of social control and exclusion. By devaluing certain individuals and groups, society can excuse itself for making decisions about the rationing of resources (e.g. HIV anti-retroviral drugs), services (e.g. health insurance exclusions), research funding/efforts and care (e.g. denying operations to individuals who are obese) to these groups. In terms of the social model of disability, stigmatization may be the main issue concerning disability.

Multidisciplinary research is needed to further explore how stigma is related to health, disability and social justice. Why is recognition of the similarities between stigmatized and non-stigmatized individuals over-ridden and obscured by perceived differences that are devalued? How do different stigmas, particularly health-related stigmas, interact? How is stigma manifested by health-care professionals and what interventions might mitigate the negative effects of stigma?

Lives Worth Living Versus the Right-to-Die

The pervasive devaluation of people with disabilities, and the negative assumptions about their lower quality of life, are central to the current debates about abortion of impaired foetuses and legalization of assisted suicide/euthanasia or the right-to-die. Disability rights organizations champion the argument that abortion decisions should not be made on the basis of foetal impairment indicators whereas they challenge the 'right-to-die' rhetoric on the basis of disability.

The disability movement argues against abortion on the grounds of potential impairment due to the eugenic implications of such a practice (Sharpe and Earle, 2002). The reason for their concern is encapsulated in Singer's quote: 'the killing of a defective infant is not morally equivalent to the killing of a person; very often it is not morally wrong at all' (1993: 184). The new genetic testing and selection technologies allow the identification of suspected foetal impairment during pregnancy and subsequent foetal termination. Shakespeare (1998: 669) argues that such technologies operate as a weak form of eugenics 'via non-coercive individual choices' based on the assumed unacceptable quality of life of disabled people. The rationales for screening and termination include assumptions that people with disabilities are more costly to society, that the lives of children with disabilities are harmful to their families and that some impairments involve a level of suffering and misery that makes life not worth living.

The way professionals describe test results and the influence of the advice they give is also a concern. There is substantial evidence that the advice given, while often subtle, most frequently encourages termination in response to potential impairment results and most testing takes place within a plan-to-abort context. There is a tension between this argument and the feminist position that women have a categorical right to make decisions about their own bodies including the decision to terminate an unwanted pregnancy. However, the disability movement position is not against abortion itself, rather it revolves around the bases upon which the decision is made. Aborting a specific foetus on the basis of a devalued attribute is different from aborting any foetus on the basis of not wanting to have a child at that time (Fine and Asch, 1982). It is unlikely that a woman would be encouraged to terminate a pregnancy because a test indicated the child is likely to have ginger hair; however, the same is not true when a test suggests a possibility of impairment. It is this difference that makes it an issue of discrimination. The disability movement also asserts the rights of disabled women to have children. This fundamental human right is denied to many women, particularly those with cognitive and emotional impairments, as the additional support and resources that they need to allow them to raise a child are often not available. In some countries, forced sterilization still occurs, including Australia, Spain and Japan.

The right-to-die debate revolves around the argument that people with severe or terminal illness and people with disabilities have the right to end their lives when they feel they have become unbearable, and that assisting them to do so should not be illegal. The taken-for-granted assumption that underlies this argument is the belief that the quality of life for such individuals is so severely reduced that it makes it unendurable and is bound up with a rhetoric of the moral imperative to relieve suffering. Such assumptions underlie the decisions of many health-care professionals concerning assisted dying.

A recent review by Gill (2000) challenges this assumption. In general, people with disabilities have rated their quality of life as good to excellent. Lower quality of life ratings may relate more to socio-demographic factors (e.g. poverty, exclusion, lack of social support) than disability per se. Consistently, research has failed to show an association between diminishing quality of life and increasing severity of physical impairment. Many factors mediate quality of life. Overall the research indicates that people with disabilities derive life satisfaction through performing expected social roles, enjoying reciprocal relationships and a sense of living in a reciprocal social world. Despite no empirical basis suggesting compromised quality of life, health-care professionals consistently and significantly underestimate it in people with disabilities. The negative attitudes of these professionals inform their own decision-making and are communicated, directly and indirectly, to their patients and patients' families. Negative attitudes about people with disabilities include underestimating quality of life, underestimating future capabilities (especially for children), overestimating depression, viewing it as a normal and inevitable response (therefore not treating it) and underestimating the functional ability to commit suicide. Health-care professionals have to make explicit decisions about whether to assist a patient who asks for help to die. They also have to make less explicit decisions around provision of life-sustaining treatment (e.g. whether to withhold heart operations for Down Syndrome children). Professionals who most underestimate quality of life also appear to be most likely not to support life-saving treatment. Life-sustaining efforts are often less rigorously applied to infants with severe impairments.

More importantly, the entrenched disability prejudices held by health-care professionals result in unsupported assumptions that the quality of life of people with disabilities is diminished in such a way that it makes it more unendurable, more hopeless and more limited than that of people for whom other factors have diminished their quality of life (e.g. someone whose family have been killed and finds life unbearable without them). In addition, assisting certain people with disabilities to die would not be countenanced. For example, it is unlikely that assisting the survivors of genocide to die would be countenanced, despite them enduring extreme suffering, pain, disability and distress. There are a number of forms of 'assisted-dying' including a person ending their own life by their choice using a tool supplied by someone else, someone else ending a person's life with their consent, someone else ending a person's life without their consent and withholding life-sustaining treatment (with or without that person's consent). All of these forms of 'assisted-dying' have been applied to people with disabilities. That 'assisted-dying' can refer to the act without the consent of the person who dies is particularly worrying. It has been suggested that many people with disabilities fear that episodes of illness may be viewed as an opportunity to 'allow' them 'merciful' release (D. Marks, 1999), and there may be some basis for this. In the Netherlands, assisted suicide has been legalized and people with physical and psychiatric disabilities have been helped to die both with and without their consent.

The argument against the right-to-die lobby, although implicitly anti-suicide, is not necessarily about whether suicide per se is right or wrong. It should be viewed as being about the differential treatment of the issue for people with disabilities and severe illnesses as opposed to 'healthy' people. Morally sanctioning assisting people with incurable terminal or non-terminal conditions to end their lives or withholding life-sustaining treatment/support, while morally opposing the right of suicidal 'healthy' individuals to end their lives (and offering them suicide prevention interventions), equates to a severe form of discrimination based on stigmatization of these individuals.

The two debates discussed above are about the differential value placed on the lives on people with versus without disabilities/illnesses. Stigmatized individuals are regarded as flawed, compromised, less than fully human (Heatherton et al., 2000) and, in the case of people with disabilities, may be thought of as worthless. Being judged as having a life not worth living may represent the most fundamental claim to injustice and inequality.

Social Justice and Health

Social justice

Critics of the research into social inequalities in health often charge that social inequalities are both an inevitable part of life and also are necessary for social progress. An alternative perspective is to consider not simply inequalities per se but inequities in health. According to Dahlgren and Whitehead (1991) health inequalities can be considered as inequities when they are avoidable, unnecessary and unfair. The issue of fairness leads us to consider the issue of **social justice** and health.

KT

A useful starting point is the theory of 'justice as fairness' developed by the moral philosopher John Rawls (1999). He identified certain underlying principles of a just society, as follows:

- Assure people equal basic liberties including guaranteeing the right of political participation.
- Provide a robust form of equal opportunity.
- Limit inequalities to those that benefit the least advantaged.

When these principles are met citizens can be confident that they are respected by others and can acquire a sense of self-worth.

Daniels et al. (2000) argue that adhering to these principles would address the basic social inequalities in health. They detail a series of implications for social organization that flow from the acceptance of these principles. First, assuring people equal basic liberties implies that everyone has an equal right to fully participate in politics. This will in turn contribute to improvements in health since according to social capital theory political participation is an important social determinant of health.

Second, providing active measures to promote equal opportunities implies the introduction of measures to reduce socio-economic inequalities and other social obstacles to equal opportunities. Such measures would include comprehensive childcare and childhood interventions to combat any disadvantages of family background (Daniels et al., 2000). They would also include comprehensive health care for all including support services for those with disabilities.

Finally, a just society would allow only those inequalities in income and wealth that would benefit the least advantaged. This requires direct challenge to the contemporary neo-liberal philosophy that promotes the maximization of profit and increasing the extent of social inequality.

Psychologists and social justice

Increasingly psychologists have recognized the link between poor social conditions and physical and mental health. In 2000 the American Psychological Association passed a landmark resolution on Poverty and Socioeconomic Status. This resolution called for a programme of research on the causes and impact of poverty, negative attitudes towards people living in poverty, strategies to reduce poverty, and the evaluation of anti-poverty programmes. This resolution has been followed by a number of initiatives.

Bullock and Lott (2001) developed a research and advocacy agenda on issues of economic justice. Such an agenda is not just concerned with describing the impact of poverty and inequality on health and well-being but also with advocating for social and economic justice.

This agenda includes challenging the victim-blaming ideology that is often adopted in psychological approaches to the study of health and illness. It also includes defining health psychology as a resource for social change (Murray and Campbell, 2003). This can involve a variety of strategies. This leads to a more politically engaged health psychology such as the one championed by Martin-Baro (1994) who challenged psychologists to adopt a 'preferential option for the poor'.

Three approaches have been suggested by Fine and Barreras (2001):

- Public policy: documenting the impact of regressive social policies and agitating against such policies.
- Popular education: challenging popular victim-blaming beliefs ('common-sense') about the causes of ill-health.
- Community organizing: working with marginalized communities and agitating for social change.

The success of such a strategy requires building alliances with social groups most negatively impacted by social inequalities. These can range from patient-rights groups to trade unions and other activist groups (Steinitz and Mishler, 2001). As Martin-Baro stressed: 'the concern of the social scientist should not be so much to explain the world as to transform it' (1994: 19).

Future Research

1 There is a need to clarify the character of the psychosocial explanations for the social inequalities in health.
2 Research on social inequalities needs to be combined with further research on ethnic and gender inequalities in health. Qualitative studies of the health experiences of people from different socio-economic backgrounds are of particular importance to our understanding of the psychological mechanisms underlying health variations. Further qualitative studies are also needed to explore the relationship between social positioning and health experience.
3 Forms of research on social inequalities in health need to explicitly consider how they can contribute to reducing them.
4 An essential aspect of future research is to consider the social and psychological obstacles to movements to alleviate social inequalities in health.

Summary

1 Health and illness are determined by social conditions.
2 There is a clear relationship between income and health leading to the development of a social gradient.
3 Psychosocial explanations of these social variations include perceived inequality, stress, lack of control and less social connection.
4 Material explanations of the social gradient in health include reduced income and reduced access to services.
5 Political factors connect both psychosocial and material explanations in a broader causal chain.
6 Lay explanations of social inequalities in health include people's immediate social and physical environment.
7 Social environment includes the character of people's social relationships and their connection with the community.
8 Social justice is concerned with providing equal opportunities for all citizens. Socio-economic status (SES) and wealth are strongly related to health, illness and mortality. These gradients may be a consequence of differences in social cohesion, stress and personal control.
9 A health psychology committed to social justice needs to orient itself to address the needs of the most disadvantaged in society.

Key Terms

Black Report

ecological approach

psychosocial explanations

sense of community

social capital

social inequality

social justice

socio-economic status

systems theory approach

4

Culture and Health

There is no such thing as human nature independent of culture. (Clifford Geertz, 1973: 229)

Outline

The way people think about health, become ill and react to illness is rooted in their broader health belief systems that are in turn immersed in culture. This chapter provides some examples from the work of historians and anthropologists who have investigated how health belief systems vary across time and space. We consider some of the different expert health belief systems that have existed historically in western society and contemporary popular belief systems. We also consider several non-western health belief systems and the concept of disability culture.

Context

We are cultural beings and an understanding of health beliefs and practices requires an understanding of the cultural and indeed of the historical and social context within which we live. It is impossible to extract humans from the context that gives them meaning. Historians and anthropologists have conducted substantial research into the historical and cultural embeddedness of health beliefs.

Culture is all around us and pervades our very being. An inclusive definition of culture has been provided by Corin who defines it as:

Above all a system of meanings and symbols. This system shapes every area of life, defines a world view that gives meaning to personal and collective experience, and frames the way people locate themselves within the world, perceive the world, and believe in it. Every aspect of reality is seen as embedded within webs of meaning that define a certain world view and that cannot be studied or understood apart from this collective frame. (Corin, 1995: 273)

An understanding of people's reactions to illness requires an understanding of these culturally specific, indigenous health belief systems.

Table 4.1   *Causal ontologies of suffering (Shweder et al., 1997)*

Causal ontologies	Explanatory references	Therapy
Biomedical	Western: genetic defects, hormone imbalances, organ pathologies, physiological impairments	Direct or indirect ingestion of special substances, herbs and roots, vitamins, chemical compounds
	Non-western: humors, bodily fluids, juices	Direct or indirect mechanical repair (e.g. surgery, massage, emetics) of damaged fibres or organs
Interpersonal	Western: harassment, abuse, exploitation	Avoidance or repair of negative interpersonal relations
	Non-western: sorcery, evil eye, black magic	Talismans, magic
Socio-political	Oppression, political domination, adverse economic or family conditions	Social reform
Psychological	Unfulfilled desires and frustrated intentions, forms of fear	Intrapsychic and psychosocial interventions, e.g. meditation, therapy
Astrophysical	Arrangement of planets, moon or stars	Wait with optimism for change
Ecological	Stress, environmental risks	Reduction of stress and environmental hazards
Moral	Transgressions of obligation or duty, ethical failure	Unloading one's sins, confession, reparation

Causal Ontologies and Moral Discourse of Suffering

Each society has developed its own understanding of health and illness. Shweder et al. (1997) have described seven general systems of understanding that they have termed ontologies of suffering. Each of these systems are locally developed ways of understanding illness and suffering that are in turn linked with ways of intervening to alleviate suffering. Table 4.1 summarizes these **causal ontologies**.

Murdock (1980) conducted a survey of the explanations of illness in 139 societies. He found that in sub-Saharan Africa there was a preference for explanations based upon moral transgressions. In East Asia, the preference was for interpersonal explanations and in the circum-Mediterranean region he found that witchcraft explanations for death and suffering were widespread. Further analysis of these data showed that on a worldwide scale, the three more common explanations are interpersonal, moral and biomedical.

In their review of this evidence Shweder et al. (1997) claimed that the **moral discourse** was the pervasive underlying explanatory framework in many societies. In light of this they conducted detailed analysis of the moral discourse of the residents of the city of Bhubaneswar, Orissa in India. From this they identified three moral dimensions that are summarized in Table 4.2.

In western societies the dominant moral discourse is that of autonomy which focuses on the rights of the individual. As Porter (1997) argued: 'the West has evolved a culture preoccupied with the self, with the individual and his or her identity, and

Table 4.2   *Moral discourses of suffering (Shweder et al., 1997)*

Discourse	Focus	Content
Autonomy	Individual	Harm, rights, justice
Community	Family and community	Duty, interdependence
Divinity	Divine design	Sacred and natural order

this quest has come to be equated with (or reduced to) the individual body and the embodied personality, expressed through body language' (1997: 7). In health care this leads to the rights of the individual patient having paramount importance. This discourse pervades much of contemporary medical ethics.

As discussed in Chapter 2, in western discourse the individualistic focus is promoted as natural, while alternative concerns are disparaged. The anthropologist Clifford Geertz (1973) describes the relative character of this focus as follows:

> The Western conception of the person as a bounded, unique, more or less integrated motivational and cognitive universe, a dynamic centre of awareness, emotion, judgement, and action organised into a distinctive whole and set contrastively both against other such wholes and against a social and natural background is, however incorrigible it may seem to us, a rather peculiar idea within the context of the world's cultures. (Geertz, 1973: 229)

The pervasiveness of the individualistic ethos in western society is also evident in a number of psychological studies that have attempted to characterize cultural variations in people's ways of thinking and acting. One frequently cited study is that by Hofstede (1980) who analysed national differences in responses to employee morale surveys conducted by a large American multinational corporation. Factor analysis of the responses identified four dimensions: power distance, uncertainty avoidance, masculinity/femininity, and individualism/collectivism. Of these four, the most investigated dimension is individualism versus collectivism.

Individualist cultures emphasize the separateness and uniqueness of its members whereas collectivist cultures emphasize group needs and interconnectedness. For example, in Hindu society the community and divinity discourses are more prominent. An understanding of these dimensions is important for understanding cultural variations in health belief systems.

Health Belief Systems

As societies have evolved they have developed various health belief systems, knowledge of which is sometimes confined to those who undergo specialized training. This has given rise to the separation of what have become known as expert or technical beliefs systems as opposed to the traditional folk or indigenous systems. These systems are not discrete but interact and are in a process of constant evolution. Although the majority of people in any society organize their world through indigenous belief systems the character of these is connected in some form with the expert belief system.

Kleinman (1980) distinguished between three overlapping sectors of any health-care system: the professional, the folk and the popular. The popular sector is 'the lay, non-professional, non-specialist, popular culture arena in which illness is first defined and health care activities initiated' (1980: 50). The professional sector comprises the organized healing professions – their representations and actions. The folk sector is the non-professional, non-bureaucratic, specialist sector that shades into the other two sectors. In view of the central role of health in our self-definition, these different health sectors both reflect and contribute to broader worldviews.

Although this threefold division is widely cited, other researchers (e.g. Blumhagen, 1980) have preferred a simpler twofold division into professional and popular realms. 'Systematicity, coherence and interdependence are aspects of the professional belief systems' (Blumhagen, 1980: 200). Conversely, the lay health belief system can appear disconnected. This broad classification avoids an accusation that certain specialized health belief systems are classified as folk when they have limited status in society although they may have an extensive codification of health complaints and treatments. These two broad belief systems interact such that the lay person can draw upon more specialized knowledge but also the specialist will make use of more popular knowledge. Further, both ways of thinking about health draw upon a more general worldview and are located within a particular local and political context. Blumhagen (1980) also argues that these two health belief systems should be considered distinct from the individual belief system that the individual uses to understand their personal experience of illness. An understanding of popular health beliefs requires an understanding of the dominant expert health belief systems.

Western Health Belief Systems

Classical views of health

In the west the classical view of health and illness derived from the Graeco-Arabic medical system. **Galenic medicine** provided an expert system developed from the Greeks, in particular the work of Hippocrates and his colleagues. Their major contribution was in offering a naturalistic explanation of health and illness. A central concept in Galen's formulation was balance that was equated with health and imbalance that implied ill-health (see also Chapter 1). Balance was conceived as a balance of bodily fluids or **humours**. They identified four main fluids: bile, phlegm, blood and black bile. These seemed to vary with the seasons such that an excess of phlegm was common in the winter leading to colds, while an excess of bile led to summer diarrhoea. Figure 4.1 shows a plan of the Hippocratic humoral system.

Not only could these four humours be linked to the four seasons, but they were also linked to the four primary conditions of hot, cold, wet and dry. Further, in Roman times they linked the four humours with the elements of air, fire, earth and water, with four types of fever, four periods of the day, four colours, four tastes. Medieval scholars added four temperaments, four Evangelists and four music tones (Nutton, 1995).

Besides a focus on understanding natural processes, the Galenic tradition also placed responsibility on individuals to look after themselves. Ill-health was a consequence of natural processes, not a result of divine intervention. In many ways Galen's ideas not only prefigured but also continue to influence much of contemporary health beliefs.

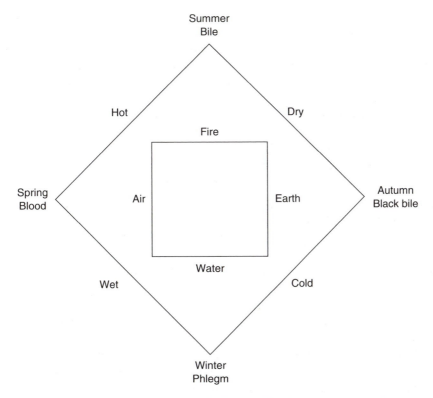

Figure 4.1   Hippocratic humoral system (Nutton, 1995: 25; reproduced with permission)

Christian ideas

Galenic ideas dominated the expert system of medicine in Europe for almost two millennia. However, during the Middle Ages in Europe, Galen's work became confined more to the learned few and other ideas based upon religion became more commonplace. Illness was often seen as punishment for humankind's sinfulness. Herzlich and Pierret (1987) in their historical study of popular beliefs about health and illness note the interweaving of naturalistic and religious explanations:

> The disorders of the body ... have their correspondence in the corruption of both the air and morals. This breakdown of order encompasses the phenomena of nature, those of the organism, and the conduct of human behaviour. But over all of this hovers the will of God. In the last analysis, it is he who sends illness to us. (Herzlich and Pierret, 1987: 103)

Indeed, this belief was written into the Book of Common Prayer: 'Whatsoever your sickness is, know you certainly, that it is God's visitation' (Anselman, 1996: 229). The Church's seven deadly sins even came to be associated with pathological conditions of the body. For example, pride was symbolized by tumours and inflammations while sloth led to dead flesh and palsy (Thomas, 1979).

Christianity drew upon different traditions. The ascetic tradition scorned concern for the body and instead promoted acts such as fasting and physical suffering, which supposedly led to spirituality. Indeed disease could be welcomed as an opportunity to purify the soul through suffering. With the Protestant Reformation this belief was replaced with the idea that the body had been given to humans by God. It was the individual's religious duty to look after and care for the body. Illness was seen as a sign of weakness and neglect. To honour God required living a healthy life and abstaining from excess, especially in terms of sex and diet.

Up until the Reformation, and later, the priest played an important role in healing. Wear (1985) noted that religious writers frequently made reference to the body. He remarked on the works of several seventeenth-century religious figures. For example, Robert Horne described the body as the 'Temple of God' that it was necessary to keep pure and clean. He quotes from the work of William Perkins (1612):

> Whereas our bodies are God's workmanship, we must glorify him in our bodies, and all the actions of body and soul, our eating and drinking, our living and dying, must be referred to his glory: yea we must not hurt or abuse our body, but present them as holy and living sacrifices unto God. (cited in Wear, 1985: 63)

These ideas were widely promulgated in the new Protestant Reformation. The way to heaven was through attention to health behaviour; it was also linked to a social morality. The poor were expected to take responsibility for their condition while at the same time the rich were wrong to indulge themselves while there was so much poverty and suffering.

Despite the authority of the Church, these religious interpretations began to decline with the growth of medical science. For example, Anselman (1996) in his analysis of the diaries of an eighteenth-century woman notes that 'her distinctive understanding of illness remains fundamentally physical rather than metaphysical' (1996: 229). While in terms of the expert belief system there has been increasing acceptance of a naturalistic view of disease, the moral basis of health continues to underlie much of contemporary health belief.

Biomedicine

Two streams of thought in knowing the world attained dominance during the Enlightenment. The first was the acceptance of the distinction between superstition and reason. The second was the emergence of positivism that emphasized that science based upon direct observation, measurement and experimentation gave direct access to the real world. This approach concentrated attention on material reality and a conception of the body as distinct from the mind. A central figure was Descartes (1596–1650) who conceived of the human being as composed of mind and body. The former was not open to scientific investigation whereas the latter could be conceived as a machine: 'I would consider myself primarily as having a face, hands, arms, and this entire machine composed of bones, and flesh, as it appears in a corpse, of which I designate through the name of body' (cited by Benoist and Cathebras, 1993: 860–1).

The eighteenth century saw the rise of individualism in western society. In previous eras the group or collective organized ways of thinking and acting, which in turn was interconnected with the physical and spiritual world. Professional understanding of health and illness became more closely entwined with knowledge of the individual physical body. Foucault (1976) described how between the mid-eighteenth and mid-nineteenth centuries the 'medical gaze' came to focus on the interior of the human body. The symptoms of illness now became signs of underlying pathophysiology. Foucault noted that the change in perspective of the physician was illustrated in the change in the patient query from 'How do you feel?' to 'Where does it hurt?' For this new physician the stethoscope became the symbol of having insight into the bodily interior. Treatment centred on changing the character of this physiology either by medical or surgical means.

Foucault argued that this concern with the passive individual body reflected wider social changes. The view of the body as 'something docile, that could be surveilled, used, transformed and improved' was reflected not only in the growth of hospitals, but also prisons, asylums and schools. As Williams and Calnan (1996) noted: 'From this perspective, modern medicine is seen as part and parcel of a wider, more extensive, system of disciplinary techniques and technologies of power that are concerned with the moral regulation and "normalization" of the population through the medical regimen' (1996: 1610).

This approach to the study of health and illness has become known as **biomedicine**, cosmopolitan or allopathic medicine (Leslie, 1976). It came to dominance for several reasons, including the fact that it was in accord with a broader view of humans, its alliance with physical science and the steady improvement in the health of the population that was attributed to medical intervention. The focus on the body is in accord with the western emphasis on the individual: 'One of the functions of the body becomes that of marking the frontiers of the individual' (see Benoist and Cathebras, 1993). Further, the separation of mind and body 'offers a subtle articulation of the person's alienation from the body in Western society, but this alienation is found, as well, in every sphere of economic and political life' (Benoist and Cathebras, 1993: 858). Biomedicine separates the person from the body.

Friedson (1970) described how the coming to dominance of the biological approach was not without resistance. It required strong political action to organize the profession of medicine and to take legal action against other health practitioners. Throughout there was the dismissal of alternative perspectives and the assertion that biomedicine was the central force that had led to the substantial improvements in society's health. Biomedicine was based upon a positivist epistemology that supposedly gave it access to an outside reality. Only this approach was the true approach. All other approaches could be disparaged.

KT

The biopsychosocial model of health

The dominance of this biomedical system has come in for substantial challenge both from the scientific establishment and the public. Initially, this was reflected in a call for more attention to the psychological and social aspects of health. This led to the development of the biopsychosocial model of health and illness (Engel, 1977). According to Engel (1980) the various aspects of health and illness can be organized in a hierarchy from the biosphere and society down through the individual's level of experience and behaviour to the cellular and subatomic level. All of these levels interact and need to be considered if we are to understand health and illness. With varying degrees of enthusiasm this model has in some respects replaced the basic biomedical model (however, see Chapter 1 for further discussion of this point).

In addition, the increasing evidence of the link between social and behavioural factors and health has led to the promulgation of a health promotion ethic by the medical establishment with an emphasis on personal responsibility for health. Crawford (1980: 365) argued that 'in an increasingly "healthist" culture, healthy behaviour has become a moral duty and illness an individual moral failing'. Admittedly, the adoption of a more biopsychosocial approach to health care, especially by general practitioners, is sometimes met with hostility by patients who have accepted the basic biomedical model. This might explain why some people feel concerned that their physician is becoming too involved in their psychosocial problems.

Criticisms of the biomedical model also led the World Health Organization to propose an extensive definition of health as a state of complete physical, mental, and social well-being, not the mere absence of disease or infirmity. This definition widened the scope of health care to consider not only the well-being of the individual but also of the community. In Chapter 1 an even wider definition was offered, encompassing the economic, political and spiritual domains. Currently, much of health care in western society is attempting to shift from a concern with bodily processes to concern with the wider concept of quality of life.

Alternative medicine

The late twentieth century has witnessed increasing criticism of medicine. Indeed it has been argued that a process of de-medicalization is taking place. In this period known as 'late modernity' there is widespread questioning of the scientific method (Williams and Calnan, 1996). This is reflected in medicine where there is evidence of increasing fracture between the high technology medicine on the one hand and the more psychosocial practice on the other.

The apparent failure of biomedicine to solve the big medical problems such as cancer and AIDS has led to an increased cynicism and a turn to alternative health systems. There has been a steady growth of the use of complementary and alternative medicine (CAM) in most western countries. In the USA, more visits are made to providers of unconventional therapy than to primary care physicians. Indeed, estimates show that Americans spend as much on complementary medicine as on hospitalizations. A recent survey in England found that 28% of adults had used one of eight types of complementary medicine or medication in the past year (Thomas et al., 2001).

In a series of studies, Furnham and his colleagues have investigated the reasons behind the growth of **alternative medicine**. Vincent and Furnham (1996) found in a survey of users of complementary medicine in Britain four main reasons for their usage:

KT

1   The perceived ineffectiveness of orthodox medicine.
2   The belief that complementary medicine would be effective.
3   Valuing the perceived emphasis on treating the whole person.
4   A desire to take an active role in maintaining their health.

In another study of a sample of German adults, those who use complementary practitioners have a more health-conscious lifestyle. Calnan and Williams's (1992) study of laypeople in Britain found a considerable degree of ambivalence about the value of modern medicine, particularly high-tech medicine. A study in Canada (Sirois and Gick, 2002) found that the key predictors of use of complementary medicine were health-aware behaviours, dissatisfaction with medical doctors, number of medical problems, and household income. The role of income probably reflects the need to pay for complementary medicine since in Canada, as in many western countries, most bio-medical services are provided by the state.

Increasingly CAM is gaining respectability in mainstream health care. An example is the UK House of Lords Select Committee report recommending the use of some CAM therapies within the health-care system (House of Lords Select Committee on Science and Technology, 2000). However, evidence suggests that established health professions are very apprehensive at the growth of complementary medicine and are insisting that it meets positivist scientific standards of safety and efficacy (Kelner et al., 2003). A study from Australia noted some evidence of convergence between orthodox medicine and CAM (Bombardieri and Easthorpe, 2000). There was also evidence that orthodox medicine was incorporating aspects of CAM into their practice while maintaining its dominant position. This move is not uncontested and the growth of CAM can be considered a symptom of our postmodern world that includes consumer demand for a wider choice in healthcare.

Popular views of health in the west

Evidence from a series of studies of popular beliefs about health and illness in western society illustrates the interaction of what can be described as the classic, the religious, the biomedical and the lifestyle approaches to health and illness. Probably the most influential study of western lay health beliefs was carried out by Herzlich (1973). She conducted interviews with a sample of French adults and concluded that health was conceived as an attribute of the individual – a state of harmony or balance. This had such components as physical well-being, plenty of physical resources, absence of fatigue, psychological well-being, evenness of temper, freedom of movement, and effectiveness in action and good relations with other people. Illness was attributed to outside forces in our society or way of life.

This concern with balance could be said to reflect an older more traditional view of health and moves beyond the individual to relationships with the social and physical world. The laypeople also referred to illness in terms of both organic and psychosocial factors. On their own organic changes did not constitute illness. Rather, for the layperson 'physical facts, symptoms and dysfunctions have, of course, an existence of their own, but they only combine to form an illness in so far as they transform a patient's life'. The ability to participate in everyday life constitutes health, whereas inactivity is considered the true criterion of illness.

Herzlich's study was seminal because it provoked further research into popular health beliefs. However, symbolic culture does not exist independently from the physical and material circumstances of the community; rather they have a complex dialectical relationship. Thus, to understand somewhat more of Herzlich's findings requires recognition of her sample, which was largely French middle-class adults supplemented with some rural workers. These health beliefs were perhaps more typical of this group of people than groups from poorer social situations.

Other studies have explored how lay perceptions of health and illness are rooted in the social experience of people, in particular sub-cultures. D'Houtaud and Field (1984) conducted a large open-ended survey of over 4,000 French adults. Content analysis of their replies revealed 6,172 responses that were subsequently coded into 41 categories and then into 10 broader themes. There was a clear pattern in the preference for these themes across the social classes. The higher and middle-class adults preferred a definition of health in terms of a hedonistic use of life, in terms of their body and in terms of equilibrium and of vitality. Conversely, those from lower more manual social classes preferred a definition in terms of the value of health, psychological well-being, hygiene and absence of sickness. In considering these variations, D'Houtaud and Field argue that 'it is not difficult to discern in such com-plementary representations of health the reflection of the corresponding roles of mastery on the one hand and of execution of social tasks on the other' (1984: 48). The health beliefs are not things in themselves but are intimately related to the immediate social experience of the adults.

Blaxter (1990) analysed the definitions of health provided by over 9,000 British adults in the health and lifestyles survey. She classified the responses into nine categories (Table 4.3).

In analysing the responses across social classes, Blaxter (1990) noted considerable agreement in the emphasis on behavioural factors as a cause of illness. Indeed, she commented on the limited reference to structural or environmental factors, especially among those from working-class backgrounds. Williams and Calnan (1996) suggest that the growth of the self-help consumer movement in health care is another symbol of popular opposition to the passive patient model of biomedicine. They noted that this opposition 'can be located within the broader socio-cultural and political frame-work of self-determination and a reclaiming of control over the body, self and wider environment' (1996: 1617).

However, indigenous health beliefs go beyond descriptive dimensions to consider underlying etiology. In a discussion of social representation theory, Moscovici (1984) suggested that people rarely confine their definition of concepts to the descriptive level.

Table 4.3 *Popular definitions of health (Blaxter, 1990)*

- Health as not-ill: the absence of physical symptoms.
- Health despite disease.
- Health as reserve: the presence of personal resources.
- Health as behaviour: the extent of healthy behaviour.
- Health as physical fitness.
- Health as vitality.
- Health as psychosocial well-being.
- Health as social relationships.
- Health as function.

Table 4.4   *Popular explanations of health (Stainton-Rogers, 1991)*

Accounts	Explanations
Body as machine	Illness is naturally occurring and 'real' with biomedicine considered the main form of treatment.
Body under siege	Illness is a result of external influences such as germs or stress.
Inequality of access	Emphasized the unequal access to modern medicine.
Cultural critique	Based upon a sociological worldview of exploitation and oppression.
Health promotion	Recognized both individual and collective responsibility for ill-health.
Robust individualism	Concerned with every individual's right to a satisfying life.
Willpower account	Defined health in terms of the individual's ability to exert control.

Rather, lay descriptions often include reference to explanations. This is apparent in a study of lay descriptions of health and illness by Stainton-Rogers (1991). Stainton-Rogers used Q-sort methodology to identify the concepts used by a sample of British adults to explain health. She identified seven different accounts of health and illness (Table 4.4)

Recent studies have explored how lay perceptions of health and illness are rooted in the social experience of people, in particular sub-cultures. A study of East and West German workers found similar findings to that of Herzlich but with an added emphasis on health as lifestyle (Flick, 1998). In a subsequent study comparing German and Portuguese women it was found that German women felt they should be responsible for their health, that they felt 'forced towards health' by the state, physicians and the media. Conversely Portuguese women have a generalized 'lack of awareness' of health. It was suggested that these differences reflected historical and cultural differences between the two groups.

In a study of Canadian baby-boomers Murray et al. (2003) found a very activity-orientated conception of health. They defined health in terms of lifestyle, functionality, social engagement and attitude as well as reserve and also in a vacuum. It was suggested that this conception reflected a greater self-responsibility for health that is promoted in Canadian culture. However, there was also evidence of a certain resistance to this stance among those from working-class backgrounds.

In western society the metaphor that is associated with health is that of self-control. This metaphor is in turn infused with moral connotations such that to become ill is not to take care of oneself (Crawford, 1980). Admittedly, health is a contested arena since release from certain controls, or even the rejection of them, can be considered a sign of good health. Conversely, the person who abides by certain controls can be perceived as unhealthy. In her study of laypeople's views of health and illness Crossley (2003) found that for some to transgress the moral imperative to health was perceived as good. A study comparing the health beliefs and practices of adults living in Japan with adults, from Japanese and Caucasian heritage, resident in Hawaii found that the Japanese residents had less concern about their health and were less likely to believe that they had control over their health (Gotay et al., 2004). These findings illustrate the close interweaving of health beliefs and practices with culture.

Non-Western Views of Health

The biomedical perspective has come to a position of dominance throughout the world, reflecting the imperialistic expansion of western society more generally. Alternative health-care systems have tended to be disparaged by biomedicine. Being based upon a positivist perspective, the practitioners of biomedicine believe that they have access to a reality that is independent of the patient's effort to understand and control the situation. As such, alternative perspectives are seen as basically wrong.

However, alternative professional systems of health care continue to exist in large parts of the world, especially in Asia. Further, as migrants have moved to other countries they have taken their health beliefs with them. In the major western metropolitan centres there is now extensive availability of health-care systems other than biomedicine. This has led to a feedback into western ways of thinking about health and illness, especially among those who are disenchanted with biomedicine.

Chinese views of health

The Chinese perspective views health as the result of a balance between and within the various systems both internal and external to the person. Disease is perceived as the consequence of disharmony or disequilibrium. This view of health and illness reflects a broader worldview that emphasizes interconnectedness and balance (Quah and Bishop, 1996).

Chinese medicine rests upon the religion and philosophy of Taoism. According to this view the universe is a vast and indivisible entity and each being has a definite function within it. Each being is linked in a chain in harmony. 'Violating this harmony is like hurling chaos, wars, and catastrophes on humankind – the end result of which is illness' (Spector, 1991: 243). The balance of the two basic powers of yin and yang governs the whole universe including human beings. Yin is considered to represent the male, positive energy that produces light and fullness. Conversely, yang is considered the female, negative force that leads to darkness and emptiness. A disharmony in yin and yang leads to illness. A variety of methods including acupuncture and the use of herbal medicines can be used to restore this harmony.

Within Chinese culture human suffering is traditionally explained as the result of destiny or ming. Cheng (1997) quotes the Confucian teacher Master Meng: 'A man worries about neither untimely death nor long life but cultivates his personal character and waits for its natural development; this is to stand in accord with Fate ... All things are determined by Fate, and one should accept what is conferred' (1997: 740). An important part of your destiny depends upon your horoscope or pa-tzu. During an individual's life, his or her pa-tzu is paired with the timing of nature. Over time these pairings change and create the individual's luck or yun.

Buddhist and Taoist beliefs are also reflected in Chinese medical belief systems; for example, good deeds and charitable donations are promoted. Heavenly retribution is expected for those who commit wrongs. This retribution may not be immediate but it will be inevitable. An important concept in this respect is pao that has two types – reciprocity and retribution (Cheng, 1997). In mutual relationships reciprocity or give and take is expected. When this does not occur some form of retribution will take place.

These views of health and illness are not only codified within Chinese medicine but influence everyday lay beliefs about health and illness both in China and in Chinese communities around the world. Several examples illustrate this. Cheng (1997) conducted interviews with a sample of Chinese workers in Hong Kong who had sustained hand injuries. He found that many of the workers, especially the older ones, explained their injuries in terms of fate or predestination. For example, one worker said: 'The injury was predestined. You were bound to be hurt no matter how careful you were. Something like a ghost blinded your eyes. No way for you to be careful! It couldn't be escaped in any way!' (p. 745).

Others referred to the role of retribution for some wrong that the individual may have committed in a previous life. One mentioned the role of his pa-tzu or horoscope. Admittedly, this did not mean he was condemned to misfortune. If he changed his life course then the pairing with his pa-tzu may become more harmonious. His belief in the role of fate enables the person to escape blame for the event but still maintain a belief that they have control over their lives. Cheng (1997) gives the example of a Mr Pang who says: 'Everything is predestined. Although my ming [fate] is not good, you know. I haven't looked down upon myself for the past years.' (p. 746).

Bishop and Teng (1992) investigated how Chinese Singaporean students describe illness. They found they used not only the dimensions of seriousness and contagiousness that were used by western students (see Chapter 11) but also a third dimension that was concerned with the extent to which the disease was perceived as related to behaviour or the Chinese concept of 'heatiness' ('hot' versus 'cold'). Further evidence is available for this three-dimensional model although, this time, the third dimension is concerned with the degree to which a disease is perceived in terms of blocked 'qi' or energy. These two findings are reconciled by suggesting that blocked 'qi' and 'heatiness' both include the concept of internal imbalance or energy that is a central concern in Chinese medicine.

In a subsequent study it was found that the preference for Chinese illness concepts and for seeking help from practitioners of traditional Chinese medicine (sinsehs) were related to the extent of Chinese culture orientation as measured by their agreement with a series of Chinese values (Quah and Bishop, 1996).

These lay belief systems remain strong within immigrant communities. For example, in interviews with Cambodian refugee women in California, it has been found that they explain health and illness within a traditional Buddhist worldview. Again, this approach emphasizes the central importance of balance and harmony within one's life. For these women a disturbance of this equilibrium results in a state of internal 'bad wind'. Using various wind releasing strategies such as 'coin rubbing', equilibrium could be restored. Equilibrium could be maintained by avoidance of competitive behaviour, respect for individuality, nurturance of the weak and peaceful co-existence with the natural world. Despite the availability of western medicine facilities, the women prefer to travel considerable distances to access a Cambodian physician.

There is evidence of this more collectivist approach to health among Koreans and Mexicans. In a large sample of American seniors from four ethnic backgrounds, Korean and Mexican Americans were found to place greater emphasis on family decision-making.

Illness was not simply a property of the individual but had implications for the whole family who should be consulted about treatment plans.

Ayurvedic medicine

The Ayurvedic system of medicine is based upon the Sanskrit words meaning knowledge (veda) needed for longevity (ayus). This system remains extremely extensive in India. It is estimated that 70% of the population of India and hundreds of millions of people throughout the world use ayurvedic medicine (Schober, 1997). According to this system that is based on Hindu philosophy both the cosmos and each human being consists of a female component, Prakrti, which forms the body, and a male component, Purusa, which forms the soul. While the Purusa is constant, the Prakrti is subject to change. The body is defined in terms of the flow of substances through channels. Each substance has its own channel. Sickness occurs when a channel is blocked and the flow is diverted into another channel. When all channels are blocked the flow of substances is not possible and death occurs. At this stage the soul is liberated from its bodily prison.

The task of Ayurvedic medicine is to identify the blockages and to get the various essences moving again. The different forms of imbalance can be corrected through both preventive and therapeutic interventions based on diet, yoga, breathwork, bodywork, meditation and/or herbs (Schober, 1997).

As with the Chinese medical system, the Ayurvedic system pervades much of popular beliefs about health and illness throughout the Indian sub-continent and among Indian communities in other parts of the world. However, Ayurvedic medicine has not gained the hegemony of western biomedicine, even within India. There is a variety of other competing health belief systems that has led to the development of a pluralistic health culture made up of several different systems. In an interview study of a community in Northern India, Morinis and Brilliant (1981) found evidence not only of Ayurvedic beliefs, but also 'unami' (another indigenous health system), allopathic, homeopathic, massage, herbalist, folk, astrologic and religious systems. They note that while these systems may formally seem to conflict, in their study participants could draw on some or all of them to help explain different health problems.

Further, the strength of these beliefs is related to the immediate social situation and the roles and expectations of the community. For example, for women in some parts of Pakistan, the health belief system is a mixture of biomedicine and 'unami' medicine that is a version of Galenic medicine.

African medical systems

In Africa, a wide range of traditional medical systems continues to flourish. These include a mixture of herbal and physical remedies intertwined with various religious belief systems. As Porter (1997) notes, belief systems that attribute sickness to 'ill-will, to malevolent spirits, sorcery, witchcraft and diabolical or divine intervention … still pervade the tribal communities of Africa, the Amazon basin and the Pacific' (1997: 9). In a more developed assessment Chalmers (1996) summarized the African view as reflecting 'a belief in an integrated, independent, totality of all things animate and inanimate, past and present' (1996: 3). As with other traditional health systems a central concept is balance: 'Disturbances in the equilibrium, be they emotional, spiritual or interpersonal, may manifest in discordance at any level of functioning' (Chalmers, 1996: 3).

Two dimensions are paramount in understanding African health beliefs: spiritual influences and a communal orientation. It is common to attribute illness to the work of ancestors or to supernatural forces. Inadequate respect for ancestors can supposedly lead to illness. In addition, magical influences can be both negative and positive, contemporary and historical. Thus, illness can be attributed to the work of some malign living person. The role of the spiritual healer is to identify the source of the malign influence.

Rather than the individualistic orientation of western society, African culture has a communal orientation. Thus, the malign influence of certain supernatural forces can be felt not just by an individual but also by other members of his or her family or community. 'The nuclear family, the extended family, the community, the living and the deceased as well as their ultimate relationship with God are intimately linked in the African view of health and illness' (Chalmers, 1996: 4). Thus intervention may be aimed not only at the sense of balance of the individual but also of the family and the community.

Four dimensions on illness causal beliefs have been identified in a large sample of Ethiopian adults: (1) psychological stressors; (2) supernatural retribution; (3) biomedical defects; and (4) social disadvantage. Psychological stressors and supernatural retribution were considered more important causes of psychological than of physical illnesses. A relationship between these causal beliefs and treatment choices, attitude to patients and demographic characteristics has been found. For example, belief in supernatural retribution is associated with use of religious prayer, holy water, consulting traditional healers and both traditional and modern medicine. Finally, there is also a relationship between education and causal beliefs such that the less educated placed more emphasis on supernatural causes. This reflects the extent of acculturation to the western biomedical model of illness.

As with other medical systems, immigrant communities have brought their health beliefs to their new countries of residence. Landrine (1997) criticized studies of North American health beliefs that have largely ignored the distinctive culture of black Americans. African slaves maintained their pre-slavery health beliefs, practices and indigenous healers. When they gained emancipation black Americans found they were denied access to medical care. As a consequence they relied on their indigenous healers and over time developed a unique African-American folk medicine. She suggests that in contemporary North America many blacks are returning to this medical system as they feel rejected or excluded by what they perceive as the racism of white American health care.

Changing cultures and health

Our modern world is a world of rapid change and interpenetration of cultural groups and belief systems. There is increasing evidence that laypeople are mixing and matching their use of health systems. Thus in a trial and error manner they will try one system and depending upon its success they may or may not try another system. There

Table 4.5   *A typology of themes relating culture, empowerment and health (MacLachlan, 2004)*

Theme	Explanations
Cultural colonialism	Comparisons of the superior 'us' with the inferior 'them' with the aim of managing 'them' in the interests of the elites.
Cultural sensitivity	Awareness of the 'them' who now live among 'us' with the aim of making 'our' healthcare accessible to 'them'.
Cultural migration	Awareness of the broad impact of migration on the health and well-being of individuals and communities.
Cultural alternativism	Acceptance of different approaches to health care.
Cultural empowerment	Empowerment of oppressed groups through cultural reawakening.
Cultural globalization	Oppression of indigenous cultures in the interests of the dominant culture/class.
Cultural evolution	Impact of the loosening of cultural connections on identities and health.

is little apparent sign of internal conflict over trying systems that are fundamentally opposed. This is the case both in developing and increasingly in developed countries. In a study of South African miners, it was found that their model of health is holistic and is concerned with the balance between the person and the environment. More importantly, they show no discomfort in moving between representatives of western biomedicine (hospitals, clinics, pharmacies) and traditional healers (diviners, herbalists and faith healers). The growth of CAM in western society is another indication of this mixing of health belief systems.

The growth of these mixed belief systems can lead to confusion among health professionals. Health psychology needs to recognize this complexity rather than assuming that health belief systems are fixed (MacLachlan, 2000). It is important to recognize that culture goes far beyond our health belief systems to include an understanding of our changing world. A typology to integrate many of the various ideas around culture and health has been developed by MacLachlan (2004). This illustrates the complexity of the connections between culture and health (Table 4.5).

Disability Culture

KT

Over the last 30 years there has been a growing interest in **disability culture**. However, the concept is even now a contested one. Disability culture developed within the disability movement; definitions (e.g. Peters, 2000) have tended to emphasize:

- shared history and experiences, particularly of oppression and resilience;
- a common purpose in the form of political resistance to devaluation and oppression;
- shared creative expression particularly through flourishing disability art and humour;
- promotion of a positive disabled identity to 'act as a means of politicising and cohering disabled people' (Barnes and Mercer, 2001: 517), and to increase self-esteem and oppose negative representations of disability in mainstream ablist cultures (e.g. supercrip, personal tragedy, sick, weak etc.).

In addition, some argue disability culture includes an evolving language and symbols, a unified worldview, and shared beliefs and values. There is no doubt that for many disabled people there is a growing affiliation with disability culture. Certainly, most, if not all, disabled people share common experiences and strive for a more positive self-identity. Disability culture may represent a powerful tool in the struggle against oppression. However, not all disability theorists accept the concept uncritically.

Some authors argue that there is an inherent risk in the promotion of a singular disability culture. Using disability as its foundation, the essentialist category that is responsible for constructing oppression risks perpetuating oppression and reinforcing dichotomous thinking rather than prioritizing the acceptance and valuing of diversity.

The desire for a separate, unifying cultural identity, while politically expedient, is ultimately a consequence of oppression, one that may conflict with the aim of complete integration and equality in society. The idea of disability pride remains problematic for many, due to the pain and distress associated with much impairment. Furthermore, different impairment groups may consider that they have little in common with other impairment groups (Davis, 2002), clearly illustrated by the Deaf community. Many deaf people refuse to define themselves as disabled, instead defining themselves as an able, linguistic and cultural minority. They emphasize that membership of Deaf culture requires voluntary affiliation with the Deaf community, fluent use of sign language and refusal to identify themselves as being disabled. The capital D is used to differentiate themselves from deaf people who do not fulfil these requirements (e.g. deaf people who don't use sign language).

The idea of a singular disability culture is therefore not universally accepted. In fact, the disability movement has been criticized for not paying enough attention to other aspects of identity that may be equally salient to the experience of disability. In particular, gender, ethnicity, sexuality and age, along with dimensions of individual suffering, have all been mentioned as receiving insufficient attention in disability research.

Not all those who could define themselves as disabled choose to do so. This is hardly surprising when disabled people represent such a vastly heterogeneous group. Disabled people can vary in all the ways that able-bodied people can vary (e.g. ethnicity, gender, etc.) and in addition vary in terms of their impairment including type (e.g. autism versus amputation), domain (physical, sensory, cognitive), time of acquisition (from birth, childhood, adulthood, old age), duration, association with illness, prognosis, severity, visibility, intermittence, and level of stigma (e.g. AIDs versus blindness).

Disability is unlikely to have the same meaning in relation to a healthy, white, middle-class, older man who was born with a missing limb, as in relation to a black, boy with autism from a lower SES family or a mixed race young woman who has severe early onset arthritis. Most disability occurs later in life when individuals have already been immersed in mainstream non-disabled cultures and consequently may be resistant to a disabled identity or affiliation with disability culture.

Deal (2003) reports the existence of hierarchies of impairment, both among disabled and non-disabled populations (including health professionals), which vary depending on whether asked about functionality or 'what-if' preferences. For example, many physically impaired people appear offended by, and reject, association with groups with learning difficulties. This holds important implications for the well-being of those lowest in the hierarchy and concerning the influence of stereotyping within the health professions. People with chronic illnesses allude to a complex existence that occupies a space between health and illness and between disability and normality. The transition from health to illness/impairment through to accepting a disabled identity is often slow, difficult, fluid and multidimensional. They may therefore consider disability culture as unavailable, inapplicable or irrelevant to them, especially as individual dimensions of their experience like pain and fatigue tend to be minimized within the movement.

Disabled people have been compared to other minority groups like those based on ethnicity, gender or sexuality. A growing body of work on disabled people with other minority statuses suggests that they have unique experiences and perspectives. Some argue that the cumulative effects of these interacting identity statuses represent double or multiple oppressions. Such groups (e.g. black disabled people) could then be the most deprived and oppressed members of society. This is termed as simultaneous oppression, where individuals may be forced to exist on the margins of each minority group they belong to. The influence of multiple minority statuses is likely to aggravate the experience of disability.

The heterogeneity of the disabled population suggests the existence of 'cultures of disabilities' rather than a singular disability culture (Brown, 2001). There is a distinct tension between fragmentation into separate multiple minority groups and cultures of disabilities, and the need to present a unified front to effect political change. Perhaps affiliation with a unified disability culture is best viewed as a fluid community of resistance that does not preclude the inherent multiplicity of identity and cultural memberships.

Many of the issues discussed above should be of concern to health psychologists including:

- How extensively does disability culture encompass shared beliefs that differ from those of non-disabled populations, in particular, health-related beliefs and health-related behaviours? For example, there is evidence suggesting that some disabled women believe everyday illnesses are a sign of weakness, which results in a refusal to 'give in' or visit their GPs.
- What are the effects of multiple minority statuses? How do they interact and influence the health of disabled people?
- What are the implications for the well-being of disabled people who are placed lowest in hierarchies of impairment? How do hierarchies of impairment reflect negative stereotyping and influence health professionals in their interactions with disabled people?
- Should health psychologists working with people with chronic illnesses promote disability culture, as a source of empowerment in the transition from health to acceptance of a disabled identity?
- Does affiliation with disability culture always result in increased self-esteem and, where it does, are there associated health-related benefits?
- Treating disabled people as a homogeneous group can result in institutional discrimination. How can health psychologists influence health and service providers to ensure the variant needs of disabled people are adequately addressed?
- How can health psychologists help to promote the acceptance and respect of diversity in their practice, and most importantly, the full inclusion of disabled people?

Culture and Health Beliefs

It is apparent that how people organize their beliefs about health is intertwined with their broader belief systems. Culture is not simply part of traditional communities but pervades all our lives. We are all cultural beings. The definition of health as a quality of the individual body is something peculiar to biomedicine. Other cultures both within and outside western society prefer a more social definition of health that emphasizes the relationship between the individual and the world. These alternative belief systems are not fixed and separate but are in a process of constant change.

Future Research

1 Through access to historical documents, psychologists can assist in expanding our understanding of the evolution of contemporary health beliefs.
2 Understanding of popular health beliefs requires an understanding of their social and cultural context.
3 The increasing development of alternative health care in western society requires ongoing research.
4 In most large industrialized societies cultural minorities make use of a variety of competing health belief systems. There is a need for research to explore how these interact with the more dominant health belief systems.
5 The implications of disability culture on health, health beliefs and practices needs to be explored.

Summary

1 Human thought and practices are culturally immersed.
2 Different ways of explaining health and illness are apparent in different societies and cultures. These are known as causal ontologies.
3 The moral discourse of suffering is a particularly pervasive health discourse.
4 Systems of health can be considered as either expert or folk. These two systems are not separate but interactive.
5 The western view of health has moved through various stages from the classic to the religious and then the scientific.
6 The scientific view of health or biomedicine is the most dominant view in contemporary society but other health belief systems remain popular.
7 In contemporary society there is increasing interest in various alternative therapies.
8 Chinese medicine is an expert health belief system that remains popular in China and among Chinese migrants in other societies.
9 Ayurvedic medicine remains popular in other parts of Southern Asia.
10 In Africa there is a wide variety of other health belief systems that emphasize spiritual aspects and a communal orientation.
11 A burgeoning disability culture may be viewed as a source of empowerment for disabled people with the potential for improved well-being, via fellowship and increased self-esteem.

Key Terms

alternative medicine

biomedicine

causal ontologies

disability culture

Galenic medicine

humours

moral discourses

5

Research Methods in Health Psychology

Outline

In this chapter we introduce the principal research methods used within health psychology. The methods fall into three categories: quantitative, qualitative and action research. Methods of all three kinds are vehicles for advancing our understanding of health, illness and health care. Research designs that are quantitative in nature place emphasis on reliable and valid measurement in controlled experiments, trials and surveys. Qualitative methods use interviews, focus groups, narratives or texts to explore health and illness concepts and experience. Multiple sources of evidence are synthesized in systematic reviews and meta-analyses. Action research enables change processes to feed back into plans for improvement, empowerment and emancipation.

Introduction

Health psychology generates a great diversity of research questions and consequently requires a wide range of methods for gathering evidence to answer them. As the field develops, the role of theory and model development is a crucial one. However, methodology is of equal importance in the testing of theories and models, in putting theory into practice, and in evaluating the consequences of doing so. In applying health psychology principles and practice in health work by making interventions or taking concerted actions designed to produce change, it is necessary to be evidence based. Interest in action research and methods of evaluation is increasing.

Many of psychology's traditional methods and research designs are quantitative in nature, placing emphasis on reliable and valid measurement in the context of controlled investigation with experiments, trials and surveys. Multiple sources of such evidence can be synthesized using systematic reviews and meta-analysis. Case studies are more suited to unique, one-off situations that require investigation. Qualitative methods use interviews, focus groups, narratives or texts to explore health and illness concepts and experience (Marks and Yardley, 2004). Action research enables change processes to feed back into plans for improvement, empowerment and emancipation. The different kinds of method complement each other, and all are necessary in painting a complete picture of psychology and health.

No method is essentially 'better' or 'worse' than any other. There is no 'royal road' to the gathering of research information. A method that suits one purpose will not suit another. Which method is to be recommended depends entirely upon the question being asked and the context of the asking. The sections below briefly describe some of the main quantitative and qualitative methods for data collection and analysis. This is followed by a section that introduces action research.

The majority of studies in health psychology have used the methods or designs described below. Progress in health psychology follows a creative problem-solving approach by many different individuals and groups using a multiplicity of skills and expertise of which implementation of sound methodology is but one. Rigour in methodology needs to be appropriately matched by rigour in theory and practice. For a more detailed exposition of research methods in health and clinical psychology, see Marks and Yardley (2004).

Quantitative Research Methods

Between groups designs

KT

KT

A **between groups design** allocates matched groups of people to different treatments. If the measures are taken at one time this is sometimes called a **cross-sectional design**, in contrast to a **longitudinal design** where the groups are tested at two or more time-points.

KT

When we are comparing only treatment groups, a failure to find a difference between them on the outcome measure(s) might be for one of three reasons: they are equally effective; they are equally ineffective; they are equally harmful. For this reason, one of the groups should be a **control group** that will enable us to dicover whether the treatment(s) show a different effect from no treatment.

Ethical issues arise over the use of control groups. Not treating someone in need of treatment is unacceptable. However, if there is genuine uncertainty about what works best, it is better to compare the treatments with a control condition than to continue for ever applying a treatment that may be less effective than another. Once we have determined which therapy *is* the most effective, this should be offered to the control group and to all future patients (see Clark-Carter and Marks, 2004).

KT

The choice of the control condition is important. The group should receive the same amount of attention as those in the treatment condition(s). This type of control is known as a **placebo control** as treatment itself could have a non-specific effect to 'please' the client and enhance his/her well-being.

If all of the various groups' responses are measured only after an intervention, then we haven't really measured change. All groups, including the control group, could have changed but from different starting positions, and failing to find a difference between the groups after the treatment could miss this. We can help to deal with this problem by using a mixed design when we measure all groups before and after the treatment. However, we would be introducing some of the difficulties mentioned above for a cross-over or within-subjects design (see Clark-Carter, 1997).

Cross-over or within-participants designs

The **cross-over or within-participants design** is used when the same people provide measures at more than one time and differences between the measures at the different times are recorded. An example would be a measure taken before an intervention (pre-treatment) and again after the intervention (post-treatment). Such a design minimizes the effect of individual differences as each person acts as his or her own control.

There are a number of problems with this design. Any change in the measure may be due to other factors having changed. For example, you may have introduced an intervention that is designed to improve quality of life (QoL) among patients in a particular long-stay ward of a hospital but the hospital has also introduced other changes, for example, a new set of menus introduced by the catering department. In addition, the difference may be due to some aspect of the measuring instrument. If the same measure is being taken on both occasions, the fact that it has been taken twice may be the reason that the result has changed. If, to get around this problem, a different version of the measure is used then the difference might be due to the difference in the nature of the measures and not the efficacy of the intervention.

Another issue is that failure to find a difference between the two occasions doesn't tell you much; in a worsening situation the intervention still might have been effective in preventing things from worsening more than they have already. Additionally, if you use a cross-over design to compare two or more treatments, the particular results could be an **artefact** of the order in which the treatments were given. Perhaps there is a carry-over effect so that later trials show improvement as a result of practice or later trials could demonstrate poorer performance as a result of fatigue and these effects would have happened even if the treatment had remained the same. To counter such order effects one can use a baseline or 'washout period' before and after treatment periods. Also one can randomly assign people to different orders or, if one is interested in seeing whether order does have an effect then a more systematic allocation of participants to different orders can be employed: e.g. if there are only two conditions participants could be alternately placed in the two possible orders, or if there are more than two conditions a Latin square design could be employed. Such systematic allocations of participants allow us to test formally whether there is an effect of order (see Clark-Carter and Marks, 2004 for further details).

Cross-sectional studies

Cross-sectional studies obtain responses from respondents on one occasion only. With appropriate randomized sampling methods, the sample can be assumed to be a representative cross-section of the population(s) under study and it is possible to make comparisons between sub-groups (e.g. males versus females, older versus younger people, etc.). Cross-sectional designs are quite common because they are relatively inexpensive in time and resources. However, there are problems of interpretation whenever there is doubt about the randomness/representativeness of the samples. Also cause and effect can never be inferred between one variable and another and it is impossible to say whether the associations that may be observed are caused by a third variable not measured in the study. Examples of cross-sectional studies and the associated problems of interpretation may be found in Chapter 12.

Direct observation

The simplest and least problematic kind of study involves directly observing behaviour in a relevant setting, for example, patients waiting for treatment in a doctor's surgery or clinic. The observation may be accompanied by recordings in written, oral, auditory or visual form. Several investigators may observe the same events and reliability checks conducted. **Direct observation** includes casual observation, formal observation and participant observation. However, ethical issues are raised by planned formal observational study of people who have not consented to such observations.

Interviews (structured)

A **structured interview** schedule is a prepared, standard set of questions that are asked in person, or perhaps by telephone, of a person or group concerning a particular research issue. A semi-structured interview is more open ended and allows the interviewee to address issues that he/she feels relevant to the topics raised by the investigator (see Qualitative research methods below).

Longitudinal designs

These designs involve measuring responses of a single sample on more than one occasion. The measurements may be *prospective* or *retrospective*. Prospective longitudinal designs allow greater control over the sample, the variables measured and the times when the measurements take place. Such designs are superior to cross-sectional designs because one is more able to investigate hypotheses of causation when the associations between variables are measured over time. **Longitudinal designs** are among the most powerful designs available for the evaluation of treatments and of theories about human experience and behaviour, but they are also the most costly in labour, time and money.

Meta-analysis

A **meta-analysis** is a systematic and integrative statistical analysis of the results from a number of research studies that may be combined because they asked a similar research question. The analysis is often based on the calculation of the mean effect size in which each study is weighted according to the number of participants. Statistical techniques are used to combine the results of primary studies addressing the same question into a single, pooled measure of effect size, with a confidence interval.

Questionnaires

Many constructs are measured using **questionnaires** consisting of a standard set of items with accompanying instructions. Ideally a questionnaire will have been demonstrated to be both a reliable and a valid measure of the construct(s) it purports to measure.

Questionnaires vary in objectives, content, especially in their generic versus specific content, question format, the number of items, and *sensitivity* or *responsiveness* to change. Questionnaires may be employed in cross-sectional and longitudinal studies. In prospective studies the same measures are taken from a number of groups of participants on a number of occasions and the principal objective will be to evaluate the differences that occur between groups across time. When looking for changes over time, the responsiveness of a questionnaire to clinical and subjective changes is a crucial feature. A questionnaire's content, sensitivity and extent, together with its reliability and validity, influence a questionnaire's selection.

Guides are available to advise users on making a choice that contains the appropriate generic measure, domain or disease of interest (e.g. Bowling, 1991, 1995). These guides are extremely useful as they include details on content, scoring, validity and reliability of dozens of questionnaires for measuring all of the major aspects of psychological well-being and quality of life, including disease-specific and domain-specific questionnaires and more generic measures.

There are hundreds of questionnaires available, measuring almost every imaginable aspect of health behaviour and clinical experience. There are some essential characteristics that should be considered in selecting or designing a questionnaire: your objectives, type of respondents, the content, question format, number of items, reliability, validity and sensitivity to change.

The investigator must ask: What is it that I want to know? The answer will dictate the selection of the most relevant and useful questionnaire. The most important aspect of questionnaire selection is therefore to *match the objective of the study with the objective of the questionnaire*. For example, are you interested in a disease-specific or broad ranging research question? When this question is settled, you need to decide whether there is anything else that your research objective will require you to know. Usually the researcher needs to develop a specific block of questions that will seek vital information concerning the respondents' socio-demographic characteristics that can be placed at the beginning or the end of the main questionnaire.

Questionnaire content may vary from the highly generic (e.g. 'How has your health been over the last few weeks: Excellent, Good, Fair, Poor, Very Bad?') to the highly specific (e.g. 'Have you had any arguments with people at work in the last two weeks?). The items may all be different ways of trying to measure the same thing, or there may be a variety of scales and sub-scales for measuring different dimensions or variables within a single instrument.

Questionnaires vary greatly in the number of items that are used to assess the variable(s) of interest. Single-item measures use a single question, rating or item to measure the concept or variable of interest. For example, the now popular single verbal item to evaluate health status, 'During the past 4 weeks ... how would you rate your health in general? Excellent, Very good, Good, Fair, Poor.' Single items have the obvious advantages of being simple, direct and brief.

Surveys

Surveys are systematic methods for determining how a sample of participants respond to a set of standard questions attempting to assess their feelings, attitudes, beliefs or

KT

knowledge at one or more times. For example, we may want to know how drug users' perceptions of themselves and their families differ from those of non-users, or to better understand the experiences of patients receiving specific kinds of treatment, how health and social services are perceived by informal carers of people with dementia, Parkinson's, multiple sclerosis (MS) or other chronic conditions, or learn more about how people recovering from a disease such as coronary heart disease feel about their rehabilitation. The survey method will be the method of choice in many of these types of study.

The survey method, whether using interviews, questionnaires, or some combination of the two, is versatile, and can be applied equally well to research with individuals, groups, organizations, communities or populations to inform our understanding of a host of very different types of research issues and questions. Normally a survey is conducted on a sample of the study population of interest (e.g. people aged 70+; women aged 20–44; teenagers who smoke; carers of people with dementia etc.). Issues of key importance in conducting a survey are: the objective(s); the mode of administration; the method of sampling; the sample size; the preparation of the data for analysis.

In running a survey it is essential to have a clear idea in mind about the objective before starting it. We must have a very clear idea about *why* we are doing our study (the theory or policy behind the research), *what* we are looking for (the research question), *where* we intend to look (the setting or domain). We must also decide *who* will be in the sample (the study sample), and *how* to use the tools we have at our disposal (the specific procedures for applying the research methods). We have to be cautious that our procedures do not generate any self-fulfilling prophecies. *Lack of clarity about purposes and objectives* is one of the main stumbling blocks for the novice investigator to overcome. This is particularly the case when carrying out a survey, especially in a team of investigators who may have varying agendas with regard to the *why, what, who, where* and *how?* questions that must be answered before the survey can begin.

The main modes of administration are: face-to face interview, telephone interview, group self-completion, and postal self-completion. These modes may also be used in combination.

Next you need to decide *who* will be the sample for your survey and also *where* you will carry it out. The first issue that needs to be addressed is who are your study population? In other words, which population of people is your research question about? And how specific can you be about the definition of this population?

The sample for any survey should represent the study population as closely as possible. In some cases, the sample can consist of the entire study population, e.g. every pupil in a school; every student at a university; every patient in a hospital. More usually however, the sample will be a random selection of a proportion of the members of a population, e.g. every tenth person in a community, or every fourth patient admitted into a hospital. This method is called simple random sampling (SRS).

A variation on SRS is systematic sampling. In this case the first person in the sampling frame is chosen at random and then every *n*th person on the list from there on, where *n* is the sample fraction being used.

In stratified sampling the population is divided into groups or 'strata' and the groups are randomly sampled, but in different proportions so that the overall sample sizes of the groups can be made equal, even though they are not equal in the population (e.g. the 40–59, 60–79 and 80–99 age groups in a community sample, or men and women in a clinical sample). These groups will therefore be equally represented in the data. Other methods include non-probability sampling of six kinds: convenience samples, most similar/dissimilar samples, typical case samples, critical case samples, snowball samples, and quota samples.

All such sampling methods are biased; in fact there is no perfect method of sampling because there will always be a category of people that any sampling method under-represents.

In any survey it is necessary to maximize the proportion of selected people who are recruited. If a large proportion of people refuse to participate, the sample will not represent the population, but be biased in unknown ways. As a general principle, surveys that recruit at least 70% of those invited to participate are considered representative. The sample size is a key issue. The variability of scores obtained from the sampling diminishes as the sample size increases. So the bigger the sample, the more precise will be the estimates of the population scores, but the more the survey will cost.

Randomized controlled trials

Randomized controlled trials (RCTs) involve the systematic comparison of interventions using a fully controlled application of one or more 'treatments' with a random allocation of participants to the different treatment groups. This design is the 'gold standard' to which much research in psychology and health care aspires. Participants are allocated randomly to one or more intervention conditions and to a control condition. The statistical tests that are available have as one of their assumptions that participants have been randomly assigned to conditions. However, when researchers move beyond the laboratory setting to real world clinical and health research, it soon becomes evident that the so-called 'gold standard' cannot always be achieved, in practice, and, in fact, may not be desirable for ethical reasons. | KT |

We are frequently forced to study existing groups that are being treated differently rather than have the luxury of being able to allocate people to conditions. Thus, we may in effect be comparing the health policies and services of a number of different hospitals and clinics. Such a design is sometimes described as '**quasi-experimental design**' in that we are comparing treatments in as controlled a manner as possible, but we have been unable for practical reasons to manipulate the independent variable, the policies, or allocate the participants ourselves. | KT |

The advantage of a randomized controlled trial is that differences in the outcome measure between the participants treated in the different ways can be attributed with more confidence to the manipulations of the researchers, because individual differences are likely to be spread in a random way between the different treatments. As soon as that basis for allocation of participants is lost, then questions arise over the ability to identify causes of changes or differences between the groups; in other words, the **internal validity** of the design is in question. | KT |

Single case experimental designs

Single case experimental designs are investigations of a series of experimental manipulations with a single research participant. | KT |

Systematic review

KT

A **systematic review** is an integration of evidence about an effect or intervention involving the summary and integration of evidence from all relevant and usable primary sources. What counts as 'relevant and usable' is a matter for debate and judgement. Rules and criteria for selection of studies and for data extraction can be agreed by those carrying out the review. Publishing these rules and criteria along with the review enables such reviews to be replicable and transparent. Proponents of the systematic review therefore see the systematic review as a way of integrating research that limits bias. Traditionally the method has been applied to quantitative data. Recently, researchers have begun to investigate ways and means to synthesize qualitative studies also.

The synthesis of research evidence has been discussed in psychology since the mid-1970s when Glass (1976) coined the term 'meta-analysis'. From the late 1980s, research synthesis was discussed in the medical sciences (Mulrow, 1987; Oxman and Guyatt, 1988). The foundation of the Cochrane Collaboration in the 1990s, an organization that prepares and updates systematic reviews, was pivotal in establishing the systematic review as the method of choice for synthesizing research in health care. The use of systematic reviews is now widespread and strongly linked to 'evidence-based practice'. Systematic reviews of randomized controlled trials (RCTs) are seen as the 'gold standard' for determining 'evidence-based practice'.

Knowing how to carry out a systematic review and how to critically interpret a systematic review report are skills that health psychologists need to acquire. They are competences that enable the psychologist to integrate and implement research findings in making improvements in clinical and health care.

Inevitably systematic reviews act like a sieve, selecting some evidence but rejecting other evidence. To retain the visual metaphor, the reviewers act as a filter or lens; what they see and report depends on how the selection process is operated. Whenever there is ambiguity in evidence, the selection process may well tend to operate in confirmatory mode, seeking positive support for a position, model or theory rather than seeking disconfirmation. It is essential to be critical and cautious in interpreting and analysing systematic reviews of biomedical and related topics. Over time systematic reviews have the potential to influence clinical and health psychology practice in many different ways. However, the criteria for the selection of studies determine the outcome of the review, and so different criteria may well lead to different outcomes.

If we want to implement new practice as a direct consequence of such reviews, we had better make certain that the findings are solid and not a mirage. This is why the study of the method itself is so important. However seductive the view that systematic reviews can produce evidence that is bias-free, systematic reviews of the same topic can produce significantly different results, indicating that bias is difficult to control. Like all forms of knowledge, the results of a systematic review are the consequences of a process of negotiation about rules and criteria, and cannot be accepted without criticism and debate. We shall see later in this book how systematic reviews of evidence may cause controversy (e.g. Chapter 17).

Qualitative Research Methods

Historical analysis

Health and illness are socially and historically located phenomena. As such psychologists have much to gain by detailed historical research (**historical analysis**) on the development of health beliefs and practices. They can work closely with medical or health historians to explore the evolution of scientific and popular beliefs about health and illness or they can work independently (see Chapter 3).

KT

An excellent example is the work of Herzlich and Pierret (1987). Their work involved the detailed analysis of a variety of textual sources such as scientific medical writings but also popular autobiographical and fictional accounts of the experience of illness. They noted the particular value of literary works because of their important contribution to shaping public discourse. Such textual analysis needs to be guided by an understanding of the political and philosophical ideas of the period.

All societies have ways of interpreting the world and defining health and illness. For example, historically people in western society attributed illness to various supernatural forces. However, with the scientific revolution ideas about illness were increasingly located within the physical body. More recently we have increased concern about a wider definition of health encompassing quality of life. An understanding of these changing ideas requires connecting them to the changing historical periods (e.g. Flick, 2002; Porter, 1997).

Health psychologists need also to be reflexive about the history of their own discipline. It arose at a particular historical period sometimes described as late modernity. Initially it was seen as providing a complement to the excessive physical focus of biomedicine. Now some see it as part of the broader lifestyle movement.

There are different approaches to the writing of history. There are those who can be broadly characterized as descriptive and who often provide a listing of the growth of the discipline in laudatory terms (e.g. Stone et al., 1987). Conversely there are those who adopt a more critical approach and attempt to dissect the underlying reasons for the development of the discipline. Within health psychology, this latter approach is still in its early stages (e.g. Stam, 2004).

Such writings can be complemented with interviews with elderly people about their health problems and their experiences with health services in their youth. This oral historical research connects with ageing and narrative research. This work can enable the researcher to identify the changing character of health beliefs and practices. In turn, this work can be connected to forms of action research (see below).

Diary techniques

In health research diaries (**diary techniques**) have been frequently used as a method for collecting information about temporal changes in health status. These diaries can be prepared by either the researcher or participant or both, and they can be quantitative or qualitative or both. They can be compared to the time charts that have been

KT

Table 5.1   *The applicability of a diary to psychological research (Reid et al., 2003)*

Diary uses	Description of use	Example of population used	References
Gold standard	Possible to validate use of questionnaires examing the same behavioural change or psychological characteristics as recorded in diary.	Chronic headache sufferers	Stewart et al. (1999)
Reflective practice/ medical documentation	Traditional use of diary to note observations and thoughts regarding illness/treatment/ research.	Health care provider	Heath (1998)
Communication device	Provides a voice for the patient and an insight into how the patient interprets illness and treatment.	Patients with longstanding illness	Stensland and Malterud (1999)
Evolving methodology	Provides an opportunity to gain qualitative data that can inform hypothesis generation and testing.	ICU patients and families	Berghom et al. (1999)
Tracking/time series	Psychological, behavioural and physiological data can be collected to map changes over time.	Sleep/wake times	Eissa et al. (2001)
Efficacy of treatment	Outcome measure.	Behavioural therapy for irritable bowel syndrome	Heyman-Monnikes et al. (2000)

used by health professionals for generations to track changes in the health status of individuals.

A useful summary of the current uses of the diary in health research has been prepared by Reid et al. (2003) and is reproduced in Table 5.1.

Diaries have been especially used as an aid to the evaluation of particular interventions. The more detailed the diary records the more detailed the evaluation. However, a major challenge is convincing the research participant to complete the diary entry on a regular basis. Often, they will be completed at irregular intervals or alternatively several entries may be completed at the same time. It is essential that the participant see the value in completing the diary.

Evidence suggests that diary keeping can have benefits for the participant irrespective of the researcher. Work by Pennebaker (1995) and others have confirmed that writing can be psychologically beneficial. A series of empirical studies have provided evidence that journal writing can lead to reduction in illness symptoms and in the use of health services (e.g. Smyth et al., 1999). There are a number of explanations for this including release of emotional energy, cognitive processing and assistance with narrative restructuring.

Narrative approaches

This approach is concerned with the desire to seek insight and meaning about health and illness through the acquisition of data in the form of stories concerning personal experiences. These **narrative approaches** assume that human beings are natural storytellers and that the principle task of the psychologist is to explore the different stories being told (Murray, 2003).

KT

The most popular source of material for the narrative researcher is the interview. The focus of the narrative interview is the elicitation of narrative accounts from the interviewee. This can take various forms. The life-story interview is the most extended form of the narrative interview. As its name implies, the life-story interview seeks to obtain an extended account of the person's life. The primary aim is to make the participant at ease and encourage him/her to tell their story at length.

More frequently, the health psychologist is interested in a particular health and illness experience such as what it is like to live with a chronic illness. In this case the focus will be more on the actual lived experience of the illness but bearing in mind that illness exists within a certain social world and cannot be extracted from it.

A particular version of the narrative interview is the episodic interview in which the researcher encourages the participant to speak on a variety of particular experiences (Flick, 2002). This approach assumes that experiences are often stored in memory in narrative-episodes and that the challenge is to reveal these without integrating them into a larger narrative. Throughout the interview the role of the interviewer is to encourage sustained narrative accounting. This can be achieved through a variety of supportive remarks. The researcher can deliberately encourage the participant to expand upon remarks about particular issues.

Narrative analysis (NA) can take various forms. It begins with a repeated reading of the text to identify the story or stories within it. The primary focus is on maintaining the narrative integrity of the account. The researcher may develop a summary of the narrative account that will help identify the structure of the narrative, its tone and the central characters. It may be useful to engage in a certain amount of thematic analysis to identify some underlying themes. But this does not equate with narrative analysis. NA involves trying to see the interconnections between events rather than separating them. Having analysed one case the researcher can then proceed to the next, identifying similarities and differences in the structure and content of the narratives.

This inductive form of analysis does not connect with the theoretical assumptions guiding the researcher. This requires deliberately identifying particular psychological processes underlying the narrative. An example of this is the work of Hollway and Jefferson (2000) who explored the unconscious defences against anxiety underlying narrative accounts of crime. Alternatively, the researcher can connect with personal narrative with the broader cultural narrative (e.g. Crossley, 1999). Some examples are given in Chapter 11.

Case studies

The term case study is used to describe a detailed descriptive account of an individual, group or collective. The purpose of such **case studies** is to provide a 'thick description' (Geertz, 1973) of a phenomenon that would not be obtained by the usual quantitative or qualitative approaches. It requires the researcher to be expansive in the type of data collected with a deliberate aim to link the person with the context, e.g. the sick person in the family.

KT

In developing the case study the researcher usually attempts to provide a chrono-logical account of the evolution of the phenomenon from the perspective of the central character. A challenge for the researcher is in establishing the boundaries of the case. These need to be flexible to ensure that all information germane to the case under investigation is collected.

The major strength of the case study is the integration of actor and context and the developmental perspective. Thus the phenomenon under investigation is not dis-sected but rather maintains its integrity or wholeness and it is possible to map its changes over time.

There are several different types of case study. The empirical case study is grounded in the data. The aim of this type of case study is to see the general in the particular. Thus the researcher tries to move from the specific to the general in an inductive manner. The theoretical case is an exemplar for a process that has already been clarified. The latter case is the one often used in clinical teaching. These clini-cal cases will be selected to provide the best examples of a particular phenomenon. The case histories provided by Freud are classic examples of this form. Often the researcher will move back and forward in his/her research identifying certain pat-terns in a particular case and then confirming and extending his/her understanding in another case.

The researcher can use a variety of techniques to collect information for the case study. Thus the researcher can conduct interviews, or repeat interviews and observe the case in different settings.

The process of analysis can be considered the process of shaping the case. Thus the researcher selects certain pieces of information and discards others so as to present a more integrated case. This is a challenge since at this stage the creative role of the researcher assumes importance.

Ethnographic methods

KT

Ethnographic methods seek to build a systematic understanding of a culture from the viewpoint of the insider. Ethnographic methods are multiple attempts to describe the shared beliefs, practices, artefacts, knowledge and behaviours of an intact cultural group. They attempt to represent the totality of a phenomenon in its complete context in its naturalistic setting.

Detailed observation is an important part of ethnographic fieldwork. The observa-tion can be either overt or covert. In the overt case the researcher does not attempt to disguise his/her identity but rather is unobstrusive such that the phenomenon under investigation is not disturbed. In this case the researcher can take detailed notes, in either a prearranged or discursive format.

In certain cases the researcher may decide that his/her presence may disturb the field. In this case two forms of covert observation may be used. In one form the focus of observation is not aware at all of the presence of the researcher. Thus the researcher may observe the person from behind a screen or record conversation unobstrusively using an audio or video-recorder. An alternative approach is when the person observed may be aware of the researcher's presence but is unaware that he/she is a researcher. To achieve this covert form of observation the researcher becomes a participant observer by which he/she engages in complementary activities to that of the case. In both of these forms the researcher needs to consider the ethics of deception.

A form of participant observation that is not covert is when the researcher accompanies the person but tries not to interfere with the performance of everyday tasks. A classic example of this is Willis's (1977) study of the entry of working-class boys into the workplace. In this study Willis sat in during classes in school and accompanied the boys during their first weeks at work. He also conducted individual and group interviews with the boys, their teachers and parents. In addition, he considered other material such as careers brochures and other printed material available to the boys. At all times the boys were aware of Willis but gradually accepted him as part of the background. To be accepted the researcher usually has to show some empathy with the study participants. Again, the researcher needs to consider the broader ethical issues of apparently espousing certain beliefs and engaging in certain activities.

Interviews (semi-structured)

Semi-structured interviews are designed to explore the participant's view of things with the minimal amount of assumptions from the interviewer. Open-ended questions are useful in this kind of interview. They have several advantages over closed-ended questions. The answers will not be biased by the researcher's preconceptions as much as closed-ended questions can be. The respondents are able to express their opinions, thoughts and feelings freely using their own words in ways that are less constrained by the particular wordings of the question. The respondents may have responses that the structured interview designer has overlooked. They may have in-depth comments that they wish to make about your study and the topics that it is covering that would not be picked up using the standard questions in a structured interview.

In preparing for the interview the researcher should develop an interview guide. This can include a combination of primary and supplementary questions. Alternatively, the researcher may prefer to have a list of themes to be explored. However, it is important that the researcher does not formally follow these in the same order but rather introduces them at the appropriate time in the interview. Prior to the interview, the researcher should review these themes and order them from the least invasive to the more personal.

Some general guides to promote discussion in the interview have been suggested by Wilkinson et al. (2004):

- Be a good listener: the researcher should show a strong interest in what the participant has to say.
- Be empathetic, not judgemental: the participant can easily be discouraged by any evidence that their viewpoint is not accepted.
- Allow the participant's worldview to develop: encourage the participant to express herself fully in her own words.
- Allow expression of feelings: the participant may be happy, sad or angry about certain experiences. The researcher should not be disturbed by this expression of feelings. It is important to remember that the focus of the interview is research, not psychotherapy, and the researcher should maintain those boundaries. If the interview becomes strained then the researcher and the interviewer should negotiate its continuation.

As with all qualitative research, preparation is essential. Thus the researcher should ensure that the participant knows what the research is about in general terms prior to the interview. Novice interviewers should always liaise closely with their mentors to ensure personal safety and to debrief fully afterwards. This will enable them to refine their interview techniques and possibly review the questions and themes they have used.

Focus groups

KT

Focus groups comprise one or more group discussions in which participants 'focus' collectively upon a topic or issue usually presented to them as a group of questions, although sometimes as a film, a collection of advertisements, cards to sort, a game to play, or a vignette to discuss. The distinctive feature of the focus group method is its generation of interactive data (Wilkinson, 1998).

Focus groups were initially largely used in marketing research. As its title implied they had a focus that was to clarify the participants' views on a particular product. Thus from the outset the researcher had set the parameters of the discussion and as it proceeded he/she deliberately guided the discussion such that its focus remained limited.

More recent use of the focus group has been much more expansive. In many cases the term *discussion group* is preferred to give an indication of this greater latitude. This approach was originally developed by Willis (1977) to explore working-class boys' views on life and work. In this case the participants have a much greater say on the direction of the group conversation and so it can be considered more naturalistic.

The role of the researcher in the focus group is to act as the moderator for the discussion. The researcher can follow similar guidelines as those with the interview. However, the researcher needs to ensure that all the group participants have opportunity to express their viewpoints.

At the beginning of the discussion the researcher should follow the usual guidelines. It is important that the group is briefed on the basic principles of confidentiality and respect for different opinions. It is useful for them to know each others' first names and to have name badges. This facilitates greater interaction. It is also useful to have some refreshments available.

Although it is usual for the moderator to introduce some themes for discussion, this can be supplemented with a short video extract or pictures relevant to the topic being investigated. As the discussion proceeds, the researcher can often take a background role, but ensuring that the discussion does not deviate too far from the focus of the research and that all the participants have an opportunity to express their views.

It is useful to have an assistant or a colleague participate in focus group research. This person can help completing consent forms, providing name-tags, organizing refreshments, keeping notes on who is talking (this is useful for transcription), and monitoring the recording equipment. The focus group recording should be transcribed as soon as possible afterwards since it is often difficult to distinguish speakers.

Discourse analysis

KT

Discourse analysis is a set of procedures for analysing language as used in speech or texts. It focuses on the language and how it is used to construct versions of 'social reality' and what is gained by constructing events using the particular terms being used. It has links with ethnomethodology, conversation analysis and the study of meaning (semiology).

Two forms of discourse analysis have evolved over the past decade. The former, now termed *discursive psychology*, evolved from the work of Potter and Wetherell (1987) and is particularly concerned with the conversational context of the discourse. According to this approach language is 'a medium of social action rather than a mode for representing thoughts and ideas' (Edwards, 1997: 84). Discursive psychology is concerned with the discursive strategies people use to further particular actions in social situations, including accounting for their own behaviour or thoughts. These strategies are not considered evidence of participants' insincerity or of impression management but rather part of the social construction of identity in everyday conversation. This approach has been used to explore the character of patient talk and the character of doctor–patient interactions. There is a particular preference for naturally occurring conversations, e.g. mealtime talk (Wiggins et al., 2001).

The other approach is known as critical or *Foucauldian discourse analysis* (FDA). This approach has been especially developed by Ian Parker (1997) who criticizes the previous approach as evading issues of power and politics. FDA aims to identify the broader discursive resources that people in a particular culture draw upon in their everyday lives. These resources not only shape the way we interpret and act in the world but also how we define ourselves. This approach has been used to explore such health issues as smoking (Gillies and Willig, 1997) and anorexia nervosa. They each are concerned with how the discourse resources that are drawn upon in turn position people in certain ways.

Grounded theory analysis

Grounded theory analysis is a term used to describe a set of guidelines for conducting qualitative data analysis. It was originally developed by Glaser and Strauss (1967) and has subsequently gone through various revisions.

In its original form qualitative researchers were asked to dispense with theoretical assumptions when they began their research. Rather they were encouraged to adopt a stance of *disciplined naivety*. As the research progresses certain theoretical concepts are discovered and then tested in an iterative fashion. In the case of the qualitative interview, the researcher is encouraged to begin the analysis at a very early stage, even as the interview is progressing. Through a process of *abduction* the researcher begins to develop certain theoretical hypotheses. These hypotheses are then integrated into a tentative theoretical model that is tested as more data is collected.

This process follows a series of steps beginning with generating data. At this stage the researcher may have some general ideas about the topic but this should not restrict the talk of the participant. From the very initial stages the researcher is sifting through the ideas presented and seeking more information about what are considered to be emerging themes. From a more positivist perspective it is argued that the themes emerge from the data and that the researcher has simply to look for them. This approach is often associated with Glaser (1992). From a more social constructionist perspective, certain theoretical concepts of the researcher will guide both the data collection and analysis. This approach is more associated with the symbolic interactionist tradition (Strauss, 1987; Charmaz, 2003).

Having collected some data the researcher conducts a detailed coding of it followed by the generation of bigger categories. Throughout the coding the researcher follows the process of *constant comparative analysis*. This involves making comparison of codes within and between interview transcripts. This is followed by the stage of *memo-writing* which requires the researcher to begin to expand upon the meaning of the broader conceptual categories. This in turn can lead to further data generation through *theoretical sampling*. This is the process whereby the researcher deliberately selects certain participants or certain research themes to explore further because of the data already analysed. At this stage the researcher is both testing and strengthening the emergent theory. At a certain stage in this iterative process the researcher feels that he/she has reached the stage of *data saturation* – no new concepts are emerging and it is considered fruitless to continue with data collection.

Interpretative phenomenological analysis

Phenomenological research is concerned with exploring the lived experience of health, illness and disability. Its aim is to understand these phenomena from the perspective of the particular participant. A challenge for the researcher is how, as it were, to get inside the head of the person being investigated through what the person has to say about the experience. This in turn has to be interpreted by the researcher. A technique that addresses this challenge is **interpretative phenomenological analysis (IPA)** (Smith, 2004).

KT

IPA focuses on the cognitive processing of the participant. Smith (2004) argues that it accords with the original direction of cognitive psychology being concerned with exploring meaning-making rather than information-processing. IPA also accepts that what the study participants have to say has to be interpreted by the researcher since their perceptions and interpretations are not directly accessible.

IPA provides a guide to conducting this interpretation. It begins by accessing the participant's perceptions through the conduct of an interview or series of interviews with a homogeneous sample of individuals. The interview is semi-structured and focuses on the particular issue of concern.

The actual data analysis suggested in IPA goes through a number of stages. Initially the researcher reads through the interview transcripts and annotates it identifying any feature of interest in the text. The researcher then re-reads the text and develops a higher order thematic analysis. The skill at this stage is to develop these more abstract categories that are clearly rooted in the text and that can be connected across cases. Having identified the key themes or categories the researcher then proceeds to look for connections between them by identifying clusters. At this stage the researcher is drawing upon her broader understanding to make sense of what has been said. Once the researcher has finished the analysis of one case he/she can proceed to conduct an analysis of the next case in a similar manner. Alternatively, the researcher can begin to apply the analytic scheme developed in the previous case. The challenge is to identify repeating patterns but also to be alert to new patterns. Further details of this form of analysis are available in Smith et al. (1999) and Smith and Osborn (2003).

Action Research

The research methods described above are concerned with the investigation of states of affairs as they exist, or are perceived to exist by the research participants. We turn now to a mode of research that occurs as part of an intervention designed to bring about change. Thus the research and the intervention are part and parcel of the same process. **Action research** is concerned with the process of change and what is decided upon to stimulate change. The investigator acts as a facilitator/collaborator/agent-of-change who works with the stakeholders in a community or organization to help a situation to develop or make a change of direction. The aim is to bring about change in partnership with the community or organization concerned. Action research is particularly suited to organizational and consultancy work when a system or service requires improvements. In a community context it aims to be emancipatory, helping participants to go through an empowering process of increasing agency, control and self-determination.

Action research stems from Kurt Lewin's studies of the 1940s (Lewin, 1947, 1948). The Lewinian perspective on social change is sometimes viewed as 'unscientific' because it does not use control groups or random samples. However this is a misunderstanding of the approach.

Lewin wrote about what he called 'Feedback problems of social diagnosis and action' (1947: 147–53) and presented a diagram (Figure 3, p. 149) of his method (see Figure 5.1 below).

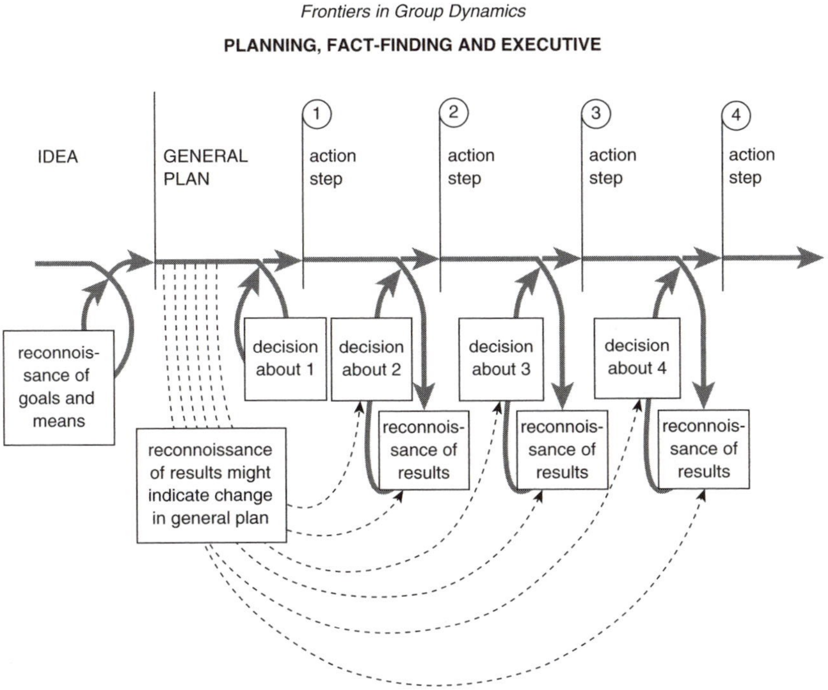

KT

Frontiers in Group Dynamics

PLANNING, FACT-FINDING AND EXECUTIVE

Figure 5.1 Lewin's model of social diagnosis and action that became known as 'action research' (Lewin, 1947: 149; reproduced with permission)

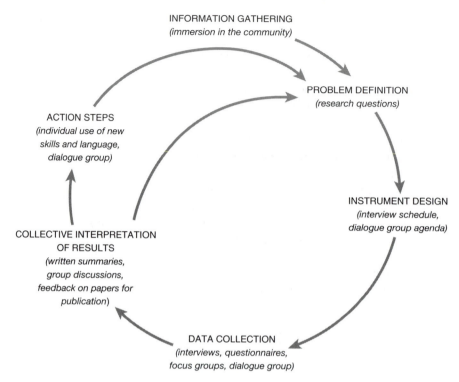

Figure 5.2   Participatory Action Research (Chataway, 1997: 753; reproduced with permission)

Figure 5.1 shows a series of feedback loops in which changes to plans might result from the preliminary results of initial actions. Disciples of Lewin (e.g. Argyris, 1975) interpret Lewin in terms of increasing participation and collaboration of community members, stakeholders and researchers in the design and interpretation of the study. Feedback of the early results to the participants often can lead to redesigning methods or theory in light of consultation meetings about the findings.

Participatory action research

Participatory action research (PAR) is a version of action research that deliberately seeks to provoke some form of social or community change (see Figure 5.2). The researcher works with the organization or community before defining an issue or research question. The researcher then works with the community in exploring the question and in seeking a solution to the problem. Together the researcher and the community begin to understand the issue and the solution through the very process of action.

Historically, this form of research has been used with socially disadvantaged or marginalized groups. It deliberately links popular education, community-based research and social action (Brydon-Miller, 2004). This focus reflects its broader political commitment to social change. Thus, while the immediate focus of concern may be a particular community issue the PAR researcher does not lose sight of the broader social inequalities within which the community is nested (Campbell and Murray, 2004).

Theoretically PAR draws much inspiration from the work of the Brazilian educator Paulo Freire (1993). Freire's work was especially developed around promoting literacy among impoverished communities in Brazil. Through this work he developed a critique of traditional education. He characterized this as a form of banking in which the teacher is the depositor and the students are the depositories. To this he counterposed the concept of *conscientization*, the process of developing a critical understanding among community members about the broader socio-political contradictions and ways of taking action against oppressive elements.

PAR is also connected with a more generalized liberation psychology. This form of psychology begins with a broad political critique of the injustices in society and locates psychology as a potential agent for change. Martin-Baro (1994) stressed that psychology should start by taking a stand alongside those most oppressed in society: 'We have to redesign our theoretical and practical tools, but redesign them from the standpoint of the lives of our own people: from their sufferings, their aspirations, and their struggles' (1994: 25).

PAR is more an approach rather than a single method. As such it can use both quantitative and qualitative methods so long as they contribute to the overall goal of increasing understanding and promoting social change. It is through the process of social change that the participants begin to understand themselves and the limitations on their social progress.

Health action research

As yet the various forms of action research have not been used extensively within health psychology. However, there is growing evidence of a certain resistance among communities and individuals at what can be characterized as research surveillance. This is reflected in the increased demand that researchers deliberately demonstrate the relevance of their work to participants and to actively share with them their findings. This can be considered a weak form of action research. Simultaneously there has been an increasing recognition of the limitations of traditional didactic approaches to health promotion (see Chapter 20 and Campbell, 2004).

Many PAR researchers have used the arts as a vehicle for promoting change. A particularly effective example is the use of photo-novella (Wang et al., 1996; Lykes, 2001) whereby community residents were provided the opportunity to reflect on their own community and to consider broader health issues through photography. Through the process of taking and displaying photographs the community members became more aware of themselves and were able to mobilize around particular local issues to campaign for greater resources. [For an in-depth discussion of the use of photo-novella within PAR, see Lykes (2000), which is Reading 25 in Marks (2002a).]

Drama can also be used as a means of creating community awareness. A study of accidents in a fishing community used this approach (Murray and Tilley, 2004). In this study interviews and group discussions were initially held with fish harvesters. Local artists then used this material to develop a variety of compositions including a song and a play. Gray and his colleagues (Gray et al., 2001; Gray and Sinding, 2002) transformed interviews with cancer patients into plays that were subsequently performed to support groups. Participatory action research can engage in direct social action to promote health-related change. An example is assisting in the organization of housing campaigns with groups for homeless people. Yeich (1996) described how such a campaign could involve assisting in the organization of demonstrations and working with the media to raise broad awareness of people's housing needs.

Action research is often a method that takes time and requires collaboration with different agencies. It is also an approach that does not follow a straight line but proceeds in a much more halting zig-zag format. Often there are many personal challenges and disappointments for the researcher who must devote substantial emotional as well as intellectual energy to the project (Brydon-Miller, 2004). Despite this it also offers much promise for a revitalized health psychology.

Future Research

1　The heavy focus on quantitative research in the research base of health psychology needs to be broadened to encompass more studies using qualitative and action research methods.
2　Methods for assessing the health experiences of children, ethnic groups, people with disabilities and older people need to be expanded to provide an evidence base that is more comprehensive than at present.
3　The evidence based on efficacy and effectiveness of psychosocial interventions needs to be strengthened by more large-scale randomized controlled trials.
4　Collaboration with health economists is necessary to carry out more studies of cost-effectiveness of health psychology interventions.
5　Policy-oriented research within health psychology is relatively under-developed. If health psychology is to achieve its full potential as an agent of change and improvement, policy-relevant research that can be applied by policy-makers must be developed.

Summary

1　The principal research methods of health psychology fall into three categories: quantitative, qualitative and action research.
2　Quantitative research designs emphasize reliable and valid measurement in controlled experiments, trials, and surveys.
3　Qualitative methods use interviews, focus groups, narratives, diaries, or texts to explore health and illness concepts and experience.
4　Action research enables change processes to feed back into plans for improvement, empowerment and emancipation.
5　All of the three types of methods are capable of advancing our understanding of health, illness and health care.
6　Multiple sources of evidence may be synthesized in systematic reviews and meta-analyses.
7　Research methods are a means to an end, not an end in themselves. Health psychology research of the highest possible quality and its applications should be disseminated to the widest possible audiences at all levels of society.

Key Terms

action research

artefact

between groups design

case studies

control group

cross-over or within-participants design

cross-sectional design

diary techniques

direct observation

discourse analysis

ethnographic methods

focus groups

grounded theory analysis

historical analysis

internal validity

interpretative phenomenological analysis (IPA)

interviews (semi-structured)

interviews (structured)

longitudinal designs

meta-analysis

narrative approaches

placebo control

quasi-experimental design

questionnaires

randomized controlled trials (RCTs)

single case experimental design

surveys

systematic review

Part Two

Health Behaviour and Experience

In Part 2 we review theory and research concerned with the health behaviours and experiences most relevant to the major causes of illness and death and the environmental influences, both physical and social, that affect them. Each chapter offers practical recommendations as to how the relevant theory and research can be applied to improve current systems of health care. In each case the focus is on behaviour and its ecological determinants. Changes in living conditions as human societies changed from hunter-gathering to post-industrial, post-electronic sedentary living have generated a toxic ecology in affluent societies.

Chapter 6 examines the part played by food and eating in the changing patterns of illnesses and death and, in particular, the rapidly increasing prevalence of obesity. The influence of diet on health is explored across the complex array of factors that determine food consumption. Environmental changes and improvements in eating habits could significantly reduce the levels of obesity, diabetes, cardiovascular diseases, cancers, osteoporosis and dental disease. The toxic environment, conditioning, culture and cuisine all play a role in shaping the high occurence of unhealthy eating. The evidence on the (in)effectiveness of interventions is critically reviewed and recommendations are given for dietary health communication, education and promotion.

Chapter 7 discusses theories and research on the psychology of drinking and the causes, prevention and treatment of alcohol problems. It begins with a brief history of attitudes to alcohol and the emergence of the theory that alcoholism is a disease that can only be cured by lifelong abstinence. An analysis of the physical and psychosocial dangers of heavy drinking is followed by an examination of contrasting theories about its causes. The chapter concludes with a discussion of the relative merits of different approaches to the prevention and treatment of alcohol problems.

Chapter 8 discusses tobacco and smoking. With the accumulation of evidence on the toxic effects of tobacco smoke, industrialized societies have introduced measures to reduce the number of people who smoke. Meanwhile smoking is increasing dramatically throughout the developing world and a large number of people continue to smoke in the industrialized world. The aim of this chapter is to document the extent of smoking and factors that help to explain its continued popularity and to discuss why people take up smoking and what steps can be taken to help people give up.

Chapter 9 discusses sexual behaviour and experience. It provides an overview of the study of sexual behaviour in historical context. Five contemporary approaches to the study of sexual behaviour are described. These revolve around a behavioural, physiological, cognitive, relationship and meaning-centred focus. These approaches are illustrated and critically evaluated.

Chapter 10 discusses exercise and activity. Recent years have seen an increased interest in and promotion of exercise and physical activity. This chapter reviews the background to this 'exercise movement' and summarizes the evidence linking exercise with health. It considers the wide variations in exercise participation and the social and psychological factors associated with these variations. It then considers the varying meanings of exercise within different social contexts and strategies that have been used to promote greater participation.

6 Food and Eating

You are what you eat.

Outline

In this chapter we examine the part played by food and eating in the changing patterns of illnesses and deaths and, in particular, the rapidly increasing prevalence of obesity. We discuss the influence of diet on health and explore the complex array of factors that determines food consumption. Our interest is motivated by the possibility that improvements in eating habits could reduce the prevalence of obesity, diabetes, cardiovascular diseases, cancers, osteoporosis and dental disease. We examine the impact of changes in lifestyle during human evolutionary history leading to the toxic ecology of eating in affluent societies. Then we consider the role played by conditioning, culture and cuisine. Finally, we review the evidence on the effectiveness of interventions and make recommendations for dietary health communication, education and promotion.

Eating and Obesity

From the cradle to the grave, many of the most significant, social and pleasurable activities in human experience are centred on eating and drinking. Eating and drinking are much more than ways of satisfying hunger and thirst, they are also social activities that are rich in symbolic, moral and cultural meanings. Changes in diet, lifestyle and social organization during our evolutionary history have produced a mixture of beneficial and deleterious effects on health. Eating the 'right' balance of foods and setting the 'right' balance between energy input from eating and drinking and energy expenditure through activity and exercise are of critical importance. Eating preferences and habits are influenced by a complex interaction of processes that include conditioning, customs and culture.

The increasing prevalence of **obesity** is a primary focus for concern. Its prevalence has risen by 74% in the past decade in the USA, with 27% of adults now classified as obese and 34% as overweight (Wadden et al., 2002). In the Middle East and North Africa, Eastern Europe and Latin America, the prevalence of overweight and obesity in

KT

women is similar to, or exceeds, that of the USA (Chopra and Darnton-Hill, 2004). There appears to be widespread agreement that the overweight and obesity epidemic requires concerted effort at all levels of health action but especially at the level of policy and regulation (e.g. Kumanyika et al., 2002; Rossner, 2002; Wadden et al., 2002; Hu, 2003; Chamberlain, 2004). As is the case with alcohol and tobacco control (see Chapters 7 and 8), voluntary agreements with industry are not working.

Overweight and obesity contribute significantly to the global burden of disease and disability resulting from heart disease, type 2 diabetes, hypertension, stroke and some cancers. There are many debilitating conditions that reduce quality of life and generate high absenteeism and health costs, e.g. osteoarthritis, gallbladder disease, respiratory difficulties, infertility, skin problems, depression, lowered self-esteem, job discrimination, and stigmatization (Kumanyika et al., 2002).

Like other 'diseases of affluence', overweight and obesity have multiple causes that include genetic predisposition, culture, family eating patterns, lack of positive role models, individual food choices and lifestyle, and in particular lack of physical activity.

The total energy (calories) supplied by food and beverages has increased as food has become more processed and more energy dense (Chopra and Darnton-Hill, 2004). In North America, fat and sugar account for more than half the total dietary energy intake. These dietary patterns are being reproduced in developing countries as a result of globalization. In developing countries, the per capita supply of beef, mutton, goat, pork, poultry, eggs, and milk rose by 50% between 1973 and 1996. This transition towards an energy dense diet is also occurring at much lower income levels. Small changes at a population level can have an immense impact on obesity prevalence levels. The rise in obesity in the United States during 1980–94 can be explained by an average daily increase in consumption of only 3.7 kilocalories (kcal) above maintenance energy requirement for 35-year-old men and 12.7 kcal for 35-year-old women (Khan and Bowman, 1999).

In the USA, 170,000 fast food restaurants and 3 million soft drink vending machines have encouraged people to eat and drink out of their homes (Chopra and Darnton-Hill, 2004). Wadden et al. refer to 'a toxic environment that implicitly discourages physical activity while explicitly encouraging the consumption of supersized portions of high-fat, high-sugar foods' (2002: 510). A survey reported by Gardner and Halweil (2000) found that only 38% of meals eaten were home made, and many people have never cooked a meal themselves using raw ingredients.

In the United States the food industry spends over $30 billion (£16.5 billion) on promotion – more than any other industry. The challenge for multinational corporations is to continue to generate growth when the market for food is already saturated in developed countries. The food supply already contains 15.9 megajoules (MJ) (3,800 kcal) for every adult and child in the US – nearly twice the daily requirement (Chopra and Darnton-Hill, 2004). The foods industry uses several strategies to maintain their profits, including the following:

- Persuading people to consume even more food, especially highly energy dense foods, through advertising and outlets.
- Increasing serving size and adding price inducements to order the larger sizes.
- Opening up markets in transitional and developing countries.

- Substituting agricultural products with efficient artificial foods, e.g. margarine as a substitute for butter.
- Adding sugar, salt, fats, oils and artificial flavourings and dyes to enhance flavour, look and competitiveness.

One part of the explanation is that people are becoming significantly less active than was previously the case. National surveys suggest that average activity and fitness levels have been declining since 1950. In the Allied Dunbar (1992) survey seven out of 10 men and eight out of 10 women were found to be taking insufficient exercise to achieve any health benefit, although 80% of the population believed themselves to be fit. However, one-third of men and two-thirds of women were unable to continue walking at a moderately brisk pace (3 mph) up a slight gradient (1 in 20) without becoming breathless, finding it very demanding and having to slow down or stop. A European survey found that obese people in the European Union (EU) are more likely to be physically inactive for longer hours in their leisure time and more likely not to participate in any physical activity (European Commission, 1999). Chapter 10 provides a more in-depth discussion of the role played by activity and exercise.

Another factor is income. Income is strongly associated with dietary quality (Low Income Project Team, 1996). This is because in low-income households the food budget often acts as a reserve when demands for other items including alcohol, tobacco or bills must be met.

Yet another factor is stress. In a study of London schoolchildren Cartwright and colleagues (2003) found that higher stress was associated with more fatty food intake, less fruit and vegetable intake, more snacking and a reduced likelihood of eating breakfast. This is a similar trend to that existing for smoking and drinking.

Effective methods of health promotion and behaviour change are needed at a population level. Such initiatives need to be created using building blocks from psychology, nutrition and epidemiology. It is necessary to build these interventions on a solid foundation which acknowledges the powerful influences of evolution, history and culture. Explanatory accounts of eating and diet in purely behavioural terms cannot be expected to succeed if these contextual factors are ignored. Evolution, history and culture are significant contextual determinants of why we eat what we eat and when and how we eat it.

An Evolutionary Perspective

The study of human evolution and pre-history provides a perspective on contemporary ways of life, especially aspects related to food, eating and energy. Early humans can be traced to sites in Africa dating approximately 2.5 million years BP (before the present) when the tool-making *Homo habilis* (or 'handy man') lived in the Olduvai Gorge in Tanzania. The Olduvai hominids were hunter-gatherers, killing and processing their food with weapons and tools fashioned from pieces of volcanic obsidian (Lamb and Sington, 1998). They may have communicated using an early form of speech. Early hominids evolved at a time when the temperature of the earth was cooling and the northern hemisphere was becoming increasingly glaciated. In fact, the ice sheets have advanced and retracted several times during the last million years when the earth's surface temperature has shifted dramatically by up to an average of 10°C every few thousand years (Lamb and Sington, 1998).

Allowing 25 years for each generation, 100,000 generations of humans separate contemporary *Homo sapiens* from our hominid ancestors *Homo habilis*. In evolutionary terms, this is not very many generations for changes to occur. Another species of hominids, *Homo erectus*, is dated from about 1.8 million years BP and contemporary *Homo sapiens* from about 130–100,000 years BP. The survival of the genus *Homo* over the last 2.5 million years can be attributed to a very high adaptability to geological and climatic variations. An efficient body temperature control system, the ability to hunt, fish, gather and process foods throughout the entire earthly terrain, a communication system and social organization to support the nomadic way of life must have all aided human survival.

For 99.5% of evolutionary history, members of genus *Homo* lived as nomadic 'hunter-gatherers'. At the start of the Holocene 10,000 years ago, following the last Ice Age 18,000 years ago (Lamb and Sington, 1998), groups of humans began permanent settlements as agricultural communities and the 'agricultural revolution' had begun.

Because phylogenetic evolution is quite slow, it is reasonable to assume that the genetic make-up of contemporary humans remains adapted to a nomadic existence of gathering and hunting (Powles, 1992). In essence we are urbanized hunter-gatherers and our afflictions and diseases reflect that. Contemporary humans are not fitted to the forms of social organization that exist today in post-agricultural, post-industrial societies. The ecological niches to which genus *Homo* became adapted to over 2.4 million years are found today in only a few inaccessible places where wheat fields, supermarkets and televisions are nowhere to be seen. Contemporary *Homo sapiens* remains phylogenetically adapted to a hunter-gatherer lifestyle in ways that are compromised by agriculture, urbanization and advanced technology.

The vast majority of human populations live in cities, towns and villages. However, our urban lifestyles, social structures and toxic ecology are generating ill-health and disease on a massive scale. The hypothesis that contemporary human beings are living as urbanized hunter-gatherers receives general support from a variety of observations.

The era of the hunter-gatherer

The hunter-gatherer hypothesis can be evaluated in the light of studies of contemporary hunter-gatherers. Four groups have been studied: Australian aboriginals; the San (or 'Bushmen') of the Kalahari Desert, especially of the !Kung language group; pygmies in the Congo Basin; and the Hadza of East Africa (Powles, 1992). There have also been studies of nomadic peoples in Siberia, Lapland and Greenland.

Hunter-gatherers typically lived in bands of 10 to 50 persons with an average band size of perhaps 25. Band composition was fluid. Temporary shelters were built near water and, when food and water supplies were abundant, a band would remain in settlement for several months. A number of bands or 'tribes' of perhaps 500 to 5,000 individuals would speak a common language. Population density was below one person per square kilometre. Property was a burden as it had to be carried manually and so, except for a few essential clothes, utensils and weapons, hunter-gatherers would have had hardly any permanent personal possessions. Concepts of ownership, scarcity and territory, and the associated psycho-social issues, were irrelevant to hunter-gatherers. Horses, camels or reindeer were used for transportation and for their milk, meat and skins. When fire was discovered, enabling heating and cooking of raw foods, remains uncertain.

It is believed that early hunter-gatherers spent less time working, building shelters and obtaining food than most humans did following the agricultural revolution. The !Kung San typically spend 2.0 hours per day and the Arnhem Land Aborigines 4.5 hours per day collecting food. It appears likely that about 75% of food energy would have been gathered from vegetable sources by women and the remaining 25% from hunting of animals mainly by men. Powles (1992) estimated the average daily **energy expenditure** for four different historical periods. These estimates suggest that the average daily energy expenditure for a 65 kg male in postindustrial society is 3.5 megajoules (MJ) compared to 4.4 MJ among hunter-gatherers, a difference of more than 25%. In comparison to the 9.3 MJ expended by a labourer in industrial society, however, the difference is much larger at 62%. Yet, the evidence suggests that nomadic, or even early post-industrial, levels of obesity were nothing like those of today.

Even larger differences in energy expenditure may have existed for women – traditionally the principal food gatherers, water collectors, cooks, cleaners, child rearers and child carriers. In most societies nearly all aspects of food getting show differential gender involvement with women being responsible for the majority of food-related activities (Fieldhouse, 1996). In pre-literate societies, three-quarters of over 200 food-related situations were the exclusive province of women. Hunting and fishing tended to be done by males while grinding grain and fetching water were done predominantly by women (Murdock, 1937). In contemporary Africa, women are responsible for 75% of agricultural production, 30% of the ploughing, 50% of planting, 50% of livestock care, 60% of harvesting, 70% of weeding, 85% of food processing, and 95% of domestic work (Fieldhouse, 1996).

A study reviewed by Powles among !Kung Bushmen observed that a child is carried by the mother for a distance of 2,400 km each year in the first two years of life, 1,800 km in year three, and 1,200 km in year four, giving a total of 7,800 km (4,900 miles) over four years. These exceed average activity levels among contemporary adult western women by a wide margin. Reductions in energy expenditure in women may have exceeded that of men; this is consistent with the observation that obesity is generally more common in women than in men (Webb, 1995).

In addition to possible differences in energy expenditure there are differences in diet. Natural ecosystems provide a diet of wild foods that is both varied and plentiful. For example, North American Indians used hundreds of plants in their diets including stinging nettle, common purslane, milkweed, clover, pond-lily, dandelions and fiddleheads (Fieldhouse, 1996). Over 13,000 insects have been classified as edible. In 1950, the Groote Eylandt Aborigines ate 19 large land animals, 76 birds, 97 fish, 39 crustaceans and 82 plants. This diet is adequate both in quality of nutrients and quantity of energy supplied. The evidence suggests that protein, mineral and vitamin intake among hunter-gatherers would have been generally above 'recommended levels'.

For hundreds of thousands of years of human evolution, the capacity to store fat easily was advantageous for survival. Ice Age hunter-gatherers needed to store fat to survive the winters and long journeys in search of food. When the ice retracted and temperatures increased, foods became more accessible and activity levels declined. Thus a metabolic feature promoting survival became a risk factor for diseases that previously had rarely existed.

The agricultural revolution

The agricultural revolution is dated at about 10,000 years BP when humans in the Middle East began settlements in fertile valleys and river deltas. This development meant that humans lived for the first time in densely populated villages and towns. Wheat, barley and other cereals were cultivated and sheep and goats were kept in captivity and slaughtered to provide a ready supply of meat. For the first time people acquired and retained ownership of property and land. The revolution spread through Europe, reaching Britain about 5,000 years ago. Population density increased dramatically from less than four persons per square kilometre to 100 or more persons per square kilometre. In fertile river valleys, densities would have increased several hundredfold. Settlement made it easier for individuals to survive protracted or severe bouts of illness or disability. New forms of social organizations could be established to promote health and provide aid to the sick. However, with the stabilizing influence of settlement and civilization came a number of adverse consequences:

• Food supplies were more dependent on local weather conditions and hazards, e.g. floods, droughts, earthquakes and volcanoes.
• The diet became less varied and balanced.
• Malnutrition, anaemia and osteoporosis become more prevalent.
• Average levels of activity and energy expenditure decreased.
• The prevalence of bowel and respiratory infections increased.
• New pathogens and epidemics were possible.
• The birth rate increased.
• Warring over territory became more likely.
• Social problems related to population density and ownership became more prevalent.
• Psychosocial and socio-economic stress related to population density, property, status and self-esteem became more significant.

The industrial revolution and beyond

About 200 years ago the next stepping stone in human social evolution was laid – the industrial revolution which came with the steam engine. Later, with the electric motor, light bulb, telephone, computer and Internet, we can now do almost everything we need to live within the comfort of four walls without moving anywhere. The internal combustion and jet engines permit one to travel everywhere on earth with minimum energy expenditure. These new systems of communication and transportation have had radical effects on lifestyles.

The contemporary era of television, computers, satellites, mobile phones and the Internet is bringing many benefits to working efficiency and communication. Labour-saving products in the form of washing machines, dryers, microwave ovens and dish-washers have brought further reductions in energy expenditure in tasks of daily living.

Food is produced ready for the supermarket. The availability of 'instant' dinners, desserts and snacks for consumption during a schedule of sedentary work and television viewing means that food preparation and cooking is increasingly being moved from the kitchen to the food-processing industry. The contribution of the food industry to the quality of food and eating in the population is becoming ever more crucial. In general the industry does not make improvements voluntarily. Health only becomes a higher priority than profit when there is a heavy consumer demand backed by policy and legislation.

An Ecological Model

In this section we consider the implications of the hunter-gatherer hypothesis for the contemporary ecology of food and eating. A primary focus for this discussion will be *fat,* in people who are perceived – or perceive themselves – to be fat, in foods, and the relationship between the two. A concern with fatness and thinness has dominated discourses of diet and dieting during the past few decades. Ogden (1992) suggested that the widespread concern with dieting among western women has become the modern-day equivalent of Chinese foot binding, corsets and breast binding. These were all ways of controlling, managing or 'mastering' the female body. Ogden stated: 'The majority of dieters have a problem with feeling fat, not with being fat, but the dieting industry does not distinguish between the two' (1992: 16).

Being, or the feeling of being, fat

A pan-European survey asked a sample of 15,239 people representative of the population to indicate which of nine figures best described their current and ideal body image. An underweight body image was chosen by 55% as their ideal, in comparison to only 37% who felt that their body image was in the underweight category. The disparity between ideal and current body image was generally greater for females than males (European Commission, 1999). The high value placed on thinness in contemporary affluent societies is not evident in Africa or the Pacific Basin, nor was it seen in previous eras when a fulsome figure was seen as attractive or a symbol of power and status.

The obesity debate has focused on two main subjects: high fat foods and overweight people. First, in most western countries the proportion of food energy derived from fat is close to 40% as compared to a recommended level of 30–35%. **Triglyceride** is the main component of dietary fats and oils and the principal form in which fat is stored in the body. Triglyceride is composed of three fatty acids attached to a glycerol molecule. These acids are saturated (S), monounsaturated (M) and polyunsaturated (P). The proportions of these three acids varies across different fats and oils, butter having 64%, 33% and 3%, olive oil having 15%, 73% and 13%, and rape seed oil (canola) having

KT

7%, 60% and 33% respectively. The P:S ratio is therefore approximately 0.05 for butter and almost 5.00 for canola.

KT

Keys et al. (1959) measured total serum **cholesterol** levels in two groups of men who were given diets that varied in the degree of saturation of fat but matched for total fat content. Diet A that had a P:S ratio of 0.16 produced a much higher serum cholesterol level than diet B with a P:S ratio of 2.79. Cholesterol has been implicated as a causal factor in

KT

coronary heart disease (Brown and Goldstein, 1984). The findings of Keys et al. led many to conclude that fats and oils with a low P:S ratio like butter or coconut oil were high risk food items while olive oil and rape seed oil were lower risk. This analysis led to a negative health image for food items containing high amounts of saturated fat (Webb, 1995) triggering health promotion campaigns with the aim of reducing saturated fat in western diets. However, it is important to distinguish between two different fractions of cholesterol that are low-density lipoprotein (LDP) and high-density lipoprotein (HDP). High levels of LDP are positively associated with cardiovascular disease while high levels of HDP are negatively associated with cardiovascular disease. The different types of fatty acids have a complex set of effects on raising or lowering LDP and HDP. This complicates the issue and presents a considerable challenge to nutritional health promotion.

KT

A second focus has been the characteristics of people who are classified overweight or obese. The excess weight of obese individuals is due mainly to **adipose tissue** mass that is 85% fat. Models of obesity have placed the cause at one of two levels: (1) individual overweight and obese people have been blamed for their 'sloth' and 'gluttony'; (2) overweight and obese people are assumed to have a genetic predisposition to lowered metabolic rate (Webb, 1995).

The first of these causes is seen as potentially controllable, but only in those people who possess 'strong will power' or high 'self-efficacy' (Bandura, 1977). In attributing responsibility to individuals, one must take into account biological, social, ecological and psychological barriers to change (see also Chapters 9 and 10). Working with obese people at an individual level is the primary activity of organizations such as Weight Watchers and has been an active area of research in clinical psychology.

The idea that there is a genetic predisposition to obesity is the second major theory. This theory provides little hope to those affected as obesity is seen as irreversible within present technology. Biological influences on body fat levels include age, sex, hormonal factors and genetics. On present evidence, biological influences on fatness appear to be unalterable and are likely to remain so in the foreseeable future.

The toxic environment

The ecological approach to obesity sees obesity in the context of the individual's relationship to the surrounding environment. Essentially it blames the environment for obesity not obese individuals themselves. Egger and Swinburn (1997) proposed three main influences on equilibrium levels of body fat – biological, behavioural and environmental. Obesity is not a pathological disorder of individuals requiring treatment but a normal end result of living in an environment that produces obesity. Contemporary

KT

society is said to be **obesogenic** because it generates too high an equilibrium level of fatness across the whole population relative to average activity levels. In order to solve the obesity problem it is necessary to understand, measure and alter the characteristics of the environment, not attempt to address the problem at the level of the individual.

This ecological theory is based on the **fat balance equation** (Swinburn and Ravussin, 1993) that states:

Rate of change of fat stores in the body = Rate of fat intake − Rate of fat oxidation

Total energy is the mediator of weight gain that, under contemporary conditions, is interchangeable with fat energy. The intake of fat is a significant component of total energy intake while total energy expenditure is the main determinant of fat oxidation. A reduction of dietary fat within an otherwise varied diet leads to weight loss. However, weight loss tends to be associated with rebound weight gain due to physio-logical defences against weight loss. In an environment that promotes obesity, there is also a high equilibrium point of fat stores.

Although the proportion of energy from fats and oils has decreased in western countries since the 1960s, this reduction is attributed mainly to reductions in food **energy intake** rather than a shift to a lower fat diet (Webb, 1995). However, the aver-age level of energy intake is falling more slowly than the average level of energy output. This imbalance has caused increases in average weight levels and prevalence of obesity.

If the prevalence of obesity is to decrease, average energy expenditure needs to be significantly increased while average energy intake is reduced. Without intervention at a policy level, the currently high prevalence of obese and overweight people is likely to remain evident for some considerable time.

There is a vast range of environmental influences that affect what and how much is eaten, by whom, and under which circumstances. As Egger and Swinburn (1997) point out, these influences are frequently underrated. Examples of these influences are shown in Table 6.1. A celebrity chef, Jamie Oliver, recently revealed that only 37 pence is spent on ingredients in school dinners in South London (Channel 4, 2005). Even some food provided by schools in the UK can be classified as 'toxic'. As a consequences of Jamie Olivers direct actions, the British government implemented measures to raise nutritional standards of school meals.

Food promotion influences on children

One primary influence in the toxic environment is food promotion. The Food Standards Agency (2003) published a systematic review examining how foods are pro-moted to children and possible links with children's eating patterns. The review exam-ined how children respond to food promotional activities and, in particular, whether it influences their food preferences, and if so, the extent of that influence. The report concluded that advertising to children does have an effect on their preferences, pur-chase behaviour and consumption, and the effects occur not only for brands but also for types of food. For the report, 29,946 potentially relevant pieces of research were initially assessed. Following relevance and quality assessment, 118 research papers describing a total of 101 studies passed the methodological criteria.

The review report found that children's food promotion is dominated by televi-sion advertising of the so-called 'Big Four': pre-sugared breakfast cereals, soft-drinks,

Table 6.1 *Environmental influences on food intake and physical activity (Egger and Swinburn, 1997: 478; reproduced with permission)*

Type of environment	Physical environment		Economic environment		Socio-cultural environment	
	Food	Activity	Food	Activity	Food	Activity
Macro	Food laws and regulation	Labour saving devices	Food taxes and subsidies	Cost of labour versus automation	Traditional cuisine	Attitudes to recreation
	Food technology	Cycleways and walkways	Cost of food technology	Investment in parks and recreational facilities	Migrant cuisines	National sports
	Low fat foods	Fitness industry policies	Marketing costs	Costs of petrol and cars	Consumer demand	Participating versus watching culture
	Food industry policies	Transport system	Food prices	Costs of cycleways	Food status	Gadget status
Micro	Food in house	Local recreation facilities	Family income	Gym or club fees	Family eating patterns	Peers' activities
	Choices at school or work cafeterias	Second cars	Other household expenses	Owning equipment	Peer attitudes	Family recreation
	Food in local shops	Safe streets	Subsidized canteens	Subsidized local events	Pressure from food advertising	School attitude to sports
	Proximity of fast food outlets	Household rules for watching TV and video	Home grown foods	Costs of school sport	Festivities	Safety fears

confectionary and savoury snacks. However, recently, advertising for fast food outlets has rapidly increased, so now we have the 'Big Five'. The advertised diet is promoted in terms of fun, fantasy and taste, rather than health and nutrition.

The review found a link between the amount of television viewing and diet, obesity and cholesterol levels. However, it could not be determined whether it is the advertising itself, the sedentary nature of television viewing or the snacking that often takes place while viewing, that cause this problem.

To summarize, the reviewers found that:

- There is a lot of food advertising to children.
- The advertised diet is less healthy than the recommended one.
- Children enjoy and engage with food promotion.
- Food promotion is having an effect, particularly on children's preferences, purchase behaviour and consumption.
- This effect is independent of other factors and operates at both a brand and category level.

These findings confirm what has been suspected for some time. This study increases understanding of how children's choices and eating habits are being moulded by large corporate interests. Action is needed to limit the power of commercial organizations in order to bring about improvements in eating habits that are established in young people. [For further discussion of the ecological approach to obesity, see Egger and Swinburn (1997), Reading 12 in Marks (2002a).]

Studies of Diet and Health

Fat and fibre

Epidemiology has contributed a large number of studies on the influence of diet on illness and mortality. Doll and Peto (1981) concluded that approximately 35% of all cancer deaths can be attributed to diet as compared to the 30% that are attributable to tobacco. Earlier ecological studies found that average animal fat intake in grams per day was strongly associated with age adjusted death rates. However, ecological studies are confounded by numerous variables that have no theoretical relationship to mortality (e.g. GNP) and yet have as strong a correlation as average daily fat intake. Recently there have been controlled prospective studies, systematic reviews and meta-analyses to draw upon.

A major focus for epidemiological research has been dietary fat and fibre in the form of meat, cereals, fruit and vegetables. Animal-derived foods are high in fat but contain almost no fibre. Fruit and vegetables contain high amounts of fibre but no fat. One approach to study the impact of contrasting amounts of fat and fibre in the diet is by comparing the mortality and illness rates of meat eaters and non-meat eaters. Although meat consumption increases the risk of cancers of the colorectum, breast and prostate, until recently the evidence of reduced illness and mortality among vegetarians has not been conclusive.

Key et al. (1998) compared the mortality rates of vegetarians and non-vegetarians among 76,000 men and women who had participated in five prospective studies. This meta-analysis analysed the entire body of evidence collected in prospective studies in western countries in the period 1960 to 1981. The original studies were conducted in California (2), Britain (2) and Germany (1) and provided data concerning 16- to 89-year-old participants for whom diet and smoking status information was available. The results were adjusted for age, sex and smoking. Vegetarians were defined as those who did not eat any meat or fish ($n = 27,808$). Participants were followed for an average of 10.6 years when 8,330 deaths occurred. The results showed that vegetarians as a group contained a lower proportion of smokers and current alcohol drinkers, a higher proportion of high exercisers and had a consistently lower **body mass index (BMI)**.

The death rate ratio for ischaemic heart disease for vegetarians versus non-vegetarians across the five studies was 0.76 (95% CI 0.62–0.94). The all cause mortality ratio was 0.95 (95% CI 0.82–1.11). The reduction in mortality among vegetarians varied significantly with age at death, younger ages at death being associated with much lower rate ratios: 0.55 for deaths under 65; 0.69 for deaths between 65 and 79; 0.92 for deaths between 80 and 89. When the group of non-vegetarians was subdivided into regular meat eaters and semi-vegetarians who ate fish only or ate meat less than once a week, there was evidence of a significant dose-response effect. The ischaemic heart disease death rate ratios compared to regular meat eaters were 0.78 in semi-vegetarians and 0.66 in vegetarians.

These data suggest that vegetarians have a lower risk of dying from ischaemic heart disease than non-vegetarians. Like any epidemiological study, this study could not control for all relevant factors and could be subject to confounding. For example, vegetarians may differ from carnivores in many ways that could not be controlled for (e.g. in exercise levels, use of drugs, religious beliefs and health values).

Other studies have found an association between diet and cancer. Block et al. (1992) reviewed the role of fruit and vegetables in cancer prevention and concluded that 132 of 170 studies indicated a significant protective effect for cancers at all sites including prostate.

Ness and Powles (1997) reviewed ecological, **case-control**, cohort studies and unconfounded trials in humans concerning fruit, vegetables and cardiovascular disease from the period 1966 to 1995. All studies in the review reported on fresh fruit and vegetables or a nutrient that could serve as a proxy. Many of the studies found a significant protective association for coronary heart disease and stroke with consumption of fruit and vegetables or surrogate nutrients. The protective effect appeared to be stronger on stroke than on coronary heart disease.

Cummings and Bingham (1998) stated: 'What is remarkable about the diet–cancer story is the consistency with which certain foods emerge as important in reducing risk across the range of cancers.' They concluded that vegetables and fruit are protective for almost all of the major cancers. Consumption of meat, especially red meat and processed meat, is linked with bowel, breast, prostate and pancreatic cancer.

Salt

Salt (sodium chloride) has long been associated with essential hypertension. Ecological studies suggest that populations with low salt intake such as the Kalahari Bushmen have low incidence of hypertension in comparison to societies such as the UK and USA

KT

KT

where salt intake and hypertension incidence are both high (Webb, 1995). However, there are many confounding variables in these ecological studies that could explain this link: high physical activity, low levels of obesity, low alcohol and tobacco use and high potassium intake in those groups with low salt diets.

In a controlled study, Law et al. (1991) correlated blood pressure and salt intake from 24 populations and found a highly significant relationship that increased with age and baseline levels. Populations with lower mean salt intake generally have a lower blood pressure and a less steep rise of blood pressure with age. Much of the salt in western diets, perhaps 80%, comes from processed food. There is a need to restrict the salt content of processed foods requiring regulation of the food industry.

Sugar

Sugar or sucrose appeared in the west in the eighth century (Mintz, 1997). Sugar is a disaccharide composed of one unit of glucose and one of fructose, which is found in fruits and vegetables, particularly sugar beet and sugar cane, from which it is extracted and purified to make white sugar, brown sugar, treacle or syrup. It is used as a sweetener and preservative by food processors. It has been strongly linked with the development of obesity, maturity onset diabetes and the rotting of teeth (dental caries). Increasing obesity rates can be attributed in part to the prominence in our diet of the 'empty' calories of sugar that carry no nutritional value.

Caffeine

Caffeine is the most popular drug on earth with more than 80% of the world's population consuming it daily (James, 1997). It is consumed in coffee, tea, drinking chocolate, cocoa and cola drinks providing a slight psychoactive effect on arousal and mood. Coffee has achieved symbolic status as a recreational and exotic beverage. Consumption varies across countries with four of the highest consumers being the UK, Sweden, Canada and the USA with average daily levels of 444, 425, 238 and 211 mg (Gilbert, 1984).

Because of its widespread usage even small increases in relative risk for heart disease or cancers could have large absolute effects. James (1997) reviews evidence from hundreds of studies concerning caffeine's psychopharmacological and epidemiological effects. James suggests that caffeine use *could* account for 9–14% of cases of coronary heart disease, 17–24% of stroke cases and could contribute to adverse reproductive outcomes when used in pregnancy. However, these estimates require further research.

Psychological, Social and Cultural Aspects of Food and Eating

Conditioning and early experience

Following Pavlov's (1927) studies of conditioned reflexes, learning and conditioning became the main focus of research on food preferences and aversions. Although experience generally determines food choices, sweet tastes and possibly fatty tastes are innately attractive while bitter tastes are innately avoided. Capaldi (1996) suggests that preferences for foods are modifiable in four ways:

1 Mere exposure.
2 Flavour-flavour learning: flavours that are repeatedly associated with an already preferred flavour such as saccharin will themselves become preferred. A sweetener produces liking in almost any other food with which it is mixed.
3 Flavour-nutrient learning: flavours that are repeatedly associated with a nutrient such as a protein become preferred.
4 Taste aversion learning: this occurs when a novel taste solution (the conditioned stimulus or CS) is followed by an unpleasant stimulus (the unconditioned stimulus or UCS) that produces transient gastrointestinal illness or vomiting (the unconditioned response or UR) (Garcia et al., 1966). This type of learning is adaptive in animals that need to learn rapidly to differentiate between positive and toxic foods. However, taste and food aversions are also quite common in humans, for example, with specific types of alcohol (gin or whisky) as a result of nausea caused by over-imbibing on the first occasion of use.

The flavour of food is conveyed by the senses of taste, smell and chemical irritation. The foetus receives its first nutrients in the amniotic fluid that is a potential carrier of flavour and odour (Mennella and Beauchamp, 1996). By term the human foetus has swallowed quite large amounts of amniotic fluid (200–760 ml daily) and has been exposed to glucose, fructose, lactic acid, pyruvic acid, citric acid, fatty acids, phospholipids, creatinine, urea, uric acid, amino acids, proteins and salts (Mennella and Beauchamp, 1996). The amniotic fluid and mother's milk are both primed by a maternal diet that is unique and so may have similar aromatic profiles providing a 'thread of chemical continuity between the pre- and postnatal niches' (Schaal and Orgeur, 1992). Studies of foetal swallowing and of preterm infant sucking even suggest that a preference for sweet flavours is evident before birth (Tatzer et al., 1985). This evidence suggests that preferences for flavour and smell are influenced very early in life. In fact the earliest and most emotional life events revolve around eating and drinking and, as Rozin states, the taking and giving of food are, from the very first, 'exquisitely social' (Rozin, 1996: 235).

Culture and cuisine

Culturally shared eating habits provide a sense of belonging; they are an affirmation of cultural and social identity, kept with pride and not readily altered. Food preferences and eating habits are acquired in the context of family dynamics, moral values, culture and cuisine. Culture is the major determinant of what and when we eat and, to a lesser degree, how much we eat. Food habits and preferences are among the last characteristics of a culture to be lost during immigration into a new culture. Rozin suggests that socio-cultural factors are so important in determining food choices that if you can ask only one question, the question should be: 'What is your culture or ethnic group?' (Rozin, 1996: 235). A second useful question would be: 'What is your religion?'.

Culture is the sum total of a group's learned behaviour and preserved traditions, especially those concerned with eating habits: 'Culture is learned. Food habits are acquired early in life and once established are likely to be long-lasting and resistant to change. Hence the importance of developing sound nutritional practices in childhood as a basis for life-long healthy eating' (Fieldhouse, 1996: 3). Moral influences concerned with power and control are also key features of family eating practices. Mintz (1997), for example, states: 'In any society, the act of eating can be encumbered with moral overtones – as can the act of not eating when others eat ... to redefine ingestion as an arena for the acting out of moral principles is a distinctively human achievement' (1997: 173).

Eating and drinking habits are central to socialization that occurs during infancy in the family and are influenced principally by mothers. The immediate family is the dominant influence on the child, establishing cultural and culinary practices and preferences and the rules by which different foods may be eaten in particular combinations or meals.

Recent studies have explored the role of family dynamics and parental influences on the food choices of adolescents. The evidence suggests that food preferences established by mid-adolescence appear to continue well into adult life (Kelder et al., 1994). Of particular interest is the establishment of preferences for snacks, sweet foods, fruit and vegetables. Boureaudhuij (1997) investigated the establishment of family food rules in infancy and its impact on food choices and consumption in adolescence. Adolescents and young adults aged 12 to 22 who reported more permissiveness in their family at age 10 were found to be eating more fat and sweet foods and more snacks. They reported more unhealthy food choices in their families.

In industrialized societies, variations in family structures have occurred as a result of social changes and new working patterns. These changes have brought more variation to traditional patterns of eating communal family meals. However, meal structures are adhered to rather inflexibly and the scope for innovations may be more limited than nutritional health education desire (Douglas and Nicod, 1974).

A significant role within these stable cultural and family influences is played by cuisine, a style of cooking with particular ingredients, flavours and modes of preparation and rules about orders and combinations (Rozin, 1982). These culinary principles tend to be culture specific to some extent. Cuisine is nationally or regionally based and so we speak of French, Italian, Indian, Japanese and Chinese cuisine, although these broad categories need to be subdivided into more specific culinary groups, e.g. Cantonese, Szechwan, etc. The type of cuisine defines written or oral rules concerning how food sources are gathered or killed, prepared and combined into meals. Fieldhouse concludes: 'Our unwillingness to accept just anything as food betrays the notion that food is consumed for nourishment of the body alone. Food also nourishes the heart, mind and soul' (1996: 76).

Stigmatization and the dieting industry

Prior to the twentieth century in the USA and Europe corpulence was a sign of status, health and happiness. The positive valuing of obesity exists to the present day in a number of cultures (e.g. in Polynesia) and in regions where food supplies are scarce (e.g. sub-Saharan Africa). For complex reasons, in contemporary western societies today thinness is perceived to be the ideal for beauty and health. This trend has stigmatized people who are overweight or obese, especially women (Price and Pecjak, 2003). Price and Pecjak state:

> At least in the US, obesity is the last stigma against which it is socially desirable to discriminate. The discrimination occurs in a wide variety of settings, resulting in emotional and physical suffering. Obese individuals are discriminated against in employment, housing, insurance coverage, education, jury selection, adoption proceedings, and healthcare ... to name just a few. (2003: 18)

In the USA obesity has been declared a disability within the Americans with Disabilities Act. According to Price and Pecjak, women are more affected by the stigma because they are judged more on the basis of appearance than are men.

Perhaps it is not surprising that overweight and obese women are more prone to take up dieting than men. This is in spite of the fact that obese people generally have little success in permanent weight loss. The consequences of dieting are often negative. Dieters are more likely to binge eat when they feel anxiety (Heatherton et al., 1991) and have a higher prevalence of eating disorders. In most cases of anorexia nervosa and bulimia nervosa, dieting had occurred prior to the development of the disorder (Price and Pecjak, 2003).

The cultural idea of thinness as beauty is almost certainly a temporary one. If and when it is replaced, the prevalence of eating disorders will quite possibly improve.

Interventions

Small-scale, individual level studies

A variety of interventions have been tried at the individual level of influence. The quality of the research used to evaluate the interventions is of varied quality but mostly rather poor. Sample sizes are small, power analyses are rarely if ever carried out, and designs are overall rather poor. Recent systematic reviews on effectiveness will be briefly summarized to illustrate the near crisis situation that exists in dealing with the obesity problem.

Campbell and colleagues (2002) systematically reviewed interventions for preventing obesity in children. The objective was to assess the effectiveness of educational, health promotion and/or psychological/counselling interventions that focused on diet, physical activity and/or lifestyle and social support which were designed to prevent obesity in childhood. Randomized controlled trials (RCTs) and non-RCTs were included where observations were taken for a minimum of three months. The preferred interval of 12 months yielded only seven acceptable studies. By going to three months a total of 10 studies could be included. The seven accepted 12-month studies were carried out during the period 1986–2001.

The results were non-significant overall. However, one long-term study and two short-term studies focusing on physical activity resulted in a slightly greater reduction in overweight.

A second systematic review evaluated interventions for treating obesity in children (Summerbell et al., 2004). Eighteen RCTs with 975 participants that used a minimum six-month period for the follow-up were studied. Five studies with 245 participants investigated changes in physical activity and sedentary behaviour; two studies with 107 participants compared problem-solving with usual care or behaviour therapy. Nine studies with 399 participants compared behavioural therapy at varying degrees of family involvement with no treatment or usual care. Finally two studies with 224 participants compared CBT with relaxation.

The authors state that most of the studies were 'too small to have the power to detect the effects of the treatment'. They were unable to carry out a meta-analysis because so few of the trials included the same comparisons and outcomes. Therefore a narrative synthesis only was used and no direct conclusions could be confidently made.

A third systematic review assessed the evidence on advice on low-fat diets for obesity (Pirozzo et al., 2004). Twelve RCTs were selected with varying periods of follow-up: four with six-months follow-up; five with 12-months follow-up; three with 18-months follow-up. No significant differences were evident at any of these three periods. The authors concluded that low fat diets do no better than low calorie diets in terms of long-term weight loss.

Larger-scale, higher-level approaches: guidelines for future health promotion practice

The very poor results obtained with small-scale individual level interventions suggest the need for large-scale, higher-level approaches. These would use legislation to control promotion of unhealthy foods and health education to better inform consumers. Diets are influenced by a multinational food industry that is continually trying to increase demand and sales. Food industry tactics are similar to those used by the tobacco industry – supplying misinformation, publication of supposedly conflicting evidence, and hiding negative data. Chopra and Darnton-Hill (2004) suggest that tactics used in tobacco control have relevance for the fight against unhealthy diets because the experience of using voluntary codes of conduct with the food industry has not worked. They suggest that international standards on marketing unhealthy food products, restrictions on the advertising and availability of unhealthy products in schools, standard packaging and labelling of food products, or potential price or tax measures to reduce the demand for unhealthy products should all be considered.

As we have seen, the 'western diet' is associated with cardiovascular diseases, cancer, diabetes, osteoporosis and dental disease. Among the six leading causes of death in western societies (e.g. see Table 1.1) at least four are associated with nutritional factors or excessive alcohol consumption. In this light, many international and national expert committees have recommended dietary standards and there have been many health promotion campaigns. Public debates about food and eating have been fuelled by scientific findings that have not always been easy to interpret, leading to food scares, distrust of authorities and other negative reactions. Before developing interventions and policy based on epidemiological studies, however, the psychological, social and cultural aspects of these epidemiological imperatives need to be considered.

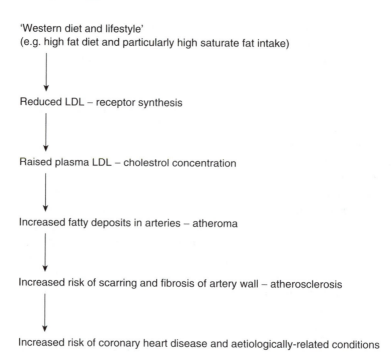

'Western diet and lifestyle'
(e.g. high fat diet and particularly high saturate fat intake)

Reduced LDL – receptor synthesis

Raised plasma LDL – cholestrol concentration

Increased fatty deposits in arteries – atheroma

Increased risk of scarring and fibrosis of artery wall – atherosclerosis

Increased risk of coronary heart disease and aetiologically-related conditions

Figure 6.1   The diet–heart hypothesis (Webb, 1995: 195; reproduced with permission)

They may create greater obstacles to and opportunities for improving the diet than is generally acknowledged.

A popular theme for health education campaigns in the latter part of the twentieth century has been the 'diet–heart hypothesis'. This is based on the evidence that coronary heart disease is associated with raised cholesterol levels (see Figure 6.1). Health education publications in the 1980s and 1990s dedicated considerable space to the desirability of a diet that is low in fat and cholesterol. However, the issue of serum cholesterol reduction is complicated by the existence of different fractions of cholesterol, as previously mentioned (see p. 120).

To effect behaviour change, health promotion messages must be *simple, clear* and *consistent*. Unfortunately, dietary health communications have sometimes been the opposite, creating much confusion. One example is the controversy over cholesterol, butter and margarine. For many years it was believed that butter was bad for health because of its high content of saturated fats causing high levels of serum cholesterol. Health-conscious consumers switched to margarine. Subsequently it was claimed that margarine could be equally unhealthy and many consumers switched back to butter. These responses were associated with confusion and distrust of health messages in the dietary field.

At the same time that all this attention was being focused on dietary fat, relatively little attention was being paid to the issues of dietary sugar, salt and caffeine. Campaigns have also ignored the possibility that a pressure to change diet can bring about deleterious physical and psychological effects including depression and even suicide if certain nutrients become deficient in particularly vulnerable people (Hartley, 1998).

Individuals acquire their knowledge about health through schooling, the media, medical practitioners, community nurses, information from industry, product labels, public health campaigns and other sources. Communication must provide accurate information in 'digestible' form so that is understood by the target audience. Dietary guidelines are usually formulated in terms of *nutrients*. However, consumers eat *foods* and should be empowered to translate recommendations into how best to purchase foods. Effective nutritional health promotion involves collaboration of nutritionists, epidemiologists, psychologists, educators, professional communicators, journalists, medical doctors, industrialists and legislators. For each target population group, it is necessary that common efforts be directed to:

- Agreeing a set of dietary guidelines based upon systematic reviews.
- Designing simple, clear and consistent health communications.
- Implementing programmes that target relevant health professionals.
- Then, supported by the relevant health professionals, targeting the relevant community groups.
- Evaluation of process and outcome.

For many reasons, a population or community level approach to disease prevention and health promotion is more effective than individual approaches. Community approaches have a higher impact, provide a more efficient use of funds and are more cost effective (Tolley, 1985). For example, a small reduction in dietary fat made by a large proportion of the population would lead to greater improvements in population health than large changes made by a relatively few people (Rose, 1992).

Boyle and Morris (1999) review community nutrition programmes in the USA. Winett et al. (1989) and Bennett and Murphy (1997) discuss community health promotion from a psychological perspective.

Future Research

1   The hunter-gatherer hypothesis could be tested by investigating the health of groups and communities who belong to similar cultures but differ with respect to hunter-gatherer characteristics, e.g. agriculturalists versus pastoralists. It should be possible to determine whether pastoralists have higher levels of well-being, lower rates of chronic illness and live longer than agriculturists, as predicted. A study in Burkina Faso found that the agriculturalist Mossi people were more stressed and marginalized than the pastoralist Fulani people (Van Haaften and Van de Vijver, 1996). Further studies with actual hunter-gatherers and matched sedentary control groups could determine how such differences translate into illness and mortality rates.
2   The quest for thinness on well-being and body weight requires further study, particularly in girls and women. The relationship between contemporary ideal images of thinness and the increasing prevalence of obesity warrants further study.

3   Much of the discussion of risk factors for coronary heart disease focuses on dietary fat, LDL and HDL cholesterol. However, many other dietary factors including fibre, several minerals and vitamins and non-nutrient substances also influence the development of this disease, as well as many non-dietary factors such as smoking and exercise. Rather than focusing on cholesterol alone, studies are needed to explore how disease prevention can best be applied with vulnerable population groups concerning all known risk factors.

4   More study is needed at a policy level to explore the best ways of working with the food industry, both manufacturing and retail, to improve the quality of food at affordable prices.

Summary

1   Much of human existence is focused on the acquisition of food, eating and drinking. Eating and drinking are symbolic, moral and culturally embedded activities.

2   Eating a balanced diet and setting an optimum balance between energy input and energy expenditure are important aspects of health.

3   Among the six leading causes of death in affluent societies, at least four are associated with nutritional factors or excessive alcohol consumption. Cancer, coronary heart disease, stroke, obesity and other 'diseases of affluence' are all associated with the western lifestyle, especially diet.

4   Obesity has multiple causes that include genetic predisposition, culture, family eating patterns, lack of positive role models, individual food choices and lifestyle, in particular lack of physical activity.

5   Human beings spent 95.5% of evolutionary history as hunter-gatherers. The genetic make up of contemporary humans remains adapted to a nomadic existence of hunting and gathering. Contemporary humans are not yet optimally fitted to the social conditions of post-agricultural, post-industrial societies.

6   The agricultural revolution brought many deleterious changes to health, diet and life-styles. Food supplies became more dependent on local weather conditions and hazards; the diet became less varied and balanced; fat consumption increased; average levels of activity and energy expenditure decreased; the prevalence of bowel and respiratory infections increased; new pathogens and epidemics were possible; the birth rate increased; warring over territory became more likely; social problems related to population density and ownership became more prevalent; psychosocial and socio-economic stresses related to population density, property, status and self-esteem became more significant.

7   Changes in industrialized societies over the last 200 years have produced a mixture of beneficial and deleterious effects on human health. One of the most significant was a reduction in energy expenditure as a consequence of labour saving devices and new forms of transportation.

8   Food preferences are influenced very early in life. The earliest and most emotional life events revolve around eating and drinking. The basic mechanisms for establishing these preferences are learning and conditioning in the context of family power dynamics, moral values, culture and cuisine. Culturally shared eating habits provide a sense of belonging, affirm cultural and social identity and are not readily altered.

9   The ecological approach analyses eating in the context of the surrounding environment. Obesity is not seen as a pathological disorder of individuals requiring treatment but the end-result of the toxic, obesogenic environment.

10 Epidemiological evidence suggests that a diet that is high in fruit, vegetables and cereals and low in meat and fat is protective against cancer. This diet helps prevent other chronic diseases, including coronary heart disease, hypertension and obesity. There are further health benefits if people consume less sugar, salt and caffeine.

11 A community approach has many advantages compared to individual-level approaches: they have a higher impact, are more efficient and more cost effective.

12 Interventions at a population level require an agreed set of dietary guidelines following systematic reviews, simple, clear and consistent health communications, targeting the relevant health professionals and then population groups and communities.

Key Terms

KT

adipose tissue

body mass index (BMI)

case-control study

cholesterol

coronary heart disease (CHD)

energy expenditure

energy intake

epidemiology

fat

fat balance equation

obesity

obesogenic

triglyceride

7

Alcohol and Drinking

Dionysus discovered and bestowed on men the service of drink, the juice that streams from the wine-clusters; men have but to take their fill of wine, and the sufferings of an unhappy race are banished, each day's troubles are forgotten in sleep – indeed this is our only cure for the weariness of life. (Euripides, The *Bacchae*, trans. P. Vellocott, 1954)

Outline

This chapter discusses theories and research on the psychology of drinking and the causes, prevention and treatment of alcohol problems. It begins with a brief history of attitudes to alcohol and the emergence of the theory that alcoholism is a disease that can only be cured by lifelong abstinence. An analysis of the physical and psychosocial dangers of heavy drinking is followed by an examination of contrasting theories about its causes. The chapter concludes with a discussion of the relative merits of different approaches to the prevention and treatment of alcohol problems.

The Blessing and Curse of Alcohol: Historical Background

Ambivalent modern attitudes to alcohol can be traced back to the eighteenth century, when distilled spirits first became widely available. In England, because of their relative cheapness, they were popular with the working class. This was the subject of deep social concern, at least among the educated middle classes. William Hogarth's prints, *Beer Street* and *Gin Lane* (Figure 7.1), illustrate the prevailing view by contrasting the pleasant and supposedly harmless effects of drinking beer with the dire consequences of drinking spirits. Notice the general sense of industriousness and well-being in Beer Street; many people are working and the only shop that is boarded up is the pawnbrokers. In Gin Lane nobody is working except the busy pawnbroker and there is a grim depiction of emaciation, death and the neglect of children.

The way in which alcohol came to be treated as a social problem is illustrated by the history of the **temperance societies**, initially in the USA and spreading to many other countries over the last 150 years. Alcohol has commonly been perceived as the

KT

Figure 7.1 Hogarth's Beer Street and Gin Lane (© The Trustees of the British Museum)

principal cause of violence, crime, sexual immorality, poverty through loss of employment, broken homes and child neglect. Temperance societies began with the Washingtonian movement of the 1840s and continue to the present day as Alcoholics Anonymous, which has branches in almost every North American and British town of any size and in many other countries. 'Temperance' is a misnomer for these societies since they usually promote abstinence and prohibition rather than moderation. They have typically been organized by reformed alcoholics with the mission to help others to become abstinent. Their influence has been enormous not only in bringing about the era of prohibition from 1920 to 1934 but also in establishing as received medical opinion the debatable hypothesis that alcoholics can never return to moderate drinking but can only be cured by remaining abstinent for the rest of their lives.

The Dangers of Drinking

In this section we will consider evidence of the health risks associated with the consumption of alcohol as well as the possible health benefits. A brief summary of the risk factors that we identify is given in Box 7.1.

BOX 7.1

RISKS INCURRED BY THE CONSUMPTION OF ALCOHOL

Risks that can be incurred on any single occasion of heavy drinking

- Driving, industrial and household accidents; falls, fires, drowning.
- Domestic and other forms of violence as perpetrator.
- Domestic and other forms of violence as victim.
- Unwanted pregnancies; HIV or other sexually transmitted diseases following unprotected sexual exposure.

Risks incurred by regular heavy drinking

- Death from liver cirrhosis and acute pancreatitis.
- Irreversible neurological damage.
- Increased risk of cardiovascular disease and certain cancers.
- Problems caused by alcohol dependence.
- Exacerbation of pre-existing difficulties such as depression and family problems.
- Loss of employment, reduced career prospects.

Risks incurred by women who drink during pregnancy

- Foetal alcohol syndrome.
- Spontaneous abortion.
- Low birth weight babies.

An analysis of the research findings on the health hazards of drinking is considerably more complicated than is the case for smoking. Whereas smoking is very dangerous at all levels, and increasingly so at higher levels, the dangers to health of alcohol consumption are not normally found at low levels of consumption. We will therefore examine the evidence for risk associated with high levels of consumption and go on to consider the somewhat vexed question of the possible benefits of low levels of consumption.

To begin with, it is necessary to be a little more precise about what is meant by 'light', 'moderate' and 'heavy' drinking. We will adopt the British system of informal measurement in which one 'unit' is assumed to equal 8 gm of alcohol or one glass of wine of average strength, half a pint of normal strength beer, and a single measure (25 ml) of spirits. It is important to bear in mind that strong wines and beers may contain up to twice this amount of alcohol. We will consider moderate drinking to be at the level of 21/14 units a week for men/women; less than half of that level will be regarded as light drinking and anything over 42/28 units will be regarded as heavy drinking.

Prolonged heavy drinking is known to be the main cause of **liver cirrhosis**, a serious condition that frequently results in death. Using recent figures provided by the British Department of Health, the Academy of Medical Sciences (2004) has noted a four- to five-fold increase in deaths from chronic liver disease in the UK from 1970 to 2000, with over nine-fold increases among young men and women. While some of these changes are attributable to increased rates of hepatitis C infection, effects that are themselves exacerbated by alcohol consumption, the main reason for the changes are increases in levels of heavy drinking.

Although it receives much less publicity than liver cirrhosis, acute pancreatitis is another frequently fatal disease that is often caused by heavy drinking. Goldacre and Roberts (2004) surveyed hospital admissions for this disease in England from 1963 to 1998, noting that they have more than doubled over the 35-year period, with particularly high increases among the younger age groups. These changes closely parallel the patterns of increased alcohol consumption. Heavy drinking is associated with a substantial increased risk of strokes. In a 21-year follow-up study of 5,766 Scottish men, Hart et al. (1999) found that those drinking 35 units or more a week were at twice the risk of death from stroke than light or moderate drinkers.

The evidence linking alcohol consumption to cancer has been reviewed in detail by Bagnardi et al. (2001). They considered the evidence for three levels of consumption, 14, 21 and 28 units a week, and found associations increasing at each level for cancers of the oral cavity and pharynx, larynx, breast, liver, colo-rectum and stomach. The association with breast cancer is of particular importance because this is the most common cause of premature death in women. Hamajima et al. (2002) conducted a detailed re-analysis of data from 53 studies with a total sample size of over 150,000. They found that there was a clear relationship with risk increasing steadily from teetotallers through to those drinking more than five units a day. However, the level of risk is quite modest and the authors note that it needs to be interpreted in the context of the possible beneficial effects of moderate alcohol consumption; but they conclude that alcohol could be the cause of about 4% of deaths from breast cancer.

KT

KT

Drinking during pregnancy has been shown to be associated with a significant risk of damage to the unborn child. Heavy drinking is the main cause of **fetal alcohol syndrome**, in which the child suffers from a particular type of facial abnormality as well as mental impairment and stunted growth. Relatively low levels of drinking have also been linked to below average birth weight and an increased risk of spontaneous abortion. It is still unclear what, if anything, constitutes a safe level of drinking during pregnancy, or whether the risks are mainly restricted to certain periods of foetal development. Current medical opinion is that the pregnant woman is best advised not to drink at all throughout her pregnancy.

The benefits of light to moderate drinking seem to be mainly associated with a reduced risk of death from heart disease, although there is also evidence of reduced risk of stroke for men over 40 (Berger et al., 1999) and of dementia for men and women over 55 (Ruitenberg et al., 2002). Doll et al. (1994) analysed data for 12,321 male British doctors born between 1900 and 1930, who have been investigated from 1978 to date, and found that regular drinkers had lower rates of heart disease than non-drinkers. They also examined all causes of mortality and concluded that this increased progressively with amount drunk above 21 units a week. Similar findings were reported on the basis of a review of the literature by Bondy et al. (1999). However figures based on average levels of weekly consumption need to be interpreted with caution since Murray et al. (2002) found that sporadic heavy drinking ('binge drinking') raises the risk of heart disease.

The results of these and other studies are not entirely consistent with each other, especially for the purpose of establishing upper limits for safe drinking, but they are at least consistent with the statement that men and women who drink up to 21 and 14 units a week respectively are not taking any significant risk with their physical health. The additional claim that light to moderate drinking is actually beneficial to health is more open to doubt. Although non-drinkers do have higher mortality rates than drinkers, this may be only because the category of non-drinkers includes a substantial number of individuals who have given up drinking because of poor health. This is a useful illustration of the statistician's dictum that *correlation does not entail causation*. It could be that not drinking causes poor health but, equally well, it could be that poor health causes not drinking.

Following an extensive analysis of data from 10 North American studies, Fillmore and her colleagues (Fillmore et al., 1998a, 1998b; Leino et al., 1998) conclude that, when appropriate statistical controls are made for confounding effects, there is no evidence that abstinence is associated with a greater mortality risk than light drinking and this has been confirmed in a Scottish study by Hart et al. (1999).

Accidents

In Britain the Department of Transport (1996) carried out an analysis of data on road traffic accidents in which one or more of the drivers involved either failed or refused a breath or blood test. In 1996 there were 10,850 drink-drive accidents including 540 deaths. Pedestrians who are killed in road accidents are also likely to have been drinking. In an earlier report (Department of Transport, 1992), it was estimated that about half of pedestrians aged between 16 and 60 killed in road accidents had more alcohol in their bloodstream than the legal drink-drive limit.

Studies conducted in a number of countries indicate that alcohol is implicated in many attendances at hospital accident and emergency departments. Williams et al. (1994) reported that 50% of adults admitted to a hospital surgery unit with a head injury were obviously drunk. Alcohol has been shown to play a significant role in deaths from falls, fires, industrial accidents and deaths from drowning.

Psychosocial problems

The regular use of alcohol often gives rise to the problem of alcohol dependence. There has been some debate about the usefulness of the concept of alcohol dependence as a clinical category, an issue that will be discussed in the next section.

Morgenstern et al. (1997) have shown that alcohol problems are often found among people with a range of personality disorders. Similarly, Miller and Brown (1997) point out that drinking problems are common among those being treated for other mental health problems, making it more difficult to provide effective therapy. Alcohol is also frequently implicated in suicide, homicide and other violent crime, both as perpetrator and as victim. The British Medical Association (1989) estimated that alcohol is associated with 60–70% of homicides (one-third of victims being intoxicated at time of death), 75% of stabbings, 70% of beatings and 50% of fights or domestic assaults.

To what extent is alcohol to blame? This raises all of the usual chicken-and-egg problems of interpreting statistical correlations. For example, does drinking incite people to commit crimes or do criminals drink to reduce their fear before carrying out the crimes which they have already decided to commit? Do people take to drink in an effort to ameliorate their psychological problems, or are these problems caused by heavy drinking? Probably the most sensible response that can be made to this latter question at the present time is to reiterate the well-known health education slogan: 'If you drink because you have a problem, then you will end up with two problems.'

Theories of Drinking and Alcohol Dependence

To understand the motivation for drinking and problems of dependence it is best to begin by considering the psychological effects of alcohol. Alcohol is popularly associated with beliefs about the loosening of inhibitions and the suppression of unpleasant emotions, especially anxiety. This explains why it is consumed in social gatherings such as parties and weddings, when people are expected to interact in a much more relaxed and informal way than they would otherwise, and also why heavy drinking is common among people with psychological problems.

The view that the major motive for drinking is to reduce anxiety is often referred to as the **tension reduction hypothesis**. Some versions of this hypothesis have focused primarily on the direct effect of alcohol on the nervous system, but in recent years there has been a shift of opinion towards models that account for the anxiety reducing effects as indirect consequences of the effect of alcohol on information processing,

KT

Table 7.1   *Theories of problem drinking*

Type of theory	Causes of problem drinking
Genetic theories	DNA variations believed to be associated with the metabolism of alcohol mean that certain individuals are much more likely than most to develop alcohol problems if they drink.
Disease theories	Individuals who drink heavily may develop the 'disease' of alcoholism, a chronic and irreversible condition which can only be treated by lifelong abstinence.
Learning theories	Mechanisms of conditioning and social learning are employed to explain the initiation and development of excessive consumption, and to explain the phenomena of dependence, craving, increased tolerance and withdrawal symptoms.

making cognitive processes more shallow and reducing awareness of information that could lead to a negative self-evaluation. Others have proposed that it works by altering responses to stress. A detailed analysis of the relationship between alcohol and emotional arousal is given by Stritzke et al. (1996).

Let us now turn from the general theoretical question of why people drink to the question as to why some people develop drinking problems. Here a number of contrasting theoretical perspectives need to be considered. They are not mutually exclusive in the sense that this can sometimes be said of theories in the natural sciences. The discerning reader will notice various ways in which elements of each can be consistent with elements of the others. They are best thought of as reference points that are useful aids to thinking about the issues. A brief summary of the main theoretical views is given in Table 7.1.

Genetic theories

Genetic theories propose that some people have an inherited predisposition to develop drinking problems. However, even if it is true, this should not be taken as implying that it is inevitable that they will do so. To take an analogy, some people may have an inherited proneness to develop heart disease, but whether or not they will do so still depends on whether they smoke, eat fatty foods and so on. The risks are just greater for some people than for others. Similarly, there could be many environmental reasons why drinking problems develop in those who have an inherited predisposition and also in those who do not.

Much depends on the relative potency of hereditary and environmental factors. At one extreme it is sometimes suggested that certain people are 'born alcoholics', destined to succumb to alcoholism as soon as they take their first drink. Organizations such as Alcoholics Anonymous see their mission as rescuing such unfortunate people by showing them how to achieve total abstinence and maintain it against all temptation. Perhaps surprisingly, this 'biological determinist' view is also attractive to manufacturers of alcoholic drinks. They can argue that the born alcoholic is bound to have a drink and become alcoholic sooner or later, however much the availability of drink is restricted. The rest of us can drink as much as we want without running the risk of becoming alcoholic. As Rose et al. (1990) point out, using many different examples, biological determinism is always attractive to those who wish to evade responsibility for creating or failing to solve social problems.

At the opposite end of the spectrum to the biological determinist view is the 'environmentalist' view that, in the same circumstances, everyone is equally likely to develop a drinking problem. This view is implicitly held by those who adopt the addiction model and place all the blame for drinking problems on alcohol, which they consider to be a highly addictive substance. The third view is that of genetic–environmental interaction: both heredity and environment play a part in determining whether people develop drinking problems. It is this view that receives most support from the research evidence.

It has been clearly established that alcohol problems tend to run in families. The children of heavy drinkers are more likely to become heavy drinkers themselves than children whose parents do not drink heavily. However, this cannot be taken as evidence of an inherited predisposition as it could equally well be that patterns of drinking are learned from parents. The key evidence for hereditary effects comes from twin and adoption studies and a useful review of the rather confusing evidence has been provided by Heather and Robertson (1997).

One way of assessing hereditary effects is to compare the concordance rates for drinking in *monozygotic* (MZ, identical) and *dizygotic* (DZ, fraternal) *twins*. The theory behind this is that both types of twin grow up in the same family environment, so that a greater concordance for the 100% genetically similar MZ twins than for the 50% similar DZ twins is evidence of genetic effects. The data turns out to be suggestive rather than conclusive. Most but not all studies found higher concordance for MZ twins. Assessment of the potency of heredity is not possible from these studies because the crucially important size of the difference between MZ and DZ concordance rates varies greatly from study to study. It also varies according to what patterns of drinking are assessed. One study found the greatest hereditary effect for chronic alcoholism, in comparison with moderate to heavy drinking, while another found the greatest effect for teetotalism in comparison with all other patterns of drinking! The shortcomings of MZ/DZ comparisons for assessing heredity have been analysed by Rose et al. (1984). For example, MZ twins spend much more time in each other's company than DZ twins and thus may be more likely to acquire the same patterns of drinking for non-hereditary reasons.

The other main way of assessing hereditary effects is to examine whether adopted children grow up to acquire similar drinking habits to their biological parents, or whether they are more influenced by their adopting parents. As with MZ/DZ comparisons, the evidence tends to confirm the existence of hereditary effects, but assessing the relative potency of heredity and environment proves to be impossible, partly because of unexplained variation in the results obtained from different studies, and partly because of inherent methodological weaknesses in adoption studies. Some studies found a strong hereditary effect for males but not for females, while others have found the reverse. Results have also varied considerably for different categories of problem drinkers.

It should be noted that the genetic pathways that predispose people towards particular patterns of drinking are unlikely to be straightforward as in the case of eye colour or blood groups. There have been attempts to demonstrate specific genetic pathways for alcohol problems but they have received only modest support from research (Cook and Gurling, 2001). As with other forms of human behaviour, there are likely to be a multitude of complex genetic routes that may make some individuals more likely than others to become problem drinkers. For example, there may be inheritable differences in the way that alcohol is metabolized, so that some people find its effects pleasant, others unpleasant, some find it takes more alcohol, others less, to achieve the same effect. There may be differences in genetic predisposition to experience anxiety, so that some are predisposed to drink more than others on discovering that it temporarily suppresses anxiety.

Finally, it is worth asking what would be the advantage of having a better assessment of hereditary influences on alcohol consumption? The obvious answer is that it could prove valuable for preventive purposes. This would certainly be true if it proved possible to identify specific genetic markers of the kind discussed by Cook and Gurling (2001). In that case DNA screening could be used to identify at-risk individuals at an early age and counsel them accordingly. But what if specific gene effects are unknown and we have only the evidence of hereditary effects from twin and adoption studies? It might still be thought useful because, if the hereditary influence is a strong one, then anyone with a heavy drinking parent would be advised to examine carefully their parent's drinking habits and their own in order to avoid making the same mistakes. But now consider what would follow if environmental influences predominate. Since we know that alcohol abuse tends to run in families, an important environmental influence would be from parent to child. Anyone with a heavy drinking parent would still be advised to reflect carefully upon their parent's drinking habits and their own in order to try to avoid making the same mistakes. Thus it appears that there is little to be gained for practical purposes by carrying out studies designed to provide better estimates of the relative importance of hereditary and environmental influences on alcohol consumption and dependence.

Addiction, disease and dependency theories

The fascinating history of these interrelated theories has been surveyed by Heather and Robertson (1997) and McMurran (1994). It appears that they all have their origins in the activities of the temperance societies and other evangelical anti-drink campaigners rather than being the natural outcome of dispassionately conducted medical and psychological research. Yet evangelical campaigners have succeeded in influencing medical opinion to the point that disease and dependency theories have become medical orthodoxy despite a lack of adequate evidence to support them.

KT   The earliest clear statements of **addiction theories** can be traced back to the classic works of Benjamin Rush of Philadelphia and Thomas Trotter of Edinburgh, published respectively in 1785 and 1804. These men replaced the view of habitual drunkards as moral degenerates by one in which they are victims of a disease of addiction. Once the disease is established, the victims lose all voluntary control over their drinking. They have become incapable of resisting their craving for the 'demon drink'. Rush and Trotter succeeded in popularizing their belief that alcohol is a highly addictive substance 70 years before the case was made for opium.

Later **disease theories** focused increasingly on the at-risk individual who has a predisposition to become alcoholic once he or she starts drinking. Although a predisposition to become alcoholic does not have to be hereditary (we have already mentioned that it may be the result of upbringing), nevertheless the concept of the born alcoholic proved attractive to disease theorists. In common with earlier addiction theories, disease theories emphasized craving and loss of control. The difference was that, for the new disease theorists, alcohol is only highly addictive for a small number of people. The rest of us can drink with impunity. This change of emphasis proved attractive, especially to a North American society that had abandoned prohibition, embraced personal liberty and responsibility and has a powerful drinks industry.

From the mid-1970s, the disease theory was being revised and extended, notably by Griffith Edwards and Milton Gross, to become the **alcohol dependence syndrome**. In this new conceptualization, the sharp distinction which had previously been made between physical addiction and psychological dependence was abolished and the syndrome was viewed instead as a psycho-physiological disorder. The descriptions given by Edwards and Gross are not always very clear and tend to change from one publication to another. Sayette and Hufford (1997) summarize Edwards's more recent accounts as including some or all of the following symptoms:

- Tolerance: a diminished effect of alcohol, usually accompanied by increased consumption.
- Withdrawal symptoms following reduced consumption.
- Consumption of larger amounts or for a longer time period than was intended.
- Persistent desire or unsuccessful efforts to cut down or control drinking.
- Excessive time spent obtaining, consuming or recovering from the effects of alcohol.
- Reduction of important activities due to drinking.
- Continued drinking despite knowing that it is causing or exacerbating a physical or psychological problem.

The concept of the alcohol dependence syndrome has been sharply criticized by Shaw (1979) who points out that much woolly thinking lies behind it. Most people, on reading the above list of symptoms, would conclude that anyone who drinks regularly would exhibit one or more of them to some degree. As a list, it seems consistent with the idea that, rather than being a disease, alcohol dependence is an arbitrary point that can be chosen on a continuum from the light social drinker to the homeless street drinker. Yet proponents of the syndrome insist that it is a clinical entity, admittedly with somewhat varying symptomatology, which only applies to a relatively small number out of all the people who drink heavily.

One should not, of course, 'throw out the baby with the bath water'. No theory of alcohol use can afford to neglect the phenomena of physical dependence associated with prolonged heavy drinking and most clearly manifested in the spectacular withdrawal symptoms that can occur. These include the most unpleasant to be found among all drugs and involve tremors ('the shakes'), sweating, nausea, vomiting, hallucinations ('pink elephants') and convulsions. In some cases, sudden withdrawal can actually prove fatal. The phenomena of psychological dependence also need to be addressed by any theory of alcohol use. While alcohol dependence syndrome may be poorly defined as a clinical entity, the psychological problems that are often associated with heavy drinking certainly need to be explained.

Learning theory and the controlled drinking controversy

Learning theorists consider drinking problems to develop as a result of the same learning mechanisms that are at work in establishing patterns of 'normal drinking'. They argue that the reasons why some people become problem drinkers and others do not lie in their particular personal histories of learning to drink, their present social environment insofar as it provides opportunities and encouragement to drink, and in physiological variables that may make the effects of alcohol more pleasurable or positively reinforcing for some people than others.

KT

Operant conditioning is the type of learning that occurs when animals are trained to respond in a particular way to a stimulus by providing rewards after they make the appropriate response. In the classic experiment, hungry rats were confined in small boxes and trained to press a bar in order to obtain food pellets. This phenomenon, which was of course well known to animal trainers, pet owners and the parents of small children long before it was 'discovered' by psychologists, has some applicability

KT

to the understanding of problem drinking. Of particular importance is the **gradient of reinforcement**, the fact that reinforcement that occurs rapidly after the response is much more effective in producing learning than delayed reinforcement. In the case of drinking alcohol, a small amount of positive reinforcement, such as reduced anxiety, that occurs fairly soon after drinking, may cause a strong habit to develop in spite of the counterbalancing effect of a large amount of negative reinforcement (hangover, divorce, loss of employment) that occurs much later.

Drinking, eating, smoking, drug and sexual addictions all have the 'irrational' characteristic that the total amount of pleasure gained from the addiction seems much less than the suffering caused by it. According to learning theorists, the reason for this lies in the nature of the gradient of reinforcement. Addictive behaviours are typically those in which pleasurable effects occur rapidly while unpleasant consequences occur after a delay. The simple mechanism of operant conditioning and the gradient of reinforcement is able, as it were, to overpower the mind's capacity for rational calculation. Bigelow (2001) discusses the applicability of operant conditioning principles to the understanding and treatment of alcohol problems. He concludes that they have considerable relevance but notes that there has been little interest in them in the alcohol field in recent years, in contrast to the field of illegal substance use where they continue to play quite a dominant role.

KT

Classical conditioning refers to the process whereby a response that occurs as a natural reflex to a particular stimulus can be conditioned to occur to a new stimulus. In Pavlov's early experiments a bell was rung shortly before food was placed in a dog's mouth, thereby eliciting salivation as a physiological reflex. After a number of pairings of bell and food Pavlov found that the dog salivated when the bell was rung unaccompanied by food.

A number of interesting models have been developed by applying classical conditioning principles to addictions, and Drummond et al. (1995) provide a useful survey of this now highly technical subject. One interesting application to explain the phenomena of drug dependence, tolerance and withdrawal is the **compensatory conditioned response model**. Initially, when a drug is taken, a physiological *homeostatic* mechanism comes into operation to counteract its effects. In the case of alcohol, which has a depressing effect, the homeostatic mechanism activates the nervous system in order to maintain the normal level of activation. In the regular drinker this gradually produces tolerance so that increasingly large quantities of alcohol are required to produce the same effect. Furthermore, the homeostatic response of nervous activation may become conditioned to stimuli normally associated with drinking, such as situations where drinking has frequently taken place in the past. If conditioned drinkers are in such situations but do not drink, the conditioned response of nervous activation will not be balanced by the effects of alcohol and the resultant unpleasant state of excessive activation is what is known as a withdrawal state. In this way classical conditioning can account for the close connection observed between the phenomena of tolerance and withdrawal.

The compensatory conditioned response model has considerable intuitive plausibility but there is a lack of convincing evidence for its applicability to problem drinking. Drobes et al. (2001) discuss this model and a range of alternative classical conditioning models with specific reference to alcohol dependence and they conclude that, in all cases, there is a lack of empirical evidence to support the approach.

Social learning theorists argue that classical and operant conditioning provide incomplete explanations of human learning, which also frequently depends on observation and imitation. Bandura (1977) has been particularly influential in emphasizing the importance of learning by imitation and linking it to his concept of **self-efficacy**, a personality trait consisting of having confidence in one's ability to carry out one's plans successfully. People with low self-efficacy are much more likely to imitate undesirable behaviours than those with high self-efficacy. Patterns of drinking by parents are observed by children who may then imitate them in later life, especially the behaviour of the same sex parent. In adolescence, the drinking behaviour of respected older peers may also be imitated, and subsequently that of higher status colleagues at work, a phenomenon that may explain the prevalence of heavy drinking in certain professions such as medicine and journalism.

Freud's concept of 'secondary gain' can also be usefully applied to alcohol problems as an extension of the learning theory perspective. Just as hypochondriacs are often seen to be using their condition to avoid work and to get people at their beck and call, so can it be seen that sufferers from many kinds of neurosis often exploit their condition in order to gain attention, avoid things that they do not wish to do and generally manipulate people around them. It is easy to see how patterns of drinking can function in this way, and not only in the regular heavy drinker: 'It's your fault for getting me drunk' or 'I only did it because I was drunk' can provide a convenient way of evading responsibility for the person who commits a sexual indiscretion or beats their partner. Here alcohol has the double function of releasing the inhibitions that might otherwise prevent the impulse from being acted on, while simultaneously being held to blame as if it were the drink that performed the action rather than the drinker. In the case of the alcoholic, it is possible to see here some dangers in adopting the medical or disease model. If alcoholics think of themselves as victims of a disease over which they have no control, not only will they avoid taking responsibility for actions carried

KT

KT

out while under the influence of drink, but they will also avoid taking responsibility for drinking, which may make it difficult or impossible to help them.

Can individuals with drinking problems ever resume moderate levels of drinking, or is total abstinence their only realistic goal? Because they regard heavy drinking as essentially a habit rather than a disease, learning theorists have taken the view that a return to moderate drinking can, at least in some cases, be a viable objective. Although not necessarily the preferred objective, moderation may sometimes be a reasonable one to pursue. This apparently modest and cautious view has provoked an extraordinary amount of criticism, especially in the USA, where a belief that lifelong abstinence is the only cure is deeply entrenched, often taking on the character of a moral crusade. The evidence that has accumulated over the last 40 years points clearly in favour of the learning theorists.

Heather and Robertson (1997) review the evidence. A number of studies have carried out long-term follow ups of patients originally diagnosed as severely alcoholic and treated with programmes aimed at lifelong abstinence. A consistent finding is that at least as many were drinking moderately as were abstinent, although it should also be noted that, even taken together, the proportion who were abstinent or moderate drinkers was considerably smaller than the proportion who had resumed heavy drinking. Other studies have looked at spontaneous changes in people's drinking habits and found considerable fluctuation between moderate drinking, light drinking and abstinence over periods of a few years. Spontaneous remission rates from problem drinking have also been reported at levels ranging from 4% to 42%.

Heather and Robertson also consider the relative merits of treatment programmes that aim for a return to moderate drinking and those that aim for abstinence. A return to moderate drinking seems to be a viable objective for people with less severe forms of dependence provided that they are well motivated. For those with severe dependence, abstinence is often preferred as the objective, although much again depends on level of motivation. In the case of homeless street drinkers with a long history of severe dependence, a reduction in daily intake is probably the only realistic goal of an intervention. A recent development in Britain has been the establishment of *wet houses* that provide accommodation and activities designed to reduce the amount of drinking that takes place, while, in contrast to traditional establishments, not actually prohibiting consumption on the premises. This form of intervention combines practical help to those who most need it together with sensible expectations of those with a severe drinking dependency.

Prevention and Treatment of Alcohol Problems

Prevention

Over the last 30 years the World Health Organization has sponsored a series of reports which have reviewed the evidence concerning public policy and the prevention of alcohol problems. The most recent of these is that of Babor et al. (2003). These reports have consistently argued in favour of the *population-based approach,* which incorporates the principle that the most effective policies for reducing alcohol problems are those that reduce overall levels of consumption. These policies include high levels of taxation for alcoholic drinks and restrictions on access, such as limiting opening hours for bars and imposing tight controls on which shops can sell alcohol and the hours during which they can do so.

Babor et al. emphasize the importance of adapting policies to local conditions in a world where overall levels of consumption and patterns of heavy drinking vary greatly from country to country. More ominously, they note the increasing influence on government policies of a drinks industry concerned to protect its commercial interests, supported by free market values and concepts. In response to recent concern about alcohol problems in Britain, where per capita consumption rose by over 50% between 1970 and 2002, the Academy of Medical Sciences (2004) has produced a report that also broadly endorses the population-based approach while at the same time discussing the difficulties of implementation in the present climate of opinion.

The population-based approach is opposed by the drinks industry because reduced overall consumption means smaller profits. Neither are the associated policies popular with governments who fear that restrictions on availability and high taxation would be unpopular with the electorate and with the drinks industry, which is a powerful pressure group. Heather and Robertson (1997) describe attempts by the Portman Group, an organization funded by the British drinks industry, to influence academic debate on alcohol policy by financial offers. The Institute of Alcohol Studies (2003) has commented on the influence of the Portman Group on the current plans of the British government to extend permitted drinking hours in England and Wales. One of the reasons given for this is that it will reduce levels of 'binge drinking' and associated public disorder, an implausible claim that is opposed by the police and medical authorities, but supported by a single report produced for the Portman Group. The Institute for Alcohol Studies counter this with extensive evidence from countries that have experienced a substantial increase in alcohol problems following liberalization of drinking regulations, notably Scotland, New Zealand and Australia. Further examples are given later in this chapter.

The British drinks industry apparently has had much more influence than any other organization on another key alcohol policy proposal, the *Alcohol Harm Reduction Strategy for England* (Cabinet Office, Prime Minister's Strategy Unit, 2004). This document is replete with positive references to the drinks industry and the Portman Group, emphasizing the value of educational programmes and other drinks industry initiatives, while rejecting any increases in taxation or legislation to control advertising and availability. Its main proposed action is to reduce the 'further increase in alcohol related harms in England'. As Plant (2004) points out, given the existing levels of problems, a policy that does not even set out to reduce them substantially is depressing. Certainly it is not a strategy that is likely to cause too much concern to the drinks industry.

Paralleling the activities of the Portman Group in the UK, Heather (2001a) draws our attention to those of the International Center for Alcohol Policies (ICAP), funded by the international drinks industry and established in the USA in 1995. Among its publications are *Alcohol and Pleasure: A Health Perspective* (Peele and Grant, 1999), a book that emphasizes the pleasurable and beneficial effects of alcohol as against attempts to undermine this view by the 'vast literature on health and social problems associated with alcohol abuse'. The activities of the ICAP have been criticized by McCreanor et al. (2000) on the grounds that they are basically designed to influence public policy in directions that will increase drinks industry profits, especially in the developing world, while having a negative impact on health.

In opposition to the population-based approach, the argument favoured by the pro-alcohol lobby can be called the 'killjoy' or 'why spoil everybody's fun?' argument. The 'killjoy' or 'freedom' argument is expanded as follows. Alcoholics are a small minority who will probably continue to drink heavily however highly it is taxed and however much access is restricted. Their condition is probably inherited and unlikely to be changed by any measures short of total prohibition. For the vast majority of the population, alcohol problems can best be prevented by educational initiatives on sensible approaches to drinking. Why, then, hit the pockets of the normally drinking majority, and restrict their opportunities to enjoy drinking, in a probably unsound strategy to protect a small minority? This argument is often associated with the slur of accusing Britain of being a 'Nanny state'.

These views may sound reasonable but they are not supported by scientific evidence. In examining the dangers to physical health of heavy drinking, we have already referred to UK evidence of the close relationship between per capita alcohol consumption and deaths from liver cirrhosis, the latter a clear indicator of prolonged heavy drinking. Saunders (1985) found similar evidence when analysing the very large changes in average levels of consumption in Finland this century as a result of periods of restrictive legislation followed by periods of liberalization. These changes were associated not only with corresponding changes in rates of liver cirrhosis, but also in hospital admissions for alcoholism, arrests for drunkenness, road traffic accidents where the driver had been drinking, and arrests for driving while under the influence of alcohol. Kendell et al. (1983a, 1983b) conducted a similar analysis of the effects in Scotland of a large increase in tax on alcohol. They found an 18% fall in consumption, equally for light drinkers and heavy drinkers, and a corresponding reduction in alcohol-related fights and road traffic accidents.

One area of legislation to control the dangers of alcohol use, which more and more countries are adopting, is strictly enforced drink-driving laws with severe penalties for offenders. It is now almost universally agreed that this has played an important role in reducing traffic fatalities. It even commands the support of the drinks industry which, in view of the high level of public support for the laws, would be foolish to oppose it.

The other main preventive measures that have been much analysed are health education initiatives with the aim of preventing alcohol misuse. Unfortunately, the evidence here indicates that they are not very effective. Health education generally appears to improve knowledge about the effects of alcohol and attitudes to it, but has no effect on the amounts actually consumed. Midford and McBride (2001) review alcohol education programmes in schools, noting that, in the USA, efforts have been hampered by excessive emphasis on abstinence, while in Europe and Australasia the emphasis has been on 'sensible drinking'. Although they detect a few promising signs in recent developments, the general finding is that these programmes have either failed to achieve any effects or, at best, have produced very small effects. Foxcroft et al. (2003) review reports of 56 interventions aimed at young people aged 25 or under with substantially similar conclusions.

The ineffectiveness of educational campaigns designed to encourage sensible drinking perhaps explains why the drinks industry is happy to support them and even participate in them. Although this may seem an unnecessarily cynical view, there are some reasons for taking it seriously. Heather and Robertson (1997) point out that the drinks industry derives a good part of its profits from very heavy drinkers. In a 1978 survey of Scottish drinking habits, it was estimated that 3% of the population were responsible for 30% of total alcohol consumption. The loss of this source of profits would be crippling to the drinks industry. Hence the continued profitability of the industry requires the existence of a substantial percentage of very heavy drinkers. This provides another salient example of a conflict of interest between good public health and profits in industry.

Agostinelli and Grube (2002) review alcohol counter-advertising, including warnings on alcoholic products, with a number of interesting proposals. Unfortunately research to date has been mainly concerned with participants' assessments of the impact of this type of advertising rather than its effectiveness in reducing misuse. It can also be argued that such efforts are a drop in the ocean in comparison with the amount of money that the drinks industry spends on product promotion. An alternative approach, deeply unpopular with the drinks industry, is the introduction of bans on advertising and sponsorship. Although earlier research has indicated that bans have little or no effect on overall consumption, Saffer and Dave (2002) argue that this research is flawed. They use an economic model to analyse pooled data from 20 countries over 26 years and conclude that there is a significant effect that indicates that bans can reduce overall consumption by 5% to 8%. They note that increases in levels of consumption often stimulate the introduction of bans, but that reductions in consumption often lead to the rescinding of bans, as has happened recently in Canada, Denmark, New Zealand and Finland.

Treatment

A brief synopsis of alternative approaches to treatment is given in Table 7.2.

One of the most striking features of the treatment of alcohol problems is the contrasting approaches taken in different countries. In the USA and Canada, treatment is usually aimed at total abstinence, while in Britain a return to moderate drinking has increasingly become the treatment goal. North American programmes are normally based on specialist treatment centres that have a strong medical orientation, dominated by psychiatrists who subscribe to a disease model of alcoholism. In Finland, on the other hand, alcohol problems are regarded as essentially social problems and dealt with primarily by social workers. These differences have been shaped by social forces and, until recently, have rarely involved any serious critical analysis of the evidence for the efficacy of the approaches. For example, Miller and Brown (1997) note that the specialist US treatment programmes for alcohol and drug problems are among those least supported by scientific evidence.

Table 7.2   *Main approaches to the treatment of problem drinking*

Type of treatment	Approach to treatment
In-patient treatment	'Drying out centres' and private clinics which focus on the alleviation of withdrawal symptoms followed by counselling and therapy to maintain abstinence following discharge.
Alcoholics Anonymous	Self-help groups run by ex-alcoholics using the *twelve step facilitation programme* to maintain lifelong abstinence. May receive individuals on discharge from in-patient treatments.
Counselling and psychotherapy	Encompasses many approaches deriving from alternative psychotherapeutic models with the shared aim of helping clients to achieve insight into the causes and effects of problem drinking, seen as an essential basis for change.
Cognitive behavioural therapies	Based on learning theories and sometimes aiming to reduce levels of drinking rather than promoting abstinence as the treatment objective. *Motivation enhancement therapy* and *relapse prevention therapy* are currently the most popular approaches.

Where the comparative efficacy of different treatment programmes has been evaluated, the predominant finding is that **cognitive-behavioural therapy** (CBT) programmes are the most cost effective and also likely to produce better results than other types of treatment, including counselling and psychotherapy (Miller and Brown, 1997). Recent evidence suggests that a particularly effective technique is **motivation enhancement therapy** (Miller and Rollnick, 2002). This approach is in direct contrast to the confrontational tactics traditionally adopted by therapists treating addictions, in which every effort is made to overcome the client's supposed resistance to acknowledging that he or she has a problem, aggressively to challenge any dishonesty and to break down his or her defences. Instead the motivation enhancing therapist tries to create a warm empathic relationship with the client and uses a gentle and indirect approach in order to elicit, rather than impose, an increase in motivation to change behaviour, improve self-esteem and develop the feeling of self-efficacy for putting changes into practice. Further effective therapeutic techniques include social skills training, not least those needed to abstain or drink moderately in situations where others are drinking heavily, and training in psychological strategies designed to prevent a full-blown relapse from occurring after a single occasion of relapse. **Relapse prevention therapy** is described in detail by Marlatt and Gordon (1985) and, in a review of outcome studies, Irvin et al. (1999) conclude that it is effective both for alcohol and drug abuse problems.

One finding that has been confirmed by a number of investigators is that brief treatments can be as effective as more extensive ones (Heather, 2001b). In a very large five-year study in the USA, known as Project MATCH, 1,726 people with drinking problems were divided into three groups receiving respectively: (a) a treatment based on the **twelve-step facilitation programme** of Alcoholics Anonymous; (b) coping skills therapy based on social learning theory; (c) **motivation enhancement therapy**. Motivation enhancement therapy proved just as effective as the other two, although it consisted of only four as against 12 sessions over a 12-week period. This finding applied equally across clients with problems of relatively high and low degrees of severity (Project MATCH Research Group, 1997).

In addition to brief treatments like these that are aimed at individuals who specifically seek help for alcohol problems, there has also been a great deal of recent interest in **opportunistic interventions**, interventions by general practitioners and other professionals to individuals who have come to seek their advice for other reasons. These were first introduced to encourage smoking cessation, and their success led to similar studies of advice to cut down on drinking (e.g. Fleming et al., 1997). The most impressive evidence comes from a World Health Organization study (Babor and Grant, 1992) in which 1,655 heavy drinkers in 10 countries were given one of: (a) an assessment only of the individual's alcohol problems (control group); (b) assessment plus five minutes' interview with a health worker who advised them to cut down; (c) assessment, advice and 15 minutes' counselling on a habit breaking plan; (d) assessment, advice and extended counselling consisting of at least three further sessions. Men in all three intervention groups performed equally well, cutting down 25% more than the control group. In the case of women, all four groups showed equally reduced consumption so that, for them, the mere fact of having been assessed was sufficient to motivate them to cut down.

These findings could have considerable significance for public policy. The cost effectiveness of brief treatments for those requesting help and very brief opportunistic interventions for those who do not appears to be relatively high and they offer health-care systems excellent value for money. It should however be emphasized that they have been designed for individuals with relatively low levels of alcohol dependence and problems, rather than for those with severe dependence.

Future Research

1 Clarification of the health risks and possible benefits of light to moderate drinking, including heart disease, various cancers and risks to the unborn child.
2 Epidemiological studies to determine the causal role of alcohol in psychosocial problems, including different types of crime, marital and family problems, suicide and psychological disorders.
3 Studies to assess the relative merits of abstinence versus controlled drinking as an objective for people with drinking problems. What types of client are best advised to aim respectively for abstinence and for moderation?
4 Investigations to establish what are the physiological and psychological characteristics of dependence, tolerance and withdrawal. Comparative testing of alternative conditioning models.
5 Evaluation of the effectiveness and cost effectiveness of interventions using long-term follow-ups and appropriate controls. Currently the most promising appear to be brief opportunistic interventions by medical practitioners and, for those actively seeking help, motivation enhancement therapy and cognitive-behavioural therapy.
6 Research into the cost effectiveness of alternative approaches to the prevention of alcohol problems, including taxation, restrictions on availability, educational and other health promotion initiatives.

Summary

1   Most cultures have had an ambivalent view of the use of alcohol, its benefits and undesirable effects.

2   There is a sharp conflict between the medical or disease model of alcoholism, particularly prevalent in North America, where lifelong abstinence is considered to be the only cure for the alcoholic, and psychological models based on learning theory, more common in Europe, where drinking in moderation is considered a viable objective, at least for some types of heavy drinker.

3   Drinking has been shown to cause liver cirrhosis, pancreatitis, strokes, various cancers and, in the case of drinking during pregnancy, damage to the unborn child. Most of these risks are confined to the heavy drinker. However, in the case of drinking during pregnancy there is evidence that risk may begin at quite low levels of consumption.

4   The greatest physical risk taken by the moderate drinker and the occasional binge drinker is the risk of accidental injury or death, especially, but not exclusively, traffic accidents.

5   It is not clear to what extent problem drinking causes psychological disorders or is a consequence of pre-existing disorders. However, whichever is the case, drinking has the effect of exacerbating these disorders and making them more difficult to treat.

6   Alcohol has been shown to be associated with a large proportion of homicides and assaults, both as perpetrator and as victim.

7   It has proved difficult to assess the relative contribution of hereditary and environmental factors to the development of different patterns of drinking; on balance, the evidence suggests that both factors make a substantial contribution.

8   The nature of physical and psychological dependence on alcohol is not well understood; at present, conditioning/learning models represent the most promising approach.

9   For heavy drinkers who have not actively sought treatment for their problems, advice to cut down or stop drinking given by general practitioners or other professionals is the most effective known intervention.

10   For those who seek help, cognitive/behavioural therapies, including motivation enhancement therapy and relapse prevention therapy are at least as effective as the combative, confrontational approach usually associated with the disease model of alcoholism.

11   The most effective methods for preventing alcohol problems are measures that have the effect of reducing overall levels of consumption, including high taxation and restricted availability. However, in most countries in the west the drinks industry acts as a powerful lobby against these measures and few politicians would risk unpopularity by introducing them.

 ## Key Terms

addiction theories

alcohol dependence syndrome

classical conditioning

cognitive-behavioural therapy (CBT)

compensatory conditioned response model

disease theories

fetal alcohol syndrome

gradient of reinforcement

liver cirrhosis

motivation enhancement therapy

operant conditioning

opportunistic interventions

relapse prevention therapy

self-efficacy

temperance societies

tension reduction hypothesis

twelve-step facilitation programme

8

Tobacco and Smoking

This vice brings in one hundred million francs in taxes every year. I will certainly forbid it at once – as soon as you can name a virtue that brings in as much revenue.
(Napoleon III, 1808–73)

Outline

With the accumulation of evidence on the negative aspects of smoking, most western governments promoted measures to reduce the prevalence. These measures have met with substantial success such that the prevalence of smoking has fallen steadily in most industrialized societies. Meanwhile it continues to increase dramatically throughout the developing world and a large number of people continue to smoke in the industrialized world. Indeed, the evidence suggests that the overall prevalence of smoking in young people in the USA and Britain started to increase again in the mid-1990s although it has since declined. The aim of this chapter is to document the extent of smoking and factors that help explain its continued popularity and to discuss why people take up smoking and what steps can be taken to reduce the prevalence.

Brief History of Tobacco and Smoking

The adventurer Sir Walter Ralegh is alleged to have introduced both potatoes and tobacco to England. Ralegh's legacy to public health in the form of fags and chips would be hard to rival. Ralegh popularized tobacco at court, and apparently believed that it was a good cure for coughs and so he often smoked a pipe. Indeed, it is alleged that Ralegh's final request before his beheading by James I at the Tower of London in 1618 was a smoke of tobacco, a legacy to all subsequent prisoners facing execution.

Cigarette smoking was reintroduced to England by British soldiers returning from Wellington's Napoleonic campaigns in the Iberian Peninsula (1808–14). Following this, veterans returning from the Crimean War (1853–56) increased cigarette smoking in Britain. In addition to bringing many millions of deaths and injuries to service personnel, war has always been a great addicter to tobacco and, in the case of the Royal Navy, to rum.

The economics and politics of tobacco are complicated with many dilemmas and contradictions. Over the last 450 years tobacco has become a major contributor to the economy. Tobacco tax makes a significant contribution to the wealth of nations (e.g. over £7 billion in the UK), exceeding the cost of treating smoking-related diseases in health systems (e.g. estimated to be £1.5–2.0 billion in the UK). Thus in this, as in other domains, government policy involves a conflict of interests. Many farms on the European continent grow tobacco. The European Union (EU) subsidizes tobacco growers by paying EU farmers £650 million each year. At the same time the EU tries to discourage the smoking of tobacco by restricting tobacco advertisements, and putting health warnings on the packets of cigarettes.

Recent Prevalence and Distribution

Although tobacco was popular during the nineteenth century, it was largely smoked using pipes and confined to men. The development of cigarettes towards the end of the nineteenth century was followed by a rapid increase in tobacco consumption. In the first half of the twentieth century, cigarette smoking became a hugely popular activity, especially among men in the western world. In the USA cigarette consumption doubled in the 1920s and again in the 1930s and peaked at about 67% in the 1940s and 1950s. In Britain it was estimated that the prevalence among men reached almost 80% during the same period (Wald et al., 1988). Since then, the prevalence has declined overall, although sex, social class, regional and other differences have developed.

The World Health Organization (2004) estimates that 47% of men and 12% of women smoke, including 42% of men and 24% of women in developed countries, and 48% of men and 7% of women in developing countries. Prevalence in developing countries is rising dramatically where there is extensive promotion of smoking by the tobacco industry.

Though fewer women than men are smokers, there have been dramatic increases in smoking among women and the gap in smoking rates between men and women is narrowing in most places. In Europe, there was a consistent decline in the prevalence of smoking among men from about 70–90% to about 30–50% between 1950 and 1990. However, among women the same period saw a rise in the prevalence of smoking followed by a slow decline reaching 20–40% in 1990. The initial rise in prevalence was led by women from professional backgrounds, but they have also led the decline such that today smoking is more common among women from poorer backgrounds.

National variations in smoking behaviour have also been found across Europe. More than 40% of men in Austria, Greece, Norway and Portugal smoked, while less than 25% smoked in Belgium, Finland, Hungary and Sweden. In general the prevalence of smoking was lower among women and lowest (10%) in Finland.

National surveys have also clearly established a growing link between smoking and various indicators of social deprivation. In Britain a national survey of health and lifestyles found that smoking is more prevalent among people on low incomes, the unemployed and those who are divorced or separated.

Health Effects of Smoking

The health effects of smoking have been studied for over 100 years. The evidence has been collated by health authorities throughout the world. There is hardly a single organ in the body that is not deleteriously influenced by tobacco smoking. Today the only people still claiming that smoking is safe is the tobacco industry.

Effects on active smokers

The classic study by Doll and Hill (1952) linking smoking with cancer was followed by reports by the Royal College of Physicians in Britain (1962) and the Surgeon General in the United States (US Department of Health, Education and Welfare, 1964) demonstrating the harmful effects of smoking. The US Centers for Disease Control and Prevention (2005) give a useful guide to the health impacts of smoking. Cigarette smoking accounts for more than 440,000 deaths each year in the United States and 120,000 deaths in the UK, nearly 1 of every 5 deaths. More deaths are caused each year by tobacco than by all deaths from human immunodeficiency virus (HIV), illegal drug use, alcohol use, motor vehicle injuries, suicides and murders combined. The risk of dying from lung cancer is at least 22 times higher among men who smoke, and about 12 times higher among women who smoke compared with those who have never smoked.

In the USA there have been no less than 28 Surgeon General's Reports on smoking and health during the period 1964–2004. Tobacco is the leading preventable cause of death in the United States, causing more than 440,000 deaths each year and resulting in an annual cost of more than $75 billion in direct medical costs. Nationally, smoking results in almost 6 million years of potential life lost each year. More than 6.4 million children living today will die prematurely because of their decision to smoke cigarettes.

In 2004 the US Surgeon General released a new report on smoking and health, revealing for the first time that smoking causes diseases in nearly every organ of the body. Published 40 years after the Surgeon General's first report on smoking – which had concluded that smoking was a definite cause of three serious diseases – the 2004 report finds that cigarette smoking is conclusively linked to diseases such as leukaemia, cataracts, pneumonia and cancers of the cervix, kidney, pancreas and stomach.

On average, men who smoke cut their lives short by 13.2 years, and female smokers lose 14.5 years. Statistics indicate that more than 12 million Americans have died from smoking since the 1964 report of the surgeon general, and another 25 million Americans alive today will most likely die of a smoking-related illness.

The report concludes that quitting smoking has immediate and long-term benefits, reducing risks for diseases caused by smoking and improving health in general. Quitting smoking at age 65 or older reduces by nearly 50% a person's risk of dying of a smoking-related disease.

Effects on passive smokers

For obvious reasons, tobacco smoke does most damage to the person who is actively inhaling. However, those nearby who are breathing second-hand or environmental tobacco smoke (ETS) also are likely to have a higher risk of cancer, heart disease, and respiratory disease, as well as sensory irritation. Smoking causes the premature death of thousands of non-smokers worldwide. Studies conducted in the 1990s confirmed the ill effects of the passive smoking of environmental tobacco smoke. The Scientific Committee on Tobacco and Health (Report of SCOTH, 1998) commissioned a review of the impact of secondary smoking on lung cancer. This review analysed 37 epidemiological studies of lung cancer in women who were life-long non-smokers living with smokers. The review found that the women had a statistically significant excess risk of lung cancer of 26%. The analysis also showed that there was a dose response relationship between the risk of lung cancer and the number of cigarettes smoked by a person's partner, as well as the duration over which they had been exposed to their smoke. The report also concluded that parental smoking caused acute and chronic middle ear disease in children. Furthermore, it concluded that sudden infant death syndrome, the main cause of post-neonatal death in the first year of life, is associated with exposure to environmental tobacco smoke. The association was judged to be one of cause and effect.

Tobacco Promotion and the Social and Economic Context of Smoking

The tobacco industry spends billions worldwide advertising and promoting tobacco products. Research shows that tobacco advertising encourages children to start smoking and reinforces the social acceptability of the habit among adults. The US Surgeon General (1989) stated that tobacco advertising increases consumption by:

- encouraging children or young adults to experiment with tobacco and thereby slip into regular use;
- encouraging smokers to increase consumption;
- reducing smokers' motivation to quit;
- encouraging former smokers to resume;
- discouraging full and open discussion of the hazards of smoking as a result of media dependence on advertising revenues;
- muting opposition to controls on tobacco as a result of the dependence of organizations receiving sponsorship from tobacco companies;
- creating, through the ubiquity of advertising and sponsorship, an environment in which tobacco use is seen as familiar and acceptable and the warnings about its health are undermined.

Hastings and MacFadyen (2000) analysed internal tobacco company documents and found that the companies worked with advertising agencies to target young people. The companies used advertising to increase overall consumption as well as brand share, in contrast to their public assertions that they only advertise to encourage existing smokers to switch brands.

Most econometric studies have found that increased expenditure on tobacco advertising increases demand for cigarettes, while banning advertising leads to a reduction in tobacco consumption. In 1991, a meta-analysis of 48 econometric studies found that tobacco advertising significantly increased tobacco sales. The UK Department of Health's Chief Economic Adviser found that there was a drop in tobacco consumption of between 4 and 16% in countries that had implemented a tobacco advertising ban (Smee et al., 1992). Details of advertising restrictions in the UK are given in Box 8.1.

BOX 8.1

ADVERTISING BANS GRADUALLY COME INTO FORCE IN THE UK (SOURCE: ASH, 2004)

From September 2001 to August 2002, tobacco advertising expenditure in the UK was £25 million, excluding sponsorship and indirect advertising. Companies traditionally have invested in sports sponsorship to promote their brands, spending an estimated £8 million a year on sponsorship of sport (excluding Formula One) and a further £70 million on Formula One. Additionally promotional offers, shop-front and point of sale advertising, and brand-stretching led to tobacco brand logos on fashion clothing and accessories. During the 1990s, the industry shifted marketing funds from billboard and print advertising to direct mail, sales promotions and other promotional activities.

Following the Tobacco Advertising and Promotion Act in 2003, most forms of tobacco advertising and promotion are now banned in the UK. An EU Directive placing a partial ban on tobacco advertising also exists throughout the European Union. The EU Directive is weaker than the UK Act and applies only to cross-border advertising (e.g. by radio, Internet) and sponsorship. It does not cover Indirect advertising.

Tobacco advertising in print media and on billboards was prohibited from 14 February 2003, and direct mail and other promotions was banned from 14 May 2003. Tobacco sponsorship of sport (other than global events) ended on 31 July 2003 but, owing to a 'special case' and a retracted contribution to Blair's Labour Party funds, sponsorship of Formula One motor racing continued until July 2005. Regulations on brand-sharing (indirect advertising) and point of sale advertising were issued in September 2003 and are likely to come into force towards the end of 2004 or early 2005.

Prior to the Tobacco Advertising and Promotion Act, tobacco advertising on television was banned under the European 'Television without frontiers' directive. Cigarette advertising was banned from UK television in 1965 under powers granted by the Television Act 1964. All other forms of advertising and promotion were controlled by two voluntary agreements that were periodically negotiated between the tobacco industry and the government. One agreement covered advertising and the other governed tobacco sponsorship of sport.

However, the voluntary agreements were ineffective in reducing advertising. Following the ban of cigarette advertising from television in 1965, companies started to sponsor sports such as motor racing, snooker and rugby to advertise their brands on television. Research has shown that children as young as six associate brands such as Marlboro with 'excitement and fast cars'.

Other sponsorship includes the funding of research and research institutions. In 1996, BAT gave £1.5 million to Cambridge University to fund a Chair in international relations. In 2000, Nottingham University accepted a grant of £3.8 million from BAT to set up an International Centre for Corporate Social Responsibility.

Some companies have covert websites to attract young smokers by stealth. These sites typically contain information about nightclubs or other events where cigarettes are heavily promoted.

Given the huge numbers of people who die from smoking related diseases, it seems illogical that tobacco companies are allowed legally to advertise their harmful products. However, many issues are intertwined and the abolition of tobacco advertising has not been as simple and straightforward as it might first appear.

First, there is the argument that there is a lack of evidence to suggest that tobacco advertising significantly influences smoking behaviour. The 'magical potency' of tobacco advertising could be questioned since most advertisements are directed to target audiences who already use the product. Researchers claimed that econometric studies have found either no overall relationship between advertising and sales or a small, statistically significant positive relationship. However, this view can be contested and the results of such studies are equivocal as much depends on who supplies data for the studies: the tobacco industry or the public health authorities.

The issue of banning tobacco advertising is further tangled when politics are included. The epitome of this can be seen within the European Union (EU) that, on the one hand, supports and finances the tobacco industry through the Common Agricultural Policy, and on the other, recognizes the health effects of tobacco in funding its 'Europe Against Cancer' campaign. However, in financial terms, the former greatly exceeds the latter. Despite this, attempts have been made to persuade tobacco growers to change their crops. Yet the fact remains that in 1994 the EU provided € 1,165 million in tobacco subsidies and a mere € 15 million to the 'Europe Against Cancer' campaign.

As we saw in Chapter 2, demographic changes are occurring with decreasing birth rates and increasing life expectancy. Smokers who die before the average life expectancy are helping to reduce expenditure on an already expensive elderly population. Between 4 and 5% of government revenue comes from tobacco sales tax. By killing off smokers early, the tobacco industry is helping the economy. Does this fact help to explain why policies to control tobacco over many years have been so weak and ineffectual?

Theories of Smoking

The resistance shown by smokers to large-scale campaigns to discourage the practice has prompted a massive amount of research to help to explain the continuing popularity of smoking. It is agreed that smoking is an extremely complex practice involving a mixture of biological, psychological and social processes. The biopsychosocial model indicates the three main contributing influences on health that are mirrored in theories of smoking.

Biological theories

Nicotine, the main active ingredient in tobacco smoke, is a substance that if taken in large quantities can be toxic. However, delivered in small amounts via cigarette smoke it has a range of psychophysiological effects including tranquillization, weight loss, decreased irritability, increased alertness and improved cognitive functioning. However, it would seem that tolerance to the effect of nicotine develops such that there is less evidence of performance improvements among regular smokers (Jarvis, 2004).

KT

The apparent conflict between the stimulant physiological effect of nicotine and reports of relaxation has been called the '**nicotine paradox**' (Nesbitt, 1973). One explanation for this paradox is that smoking appears relaxing because the smokers are often in a state of mild nicotine withdrawal that is relieved by the cigarette that returns the nicotine level in the body to 'normal'.

KT

Over time the smoker seems to develop a **physical dependence** on nicotine. In the USA several tobacco companies have publicly admitted that smoking is addictive. In 1997 the smallest of the big five US tobacco companies (the Liggett Group) admitted that it had raised the nicotine content in cigarettes to increase their addictiveness.

Nicotine is a naturally occurring colourless liquid that turns brown when burned and smells of tobacco when exposed to air. It has complex but predictable effects on the brain and body. Most cigarettes contain 10 milligrams (mg) or more of nicotine. The typical smoker takes in 1 to 2 mg nicotine per cigarette. Nicotine is absorbed through the skin and lining of the mouth and nose or by inhalation in the lungs. In cigarettes nicotine reaches peak levels in the bloodstream and brain very rapidly, within 7–10 seconds of inhalation. Cigar and pipe smokers, on the other hand, typically do not inhale the smoke, so nicotine is absorbed more slowly through the mucosal membranes of their mouths. Nicotine from smokeless tobacco also is absorbed through the mucosal membranes.

Nicotine is addictive because it activates brain circuits that regulate feelings of pleasure, the 'reward pathways' of the brain. A key chemical involved is the neurotransmitter *dopamine* that nicotine increases. The acute effects of nicotine disappear in a few minutes, causing the smoker to repeat the dose of nicotine to maintain the drug's pleasurable effects and prevent withdrawal symptoms.

The cigarette is an efficient and highly engineered drug-delivery system. By inhaling, the smoker can get nicotine to the brain very rapidly with each and every puff. A typical smoker will take 10 puffs on a cigarette over a period of 5 minutes that the cigarette is lit. Thus, a person who smokes 30 cigarettes daily gets 300 'hits' of nicotine every day. That is over 100,000 hits a year or one million every ten years! This is why cigarette smoking is so highly addictive. Smoking behaviour is rewarded and reinforced hundreds of thousands or millions of times over the smoker's lifetime.

An enzyme called monoamineoxidase (MAO) shows a marked decrease during smoking. MAO is responsible for breaking down dopamine. The change in MAO is caused by an ingredient other than nicotine, since it is known that nicotine does not dramatically alter MAO levels. The decrease in MAO results in higher dopamine levels, reinforcing smoking by keeping high satisfaction levels through repeated tobacco use.

There is evidence that tobacco is the most addictive drug available. More than 30% of people who try tobacco for the first time develop a dependency on tobacco, while for other drugs, this percentage is generally lower. However, there are variations in the

KT

speed and strength of **addiction** to nicotine among smokers. One obvious way to explain individual differences in smoking is our genetic makeup. Genetic factors could play a role in several aspects of nicotine addiction, from the tendency to begin smoking, to the chances of quitting.

A number of twin studies have produced evidence of a genetic link in the risk of smoking. Heath and Madden (1995) reviewed the evidence from national twin studies in Scandinavia and Australia. In their predictive model genetic factors increased both the likelihood of becoming a regular smoker ('initiation') and of these smokers becoming long-term smokers ('persistence'). In a large follow-up survey of the smoking practices of male twin pairs from the US Vietnam Era Twin Registry, True et al. (1997) found that genetic factors accounted for 50% of the risk of smoking and environmental factors accounted for a further 30%. In addition, genetic factors accounted for 70% of the risk variance of becoming a regular smoker whereas environmental factors were not important. Evidence for a genetic component was stronger among light smokers.

According to evolutionary psychologists, the persistence of behaviour patterns such as smoking must reflect some evolutionary value. With the decline in the overall prevalence of smoking there has emerged what Pomerlau (1979) has described as a group of 'refractory' smokers who are more likely to have a variety of other problematic patterns of behaviour and cognition such as depression, anxiety and bulimia/binging. In ancient times these patterns may have been biologically adaptive or neutral. However, in contemporary society, a more active fight or flight response is inappropriate. Smoking would be valuable to this population because it can produce small but reliable adjustments to levels of arousal. While smoking may be hazardous to health, Pomerlau suggests that the introduction of other forms of nicotine administration raises new questions. In countries where the prevalence of smoking is still high, the smoking population presumably includes many less dependent smokers. These less dependent smokers would have less physiological need for smoking. Evolutionary approaches to addictions tend to ignore the psychological and social influences that create the conditions for tobacco use (Marks, 1998). It is to these influences that we now turn.

Psychological theories

Probably the most frequently used model of smoking is that based on learning theory. Basically, it argues that people become smokers because of the positive reinforcement they obtain from smoking. The mechanisms are similar to those described in Chapter 7 in reference to alcohol drinking. Initially, smoking is physically unpleasant (to a greater extent than is the case for alcohol) but this is overruled because of the social reinforcement from peers. The pleasant associations of smoking then generalize to a range of other settings. In addition, the smoker learns to discriminate between those situations in which smoking is rewarded and those in which it is punished. He or she also develops responses to a number of **conditioned stimuli** (both internal and external) that elicit smoking. Smoking can be conceptualized as an escape/avoidance response to certain aversive states (Pomerlau, 1979). The smoker will light up a cigarette to escape or avoid an uncomfortable situation.

KT

In 1966 Tomkins proposed his 'affect management model' of smoking that was subsequently revised and extended by Ikard et al. (1969) who conducted a survey of a national (US) probability sample. In a factor analysis of the responses they identified six smoking motivation factors: reduction of negative affect, habit, addiction, pleasure, stimulation and sensorimotor manipulation. Subsequent surveys produced similar factors. Women more than men report that they smoked for reduction of negative affect and pleasure.

In their study of smoking among young adults, Murray et al. (1988) added two additional reasons: boredom and nothing to do. In a survey they asked young adults to indicate which of these factors were important reasons for smoking in different situations. In all situations relaxation and control of negative affect were considered the most important reasons. At home boredom was also considered important, perhaps reflecting these young people's frustration with family life. At work addiction was considered important, perhaps reflecting the extent to which it disrupted their work routine, while socially habit was rated important.

KT

According to Zuckerman (1979) individuals engage in **sensation seeking** so as to maintain a certain level of physiological arousal. More specifically, Zuckerman emphasized that sensation seeking was designed to maintain an optimal level of catecholaminergic activity. In a French sample, smokers score higher on a measure of sensation seeking, in particular on disinhibition, experience seeking and boredom susceptibility subscales. From a physiological perspective these sensation seekers have a low level of tonic arousal and seek exciting, novel or intense stimulation to raise the level of cortical arousal. This argument is very similar to that of Eysenck et al. (1960) who found that smokers scored higher on measures of *extraversion*. This personality dimension is also supposed to reflect a lower level of cortical arousal that could be raised by engaging in risky activities such as smoking.

Besides sensation seeking and extraversion, a variety of personality characteristics have been found to be associated with smoking. In a sample of Scottish adults, Whiteman et al. (1997) found that smoking was associated with hostility. However, they accept that 'presence of an association does not help in determining if the relationship is causal'. Indeed, they hypothesize that deprivation of smoking that was required for the study may have increased hostility.

A variety of different types of studies have found that stress is associated with smoking. For example, among smokers, consumption is higher in experimental stressful laboratory situations. In surveys, people with higher self-reports of stress are more likely to be heavy smokers. In a study of nurses' smoking practices, Murray et al. (1983) found that those who reported the most stress were more likely to smoke. This relationship remained after controlling for the effect of family and friends' smoking practices. Finally, in a macro-social study, US states that have the highest levels of stress as measured by a range of social indicators also have the highest levels of smoking and of smoking related diseases.

Other researchers have looked for evidence of personality differences between people who smoke and non-smokers. Sensation seeking, neuroticism and psychoticism are all correlated with smoking (Marks, 1998). However the relationships are fairly weak and it can be concluded that anybody has the potential to become addicted to nicotine.

Social theories of smoking

Smoking is a social activity. Even when the smoker smokes alone he or she still smokes in a society where cigarettes are widely available and promoted. A number of qualitative studies have considered the social meaning of smoking. Murray et al. (1988) conducted detailed interviews with a sample of young adults from the English Midlands. These suggested that smoking had different meanings in different settings. For example, at work going for a cigarette provided an opportunity to escape from the everyday routine. For these workers, to have a cigarette meant to have a break and conversely not to have a cigarette meant not to have a break. The cigarette was a marker, a means to regulating their work routine.

Outside work, smoking was perceived as a means of reaffirming social relationships. For those young people who went to the pub, the sharing of cigarettes was a means of initiating, maintaining and strengthening social bonds. Those who did not share cigarettes were frowned upon.

Graham's (1976) series of qualitative studies has provided a detailed understanding of the meaning of smoking to working-class women. In one of her studies, she asked a group of low-income mothers to complete a 24-hour diary detailing their everyday activities. Like the young workers in the study by Murray et al. (1988), smoking was used as a means of organizing these women's daily routine. Further, for these women smoking was not just a means of resting after completing certain household tasks but also a means of coping when there was a sort of breakdown in normal household routines. This was especially apparent when the demands of childcare became excessive. Graham describes smoking as 'not simply a way of structuring caring: it is also part of the way smokers re-impose structure when it breaks down' (1987: 54).

Graham (1987) argues that for these women smoking is an essential means of coping with everyday difficulties. It is also a link to an adult consumer society. Through smoking the women were reaffirming their adult identity. Similarly, in Bancroft et al.'s (2003) Scottish study, both men and women reported integrating smoking into contrasting periods of their lives. They smoked as a means of coping with stress at work and often because of boredom at home.

Smoking is not only embedded in the immediate material circumstances in which the smoker lives, but also in the wider social and cultural context within which smoking is widely promoted. Admittedly, in most western societies there are considerable restrictions on the sale and promotion of cigarettes. Despite these, tobacco manufacturers continue to find ways to promote their products, e.g. through the sponsorship of sporting and cultural activities. In the USA it is estimated that the tobacco companies spend approximately $6 billion per annum on advertising and promotion. As illustrated above, the tobacco industry is a powerful lobby group having considerable influence on government and policymaking.

Further, it has been suggested that smoking fits with the biocultural demands of late modernity (Nichter, 2003). Cigarettes have been engineered to provide a fast and effective system of nicotine delivery and as such it is particularly suitable for mood-control in our rapidly changing lifestyle. Nichter also suggested that as such the continued popularity of smoking can be considered a symptom of our times as well as a reflection of a form of capitalist ideology based upon the promotion of dependence.

Starting Smoking

Conrad et al. (1992) conducted a review of the findings of 27 longitudinal studies of the onset of smoking that were conducted between 1980 and 1990. They organized several hundred predictors of smoking identified under six domains into a hypothetical model

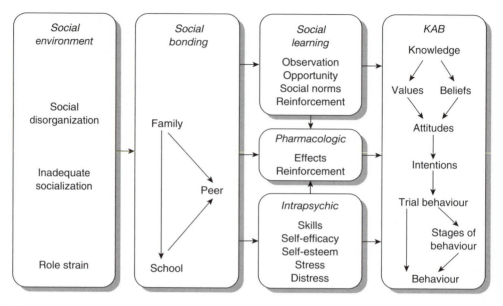

Figure 8.1   Six domains of the determinants of tobacco use (Conrad et al., 1992: 1714; reproduced with permission)

that is illustrated in Figure 8.1. This provides some indication of the many factors involved in the recruitment of teenagers to smoking. The model attempts to integrate the large amount of information.

This model is derived from large-scale survey data. Despite proposing links between domains within this hypothetical model, Conrad et al. concluded: 'Few researchers have tested competing theoretical models ... Most studies have been based on different, unstated, or atheoretical orientations, so it is difficult to see a consistent pattern across studies' (p. 1720). Other researchers have also been critical of the inadequacy of much survey-based research. A major problem with the urge to find a predictor is that the endpoint is not fixed.

As Murray et al. (1988) stated earlier: 'While epidemiological surveys have provided a wealth of detail about the characteristics of young smokers and about the situations in which they smoke their methodology has tended to reify smoking. Smoking has been considered a fixed individual characteristic rather than an ongoing social and psychological process' (1998: 10). Thus, to understand the **acquisition** of smoking requires a more fine-grained analysis. However, attention to these 'determinants' or predictors of smoking during adolescence can inform us as to the character of those who adopt smoking during this period.

Biological factors in recruitment to smoking

Pre-adolescence is the period of preparation. During this period children become increasingly aware of the character of cigarettes and why people smoke. Eiser et al. (1986) conducted interviews with a small sample of 7- to 8- and 10- to 11-year-olds. They found that both groups of children were aware to some extent not only of the health hazards of smoking but also of the social reasons for smoking. Further, more of the older children spoke of the supposed psychological relief provided by smoking.

Although the initial reaction to tobacco smoke is usually negative, teenagers rapidly develop a taste for it. There is also evidence that from an early stage, pharmacologic factors begin to play a role in the establishment of regular smoking. Young smokers report that smoking has a calming effect and that they crave cigarettes if they cannot smoke. Admittedly, while this self-report of craving may be an exaggeration there is supportive evidence in that reports of craving are strongly associated with nicotine intake as measured by saliva analysis. Further, within two or three years of smoking onset teenagers report difficulties in stopping. Indeed, there is evidence that the tobacco industry collected data showing that signs of dependence are apparent among teenagers and they find it difficult to quit. In a study of high school students, 52% of those who smoked feel that they are 'hooked' on cigarettes or that they would become addicted to them. Indeed, six out of ten of these young smokers feel that even giving up for three days would be difficult. Further, teenagers who are dependent on smoking report the same symptoms as dependent adult smokers including craving, withdrawal, tolerance, and a desire to cut down on smoking (Colby et al., 2000).

Psychological factors in recruitment to smoking

This domain includes a range of more psychological, interpersonal and behavioural factors. Although Conrad et al. (1992) identify an association between these factors and smoking among adolescents, other reviewers suggest caution. For example, it has been argued that despite the large number of studies on the role of attitudes the evidence remains insufficient. Stacy et al. (1994) found that while attitudes were associated with smoking they did not predict smoking as measured 12 months later. They concluded that 'it is possible that attitude toward health behavior is useful empirically, theoretically, and practically only in the context of a more general theory' (1994: 82).

Research based on the **theory of reasoned action** (TRA, Ajzen, 1985) and the **theory of planned behaviour** (TPB, Ajzen, 1991) argues that smoking behaviour is predicted by behavioural intention that in turn is predicted by attitudes, social norms and perceived self-efficacy. Several studies have considered the value of all or parts of these models for predicting the uptake of smoking. In a longitudinal study of teenage smoking behaviour Flay et al. (1994) found that smoking initiation was predicted by intentions that were in turn predicted by negative outcomes expectation regarding smoking and ill-health (a measure of attitudes), parents' and friends' social behaviour (an indirect measure of social norm) and refusal self-efficacy.

KT

Several studies have found that perceptions of smoking norm predicted smoking. For example, teenagers who had an overestimate of the prevalence of smoking are more likely to adopt smoking. A related factor is the availability of cigarettes. Teenagers who had ready access to cigarettes are at greater risk of becoming smokers. Pierce et al. (1996) examined in some detail the role that perceived susceptibility plays in the transition from pre-experimentation to actual experimentation. They argued that adolescents who adopt smoking would be 'cognitively predisposed to smoking' (1996: 358). By this they meant that they would both intend to and expect to adopt smoking. They found that those adolescents who were classified as susceptible in terms of their smoking expectations were more likely to be smoking four years later.

A number of studies have asked children and teenagers why they smoke. One study found curiosity as the most common reason. Another found that pleasure, improvement in emotion and habit are common reasons. In a large survey of tenth grade students, curiosity, social norms and social pressure are most frequently given for initiation while pleasure and addiction are mentioned by current smokers. More girls than boys mentioned social norms and pressure to adopt smoking.

Researchers have also considered the teenagers' awareness of health hazards of smoking. They have found that not only do teenage smokers underestimate the health risk of smoking, especially in the first few years (Slovic, 2000), but they also believe that they will stop before serious damage is done to their health (Arnett, 2000). It would seem that teenagers smoke in spite of the perceived health hazards. In addition, teenagers tend to define health more in terms of fitness and beauty (Murray and Jarrett, 1985). In the early stages, smoking is not often seen as harming these features.

A variety of other intrapsychic variables have been found to predict smoking onset. In particular, indicators of rebelliousness and risk taking have frequently been found to predict smoking. Research show that people who subsequently began smoking score higher on measures of rebelliousness, impulsivity, sensation seeking and hostility. A related factor is pubertal timing. Early maturers and those adolescents who report emotional distress are more likely to be smokers.

Since adolescence has frequently been characterized as a period of stress it is not surprising that several researchers have considered the role of smoking as a means of coping with stress during adolescence. It has been suggested that people low in personal resources such as self-esteem, feelings of mastery and social support turn to smoking or other substance use because it is the only available means of coping with stress.

Social factors in recruitment to smoking

These factors are relevant to the *social learning*, *social bonding* and *social environment* domains. Having parents, siblings and peers who smoke strongly increases the risk of smoking among adolescents. There is a certain difference between studies in the reported relative effect of family members versus peers but all agree on the overall effect. It has been suggested that parents are more important at the preparation stage while peers become more important as the adolescents begin to experiment with cigarettes. Chassin et al. (2000) found that parental smoking was associated with early onset among teenagers, escalation to heavy smoking, and persistence over time. Murray et al. (1985) found some evidence of sex linking in this relationship, indicating that an important process of adopting smoking was modelling the behaviour of the same sex parent. Further, this and other studies have found a relationship between smoking and family structure with children from single parent families being more at risk. Conrad et al. also suggest that there may be a secular effect with parents having a lesser influence today than they did in previous years. These associations between adolescent smoking and smoking by their parents and peers has been explained as due to such processes as modelling, accessibility, peer pressure and perceived social norm.

Various indicators of poor social attachment with parents have been found to be associated with increased risk of smoking. Strong attachment with parents is associated with a better sense of well-being and a greater capacity to handle stressful events. It has been suggested that teenagers with poor social attachment have a weaker self-image and a greater need to portray themselves to their peers as 'tough' or 'cool' through, for example, smoking (Leventhal and Cleary, 1980). In a longitudinal study of Scottish adolescents Glendinning et al. (1997) found that perceptions of family support were inversely related to smoking. This effect was raised when there was evidence of fewer parental controls.

The social environment includes a group of distal variables described as social disorganization and role strain which are more common in families from low SES. This broad social category is sometimes expanded to include the public marketing of cigarettes. There is evidence linking adolescence cigarette consumption to advertising of particular brands. For example, a study of cigarette brand preferences among teenagers in the USA in the period 1989–93 found that the most significant change was an increase in the proportion of youth purchasing the three most heavily advertised brands. Several other historical analyses have identified a clear association between increases in adolescent smoking and cigarette advertising campaigns. In a three-year follow-up study, it was found that those who are aware of cigarette advertisements at baseline are more likely to experiment with cigarettes in the follow-up period.

Smoking Cessation

It was estimated that the proportion of ever-smokers who quit smoking increased from 30% in 1965 to 45% in 1987 (US Public Health Service, 1990). However, the speed of the decline seemed to have slowed in the 1990s, suggesting that smoking rates will finally asymptote at about 15–20%. The evidence from both clinical and community smoking cessation programmes has been disappointing. This has led to attempts to develop a more sophisticated understanding of the process of giving up smoking.

Biological aspects of cessation

It is well established that **cessation** of smoking by regular smokers leads to a variety of symptoms such as irritability, difficulty concentrating, anxiety, restlessness, increased hunger, depressed mood and a craving for tobacco. Important evidence that these withdrawal symptoms are due to the loss of nicotine is the finding that it is relieved by administration of nicotine but not of a placebo.

This evidence has led to the development of a variety of pharmacologic products aimed at aiding smoking cessation. These are designed to deliver nicotine directly rather than through cigarette smoke. The techniques developed include nicotine chewing gum, nicotine transdermal patch and a nasal spray or inhaler. Evidence from clinical trials has demonstrated that these techniques are effective (Stolerman and Jarvis, 1995). However, the individual smoker must still have the psychological motivation to use them.

Psychological aspects of cessation

Possibly the most influential psychological model that has been used in the design of health behaviour change programmes over the past decade has been the **transtheoretical model of change** (TTM). Historically, this model evolved from a review of over 300 theories of psychotherapy that led to the identification of 10 distinct 'processes of change' underlying these theories. In a subsequent empirical study with a sample of smokers the participants reported that they used different change processes at different times. From this work DiClemente and Prochaska (1982) developed a series of **stages of change**. Subsequent research has provided more detail on the character of the different stages and the processes that connect them. The following are the most important components of the model:

1   Processes of change: the character of the ten change processes and possible intervention strategies derived from them are summarized in Table 8.1. These processes have been grouped into two broad blocks: experiential (consciousness raising, self-re-evaluation, emotional arousal, environmental re-evaluation and social liberation) and behavioural (counter-conditioning, stimulus control, reinforcement management, self-liberation and helping relationships).

2   Stages of change: the TTM argues that change proceeds through six stages that are summarized in Table 8.2. DiClemente and Velicer (1997) note that initially they

Table 8.1   *Processes of change: definitions and representative interventions identified in the transtheoretical model (DiClemente, 1993: 102; reproduced with permission)*

Process	Definition	Interventions
Consciousness raising	Increasing information about self and the problem.	Observations, confrontations, interpretations, bibliography.
Self-re-evaluation	Assessing how one feels and thinks about oneself with respect to the problem behaviours.	Value clarification, imagery, corrective emotional experience, challenging beliefs.
Self-liberation	Choosing and committing to act or believing in ability to change.	Decision-making therapy, New Year's resolutions, logotherapy techniques, commitment enhancement techniques.
Counter-conditioning	Substituting alternatives for anxiety related to addictive behaviours.	Relaxation, desensitization, assertion, positive self-statements.
Stimulus control	Avoiding or counter stimuli that elicit problem behaviours.	Restructuring one's environment (e.g. removing alcohol or fattening foods), avoiding high-risk cues, fading techniques.
Reinforcement management	Rewarding oneself or being rewarded by others for making changes.	Contingency contracts, overt and covert reinforcement, self-reward.
Helping relationships	Being open and trusting about problems with people who care.	Therapeutic alliance, social support, self-help groups.
Emotional arousal	Experiencing and expressing feelings about one's problems and solutions.	Psychodrama, grieving losses, role playing.
Environmental re-evaluation	Assessing how one's problems affect the personal and physical environment.	Empathy training, documentaries.
Social liberation	Increasing alternatives for non-problem behaviours available in society.	Advocating for rights of the repressed, empowering, policy interventions.

Table 8.2   *Stages of behaviour change (DiClemente and Velicer, 1997a: 39)*

Stage	Definition
Precontemplation	Not intending to take action in the foreseeable future.
Contemplation	Intending to change.
Preparation	Intending to take action in the immediate future and have developed a plan of action.
Action	Have made specific overt modifications.
Maintenance	Working to prevent relapse but do not apply change processes as frequently as in the Action stage.
Termination	Behaviour change successful and individuals have zero temptation and 100% self-efficacy.

viewed **relapse** as a separate stage but now they accept that relapse is a process of reversal that can occur between any two stages. The experiential processes are more active in the early stages and the behavioural processes in the later stages. Of particular importance to interventions is the recruitment of smokers who are at the **action stage** and the ability to support recent ex-smokers during the **maintenance stage**.

3   Decisional balance: this reflects the relative weighting of the pros and cons of changing the behaviour. As the individual moves from the precontemplation stage to the preparation stage the pros of smoking decrease and the cons of smoking increase.

4   Self-efficacy: this concept, derived from Bandura (1977), is the situation-specific confidence that individuals have that they can maintain behaviour change. Individuals at the preparation stage have a higher sense of situational self-efficacy than those at the precontemplation stage.

5   Temptation: this is a measure of the intensity of urges in a particular situation to engage in a particular behaviour. The most common types of tempting situations are negative affect, positive social situations and craving. It is posited that situational temptation to smoke is higher among those at the precontemplation stage compared with those at the preparation stage.

Recently, the transtheoretical model has been extended into four stages: immotives, precontemplators, contemplators and preparers. As their name implies, immotives are stuck in the sense that they are planning never to quit, at least in the short term. They also differed from precontemplators in the sense that they anticipated fewer long-term health consequences of smoking and had lower levels of self-evaluation. 'Precontemplators' do have some desire to quit but not within the next six months.

In a large follow-up study of a large sample of smokers Dijkstra et al. (1998) found further evidence of these four stages. In a factor analysis they identified four pros of quitting: long-term health consequences; short-term health consequences; social consequences; self-evaluative consequences. They identified one con of quitting factor that emphasized various perceived negative consequences; and two quitting self-efficacy factors – one with regard to social situations and one regarding emotional situations. The precontemplators scored higher on all the pros of smoking and on the measures of self-efficacy. When these smokers were followed up three and 14 months later their initial stage of readiness was found to predict their subsequent smoking behaviour.

The TTM has attracted considerable debate. For example, it has been argued that the stages are artificial and do not reflect the constant process of change. Nevertheless, the stages are not a substitute for processes but rather an attempt to specify when and where such processes operate. In a prospective study, it has been found that a measure of addiction is a better predictor of subsequent smoking status than the initial stage of change. Most researchers feel that despite various criticisms the model is still a useful and robust approach to understanding smoking cessation. There have been various attempts to deepen the theoretical base of the model. However, there still remains the concern that this model does not sufficiently consider the social aspects and meaning of smoking.

Social Aspects of Cessation

Smoking activities are deeply embedded in everyday social activities and a society where cigarettes are widely promoted. Cessation attempts must take these aspects into consideration, including the increasing social gradient in smoking prevalence. Smoking is becoming confined to people who live in poor circumstances. As Graham has demonstrated, for many of these people smoking serves an immediate positive social function such that attempts to discourage smoking among them will be resisted.

Stewart et al. (1996) conducted a qualitative study of the role of smoking in the lives of such women and their perception of smoking cessation efforts. In reading the interviews with these women Stewart et al. felt that 'due to the pressing nature of the participants' life circumstances, many were caught in a daily struggle for survival. Consequently, the long-term benefits of quitting had little relevance for them' (p. 45). Smoking was a means of coping with the 'stress, chaos and crises in their lives'. In addition, the women felt that they did not have the self-esteem and confidence to quit smoking.

As regards attempts to quit, the women mentioned lack of social support from their partners, immediate family and friends. They felt that if there were peer support groups it would be easier to quit. In concluding, Stewart et al. emphasized the disempowering character of the immediate social circumstances of these women's lives. Smoking cessation efforts need to provide not only social support but also attempt to enhance the women's sense of control and mastery through changing their social conditions.

Finally, social attempts at smoking cessation need also to address the widespread promotion and availability of cigarettes. Reviews of the impact of national bans on cigarette advertising in countries like Norway and Finland found they were followed by a decline in tobacco consumption (Laugesen, 1992). As regards availability, there is a clear association between the price of cigarettes and consumption. Further, it was smokers from lower incomes who were most affected by increase in the price of cigarettes. They suggest that social policy should take into consideration the effect on their living conditions of increased price.

Psychological Therapy for Smokers

Quitting smoking or, if that is impossible, reducing cigarette consumption, adds years to the lives of young or middle-aged smokers. There are also substantial social and socio-economic benefits when measured across the entire population. Thus, quitting smoking or, if that fails, reducing smoking, are both viable targets for a smoking cessation programme. In order to achieve these aims, it is necessary for an intervention to help smokers to control both their physical and **psychological dependency** on smoking.

| KT |

Research in the UK has shown that smoking cessation interventions are very cost effective, both absolutely and relative to other kinds of health promoting activities. The cost per life year gained ranges from £94 to £711 depending upon the method used.

There has been increasing interest in the development of cognitive behavioural therapy (CBT) for the control of smoking and other health-related behaviours. These therapies can be delivered as a brief intervention of one or more sessions to groups of smokers who are at the action stage. An example of a brief intervention using CBT is the **QUIT FOR LIFE (QFL) Programme** (Marks, 2005). QFL encourages a steady reduc-

| KT |

tion of cigarette consumption over seven to 10 days followed by complete abstinence. The QFL programme is delivered in several alternative ways: as a group therapy of 10 sessions, as a self-help programme following a single, one-hour group therapy session, or on the Internet.

A preliminary observational study suggested that the therapy could be particularly effective when delivered to groups of self-referring smokers (Marks, 1992). Randomized controlled trials carried out in the 1990s showed that the QFL programme is capable of delivering relatively high quit rates. These results suggest that this CBT intervention has the potential to reduce the prevalence of smoking among lower SES smokers at relatively low cost.

Future Research

1   There is still limited understanding of the social basis of cigarette smoking among young people. In particular, there is a need for increased understanding of the social, ethnic and gender variations in the dynamics of smoking among young people.
2   Although there have been a plethora of prevention programmes there is still a need for greater understanding of the variations in their effectiveness.
3   More research on the influence of tobacco advertising on the uptake of smoking in young people is necessary in those countries where advertising is still permitted. The evidence is likely to be significant in eventually gaining a worldwide advertising ban.
4   Randomized controlled trials of psychological therapy in comparison to nicotine replacement therapy are necessary to determine their relative efficacy and cost effectiveness.

Summary

1   About 25% of adults in most western societies smoke, while prevalence rates in the developing world are higher than this and are increasing. The prevalence of smoking varies according to sex, social class and ethnicity.
2   Biological, psychological and social factors contribute to the continued popularity of smoking.

3   The uptake of smoking occurs largely in adolescence and appears to be associated with parental and peer smoking. Various social and psychological factors are of prime importance in understanding the recruitment of teenagers to smoking.
4   Most smokers report difficulty in quitting the habit. The transtheoretical model describes the process of quitting as progressing through several stages.
5   Social, biological and psychological factors are involved in the process of smoking cessation. Brief psychological therapies for smoking cessation based on cognitive behavioural therapy are showing considerable promise.
6   The final solution to tobacco control will require a multi-level approach consisting of economic, political, social and psychological interventions.

KT Key Terms

acquisition

action stage

addiction

cessation

conditioned stimulus (CS)

maintenance stage

nicotine paradox

psychological dependency

QUIT FOR LIFE (QFL) programme

relapse

sensation seeking

stages of change

theory of planned behaviour (TPB)

theory of reasoned action (TRA)

transtheoretical model of change (TTM)

9

Sexual Behaviour and Experience

Discourses of sexuality … are often inadequate, contradictory and fragmented, leading to unexpected and often undesirable (and undesired) material outcomes whether they meet in Parliament, the classroom, the parking lot or in bed. (Ingham and Kirkland, 1997: 173)

Outline

This chapter provides a brief overview of the study of sexual behaviour in its historical context. This is followed by a discussion of five contemporary approaches to the study of sexual behaviour. These revolve around a behavioural, physiological, cognitive, relationship and meaning-centred focus. These approaches are illustrated and critically evaluated.

Sexuality and Health

Sexual behaviour is of relevance to health psychologists for a number of reasons. First, sexual behaviour constitutes an excellent example of the mind–body interdependence which interests health psychologists. Second, sexual behaviour can have very serious physical and emotional consequences such as pregnancy or sexually transmitted disease. These consequences have major implications for the individual's psychological well-being. Third, sex is very much a social activity during which two (or more) individuals' minds and bodies meet. Since much of health psychology's theorizing is derived from social psychology, health psychologists can be expected to have something to say about sexual interaction. However, the study of sexual behaviour (or **sexology**) has historically been a truly interdisciplinary field in which epidemiologists, medics, sociologists, psychologists and other social scientists work together.

KT

Sexology in Historical Context

Preceding the nineteenth century a purely moral approach to sex prevailed. A fundamental divide between reproductive and non-reproductive sexuality meant that reproduction was the only moral justification for sexual indulgence. Any non-reproductive sexual act was referred to and condemned as 'sodomy'. (The meaning of this term has changed since then and it is now taken to refer to anal sex.) However, it was acknowledged that sodomy could potentially be practised by anyone. Thus, it was perceived as a temporary aberration rather than a stable preference or even identity.

A more medico-scientific approach to sex emerged in the nineteenth century. This involved classification of sexual practices into 'normal/healthy' and 'abnormal/unhealthy'. It also meant that sexual practices were seen as an expression of an inherent trait rather than as aberrant behaviours. As a result, sexual types were constructed: the 'homosexual', the 'sadist', the 'masochist', the 'transvestite', and so forth. Krafft-Ebbing's *Psychopathia Sexualis* (1887) presents an inclusive catalogue of sexual perversions.

Weeks (1985) shows how the emergence of sexology in the nineteenth century served to replace religious authority (and its concern with morality) with scientific authority (and its concern with disorder and abnormality). However, the new focus upon sexual pathology and perversion was based upon widespread assumptions of what constituted 'normal sexuality'. Sexologists studied those individuals who did not conform to sexual norms and expectations. They did not explore what 'ordinary people' actually did sexually, that is, to what extent norms and expectations actually reflected the lived reality of people's sexual lives.

KT

It was only in the middle of the twentieth century that researchers began to describe, rather than judge or pathologize, human sexual behaviour. Scientists became aware that there was a profound lack of knowledge about normal **sexuality**. On the basis of their literature review preceding their large-scale survey of Americans' sexual behaviours, Kinsey and his colleagues noted that 'the scientific understanding of human sexual behaviour was more poorly established than the understanding of almost any other function of the human body' (Kinsey et al., 1953: 5). Even today, the study of sexual behaviour remains one of the most under-developed fields in the human sciences (Johnson and Wellings, 1994).

Researchers have used a range of different methods in order to find out about people's sexual experience. The following five approaches have informed contemporary psychosexual research:

1　Sex surveys.
2　Laboratory studies of sexual activity.
3　Study of social cognitions about sex.
4　Study of sexual experience within close relationships.
5　Study of sexual meanings.

Sex Surveys

KT

Sex surveys adopt a behavioural focus. They employ large-scale survey methods in order to provide descriptive data about a population's sexual habits. Sex surveys usually involve the collaboration of researchers from a variety of disciplines, including epidemiologists, sociologists and psychologists. Sex surveys are designed to obtain descriptive information about a particular population's sexual behaviour patterns.

Such surveys typically include questions about age at first sexual intercourse, frequency of intercourse, sexual orientation, use of contraception and number of sexual partners. Many surveys also include questions about sexual knowledge (e.g. about reproductive processes and sexually transmitted diseases) and attitudes (e.g. towards pre-marital sex, homosexuality and monogamy).

Sex surveys tend to be carried out in response to particular social and/or medical concerns of the day such as teenage pregnancies in the 1970s or the spread of the human immunodeficiency virus (HIV) in the 1980s. The choice of questions included in any one survey tends to reflect such concerns. For example, earlier studies (e.g. Kinsey et al., 1948) are characterized by a focus upon the experience of orgasm, whereas later studies (e.g. Johnson et al., 1994) are more interested in the use of sexual risk reduction strategies (i.e. contraception and **safer sex practices**).

KT

Sex surveys are a relatively recent development. The short history of sex surveys is characterized by two attributes. First, researchers have encountered strong resistance from powerful individuals and institutions who argued that sexual surveys were socially and/or morally inappropriate. For example, Kinsey et al. (1948, 1953) encountered public and official opposition to their study of sexual behaviour of American males and females, including the threat of lawsuits by a medical association. Forty years later, in Britain, Johnson et al. (1994) were refused government funding of a large-scale study into sexual attitudes and lifestyles on the grounds that it was intrusive and unacceptable to the British people. Similarly, in the USA, funding for a national survey of sexual behaviour was withdrawn in response to government opposition to the nature of the survey (Aldhous, 1992).

The second characteristic of sex surveys is that they tend to reveal much greater diversity of sexual practices than is publicly acknowledged within the culture. It appears that human sexual behaviour is extremely flexible and that people have a wide range of sexual preferences, both with regard to the types of activities as well as the frequencies with which these are engaged in.

The Kinsey reports (Kinsey et al., 1948, 1953)

Alfred Kinsey, an American biologist, instigated the first mass sex survey. He and his colleagues analysed data obtained from interviews with 5,300 males and 5,940 females. These interviews covered between 300 and 500 questions about a wide range of aspects of sexual experience, lasting an average of two hours each. The interview agenda covered social and economic data, marital histories, sex education, physiological data, masturbation, nocturnal dreams, heterosexual and homosexual histories, as well as animal contacts. The researchers also examined materials such as sexual diaries, calendars, personal correspondence, scrapbooks and photographic collections, paintings and drawings as well as toilet wall inscriptions and graffiti.

Kinsey and his colleagues were keenly aware of the lack of scientific studies of human sexuality. The reason for this absence was, they felt, the 'almost universal acceptance, even among scientists, of certain aspects of [sexual] behaviour as normal, and of other aspects of that behaviour as abnormal' (1948: 7). By contrast, Kinsey et al. set out to chart sexual practices without preconceptions as to what was rare or common, normal or abnormal, or socially or morally desirable or significant.

Findings   The findings vindicated their non-judgemental approach. They found high incidences and considerable frequencies of sexual behaviours which had been publicly regarded as both rare and abnormal. For example, they found that more than a quarter of teenage males had experienced homosexual activity to the point of orgasm. Of male teenagers and men in their early twenties 10% had had extramarital homosexual contacts. By the age of 45, 37% of men and 13% of women had experienced homosexual activities to orgasm. Again, challenging socio-moral assumptions, Kinsey et al. found that by the age of 40, 50% of males and 26% of females had experienced extramarital coitus.

Overall, the authors stressed the similarity of the sexual response in men and women, particularly with regard to the physiological nature of orgasm. The major difference between males and females was that women's sexual activities were more discontinuous, that is they were found to occur more sporadically. In addition, there was more variability of sexual behaviour within the female sample, that is women were found to differ more among themselves than did men.

Evaluation of the Kinsey survey

Representativeness   Even though the Kinsey sample included a wide range of participants varying in age, education levels, religious affiliation, occupation and geographical location, there was a bias towards better educated, professional, urban Protestants living in the northeastern quarter of the USA. In addition, the authors excluded data obtained from black respondents on the grounds that this sample ($n = 934$) was too small to allow for comparative analysis of sub-groups within the sample, as well as from white women who had served prison sentences ($n = 915$) on the grounds that this sample's responses were so different from the rest that its inclusion would have distorted the data.

Participants were selected on the basis of their membership of social groups such as religious, community, professional or trade union groups or educational or penal institutions. Although this method of sampling avoided problems associated with the low response rates in probability sampling as well as self-selection biases associated with recruiting volunteers, it excluded individuals who were not members of social groups. This is a major problem in a sex survey since social group membership may well be a relevant variable in the determination of sexual practices. In addition, many respondents came from single-sex institutions such as colleges, prisons and the armed forces which may have inflated the reporting of homosexual encounters (Tatchell, 1996).

Reliability and Validity   Reliability and validity checks were carried out on the data by way of internal consistency assessments and re-takes of histories (reliability), as well as comparisons of spouses' and male–female data (validity). Both reliability and validity were found to be good, with the exception of a large discrepancy found between males' and females' reportings of pre-marital coitus.

The interviews were conducted by the four researchers themselves. Kinsey alone carried out 57.6% of the interviews, taking 7,036 sexual histories. This ensured that interviewers were well trained as well as experienced. However, the four researchers were all male which almost certainly influenced the responses obtained from the female respondents. Recent researchers noted that both male and female respondents prefer to be interviewed about sexual matters by a female interviewer (e.g. Johnson et al., 1994).

National survey of sexual attitudes and lifestyles (Johnson et al., 1994)

The emergence of the sexually acquired infection with the human immunodeficiency virus (HIV) and its continuing spread throughout the 1980s and 1990s highlighted the importance of scientific studies of sexual lifestyles and attitudes. Johnson et al. (1994) carried out the largest representative sample survey of sexual lifestyles ever undertaken in the British population. A total of 18,876 women and men aged between 16 and 59 took part in the survey. Its objectives were twofold:

- to provide data which would increase understanding of transmission patterns of HIV and other sexually transmitted diseases (epidemiological focus);
- to obtain information which would be helpful in designing effective HIV/AIDS education interventions (psychosocial focus).

In order to obtain relevant data, a team of trained interviewers administered the questionnaire within the context of a personal interview. Core questions about sexual lifestyle covered age at first intercourse, numbers of heterosexual and homosexual partners, frequency of sex, experience of different practices and so on. Attitudinal questions, administered to a subsection of the sample (*n* = 5,000), assessed attitudes towards pre-marital, extramarital as well as homosexual sex. Particularly sensitive questions were administered by way of self-completion booklets.

Findings   Pre-marital sex was found to be near universal. Median age of first intercourse decreased from 21 for the oldest female cohort to 17 for the youngest. The ages were 20 and 17 for male cohorts respectively. Non-use of contraception at first intercourse has declined steadily over recent decades, and was reported by fewer than a quarter of women and a third of men aged 16 to 24. However, when intercourse occurs before age 16, contraception is much less likely to be used.

Condoms are the most popular form of contraceptive at first intercourse. There was marked variability between individuals in the number of sexual partners they reported. Over the last five years, 65.2% of men and 76.5% of women reported no or only one sexual partner, whereas 1% of men reported more than 22 partners and 1% of women more than 8. The range of the number of sexual partners over a lifetime was zero to over 4,500 for men and zero to 1,000 for women. Men and women in the 16 to 24 age group reported the greatest number of sexual partners, with 11.2% of men and 2.5% of women of this age group reporting over 10 partners in the last five years. The authors argue that the large difference between numbers of heterosexual partners reported by males and females suggests that there must be some over-reporting by men and/or under-reporting by women.

Extramarital sex: 4.5% of married men and 1.9% of married women reported more than one sexual partner in the last year. Among single people the figures were 28.1% of men and 17.5% of women. Among cohabiting couples, 15.3% of men and 8.2% of women

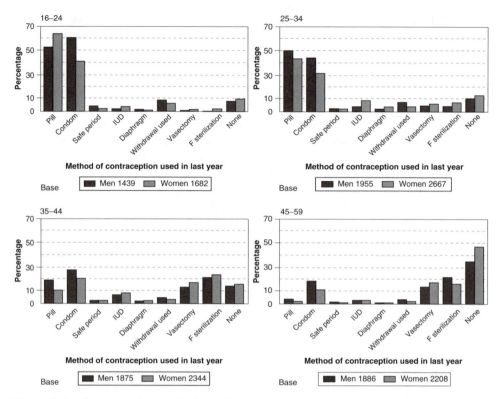

Figure 9.1   Contraceptive method used in the last year by age group (Johnson et al., 1994: 300; reproduced with permission)

reported more than one sexual partner in the last year. Among separated, widowed or divorced respondents aged 25 to 44, the figures were 40% of men and 16% of women.

Homosexual behaviour: 92.3% of men and 95.1% of women reported exclusively heterosexual experiences. Some kind of homosexual experience was reported by 6.1% of men and 3.4% of women, with 3.6% of men and 1.7% of women reporting genital contact. Within the last two years 1.4% of men and 0.6% of women had had a same-sex partner. Men aged 35 to 44 were most likely to have had homosexual experience at some time in their lives (over 7%). Exclusively homosexual behaviour appears to be rare. Over 90% of both men and women who reported same-sex partners also had experience of heterosexual sex.

Contraception (see Figures 9.1 and 9.2): 17.6% of sexually active men and 21.1% of sexually active women reported no use of contraception in the past year. Contraceptive use decreases with age. The three contraceptive methods most commonly relied on are the pill (28.8% of women and 30.4% of men); the condom (25.9% of women and 36.9% of men); and male or female sterilization (23.3% of women and 21.4% of men). Even though contraceptive use increases with numbers of partners, a substantial minority of those with five or more partners in the past year do not report condom use (39.6% of women and 28.4% of men). This gives cause for concern within the context of HIV transmission.

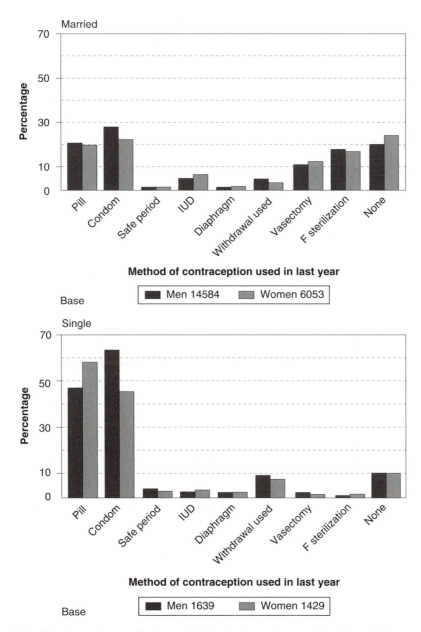

Figure 9.2 Contraceptive method used in the last year by marital status (Johnson et al., 1994: 301; reproduced with permission)

Sexual attitudes (see Table 9.1): pre-marital sex is fully accepted by three-quarters of respondents, whereas extramarital sex was considered to be always or mostly wrong by nearly 80% of the sample. Monogamy was seen to be the appropriate form of sexual expression within a regular relationship for all age groups. The views of men and women were most divided on the question of casual sex: 35.8% of men regarded one-night stands as always wrong, whereas 62.45% of women were of this view.

Table 9.1   *Views on selected sexual relationships and encounters (Johnson et al., 1994: 237; reproduced with permission)*

	Always wrong (%)	Mostly wrong (%)	Sometimes wrong (%)	Rarely wrong (%)	Not wrong at all (%)	Base
Sex before marriage						
Men	4.7	3.5	10.7	7.6	73.5	8,242
Women	5.8	5.0	15.0	8.1	66.1	10,191
Sex outside marriage						
Men	47.0	31.8	17.4	1.1	2.7	8,155
Women	55.6	28.6	13.7	0.9	1.2	10,258
Sex outside live-in relationship						
Men	35.8	32.7	19.6	2.9	9.0	8,083
Women	46.9	32.7	14.3	1.6	4.5	10,210
Sex outside regular relationship						
Men	28.9	30.6	22.5	5.5	12.6	8,082
Women	37.6	32.4	18.2	3.9	8.1	10,178
One-night stand						
Men	35.8	21.7	17.8	6.5	18.2	8,067
Women	62.4	20.3	10.6	2.3	4.4	10,251
Sex between two men						
Men	60.8	9.4	6.4	3.9	19.6	8,022
Women	46.2	11.7	10.7	6.1	25.3	9,629
Sex between two women						
Men	51.2	13.3	9.2	4.7	21.7	7,951
Women	46.6	12.2	10.2	5.9	25.0	9,667
Abortion						
Men	16.8	16.3	41.2	8.0	17.7	7,642
Women	17.7	19.9	42.1	7.5	12.8	9,458

Views on homosexuality were the most polarized within the sample: 70.2% of men and 57% of women regarded sex between two men to be always or mostly wrong (64.5% and 58.8% for sex between two women). One in five respondents believed homosexual sex to be not wrong at all. Abortion is seen as always or mostly wrong by 37.7% of women and 33.1% of men.

Overall, those without experience of a particular behaviour are more likely to perceive it as being wrong.

Evaluation of the survey

Representativeness   The survey obtained a systematic probability sample of around 20,000 people using the postcode address file as the sampling frame, with an acceptance rate of 71.5% (among households where an eligible respondent could be identified and interviewed). The postcode address file is the file of current postal addresses kept by the Royal Mail and is likely to have generated a reasonable level of representativeness of the general population. However, this method of sampling excludes the homeless and its use of self-completion booklets required literacy among participants (Stanley, 1995).

Reliability and Validity   Administration of the survey was preceded by a two-year development period during which qualitative work, piloting as well as a feasibility study were carried out. This ensured that terminology, question formulation and ordering, accuracy of memory and willingness to disclose intimate information using different formats (e.g. face to face, self-completion booklet, showcards) had been thoroughly explored before the questionnaire was designed. However, the choice of formal as opposed to vernacular terms to refer to sexual organs and practices, together with precise, technical definitions, though preferred by both interviewers and respondents, may have inhibited (some) respondents in their talk. The use of formal terminology tends to locate the interview within a clinical context, with its connotations of health and illness. This may have led respondents to simplify and homogenize their answers.

In addition, some of the questions included in the survey need to be placed within their social contexts. For example, the widespread condemnation of homosexual sex identified by the survey highlights the hostile social environment within which reporting of such activities is still taking place. This may have resulted in under-reporting of experiences of same-sex contacts.

NATSAL 2: an update of sexual behaviour in Britain

Ten years after the first national survey, a second, smaller survey was carried out in order to trace changes in sexual behaviours and attitudes over time (Johnson et al., 2001). For this survey, 11,161 respondents (4,762 men and 6,399 women) answered similar questions; however, in the second survey, computer-assisted self-interview was substituted for the pen-and-paper self-completion booklets.

The researchers observed significant increases in reporting a range of behaviours including numbers of heterosexual partners, homosexual partnerships and concurrent partnerships. The increase in reporting these behaviours was significantly greater among women than among men. There was also an increase in reported condom use among both men and, to a lesser extent, women. In line with the reported changes in behaviour, respondents reported greater tolerance in relation to both male and female homosexuality and to casual partnerships.

The researchers attribute the observed changes over time to a combination of true behavioural change and a greater willingness to report sensitive behaviours due to improved survey methodology and more tolerant social attitudes.

General problems with sex surveys

There are a number of methodological problems shared by all sex surveys. First, people who agree to answer questions about their sexual habits, whether verbally or in writing, may well differ systematically from those who refuse. As a result, sex surveys do not access the full range of sexual information potentially available and are therefore limited in their representativeness.

Second, strong socio-cultural norms and expectations with regard to sexuality may lead respondents to misrepresent their sexual habits and experiences. It has been suggested that women downplay the nature and extent of their sexual activities, whereas men exaggerate theirs (e.g. Kinsey et al., 1948, 1953; Johnson et al., 1994).

Third, the identity of the interviewer may influence the validity of the responses obtained. For example, Davis (1992) suggests that around one-third of gay men would not disclose their sexual identity within the context of a large-scale sex survey. Thus, social desirability biases may limit the validity of a sex survey's findings.

Fourth, another concern with validity arises from the formulation of the questions included in a sex survey. There appears to be a great deal of ambiguity surrounding sexual terminology. For example, Hunt and Davis (1991) found that the term 'sexual partner' was interpreted in many different ways by their gay male respondents, ranging from describing someone with whom genital contact had occurred (48.2%) through someone orgasm had been experienced with (25.9%), to someone with whom a bed has been shared, naked (22.3%). Furthermore, the range of response options including presuppositions implied by question formulations (e.g. 'Have you ever' as opposed to 'When did you last') can restrict information obtained.

Fifth, the choice of sexual vocabulary, such as vernacular or medical, provides a discursive context within which sex is considered. Such a context may facilitate the revelation or withholding of particular types of information. Kinsey et al. (1953) drew attention to the ways in which terminology can shape responses obtained: 'Syphilis may be rare ... although bad blood may be more common ... The existence of prostitutes in the community may be denied, although it may be common knowledge that there are some females and males who are hustling' (1953: 61–2).

Finally, it is important to remember that sex surveys can only provide information about that which they have been designed to measure. As a result, those sexual practices and experiences which the researchers were not aware of at the design stage of the survey cannot emerge through the survey. Thus, sex surveys using forced choice or multiple choice questions preclude the identification of the unexpected. Such procedures therefore provide, at best, an incomplete account of the sexual experiences of the population. In addition, because the extent of biasing is unknown, the statistical reliability of the findings remains uncertain.

Laboratory Studies of Sexual Activity

These studies adopt a physiological focus. They aim to obtain accurate descriptions of the physiological processes which accompany human sexual activity. Laboratory studies of the **human sexual response** constitute a later development in the scientific study of human sexuality. Such studies involve observation and physiological measurement of the body's response to sexual stimulation. This requires the presence of researchers and/or measurement instruments during human sexual activity. Levels of arousal and other physiological changes can be measured by attaching electrodes to relevant body parts as well as insertions of micro-cameras into the body.

KT

One major problem with laboratory studies of this type is the inevitability of obtaining biased (i.e. non-random) samples of participants through self-selection: the willingness to be observed during masturbation or intercourse is unlikely to be randomly distributed across the population.

Study of the human sexual response (Masters and Johnson, 1966)

The best-known laboratory study of the human sexual response is Masters and Johnson's (1966) pioneering work. They set out to answer two general questions:

- What happens to the human male and female as they respond to effective sexual stimulation?
- Why do men and women behave as they do when responding to effective sexual stimulation? (Masters and Johnson, 1966: 10).

The authors recruited 382 women and 312 men, most of whom were between 21 and 40 years of age, to take part in their study. Over a period of 11 years, they observed more than 10,000 sexual response cycles in the context of various forms of masturbation and heterosexual penetrative intercourse. A major focus of the study was orgasmic expression in women.

Masters and Johnson identified the sexual response cycle, a sequence of stages of sexual arousal taking the individual from initial excitement to a plateau phase, on to orgasm and finally into a resolution phase. Male and female sexual response cycles were found to follow the same pattern. Masters and Johnson provide detailed descriptions of physiological changes in various organs which take place during the sexual response cycle. They observe that the human physiological reaction to elevated levels of sexual tension is not confined to the primary or secondary organs of reproduction. Rather, there is evidence of sexual arousal throughout the entire body. This takes the form of widespread vasocongestion as well as myotonia (muscle tension). For both women and men, physiologically more intense orgasms were obtained through masturbation. For women, orgasms were also more frequently and more consistently produced through self-manipulation.

Evaluation of the study

The major shortcoming of the study revolves around the selection of participants. Masters and Johnson's sample was drawn from the academic community associated with a large university hospital complex in the USA. In addition, a precondition for participation in the study was 'facility of sexual responsiveness' and 'essential normalcy of the reproductive viscera' (ibid: 12). This meant that those people who did not experience what the researchers defined as 'normal' or 'healthy' sexual responses were not included in the study. Furthermore, participants had to have a 'positive history of masturbatory and coital orgasmic experience' (ibid: 311). In this way, the researchers prejudged the very categories they set out to investigate.

Masters and Johnson's research questions refer to responses to 'effective' sexual stimulation. Tiefer (1995), in a thorough deconstruction of Masters and Johnson's sexual response cycle, draws attention to the inherent circularity of the research questions: 'effective' sexual stimulation is defined as that which induces the complete sexual response cycle. As a result, the researchers' finding that the cycle is a universal human phenomenon follows almost by definition. It appears that rather than researching what actually happens to a wide range of men and women during sex, Masters and Johnson demonstrated what could be achieved by a selected group of enthusiastic volunteers who fulfilled a set of predetermined criteria. Thus, Masters and Johnsons's sexual response cycle constituted a physiological potential rather than a universal reality.

However, it is important to remember that an awareness of a human potential, of what it is possible to do or experience, can motivate people to bring about a desired change in their performance and/or competency. Masters and Johnson did not claim that their sample was representative of the general population or that most people did experience the complete sexual response cycle regularly. Rather, they saw their research as a way of providing information which could help individuals to learn how they could gain access to sexually satisfying experiences (see also Masters and Johnson, 1966). However, what they described was restricted to two particular kinds of sexual activity – penetrative heterosexual intercourse and masturbation.

General problems with laboratory studies

KT

Laboratory studies of sexual activity lack **ecological validity**. This is to say, the social and physical environment within which sexual activity takes place in these studies is so far removed from its real-life context that their findings must be treated with caution. In addition, individuals who agree to take part in such studies are unlikely to be representative of the general population. They are likely to be more confident about their sexual performance and more liberal in their sexual attitudes than those who do not take part.

KT

On a more conceptual level, it has been argued that laboratory studies of sexual behaviour contribute to the **medicalization** of sexuality (e.g. Tiefer, 1995). Here, sex is perceived as a simple and universal biological function which all humans are expected to perform in the same way. If they do not, treatment is required in order to re-establish what is considered to be the natural sexual response. As a result, those whose sexual experiences do not match the 'healthy human sexual response' identified in the laboratory are diagnosed as suffering from sexual dysfunction. This can undermine people's acceptance and enjoyment of alternative forms of sexual pleasure such as those which do not involve penile penetration. Ironically, just as homosexuality was removed from the Diagnostic and Statistical Manual for the categorization of mental illness in the early 1970s, sexual dysfunctions have been defined as psychiatric disorders by the American Psychiatric Association.

Study of Social Cognitions about Sex

These studies use questionnaires in order to measure beliefs, attitudes and perceptions held by individuals. They are theoretically informed and aim to predict sexual behaviour, or at least behavioural intentions.

Psychological studies of sexual behaviour are often informed by theories and methods associated with the social cognition framework (see Chapters 12 and 13). Such studies seek to obtain information about individuals' cognitions concerning sex and to explore the relationship between these cognitions. For example, researchers may investigate the extent to which a person's attitudes towards particular sexual practices allows us to predict their intention to engage in these practices. Cognitive studies of sexual behaviour frequently set out to test existing models of health behaviour within the context of sexual health. They are usually motivated by the desire to understand why people take sexual risks, such as unprotected sexual intercourse, and how such risk taking may be reduced. In recent years, numerous studies of young people's knowledge and attitudes regarding HIV/AIDS and safer sex practices have been published.

Researchers using social cognition models within the context of sexual risk taking argue that people's sexual behaviour is mediated by attitudes rather than knowledge. This is said to explain why widespread awareness of the mechanisms for sexual transmission of HIV has not led to a correspondingly widespread change in sexual practices. A number of social cognition models have been used to study contraceptive use and/or safer sex practices. The health belief model, protection motivation theory and the theory of reasoned action/planned behaviour have all informed studies of sexual risk taking (e.g. Van der Velde and Van der Pligt, 1991; Terry et al., 1993; Abraham and Sheeran, 1994).

It appears that the theory of reasoned action is better suited to account for sexual choices than the health belief model or protection motivation theory because social norms and interpersonal considerations play an important role in sexual behaviour (Sheeran and Abraham, 1995). Also, it has been found that more positive attitudes towards condoms are associated with greater past and/or intended future use of condoms (Pleck et al., 1990).

Example of a study of social cognitions about sex: attitudes and experiences of heterosexual college students

Campbell et al. (1992) investigated the relationship between attitudes towards condom use and actual condom usage. Participants were 393 unmarried, heterosexual American undergraduate students, aged 18 to 24. A 20-item measure of condom attitudes assessed beliefs about condoms in four domains: comfort and convenience, protective effectiveness, interpersonal aspects and sexual sensation (see Table 9.2 for all items). There was also a single item measure of general attitudes towards condoms ('How positive or negative are your personal feelings about you/your partner using a condom?'). Students with sexual experience (66%) were also asked whether they had ever used condoms and whether they had used condoms the last time they had sex. Intention to use condoms in the future was measured by asking the subjects to assess the likelihood of them using condoms with a hypothetical new sexual partner.

The results showed that women had more positive attitudes towards condoms. Men were concerned about the effects of condoms on sexual sensation. Women worried more about getting a sexually transmitted disease from a new partner. For women, past condom use was best predicted by positive general attitudes towards condoms as well as less negative attitudes towards the effects of condom use on sexual sensation. For men, feeling positive about the interpersonal aspects of condom use as well as having positive general attitudes towards condoms were significant predictors of past condom use. For both women and men, intended condom use in the future was best predicted by positive general attitudes towards condoms and positive views about the interpersonal aspects of condom use. In addition, those students who had had fewer sexual

Table 9.2   *The condom attitudes items (Campbell et al., 1992: 278; reproduced with permission)*

Comfort and convenience

1   Condoms are easy to obtain.
2   Condoms are expensive. (R)
3   An advantage of condoms is that you don't need a prescription from a physician.
4   It would be embarrassing to be seen buying condoms in a store. (R)
5   Modern condoms are reasonably comfortable for the man to wear.
6   Condoms are messy and awkward to dispose of. (R)
7   Condoms are convenient and easy to carry.
8   Condoms are difficult for a man to wear.

Efficacy

9   The use of a condom is an effective method of birth control.
10   Condoms are not effective because they often break easily. (R)
11   The use of a condom is a good way to prevent getting sexually transmitted diseases.
12   Condoms do not offer reliable protection. (R)

Interpersonal

13   Discussing the use of a condom with a partner can improve communication.
14   The use of a condom might be embarrassing to me or to my partner. (R)
15   The peace of mind gained from using a condom can improve a sexual relationship.
16   Interrupting lovemaking to use a condom spoils the mood. (R)

Sexual sensation

17   A problem with condoms is that they reduce sexual stimulation. (R)
18   The use of a condom can actually enhance sexual pleasure for both myself and my partner.
19   Sex doesn't feel as natural with a condom. (R)
20   The thinking ahead that is needed when using a condom adds excitement to lovemaking.

Scores for items followed by (R) were reversed before computing means, so that higher scores indicate more positive attitudes. Each item was rated on a 5-point scale from 1 (strongly disagree) to 5 (strongly agree). Items were presented in a random order without headings.

partners were more likely to say that they would use a condom in the future. For women only, increased worry about contracting a sexually transmitted disease (STD) also predicted intention to use condoms in the future (see Table 9.3).

   This study suggests that there are gender differences regarding attitudes towards condoms as well as condom usage. Women and men worry about different aspects of condom use and have different reasons for using (or not using) condoms in the past. However, intended condom use was associated with similar considerations for both men and women.

General problems with the cognitive approach

There are several problems with the cognitive approach. Studies measuring social cognitions about sexual practices rely upon questionnaires which presuppose that cognitions are stable entities residing in people's heads. They do not allow for *contextual variables* which may influence social cognitions. For example, an individual's attitude towards condom use may well depend upon the sexual partner with whom they anticipate having sexual contact. It may depend upon the time, place, relationship and

Table 9.3 *Regression analyses predicting expected use of a condom with a new partner (Campbell et al., 1992: 284; reproduced with permission)*

Predictor	Women			Men		
	Standard coefficient	SE	t	Standard coefficient	SE	t
Single-item condom attitude rating	.15	.03	4.82***	.27	.04	6.22***
Comfort and convenience	.06	.11	0.52	.12	.11	1.05
Efficacy	.09	.07	1.31	.06	.10	0.64
Interpersonal	.21	.08	2.82**	.35	.10	3.66***
Sexual sensation	.10	.05	1.88	−.02	.08	−0.28
Worry about disease	.24	.04	5.74***	.03	.05	0.62
Number of sexual partners	−.13	.03	−4.19***	−.11	.04	−2.77**
		$R^2 = .53$			$R^2 = .50$	
		$F = 19.05***$			$F = 17.23***$	

* $p < .05$. ** $p < .01$. *** $p < .001$.

physiological state (e.g. intoxication) within which sex takes place. As a result, the attempt to predict actual behaviour from decontextualized attitude measures is unlikely to succeed. In addition, it can be argued that sexual intercourse, which is a joint activity, is less likely to be shaped by individual cognitions than solitary health behaviours such as flossing or exercising. The variance in sexual behaviour controlled by social cognition variables is generally modest (around 20% or less) (e.g. Abraham et al., 1992).

Another problem with the cognitive approach is its reliance upon self-reports for past sexual behaviour. As discussed within the context of sex surveys, there are limitations to the accuracy with which individuals report their own sexual practices. Most social cognition studies measure behavioural intentions rather than actual behaviour. This may generate higher correlations between attitude and behavioural measures. However, the relationship between intentions and behaviours is by no means a direct one. More research needs to explore the ways in which intentions are/are not translated into behaviours.

Finally, the vast majority of social cognition studies of sexual behaviour has focused upon young heterosexual people and gay men, who are perceived to be most vulnerable to HIV infection. However, Johnson et al. (1994) found that people who are divorced, widowed or separated report higher rates of risky sexual practices than those who are single. Also, most heterosexual women in the USA suffering from STD infections have become infected by a partner with whom they have had a long-term involvement (Reiss, 1991). Thus, there is a need for studies of older and/or cohabiting/married heterosexuals' sexual decision-making.

Study of Sexual Experience within Close Relationships

Studies of this type use questionnaires, interviews, diaries and observation in order to investigate sexual experience and behaviour in close relationships. They explore how a sexual relationship begins, how partners come to have sex for the first time and how sexual partners communicate about sex. They also assess frequency of sex and sexual satisfaction within different types of relationship. Finally, a relationship focus allows researchers to examine the role played by sexuality within a close relationship and its part in relationship processes such as conflicts or break-ups.

Sexual satisfaction within a particular relationship has been the focus of many studies. For example, Kurdek (1991b) found no significant differences between sexual satisfaction among gay, lesbian, heterosexual unmarried and heterosexual married couples. Greeley (1991) observed that sexual satisfaction was higher for younger respondents. However, earlier studies suggested reverse trends, with married adults enjoying sex more in middle age than in the earlier years of their marriage (e.g. Brown and Auerback, 1981), and lesbians being more satisfied with the sex in their relationships than heterosexual women (e.g. Coleman et al., 1983). Frequency of sex within a relationship has consistently been found to be associated with sexual satisfaction (Greeley, 1991).

It is important to bear in mind that such associations do not imply a causal relationship between the two variables. For example, it is possible that both frequency of sex and sexual satisfaction are not directly causally related, and that another third variable (such as overall relationship satisfaction or conflict) gives rise to both. There appears to be a positive association between sexual satisfaction and relationship satisfaction (Sprecher and McKinney, 1993). Greeley (1991) suggests that sexual satisfaction is a contributing factor to marital happiness. This claim is compatible with the finding that sexual problems play an important role in relationship break-ups for both heterosexual and homosexual couples (Kurdek, 1991a). However, it is possible that post break-up studies artificially increase sexual explanations of the break-up. This could occur either because people remember deteriorating sexual relations most vividly and therefore identify them as the cause of the break-up, or because references to sexual problems are a socially acceptable way of accounting for relationship break-ups.

General problems with the study of sexual relationships

Studies of sexual behaviour with a relationship focus have generated a wide range of findings which can help to answer questions about sex in close relationships. However, there are a number of conceptual and methodological problems with such studies. First, key variables used in such studies are based upon rather narrow definitions at best, and remain unspecified at worst. For example, 'satisfaction' is a key concept investigated by numerous studies. It is either left undefined and assessed with a single question, such as 'How much sexual satisfaction do you get out of your sexual relationship?' (e.g. Greeley, 1991), or it is measured with multi-item scales which assess different dimensions of sexual satisfaction, such as levels of fun, closeness, excitement or enjoyment experienced (Pinney et al., 1987). In both cases, participants respond on Likert-type scales (e.g. from 1 'very much' to 5 'not at all').

The problem with both types of measures is that they do not allow researchers to find out what 'sexual satisfaction' may mean to respondents, and how these meanings may vary between groups and across contexts. For example, it may be that women and men differ in their definitions of 'satisfaction' or even in the extent to which they perceive sexual satisfaction to be important. For some people, satisfaction may be synonymous with having experienced an orgasm, whereas for others it may signify feeling happy and relaxed, or it may simply mean that they do not experience any sexual dysfunctions. Furthermore, questionnaire items tend to ask very general and abstract questions, divorced from particular contexts. This obscures the fact that people's sexual relations take place within specific settings and that these may give rise to varied sexual experiences which cannot be evaluated globally. For example, the item 'Sex is fun for my partner and me' (from Hudson et al., 1981) does not allow a respondent to report great sex on Sunday mornings and lousy sex on weekday nights. Quantitative averaging of such varied experiences does not capture the diverse range of experience of an individual's sex life.

Sprecher and McKinney (1993) note a number of further shortcomings with this research method. They draw attention to the fact that the widely used questionnaire-based self-report measures are vulnerable to self-report bias (under- and over-reporting) as well as memory problems. Much of what participants report may be reconstructions of events based on culturally available sexual scripts rather than accurate reports of what actually occurred. Another problem concerns generalizability. Much of the research has been conducted with predominantly white, middle-class, heterosexual volunteers, often college students. Findings cannot, therefore, be generalized to other socio-cultural groups.

Study of Sexual Meanings

Since the mid-1980s, studies of sexual behaviour have emerged which focus upon **sexual meanings**. This approach is informed by a social constructionist perspective. Here, the objective is to understand what people do by reference to the *meanings which they attribute to their actions*. Thus, a focus upon sexual meanings moves beyond attempts to describe sexual habits or to identify and measure relevant cognitions about sex. Instead, these studies aim to understand how people 'make sense' of their sexual experience and how people's lay theories about sex inform their sexual practices.

KT

For example, Plummer (1996) argues that people's sexual experiences are organized by culturally available 'sexual stories'. These change throughout history and thus allow different sexual meanings to be constructed at different times. Sexual stories provide interpretative frames which make particular sexual identities available. For example, the identity of the gay man/lesbian woman becomes available in the 'coming out' story. Social constructionist studies of sexuality do not aim to reveal the truth about people's sexual lives; rather, they explore how people construct or make a particular sense of their sexual lives. In order to do this, researchers examine transcripts of semi-structured interviews, letters, diaries and/or naturally occurring conversations about sex.

The continuing spread of AIDS has prompted social constructionist researchers to use these methods in order to find out why even those people who know the facts about the transmission of HIV are still reluctant to adopt safer sex practices. For example, Holland et al. (1991) found that young heterosexual women's conceptualization of sex in terms of love and romance informed their choice of sexual practices, namely penetrative sex without condoms. The authors suggest that condoms carry symbolic meanings which undermine their use in heterosexual love relationships.

Similarly, Ingham et al. (1992) observed that a social construction of sex as something mystical and uncontrollable allows people to justify and accept unsafe sexual behaviour as 'natural'. Safer sex practices are not easily compatible with the notion of 'passion' which involves the loss of control and rationality. From within this discourse, a sexual encounter which requires planning and negotiation is perceived as premeditated and therefore not consistent with love and passion (Willig, 1994). Discursive constructions of sexual activity, safer sex and contraception position those who use such constructions in particular ways, and these positionings have implications for sexual practice (Willig, 1998). For example, Harden and Willig (1998) found that young people's discursive construction of contraceptive methods was gendered, which meant that they were reluctant to use the male pill or the female condom.

KT

The social constructionist approach is an ***anti-essentialist*** **view of human sexuality** because it conceives of human sexuality as a set of potentialities which may or may not be realized within differing social, cultural and historical contexts. In this sense, sex is not 'a natural act' (see Tiefer, 1995), but rather a social practice. A social constructionist approach can also be applied to the reading of published research into sexual behaviour and experience, demonstrating how particular versions of human sexuality are constructed through research and writing about them. Stainton-Rogers and Stainton-Rogers' (2001) review of psychological theorizing about sex and gender provides a clear illustration of such an approach.

Example of a study of sexual meanings: constructions of condom use and their implications for sexual practice

Willig (1995) investigated the question: How is 'condom use' discursively constructed by heterosexual adults, and how do such constructions position speakers? The participants were 14 heterosexual British adults aged 22 to 56. Semi-structured interviews included questions about the nature of HIV disease, its social and political implications, as well as the participants' personal feelings about HIV and AIDS. Interview transcripts were analysed using Parker's (1992) version of the discourse analytic method. This facilitated a systematic exploration of the ways in which the discursive object, in this case 'condom use', was constructed in the texts.

The results showed that participants framed their accounts of condom use almost exclusively within a marital discourse. This discourse constructs marriage and its equivalent, the 'long-term relationship', as a condition incompatible with condom use. Participants' assumptions regarding the nature of such relationships – as safe by definition and based upon trust – together with their awareness that relationships can 'go wrong', positioned them in such a way that they felt unable to request safer sex from their partners. In order to communicate to their partner that they could be trusted not to engage in extramarital sex, respondents took the risk of unprotected sex with their partner.

It was concluded that 'condom use' was constructed as incompatible with the 'long-term relationship'. The practice of unprotected sex fulfils a communicative function which is perceived to be instrumental to the maintenance of long-term sexual relationships.

General problems with the study of sexual meanings

Studies of sexual meanings tend to be based on small samples. Semi-structured interviewing is a very time-consuming method of data collection. Transcription of one hour's worth of interviewing takes approximately 10 hours. As a result, it is hard to tell how widespread discursive constructions identified in any one study might be within a particular population. Small-scale qualitative studies of this kind can only demonstrate the availability and contextualized deployment of particular discursive formations. Ideally, studies of sexual meanings ought to be conducted in clusters, whereby constructions identified in one study are then traced in further studies with different respondents, in different contexts. For example, marital discourse described by Willig (1995) may or may not be available to gay men and lesbians. It may or may not be deployed in naturally occurring conversations. However, most studies of sexual meanings remain isolated and consequently fail to integrate findings from diverse research projects.

At a more theoretical level, it has been argued that social constructionist approaches to the study of sexuality fail to address questions about bodily and psychic processes and their role in the constitution of sexual desire (e.g. Segal, 1994). By exclusively focusing on discourse and representation, the body is reduced to a blank slate inscribed with meanings.

Future Research

1 It has been pointed out (e.g. Giddens, 1992) that social scientific research, as it reaches the public domain, establishes a new context within which social behaviour takes place. This is to say, social research feeds back into and so changes that which it studies. For example, survey information about sexual habits can change social and moral norms in society. Johnson et al. (1994) note that the Kinsey reports sold 200,000 copies in the first two months after publication and that their exposure of sexual diversity in the USA had major implications for sexual ethics. Thus, the study of sexual behaviour ought to include studies which reflexively explore the ways in which the dissemination of research findings are taken up and assimilated into their surrounding culture.

2 Segal (1994) draws attention to sexology's failure to theorize desire. She argues that a pervasive biological reductionism has informed studies of sexual behaviour which have consequently sought to measure orgasms and sexual satisfaction, thus reducing the sexual encounter to 'joint masturbatory homework' (ibid: 113). Little research has attempted to find out what attracts us sexually to particular others, how sex acts are experienced subjectively, what constitutes sexual pleasure, the role of fantasy in desire, what 'sexual passion' means and how it comes about. More work is needed which addresses these questions.

3 Tiefer (1995) expresses her concern about the colonization of sex research by a discourse of health and illness. She shows how the location of sexuality within the conceptual model of health and the health industry constitutes a particular choice. This, she argues, results in the construction of sexual activity as a fundamentally biophysical phenomenon which is studied by those who are trained medically rather than those who know about culture and learning. Tiefer suggests that this serves to individualize sexual

problems, such as impotence, by locating their cause within the sufferer's body, rather than to explore their social causes. Further work is needed which attempts to link individual sexual experiences to wider social discourses about sex and sexuality.

4   Some types of sexual activity have outcomes that are of concern from a public-health perspective. These activities, their causes and consequences, are the subject of much public debate, particularly when it is felt that various attempts at managing them have been unsuccessful. High rates of teenage pregnancy and upward trends in sexually transmitted infections (STIs) are examples of such problematic outcomes (Fenton et al., 2001). Since it has become clear that awareness of the possible adverse consequences of risky sexual behaviour is not enough to prevent its occurrence, researchers need to adopt methodologies which allow them to explore the ways in which social, psychological and material factors interact in the facilitation of risky sex. This includes acknowledging the element of pleasure that may be associated with risky sex and with the transgression of social and/or physical boundaries involved in taking sexual risks (Crossley, 2002).

Summary

1   In the nineteenth century a medico-scientific approach to sexuality emerged in the industrialized world. This approach involved the classification of sexual behaviours as either 'healthy' or 'unhealthy' and the construction of sexual types. Research was generally prescriptive and much of sexology pathologized those whose sexual preferences deviated from social norms.

2   Contemporary psychosexual research focuses on the behavioural, physiological, cognitive, relationship and meaning-centred dimensions of human sexual experience. Research methods include large-scale surveys, laboratory experiments, questionnaire studies and interviews.

3   Sex surveys adopt a behavioural focus. They employ large-scale survey methods in order to provide descriptive data about a population's sexual habits. They reveal much greater diversity of sexual practices than is publicly acknowledged within the culture.

4   Methodological problems with sex surveys include limited representativeness of samples, strong effects of desirability bias and demand characteristics, ambiguity surrounding sexual terminology and the limitations of closed-question formats.

5   Laboratory studies of sexual activity adopt a physiological focus. They aim to obtain accurate descriptions of the physiological processes which characterize human sexual activity. Laboratory studies allow researchers to identify and map human potential rather than to describe habitual behaviours.

6   Laboratory studies of sexual behaviour have limitations. They lack ecological validity. Participants are unlikely to be representative of the general population. In addition, laboratory studies tend to reduce human sexual experience to its purely biological function.

7   Cognitive studies of sexual behaviour are concerned with people's beliefs about and attitudes towards sexual matters. They tend to utilize social cognition models in order to study the relationship between cognitions about sex and sexual behaviour.

8   Social cognitions control only around 20% of the variance in sexual behaviour. Cognitive studies are limited because they do not consider the role of contextual variables, the importance of negotiation with a sexual partner and the mechanisms by which behavioural intentions are translated into actual behaviour.

9 Some studies of sexual experience have a relationship focus. They explore the role of sex in close relationships. Sexual satisfaction within close relationships has been the object of many studies. There appears to be a positive association between sexual satisfaction and relationship satisfaction.

10 Methodological problems with relationship-focused studies include narrow definitions of key variables, self-report bias, reliance on participants' memories of events and limited generalizability due to restrictive sampling.

11 Recent studies of sexual experience have focused on the sexual meanings people attribute to their actions. Diverse and changing sexual 'stories' and 'discourses' have been identified and their implications for sexual practice have been explored.

12 Studies of sexual meanings can be criticized for their limited generalizability due to small sample sizes and their heavy dependence upon context. In addition, their exclusive focus on discourse and representation ignores the materiality of the human body and its role in sexual experience.

Key Terms

KT

anti-essentialist view of human sexuality

ecological validity

human sexual response

medicalization

safer sex practices

sex survey

sexology

sexual meanings

sexuality

10

Exercise and Activity

By equating certain types of behaviour with virtue and others with vice, the secular moralists ... threaten to undermine the critical task of educating the public in general ... to the very real dangers lurking behind everyday behavioural choices. (Howard M. Leichter, 1997: 359)

Outline

Recent years have seen an increased interest in, and promotion of, exercise and physical activity. This chapter reviews the background to this 'exercise movement' and summarizes the evidence linking exercise with health. We consider the wide variations in participation in exercise and the social and psychological factors associated with these variations. We then consider the varying meanings of exercise within different social contexts and strategies that have been used to promote greater participation.

Physical Activity and Health

The enthusiasm for physical activity as a means of promoting health has waxed and waned over the centuries. In ancient China exercise was encouraged as a means of improving health. Similarly, in ancient Greece gymnastic activity was considered a means of treating disease. However, others urged caution about exaggerating the benefits of physical activity. For example, the famous physician Galen (c. 200–129BC) who had so much influence on western medicine, cautioned against excessive involvement in athletics:

> While athletes are exercising their profession, their body remains in a dangerous condition, but when they give up their profession they fall into a condition more powerless still; as a fact, some die shortly afterward; others live for a little time, but do not arrive at old age ... Athletes live a life quite contrary to the precepts of hygiene, and I regard their mode of living as a regime far more favourable to illness than to health.

The advent of scientific medicine in the last century provided an opportunity to clarify the value of sustained exercise on health. For example, John Morgan (1873) studied the longevity of oarsmen who participated in the Oxford and Cambridge boat race. He found that their life expectancy was 2.2 years longer than that predicted from contemporary life tables, thus disputing popular wisdom of those days. Since then there have been sustained attempts to identify the relative contribution of physical exercise on physical and mental health.

Physical health

There has been a steady accumulation of evidence confirming the benefits of exercise in terms of physical health. Initially, this evidence was correlational but now there is experimental evidence. A meta-analysis of the contribution of physical activity to the prevention of coronary heart disease (CHD) concluded that physically inactive individuals are twice as likely to develop coronary heart disease as people who engage in regular physical exercise.

In 1991 the American Centers for Disease Control and Prevention and the American College of Sports Medicine convened a panel of experts to review the evidence. In their report (Pate et al., 1995) they concluded that 'cross-sectional epidemiologic studies and controlled, experimental investigations have demonstrated that physically active adults, as contrasted with their sedentary counterparts, tend to develop and maintain higher levels of physical fitness' (1995: 403). They added that research demonstrated a clear link between physical fitness and reduced risk for several chronic diseases. In 1996 the US Surgeon General published a special report (DHHS, 1996) on physical activity and health. It estimated that physical inactivity contributes to 400,000 preventable deaths (17% of total deaths) per year in the United States. In view of this evidence, it recommended that every US adult should (daily) accumulate 30 minutes or more of moderate-intensity physical activity that can be accumulated in relatively short bursts.

This recommendation emphasized that it was not necessary to engage in prolonged vigorous exercise. Rather 'gardening, housework, raking leaves, and playing actively with children can also contribute to the 30-minute-per-day total if performed at an intensity corresponding to brisk walking. Those who perform lower-intensity activities should do them more often, for longer periods, or both' (DHHS, 1996: 404). These recommendations emphasized the importance of what could be described as everyday physical activity that was within the grasp of most people rather than the more intense vigorous activity often rejected by lay people.

Subsequent reports provided further evidence of the beneficial effects of regular moderate physical activity. In 1996 the US National Institute of Health convened a consensus conference to review the evidence. The report (NIH Consensus Development Panel, 1996) concluded that 'accumulating scientific evidence indicates that physical inactivity is a major risk factor for CVD'. They recommended similar guidelines as the previous report and affirmed that 'intermittent or shorter bursts of activity (at least 10 minutes), including occupational, non-occupational, or tasks of daily living, also have similar cardiovascular and health benefits if performed at a level of moderate intensity (such as brisk walking, cycling, swimming, home repair, and yard-work) with an accumulated duration of at least 30 minutes per day' (1996: 23). Further, they suggested that the low rate of participation in regular physical activity may be due to the misperception that vigorous continuous activity was necessary to reap the health benefits. They caution that risk of injury increases with increased intensity and frequency of activity.

Mental health

As with physical health the past decade has seen a series of reports of experimental studies confirming the beneficial effects of exercise on mental health. Plante and Rodin (1990) reviewed the impact of physical activity on the psychological health and well-being of non-clinical populations. They concluded that exercise improves mood and well-being and reduces anxiety, depression and stress. They also reported positive effects on self-concept, self-esteem and self-assurance. They suggested five biological mechanisms underlying the connection between physical activity and mental health that are detailed in Table 10.1.

However, it is not simply biological processes but also psychological processes which explain the connection between exercise and mental health. Plante and Rodin (1990) suggest eight psychological processes that may be involved in explaining the improvement in mood following exercise (Table 10.2).

Although, most contemporary evidence confirms the beneficial psychological effects of even limited physical exercise, there is still contrary evidence from laboratory research. For example, a carefully designed study showed that an acute exercise programme administered to a sample of physically inactive participants has no mood-enhancing effects. Since much of the previous research was conducted using volunteers, it has been suggested that future research should consider the effect of exercise on different populations, including those with sedentary lifestyles.

Table 10.1   *Physical activity and mental health: biological mechanisms (based on Plante and Rodin, 1990)*

- Increases in body temperature due to exercise result in short-term tranquillizing effects.
- Regular exercise facilitates stress adaptation because the increase in adrenal activity increases steroid reserves that can then be available to counter stress.
- Reduction in resting muscle activity potential after exercises helps release tension.
- Exercise enhances neurotransmission of noradrenalin (norepinephrine), serotonin and dopamine leading to improved mood.
- Exercise leads to the release of endogenous morphine-like chemicals synthesized in the pituitary gland leading to enhanced feelings of well-being.

Table 10.2   *Physical activity and mental health: psychological processes (based on Plante and Rodin, 1990)*

- Improved physical fitness provides people with a sense of mastery, control and self-sufficiency.
- Exercise is a form of meditation that triggers an altered and more relaxed state of consciousness.
- Exercise is a form of biofeedback that teaches exercisers to regulate their own autonomic arousal.
- Exercise provides distraction, diversion, or time out from unpleasant cognitions, emotions, and behaviour.
- Since exercise results in the physical symptoms associated with anxiety and stress (e.g. sweating, hyperventilation, fatigue) without the subjective experience of emotional distress, repeated pairing of the symptoms in the absence of associated distress results in improved psychological functioning.
- Social reinforcement among exercisers may lead to improved psychological states.
- Exercise may act as a buffer, resulting in decreased strain caused by stressful life events.
- Exercise competes with negative affects, such as anxiety and depression, in the somatic and cognitive systems.

Participation in Physical Activity

Modern lifestyle

We discussed in Chapter 6 the evidence that human beings traditionally required considerable energy expenditure for survival. In ancient times the hunter-gatherer needed to expend substantial energy on a regular basis so as to ensure access to food and shelter. This need to expend substantial energy remained well into this century and continues in much of the developing world. However, the rapid increase in technology in industrialized societies over the past generation has led to a much more sedentary lifestyle. This decline in physical activity is a consequence of the reduced need for energy expenditure in all spheres of human life, including work, transportation and home maintenance. Technological developments in entertainment have reduced the role of physical activity in leisure time. In describing the implications of this change in lifestyle Blair et al. (1992: 103) remarked that 'humans evolved to be active animals and may not be able to adapt well to the modern sedentary lifestyle'.

The steady accumulation of evidence linking physical activity with improved health status has been followed by a 'fitness boom' (King, 1994). Superficially, it would seem that involvement in physical activity and exercise has increased substantially in popularity. However, results of large national surveys indicate that most adults in industrialized societies still prefer a sedentary lifestyle although with substantial regional variations.

In the USA the National Health Interview Survey estimated that only 14% of American adults engage in vigorous physical activity 3 or more times a week, a further 24% engage in moderate physical activity 5 or more times per week and 24% engaged in no physical activity (National Center for Health Statistics, 1994). The Behavioral Risk Factor Surveillance System (US Centers for Disease Control and Prevention, 1993) estimated that 58% of American adults are sedentary (i.e. engage in no or irregular leisure-time activity).

In Britain, according to the *Allied Dunbar National Fitness Survey* (Allied Dunbar et al., 1992) only 20% of women and 30% of men are taking sufficient physical exercise to benefit their health. In a survey of over 4,000 Australian adults, it has been found that 22% are physically inactive, 40% exercised occasionally and only 38% exercised regularly and planned to continue. Admittedly an indication of the popular belief in the benefits of exercise was apparent in the finding that about half of those who did not exercise regularly were thinking about doing it. Scandinavian countries would seem to have a more active lifestyle.

Since reduced physical activity can contribute to overweight/obesity, it is not surprising that public health officials are concerned at the low rate of participation. In North America, the rates of obesity continue to climb. It was estimated that 61% of adults in the US were overweight or obese in 1999 (DHHS, 2001). Rates in other western countries also show evidence of increases.

Variation in participation

Most studies confirm that there are substantial age and sex variations in participation in physical activity. For example, in 1985, there was a steady decrease in participation in outdoor activities from 55% and 36% among 16- to 19-year-old males and females to 17% and 6% of 70+ year olds. During adolescence there is a steady decline in participation in physical activity. North American surveys have estimated that while 70% of 12-year-olds report participation in vigorous physical activities, this declines to 42% of men and 30% of women by 21 years (NIH Consensus Development Panel, 1996).

Participation in physical exercise is also linked to socio-economic and educational background. In the British Whitehall study it was found that while only 5% of men in the highest grade did not participate in moderate or vigorous exercise, 31% of those in the lowest grade did not. The Health Survey for England (Prescott-Clarke and Primatesta, 1998) found that men from manual social classes are more active but this was due to greater occupational activity. In general, adults from manual social classes participated less in sporting and exercise-related activities. The proportion of adults in the US National Health Interview Survey (National Center for Health Statistics, 1994) reporting a sedentary lifestyle was 32% among lower-income people compared to 24% in the general population.

There is also evidence of significant ethnic variations although these are often confounded by socio-economic and educational variations. In the USA several studies have found that black women are less active than white women. The Behavioral Risk Factor Surveillance System (USCDCP, 1993) found that in general ethnic minorities were less involved in physical activities. Among women a sedentary lifestyle was reported by 68% of African Americans compared to 56% of non-Hispanic whites. A similar pattern was apparent among men.

Psychological Factors Associated with Adult Physical Activity

An increasing amount of psychological research is being aimed at explaining the variations in the extent of participation in physical activity among adults. Frequently, these studies have used various social cognition models of health behaviour. The most popular have been the Health Belief Model and the theories of reasoned action and planned behaviour. Recently, there has been a rapid increase in the number of reports using the transtheoretical model of change. These **social cognition** models are used to explain multiple health practices that are detailed in other chapters. In this chapter we consider the details of the main models and their application to explaining physical activity.

Health belief model

 The **health belief model (HBM)** was originally developed by Rosenstock (1966). According to the model (Figure 10.1), a person's readiness to take a health action is determined by four main factors:

- perceived susceptibility to the disease;
- perceived severity or seriousness of the disease;
- perceived benefits of the health action;
- perceived barriers to performing the action.

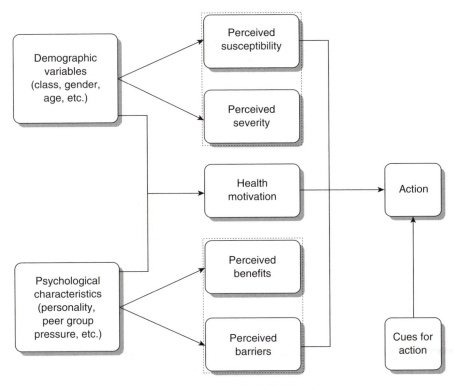

Figure 10.1   Original components of the Health Belief Model

In addition, Becker and Mainman (1975) included general health motivation as a fifth factor. More recent revisions of the theory (Becker and Rosenstock, 1984) have also included three further factors in the HBM. These supplementary factors are demographic variables, psychosocial variables and structural variables, in particular knowledge of the disease and contact with the disease. More recently 'cues to action' has been added as an additional explanatory variable. This proliferation of variables led Oliver and Berger (1979) to describe the HBM as 'more a collection of variables than a formal theory or model' (1979: 113).

Several studies have used all or, more usually, portions of the HBM to explain participation in physical activity. In particular, researchers have considered to what extent perceived benefits of and barriers to physical activity explain participation. Dishman (1986) classified the main perceived barriers into four categories: effort, time, health limitations and obstacles. However, it is possible that these barriers are more justifications for lack of participation rather than explanations of it. Furthermore, when these benefits of and barriers to exercise are considered along with a host of other predictive factors they do not emerge as important.

Theories of reasoned action and planned behaviour

The **theory of reasoned action (TRA)** was developed by Ajzen and Fishbein (1980). This model proposes that exercise behaviour is predicted by intention to engage in

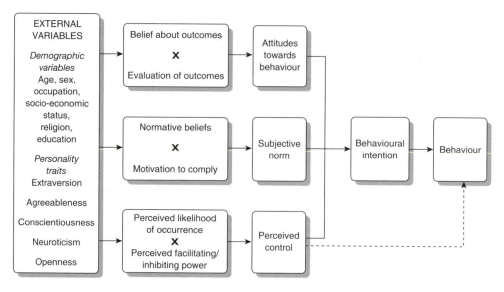

Figure 10.2 The theory of planned behaviour

such behaviour that in turn is predicted by the individual's attitude towards exercise and the perceived social norm. The attitudinal component is in turn a function of the perceived consequences of participating and a personal evaluation of those consequences. Further, the perceived norm is a function of the perceived expectations to participate and the motivation to comply with those expectations. Godin (1994) conducted a review of physical activity studies adopting the TRA and concluded:

> It has proven to be very helpful in understanding the decision-making process underlying exercise behavior ... approximately 30% of the variance in intention to exercise seems to be explained by the attitudinal component. The normative component is less consistently associated with intention to exercise and does not appear to be a stable variable for the interpretation of exercise behavior. (Godin, 1994: 1392)

The theory of planned behaviour (TPB) developed by Ajzen (1985) introduced perceived behavioural control into the basic model and suggested that, besides the attitudinal and social norm components, whether someone intended to behave in a certain way depended upon the extent to which they believed they had control over a particular behaviour (Figure 10.2). This concept was derived from Bandura's (1977) concept of self-efficacy. Godin (1994) found that the introduction of the behavioural control variable in studies of exercise participation increased the proportion of the variance explained.

Godin and his co-workers (Colette et al., 1994) also applied an extended version of this model to explain the intention of a sample of adults to take up a physical exercise. In a survey of over 350 Canadian adults they found that the four best predictors of intent to participate were current physical activity, age, attitude towards exercise and personal normative belief. With regard to the attitude, the high intenders were more likely to consider exercise enjoyable, interesting, exciting, pleasant, good and useful. Colette et al. (1994) suggested that the significance of personal normative belief reflects the individuals' belief that they are the ones who decide whether or not to take action. Unlike other studies self-efficacy did not predict intention to participate.

Hawkes and Holm (1993) combined elements of the HBM with the TRA and with Cox's (1982) theory of client health behaviour (TCHB) to examine gender differences in exercise determinants. They found that for both men and women the most important statistical predictors were social influences and health self-determinism. The social influence concept was derived from the TRA while health self-determinism was a measure of intrinsic health motivation derived from the TCHB. However, the various model variables still only explained a small proportion of the variance in long-term physical activity participation, suggesting that other factors are important.

Finally, in view of criticisms of the overemphasis of cognitive factors in the TRA/TPB, recent extensions of the model have attempted to investigate the role of such additional factors as emotions and self-identity. An example is the study by Abraham and Sheeran (2004) who found that anticipated regret explained an additional proportion of the variance besides the core variables in a study of the predictive power of the TPB in explaining exercise intentions.

Self-efficacy

Bandura's (1986) social learning theory has been used extensively to explain participation in physical activity. In particular, Bandura's argument that perceived self-efficacy is the common cognitive mechanism that mediates behavioural responses has been applied. Bandura argued that whether a person persists in a particular behaviour in different circumstances depends upon his/her perception of individual mastery over the behaviour. Bandura suggested that this sense of self-efficacy develops through personal experiences of success, but also from verbal support from others and the perceived level of physiological arousal. Thus, unlike the previous models, this self-efficacy theory is bidirectional such that not only can self-efficacy contribute to increased behavioural effort but also success in the behavior can contribute to increased self-efficacy.

In physical activity and exercise research it has been found that self-efficacy predicts greater involvement. A number of variants of self-efficacy have been found to predict involvement. These include barrier self-efficacy or the confidence in one's ability to overcome barriers to regular exercise attendance, scheduling self-efficacy, and exercise self-efficacy. Some studies have found a negative relationship such that lower levels of self-efficacy statistically predicted more physical activity. Rimal (2001) in a longitudinal study found evidence of this and suggested that those with lower self-efficacy improved their self-efficacy over time which in turn led to greater exercise behaviour. Together these findings would confirm the interactive nature of self-efficacy beliefs and physical activity.

An interesting extension of self-efficacy theory is proxy efficacy or the belief in the role of others in aiding achievement of desired outcomes. Although at first this might seem to be the converse of self-efficacy, evidence suggests that it can be an important complement. A study of participants in a fitness class found that fitness instructor efficacy as well as self-efficacy beliefs were predictive of class attendance for class initiates (Bray et al., 2001).

Transtheoretical model (TTM)

KT

The **transtheoretical model of change** was originally developed by Prochaska and DiClemente (1983) to explain why anti-smoking messages were more successful for some people than for others (see Chapter 8). According to the TTM, people adopting a new behaviour move through a series of stages of change within which they utilize different processes to support the changes. These stages are described in Chapter 8. Movement across the stages is dependent on decisional balance and perceived self-efficacy. Decisional balance is a cognitive assessment of the relative merits of the pros and cons of the exercise behaviour while self-efficacy is the belief in one's ability to perform the exercise.

Some evidence for the importance of decisional balance was provided in a study that compared the reasons for and against participation in exercise given by a group of non-exercisers and regular exercisers. It found that the pre-contemplators provided relatively more con reasons while the maintainers provided relatively more pro reasons. It was concluded that one reason why people do not exercise is that they cannot think of reasons to do so (Cropley et al., 2003).

There is evidence of the importance of self-efficacy. Research shows that those who are regularly participating in physical activity (action or maintenance stages) score higher on this measure. This suggests that those who are at the early stages (pre-contemplation and contemplation) have little confidence in their ability to exercise.

KT

A related factor to self-efficacy is **self-determination**. According to the self-determination theory, people will engage in many activities simply because of pure enjoyment or intrinsic motivation. A study in Wales (Ingledew et al., 1998) found that participants in the early stages of exercising attributed participation more to extrinsic motives (e.g. appearance/weight management) whereas in the later stages they referred to intrinsic motives such as enjoyment. It was concluded that intrinsic motives are important for progression to and maintenance of the exercise.

What's wrong with social cognition models of exercise?

Social cognition models (SCMs), such as those described above, have focused on identifying the determinants of physical activity. These models have attracted increasing criticism for their methodological and theoretical short-comings. Methodologically they have been criticized because of their limited success in predicting health practices. For example, Ogden (2003) identified three main weaknesses of these models:

- the theories cannot be disconfirmed;
- the models only explain a limited amount of statistical variance;
- many of the studies use self-reports of health behaviors and so are unreliable.

The authors of the TRA (Ajzen and Fishbein, 2004) reject these criticisms but there remain more fundamental concerns that the models are too mechanistic in conceptualization. Stainton-Rogers (1991) provided a coherent critique of these models describing them as portraying 'thinking as a passive, mindless activity rather than an active striving after meaning, and portray people as thinking-machines rather than as aware and insightful, open to being beguiled by convincing tales and rhetoric, and inventive story-tellers' (1991: 55).

More than this they locate the thinking in the head of the individual rather than as something that unfolds in interaction with others leading to an individualistic focus in health promotion. A social interactionist views the individual as part of a group and of a society. His or her behaviour, thoughts and beliefs can be considered as unfolding in interaction with the groups and society as a means of adapting to changing circumstances. Their decision to become involved in physical activity is the result of an ongoing engagement with their immediate social world. Further criticisms of SCMs can be found in Chapters 9 (pp. 186–7) and 11 (pp. 223–4).

Context of Physical Activity among Adults

Social context of physical activity

There have been attempts to develop a more social interactionist understanding of physical activity. These argue that the extent to which people engage in physical activity is related to the character of their everyday social experience. Calnan and Williams (1991) conducted detailed interviews with a sample of middle-aged men and women from the southeast of England. The participants were from different social backgrounds. They found clear social class differences in perceptions of exercise. Those from working-class backgrounds perceived exercise in relation to everyday tasks, activities and duties at home and at work. They adopted a functional definition of health and fitness. For them their ability to 'exercise' their everyday tasks both confirmed and reaffirmed their health. For example, one farm-worker said: 'I get enough exercise when I am working on the farm shoveling corn all day, you get enough exercise. In the garden out there, I take the dog for a walk, yet I get enough exercise' (1991: 518). They tended to be satisfied with their physical health that they could enhance during their everyday activities.

Middle-class people tended to perceive exercise as not being part of their everyday activities. They preferred to define it with reference to recreational or leisure activities that they sometimes felt they could not engage in because of lack of time. Fitness for these individuals was defined in terms of athleticism, not in ability to perform everyday tasks. This group also made more reference to the health-promoting effects of exercise in terms of 'well-being' and relief from routine daily obligations. In discussing these class differences in perceptions of exercise Calnan and Williams (1991) referred to the work of Bourdieu (1984) who suggested that whereas working-class people express an instrumental relation to their bodily practices, middle-class people engage in health practices which are 'entirely opposed to (such) total, practically oriented movements' (1984: 214).

In a similar type of study, Mullen (1992) explored the meaning of health behaviour such as exercise within the context of work. He interviewed a sample of Scottish men from different social backgrounds. It is apparent that the men from working-class backgrounds spoke of work as exercise and as often being good for their health. For example, one man said: 'Ah think working has a good effect, hard work; it hasn't done me any harm. Ah think if you do anythin' that keeps you fit you ... you're usin' your muscles all the time you know an' ye get up the next day fresh an' ye enjoy yer, ye look forward to a holiday then right enough' (1992: 77).

Mullen (1992) does not specifically explore social class differences although he does note that sedentary (more middle-class) occupations were described in terms of lack of exercise, e.g. 'desk bound' or 'spending a lot of time in the car'. Thus exercise was defined by more middle-class people as an activity outside work.

In a large-scale survey of young people's physical activity in Norway, Oygard and Anderssen (1998) also considered the importance of the meaning of exercise and the physical body. In discussing the relationship between social class and exercise they also refer to the work of Bourdieu (1984) who suggested that this relationship derives from social class differences in attitude towards the body. In our society the legit-imized body emphasizes both inner and outer characteristics. While the former is con-cerned with the healthy body, the latter refers to the fit and slim body. The middle and upper classes are more able to produce this legitimized body since it requires invest-ment in time and money. Working-class people with less time free from necessity have a more instrumental view of their body and view concern with exercise and fitness as pretentious. Conversely, middle-class people with more leisure time and resources to expend promote a cult of health and a concern with physical appearance.

Murray and Jarrett (1985) examined gender differences in perceptions of health and health maintenance. They conducted detailed interviews with a sample of young people and found that young men were more likely to define health in terms of fitness and health maintenance in terms of physical activity that improved their ability to perform. Young women preferred diet and weight control which improved their phys-ical image. Other studies have found that concern for bodily appearance is the most important reason for physical activity among females. However, this concern with bodily image is closely linked with social position.

In their survey Oygard and Anderssen found that level of education was positively associated with extent of participation in physical activity among females but not among males. In reviewing this finding, they refer to the suggestion that concern with the body is more common among those belonging to the cultural elite who are more anxious about their appearance and their 'body for others' (Bourdieu, 1984: 213). Oygard and Anderssen concluded: 'For females in higher social positions, it may be of importance to show others who they are by developing healthy and "delicate" bodies, i.e. they are more concerned with the inner and outer body than females in lower social positions' (1998: 65). However, they also added more prosaically that the lesser involvement of less educated females may be due to them having limited access to leisure facilities. They found little relationship between education and physical activ-ity among males and suggest that this may reflect the greater promotion of male sport-ing activities and the greater integration of physical activity into male culture.

It is well established that participation in physical activity declines steadily with age. This may reflect a variety of factors including limited socialization into physical activ-ity among that generation to perceived social exclusion. A study in New Zealand found that older people who participated in sporting activities reported that they were often confronted by a discouraging stance from younger people. This negative social value regarding seniors and sports would seem to be internalized such that many elderly people report limited participation for fear that they might incur an injury.

Environmental and policy context of physical activity

There is increasing interest in the settings within which people live and work and the extent to which it either promotes or discourages physical activity. We have already mentioned how our modern lifestyle encourages sedentary practices. Ecological psychologists propose that to understand human behaviour we need to consider the 'behavior setting' or the physical and social context within which the behaviour occurs. This includes the buildings in which we live and work and the communities in which we reside. Modern buildings are not designed with physical activity in mind. For example, stairways are often more difficult to access than either escalators or elevators. Communities often have poor play facilities. This is especially the case in low-income neighbourhoods. The most common means of transport are cars such that cycling and walking are discouraged or dangerous.

However, there is evidence that personal considerations can outweigh environmental barriers to physical activity. For example, in a study of Australian adults it was found that personal barriers such as lack of time, other priorities, work and family commitments predicted extent of involvement in physical activities more than environmental barriers such as weather, cost and safety (Salmon et al., 2000). It is worth noting that these personal barriers are a reflection of broader social demands. Another Australian study by Giles-Corti and Donovan (2003) also found that individual and social environmental factors were more important than physical environmental factors in predicting exercise participation. They found that the most important predictors of participation in recreational physical activity were perceived behavioural control, behavioural intention, habit and exercising peer. The most important environmental predictor was accessibility to recreational facilities.

A related contextual factor is the extent to which a society implements policy to promote physical activity. It is undoubtedly the case that governments in most western societies have publicly recognized the health hazards of a sedentary lifestyle. This has led to a variety of health promotion activities (see below) designed to promote greater participation in physical activity. The Australian studies would suggest that while access to recreational facilities are important there must be other measures to promote use of these facilities.

Cultural context of physical activity

It is important to note that physical activities are conducted within a wider social and cultural context that promotes different ideals. For example, participation in sport is particularly promoted in North American society. There the muscular physique is presented as the ideal male form. Luschen et al. (1996) note that the emergence of those body-building exercises that are aimed at building muscular strength and fitness 'reflects a bodily culture that is in line with American values of masculine prowess' (1996: 201). They add that 'activities like American football, weightlifting, and boxing set a premium on brute physical force and place much less emphasis on endurance and relaxation' (1996: 202). Ability to attain this physical shape is promised to those who participate in various fitness gyms. However, access to these somewhat elite facilities is often restricted to those with money. In addition, aggressive sporting activities are also promoted among the middle class as a training ground for developing an aggressive business attitude, not to mention the making of useful social contacts.

A related issue is the role of religion. Certain forms of Christianity have traditionally held a negative view of excessive concern about the body (see Chapter 3). It has been suggested that this is a reason for the poorer performance of athletes from more Catholic countries in sporting events. Conversely, in more Protestant or secular societies concern with body shape and performance is promoted. Indeed, Turner (1984) argues that contemporary concern for the body could be described as the new Protestant ethic:

> The new ethic of managerial athleticism is thus the contemporary version of the Protestant ethic, but, fanned by the winds of consumerism, this ethic has become widespread throughout the class system as a lifestyle to be emulated. The commodified body has become the focus of a keep-fit industry, backed up by fibre diets, leisure centres, slimming manuals and outdoor sports. (Turner, 1984: 112)

An understanding of the variations in the extent of participation in physical activities requires attention not only to the various psychological processes but also to the socio-cultural context within which they have meaning and which promote or discourage involvement in such pursuits.

Exercise among Children

There is increasing concern at the apparent decline of involvement of children in physical activity and exercise. In the UK it was estimated that among 2–15-year-olds, four out of 10 boys and six out of 10 girls are not participating sufficiently in physical activity (Prescott-Clarke and Primatesta, 1999). Similarly, in the USA it was estimated that approximately 50% of teenagers are not vigorously active on a regular basis (DHHS, 1996). During adolescence the proportion involved in physical activity dramatically declines. Further, between 1991 and 1995 the proportion of high school students enrolled in physical education classes declined from 42% to 25%.

There are substantial variations in the extent of participation of children in physical activity. Sex, socio-economic and ethnic variations are apparent from an early age. A large survey of over 2,400 third grade (8–9-year-old) children in four US states found that not only do boys participate significantly more in moderate to vigorous physical activity but they also participate more in sedentary activities. Specifically, boys spend more time than girls watching television and playing video games. The ethnic differences in physical activity are not significant after controlling for other demographic variables. However, there are differences between states with California students reporting most moderate to vigorous physical activity and Louisiana students reporting the least.

Gottlieb and Chen (1985) considered the character of physical activity among a sample of 2,695 seventh and eight grade students (12–14-year-olds) in Texas. They found that the female students were more likely than the males to participate in running, swimming, dancing, skipping, tennis, roller-skating and volleyball. These activities were largely classified by sporting experts as individual, non-competitive and potentially aerobic activities. The male students preferred team, competitive, non-aerobic activities. Gottlieb and Chen concluded that this evidence of sex typing in sporting activities reflected 'the importance of socialization within the family unit and later through the peer group for gender differences'. They also found evidence of ethnic differences. After controlling for father's occupation, Anglos were more likely to engage in individual, non-competitive, aerobic type activities. Blacks favoured competitive team sports such as basketball and also dancing, while Mexican-Americans preferred baseball. Gottlieb and Chen suggest that this reflects the varying ethnic-related opportunities for success in sporting activities in the USA and the availability of role models.

Gender differences have been found in sporting participation interacted with socio-economic status. Among girls, those from poorer social backgrounds are less likely to participate in physical activity whereas among boys there is no relationship with social position. It has also been found that teenage girls with higher levels of education are more physically active whereas again among boys there is less evidence of a relationship with level of education.

There is evidence of increasing involvement of girls in sporting activities. It is estimated that in the USA girls now comprise 37% of high school athletes. This is an increase from 1 in 27 girls in 1971 to 1 in 3 girls in 1994. Girls were particularly active in basketball and soccer.

Explanations of children's and teenagers' physical activity

There have been a large number of quantitative studies of the factors associated with the participation of children and adolescents in physical activity. A recent comprehensive review of studies published between 1977 and 1999 classified the significant correlates into five ecological categories. These are summarized in Table 10.3. Not surprisingly in the demographic category, the most consistent finding was that boys are more likely to participate in physical activity. There was also some evidence that among adolescents, whites were more involved in PA activities.

In terms of psychological variables, the association between academic achievement and PA participation is probably a reflection of a rejection of organized physical activities by those who perform poorly academically. The importance of intention to participate is the same as with adult studies.

In terms of social variables, it would seem that parental support is of importance and would indicate the central role that parents can play with adolescents. It should be noted that it was not parents' own behaviour that was important but rather the extent of support and help they provided.

Finally, the importance of facility access and opportunities and time to participate indicate the need to ensure the availability of physical activity facilities for teenagers and children.

Table 10.3　*Correlates of child and adolescent physical activity (Sallis et al., 1999)*

Category	Child	Adolescent
Demographic	Male Parent Overweight	Male White Young
Psychological	PA preference Intention Few barriers	Achievement-oriented Intention Perceived physical competence Low depression
Behavioural	Previous PA Healthy diet	Previous PA Community sports Sensation seeking Not sedentary
Social	None	Parent support Significant other support Sibling PA Parental help
Physical environment	Facility access Time outdoors	Opportunities to exercise

PA, physical activity

Social meaning of sport for young people

Most of the above research into the development of physical activity among children and adolescents has adopted a deterministic model such that it is assumed that participation is 'caused' by a combination of social and psychological variables. This approach ignores the active role of the young person in deciding whether or not to become involved and the social context within which physical activity occurs. A limited number of studies have adopted this more social perspective.

Kunesh et al. (1992) conducted a detailed investigation of the school play activities of a sample of 11- to 12-year-old girls in the central USA. In interviews the girls reported that they found physically active games at home and at school enjoyable. However, in the school playground the girls preferred to stand in a group and talk while the boys participated in various games. When the girls did participate in games they were often criticized by the boys for their supposed inferior skill performance. To avoid this negative treatment the girls excluded themselves. The girls reported that when playing at school they felt nervous and embarrassed. These findings would suggest that while at an early age boys and girls both enjoy physical activities by the time they reach puberty the girls feel that they are being excluded.

As they enter adolescence the gender difference in participation in physical activities becomes more pronounced. From a series of interviews with young people from southeast London, Coakley and White (1992) identified five factors that help explain young people's decisions about participation in sporting activities (Table 10.4).

This study emphasized that perceived identity was a central concern in the extent and character of sports preferred. Young people actively sought out or rejected involvement in certain physical activities dependent upon a variety of factors including previous experiences and ongoing changing circumstances. As Coakley and White

Table 10.4 *Young people's decisions about sport participation (based on Coakley and White, 1992)*

1 *Consideration of the future, especially the transition to adulthood*: certain sports are accepted and others rejected depending upon their perceived adultness. Teenagers reject those games that they perceive as childish. Young women in particular become less involved in sporting activities that they perceive as having little connection with the female role.

2 *Desire to display and extend personal competence and autonomy*: young people become involved in sporting activities to the extent to which it extends their feeling of competence and autonomy. Again, there are gender differences with the young women being less likely to define themselves as sportspersons even if they are actively involved in physical activities. For them, sports are often perceived as a more masculine activity.

3 *Constraints related to money, parents and opposite-sex friends*: access to material resources is an important factor in explaining whether young people participate in certain sporting activities. In addition, the young women emphasize the importance of parents who seem to adopt a much more controlling influence on their general social lives. Further, the extent of participation in sporting activities is affected by whether or not the young women have a boyfriend. It is often the boyfriend who initiates leisure activity.

4 *Support and encouragement from parents, relatives, and/or peers*: young people report that they are often actively encouraged by family or friends to participate in certain physical activities. The young women in particular note the importance of having a friend to accompany them to sporting activities.

5 *Past experiences in school sports and physical education*: many young people report certain negative school experiences that colour their attitudes to physical activities. In particular, young women comment on how school physical education was associated with feelings of discomfort and embarrassment. Young men seem to have more pleasant memories of school sport.

(1992) state: 'young people become involved in sport through a series of shifting, back-and-forth decisions made within the structural, ideological, and cultural context of their social worlds' (p. 21). Further:

> Young people do not get socialized into sport in the sense that they simply internalize or respond to external influences; nor do young people get socialized out of sport in the sense that they drop out in response to external influences. Instead, sport participation (and nonparticipation) is the result of decisions negotiated within the context of a young person's social environment and mediated by the young person's view of self and personal goals. Neither participation nor nonparticipation is a 'once and for all time' phenomenon explainable in terms of a quantitative, cause-effect methodological approach. (Coakley and White, 1992: 34)

Declining participation in physical activity by children

There are a variety of factors contributing to the apparent reduced involvement of children in physical activity. One contributory factor is that parents are not modelling and not actively promoting this behaviour. Thus children perceive their parents as preferring a sedentary lifestyle and adopt a similar routine.

This is compounded by the evidence of the reluctance of many parents to encourage independent activities among their children. Thus many children are transported to school by their parents who often are reluctant to allow them to play independently after school. Perceived safety is an important issue. Parents are particularly concerned about the safety of their children and will restrict play activities if they perceive them to be unsafe. For example, it was found that the perceived safety of parks was identified as the most important factor in deciding whether parents allowed their children to use parks.

Other factors include promotion of sedentary activities by toy and game manufacturers and limited opportunity to participate in organized physical activities because of time constraints, cost or limited play facilities.

Promoting Physical Activity

With the increase in evidence demonstrating the physical and mental benefits of physical activity and exercise, governments and health authorities have become keen to promote greater participation. Unfortunately, the evidence suggests that many of these campaigns have not been very successful. Large-scale media campaigns have not proven very effective in increasing participation. This has led to the development of more focused interventions aimed either at the whole community or particular groups within the community.

Population-based strategies

A series of recent interventions that have attempted to increase participation in communities have been based upon various psychological models, especially the transtheoretical model. Marcus et al. (1992) designed an exercise intervention for volunteers recruited from a community. The character of the intervention was matched to the initial stage of change of the volunteers. On follow-up there was evidence of a significant increase in involvement in exercise commensurate with the initial stage. Admittedly, this study was not a controlled trial. In a subsequent randomized controlled trial, however, they found further supportive evidence. At three months follow-up the participants in the stage-matched group showed stage progression (i.e. greater interest or involvement in exercise) while those in the standard group showed stage stability or regression.

A review of randomized controlled trials of physical activity promotion in general populations provided evidence for the effectiveness of various intervention strategies. Those trials that were most effective have the following common features:

- home-based programmes;
- unsupervised, informal exercise;
- frequent professional contact;
- walking as the promoted exercise;
- moderate intensity exercise.

The character of the interaction between the professional and client might be more important than the actual behavioural technique.

Interventions aimed at high-risk groups

Alternatives to the large-scale interventions aimed at the general population are those that focus on high-risk groups. There is increasing interest in the value of exercise for elderly people or those who suffer from particular health problems. The initial interventions were often opportunistic but more recent attempts have been carefully designed to identify the characteristics of effective programmes.

Several psychological characteristics have been found to be associated with involvement of particular groups of patients in exercise programmes. Dishman and Gettman (1980) found that self-motivation was associated with participation. Wilhelmsen et al. (1975) found that social support increased involvement. Other studies which have investigated the role of health beliefs and attitudes have found inconsistent results. For example, there was little difference between exercise adopters and non-adopters in their responses to questions from the Health Belief Model.

A retrospective study that assessed the value of the Health Belief Model for explaining participation in a coronary heart disease exercise programme found that while general health motivation and perceived severity of CHD positively predicted attendance, the perceived benefits of exercise did not.

Clarke and Eves (1997) found partial support for the value of the transtheoretical model to explain the willingness of a sample of sedentary adults to participate in an exercise programme prescribed by their family doctor. They classified the participants into the pre-contemplation, contemplation and preparation stages reflecting the fact that at this stage they had not begun the programme. The cons of participation in the exercise programme decreased across the stages as predicted although there was little change in the pros. The barriers to participation identified were lack of support, lack of facilities, dislike of exercise and lack of time. The importance of dislike of exercise declined across the stages while the importance of lack of facilities increased. The finding that lack of time was used as frequently by those in the pre-contemplation as those in the preparation stage was interpreted as evidence that it is more a justification for lack of participation rather than a convincing reason.

Adherence to exercise programmes

A common problem with exercise programmes is that while many people sign up for such programmes it has been estimated that 50% or more drop out after a short period of participation (Dishman, 1986). Table 10.5 provides a summary of four behavioural strategies associated with increased adherence. However, this is a very schematic outline and there is a need for further research into the dynamic nature of the exercise behaviour change process (Robinson and Rogers, 1994).

Further, these strategies are largely focused at the individual level. They ignore the social context and the social meaning of exercise and physical activity. Social approaches attempt to widen the traditional individual change approach to include: 'changes in social networks and structures, organizational norms, regulatory policies, and the physical environment as a means of enhancing long-term maintenance of the target behavior' (King, 1994: 1406).

Table 10.5   *Behavioural strategies to improve adherence to exercise programmes (Robinson and Rogers, 1994)*

- *Stimulus control*: providing cues that remind people of the programme.
- *Consequent control*: providing rewards and punishments for participation.
- *Cognitive behaviour modification*: increasing people's belief that they have control over the design and conduct of the programme.
- *Behavioural treatment packages*: combining behavioural and cognitive strategies.

Environmental and policy-based strategies

An increasing awareness of the limited return on health education campaigns designed to promote physical activity has encouraged researchers and policymakers to explore more fully the social and physical context within which people live and work. Evidence from an increasing number of studies focusing more on intervening at this level has reported success.

In public buildings a number of strategies have been employed to promote greater use of stairs. It has been found that simply displaying posters near stairwells promotes greater usage. A variant of this is the positioning of health promotion messages on the actual stair rises. A study of a shopping centre in England found that such an initiative more than doubled stair usage.

Other environmental strategies to promote physical activity include restricting motor vehicle traffic in certain areas so as to promote walking and cycling; including side-walks/footpaths and cycle-ways in new housing developments; and reducing traffic speed so as to increase pedestrians' and cyclists' safety (Salmon et al., 2000). Although these measures have been introduced at a community level, attempts to introduce them more widely will involve considerable political effort. In addition, provision of facilities is insufficient without the opportunity or incentive to make use of them.

For example, walking is the most common physical activity but the physical and social organization of modern cities discourages it. For example, a study in Chicago found that residents of suburbs are less likely to walk while those who had high levels of fear about their neighbourhoods are also less likely to walk.

This brings us to the move to promote healthy public policy. Public policy can promote greater exercise participation through individual, community and environmental measures. A survey of European countries found that residents of those countries who perceived that public policy was promoting physical activity were more likely to report participating in such activity (Von Lengerke et al., 2004).

However, these moves to promote exercise through healthy public policy must be distinguished from the further promotion of the ideology of individualistic self-control (Murray et al., 2003). While middle-class adults may be attracted to this message, many people from working-class and more deprived backgrounds may treat it with deserved cynicism (Crossley, 2003). Healthy public policy must connect with the material circumstances of people's everyday lives if it is to achieve an echo (Murray and Campbell, 2003). Otherwise, it invites the same 'victim-blaming' criticism as traditional health education.

Future Research

1 Despite the evidence linking exercise with various indicators of health there is still a need to explore the specific impact of exercise interventions on different populations.
2 There is evidence of a changing involvement of children and youth in physical activity. Research should consider the character of these changes.

3 Physical activity has different meanings for different sub-groups of the population. Research is needed to develop our understanding of these different meanings.
4 Involvement in sporting and physical activity is closely linked to people's social and economic circumstances and the socio-cultural context. There is scope for further research on the social embeddedness of exercise.
5 Programmes to promote greater participation in physical exercise are often based upon limited understanding of the different meanings of exercise. Participatory action research offers an opportunity to increase our understanding of different groups' perceptions of physical activity programmes.

Summary

1 Interest in exercise has waxed and waned over the years. The past generation has witnessed increasing interest in the health benefits of exercise.
2 Results of several comprehensive surveys indicate that moderate degrees of physical activity have both physical and psychological benefits.
3 There is some evidence to suggest that excessive exercise can have negative health effects.
4 A large proportion of the populations of western societies are sedentary.
5 The degree of participation declines during adolescence, especially among girls.
6 In adulthood, participation is lesser among females, those from poorer social positions and those from ethnic minorities.
7 Various psychological factors have been found to be associated with participation in both childhood and adulthood.
8 The meaning of exercise is linked to the varying social contexts.
9 Exercise participation programmes can be either population based or aimed at high risk groups. The main problem with both forms of programme is adherence that is generally low.

Key Terms

KT

extrinsic motives

Health Belief Model (HBM)

intrinsic motives

self-determination

social cognition models

Part Three

ILLNESS EXPERIENCE AND HEALTH CARE

Part 3 provides an account of psychological theory and research on the principal topics concerning illness and health care. Whenever possible we provide recommendations for improving health care and patient experience.

Chapter 11 explores illness beliefs and explanations. The traditional biomedical approach to illness defines it in terms of physical symptoms and underlying physical pathology. Health is defined as the absence of such symptoms and pathology. However, as historians of medicine have emphasized, this is not the only approach. Psychologists have used a variety of theoretical perspectives to investigate popular beliefs about illness. This chapter summarizes some of this research. In particular, it contrasts the research that has used a cognitive perspective with that using a social and experiential perspective.

Chapter 12 examines illness and personality. Beginning with the history of the distinction between physical and psychological disorders, it considers various ways in which Freudian theories became applied to organic illness by the psychosomatic schools of psychoanalysis. An analysis of the problems involved in investigating and explaining links between personality and physical illness is followed by an assessment of contemporary research with particular reference to coronary heart disease and cancer.

Chapter 13 discusses theoretical models of stress and coping and research on stress as a cause of physical illness. It begins with a critical discussion of the stress concept and gives an account of stimulus, response and interactional models of stress and coping. Consideration is given to how stress affects the immune system and to the ways in which people react to trauma and stress. A discussion of the methodological problems involved in research on stress and illness is followed by an examination of the evidence linking stress to cardiovascular disease, cancer and infectious diseases.

Chapter 14 focuses on interpersonal health communication. Three approaches to the study of doctor–patient communication are described: the 'deviant patient' perspective, the 'authoritarian doctor' perspective, and the 'interactive dyad' perspective. Three widely used research tools are examined, illustrated and critically evaluated: interaction analysis systems, questionnaires and qualitative textual analysis. Recent trends in the study of health communication are introduced. They are gender and culture, 'compliance', the impact of computer technologies, non-verbal communication, the role of communication in coping with illness, and counselling.

Chapter 15 explores treatment adherence and patient empowerment. Adherence and compliance are terms used to describe the extent to which patients adhere or comply with recommended treatment regimens, one of the most widely researched forms of health-related behaviour. The connotations of the term 'compliance' imply an authoritarian stance on the part of the physician or other health professionals that are challenged by recent ideas about the nature of effective healthcare. It discusses the patient-centred formulation of health care that highlights the benefits of shared decision-making and patient empowerment.

Chapter 16 examines the prevention and control of pain, the nature of pain and the distinction between acute and chronic pain. The chapter focuses on chronic pain. The major theories, including direct line of transmission theories and multidimensional gate-control theory are discussed. A range of psychosocial factors implicated in the mediation of the pain experience is considered. Pain assessment methods are described. The issue of pain management using psychological and other techniques is discussed.

Chapter 17 focuses on cancer and chronic diseases. Three life-threatening and disabling diseases are discussed: cancer, coronary heart disease and HIV/AIDS. In each case we consider five issues: 'What is…?'; 'Interventions for…'; 'Living with…'; 'Adaptation to…' and 'Caring for someone with…'. The contribution of psychosocial interventions for patients suffering from these conditions has been evaluated in systematic reviews. Review of this evidence suggests that psychosocial interventions have not yet demonstrated their full potential. The quality of evaluation research with psychosocial interventions has generally been rather poor and the findings inconclusive. Further research to consolidate psychological knowledge and understanding of treatment and health care for these conditions is recommended.

11

Illness Beliefs and Explanations

The description of health beliefs obtained from accounts shows that these do not constitute a logically tight system, but often operate in an apparently inconsistent fashion.
(Alan Radley, 1994: 60)

Outline

The traditional biomedical approach to illness defines it in terms of physical symptoms and underlying physical pathology. Health is defined as the absence of such symptoms and pathology. However, as historians of medicine have emphasized, this is not the only approach. Psychologists have used a variety of theoretical perspectives to investigate popular beliefs about illness. This chapter summarizes some of this research. In particular, it contrasts the research that has used a cognitive perspective with that which has used a more social and experiential perspective.

Cognitive Approaches

Illness perceptions

The most developed cognitive model of illness was initially proposed by Howard Leventhal and his colleagues (Leventhal et al., 1989). This was derived from their work on the impact of fear communication. They found that, irrespective of the level of fear, the message was effective if it produced a plan of action. This led them to infer that the key factor was the way the threat was represented or understood. They developed a **dual processing model** to accommodate the cognitive and emotional representations of the threat (Figure 11.1), an influential model that has undergone some elaboration by Leventhal (1999).

KT

This model led the Leventhal group to explore how lay people represented specific threats such as illness. They conducted open-ended interviews with a sample of patients suffering from various diseases. From this information they proposed a **self-regulatory model** of illness that suggested that lay people's thoughts on illness could be organized along four dimensions. Lau and Hartman (1983) suggested that since

KT

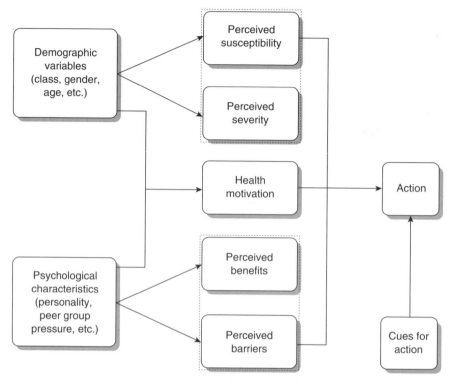

Figure 11.1   A self-regulatory model for coping with illness (Leventhal, 1999)

these dimensions were derived from a sample of patients with an acute, time-limited illness experience it was necessary to introduce a fifth dimension to cover those illnesses which were resistant to treatment (Table 11.1).

The Illness Perception Questionnaire (IPQ) was developed by Weinman et al. (1996) to measure the original five illness dimensions identified by Leventhal and Lau. This measure was used in a longitudinal study to investigate the relationship between illness representations and work behaviour after myocardial infarction (Petrie et al., 1996). Subsequent attendance at a rehabilitation course was significantly predicted by a stronger belief during admission that the illness could be cured. Return to work was predicted by perception that the illness would last a short time and have less serious consequences. In conclusion, they noted that these popular illness beliefs 'seem to be largely formed by information before becoming ill [and] are quite consistent over time'.

These findings have contributed to a steady growth of research on illness representations, in particular using versions of the IPQ (Weinman and Petrie, 1997). An example is the recent study of illness representations of diabetics (Lawson et al., 2004). It was found that patients who did not attend a diabetes clinic had more negative representations than those who did seek specialist care. The non-attenders had less perceived control, less belief in the effectiveness of treatment, perceived more serious consequences and had a more pessimistic timeline. Together, these findings would suggest that illness representations predict diabetic care-seeking practices.

Table 11.1   *Dimensions of illness perceptions (Leventhal et al., 1980; Lau and Hartman, 1983)*

- *Identity*: the signs, symptoms and the illness label.
- *Consequence*: the perceived physical, social and economic consequences of the disease and the felt emotional consequences.
- *Causes*: the perceived causes of the disease.
- *Timeline*: the perceived time frame for the development and duration of the illness threat.
- *Cure/Control*: the extent to which the illness is responsive to treatment.

Subsequently, a series of studies have used the IPQ with success to explore the character of a variety of illnesses and the relationship between illness perceptions and coping (e.g. Whitmarsh et al., 2003). Some of the dimensions were found to be inter-related. For example, among individuals with chronic fatigue syndrome (CFS), those with a strong belief in the number and seriousness of the symptoms (illness identity) also have a strong belief in serious consequences and a lengthy timeline. Similarly, in a study comparing illness perceptions of patients with Addison's Disease with those with CFS, it was found that those who report more symptoms and who judge their disease as more severe also report more serious consequences, find it difficult to adapt to their illness and believe less in possibilities for control or cure.

There have been few studies of cultural differences in illness representations. An exception is a recent study of lay representations of vertiligo, a skin disorder leading to loss of skin pigmentation (Papadopoulos et al., 2002). This study compared the illness representations of Indian/Pakistanis, Afro-Caribbeans, and Causasians with this disease who were resident in the UK. It was found that the Indian/Pakistanis identified many more negative consequences of the disease. This was not simply due to the darker colour of their skin since a similar finding was not obtained with Afro-Caribbeans. It was suggested that a much more culture-bound explanation was needed.

A recent revision of this questionnaire (Revised Illness Perception Questionnaire, IPQ-R) introduced a measure of illness coherence and of emotional representations of illness (Moss-Morris et al., 2002). The former considers how the illness 'makes sense' as a whole to the patient. The emotional representations had been ignored in the previous model although they were explicit in the original formulation of the self-regulation model of illness (Leventhal, 1999).

Illness identity and disease prototypes

The illness identity includes its label, symptoms and seriousness. As shown in the inclusion of a measure of illness coherence in the development of the IPQ-R (Moss-Morris et al., 2002), a central feature is the overall impression of the particular health problem. An important feature of medical investigation of disease is the drawing together of symptoms that occur together and the identification of symptom clusters. There is evidence to suggest that the lay person follows a similar strategy.

It has been suggested that lay people bring meaning to physical symptoms by relating them to *disease prototypes*. They are able to provide a disease label for sets of physical symptoms and vice versa. During socialization we learn which symptoms are associated together such that when we are giving minimum symptomatic details of a particular illness, we can confidently predict other symptoms.

Bishop (1987) identified certain dimensions that lay people use to organize physical symptoms. Using multidimensional scaling he identified four dimensions which he termed contagiousness, location in body, psychological cause, and degree of activity disruption. He subsequently refined these to two basic dimensions: seriousness and contagiousness. He suggested that lay people use these two basic dimensions to organize their impressions of different symptoms associated with various diseases. However, these models assume that symptoms are clearly identified and recognized as signs of illness. This is not always the case. Rather, some illnesses have few symptoms while some individuals do not perceive a cluster of symptoms as illness. An example is the case of gynecological cancers that, at least in the early stages, have few obvious symptoms.

In a study of women who had received treatment for early stage gynecological cancer it was found that the women recall the symptoms as vague and non-threatening. Indeed, there was a deliberate attempt to normalize the symptoms by considering them signs of growing old rather than of a disease. According to the **symmetry rule** (Diefenbach and Leventhal, 1996), we search for a label if we experience bodily changes and conversely we expect to suffer symptoms when we feel ill. Since the initial symptoms were perceived as vague or even normal, there was no search for a disease label. Since they had been defined as having cancer these women now felt vulnerable and particularly sensitive to any bodily change. Although they had been treated successfully, their previous experience of having a disease that had few obvious symptoms meant that they retained a lingering suspicion that they might still have the disease.

Causes of disease

According to the basic tenets of attribution theory, people attempt to provide a causal explanation for events in their world particularly if those events are unexpected and have personal relevance (Heider, 1958). Thus it is not surprising that people will generally seek a causal explanation for an illness, particularly one that is serious.

Weiner et al. (1972) suggested that we could classify causal attributions along three dimensions:

1 *Locus*: the extent to which the cause is localized inside or outside the person.
2 *Controllability*: the extent to which the person has control over the cause.
3 *Stability*: the extent to which the cause is stable or changeable.

Various researchers have used these dimensions to explore illness cognitions with greater or lesser success.

Considering the character of the causal explanations of various physical symptoms, the initial classification of the suggested causes reveal 14 categories. A revised version of these was then rated by another sample of students. Multidimensional scaling analysis of the scores suggests three dimensions: non-physical–physical, stable–unstable, and controllable–uncontrollable. The latter two labels are comparable to two of the original attributional dimensions. However, the physical–non-physical dimension has not been previously identified. Physical causes included 'physical activity' and 'physical constitution' while non-physical causes included personality, mood and stress.

Murray and McMillan (1993a) asked a sample of over 700 adults to rate the relative importance of 24 potential causes of cancer. Factor analysis of their ratings revealed five factors that were labelled:

- Stress (which contained items referring to stress, worry, loneliness, unemployment).
- Environment (including such items as air pollution, work conditions, asbestos, nuclear radiation, a knock or hurt, X-rays and promiscuity).
- Health-related (such factors as childbirth, antibiotics, breast-feeding, virus or infection).
- Behaviour (fatty foods, smoking, drinking).

Heredity and chance did not load heavily on any of these factors. Although some of these factors could be redefined along the classic attributional dimensions, others (e.g. health-related) were more specific and would suggest that people combine general and specific casual explanations.

In the development of their revised illness perception questionnaire (IPQ-R) Moss-Morris et al. (2002) identified four causal dimensions: psychological attributions, risk factors, immunity, and accident or chance. They stressed that these four factors should not be considered universal or prescriptive but that 'researchers should feel free to modify the causal [and identity] scales in order to suit particular illnesses, cultural settings or populations' (2002: 13).

One feature of these causal explanations is their broad acceptance of a medical or largely rational model of illness. Studies of non-western populations are more likely to identify religious or supernatural factors as causes of disease. For example, Furnham and Baguma (1999) in a cross-cultural study of illness attributions found that residents of Uganda more frequently referred to supernatural causes.

Research would indicate that not only there are differences in the character of causal attributions for particular illness, but there are also differences depending upon who is making the attribution. This derives from the basic attribution research that indicate the existence of an actor-observer difference. This suggests that actors have a tendency to attribute the cause of their own action to situational causes whereas observers attribute them to dispositional causes. A systematic review provided some support for this with illness attributions with the suggestion that patients are more likely to attribute the cause of illness to situational factors (e.g. stress and luck) while observers tend to attribute it to dispositional factors (e.g. overweight). However, some recent research has suggested that this distinction may not be so clear-cut but it depends upon the method of research and whether the participants were asked to attribute causes to particular or general cases of illness (French et al., 2004).

Causal attributions are not things in themselves but are the basis of plans for action. How the person explains an event partly determines how that person subsequently copes with that situation. An important factor is the perceived controllability of the cause. Interviews from a sample of men who had been hospitalized for a heart attack showed that the most common causes for the heart attack are stress and personal behaviour. Attributing the cause to stress (external, uncontrollable) is predictive of greater morbidity over the following eight years. Similar findings were obtained in a study of angina patients. In patients suffering from myocardial infarction, those who attribute the cause to lifestyle factors are more likely to make lifestyle changes subsequently. In their IPQ-R study Moss-Morris et al. (2002) found that the causal attributional dimensions were generally unrelated to illness outcome. However, they combined uncontrollable causes (e.g. heredity and medical care) with controllable causes (e.g. smoking and diet). Perceived personal control was found to be an important predictor of illness adjustment.

Finally, causal attributions do not exist in themselves but can be considered part of a larger narrative account of illness. While this is discussed further below it is sufficient to give an example of this integration here. A study of older widowed women's accounts of their husband's death found that the women gave a variety of causal attributions (Bennett, 2004). These were classified as health-related and medical, lifestyle, stress and magical. However, while interesting in themselves, the causal attributions were also part of a larger narrative account of their husband's death. The creation of these narratives was part of the process of making sense of the death.

Treatment of disease

What are the implications of the illness for the person? In their model Leventhal et al. (1989) considered not only the physical consequences but also the psychological and social. It would seem that the perceived consequences of a disease actually predicts the actual consequences. Weinman and Petrie (1997) found that the illness dimension that best predicted return to work among a sample of patients with heart attack was the perceived consequences of the illness. Moss-Morris et al. (1996) found a similar finding with patients suffering from chronic fatigue syndrome.

One consequence that is partly ignored is the character of the treatment. For many lay people the treatment is the illness and vice versa. For example, when lay people were asked to define cancer, one of the most important definitions was the character of its treatment.

An extension of the research into illness representations concerns medication representations. This research is discussed further in Chapter 15. It is sufficient here to note that medication representations of most patients indicate that they accept their necessity. However, for some patients this belief is tempered by concerns about the harm potential of certain medications and apprehension about their overuse by some physicians. These concerns depend upon a wide variety of factors including the background of the patient, the type of medication prescribed, and the relationship with the physician. But medication is only one form of treatment and there is a need for greater research into lay beliefs about different forms of treatment.

Illness cognitions among children

Several researchers have explored the development of illness concepts among children from the cognitive perspective. Bibace and Walsh (1980) interviewed children of different ages about their concepts of illness. They then coded the children's replies into Piaget's (1930) stages of cognitive development. Children between the ages of 2 and 6 years provided more pre-logical explanations. At this age the most common explanation for illness was contagion. People became ill because they were close to certain contagious objects or persons. Between 7 and 10 years children offer more concrete-logical explanations. At this age the children explain illness in terms of internalization and contamination. The person is required to come into physical contact with the source of the illness and possibly to ingest it. Finally, 11-year-olds' explanations were more formal-logical. The children offer a more physiological explanation referring to internal physiological processes. It was also suggested that young children explain illness in terms of 'immanent justice' – a form of punishment for a transgression.

Several commentators have questioned the methodological adequacy of these and comparable studies. Siegal et al. (1990) found that young children were reluctant to use contagion to explain toothache but correctly used it to explain getting a cold. They suggested that in previous work 'rather than lacking knowledge of the causes of illness, [the children] may simply have misunderstood the procedural requirements of the interview. They also found no evidence that illness is described in terms of immanent justice. They suggested that in previous research the children may have attempted to comply with the suggestion of an adult interviewer that adults may be so powerful that children who are naughty will be inevitably punished' (1990: 160).

The apparent age differences in children's illness beliefs may be more a function of access to knowledge than to cognitive development. Bird and Podmore (1990) interviewed children about health and illness and found that their replies were not detailed enough to allow reliable coding into Piagetian stage categories. They found little support for the claim that younger children prefer external contamination and that older children are more aware of internal processes. Older children were found to mention a broader range of knowledge sources such as parents, television and school.

An extension of this concern was the idea that children develop content-specific (rather than domain general) systems of knowledge that they use to make predictions using naïve theories about such phenomena as specific diseases. According to this 'theory' approach children are portrayed as theorists who interpret the world using their particular cognitive theories. There is evidence that children develop biological theories of illness at a relatively early age, although this depends upon their exposure to biological knowledge. In a study of the impact of a biology educational intervention, it was found that there is a significant increase in 4-year-old children's use of biological explanations for specific diseases.

Another approach to children's conceptions of illness considers its location within their everyday life experiences. An example of this is the work of Jutras and her colleagues. They conducted a study of 5–12-year-old children and found that they defined health along three everyday dimensions: functionality (e.g. playing sports), mental health (e.g. sense of enjoyment of life), and adherence to a healthy lifestyle. Conversely, illness was defined in terms of restrictions. In a study of conceptions of diabetes it was found that children and their mothers defined it especially in terms of repercussions affecting daily life (Jutras et al., 2003).

Collecting information about illness cognitions

One problem with the social cognitive approach to the study of illness beliefs is that it tends to ignore the context within which the beliefs are expressed. Culture-bound, self-presentational processes influence the character of the replies that people give in such studies. However, it is possible to take account of these processes.

Further research has attempted to control for this self-presentation effect. It has been suggested that studies of causal explanations of illness often neglect supernatural causes because people feel embarrassed to admit belief in such causes. When a sample of American college students was asked to generate causes of illness, supernatural causes were freely mentioned by only 4.7% of the sample whereas 66.4% of the sample rated such causes as important when they were provided.

This suggests that illness beliefs are not located in the heads of the individuals but that rather they are joint creations that partly reflect the character of the relationship between the individual and the interviewer. This criticism connects with the criticisms of other cognitive models of health practices (see Chapters 9 and 10) and has led to the development of other more social and experiential approaches.

Social and Experiential Approaches

Illness discourse

A major problem with cognitive approaches to the study of illness perceptions is that it presents them as static and asocial phenomena that exist within the minds of the individual, i.e. it abstracts the perceptions out of the meaning-making context within which they must be generated. An alternative perspective that attempts to present a more dynamic and social approach is that offered by various discursive psychologists. Their focus is on the character of the discourse and the context within which it occurs rather than on the structure of the inferred beliefs. They deliberately consider the immediate and broader social context within which beliefs are articulated. For them the communicative nature of language is the focus of attention rather than inferred underlying beliefs (Potter and Wetherell, 1987).

Two orientations have been identified in contemporary discourse analysis – discursive psychology and Foucauldian discourse analysis (Willig, 2004). The former places emphasis on unpacking the various discursive strategies such as 'footing' and 'disclaiming' and their functions within a particular discursive context. The focus of this approach is on what the discourse is doing. The latter more critical form focuses on the particular discursive resources available within a culture and the implications for those who live there. These resources enable us to construct and live in the world in particular ways. It has been argued that these two orientations should not be seen as distinct approaches but rather complementary (Potter and Wetherell, 1987). Individuals are both producers and the products of discourse. More critical psychologists are wary at the assumed autonomy of the individual actor and the ignorance of issues of politics and power by discursive psychologists.

Middleton (1996) used the discursive psychology approach to explore talk in a parent group for children with chronic renal failure. He argued that this talk is more than 'a display of inner workings of minds' but is 'part of the process of making [their] health care experiences socially intelligible' (1996: 244). Rather than breaking the talk down into elemental beliefs, he attempted to understand it as part of the process of making sense of illness within a social context. Middleton suggests that an important component of such talk is that it contains many contradictory elements and expressions of uncertainty. These elements are not deficiencies but rather are seen as being 'used to establish common understandings concerning what it is to care for chronically ill children' (1996: 257). Further, the talk is more than self-presentation that can be ironed out by careful assessment but rather part of the broader collective process of meaning-making.

Another example of the use of discursive psychology is the study by Radtke and Van Mens-Verhulst (2001) of mothers with asthma. Interviews with a number of these women revealed the dominance of the traditional medical discourse to describe asthma. Further, they identified certain causes of the disease in their everyday lives but distinct from their role as mothers. In discussing an exemplar case the authors note that avoiding any suggestion of a link between her asthma symptoms and mothering allowed the woman to do two things: 'first she positioned herself as a competent mother despite living with asthma' and 'second, it justified her claim that her previous employment situation and problems with her extended family were unjust and harmful and thereby had contributed to her illness'. In interpreting these findings Radtke and Van Mens-Verhulst emphasize that the women are both producers and products of discourse: 'As producers of discourse, the women do not draw upon the cultural resources available to them in some straightforward way, but rather use them strategically to accomplish certain actions' (2001: 381).

This strategic use of discourse in everyday social interaction was developed further by Radley and Billig (1996) in their detailed commentary on the discursive context within which talk about health and illness is generated. In particular they contrast the different positionings of healthy and sick people: 'the healthy have much to say about their illness experience, while the sick are often at pains to show their "normality"' (1996: 225). Since the interviewer is usually a healthy person, the sick person feels strongly 'the need to **legitimate** [their] position'. This emphasizes that the 'accounts are situated in a rhetorical context of potential justification and criticism' (1996: 226). Although this commentary was aimed at qualitative interview research, a similar comment can be made about quantitative questionnaire studies of health and illness beliefs.

Other studies have explored the dominant discourses that we draw upon to construct our sense of particular health issues. Drawing upon the concept of **interpretative repertoire** (Potter and Wetherell, 1987: 139), Benveniste et al. (1999) explored lay theories of anorexia nervosa. Interviews with five men and five women in Australia revealed three dominant themes that were labelled as a socio-cultural discourse, a discourse of the individual and a discourse of femininity. Drawing upon the socio-cultural discourse enabled participants to attribute a source of blame for anorexia nervosa to factors external to the individual. Conversely, the individual discourse located the cause of anorexia within the individual. However, both of these discourses are premised upon a humanist conception of the individual as an autonomous rational being. This separation of socio-cultural factors from individual psychology maintains the idea that anorexia nervosa is a manifestation of psychopathology.

The internalization of dominant discourses of health and illness can be considered part of disciplinary power by which social norms are accepted (Foucault, 1979). Deviation from such norms can cause severe distress to the individual concerned. An example is the case of hirsutism: a medical term used to describe an excess of sexual hair in the female. Western women spend a substantial amount of money to remove such bodily hair. A study of women who had self-perceived hirsutism found that the women had strongly internalized the dominant discourse of female hair and adopted a range of personal strategies to reduce the associated distress (Keegan et al., 2003). 'Through self-surveillance and correction to such norms, and the regulation of bodies through body practices such as depilitatory regimes, women are rendered less socially oriented and more focused on self-modification' (2003: 338). A particular point of interest was the way removal of hair was perceived as 'looking-after', an example of how body regulation is seen as self-care rather than a process of gender control.

A similar study of women with bulimia (Burns and Gavey, 2004) revealed the importance of the dominant discourse of healthy weight. This interacted with the dominant discourse on female body shape. The authors argue that both 'bulimic' and 'healthy' female bodies are underwritten by 'normalizing discourses that derogate female fat and amplitude and that promote engaging in regulatory practices designed to promote a slender body'. They continue that by focusing on healthy weight rather than a broader concept of health, current health promotion campaigns are 'paradoxically implicated in the shaping and production of subjectivities, practices and bodies for some women in ways that are antithetical to an overt health message' (2004: 562).

Overall, these discursive approaches argue that illness discourse is an active and social creation that reflects the attempts of the person or persons to make sense of a problematic situation. The character of the discourse is variable and needs to be considered with reference to the immediate and broader social context within which it is generated.

Illness experience

A criticism of the discursive approaches is that they have lost sight of the subject – the person who is actually discoursing. One attempt to recover the person is the phenomenological approach. Here we will briefly consider two forms of this approach – interpretative phenomenological analysis and hermeneutic phenomenology.

Phenomenology is concerned with exploring the participant's perspective on the world rather than confirming that of the observer/researcher. However, one challenge faced by the researcher is how, as it were, they could get inside the head of the participant. Various strategies were suggested including deliberately clarifying the researcher's own perspective and then 'bracketing' that from further engagement with the participant. An alternative approach is to make the researcher's own conceptions explicit. This approach is known as **interpretative phenomenological analysis (IPA)** (Smith et al., 1999). The focus of this approach is the cognitions or what the research participant thinks or believes about the particular issue: 'Thus, IPA, while recognizing that a person's thoughts are not transparently available from, for example, interview transcripts, engages in the analytic process in order, hopefully, to be able to say something about the thinking' (1999: 219). A series of studies have illustrated the value of this approach for exploring the experience of illness.

A study of the experience of men with lower urinary track infections (LUTS) used the IPA approach (Gannon et al., 2004). Interviews with the men identified four superordinate themes: uncertainty/trying to understand, implications, ways of coping,

KT

and self-evaluation/uncertainty. The researchers constructed these themes after a more thorough thematic analysis of what the men had to say about the experience.

In a comparable study, this time with young people who had developed Type 1 diabetes, two broad superordinate themes were identified: developing a relationship with diabetes and managing threats from diabetes. Under the first theme there were three sub-themes: the shock of diabetes, learning to live with diabetes, and seeking an optimal relationship with diabetes. Under the second broad theme were four sub-themes: intrapersonal threats and self-protective strategies, interpersonal threats, and self-protective strategies. As with the previous study, it is important to consider the character of the study participants. Comparable studies with participants from different backgrounds might produce different findings.

The **hermeneutical phenomenology approach** considers illness as a social performance (Kugelmann, 2004). The term performance is preferred to behaviour since the former has active and reflexive characteristics whereas the latter is passive and unreflexive. The term hermeneutical refers to the focus on what the participant has to say about the phenomena under investigation. Consider the case of pain – in what way is its meaning linked to physicality? An interview study of people with either physical or psychological pain found many similarities but also differences. Both sufferers begin their experience with some sort of wounding that they felt. This alters their existential world leading to some form of disability and isolation. The pains are different to the extent to which there is clear corporeal intrusion and medical consequences. The latter difference is variable since people suffering from psychological pain often seek some form of medical support. From the HP perspective, both types of pain are performances of affliction. These performances are not fixed but depend upon the context of the participants' lives.

Working within a symbolic interactionist framework several researchers have explored the meaning of illness for the sufferer. This framework derives from the work of George Herbert Mead (1934) and emphasizes the importance of social interaction, how meanings are socially constructed and the importance of the self in mediating between subjective experiences and the social and physical world. One of the most influential researchers using this framework has been Kathy Charmaz (1983). She has argued that the central psychological feature of chronic illness is the 'loss of self'. She interviewed people who were severely incapacitated because of chronic illness. These people described their experience whereby 'former self-images crumble away without a simultaneous development of equally valued new ones' (1983: 168). They felt that they were socially isolated, were discredited by others and felt humiliated by being a burden on others. Charmaz described the cascade effect of social isolation leading to further loss of self since they were excluded from the benefits of social interaction.

Some researchers deliberately attempt to connect their analyses of the lived experience of illness with broader social concepts such as gender or ethnicity. An example is the study of men's experiences of prostate cancer (Fergus et al., 2002). In view of the close intertwining of sexual prowess with standards of masculinity in western culture it is not surprising that the treatment for prostate cancer with its physical impact on sexual functioning can be devastating for men. In this study they found that the men adopted a variety of strategies to retain their masculine identity in the face of this experience. These included:

- emphasizing the importance of choosing life over sex;
- perception of sexual dysfunction as disrupting a core aspect of their identity;
- experience of stigmatization as a result of impaired sexual ability;
- perceived pressure to continue to perform sexually;
- efforts to minimize the loss.

Together these findings emphasize that an understanding of the experience of illness requires an understanding of it within its social and cultural context.

Illness narratives

KT

Recently, there has been a growth of interest in the stories that people tell about illness experiences. Narrative psychologists argue that **narrative** construction is an intrinsic part of making sense of the world. The process of creating a narrative enables the person to give meaning to a crisis. Before the narrative there is merely a disjointed sequence of events. In creating the narrative the person selects some pieces of information and ignores others and pieces a story together. Admittedly this process is not conducted in isolation but as part of a wider process of social engagement. As such, many narrative psychologists would locate their work within the broader framework of discursive psychology in the sense that it is concerned with language as a social phenomenon (Murray, 1997a). However, it is distinct in that it does not lose sight of the narrator who constructs the narrative accounts.

According to narrative psychology people generate stories about illness experiences (Murray, 1997a). The construction of these narrative accounts enables the person to grasp its meaning and to begin to exert some control over it. The character of these stories varies depending upon a variety of factors such as previous experience and public repertoires (Murray, 1997b). Some stories may offer the prospect of advancement, while others offer decline. Several psychotherapists have suggested that the aim of therapy is to assist the client in developing a new more personally enhancing story.

Murray (1997b) analysed the written accounts of a sample of women who had breast cancer. He found that the accounts were organized into a similar storyline with a beginning, a middle and an end. The beginning was the period before cancer that was often characterized as a time of innocence. The middle of the story was the diagnosis and the subsequent medical treatment. The end was the period of reassessment of identity and reintegration into society. In closing their story the women frequently emphasized the positive features of having cancer – it had given them an opportunity to reassess their lives. It was also apparent that the women were aware of the therapeutic benefits in telling their stories. They explicitly referred to this process of sense making. Through the process of *emplotment,* the women were able to take control over a crisis event and transform it into a life-enhancing moment.

The increasing visibility of published accounts of the varying experience of illness can be considered an attempt to challenge medical hegemony in the health arena. Such accounts are valued since they provide an opportunity to make women's experiences visible and they also provide an opportunity to hear women's experiences in their own words.

The onset of serious illness has been characterized as a period of *biographical disruption* – for example, the experience of people diagnosed with rheumatoid arthritis (RA). The onset of this disease disrupted plans and hopes for the future. For these people their life-story no longer fits with their everyday experiences and it needs to be recast. This process of reworking the parameters of the self has been termed *narrative reconstruction* by Williams (1984). Again working with people suffering from RA, Williams identified a pattern in the casual reasoning adopted by these individuals. They were attempting to integrate RA into their life plans. According to Williams this process of narrative reconstruction helped the sufferers 'reconstitute and repair ruptures between body, self, and world by linking and interpreting different aspects of biography in order to realign present and past and self and society' (1984: 197).

A study of people with cancer found that their narratives are structured around three major themes: disrupted feelings of fit, renegotiating identity and biographical work. The biographical work centres on the process of integrating the illness events into the larger narrative identity. A challenge faced by the cancer patient is that they feel rejected by their peers because of the social and moral stigma still attached to cancer. In this context they are deprived of the conversations within which they can conduct their biographical work. One place that provides a forum for narrating their changing stories is within support groups. A study of the talk within these groups (Yaskowich and Stam, 2003) found that an important theme was the biographical work. The patients spoke of their lives being changed and their attempts to get their lives back together.

Robinson (1990) invited people with multiple sclerosis (MS) to write about their illness. They provided a range of stories that varied substantially. It is possible to identify a pattern in them. The majority of the narratives could be classified as 'progressive' in that the patients described their disease as providing an opportunity for personal advancement. Others were classified as 'stable' and a minority as 'regressive'.

This preference for a progressive narrative reflects both social and personal processes. In western society the dominant health narrative is that not only can illness be positive but that also the person can exert control over their illness. Adopting a progressive narrative allows the patient to transcend the physical infirmity of MS. DelVecchio et al. (1994) in their study of patients with epilepsy also suggest that in organizing their narrative accounts the patients can 'negotiate right action in the face of uncertainty' (1994: 858).

Frank (1993) suggested that the central point in any crisis narrative is an epiphany when the actor begins to reassess their position in the world. This can occur at any time during the course of an illness but subsequently the sick person sees the illness in a new light. It is at this stage that the illness story turns from a regressive narrative into a progressive narrative. Admittedly not all sick persons encounter such an epiphanous moment. As Frank (1993) stated: 'Insofar as changing your life is a historically defined project, so the general possibility of epiphanies is also socially constructed. To experience an epiphany requires a cultural milieu in which such experiences are at least possibilities, if not routine expectations' (1993: 42).

The temporal character of the illness narrative does not have to be coterminous with the physical character of the illness. For example, Robinson (1990) noted that for some people, the diagnosis of illness meant the end of their lives – their life narrative ended; there was no prospect of progression. As he points out for some people 'a personal story may be ended before a life has physically finished'. For these people the suffering and dislocation of illness provide no prospect of renewal.

In her study of HIV-positive individuals Crossley (1999) identified three temporal orientations in their narrative accounts:

1   *Living with a philosophy of the present*: a common concern was the difficulty of making plans for the future. This was especially the case for those who had been recently diagnosed. The recent developments in treatment offer the prospect of survival but there remains the uncertainty. However, this 'provisional existence' opens up new possibilities for these HIV-infected individuals as they begin to reflect upon life and to reconsider their personal values. This orientation was associated with the more general cultural story of 'conversion/growth' that highlights the growth potential of adversity.
2   *Living in the future*: this orientation was characteristic of the narrative accounts of those who denied the impact of their disease and were determined that it would not threaten their plans. The cultural story connected with this orientation was the 'normalizing' narrative that minimized the impact of the disease on their lives;
3   *Living in the empty present*: this was the orientation of those who had been devastated by the HIV diagnosis and who could not see any future hopes or prospects. The cultural story associated with this orientation was that of loss.

Together these narrative accounts are evidence of the process through which wounded individuals attempt to maintain and to develop some form of narrative continuity in their life-stories.

Three types of illness narratives have been proposed. The first type, illness as narrative, is the process whereby illness is expressed and articulated through narrative. The second type, narrative about illness, is the way physicians and others organize their knowledge about illness. The third type is narrative as illness. This is the process by which a narrative or an insufficient narrative generates an illness. It is this third type that has led to the suggestion that therapy can be construed as narrative reconstruction – the development of a more healthy story.

An important aspect of the illness narrative is that it integrates and situates much of the information that is considered in a rather isolated and fragmented manner by the cognitive psychologists. Blaxter (1993) makes a similar point in her description of lay people's descriptions of illness: 'a ... notable feature of the accounts was the strain to connect, to present a health history as a chain of cause and effect, with each new problem arising from previous ones' (1993: 137). Further, one of the defining characteristics of narratives is that they can accommodate inconsistencies. Similarly, Blaxter (1993) notes that the lay people in her study 'were perfectly capable of holding in equilibrium ideas which might seem opposed: the ultimate cause, in the story of the deprived past, of their current ill-health, but at the same time their own responsibility for "who they were"; the inevitability of ill-health, given their biographies, but at the same time guilt if they were forced to "give in" to illness' (1993: 141).

A further feature of narratives is that they serve to orient the individual towards the illness and the social world. Narratives can be considered as conveying an argument. As with the discursive psychologists, narrative psychologists emphasize the importance of the social context within which the story is being told (Murray, 1997b). The ill person can tell a different story to the doctor, to her peers and to the researcher – it depends on what message she is trying to convey. The story-telling can be characterized as a social performance in which the narrator is asserting a certain identity. The illness narratives require a listener and so are, to an extent, shaped by the listener. They are joint productions. Thus the very narrative accounts provided in the research interview context are partly dependent upon that context and may not reflect the everyday experience of illness (cf. Lawton, 2003)

Finally, narratives can move from the level of the personal to that of the societal or political and vice versa. Farmer (1994) noted how stories are involved in the creation of **social representations**. Specifically, he noted in his study of social representations of AIDS in Haiti that as specific stories began to circulate about cases of people with AIDS, social representations about the disease developed. Further, public stories about illness that are circulated through the media impinge on the individual who in turn interprets and experiences illness through them. Public distribution of written autobiographies is also contributing to a shared illness narrative. The readers of these autobiographies learn a language for describing their illness.

KT

Social representations of health and illness

Illness beliefs do not simply exist within the heads of individuals but emerge and change in everyday social interaction. To understand their nature requires an understanding of these broader societal belief systems. Social representation theory is concerned with both the content of these broader belief systems and how they operate to shape our interpretation of the world. 'They do not represent simply "opinions about", "images of" or "attitudes towards", but "theories" or "branches of knowledge" in their own right, for the discovery and organization of reality' (Moscovici, 1973: xiv).

Several studies have used social representation theory to explore popular beliefs about health and illness. The most influential has been the classic study by Claudine Herzlich (1973). From her interviews with a sample of French adults Herzlich concluded that a central concept in the popular definitions of health and illness is activity. For most lay people to be active means to be healthy while to be inactive means to be ill. Herzlich distinguished between three lay reactions to illness:

1   *Illness as destructive*: the experience of those actively involved in society.
2   *Illness as liberator*: the experience of those with excessive social obligations.
3   *Illness as an occupation*: the experience of those who accept illness and feel they must contribute to its alleviation.

People are aware of these different reactions and not only adopt one or another of these strategies depending upon time and circumstance, but also characterize other individuals as belonging to a particular category.

An important characteristic of social representations is that they are not passive characteristics but part of the dialectic process of engagement between the individual and the social world. Moscovici (1984) refers to two particular processes, **anchoring** and **objectification**, which organize social representations. The first is the process whereby unfamiliar concepts are given meaning by connecting them with more familiar concepts,

KT

whereas the second is the process whereby a more abstract concept acquires meaning through association with more everyday phenomena.

The original formulation of SR theory emphasized the important role of science in shaping everyday common sense (Moscovici, 1984). More recent formulations have indicated a much more dynamic interaction between science and common sense. In western society, biomedicine is extremely important in shaping our understandings of health and illness. As Herzlich and Pierret stress: 'in our society the discourse of medicine about illness is so loud that it tends to drone out all others' (1987: xi). The media plays a very important role in acting as a conduit of scientific medical ideas to the general public. As such, SR researchers are interested in both what lay people have to say about illness but also in how the media reports these ideas. The media helps to transform scientific thinking into more everyday terms. In doing so they transform illness from something that is impersonal into something that is personal and is infused with particular cultural norms and values. Of course, since scientists are also lay people their language can also reflect these values.

Several researchers have used these concepts to explore popular views of particular illnesses. Joffe (1996) conducted detailed interviews about AIDS with a sample of young adults from London and from South Africa. She also conducted a content analysis of media campaigns. She notes that historically mass incurable illnesses have been anchored to the 'other'. In the case of AIDS this process is shown in the anchoring of that disease in the supposed aberrant behaviour of others. This process serves a protective function by distancing the person from the risk of contracting the disease. However, a certain amount of 'leakage' has occurred as it became apparent that AIDS could be spread via the blood supply and among heterosexuals. The process of objectification transforms an abstract concept into an image. Joffe (1996) noted that the media images of tombstones and coffins concretized the fear associated with AIDS.

The potential for modifying social representations of disease is limited since they serve the function of preserving the status quo in a culture (Joffe, 1996). They not only make the social world remain familiar and manageable but also maintain the dominance of certain ideas. Admittedly, certain organized groups within society can subvert these dominant ideas. The gay movement in Britain contributed to a reassessment of the dominant image of AIDS as belonging to a supposedly deviant minority group that in terms of religious beliefs were themselves to blame for contracting the disease. Instead, it was re-characterized as a disease that could affect heterosexual as well as gay individuals. SR theory is not just concerned with language but also with non-linguistic representations of phenomena such as illness. Joffe (2003) links this broader concern with the use of images and symbols to understand health and illness. For example, the ribbons used to convey support for particular diseases or the various metaphors that are associated with illness. The classic analyses by Sontag (1988) of the metaphors used to describe cancer and AIDS illustrate how almost impossible it is to talk and think about illness without reference to certain metaphors.

Forming social representations helps to define a group and also to promote in-group solidarity and to defend group members from out-group threats. Consider the case of the Ebola virus that is deadly if contracted. Interviews conducted in Britain about this virus found that most lay people portrayed it as an African disease and that they are very unlikely to contract it. As one woman said: 'It just seemed like one of those mythical diseases, sort of thing, science fiction like thing, that happens in places like Africa and underdeveloped countries and doesn't come here' (Joffe and Haarhoff, 2002: 965). By clearly characterizing the disease in fantastical terms the lay public is symbolically protecting itself from this outside threat.

In a comparable study of representations of AIDS in Zambia (Joffe and Bettega, 2004) it was found young residents distanced themselves from the risk of the disease by representing it as originating in western society and in deviant sexual and scientific practices. These findings highlighted the challenge of encouraging young people to take personal action to protect themselves against AIDS. Health campaigns designed to curtail the spread of AIDS must begin to challenge these social representations.

Integration

One way of integrating these more social approaches to the study of illness beliefs is by considering the levels of psychological analysis proposed by Doise (1986). Doise suggested that a reason for the confusion between different social psychologists was that they operated at different levels of analysis. He suggested that we should distinguish between research which was conducted at the *intrapsychic* level of analysis from that which is conducted at the *interpersonal, group* and *societal* levels.

The value of these different levels for organizing research on representations of illness has been considered. At the intrapsychic level are the descriptions of the phenomenological meanings and to a lesser extent the narrative accounts of the lived experience of illness. At the interpersonal and positional levels are the discursive and narrative accounts while at the societal level are the social representations. The challenge is to explore the connection across these levels.

An example of the integration of the different levels was the study by Crossley (1999) who noted the connection between personal and cultural stories. Similarly Murray (2003) explored the connection between narrative and social representation theory. Detailed analysis of the threefold typology of illness representations reveals their narrative structure. Conversely, narratives can also be explored at different levels of analysis (Murray, 2000). The challenge is to see the social and political in the personal accounts of illness and to explore the implications of this for strategies to improve health (Campbell, 2004).

Future Research

1   Illness beliefs evolve over time and place. There is a need for a greater understanding of the evolution of health beliefs.
2   Illness beliefs are not fixed but constantly changing. Health psychologists need to be involved in mapping these changes within specific sub-cultures.
3   Theoretically, health psychologists need to explore the conceptual connections between illness and health discourse.
4   The interconnectedness of illness discourse and bodily processes is still poorly understood. There is a need for a concerted programme of theoretical work in this area.

Summary

1   Psychologists have used a variety of theoretical perspectives to investigate popular beliefs about illness. Two major approaches have been a cognitive perspective which analyses the way individuals think about health and illness as processes and a social perspective, which includes discursive, narrative and social representation approaches.

2   Cognitive approaches have consisted of asking patients to rate aspects of illness experience along scales and then to factor analyse the scale ratings to develop illness dimensions such as 'identity', 'causes', 'timeline', 'consequences' and 'cure'.

3   The power of the cognitive approach is that causal attributions can be assumed to be the basis of plans for action. How the person explains an event partly determines how that person subsequently copes with that situation. This has many implications for the communication and delivery of health care.

4   However, illness beliefs are not located in the heads of individuals as stable, fixed entities, but rather they are joint creations partly reflecting the character of the relationship *between* the individual and the interviewer and the broader context within which they develop.

5   An alternative perspective attempts to present a more dynamic and social approach to representations of illness and health.

6   Discourse analysis focuses on the character of the illness discourse and the context within which it occurs rather than on the structure of inferred beliefs. Discourse theorists consider the immediate and broader social context within which beliefs are articulated. For them the communicative nature of language is the focus of attention rather than inferred underlying beliefs.

7   Phenomenologists are concerned with the lived experience of illness. These experiences are accessed through interpretation of the discursive accounts of the sick person.

8   The narrative approach analyses stories about the illness experience. The construction of narrative accounts enables the person to grasp its meaning and to begin to exert some control over it.

9   Social representation theory is concerned with exploring the broader societal beliefs about health and illness.

KT   # Key Terms

anchoring

dual processing model

hermeneutic phenomenological approach

interpretative phenomenological analysis (IPA)

interpretative repertoire

(to) legitimate attributions

narrative

objectification discourse

self-regulating model

social representations

symmetry rule

12

Illness and Personality

Ills of the body may be cured by physical remedies or by the power of the spirit acting through the soul. (Paracelsus)

Outline

This chapter examines the influence of individual differences in personality and other psychological characteristics on illness. Beginning with the history of the distinction between physical and psychological disorders, it goes on to consider Freud's work on hysteria and the various ways in which his theories became applied to organic illness by the psychosomatic schools of psychoanalysis. An analysis of the problems involved in investigating and explaining links between personality and physical illness is followed by an assessment of contemporary research with particular reference to coronary heart disease and cancer.

Psychological and Physical Disorders

Let us begin by making a rough and ready distinction between psychological disorders, such as anxiety and depression, and physical disorders, such as infectious diseases and cancer. A straightforward and natural way of understanding their causation is to propose that psychological disorders are best explained by psychological causes, such as stress, traumatic experiences, childhood problems and the like, while physical disorders are attributable to physical causes, such as viruses, bacteria and carcinogenic agents. Following on from this it seems natural that psychological disorders should be treated by psychological means, such as psychotherapy and behaviour therapy, while physical disorders are best treated medically.

Nowadays everybody knows that this is an oversimplification. Psychological disorders ranging from serious mental illness to relatively mild cases of depression are commonly attributed to biochemical imbalances, often thought to be genetic. Some of these views are supported by DNA research and there is an increasing vogue for drug treatments in preference to psychotherapy. On the other hand, it also remains fashionable to believe that people with certain kinds of personality may be particularly susceptible to heart disease or cancer and that stress is a cause of much physical illness. Holistic treatments and complementary therapies for physical diseases frequently have a large psychological component including stress management programmes, relaxation, breathing exercises and meditation. It is often claimed by proponents of such treatments that they are capable of correcting 'psychic' or 'energy' imbalances that have triggered the symptoms in the first place.

Historically the most influential doctrine has been the Hippocratic one which presupposes that there is a physical basis for all disorders, whether physical or psychological, and which dates back to the fifth century BCE. As we saw in Chapters 1 and 4, according to Galen, a key figure in the Hippocratic tradition, psychological and physical disorders are both attributable to an imbalance of the four bodily humours, blood, phlegm, black bile and yellow bile. Little scope was left for psychological causation and this theory only really lost its hold on western thinking in the 1850s. When Galen noted that *melancholy* women were more likely to get breast cancer than *sanguine* women he was not putting forward a psychological hypothesis. Although the psychological characteristics of melancholy correspond roughly to the modern concept of depression, Galen took the view that breast cancer and melancholy were jointly attributable to humoral imbalance, in this case to an excess of black bile (see Sontag, 2002).

As an indication of the grip these ideas had on medical thinking in western Europe, the black bile theory of depression was still being articulated in 1836 by Johannes Freidreich, professor of psychiatry in Würzburg, together with the view that mania was caused by an excess of yellow bile, psychosis by an excess of blood, and dementia by an excess of phlegm (see Shorter, 1992). One feature of the doctrine of the four humours that even today finds its echo in psychological theory is Galen's description of the four *classical temperaments* (see Box 12.1).

BOX 12.1

THE FOUR HUMOURS AND MODERN PERSONALITY THEORY

Anaximander (610–546 BCE) described the underlying condition of the universe as being boundless in time and space. The ancient Greeks believed that everything in the world was made of four elementary substances, Earth, Air, Fire, and Water, in primary opposites. These supported the four bodily humours and temperaments described by Galen in the second century AD. The temperaments characterized individuals possessing an excess of each of the four humours. The *sanguine* has an excess of blood, the *choleric* of yellow bile, the *phlegmatic* of phlegm and the *melancholic* of black bile. As descriptions of personality types they were still in use during the second half of the twentieth century. In his influential theory of personality the late Hans Eysenck proposed two basic dimensions of personality, extravert–introvert and stable–unstable, and developed a personality test to measure them. Both dimensions were assumed to be measurable along a continuum with extreme examples towards either end and the average person in the middle. Although he considered the reduction of personality to four qualitatively different types to be an oversimplification, Eysenck (1970) pointed out that the classical temperaments do correspond quite closely with four extremes that can be identified using his personality test: the *stable extravert* (sanguine), *unstable extravert* (choleric), *stable introvert* (phlegmatic) and *unstable introvert* (melancholic) an interesting convergence of classical and contemporary personality theories.

The humoral theory was eventually abandoned following the founding of the modem science of cellular pathology by Rudolf Virchow in the 1850s. This was the key that opened the door to our contemporary understanding of physical diseases. Since there were no obvious indications that cellular pathology could account for psychological disorders, the door was also open for the development of purely psychological explanations, notably by Sigmund Freud.

In recent years the wheel has come full circle. Advances in our understanding of neurotransmitters and the development of DNA research, together with criticism of the cost and efficacy of psychotherapy, has led to an increased enthusiasm for physiological explanations of psychological disorders. However, the historical dominance of the humoral theory and the modern ascendancy of organic medicine has not entirely inhibited speculation of the opposite kind, that psychological factors may play a part in causing physical diseases and influencing recovery. This is evident in the freedom with which modern medical practitioners and the general public deploy the concept of *stress-related disease*. A good historical example is provided by Dogen (1200–1253), the founder of the Soto school of Japanese Buddhism. Admonishing his pupils not to regard illness as a hindrance to performing their spiritual practices, he remarked:

> I suspect that the occurrence of illness stems from the mind. If you lie to a hiccuping person and put him on the defensive, he gets so involved in explaining himself that his hiccups stop. Some years ago when l went to China, 1 suffered from diarrhoea while aboard ship. A violent storm arose, causing great confusion; before I knew it, my sickness was gone. This makes me think that if we concentrate on study and forget about other things, illness will not arise. (Dogen's *Shobogenzo Zuimonki* quoted in Masunaga, 1972: 91)

Sontag (2002) provides many European and North American examples. In England in the late sixteenth and seventeenth centuries it was widely believed that the happy man would not get plague. In 1871 the physician who treated Alexander Dumas for cancer wrote that, among the principal causes of cancer, were 'deep and sedentary study and pursuits, and feverish and anxious agitation of public life, the cares of ambition, frequent paroxysms of rage, violent grief'. At about the same time in England, one doctor advised patients that they could avoid cancer by being careful to bear the ills of life with equanimity; above all things, not to 'give way' to any grief. At this time also, TB was often thought to come from too much passion afflicting the reckless and sensual, or else to be a disease brought on by unrequited love. In fact TB was often called consumption, and hence the appearance in the English language of metaphors such as 'consuming passion'.

Psychoanalysis and Psychosomatic Medicine

The rapid development of organic medicine from the 1850s led to a declining enthusiasm among medical practitioners for speculation about possible psychological causes of organic diseases. A revival came about from the 1920s to the 1950s when the theories of Freud were developed by the *psychosomatic schools* of psychoanalysis.

Having had a medical education that was second to none in the 1880s, Freud himself was always careful to avoid any temptation to propose psychological explanations for organic disorders. His psychoanalytic theories, which were eventually to encompass the whole of human psychology, originated in the study of cases of **hysteria**, patients who had symptoms that appeared to indicate serious neurological or other physical disorder, but for which there appeared to be no underlying physical cause (see Box 12.2). He insisted that psychoanalytic training should be restricted to those already qualified in medicine, on the grounds that only the medically trained psychoanalyst would have the skills necessary to decide whether or not a patient's symptoms needed to be investigated as indicating possible organic disorder.

BOX 12.2

HYSTERIA: THE CASE OF ANNA O

Psychological theories of hysteria first came to prominence as a result of the collaboration between Sigmund Freud and the Viennese physiologist Josef Breuer. From 1880 to 1882 Breuer treated a patient who became known as 'Anna O' and who proved to be of great importance in the history of psychoanalysis. Anna suffered from a spectacular range of hysterical and other symptoms, including paralysis and loss of sensation mainly on the right side of her body, disturbances of eye movements and vision, occasional deafness, multiple personality and loss of the ability to speak her native German. As a result of this last symptom, Breuer was obliged to talk to her in English over which she retained a perfect command. When she was asked to recall previous occurrences of each of her symptoms while under hypnosis, Anna invariably arrived at previously forgotten memories of distressing incidents that had occurred while she had nursed her dying father. As a result of this the symptom temporarily disappeared. For example, the paralysis of Anna's right arm disappeared after she recalled having had the hallucination of a large black snake while sitting at her father's bedside. Anna O's true identity was much later revealed to be Bertha Pappenhiem and she went on to become a well-known feminist who campaigned on problems of single mothers, children in orphanages, prostitution and the white slave trade. Just how successful was her treatment for hysteria is still a matter of controversy and she herself remained ambivalent about the value of psychoanalysis, once remarking that it depends very much on the ability of the psychoanalyst whether it is a good instrument or a double-edged sword. For further details, see Sulloway (1980).

The term hysteria is not very often used nowadays, having been largely replaced by **psychosomatic** (or **somatoform**) **disorder**, but it remains implicit in the new terminology that sufferers are somehow *somatizing* problems that are intrinsically psychological in nature. Freud found it difficult to convince his patients that they were not suffering from an organic disease and it is equally true today that sufferers from a variety of conditions are hostile to suggestions that these conditions may be psychological rather than organic in origin.

Among the conditions that provoke controversy are **myalgic encephalomyelitis (ME)** or **chronic fatigue syndrome (CFS)**, irritable bowel syndrome, repetitive strain injury, fibromyalgia, Gulf War syndrome, total allergy syndrome, migraine, and a variety of types of pain in the back, chest, abdomen, limbs and face. Arguments for believing that these are all contemporary forms of hysteria have been forcefully put by

Shorter (1992) and Showalter (1997). On the other hand, there are many who share the views of the sufferers themselves that a failure to find an organic basis for a condition is not a convincing reason for asserting that one does not exist.

Let us now move on to consider psychological influences on the development of disorders that have a clear organic basis, such as cancer, coronary heart disease and infectious diseases. Bearing in mind the long history of the search for psychological explanations of organic diseases (Sontag, 2002), it is not really surprising that Freud's ideas were developed in this way by some of his followers.

One of the most extreme examples of the psychosomatic tradition in psychoanalysis is the work of George Groddeck, who believed that all illness is unconsciously motivated and has a meaning for the sufferer. Just as a hysterical pregnancy might be motivated by an unconscious wish to have a baby, so might a case of laryngitis be motivated by a desire not to speak. To take an extreme example, a heart attack might be viewed as an unconscious attempt to commit suicide. An alternative approach was that of Wilhelm Reich, who believed, among many other extraordinary things, that repressed sexual feelings could lead to a blocking of mysterious forms of organic energy leading to the development of cancer.

Reich's cancer theories were pseudoscientific and absurd, but his idea that cancer may be caused by some block in the individual's normal flow of emotional energy has proved influential. The belief that psychological factors play an important part in the initial causation and subsequent disease course of cancer was widely held by many psychosomatic thinkers. By the mid-1950s when their influence was at its height, Leshan and Worthington (1956), reviewing research in this area for the *British Journal of Medical Psychology*, drew the following conclusions:

> As one examines these papers, one is struck by the fact that there are consistent factors reported in studies that gathered material in different ways. There appear to be four separate threads that run through the literature. These are (1) the patient's loss of an important relationship prior to the development of the tumour; (2) the cancer patient's inability successfully to express hostile feelings and emotions; (3) the cancer patient's unresolved tension concerning a parental figure; (4) sexual disturbance. (Leshan and Worthington, 1956: 54)

Views such as these are still widely held, although seldom by cancer specialists. They are often used to justify complementary therapies that aim to teach sufferers how to beat cancer by the power of the mind. This is all very well if they work, if psychological dispositions really do play a significant part in the causation and development of cancer. If not, as Sontag and others have pointed out, the propagation of these beliefs may be profoundly undesirable:

> In Karl Menninger's more recent formulation: 'Illness is in part what the world has done to a victim, but in larger part it is what the victim has done with his world, and with himself ...' Such preposterous and dangerous views manage to put the onus of the disease on the patient and not only weaken the patient's ability to understand the range of plausible medical treatment but also, implicitly, direct the patient away from such treatment. (Sontag, 2002)

Of all the theorists in the psychosomatic tradition, the one who has contributed most to modern Health Psychology is Franz Alexander, the Chicago psychoanalyst who, in *Psychosomatic Medicine* (1950), combines psychoanalytic theory with hypotheses about physiological mechanisms, principally those involving the *autonomic nervous system (ANS)*. He emphasizes the distinction between the *sympathetic* division of the ANS that, roughly speaking, controls emotional arousal and the fight-or-flight emergency reactions of the organism, and the *parasympathetic* division that, again roughly speaking, controls relaxation and the slowing down of functions activated by the sympathetic division.

According to Alexander, sustained activity in either branch of the ANS without the counterbalancing effect of the other can have disease consequences. Excessive sympathetic activity contributes to cardiovascular disease, diabetes and rheumatoid arthritis, while excessive parasympathetic activity contributes to gastrointestinal disorders including dyspepsia, ulcers and colitis. Excessive sympathetic activity may occur as a consequence of prolonged stress, a point to which we will return in the next chapter, but Alexander also thought that some personalities may be predisposed to the excessive activation of one of the two branches of the ANS at the expense of the other.

Alexander's theories led to the development in contemporary health psychology of the distinction between the **Type A** and **Type B personalities** and their differential susceptibility to cardiovascular disease, and to recent related work on hostility and cardiovascular disease. We will consider this work shortly but, before doing so, it is necessary to examine the logic underlying empirical research linking personality to physical disease and some of the pitfalls in its interpretation.

Explaining Links between Personality and Disease

It is generally agreed today that the psychosomatic approach in psychoanalysis and the proponents of **psychosomatic medicine** failed to produce convincing evidence of causal connections between psychological characteristics and physical illness, or to demonstrate that their therapeutic interventions were effective (Holroyd and Coyne, 1987). They were criticized for much the same reasons that psychoanalysis has been criticized more generally (Webster, 1995). Their theories were highly speculative and relied on elaborate interpretations of clinical data rather than controlled statistical studies. They also suffered from the defect of being retrospective, seeking to 'explain' patients' illnesses as 'caused' by psychological characteristics already known to the clinician, rather than prospective, making predictions about future illness on the basis of present psychological assessments.

The period since the 1960s has seen the growth of a large empirical literature on the statistical relationship between personality, as assessed by a wide variety of standardized tests, and physical illness. These studies often derive their hypotheses from the earlier speculations of the psychosomatic approach but seek to rectify its defects by carefully analysing statistical evidence. There is, however, one major defect that cannot be overcome because it is intrinsic to this type of research. The evidence is obtained from correlational investigations rather than true experiments and, as a consequence, findings are open to a wide range of interpretations. Obviously no investigator can assign personalities at random to experimental participants and then study their subsequent proneness to illness. All that the investigator can do is to administer personality tests to the participants and obtain measures of their illness status. Statisticians constantly remind us that it is not possible to infer causation from correlation and, in the case of personality–illness correlations, it is possible to illustrate this by considering a range of important problems of interpretation. The issues are perennial problems in the health psychology literature

Table 12.1   *Problems of explanation in research on personality and illness*

Type of problem	Statement of the problem
Correlation versus causation	Cross-sectional studies are correlational and so there can be no certainty as to the direction of causality, as to what may be a cause and what may be an effect.
Background variables	Two variables (A and B) that are associated together may both be related to a third, background variable (C) that has not been measured and may not even be known to be relevant.
Self-reporting of illness	Health psychology research often relies upon self-reported illness that has not been verified by objective medical tests.
Dimensions of personality	The number of personality dimensions to evaluate remains controversial.
Physiological mechanisms or health behaviour	Whether it is health behaviour or physiological differences that are causing illness is uncertain.

and are essentially logical in nature. We have summarized these in Table 12.1. These problems will now be considered in more detail.

Direction of causality

Psychological characteristics may be a cause of physical illness but they are also a consequence of it. This is a particular problem for cross-sectional studies that assess personality traits and illness status (present illness or illnesses experienced in the past) at the same time. For example, if patients with a history of coronary illness have higher scores on anxiety and depression than healthy controls, should we conclude that anxiety and depression are risk factors for coronary illness or that a history of coronary problems can cause people to become more anxious and depressed? Obviously the causal direction cannot be inferred from this type of study. The flaw may seem trivially obvious but it is surprising how many cross-sectional studies are to be found in the research literature on associations between personality and illness.

The problem cannot always be resolved by conducting prospective studies to investigate the extent to which the current personalities of healthy volunteers are predictive of future illness. The reason for this is that many major illnesses take a long time to develop and it is frequently the case that patients have experienced unusual and disturbing symptoms for some time before a diagnosis is given. It is therefore possible that psychological characteristics that appear to be a cause of subsequent illness are in fact a consequence of symptoms of developing illness occurring prior to diagnosis. Prospective studies are clearly far superior to cross-sectional studies but they do not necessarily eliminate the problem of the specification of causality.

Background variables

A correlation may be found between two variables A and B when there is neither a direct effect of A on B, nor of B on A, but because a third *background variable X* has an effect on both. Galen's explanation for the association he believed to exist between melancholy and breast cancer is a good illustration. Here an excess of black bile is the background variable that he hypothesized to be a cause of both melancholy and breast cancer. As a further illustration, suppose that some people have a history of childhood illness that leaves them constitutionally weak and prone to further illness. Suppose also that this history of childhood illness has had a deleterious effect on their personality development, perhaps by limiting their opportunities for social development. The inclusion of a number of such individuals in a sample along with constitutionally stronger individuals who have had a healthy childhood could produce a non-causal correlation in the sample between adult personality and adult proneness to illness, because both are influenced by childhood illness. Further examples of background variables, notably genetic predispositions, are discussed by Holroyd and Coyne (1987) and Suls and Rittenhouse (1990).

Self-reported illness and the distress-prone personality

Stone and Costa (1990) and Cohen and Williamson (1991) point out that much health psychology research relies on self-reported illness rather than biologically verified disease. This does not only apply to minor ailments such as colds and flu. The diagnosis of angina pectoris, for example, is frequently based solely on patients' reports of chest pain.

Stone and Costa argue that this reliance on self-reported illness is particularly unsatisfactory when considering research into links between personality and illness. They point out that there is extensive evidence that psychological distress is associated with somatic complaints but not with organic disease. Since many personality tests scores may be interpreted, at least to some extent, as measures of distress, it follows that correlations between test scores and self-reported illness may provide a false indication of a link between personality and disease when all that they really show is that neurotic individuals are the ones most likely to complain of being ill.

However, it should not be assumed that any discrepancy between self-reported illness and biologically verified illness is necessarily an indication of neuroticism. Adler and Matthews (1994) note that there is evidence that perceived health predicts mortality independently of biological risk factors, leading them to conclude that self-reported health provides useful information over and above direct biological indications.

Dimensions of personality

Personality testing is not an exact science and there is little agreement as to what the basic dimensions of personality really are, or even whether the question is worth asking. Three influential theories have been those of Eysenck, who argued initially that there were only two dimensions, extraversion and neuroticism (see Box 12.1), and subsequently added a third, psychoticism, Cattell, who believed he had identified 16, and McCrae and Costa (1985) who settled for five. These so-called 'Big Five' personality traits consist of extraversion/introversion, agreeableness/antagonism, conscientiousness, neuroticism/emotional stability, and openness to experience.

A problem that arises in research using personality tests is that similar items can often be found included in tests that are supposed to be measuring different traits so that, not surprisingly, scores for the same group of individuals given both tests may be highly intercorrelated. Consider some of the measures that are frequently used in research into the links between personality and illness. The individual who scores high on anxiety is also likely to score high on depression, neuroticism and **pessimistic explanatory style**, and correspondingly low on self-esteem, self-efficacy, **hardiness**, internal **locus of control** and **sense of coherence**. The common element that may run through all of these measures is probably best labelled, following Stone and Costa, as *distress proneness*. Further factors may also be common to some but not all of the tests. Given that the tests used vary from study to study as do the measures of physical illness, anyone seeking to understand the mechanisms by which personality may be linked to illness is confronted with major problems of interpretation. A useful attempt to resolve this issue has been undertaken by Yousfi et al. (2004), who factor analysed a range of personality measures which have been linked to health outcomes in order to arrive at a number of independent, uncorrelated traits. Their study will be considered later in this chapter.

Physiological mechanisms versus health behaviour

Psychological characteristics may be linked to illness, either by way of physiological variables with which they are associated, or more indirectly, by way of their relationship to health behaviour. The proponents of psychosomatic medicine, especially Franz Alexander, believed in the existence of physiological mechanisms linking personality to illness, usually involving differences in the functioning of the sympathetic and parasympathetic divisions of the autonomic nervous system. Health psychologists who conduct research into the relationship between personality and illness are also primarily interested in physiological pathways. However, it is generally acknowledged that more prosaic explanations for correlations between personality and illness may be derived from the fact that personality differences are often associated with differences in health behaviour (Miller et al., 1996; Suls and Rittenhouse, 1990).

Jerram and Coleman (1999) assessed whether the 'Big Five' personality traits (McCrae and Costa, 1985) could be related to health behaviour in a sample of 50 British older people. Neuroticism was associated with a higher number of reported medical problems, negatively perceived health status and a higher frequency of visits to the doctor. Openness and agreeableness were associated with positive health perceptions. The authors conclude that, since associations are evident for each of the personality traits, the 'Big Five' personality traits should be included in research on health behaviour.

Characteristics such as anxiety, depression, neuroticism and hostility have been variously shown to be associated with levels of smoking and alcohol consumption, diet and exercise, sleep disturbance, likelihood of seeking medical advice in the early stages of a disease and the likelihood of adhering to recommendations subsequently. Any of these variables, or some combination of them, could be invoked to account for an empirical correlation between personality and illness.

Further problems arise if we consider the relationship between personality and *stress* and *social support*, two variables that have also been shown to be associated with physical illness. Stress and social support are normally thought of as environmental influences on the individual, as distinct from personality which, as it were, comes from the inside. But the two types of variables cannot be so easily separated. The competitive individual is likely to seek out stressful situations while the anxious individual avoids them; the individual with high self-esteem may attract social contact while the depressive discourages it. Once again, associations between psychological characteristics and physical illness may be found, not because of the existence of direct underlying physiological mechanisms, but as an indirect consequence of associations between personality and other variables that influence physical health. The relationship between stress, social support and illness will be discussed in the next chapter.

The Type A/B Personality, Hostility and Coronary Heart Disease

Type A and B personality

Speculation about an association between the Type A and B personalities and coronary heart disease (CHD) has a history which dates back at least 50 years (Riska, 2000). The distinction between the two personalities was introduced in the mid-1950s by the cardiologists Meyer Friedman and Ray Rosenman, although, as we have already noted, their ideas can be traced back further to the work of Alexander in psychosomatic medicine. The Type A personality, thought to be at greater risk of CHD, is described as highly competitive and achievement oriented, not prepared to suffer fools gladly, always in a hurry and unable to bear delays and queues, hostile and aggressive, inclined to read, eat and drive very fast, and constantly thinking what to do next, even when supposedly listening to someone else. In contrast to this the Type B personality is relaxed, laid back, lethargic, even-tempered, amiable and philosophical about life, relatively slow in speech and action, and generally has enough time for everyone and everything. The Type A personality has much in common with Galen's choleric temperament, the Type B with the phlegmatic (see Box 12.1). It is well known that men are at greater risk of CHD than women, and Riska (2000) makes an interesting argument for the view that the concept of the Type A personality was an attempt to 'medicalize' traditional concepts of masculinity.

The classification of individuals as Type A or B was initially made on the basis of a structured interview in which people were not only asked questions about their Type A/B modes of behaviour, but also provoked into directly manifesting such behaviour by being subjected to pauses and delays in the interview, deliberately interrupted and challenged about their answers to questions. Their responses to these provocations enabled the interviewers to refine their ratings of Type A/B characteristics. The structured interview (SI) is generally considered to be the best method of assessment but many later researchers have adopted the less time consuming approach of using standardized self-report questionnaires of which the *Jenkins Activity Survey (JAS)* has been most commonly used. This simply asks questions about Type A/B modes of behaviour.

The key pioneering study of Type A/B personality and CHD was the Western Collaborative Group Study (WCGS) in which over 3,000 Californian men, aged from

39 to 59 at entry, were assessed using the SI and followed up initially over a period of eight and a half years, and later extending over 22 years. When results were reported at the eight and a half year follow-up, it appeared that Type As were twice as likely as Type Bs to suffer from subsequent CHD. Of the sample 7% developed some signs of CHD and two-thirds of these were Type As. This increased risk was apparent even when other risk factors assessed at entry, such as blood pressure and cigarette smoking, were statistically controlled for.

Similar results were subsequently published from another large-scale study conducted in Framingham, Massachusetts, this time with both men and women in the sample and, by the early 1980s, it was confidently asserted that Type A characteristics were as much a risk factor for heart disease as high blood pressure, high cholesterol levels and smoking. However, subsequent research failed to support these early findings. When Ragland and Brand (1988) conducted a 22-year follow-up of the WCGS they painted a different picture. The early reports appear to have exaggerated the significance of the Type A risk, and three subsequent follow-ups yielded inconsistent findings. Using mortality as the crucially important measure, Ragland and Brand found:

> Type A/B behaviour was positively but not significantly associated with coronary heart disease in the first and third intervals, significantly negatively associated ... in the second interval and not associated in the fourth interval. The results confirm the importance of the traditional coronary heart disease risk factors, and raise a substantial question about the importance of Type A/B behaviour as a risk factor for coronary heart disease mortality. (Ragland and Brand, 1988: 66)

This result and a number of other negative findings, as well as some positive ones, led to a re-evaluation of Type A/B research at the end of the 1980s when the burgeoning literature was extensively reviewed (e.g. Evans, 1990). It became clear that the bulk of the positive findings came from cross-sectional studies rather than prospective studies. Positive prospective findings also tended to come from population studies of initially healthy volunteers, while studies of high risk individuals who already had symptoms of coronary disease either failed to show a relationship with the Type A/B personality or produced a reverse finding with Type As actually having better outcomes than Type Bs. Evans (1990) considers a number of statistical artefacts that may account for this as well as the engaging hypothesis that, while healthy Type As may be more at risk than Type Bs, following an initial diagnosis Type As are more likely than Type Bs to modify their risky health behaviours, thereby giving themselves a better long-term prognosis.

Reviewers also discovered that studies using the SI to assess personality were much more likely to produce positive results than those using questionnaires, especially the JAS. In seeking to explain this, it was noted that the SI assessments only correlate modestly with those based on the JAS. Further analysis of the component scales, which contribute to the SI assessments, revealed that only one of these components, which mainly indicated hostility, was implicated in the relationship between Type A/B and CHD. Since the JAS does not include items assessing hostility, this also explains the generally negative findings from research using it to predict CHD. This last finding led to a rapid decline in Type A/B research in the 1990s together with a new enthusiasm for research into the relationship between hostility measures and subsequent illness. Recent reviews and meta-analyses of Type A/B research all conclude that there is little or no evidence of a relationship with CHD (Hemingway and Marmot, 1999; Rozanski et al., 1999; Myrtek, 2001).

Hostility

As in the case of the Type A/B personality, research on hostility and health is divided between studies using SI methods to assess hostility and those using questionnaires, usually the *Cook-Medley Ho Scale* (for details of these and other assessment methods, see T.W. Smith, 1992). Corresponding to the findings of Type A/B research, research using the SI has produced more positive findings than research using self-report questionnaires. In a detailed review of the literature Miller et al. (1996) located eight studies using SI methods and combined the results to yield a small positive relationship between hostility and CHD. Research using the Ho scale usually failed to find a significant relationship with CHD although, curiously, the Ho scale was rather more predictive of all-cause mortality, at roughly the same level as that between the SI and CHD.

Further reviews (Hemingway and Marmot, 1999; Rozanski et al., 1999; Myrtek, 2001) all indicate that existing studies are of very mixed quality, with inconsistent results. Myrtek conducted a sophisticated meta-analysis and concluded that there was evidence of a statistically significant but very weak relationship for prospective studies of initially healthy individuals, but not for studies that have followed up patients already diagnosed with CHD. It should be emphasized that the statistical relationship between measures of hostility and health is, at most, a weak one. Certainly hostility cannot be regarded as a substantial health risk of similar magnitude to that of cigarette smoking or high blood pressure, for instance.

There are many echoes of earlier discussions about Type A/B research to be found in those concerning hostility and health. In analysing possible explanations for the statistical relationship, both T.W. Smith (1992) and Miller et al. (1996) consider differences in physiological reactivity and the tendency of hostile people to indulge more in high risk health behaviours, to be subjected to higher levels of stress and to attract less social support than average. Again mirroring earlier discussions of the Type A/B personality dimension, they point out that hostility has many distinct sub-components, including cynicism, mistrust, verbal and physical aggressiveness, overt and experienced aggressiveness. They propose that more attention should be given to sub-components in order to discover which are most health hazardous.

Given the generally weak statistical associations that have been found so far between hostility measures and health outcomes, it remains an open question whether researchers in this field are engaged on an exciting search for the truly toxic dimension of personality, as far as CHD is concerned, a dimension with demonstrable physiological pathways to heart disease, or whether they are on a wild goose chase. In the next section we will consider prospective studies of the association between anxiety and depression and CHD, studies that have demonstrated rather stronger associations than is the case for the Type A/B personality and hostility.

Further Studies of Links between Personality and Illness

Affect, anxiety and depression

Much of the research on links between personality and illness is concerned with what might be termed positive and negative prevailing moods, or 'affectivity'. Researchers have sought to demonstrate that positive characteristics (e.g. optimism, high self-esteem, sense of coherence) are associated with good health, while negative characteristics (e.g. depression, pessimistic explanatory style) are associated with poor health. As we have already pointed out, these measures are frequently intercorrelated so that it is misleading to consider research under separate headings for distinct dimensions of personality. It amounts to much the same thing to show, for example, that persons scoring high on a scale measuring depression have an increased risk of heart disease as it is to show that those scoring high on a scale measuring optimism have a reduced risk. It is also important to bear in mind that persons with negative characteristics are more likely than those with positive characteristics to report illness when not actually ill, and also to indulge in hazardous health behaviours, such as cigarette smoking and heavy drinking. With these cautions in mind we will now consider the research findings.

There have been a number of recent reviews that have concluded, on the basis of prospective studies, that there are substantial associations between both anxiety and depression and subsequent CHD (Hemingway and Marmot, 1999; Rozanski et al., 1999; Krantz and McCeney, 2002; Kiecolt-Glaser et al., 2002). This applies to studies of patients with clinically diagnosed distress and to general population studies. Anxiety seems to predict sudden cardiac death rather than other types of CHD, and phobic, panic-like anxiety is a particularly strong predictor: Haines et al. (1987) found that sufferers were three times more at risk of sudden cardiac death over the next seven years compared with non-sufferers. Very similar results were subsequently found by Kawachi et al. (1994) in a two-year follow up of 33,999 initially healthy US male health professionals.

Depression is predictive of a wider range of CHD than anxiety and, in a recent three-year follow-up of 498 initially healthy men, Todaro et al. (2003) found that a composite negative emotion score, including symptoms of depression and anxiety, was significantly predictive of subsequent CHD. In a very large prospective study of 96,376 post-menopausal women, Wassertheil-Smoller et al. (2004) report that depressive symptoms were substantially associated with death from cardiovascular disease after adjusting for age, race, education, income, diabetes, hypertension, smoking, cholesterol level, body mass index and physical activity. These findings for anxiety and depression are impressive, but they should be considered alongside our earlier discussion of problems in interpreting personality–illness correlations. Hemingway and Marmot (1999) point out that these problems are particularly acute in this area. Anxiety and depression are certainly consequences of CHD as well as possible causes of it. Furthermore, symptoms of incipient CHD, such as breathlessness and chest pains, may occur for years prior to diagnosis, and lead in turn to experienced anxiety and depression. In this way, prospective studies could give the impression that anxiety and depression are causes of CHD when in fact the direction of causality is the other way round.

The widely held belief that depression is an important factor in the onset and subsequent development of cancer has received little support from research. Adler and Matthews (1994) reviewed three large-scale prospective studies of the relationship between depression and both the incidence of and mortality from cancer. In these studies, initially healthy samples of up to 9,000 were followed up over periods ranging from 10 to 20 years and no associations were found between depression and either cancer onset or mortality. Since then two large-scale studies have produced conflicting results. Penninx et al. (1998) carried out a prospective study of 1,708 men and 3,117 women aged 71 and over. They found a significantly increased incidence of cancer for those who were diagnosed as suffering from chronic depression, indicated by repeated assessments of symptoms over six years. On the other hand, Whooley and Browner (1998) undertook a prospective study over six years of 7,519 women aged 67 or over and analysed the relationship between depression and subsequent mortality from (a) cancer, (b) cardiovascular disease and (c) all other diseases. They found no relationship between depression and cancer but a strong relationship with both cardiovascular disease and all other diseases.

Negative findings have usually been reported from follow-up studies of patients who have been treated for cancer. For example, Barraclough et al. (1992) followed up 204 patients who had received surgery for breast cancer over 42 months after surgery. They used a very detailed interview schedule, which included the assessment of prolonged major depression before surgery and during the follow-up period. They found no relationship at all between depression and relapse. Relapse was also unrelated to stress, including bereavement, long-term social difficulties and lack of a confiding relationship.

A spectacular exception to the general run of negative findings on personality and cancer was the research of the late H.J. Eysenck, R. Grossarth-Maticek and their associates. They argued that personality variables are much more strongly related to death from cancer than even cigarette smoking, and they claimed to have identified personality types that increase the risk of cancer by about 120 times and heart disease by about 25 times. They also claimed to have tested a new method of psychological treatment that can reduce the death rate for disease prone personalities over the next 13 years from 80% to 32%.

These remarkable reports were not received favourably by others working in this field. In a comprehensive and highly respected review of the literature, Fox (1988) dismissed early reports by Eysenck and Grossarth-Maticek as 'simply unbelievable', and the first detailed accounts of their research, published in 1991, were subjected to devastating critiques by Pelosi and Appleby (1992, 1993) and by Amelang and Schmidt-Rathjens (1996). The 'cancer prone personality' was not clearly described and seems to have been an odd amalgam of emotional distance and excessive dependence. After pointing out a large number of errors, omissions, obscurities and implausible aspects of the data, in a manner reminiscent of Leon Kamin's now legendary analysis of Cyril Burt's twin data (Kamin, 1977), Pelosi and Appleby comment:

> It is unfortunate that Eysenck and Grossarth-Maticek omit the most basic information that might explain why their findings are so different from all the others in this field. The methods are either not given or are described so generally that they remain obscure on even the most important points; ... Also essential details are missing from the results, and the analyses used are often inappropriate. (1992: 1297)

Turning to less contentious research, Adler and Matthews (1994) reviewed findings linking positive and negative characteristics to illness generally and they report a fairly perplexing set of contrasting findings. For example, Peterson et al. (1988), in a 35-year follow-up of 99 graduates of the Harvard University classes of 1942–44, found that pessimistic explanatory style, as assessed in tests taken by the participants while undergraduates, was predictive of poor physical health in later life assessed by physicians. Yet in stark contrast to this, Friedman et al. (1993) found that children who had been rated by their parents and teachers as having a good sense of humour and being optimistic and cheerful were more likely than other children to die early in adulthood.

Sense of coherence, locus of control and other variables

More recently, in the UK, Surtees et al. (2003) carried out a prospective study over six years of the relationship between sense of coherence and mortality from all causes for a very large sample of 20,579 participants aged 41–80 years. Sense of coherence (Antonovsky, 1979) is described as the ability to perceive one's world as meaningful and manageable, the exact opposite, one supposes, of Macbeth's eventual view of life as '... a tale told by an idiot, full of sound and fury, signifying nothing'. Surtees et al. found that a strong sense of coherence was associated with a 30% reduction in mortality from all causes and also more specifically for cardiovascular disease. For cancer there was a similar reduction in mortality for men but not for women. In view of the size of the sample and the effect size, this remarkable finding can be expected to provoke considerable critical discussion and further research.

We have already mentioned a study by Yousfi et al. (2004) who factor analysed a range of personality measures that have been associated with health outcomes. This was based on a sample of 5,133 men and women aged between 40 and 65, recruited in Heidelberg, Germany. They arrived at five statistically independent factors. They then investigated the correlations between these factors and a range of illnesses, and found a number of small but statistically significant correlations, the most substantial of which was between **emotional lability** and general disease vulnerability. However, as they point out, the interpretation of the correlations is problematic because the study was cross-sectional and relied on self-reported illness. We have already discussed the limitations of such studies. It is to be hoped that prospective studies will now be carried out to investigate the extent to which these factors, assessed in an initially healthy sample, can predict subsequent clinically verified illness.

KT

An interesting and somewhat counter-intuitive finding is that of Reed et al. (1994) who investigated the relationship between realistic acceptance and survival time of men suffering from AIDS. They found that those who were assessed as showing a realistic acceptance of their deteriorating condition and eventual death had a mean survival time that was nine months less than those who were assessed as being unduly optimistic. In an earlier review of research concerning mental health, Taylor and Brown (1988) concluded that overly positive self-evaluations, exaggerated perceptions of control and mastery and unrealistic optimism, far from being associated with psychological difficulties, were actually associated with good mental health. Reed et al. appear to have shown that this surprising result extends even into the field of physical health.

KT

Another personality variable that has been of interest to health psychologists over the last 20 years is the notion of locus of control. This concept was applied to health beliefs by Wallston et al. (1978) who developed the **Multidimensional Health Locus of Control (MHLC) Scale**. This questionnaire has three sub-scales measuring the extent to which people attribute their state of health to their own behaviour (internal locus), and/or external factors including both powerful others, especially medical professionals, and chance or fate. The internal locus of control scale has much in common with the concept of self-efficacy (Bandura, 1977). In both cases the main focus of research interest has been not so much to investigate direct links with physical health, but rather to show that they are predictive of the adoption of positive health behaviours and the avoidance of negative ones.

In a detailed review of research on the topic, Norman and Bennett (1996) found that the results were mixed, and they concluded that the relationship between locus of control and health behaviour is a weak one, a conclusion that was confirmed by a large-scale study of a representative sample of 11,632 people who completed the MHLC in Wales (Norman et al., 1998). In this study, all three health locus of control dimensions were found to correlate significantly with a health behaviour index, with those engaging in more positive health behaviours scoring higher on the internal dimension ($r = 0.05$), lower on powerful others ($r = 0.09$) and lower on chance ($r = 0.16$). These are low correlations indicating a very weak predictive relationship and leaving more than 95% of the variance in health behaviour unaccounted for. Self-efficacy appears to be a rather better predictor of health behaviour and it has been argued that it is the best available predictor (Schwarzer, 1992).

Conclusions

In conclusion, the evidence indicates that associations between personality and illness are quite modest. In the case of coronary heart disease, the strongest predictors appear to be phobic, panic-like anxiety and depression, with a weak role also for hostility. In the case of cancer, there is very little evidence to support a role for personality variables in predicting onset, development or relapse. There are, however, two recent studies indicating that chronic depression and sense of coherence may be factors; but, bearing in mind the great preponderance of negative findings in this area, these two positive findings must be treated with caution, as awaiting further confirmation. The recent finding of an association between sense of coherence and all cause mortality deserves further investigation, although it should be noted that sense of coherence is likely to be correlated with the more thoroughly investigated variables of anxiety and depression. The indication that unrealistic optimism is associated with an increased survival time for AIDS sufferers could also be extended by investigating its relevance to other frequently fatal conditions including cancer.

Associations between personality and illness may be the result of direct physiological pathways, but we have pointed out that there are many other possible interpretations. One important issue is whether changes in psychological characteristics, such as anxiety and depression, may have occurred prior to the diagnosis of illness as a reaction to disturbing physiological symptoms that could have been occurring for some time before seeking medical advice. This is a very real possibility when the illness is coronary heart disease or cancer. Another issue is the extent to which links between personality and illness are mediated through health behaviour, especially since there is substantial evidence for the existence of links between personality and health behaviour. The modern trend in health psychology to focus more directly on health behaviour, how it becomes established and what causes change, seems potentially a more productive approach. This in turn suggests that levels of analysis beyond that of the individual and towards populations and population groups may be the best way forward.

Future Research

1   Studies to assess the role of psychological factors in conditions such as chronic fatigue syndrome, where there is controversy as to whether or not they have an organic basis.
2   Research to clarify the structure of personality with particular reference to health, in order to reduce or eliminate the problem of overlapping measures.
3   Investigations to distinguish between personality variables that are associated with biologically verified illness, as distinct from those that are associated with reported illness for which there appears to be no organic basis.
4   Studies to establish which dimensions of personality are directly associated with health-relevant physiological variables, and to distinguish them from those that are primarily associated with health behaviours.
5   Outcome studies to assess the effectiveness of interventions designed to modify psychological characteristics that are suspected of being health hazardous. It would be particularly valuable to assess whether interventions can improve the prognosis for those already diagnosed as suffering from organic disease. In the case of anxiety and depression, interventions would obviously be worthwhile if they relieve these conditions, whether or not they influence health outcomes.
6   Where personality variables are linked primarily to health behaviours, it would be useful to establish whether interventions designed to modify health behaviour (e.g. smoking cessation programmes) could be more effective if they took account of personality assessments of participants.

Summary

1   From the Ancient Greeks to modern times orthodox medical practitioners have usually believed that there is a physical basis to all illness, including psychological disorders. Traditional explanations based on the Galenic doctrine of the four humours have now been replaced by the *medical model*, the science of pathology and the belief that psychological disorders are caused by biochemical imbalances, often thought to be genetic in origin. Criticisim of this model has led to a biopsychosocial model.
2   The modern history of psychological explanations for physical symptoms begins with Freud's theories of hysteria, physical symptoms of illness for which no organic basis could be discovered.
3   The psychosomatic approach was developed by psychoanalysts who extended Freud's theories of hysteria to provide psychological explanations for the causation of real organic disorders such as heart disease and cancer.

4 Proponents of the psychosomatic approach generally failed to produce convincing evidence in support of their hypotheses. However, the theories of Franz Alexander on the physiological mechanisms that could underlie the relationship between the psychology of the individual and organic disease have led to modern conceptions of the Type A personality and stress as contributors to cardiovascular disease.

5 Health psychologists have found it very difficult to determine whether personality is associated with susceptibility to physical disease directly through physiological mechanisms, indirectly by way of health behaviour, or whether the data are best explained by statistical artefacts and flaws in the design of the studies from which they are obtained.

6 Early indications that the Type A personality is a risk factor for cardiovascular disease were not confirmed by later studies. Attention has shifted to hostility which does seem to be a risk factor, although much less so than traditional risk factors such as high blood pressure or cigarette smoking.

7 Anxiety, especially phobic panic-like anxiety, and chronic depression are both associated with an increased risk of coronary heart disease, although a number of different interpretations of these associations are possible.

8 There is very little clear-cut evidence to support the view that personality variables are associated with risk of cancer or of relapse following treatment.

9 Studies investigating the long-term effects on health of optimism and pessimistic explanatory style have yielded conflicting findings.

10 There is some recent evidence that sense of coherence may be associated with coronary heart disease, cancer and all cause mortality.

11 Realistic acceptance has been found to be associated with decreased survival time of men suffering from AIDS.

12 Internal locus of control is only very weakly associated with positive health behaviours. Self-efficacy shows an overall stronger relationship, yet the level of prediction is still relatively modest.

KT Key Terms

chronic fatigue syndrome (CFS)

emotional lability

hardiness

hysteria (conversion hysteria)

locus of control

Multidimensional Health Locus of Control (MHLC) Scale

myalgic encephalomyelitis (ME)

pessimistic explanatory style

psychosomatic medicine

psychosomatic (or somatoform) disorder

sense of coherence

Type A/B personality

13

Stress and Coping

Though the faculties of the mind are improved by exercise, yet they must not be put to a stress beyond their strength. (John Locke, 1690)

Outline

This chapter discusses theoretical models of stress and coping and research on stress as a cause of physical illness. It begins with a critical discussion of the stress concept and gives an account of stimulus, response and interactional models of stress and coping. Consideration is given to the effects of stress on the immune system and to the ways in which people react to traumatic stress. A discussion of the methodological problems involved in research on stress and illness is followed by an examination of the evidence linking stress to cardiovascular disease, cancer and infectious diseases.

What is Stress?

It is frequently asserted that **stress** has become a major feature of modern living, caused particularly by changes in the type of work that we do, by the breakdown of traditional family structures, and by many features of the contemporary urban environment. Stress is thought to be a principal cause of psychological distress and physical illness and millions of working days every year are believed to be lost as a consequence of this. The ability to cope successfully with stress is frequently held to be the key to human happiness (Figure 13.1).

But what exactly do we mean by the term 'stress', and how convincing is the evidence in support of these popular beliefs? If you ask people what they mean by stress you will find that their answers fall into one of three categories, each of which finds its echo in the academic literature on theories of stress.

The first type of answer is that stress is 'when you are under a lot of pressure', or 'when things are getting on top of you'. This is essentially the position taken up by theorists who put forward *stimulus models* of stress. These models derive, to some extent, from the engineering approach to the elasticity of materials, where *stress* refers to a load

KT

"Keep blowing"

Figure 13.1   Coping with stress (*Private Eye*, 4 October 1996: 22; reproduced with permission)

applied to an object or structure, setting up a force, known as *strain*, which can result in damage once the *elastic limit* is exceeded. Applied to human beings, it is assumed that individuals have a certain tolerance to stress but will become ill when the stress is too great. Stimulus theorists have tried to catalogue and present a taxonomy of types of stress or to devise measures of the relative stressful impact of life events ranging in severity from bereavement, divorce and job loss to problems in personal relationships, environmental disturbances and work pressures. These life event measures have in turn been used to investigate the role of stress as a cause of physical illness. Stimulus models are associated with approaches to stress management that seek to reduce levels of stress produced by the physical environment and at the workplace.

The second type of answer concentrates on the physical and psychological feeling of 'being stressed' or 'completely stressed out' with symptoms such as anxiety, poor concentration, insomnia, bodily tension and fatigue. This position is taken by theorists who develop *response models* of stress, theorists who concentrate on the psychophysiology of stress and who investigate possible mechanisms linking stress to physical illnesses such as coronary disease and viral infections, by way of the cardiovascular and immune systems respectively. Response models have also provided the impetus for the introduction of stress management programmes that focus on controlling the psychophysiology of stress using techniques such as relaxation and breathing exercises, yoga, meditation, aerobics and other forms of physical exercise.

The third type of answer is that stress is 'when you think you can't cope' or when you have too much strain put on you and you don't have the resources to deal with it'. This is the position developed in *interactional models* of stress by theorists who argue that stress occurs when there is an imbalance between the perceived demands placed on the individual and the ability to meet those demands, often described as *coping resources*. These models are attractive because they overcome a problem inherent in stimulus and response models, that individuals differ as to what events or demands they find stressful and in the way that they respond to them. Interactional models have led to the study of coping and to the development of techniques aimed at helping individuals to overcome stress by increasing the effectiveness of their coping methods. These are taught in **stress management workshops** and **stress innoculation training**.

KT

Not everyone agrees that the development of general theories of stress is a viable scientific objective. For example, while it seems worthwhile to study the effects respectively of bereavement, living in noisy environments and of poor role definition at the workplace, it is not necessarily the case that such studies would yield results that have enough in common to be incorporated into a general theory of stress. Critics such as Brown (1996) have pointed out that stress is an umbrella term that has been applied to so many quite different phenomena as to become virtually meaningless from a scientific point of view. In an effort to encompass such diverse phenomena theories may have become so vague and ambiguous that they lack any practical value. But if the stress concept is such a nebulous one, why has it come to play such a significant role in popular discourse and media presentations? This question can perhaps be answered by analysing stress as a social construct. Consider, for example, the following two illustrations of the way in which a social analysis can be useful.

First, stress is often used as a device for legitimating behaviour that might otherwise be seen as the result of anxiety, neurosis or personal inadequacy. For example, to phone up your workplace to say that you will not be coming in today, or to excuse yourself for not sitting an examination on the grounds that you are too worried, not sleeping well, too tired, or simply feel inadequate would not be considered acceptable. To give as the reason that you are suffering from stress, preferably supported by a letter from a doctor or counsellor, could be considered perfectly reasonable. In spite of the differences between stimulus, response and interactional models of stress, what they all have in common is that they draw attention to current events in one's life or one's immediate environment as provoking a reaction, rather than focusing exclusively on the individual. But it may very well be that an inability to cope with the demands of everyday life may be more appropriately seen as indicative of a longstanding psychological problem such as anxiety or depression.

Second, stress often has the function of explaining the otherwise inexplicable, whether this be psychological or physical symptoms or actual illness. Suppose that someone has a consultation with the doctor after suffering a heart attack. The doctor is expected to provide an explanation as to why the heart attack occurred. Does the patient smoke, drink a lot of alcohol, eat too much, especially fatty foods, have a history of high blood pressure, or avoid exercise? If the answer to all these questions is 'no', the next question is likely to be, 'have you been experiencing a lot of stress lately?', a question to which most people are likely to reply 'yes', especially if they are urgently seeking an explanation for an otherwise inexplicable complaint. But is the explanation a valid one or merely a convenient pseudo-explanation? Clearly the role of stress in the aetiology of physical illness needs to be investigated just as carefully as any other proposed causal agent.

Stress as a Stimulus

KT

Holmes and Rahe (1967) conducted some influential pioneering research into the types of life events that people rate as being most stressful. They began by choosing 43 probably stressful life events, and then asked 400 US adults to rate the relative amount of readjustment that they judged would be required by each of the 43 events. The 10 highest rated of these are listed in Box 13.1. Holmes and Rahe then used their results to construct a **social readjustment rating scale (SRRS)** that assigns points values to different kinds of stress and which has subsequently been used in research on the relationship between stress and physical illness.

BOX 13.1

STRESSFUL LIFE EVENTS AND DAILY HASSLES SCALES

Listed below in order of severity are the 10 life events rated as highly stressful by a sample of the US adult population studied by Holmes and Rahe (1967), and the 10 daily hassles endorsed most frequently by a New Zealand student population studied by Chamberlain and Zika (1990) using a scale derived from Kanner et al. (1981).

Life events	Daily hassles
1 Death of spouse	1 Not enough time
2 Divorce	2 Too many things to do
3 Marital separation	3 Troubling thoughts about future
4 Jail term	4 Too many interruptions
5 Death of close family member	5 Misplacing or losing things
6 Personal injury or illness	6 Health of a family member
7 Marriage	7 Social obligations
8 Fired at work	8 Concerns about standards
9 Marital reconciliation	9 Concerns about getting ahead
10 Retirement	10 Too many responsibilities

KT

Some researchers felt dissatisfied with the SRRS because many of the events listed in it occur relatively rarely in anyone's life. There was a desire for a scale that reflected to a greater degree the day-to-day variation experienced by people in the levels of the stress to which they are exposed. This led Kanner et al. (1981) to devise, using similar techniques to those of Holmes and Rahe, two further scales, a **hassles scale** consisting of everyday events that cause annoyance or frustration, and an **uplifts scale** consisting of events that make them feel good. Of the two, the hassles scale has been the more widely used for research that parallels that using the SRRS. Box 13.1 lists as an example the findings of Chamberlain and Zika (1990), using an adaptation of the

Kanner et al. scale, of the 10 most frequently endorsed hassles by a sample of 161 students in New Zealand.

The SRRS, the hassles scale and research using them have been the subject of extensive criticism since their original publication (e.g. Schroeder and Costa, 1984). These criticisms focus on the choice of items for inclusion in the scale, items that often seem highly arbitrary, vague, ambiguous, insensitive to individual differences and sometimes likely to assess the individual's level of neuroticism rather than experienced life event stress.

The arbitrariness of items included in the scales is probably inevitable. It is trivially easy to think of stressful life events and hassles that have not found their way into the existing scales, but a complete listing of all such events would be endless. The vagueness and ambiguity of some items is a more serious problem. Items such as *change in recreation* or *change in responsibilities at work*, taken from the SRRS, and most items on the hassles scale can be criticized in this way. Items such as bereavement may also create problems because bereavement may have very different stressful impacts on different people as a function of length and quality of relationship, whether or not the death was unexpected, and so on.

Much of the research linking physical illness to stressful life events has consisted of retrospective studies in which participants are asked about events occurring prior to the onset of physical illness. These studies have been criticized because, as noted above, people who have recently been ill may very well be predisposed to recollect and report recent stressful events to a greater extent than control group individuals who have remained well. Any such tendency will obviously lead to an overestimation of the association between stress and illness. The inclusion of vague and ambiguous items in the scales is clearly likely to maximize the differential reporting of stressful events.

The question as to whether the scales may be partially measuring neuroticism arises because they include a lot of items such as *too many things to do* or *troubling thoughts about the future* which could equally find a place in scales designed to measure anxiety or depression. This leads to a problem in interpreting the results even of prospective studies that investigate the association between scores on life events and hassles scales and subsequently occurring physical illness over a period of time. In principle this can establish whether stress really does predict the development of illness. Most prospective studies have relied on self-reports of illness; but it is highly probable that neurotic individuals will not only give high scores on life events and hassles scales but also be more likely to interpret minor symptoms as indicative of physical illness than individuals low on neuroticism. Here an empirical association between stress and illness may occur as a result of a reporting bias rather than a genuine causal link. A better approach is to rely on biologically verified assessments of illness.

Recent researchers investigating stress–illness links have shown a trend away from the use of standardized checklists in favour of the structured interview techniques developed by Brown and Harris. Their *life events and difficulties schedule (LEDS)* is used to assess, classify and rate the severity of each stressful event, making allowance for individual circumstances. Originally developed to study the social origins of depression in women, the LEDS has since been used to study links between life event stress and physical illness (Harris, 1997).

Stress as a Response

Since any catalogue of potentially stressful events is endless and individuals differ greatly as to what they find stressful, an alternative is to seek to identify a characteristic stress response that occurs whatever the nature of the stress. This could theoretically include physiological, psychological and behavioural consequences of stress, although in practice researchers have tended to concentrate on physiological effects, especially those that may be associated with the development of physical illness.

An influential pioneer was Hans Selye, who began a programme of animal experimentation into the physiological effects of noxious stimuli and other types of stress from the early 1930s until shortly before his death in 1982 (Selye, 1976). He argued for the existence of a generalized response, known as the **general adaptation syndrome (GAS)**, which occurs whenever the body defends itself against noxious stimuli. The GAS occurs primarily in the pituitary–adrenocortical system and consists of three stages, an *alarm reaction* in which the body's defences are mobilized, a *resistance stage* in which the body adapts to the cause of stress, and an *exhaustion stage* in which the body's capacity to resist finally breaks down. The GAS may be likened to the process whereby an individual, confronted by sudden unexpected financial demands, takes out a bank loan (alarm reaction), and uses it to meet these demands (resistance stage) until further income is received and the loan repaid (recovery) or bankruptcy results (exhaustion stage). Selye particularly drew attention to the abnormal physiology of the animal during the resistance stage that, if protracted, could lead to what he called the *diseases of adaptation*. These include ulcers, cardiovascular disease and asthma.

Although Selye's views have been very influential in the history of stress research, they are no longer widely accepted following extensive criticism by Mason (1971, 1975). He argued that the body's reaction to different types of stress is not uniform at all. Those common physiological reactions that are found are caused by the emotional reaction of the animal to the stressful event rather than to a direct physiological effect. In many studies of the effects of stress, laboratory animals have been exposed to some highly unpleasant conditions (to put it more bluntly, they have been tortured) and it seems likely that the researchers have been, and perhaps still are, effectively studying the physiology of fear. It is not easy to find an ethical justification for this type of animal experimentation and such studies will not be considered any further.

The tradition of psychosomatic medicine, which was introduced in the last chapter, spans a similar historical period as the work of Selye but focuses much more on the human response to stress. Franz Alexander and his associates drew a distinction between the temporary and biologically adaptive changes in the physiology of the animal facing an emergency necessitating flight or fight and the protracted and maladaptive physiological changes taking place in the anxious or stressed human being. Of particular significance are the physiological changes that are activated by the sympathetic branch of the autonomic nervous system.

KT

The proponents of psychosomatic medicine emphasized the effects of stress and anxiety on the cardiovascular, gastro-enteritic and respiratory systems. Some of their theories have an attractive plausibility, but their broad theoretical sweep and the range of physiological mechanisms proposed was never matched by an appropriate level of careful empirical research. Health psychologists have made some progress in investigating the relationship between stress and cardiovascular disease, but other areas considered by the schools of psychosomatic medicine remain, from a research point of view, largely virgin territory. At present the two most active areas of investigation into responses to stress are, first, the study of the effects of stress on the immune system, usually referred to as **psychoneuroimmunology (PNI)** and, secondly, the study of the long-term effects of extreme or traumatic stress, usually referred to as **post-traumatic stress disorder (PTSD)**. We will now consider these two areas of research.

Psychoneuroimmunology (PNI)

The AIDS epidemic was one reason for an increased interest in psychological influences on the immune system, but there are also other considerations. The immune system is implicated not only in the body's defences against all infectious diseases but also in cancer and in *autoimmune diseases* such as rheumatoid arthritis. If psychological factors can be shown to have a significant role as causes of *upregulation* and *down-regulation* of the immune system, then it is possible that psychological interventions could play an important role in the treatment of a very wide range of diseases.

O'Leary (1990) provides a useful critical analysis of research into stress, emotion and human immune function and further reviews are given by Evans et al. (2000) and Segerstrom and Miller (2004). Maier and Watkins (1998) attempt to synthesize current knowledge from an evolutionary perspective to account for psychological and behavioural effects of physical illness as well as the effects of stress on the immune system. These authors all emphasize that the immune system is a very complicated one involving a range of different types of cell with distinct functions. A brief synopsis of these is given in Box 13.2.

BOX 13.2

CELLS OF THE HUMAN IMMUNE SYSTEM

The main cells of the immune system are *leucocytes*, usually known as white blood cells. The three most important types of leucocytes are *granulocytic cells*, *monocytes/macrophages* and *lymphocytes*. These in turn divide into the following categories:

- **granulocytic leucocytes**: the main types are *neutrophils*, which are *phagocytes* (eating cells) that engulf and destroy bacteria, *eosinophils*, which similarly engulf antigen-antibody complexes, and *basophils*, which have effects that promote the migration of other immune cells to the region.

(Continued)

> **BOX 13.2   (Continued)**
>
> - **monocytes/macrophages**: these cells have a number of functions including 'recognition' of certain carbohydrates on the surfaces of micro-organisms.
> - **lymphocytes**: these cells have the function of attacking specific targets. They can be subdivided into *B cells*, *NK cells* and *T cells*. B cells produce antibodies that proliferate rapidly, thereby controlling infection. NK (natural killer) cells destroy virus-infected and tumour cells. T cells further subdivide into *T helper cells*, which enhance immune responses by stimulating the replication of immune system cells and antibodies, *cytotoxic T cells*, which destroy virus, parasite and tumour-infected cells, and *T suppressor cells*, which inhibit immune responses.

It can be seen that the human immune system is not simple. Much as one might like to do so, it is not possible to talk in a general sense of heightened or reduced immunity, because the immune system is volatile with changes constantly taking place in one or more of its parts. At any particular time one measure may indicate heightened immunity while another may indicate reduced immunity. An important example is the distinction between *cell-mediated immunity* and *humoral immunity*. In recent years there has been considerable interest in the relationship between psychological stress and increases in levels of the hormone cortisol which has the effect of inhibiting cell-mediated immunity while enhancing humoral immunity (Evans et al., 2000; Dickerson and Kemeny, 2004). This provides some support for the much earlier conjecture of the psychosomatic schools (see Chapter 12) that asthma and other allergic conditions can have psychological origins. High levels of cortisol are associated with these conditions (Evans et al., 2000).

One further complication when interpreting PNI research is that the preponderance of different kinds of immune cells varies considerably among healthy individuals and in the same healthy individual from day to day. As O'Leary (1990) points out, the demonstration of a statistically significant effect of stress on one or more parameters of the immune system does not necessarily entail that that these changes have clinical significance as regards disease outcomes.

Research on stress and immunity can be broadly divided into studies of the short-term effects of *acute stress* and of the longer term effects of *chronic stress*. Types of acute stress that have been studied include sleep deprivation, space flight, taking examinations, exposure to the objects of phobias such as snakes, violent exercise, loud noises, electric shocks and attempting to solve difficult or impossible problems. Types of chronic or long-term stress that have been studied include bereavement, unemployment, marital conflict, separation and divorce, and caring for relatives suffering from Alzheimer's disease. No study has investigated the effects of any one kind of stress on all aspects of immune function and it is therefore necessary to piece together findings from different studies in order to obtain a general picture.

It has been a fairly consistent finding that chronic stress is associated with some degree of down regulation of immune systems with changes found particularly in the number of NK cells, the total number of T cells and the proportion of T helper cells to T suppressor cells. Findings for the effects of acute stress have been more variable, with some indications of upregulation, some of downregulation, and some null findings (Evans et al., 2000; Segerstrom and Miller, 2004). Segerstrom and Miller also note that subjective reports of stress are not usually associated with immune changes.

While most of the research in this field has been concerned with establishing the effects of stress on the immune system, there have also been a number of studies investigating the effects of psychological interventions, including stress management, on immune measures. If successful these interventions could obviously have considerable potential benefit in reducing susceptibility to disease and improving recovery rates. Miller and Cohen (2001) reviewed 85 studies with rather disappointing conclusions. Positive findings were mainly for interventions using hypnosis and conditioning while stress management and relaxation techniques rarely produced substantial effects. However they warn against jumping to the conclusion that the immune system cannot be much influenced by psychological interventions, pointing out a range of research problems that need to be overcome before firm conclusions can be drawn.

There is general agreement that a number of methodological difficulties need to be overcome before we can safely conclude that stress has direct effects on the immune system with disease consequences. First, it is important to distinguish between direct effects of stress and other physiological pathways that may be activated by stressful experiences such as sleep deprivation and space flight. Second, it is necessary to rule out indirect effects that may be obtained when stress provokes health hazardous behaviour, such as smoking and alcohol consumption, which may in turn have effects on the immune system. Third, where significant effects of stress on immune function have been adequately demonstrated, it is also necessary to show that these effects have clinical significance as regards disease outcomes. We shall return to this last point later in this chapter when we examine research on the relationship between stress and biologically verified disease.

Post-traumatic stress disorder (PTSD)

The term 'PTSD' was introduced by researchers studying psychological symptoms reported by soldiers returning to the USA from the Vietnam War and it was subsequently extended to studies of other types of traumatic stress. It was first accepted as a diagnostic label by the American Psychiatric Association in 1980. The symptoms that are most often used to characterize PTSD are insomnia, nightmares, flashbacks, problems of memory and concentration, acting or feeling as if the event is recurring and a greatly increased sensitivity to new stressful events (Baum and Spencer, 1997). A variety of physiological changes have also been found in persons suffering from PTSD.

As in the other areas of enquiry that focus on reactions to stress, our understanding of PTSD is complicated by the existence of large individual differences. Not everyone exposed to traumatic stress develops the symptoms of PTSD. Prevalence rates among individuals exposed to extreme stress vary widely according to the nature of the stress, most commonly from 10% to 30%. There are also large individual differences in the types of symptoms encountered and their severity. Some recent attempts have been made to review the voluminous literature on PTSD to establish whether differences in emotional reactions occurring at the time of and immediately after traumatic stress can predict the subsequent development of PTSD, although so far with little agreement

(Harvey and Bryant, 2002; Ozer et al., 2003). Neither is it clear whether reactions to different kinds of traumatic stress are basically the same or whether they depend on the particular type of stress involved.

The psychophysiological differences found between those who suffer from PTSD and those who do not are real enough, but it has not been established whether they have occurred purely as a result of exposure to traumatic stress, or whether they are at least partly determined by pre-existing characteristics of the individuals who develop PTSD. It is quite often found that these individuals have a history of psychological problems, including substance abuse, lifetime major depression, panic attacks and other anxiety disorders (Baum and Spencer, 1997). This in turn raises the question, in any particular case, as to whether the traumatic stress is the primary cause of subsequent psychological reactions or the straw that breaks the camel's back.

While there has been at least one recent attempt to develop a theoretical model of PTSD (Brewin et al., 1996), others question its usefulness as a clinical diagnosis. A trenchant critique is given by the Canadian anthropologist Allan Young (1995) who combines a historical analysis of the concept with an ethnographic study conducted in a psychiatric unit specializing in the treatment of PTSD. He argues that PTSD is not, as its proponents would have us believe, a psychiatric condition that has been vividly described throughout human history, but a cultural phenomenon of the modern era. He traces it to the work of Freud and others in the late nineteenth century, work that has contributed to the **medicalization** of certain types of human unhappiness. While not disputing the extent of the suffering that is caused by traumatic experiences, he does challenge the usefulness of the diagnosis of PTSD as a step towards helping people to deal with their suffering.

Summerfield (2001) takes some of these criticisms further. He points out that the diagnosis of PTSD now has an important legal advantage for people seeking financial compensation for distress suffered while performing functions that might be thought to be part of their job, such as ambulance personnel attending road accidents and police officers on duty at disasters. He comments:

> There is a veritable trauma industry comprising experts, lawyers, claimants and other interested parties. It is a kind of social movement trading on the authority of medical pronouncements. An encounter between a sympathetic psychiatrist and a claimant is primed to produce a report of post-traumatic stress disorder if that is what the lawyer says the rules require and what has, in effect, been commissioned. In the United Kingdom awards for psychological damage based on the diagnosis can be several times higher than, say, the £30,000 to £40,000 limit that the Criminal Injuries Compensation Authority applies for the traumatic loss of a leg. (Summerfield, 2001: 95)

Mezey and Robbins (2001) challenge Summerfield's view. While agreeing that the diagnosis of PTSD has been used indiscriminately in civil litigation, they argue that PTSD involves a level of distress that transcends ordinary human misery and unhappiness and that the diagnosis has the positive function of taking away blame from the sufferer who experiences guilt, shame and failure, so that the symptoms can be experienced as a normal response to an abnormal event rather than a pathological condition. They also argue that the psychophysiological characteristics of PTSD can be clearly distinguished from those associated with other psychiatric diagnoses.

KT

The current approach to the treatment of PTSD usually involves a combination of pharmacological treatment and cognitive behaviour therapy. Studies of cognitive behavioural therapy over periods ranging from 6 to 16 weeks have indicated a substantial improvement in 20% to 50% of patients.

Interactional Models of Stress

A number of theorists have sought to overcome the problems of stimulus and response models by conceptualizing stress as a relationship between the individual and the environment and developing *interactional models*. The most influential of these was first put forward by Lazarus and developed by Lazarus and Folkman (1984). In this model psychological stress is defined as 'a particular relationship between the person and the environment that is appraised by the person as taxing or exceeding his or her resources and endangering his or her well-being' (p. 10). A distinction is made between *primary appraisal* whereby an event may be perceived as benign and non-threatening, potentially harmful, threatening to one's self-esteem, or challenging, and *secondary appraisal* in which an assessment is made of one's ability to cope with the threat or challenge. Stress occurs whenever there is a mismatch between perceived threat and perceived ability to cope.

These ideas have been developed at considerable length in a number of books and articles, but they do raise the question as to whether they amount to much more than just another way of saying that stress is when you think you cannot cope. Although this may seem a modest enough assertion, it can in fact be criticized for its implication that stress results only from a purely subjective mismatch between demands and coping resources. One can ask, what about the person who thinks that they can cope when objectively the demands of the situation exceed the person's actual ability to cope? Are such optimists not stressed?

This problem is partially solved by Trumbull and Appley (1986) who extended the model of Lazarus and Folkman by proposing that stress can occur whenever either the real or the perceived demands exceed either the real or the perceived capacity to cope. However, it might be felt that Trumbull and Appley's definition is so broad and all-encompassing that it amounts to no more than a statement of the obvious. A critical question might be, what is the relative importance of mismatches between real demands and coping resources and those between perceived demands and coping resources in determining whether an individual suffers the effects of stress?

Using the terminology introduced in Chapter 1, it is probably better to think of interactional models of stress as frameworks for thinking about the subject rather than specific theories or models. Another way of representing an interactional framework is the flowchart model of Cox (1978) shown in Figure 13.2. One of the useful features of this flowchart is that it incorporates feedback between responses, demands and appraisal. For example, behavioural responses, depending on whether they are appropriate or inappropriate, may result in a reduction or an increase in actual demand; psychological defence mechanisms may become activated leading to changes in the cognitive appraisal of mismatches between perceived demand and perceived capability, and so on.

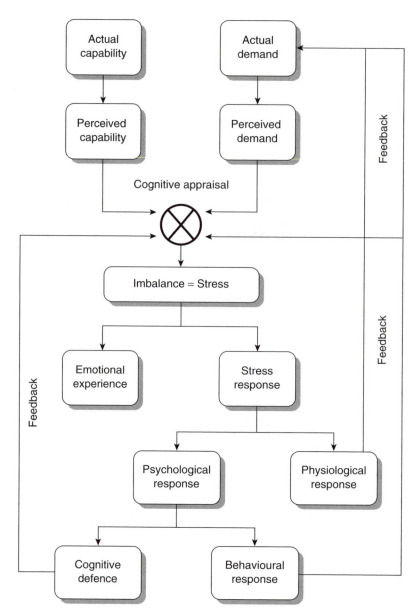

Figure 13.2 Flowchart for an interactional model of stress (Cox, 1978: 19; reproduced with permission)

One consequence of the emergence of interactional models of stress has been the development of checklists designed to assess the individual's predominant coping strategies. An example is the COPE questionnaire devised by Carver et al. (1989) that consists of 14 sub-scales each consisting of a number of items for which the individual indicates agreement or disagreement on a four-point scale. The 14 sub-scales with an example of a checklist statement from each are shown in Box 13.3.

BOX 13.3

ASSESSING COPING STRATEGIES: THE *COPE* SCALE (CARVER ET AL., 1989)

In the COPE scale, you are asked how you respond when confronting difficult or stressful events in your life. To each item you use the following rating system:

1 I usually don't do this at all.
2 I usually do this a little bit.
3 I usually do this a medium amount.
4 I usually do this a lot.

The 14 COPE sub-scales with an example of a checklist from each (the complete version contained four items per sub-scale) are:

1 **Active coping**: I take additional action to get rid of the problem.
2 **Planning**: I try to come up with a strategy about what to do.
3 **Suppression of competing activities**: I put aside other activities in order to concentrate on this.
4 **Restraint coping**: I force myself to wait until the right time to do something.
5 **Seeking social support for emotional reasons**: I ask people who have had similar experience what they did.
6 **Seeking social support for instrumental reasons**: I talk to someone about how I feel.
7 **Positive reinterpretation and growth**: I look for something good in what is happening.
8 **Acceptance**: I learn to live with it.
9 **Turning to religion**: I seek God's help.
10 **Focus on and venting of emotions**: I get upset and let my emotions out.
11 **Denial**: I refuse to believe that it has happened.
12 **Behavioural disengagement**: I give up the attempt to get what I want.
13 **Mental disengagement**: I turn to work or other substitute activities to take my mind off things.
14 **Alcohol-drug disengagement**: I drink alcohol, or take drugs, in order to think about it less.

Coping scales have been criticized for adopting a 'blunderbuss' approach to the complex mechanisms involved in coping with different types of stress, and failing to take account of the fact that individuals may vary greatly in the way they cope with different stressful situations (Somerfield, 1997; Aldwin and Park, 2004). They may also be criticized for relying too much on introspective judgements unsupported by other types of evidence. If it is a feature of the psychology of stress that people tend to behave irrationally when exposed to high levels of stress, then the reports of individuals about their personal ways of coping may be particularly inaccurate. For example, *denial*, the refusal to acknowledge the existence of a real danger, may be observed when an individual ignores or denies the significance of symptoms of life-threatening disease, but it is unlikely to be a fully conscious process. How is such an individual likely to respond to the denial items on the COPE questionnaire when asked, for example, how often when confronted with stressful life events, he or she 'refuses to believe that it has happened'?

Does Stress Make Us More Susceptible to Physical Illness?

This question has generated a great deal of research and it is easy to see why. If stress can be shown to be an important factor influencing susceptibility to disease, then the possibility exists that interventions designed to reduce stress, or to help individuals to cope better with unavoidable stress, may lower the incidence of disease and assist the recovery of those who are already ill.

The popular belief that stress is a major cause of physical illness is not convincingly supported by existing research findings, but neither is the opposite belief that stress plays only an insignificant role. The problem is that it is extremely difficult to carry out well-controlled research in this area and most of what has been done is open to a range of possible interpretations. We have already noted two shortcomings that apply to the majority of studies. First, retrospective studies may have a substantial response bias because people are more likely to recall experiencing stress in periods preceding illness than at other times. Second, all studies that rely on self-reports of illness may have a response bias because people who consider themselves to be suffering from stress are more likely than non-stressed individuals to interpret minor ailments as symptoms of illness.

The better designed studies that investigate the association between exposure to stress and subsequent and biologically verified illness may still present problems of interpretation. It has been shown that people who are experiencing stress are more likely than others to indulge in health hazardous behaviour such as heavy smoking and drinking, drug taking, poor diet, inadequate sleep and lack of exercise. Thus it could be that stress acts only indirectly as a cause of illness insofar as it influences health behaviour.

The methodological problems that we have discussed so far are all likely to lead to inflated estimates of the strength of the association between stress and illness. Further issues have been raised that point in the opposite direction, to the possibility that current research may produce underestimates. These issues derive partly from work on the relationship between personality and illness considered in Chapter 12. One argument is that some individuals possess personal characteristics that make them resistant to the effects of stress. Among the personal characteristics that have been suggested as having this function are *internal locus of control, self-efficacy, hardiness* and *sense of coherence*. If stress only causes illness in people with vulnerable personalities, then it may be misleading to calculate the size of the effect of stress on illness by using general population samples that include many who are relatively insensitive to these effects.

KT

A further issue is the potential mediating effect of **social support** on the relationship between stress and illness. There is extensive evidence that people with strong networks of social support live longer and enjoy better health than relatively isolated individuals. Uchino et al. (1996) note that high quality social support appears to have beneficial effects on aspects of the cardiovascular, endocrine and immune systems. In seeking to explain this relationship, one influential hypothesis is that social support has a *buffering effect* against the effects of stress, so that stress is only likely to cause illness among individuals with relatively low levels of support (Cohen and Wills, 1985). Uchino et al. argue that evidence from a number of studies demonstrates the existence of such stress-buffering effects.

If the above considerations are valid, then stress is only likely to have a strong effect on susceptibility to illness among individuals who score low on internal locus of control, self-efficacy, hardiness and sense of coherence, and who have a low level of perceived social support. Therefore, studies of stress–illness links that are based on representative population samples may greatly underestimate the potential effects of stress because they include many individuals for whom the effect is likely to be small. Would-be researchers, who consider these issues alongside our previous observations on factors that may lead to overestimates, could be excused if they were to throw up their hands in despair. As a research topic it is not an easy one and certainly no study published to date has succeeded in overcoming all or even most of the potential problems. Nevertheless, recent and relatively well-designed studies have thrown up a number of interesting findings, particularly in the areas of coronary heart disease (CHD), cancer and infectious diseases, and to these we now turn.

Coronary heart disease (CHD)

Studies of the relationship between stress and subsequent CHD have produced a mixture of positive and negative findings. In a 12-year follow-up study of 6,935 healthy men, Rosengren et al. (1991) found that those who had initially reported substantial stress were more likely to experience coronary artery disease subsequently, after controlling for the effects of smoking, alcohol consumption and lack of physical exercise. In contrast, in a six-year follow-up of 12,866 men who were at high risk, Hollis et al. (1990) found no relationship between stress and subsequent mortality. Macleod et al. (2002) describe a 21-year follow-up study of 2,623 Scottish men in which self-reported stress was strongly associated with subsequent angina but not with objective measures of CHD, including mortality. We have already noted in Chapter 12 that the diagnosis of angina is usually based on self-reported chest pain and Macleod et al. conclude that the stress–angina relationship probably results from a tendency of participants reporting higher stress to also report more symptoms.

There has also been extensive research into the possible relationship between occupational stress and CHD. Studies of workers in European countries, with follow-up periods ranging from 5 to 10 years, have usually found an association between assessments of job strain and subsequent risk of CHD (e.g. Kivimäki et al., 2002, and Kuper and Marmot, 2003), but Eaker et al. (2004) found no association in a 10-year follow-up of 1,711 men and 1,328 women in the USA.

In view of the conflicting nature of the findings to date, it is obviously not possible to draw any definite conclusions as to whether or not stress increases susceptibility to CHD. It is to be hoped that future studies will clarify the picture. It is apparent that such future studies should rely on objective measures of heart disease rather than the diagnosis of angina and attention will need to be given to possible differences between results for self-reported stress and life event measures, for gender, sociocultural and national differences, and for different kinds of stress.

Cancer

Studies that have considered that the subsequent occurrence of all forms of cancer following periods of stress have generally failed to find evidence of an association. The few positive findings have come from small and poorly designed studies, which have low power, whereas large prospective studies have produced negative findings. There is, for example, no indication of a higher cancer rate among the bereaved (Fox, 1988), and Keehn (1980) found no increased rate of cancer among former prisoners of war, men who had suffered extreme forms of mental and physical hardship. With regard to the prognosis for individuals already suffering from cancer, the most impressive study involved over 14,000 women in Norway and found no increased risk of recurrence or death for those who had lost a spouse or had been divorced (Kvikstad et al., 1995) or who had lost a child (Kvikstad and Vatten, 1996). Reviewing the evidence from 26 studies on coping styles and survival and recurrence in people with cancer, Petticrew et al. (2002) conclude that there were few indications of significant associations.

Over the last 20 years particular attention has been given to the possible relationship between stress and breast cancer. This is understandable because breast cancer is the most common cause of premature death in women and epidemiological studies have so far failed to establish its causes. McGee (1999) notes that speculation about stress as a cause of breast cancer may be found in medical opinion at least as far back as 1893. He gives examples of recent poorly designed studies, which sometimes produce dramatic positive findings, while large prospective studies have not found an association. In a recent review Duijts et al. (2003) confirmed this conclusion but with the single interesting exception that there was a significant albeit modest association with death of spouse. Given the preponderance of negative findings in this field, this particular positive finding needs to be treated with caution. It is also in conflict with the earlier findings of Fox (1988) mentioned above; but, in view of the fact that breast cancer and loss of spouse are both relatively common among women over 60, it is a result worthy of further research.

In addition to research into the relationship between stress and the subsequent diagnosis of breast cancer, there has also been a good deal of recent interest in studies of the relationship between stressful life events and survival and recurrence for women who have already been diagnosed and treated. Some dramatic findings of a poorer prognosis for patients who experience stressful events after diagnosis were initially given considerable publicity although other researchers were reporting negative findings (see Petticrew et al., 1999). All of these studies had serious methodological flaws that have been largely overcome in a major recent prospective study by Graham et al. (2002). They carried out a five-year follow-up of 170 women patients who had received surgery for breast cancer and found no evidence of a relationship between stressful events and increased risk of relapse.

In view of the amount of publicity that is given to positive findings, it is unlikely that researchers will be deterred by the preponderance of negative findings from carrying out further research into the possible association between stress and cancer. Research in psychoneuroimmunology discussed earlier in this chapter suggests that the most promising field of enquiry would be the effects of chronic long-term stress rather than the effect of stressful life events, which has featured in most of the research to date.

If stress causes changes in the immune system, then this could obviously lead to altered susceptibility to infectious disease. We have already seen that there is extensive evidence that stress does have statistically significant effects on a variety of measures of immune functioning, but that these effects are generally well within the range of normal variation for healthy people. This leaves the question open as to whether they are sufficiently large to lead to altered susceptibility to disease. The obvious way to find out is to examine the evidence for a direct relationship between stress and the incidence of infectious disease. Over the last 20 years Sheldon Cohen and his associates have been conducting a thorough and detailed analysis of this issue.

Cohen and Williamson (1991) dismissed evidence drawn from retrospective studies and all studies that rely on self-reported illness for reasons which we have already explained. Much of the research in this area is concerned with minor viral infections, such as the common cold, and these are likely to be particularly susceptible to reporting bias. For example, a mild sore throat and headache may be self-diagnosed as a viral infection by the more hypochondriacal individual while others will attribute the same symptoms to staying up too late at a party in a smoky atmosphere. It is easy to see how correlations may occur between such self-reported illness and perceived levels of stress, even if there is no true causal relationship between stress and susceptibility to viral infections.

A further problem pointed out by Cohen and Williamson is that stress may be associated with greater exposure to viruses, perhaps because stressed individuals seek the company of others to a greater extent than non-stressed individuals. An ingenious way of avoiding the difficulty comes from **viral challenge studies** in which volunteers are deliberately exposed to viruses, usually cold viruses, and then followed up to determine whether those reporting high levels of stress prior to exposure are more likely than others to catch the virus, biologically verified by the researchers.

KT

Since 1986 Cohen and his associates have been conducting viral challenge studies on stress and the common cold, and Cohen and Miller (2001) summarize their findings. The first major study was conducted in the UK, where 394 participants were exposed to one of five different cold viruses. It was found that stress levels predicted increased likelihood of catching a cold, that this was equally true for all five viruses, and that the higher the level of reported stress, the greater the susceptibility. They also found that this relationship remained the same after controlling for the effects of smoking, drinking, diet, exercise and sleep quality.

In a second major study, this time conducted in the USA, 276 participants were exposed to one or other of two types of cold virus, after completing the LEDS semi-structured interview, described earlier in this chapter. The main purpose of the study was to ascertain what types of stress were associated with increased susceptibility to the cold viruses. It was found that, the longer the duration of stress, the greater the probability of catching a cold, and that interpersonal problems with family and friends and work problems were the main culprits. Short-term acute stress did not appear to increase susceptibility. Cohen and Miller (2001) describe research in progress by the group, now seeking to establish which parameters of the immune system mediate the relationship between stress and susceptibility.

A question discussed frequently in recent years is whether stress is a factor in the onset or development of HIV/AIDS. Not everyone exposed to the HIV virus becomes infected and the rate at which the disease progresses varies from person to person. Since much of this variability is currently unexplained it is not surprising that there has been considerable interest in the possibility that stress is a factor. Unfortunately the topic is an extremely difficult one to investigate. It is rarely possible to know when an individual was initially exposed to the HIV virus with any degree of precision and subsequent diagnosis and disease progression is associated with much stress, lifestyle changes and the occurrence of other infections, so that it is not easy to disentangle the variables.

Cohen and Herbert (1996) reviewed the evidence on stress and HIV progression, and concluded that, although stress could not be ruled out as a factor, they were unable to find any convincing evidence that it is. However, since then there has been one notable study indicating that stress and social support may both influence progression. Leserman et al. (2000) studied disease progression over 7.5 years for 82 HIV positive homosexual men, none of whom had AIDS symptoms initially. They found that progression to AIDS was considerably faster for those reporting more stressful life events and additionally for those reporting low levels of satisfaction with social support. They conclude that research is now needed to discover whether interventions based on these findings can alter the clinical course for HIV infection. Further discussion of psychosocial aspects of CHD, cancer and HIV/AIDS is provided in Chapter 17.

Future Research

1 Analysis of *stress discourses* among and between people and health professionals to establish more clearly the ways in which the concept of stress functions in society.
2 Studies focusing on the psychological and physiological effects of different types of stress (e.g. bereavement, excessive workload, physical assault). Such research need not proceed on the assumption that very general psychophysiological models of stress are being tested.
3 Research into the effects of stress on the gastro-enteritic and respiratory systems in addition to its effects on the cardiovascular and immune systems.
4 Assessment of the effectiveness of therapeutic interventions including especially those designed to alleviate the psychological effects of traumatic stress and the physiological effects of stress for those already suffering from or at risk for *stress-related diseases.*
5 Prospective stress-disease studies that combine measures of a wide variety of physiological characteristics (e.g. of the immune system) with biologically verified assessments of disease status.
6 Clarification of the relationship between stress, physiological reactions, health behaviours, social support and *stress immunizing* personality characteristics using large-scale population-based studies.

Summary

1 Stress is sometimes conceptualized as environmental stimuli or life events that impinge on the individual, sometimes as a particular type of response or reaction to stressful events, and sometimes as a mismatch between demands placed on the individual and the perceived ability to cope with these demands.

2   Various methods have been proposed for assessing life events stress. The main problem is that individuals differ greatly as to what they find stressful. For this reason structured interviews are to be preferred to standardized questionnaires.

3   Investigations into physiological reactions to stress have identified many different types of reaction. Physiological reactions vary considerably from individual to individual and according to the nature of the stressor.

4   Significant effects of stress on the immune system have been demonstrated although it is not yet clear whether these effects are large enough to alter susceptibility to disease.

5   A variety of physiological and psychological effects associated with exposure to traumatic stress have been shown to exist, although it is arguable whether they can be used to establish post-traumatic stress disorder as a psychiatric condition.

6   Interactional models of stress are intrinsically attractive because they take account of individual differences in reactions to stress and methods of coping. They have the disadvantage that they depend very much on the reliability of subjective assessments and, for this reason, may not be scientifically testable.

7   Empirical studies of the relationship between stress and disease have frequently been unsatisfactory because they are retrospective and rely on self-reported stress and illness. They also frequently fail to distinguish between physiological effects of stress and influences on health behaviour.

8   Theoretical models of the relationship between stress and disease are difficult to test because they involve complex interactions between stress, social support and personality variables.

9   There is conflicting evidence as to whether stress does or does not contribute to risk of coronary heart disease.

10 There is no convincing evidence for a significant role of stress in the aetiology and prognosis for cancer.

11 Viral challenge studies have established that stress does increase susceptibility to some infectious diseases, especially colds and flu. It has not yet been established whether this association is the direct result of effects on the immune system or indirectly caused by changes in health behaviour.

12 There is some recent evidence that high stress and low social support is associated with faster disease progression from HIV to AIDS. It remains to be determined whether interventions based on these findings can alter the clinical course for HIV infection.

Key Terms

KT

general adaptation syndrome (GAS)

hassles scale

medicalization

post-traumatic stress disorder (PTSD)

psychoneuroimmunology (PNI)

social support

social readjustment rating scale (SRRS)

stress

stress innoculation training

stress management workshops

uplifts scale

viral challenge studies

14

Communication: Messages and Meanings

Words and language are not wrappings in which things *are packed for the commerce of those* who *write and speak. It is in words and language that things first come into being and are.* (Steiner, 1978: 41)

Outline

This chapter focuses on interpersonal health communication. Three approaches to the study of doctor–patient communication are described: the 'deviant patient' perspective; the 'authoritarian doctor' perspective; and the 'interactive dyad' perspective. Three widely-used research tools are examined, illustrated and critically evaluated: interaction analysis systems, questionnaires and qualitative textual analysis. Recent trends in the study of interpersonal health communication are introduced. They are concerned with gender and culture, 'compliance', the impact of computer technologies, non-verbal communication, the role of communication in coping with illness, and counselling.

Health Communication

KT

Health communication is communication in any form that contributes to the promotion of health. Thus, health promotion is the objective, whereas **health communication** is the means through which this objective is to be achieved. Not all measures that aim to promote health depend upon communication (e.g. fencing around dangerous sites; fitting cars with seatbelts). However, health psychologists' involvement with health promotion has been primarily concerned with communication. Thus, from a health psychology point of view, health promotion and health communication cover very similar, if not the same, ground. This is reflected in the editor's introduction to the *Journal of Health Communication*: 'Health communication is concerned with the use of ethical, persuasive means to craft and deliver campaigns and implement strategies that promote good health and prevent disease' (Ratzan, 1996: v).

Thus, the study of health communication is relevant to public health promotion efforts such as media campaigns as well as to the health promotion activities of health-care professionals including doctors. Public health communication will be discussed in Chapter 20; this chapter focuses upon interpersonal health communication. The bulk of the literature in this field is concerned with doctor–patient communication within the surgery setting. However, it is necessary to bear in mind that health promotion activities are carried out in some form by all health-care professionals (HCPs) and HCP–patient communication is a key issue for health psychologists. This chapter critically reviews the major theories and research methods, and introduces recent trends and future directions.

Doctor–Patient Communication

Why is it important?

Communication is an essential, and sometimes the only, route to information about the patient's physical and/or mental state. Early identification of symptoms and thus diagnosis and treatment are made possible through the patient's verbal descriptions of the discomfort they experience. In turn, the doctor, nurse or counsellor provides the patient with crucial information about necessary adjustments in lifestyle as well as treatment directives. All of these can be lifesaving. Also, it has been suggested that effective communication can have a therapeutic effect in itself (e.g. Radley, 1994). Although the major focus has been on verbal communication, non-verbal communication can also be important in interpersonal settings.

Limitations of doctor–patient communication

Despite its importance in the healing process, doctor–patient communication is not always effective. According to Ley (1982) communication is the least satisfactory aspect of the doctor–patient encounter: about one-third of patients in the UK say they are dissatisfied. Furthermore, patients' understanding and memory of what they have been told by the doctor is limited. In addition, and possibly as a consequence, one-third to one-half of outpatients do not comply with doctors' advice (Office of Inspector General, 1990, Chapter 8). Finally, a substantial proportion of patients' problems remain undisclosed and undetected (Maguire, 1984). In spite of a huge amount of research published in journals that are highly accessible to health-care professionals, the proportion of dissatisfied patients remained surprisingly, and disappointingly, constant over 25 years (Ong et al., 1995).

Improvements in the quality of doctor–patient communication could generate significant benefits for both patients and service providers. These include greater **patient satisfaction** with health-care services, increased patient adherence to treatment regimens, decreases in anxiety and distress on the part of patients, better mental health in doctors as well as improved health promotion. In addition, improved disease prevention, quicker recovery from surgery as well as shorter lengths of stay in hospital would benefit the tax payer.

KT

Approaches to the Study of Doctor–Patient Communication

The 'deviant patient' perspective

Early studies focused on patient characteristics in their attempt to account for failures in doctor–patient communication. For example, Balint's (1964) psychoanalytic approach assumed that in their presentations to the doctor, patients were routinely masking the 'real' problem and that it was the doctor's task to uncover it. Another popular early research question was 'what is it about the patient that makes him/her a defaulter?' (see Box 14.1).

BOX 14.1

APPROACHES TO THE STUDY OF DOCTOR–PATIENT COMMUNICATION

Perspective:	Methods:
'Deviant patient'	Questionnaires
	Interaction analysis systems
'Authoritarian doctor'	Interaction analysis systems
	Questionnaires
'Interactive dyad'	Conversation analysis
	Discourse analysis

However, the search for patient characteristics responsible for non-adherence to treatment regimens met with little success. Instead, it was found that there was a link between patient satisfaction and **compliance (or adherence)** (e.g. Ley, 1982): satisfied patients were more likely to co-operate with their doctor's advice (see Chapter 15). This, together with wider social developments of the late 1960s that challenged traditional concepts of 'authority', led to a shift of focus onto the role of the doctor.

The 'authoritarian doctor' perspective

In this approach researchers looked at the ways in which doctors use their authority in order to control the doctor–patient interaction. Much emphasis was placed upon the inbuilt asymmetry in the doctor–patient interaction. In a classic study, Byrne and Long (1976) identified different doctors' styles of communicating with patients. They analysed audio-taped interactions from 71 general practitioners (GPs) and approximately 2,500 patients and identified four diagnostic styles and seven prescriptive styles used by the doctors. These styles constitute a continuum from 'patient-centred' to 'doctor-centred' styles. A **patient-centred communication style** makes use of the patient's knowledge and experience through techniques such as silence, listening and reflection, whereas a **doctor-centred communication style** makes use of the doctor's knowledge and skill, for example, through asking questions. Byrne and Long observed that doctors adopted a habitual style that they tended to use with most patients. Some doctors were more controlling than others.

The major criticism of doctors' traditional communication style was that it was characterized by working to rigid agendas, little listening to patients' accounts and little open discussion of treatment options. A more patient-centred approach was called for. It was suggested that patient-centred styles increase patient adherence as well as satisfaction (e.g. Stewart, 1984). One corollary of this approach was the attempt to provide medical students with effective training in doctor–patient communication (e.g. Maguire, 1984; Maguire et al., 1989).

However, success has been limited. Recent studies have also not found as strong and positive a relationship between patient-centredness and satisfaction (Winefield et al., 1996). Kreps (1996) advocated a consumer orientation to health care and health promotion in order to address the imbalance of power between providers and consumers. Until this power imbalance is corrected, training in communication skills is unlikely to succeed (Meeuwesen et al., 1991). [Kreps (2001) provides further discussion of issues relevant to health communication, Reading 18 in Marks (2002a).]

The 'interactive dyad' perspective

In the 1990s the focus on doctor–patient communication shifted again. Researchers began looking at the **communicative event** to which both doctor and patient contribute. Thus, both doctor and patient are seen to be shaping the conversation as they make use of culturally available discursive resources. Both doctor and patient use language in order to achieve interpersonal objectives, such as disclaiming or attributing responsibility for the patient's ill-health or projecting a 'brave face' to avoid categorization as a hypochondriac. The 1990s ended with the assertion that 'doctor (or nurse) knows best' should have no place in modern health care (Coulter, 1999).

KT

A focus on the communicative event as a joint achievement can shed light on the reasons for communication failure. For example, serious misunderstandings can arise when the doctor takes at face value patient statements that are in fact designed to communicate relational or self-presentational meanings, such as responding 'Fine, thank you' when being asked 'How are you?' (e.g. Coupland et al., 1994).

The importance of non-verbal communication in the form of eye contact, facial expression, gestures and other forms of communication has also been highlighted (Bensing, 1991). A focus on the communicative event, as opposed to the individual characteristics of doctors and/or patients, also allows the role of culture specificity in doctor–patient interactions to be explored.

Methods Used to Study Doctor–Patient Communication

Three methods for the study of doctor–patient communication can be identified: interaction analysis systems; questionnaire studies; qualitative textual analysis.

Interaction analysis systems

KT

Researchers in the field have used a range of methods to explore doctor–patient communication. The most widely used research tool to date is the **interaction analysis system (IAS)**. This is an observation instrument that allows the researcher to identify, categorize and quantify features of the doctor–patient encounter. A large number of different interaction analysis systems have been developed. The most commonly used IASs include those devised by Bales (1950) and Roter (1977). Here, audio- or video-recorded doctor–patient interactions are analysed by categorizing each statement into one of a large number of mutually exclusive and exhaustive content categories. For example, a doctor's statement could be classified as 'information giving', 'information seeking' or 'social conversation'. A related analytic approach is Stiles' Verbal Exchange Structure (Stiles, 1996) that identifies sets of speech act categories that tend to occur together and that are designed to achieve certain objectives within an encounter.

In a meta-analysis of IAS studies of doctor–patient communication Roter (1989) identified six broad communication variables addressed in the studies. These include information giving, information seeking, social conversation, positive talk, negative talk and partnership building. Roter also notes that IASs were predominantly used to study the doctors', rather than the patients', **communication styles**. Thus, IAS research is most closely associated with the 'authoritarian doctor' perspective.

KT

Example of a study using an IAS: Street (1991)   The objective of this study was to explain systematic differences in information giving by doctors. It has been found that patients who are upper middle class, more seriously ill, more educated and middle aged receive more information from their doctors (Waitzkin, 1985). In order to identify possible causes of these differences, Street (1991) measured the following variables:

1   Patients' communicative style (e.g. question asking, affective expressiveness and opinion giving).
2   Patient characteristics (e.g. education, age, sex, anxiety).
3   Physicians' 'partnership-building' utterances (i.e. utterances that solicit/invite patients' questions, concerns and opinions).

Video-recordings of doctor–patient interactions at a family practice clinic at a teaching hospital in the USA were transcribed. The following five verbal behaviours were coded:

1   Physicians' information giving.
2   Physicians' partnership building.
3   Patients' opinion giving.
4   Patients' affective expressions.
5   Patients' question asking.

Patients were found to ask few questions (only 4.1% of all patient utterances) and to offer few opinions (6.4%). Physicians rarely solicited the patients' concerns, opinions and questions (only 2.3% of all physician utterances were partnership building). The most powerful predictor of doctors' information giving was patients' question asking. Also, anxious patients received significantly more information from their doctors than did less worried patients. There was also a tendency for younger and more educated patients to receive more diagnostic information.

Thus, this study's findings suggest that differences in physicians' information giving are partially mediated by differences in patients' communicative style (i.e. via question asking). However, it would be wrong to conclude that patients' communicative style is the 'cause of' physician information giving, since patients' question asking is largely a response to physicians' partnership-building utterances.

Even though IAS studies are able to identify and quantify relevant communication variables in doctor–patient interactions, there are a number of shortcomings associated with this approach. First, it does not allow us to analyse sequencing in conversation. IASs can only tell us what types of utterances were made, by whom and how often. It does not allow us to explore who initiates particular turns and with what consequences. Second, it relies upon a literal reading of statements. As a result, rhetorical strategies such as irony or sarcasm and their communicative functions cannot be identified and analysed. These concerns have been taken up by more recent methods of analysis, such as conversation analysis or discourse analysis, to be discussed later in this chapter.

Questionnaire studies

A number of questionnaires have been developed to measure patients' perceptions of doctors' communication style. Such questionnaires tend to be administered after a clinic visit, and they therefore rely upon the patient's memory of the actual interaction. Questionnaire items include statements about the manner in which the doctor interacted with the patient (e.g. 'The doctor deliberately reacts in such a way that I know s/he is listening') that the patient is asked to rate on a Likert-type scale. Questionnaires are also used to measure patient satisfaction. A combination of questionnaires can be used in order to investigate the relationship between doctor's communication style and patient satisfaction (e.g. Buller and Buller, 1987). Questionnaires are predominantly used to study the doctors' rather than the patients' communication styles. Thus, questionnaire research tends to come from within the 'authoritarian doctor' perspective.

Example of a questionnaire study: Makoul et al. (1995) As part of a wider study of communication and decision-making about prescription medication, Makoul et al. (1995) used questionnaires in order to study discrepancies between perceived and actual communication. They video-recorded 903 consultations involving 39 GPs and their patients in Oxford, UK. After the consultation, patients were asked to complete a questionnaire that included a section about their perceptions of communication during the consultation. Doctors' questionnaires included questions about their patients' characteristics as well as their own communication styles. Analysis of the video-recordings involved the use of checklists that allowed the researchers to record mention of a particular topic (e.g. risk, benefit of medication) as well as who initiated discussion of the topic.

The results showed that physicians most frequently mentioned the product name (in 78.2% of consultations) and instructions for use of the medication (86.7%), whereas patients remained extremely passive. There was little discussion of issues such as side effects or the patient's opinion about the medication. For example, physicians initiated discussion about the patient's ability to follow the treatment plan in only 4.8% of the consultations. However, analysis of the questionnaires revealed that both doctors and patients overestimated the extent to which these issues had been discussed during the consultation. The authors concluded that the observed pattern of communication about prescription medication does not contribute to the development of patients' decision-making competencies. In addition, they point out that the observed discrepancies between interactants' perceptions and actual communication cast doubt on communication studies that use self-report methods alone.

Questionnaire-based studies of doctor–patient communication rely upon participants' memories of their perceptions of the interaction. This introduces two sources of bias. First, memory may be faulty. Second, participants' perceptions at the time of the interaction may have been distorted. In addition, the use of closed, multiple-choice items does not allow participants to generate their own criteria for evaluating doctor–patient communication. This is to say, questionnaires may be of limited validity for individuals or groups of participants. Finally, patients may be reluctant to be critical of their doctors.

Qualitative textual analysis

Researchers have also employed qualitative methods of text analysis such as discourse or conversation analysis. These methods require accurate and detailed transcription of recordings of doctor–patient interactions. Interview transcripts are then subjected to fine-grained linguistic analysis. The aim is to identify the procedures that speakers use in order to manage their discursive objectives (e.g. changing topics, disclaiming responsibility, delivering advice, etc.). This involves paying close attention to turn taking and transitions from one topic to another. In addition, a transcript is read as a whole, with a focus upon the indexicality of language, rather than as a collection of independent statements. Researchers are thus able to explore the ways in which meaning is constructed and negotiated by participants and trace the consequences of such constructions in the text. This approach is informed by the 'interactive dyad perspective'.

Example of a discourse analytic study: Coupland et al. (1994)   Coupland et al. were interested in the relationship between medical and socio-relational dimensions of doctor–patient talk. In particular, they wanted to know how the opening phases of consultations between doctors and elderly patients are achieved and how participants enter a medical frame of talk. An analysis of 85 audio-taped consultations at a geriatric outpatients clinic in the UK was carried out for this purpose. It was found that, typically, consultations were initiated by some form of socio-relational talk, however brief. Consultation openings tended to take the following form:

- Summons/approach (e.g. 'Come in.').
- Greetings (e.g. 'Hello there.').
- Dispositional talk (e.g. 'Do sit down. Won't keep you a minute.').
- Familiarity sequence (e.g. 'I think I saw you two weeks ago, didn't I, Mrs Smith?').
- Holding sequence (e.g. 'Let's have a look at your notes.').
- How-are-you type exchange (e.g. 'How are you feeling?').

In the vast majority of cases, all of the above were initiated by the doctor. Other exchanges, such as apologies (e.g. 'Sorry I'm late'), compliments (e.g. 'You look very smart today') or environmental talk (e.g. 'It's hot, isn't it?') can be inserted into the typical consultation opening sequence by either doctor or patient. The doctor's 'How-are-you?' (HAY?) commonly occurs after a holding sequence and constitutes the transition from preliminary talk to the medical frame. However, Coupland et al. identified a number of alternative formulations of the HAY? as well as different patient interpretations of the HAY? For example, a 'How are you today?' can elicit a socio-relational 'I'm fine, thanks' instead of the intended account of the patient's current medical complaint.

In general, Coupland et al. found that patients and sometimes also doctors did not immediately and categorically orient to the medical agenda. They conclude that patients as well as doctors played significant parts in negotiating how and when they should move into medically framed talk. This, they argue, is vital within the context of geriatric care since many of the consequences of illness for elderly patients are experienced socially (e.g. reduced mobility or reduced independence).

Qualitative textual analysis is extremely time consuming. Detailed transcription, including pauses, interruptions and repetitions as they take place in naturally occurring conversations, takes up to 10 hours per one-hour recording. Line-by-line linguistic analysis of discourse requires careful reading and re-reading of the text. Researchers tend to analyse small numbers of transcripts in great detail. As a result, it is impossible to ascertain how common the discursive strategies and practices identified by any one study might be in a particular population. In other words, qualitative textual analysis does not allow us to generalize.

Another criticism of this method is that it conceives of the doctor–patient interaction as an entirely localized event. This fails to take into account power relations that pre-exist the doctor–patient encounter. That is to say, what is said by patient and doctor is not simply a product of their interaction but it reflects their respective roles and status within society. We need to look beyond the text in order to identify such factors.

Triangulation: combining methods of analysis

Even though the three methodological approaches to the study of doctor–patient communication have been discussed separately, there is no reason to believe that they are mutually exclusive alternatives. To the contrary, it could be argued that the best studies of communication would have to use a combination of methods in order to provide a comprehensive account of conversational dynamics and their outcomes. For example, the discovery by Makoul et al. (1995) that both patients and doctors overestimated the extent to which certain topics had been discussed during the consultation was only possible on the basis of a combination of questionnaire data and transcripts of the actual consultation.

Triangulation of methods of data collection and analysis allows the researcher to obtain more than one perspective on the same phenomenon. In triangulation different methods are used to explore the same research issue from different perspectives to determine whether there is consistency and coherence across the results obtained.

KT

Questionnaires reflect participants' perceptions of the interaction. IASs provide quantitative information about prominent features of the interaction. Textual analyses trace the discursive constructions and negotiations of meanings that constitute the interaction. As a result, triangulation can shed light on the limitations of any one method. For example, Makoul et al. (1995) were able to conclude that self-report methods alone are unlikely to provide accurate information about the communicative contents of a consultation.

Example of a study using a combination of quantitative and qualitative methods: O'Brien and Petrie (1996)   O'Brien and Petrie (1996) examined the nature of patient participation in the medical consultation and its effect on patient understanding, recall and satisfaction. The authors used both quantitative and qualitative methods in order to obtain information about frequencies of types of patient participation (quantitative) as well as about the content of patient participation (qualitative). The consultations of 99 patients with joint pain from two hospitals in New Zealand were audiotaped and transcribed. The transcripts were coded using the Verbal Response Mode (VRM) coding system (Stiles et al., 1979) in order to determine the frequency and type of patient participation in each section of the medical interview. Patients' ability to remember and understand information presented during the consultation as well as patient satisfaction with the consultation were assessed immediately after the consultation via two verbally administered questionnaires. Transcripts from patients with the highest ($n = 10$) and the lowest ($n = 10$) scores on participation were selected for a qualitative analysis of the content of their consultations.

The quantitative analysis of consultation transcripts revealed that the majority of patient utterances in the history-taking section of the consultation provided information (i.e. edification and disclosure). The doctors' contribution to this part of the consultation consisted largely of questions and reflection. During the examination section, patients continued to offer information while doctors began to move from questions to edification, disclosure and interpretation. Patients asked more questions in the conclusion section than in any other part of the consultation. However, the overall number of questions asked by patients was small (13 on average per consultation). The conclusion section contained most of the doctors' information provision utterances (edification). On the basis of VRM coding, a patient participation score was obtained for each patient.

Analysis of the questionnaires revealed that patients best recalled medication name, other treatment instructions (such as X-rays and blood tests) and diagnosis, while instructions for taking medication, information about the diagnosis and the purpose of the prescribed medication were less well remembered. Understanding of medical information was also limited. There was no relationship between patient participation and recall and understanding. However, there was a significant negative correlation between patient participation in the history section of the consultation and satisfaction with treatment.

Qualitative analysis of interview transcripts suggested that patient participation was not necessarily constructive. Patients with high levels of participation tended to report symptoms in a random, unfocused manner and expressed anger and frustration. These consultations were also characterized by tensions and misunderstandings between doctor and patient, low levels of patient satisfaction and low levels of recall scores. By contrast, patients with the lowest participation levels showed very little emotion, complained little and confined their comments and questions to the specific symptoms that brought them to the clinic. In this way, the qualitative analysis was able to shed light on the negative relationship between high patient participation and satisfaction with treatment. High levels of participation often reflected an individual in distress, who was suffering from several health problems and who reported a history of unsatisfactory medical care. The authors suggest that there may be an optimal level of patient participation required for a constructive medical interview. They conclude by discussing possible ways in which constructive patient participation may be facilitated.

The use of triangulation constitutes a methodological challenge for most researchers. Such an approach requires considerable research skills in more than one research method. This is particularly important where researchers combine qualitative and quantitative methods. One of the risks associated with such triangulation is that researchers use a methodological approach with which they are not familiar and of which they have limited experience. As a result, a study using a combination of methods can be 'lopsided' in the sense that only one part of the study carries any scientific weight. For example, O'Brien and Petrie's (1996) qualitative analysis of consultation transcripts is not based upon any of the recognized forms of qualitative textual analysis. The authors do not provide any information about the way in which the texts were analysed or even which approach to the analysis of conversations had been adopted. As a result, their qualitative findings are difficult to evaluate.

General Criticisms of Work in Doctor–Patient Interaction

A number of general criticisms can be made of the dominant trends in doctor–patient communication research to date. First, much of the research has attempted to identify general laws or categories that are applicable to doctor–patient interactions in general. However, Silverman (1987) points out that this may be an inappropriate goal given that a wide range of factors influence the nature of the interaction between doctors and patients. The patient's illness 'career' (i.e. early or late stage), the severity of the illness, the social status of the condition (i.e. Is it stigmatized? Does it attract research funds?), the technologies involved in treatment, the complexity of medical issues involved, as well as the location of the interaction (e.g. GP's surgery, hospital ward, specialist clinic) all shape the communicative event. In addition the individual's health status (e.g. healthy, healthy disabled, ill), the history of the doctor–patient relationship and the purpose of the contact (e.g. to gain access to non-medical services, emotional support, treatment) may also influence the interaction. As a result, it may be necessary to develop different theories and recommendations for these different types of doctor–patient interactions. Furthermore, diverse patient groups are likely to have diverse communication needs (e.g. children, the elderly, people with AIDS, disabled people in general and people with cognitive, sensory and communication disabilities in particular) which again need to be recognized.

BOX 14.2

GENERAL CRITICISMS OF WORK IN DOCTOR–PATIENT COMMUNICATION

Criticism: the search for universal laws and general categories.
Recommendation: include consideration of diverse patient communication needs.

Criticism: the focus upon general practice settings.
Recommendation: include other relevant health service settings.

Criticism: limited outcome measures.
Recommendation: include further measures of health status and quality of life.

For example, Silverman (1987) found that some parents of child patients actually want and expect the doctor to control the interaction and to make diagnostic and prescriptive decisions for them, in order to relieve them of the responsibility for their child's health. By contrast, people with AIDS constitute an extremely well-informed patient group whose knowledge about their condition often surpasses that of their doctors. Similarly, disabled people are often the greatest experts concerning their own impairment. Clearly, these two categories of clients require different communication styles from their doctors.

Second, the vast majority of research in the field takes place in the GP's surgery. Other relevant settings such as hospital wards, home visits or family planning clinics are left relatively unexplored and so are patient interactions with other health professionals such as nurses, health visitors, midwives, dentists, receptionists, therapists, benefit agency assessment doctors and hospital doctors. There is no reason to believe that we are justified in extrapolating from findings from GPs' surgeries to other medical settings.

Third, researchers have tended to use patient satisfaction, adherence, as well as recall and understanding of information as *outcome measures* in order to assess the effectiveness of doctor–patient communication. However, it could be argued that a more relevant outcome measure would be actual health status as well as quality of life of the patient in the long term (Ong et al., 1995). These have been used least in empirical studies of doctor–patient communication to date.

Recent Trends

The role of gender

A number of studies have identified gender differences in doctors' communication. Female doctors are generally found to adopt more patient-centred communication styles whereas their male colleagues tend to be more directive and controlling (Van der Brink-Muinen et al., 2002). Both male and female patients seem to feel more empowered by communicating with female doctors (Hall and Roter, 2002). For example,

often assumed to be unable to manage their own affairs or communicate symptom information reliably or meaningfully and doctors therefore direct their talk towards parents and carers rather than the individual (Begum, 1996). Such interactions can reinforce a sense of stigma and poor self-esteem. In addition, many of these individuals exhibit challenging behaviours like aggression (e.g. it is estimated 10–15% of people with learning disabilities exhibit challenging behaviours). Such behaviour represents a barrier to effective communication and few health professionals are adequately trained in how to handle this, preferring to make referrals to community learning disability or mental health teams. Appointment time limitations can mean the extra time and effort required, to allow appropriate communication to be reached, is lacking. Information is rarely available in sufficiently diverse formats (e.g. Braille). The presence of third parties (e.g. interpreters, personal assistants/carers, community team members etc.) can further disrupt communication with people with these impairments. Cultural and language issues may interact with the other aspects of communication. Issues regarding informed consent also become problematic.

Various relationships, other than those with doctors, may be highly significant for disabled people including benefit agency doctors, therapists, social workers and personal assistants, yet they have been ignored in the disability literature. It is very likely that such relationships are influenced by power inequity. The interaction with benefit agency doctors, for example, is unlikely to be the same as with ordinary doctors, as they have the power to allow or deny access to necessary resources (finance, assistive technologies, housing etc.).

Communication between disabled people and doctors or other professionals has rarely formed a main focus of research, although it does receive some coverage in qualitative experiential work on disability. Studies looking at the communication experiences of disabled people in a range of contexts are urgently required.

Reconceptualization of 'compliance'

Patient compliance with medical instructions has been a major focus of research in doctor–patient communication. Compliance, defined as 'the extent to which the patient's behaviour … coincides with medical or health advice' (Haynes, 1979: 1), is generally seen to be one of the key objectives of doctor–patient communication. Compliance has been measured and its determinants have been explored by numerous researchers over the past 30 years or so. However, researchers have also questioned traditional conceptualizations of compliance. For example, Trostle (1988) argues that concordance research has defined patient behaviour in terms of professional expectations alone, thus reflecting (and reinforcing) the growing monopoly of the medical profession over the past century. Compliance research, according to Trostle, is ideological in that 'the very notion of compliance requires a dependent layperson and a dominant professional' (1988: 1301). As a result, it fails to understand the complexity and legitimacy of patient behaviours that differ from clinical prescriptions.

In a study of 54 rheumatology patients Donovan and Blake (1992) found that noncompliance was largely the result of reasoned decision-making. Qualitative analysis of semi-structured interviews with patients and audio-taped consultations with rheumatologists revealed that patients experimented with drug dosages and timing in order to manage side effects and effectiveness of drugs. Patients made decisions about compliance based on information gleaned from sources other than the rheumatologist, including their GPs, the media, as well as family and friends. The authors propose that researchers and practitioners ought to be concerned with the provision of information that would allow patients to make informed decisions, rather than with compliance per se. Today the term 'concordance' is thought to be a more appropriate term than 'compliance'. More detailed discussion of this topic follows in Chapter 15.

The impact of computer technologies on communication

In recent years the use of computers during the consultation process has become increasingly widespread. Many surgeries are now equipped with interactive computer systems that allow the doctor or nurse to update patient records, obtain patient histories as well as print out prescriptions in the presence of the patient. The impact of the presence of computers on communication in the medical context has only just begun to be explored.

So far, studies (e.g. Greatbatch et al., 1995) suggest that the use of the computer does indeed change the nature of the interaction. Through prompts and fixed sequencing of questions, the computer directs the flow of the interview. As a result, interviews can be longer and more detailed, but do not allow for 'small talk' that may reveal psychosocial concerns on the part of the patient. For example, Greatbatch et al. (1995) video-recorded consultations with general practitioners at an inner city practice before ($n = 100$) and after ($n = 150$) the introduction of a computer system. They found that the use of the computer was more prominent during the consultations than the prescription pad and pen had been. The presence of the computer led doctors to delay their responses to patients' utterances until after keystroke sequences had been completed. They confined their visual attention to the computer screen and restricted their contributions, particularly socio-relational ones such as expressions of sympathy and surprise and non-verbal ones such as laughter. Patients attempted to synchronize their conduct with the visible (changes on the screen) and audible (warning bleeps) manifestations of the workings of the computer system. Doctors' increasing familiarity with the system did not lead to changes in these practices. The authors conclude that use of the computer system adversely affected doctors' communication with their patients. Future research needs to assess the impact of computers on patient satisfaction as well as other outcome measures.

The use of e-mail in doctor–patient communication constitutes another example of how computer technologies can impact doctor–patient communication. Baur (2000) suggests that if e-mail is used as an extension of face-to-face communication between doctor and patient (e.g. to allow the patient to follow up a visit with further queries or to reveal further information that it was felt uncomfortable to reveal face-to-face), then it can deepen the relationship and provide opportunities for patient control and self-disclosure that may not be present in traditional face-to-face encounters. In addition e-mail may be used to substitute for office visits in cases where patients are unable to attend or where they are finding face-to-face encounters with a physician uncomfortable. However, Baur (2000) suggests that research about the way in which physicians and patients are already using e-mail indicates that many of the problems associated with face-to-face communication between physicians and patients are being transferred into the electronic environment. For example, e-mail allows physicians to focus largely on technical matters and to neglect socio-relational aspects of communication. Confidentiality can also be an issue, especially if employer-provided e-mail accounts are used. For further discussion of 'e-health communication', see Kreps (2003).

Non-verbal communication

Non-verbal communication in the health-care setting has received surprisingly little attention to date. Non-verbal communication channels include body posture, facial expressions including nods and blinks, voice quality and tone, hand gestures, gaze/eye-contact, laughter/crying, proximity, touch, and minor activities (e.g. blowing one's nose, fiddling with one's watch, biting one's nails). Miller (2002) notes that non-verbal dimensions of the doctor–patient interaction can contribute to the quality of the patient experience by generating a sense of comfort, relaxation and/or pleasure. This is why it is recommended that bad news, for example, should be broken in person so that the physician can sit close to the patient, minimize physical barriers and use touch when appropriate (see Ptacek and Eberhardt, 1996). The use of non-verbal channels of communication allows for the use of supportive gestures such as offering the patient a tissue as well as for expressions of empathy through, for example, leaning forward or moving one's chair closer to the patient. It appears that non-verbal communication has the potential to increase patient satisfaction.

Ruusuvuori (2001) examined the ways in which patients respond to doctors' gaze aversions as they shift their attention from the patients themselves to patient records on the desk in front of them. Conversation analytic research has demonstrated that direction of gaze constitutes a display of attention on the part of the listener. Given that doctors need to divide their attention between the patient him/herself and their medical records, it is important that such shifts of attention are timed in a way that minimizes disengagement. Ruusuvuori (2001) observed that patients often became dysfluent in their delivery of information (i.e. cutting off an utterance or pausing in the course of its production) when doctors disengaged from the interaction and looked at their notes. Closer examination of her data indicated that there are critical points in a patient's narrative that require continuing gaze for its smooth completion. It appears that it is important for doctors to learn to discriminate between moments that require sustained attention and those that do not.

The role of communication in coping with illness

Recently, health psychologists have begun to explore the ways in which communication mediates the illness experience itself. For example, the Relational Model of Health Communication Competence (Query and Kreps, 1996) proposes that physiological and psychological health outcomes are influenced by health-care participants' level of communication competence. Competence is characterized by provider and consumer skills, such as empathic listening, verbal and non-verbal sensitivity, encoding and decoding skills and interaction management. Query and Kreps (1996) examined the relationship between lay caregivers' communication competence and their health outcomes within the context of Alzheimer's disease. Health outcome measures included social support and cognitive depression. Ninety caregivers for patients with Alzheimer's disease completed three questionnaires measuring social support, communication competence and depression. Relationships between communication competence and social support (both extent of network and satisfaction) as well as competence and depression were non-significant. However, a linear combination of social support satisfaction and number of social supports significantly discriminated between caregivers high in communication competence and those low in competence. Thus, the results provide partial support for the Relational Model of Health Communication Competence.

Frey et al. (1996) discussed the ways in which communication practices within a residential facility for people with AIDS help residents cope with the loss of fellow residents. The use of particular discursive constructions (e.g. 'the military myth', 'the journey myth'), as well as collective and private bereavement rituals, allow residents to manage the tensions of living and dying with AIDS. The authors argued that such communication practices can help residents avoid further depression of their immune system and cope better with their illness. More research into the effects of communication practices upon quality of life as well as physical health outcomes is needed.

Counselling within a medical context

The development of increasingly sophisticated diagnostic tests and screening procedures has highlighted the need for informed consent and patient choice. Genetic screening and the HIV antibody test, for example, provide the healthy individual with information that has major implications for their future health status. It may also require them to make significant lifestyle changes. The identification of an 'at risk status', therefore, has psychological consequences that need to be considered when testing is carried out. Pre-test counselling provides an opportunity for patients to consider advantages and disadvantages of testing and to make an informed decision about whether or not to do it. Post-test counselling helps the individual to make sense of the test result and to discuss ways in which they may cope with its implications.

Michie et al. (1996a) analysed 131 routine consultations conducted in a genetics centre in the UK in order to find out what constitutes effective genetic counselling. Their study was designed to examine the extent to which genetic counselling influences outcomes. The authors used self-report questionnaires in order to measure inputs (e.g. the nature of the genetic problem, patient expectations and directiveness of the counsellor's consultation style) and outcomes (e.g. patient anxiety and patient satisfaction). The process of the consultation was examined on the basis of transcripts of audiotapes of the consultation. It was found that what both patient and counsellor bring to the consultation influences patient satisfaction and mood after the consultation. No causal association between what happens during the consultation and patient outcome was identified. However, the authors caution against the conclusion that genetic counselling is ineffectual and unnecessary by drawing attention to the possibility that responsive counsellors may be modifying their consultation style according to their perception of patient needs and expectations. As a result, associations between process and outcome variables would be masked.

Future research needs to include a comparison of matched recipients and non-recipients of genetic counselling. As new forms of screening and treatment emerge, health psychologists need to study the ways in which communication is used in their management. This is particularly important when screening practices and policies are still new and undeveloped and potentially open to psychological input.

Future Research

1 Future research in doctor–patient communication must explore the communication needs of different patient groups, as well as the relationship between physician characteristics (e.g. gender, communication style, culture) and patient needs.
2 More attention needs to be paid to medical settings other than the doctor's office.
3 The relationship between doctor–patient communication and patient health status/quality of life also requires further work. In order to understand why patients do not follow physicians' advice, the notion of 'compliance' needs to be further unpacked.
4 Qualitative work can shed light on patients' reasons for not adhering to medical regimens.
5 The emergence of new technologies constitutes a challenge to health psychologists. Studies need to be designed and carried out in response to new developments in information technology, screening methods and treatment in order to trace their psychological implications.
6 The study of communication within a medical context has great potential for informing and improving communication practice. It is crucial that researchers spell out their findings implications for medical practice in a way that is accessible to practitioners.

Summary

1 Communication is an essential and sometimes the only route to information about a patient's physical and/or mental state. However, communication is the least satisfactory aspect of the doctor–patient encounter and many studies have found that its effectiveness is limited.
2 There are three major approaches to the study of doctor–patient communication: (1) the 'deviant patient'; (2) the 'authoritarian doctor'; (3) the 'interactive dyad'. Questionnaires, interaction analysis systems and qualitative textual analysis are methods with which to study doctor–patient communication.
3 The interaction analysis system (IAS) is the most widely used research tool in doctor–patient communication to date. It is an observation instrument that allows the researcher to identify, categorize and quantify features of the doctor–patient encounter. Such features include 'information giving', 'information seeking' and 'social conversation'.
4 Both doctors' and patients' communicative styles, demographic as well as personal characteristics, can influence the nature and quality of the communicative event. For example, patients' question asking, anxiety state and educational background are associated with physicians' information giving (Street, 1991).
5 Typically, patients ask few questions and rarely offer their opinions during consultations with the doctor. Doctors do little to solicit patients' questions, concerns and opinions. In Byrne and Long's terms, doctor–patient communication remains doctor-centred.

6 Qualitative approaches to doctor–patient communication recognize that both doctor and patient shape the communicative event. Qualitative textual analysis aims to identify the discursive strategies that speakers use in order to manage their discursive objectives and to explore the ways in which meaning is constructed and negotiated by participants.

7 Studies have identified gender differences in doctors' communication styles. Female doctors adopt more patient-centred styles whereas their male colleagues tend to be more directive and controlling. These findings are in line with the general literature on gender differences in communication.

8 In recent years the use of computers during the consultation has become increasingly widespread. Studies suggest that the use of the computer changes the nature of the doctor–patient interaction. Computer-aided interviews tend to be longer and more detailed, but they reduce opportunities for socio-relational talk.

9 Health psychologists have begun to explore the ways in which communication mediates the illness experience. It has been suggested that physiological and psychological health outcomes can be influenced by health-care participants' communicative style, skills and practices.

10 Future research in doctor–patient communication should focus on the communication needs of different patient groups, the role of the setting in which communication takes place, the relationship between communication and health status and the implications of new technologies for doctor–patient communication.

 Key Terms

authoritarian doctor

communication styles

communicative event

compliance (or adherence)

deviant patient

doctor-centred communication style

health communication

interaction analysis system (IAS)

interactive dyad

patient satisfaction

patient-centred communication style

triangulation

15 Treatment Adherence and Patient Empowerment

Non-compliance is an unavoidable by-product of collisions between the clinical world and other competing worlds of work, play, friendship, and family life. (Trostle, 1998: 1305)

Outline

Adherence and compliances are terms used to describe the extent to which patients adhere or comply with recommended treatment regimens. It is one of the most widely researched forms of health-related behaviour. The assumptions underlying the term compliance implies an authoritarian stance on the part of the physician or other health professional that are challenged by recent changes within health-care systems. In this chapter we consider the extent and character of treatment non-adherence and the issue of medical error. We also consider the patient-centred formulation of health care that focuses on shared decision-making and patient **empowerment**.

Character of Adherence

Medical adherence can take a variety of forms and include those which are concerned specifically with medication including: having prescriptions filled, taking the correct dosage, taking the medicine at the correct times, remembering to take one or more doses and stopping the medication on time. The extent of adherence varies across the different forms of recommended behaviours. In general, most people do not adhere to specific medical or health-care directives – at least not fully. While non-adherence would seem to be the norm, its extent varies. A recent review article (Wertheimer and Santella, 2003) estimated that 50–75% of patients do not adhere to medical advice. They also provided the following estimates:

- 14–21% of patients do not fill their prescriptions;
- 60% of all patients cannot identify their own medication;
- 30–50% of all patients ignore or compromise medication instructions;
- 12–20% of patients take other people's medication.

Consequences of non-adherence

In health terms it would seem that non-adherence has an overall negative impact on the health of society. The following estimates of the negative impact of non-adherence were provided by Wertheimer and Santella (2003):

- approximately 125,000 people with treatable ailments die each year in the USA because of inappropriate medication usage;
- approximately one-quarter of nursing home admissions are due to inappropriate medication usage;
- hospital costs due to medication non-adherence is estimated at $8.5 billion annually in the USA.

Certain forms of non-adherence are potentially more dangerous than others. One common health problem that has a high rate of non-adherence is asthma. Despite the large number of drug education programmes the proportion of people with asthma who do not comply with the recommended treatment remains high. In the USA it has been estimated that the direct and indirect costs of asthma in 1990 were over $6 billion. It has been suggested that a large proportion of this cost could be eliminated if adherence with medication was improved.

Factors Associated with Non-Adherence

Patient characteristics

There has been some success in identifying the social and personal characteristics of the non-adherent patient. In general, the less social support and the more socially isolated the patients are, the less likely they are to follow medical directives. For example, in a study of treatment adherence in an outpatient clinic for people with tuberculosis, it was found that homelessness was the only factor that predicted non-completion of therapy. Further, individuals who came from unstable families were also found to be less compliant with medical treatment. A study of adherence among diabetes patients found that adherence to medication was associated with higher levels of social support.

There has been much effort to identify the so-called 'non-compliant' personality. However, like much personality research in general (Mischel, 1968; see also Chapter 11), this effort has met with limited success. In reviewing the evidence, Hulka (1979) found no consistent relationship between age, sex, marital status, education, number of people in the household, social class and adherence. Admittedly, this is not to deny that specific groups of patients may be resistant to accepting certain types of treatment. For example, certain cognitive deficits or emotional upsets may reduce adherence. There is also evidence that people with a range of psychological problems are less likely to adhere to treatment. Table 15.1 summarizes some of the patient characteristics associated with adherence.

The more the prescribed medication accords with the patients' belief systems, the more likely they are to comply with the treatment. Many studies have confirmed the association between patients' health beliefs and adherence. In an attempt to bring some order to this plethora of research, some investigators have turned to the popular

Table 15.1   *Patient characteristics associated with adherence (Meichenbaum and Turk, 1987: 43)*

Social characteristics	Personal characteristics	Health beliefs
Characteristics of individual's social situation	Demographics Sensory disabilities	Inappropriate or conflicting health beliefs
Lack of social supports	Type and severity of psychiatric disorder Forgetfulness	Competing socio-cultural and ethnic folk concepts of disease and treatment
Family instability or disharmony	Lack of understanding	Implicit model of illness
Parent's expectations and attitudes toward treatment		
Residential instability		
Environment that supports non-adherent behaviour		
Competing or conflicting demands		
Lack of resources		

social cognitive models. Probably the most frequently used such model has been the Health Belief Model (HBM). Indeed, this model was originally formulated to explain compliance with medical recommendations (Becker and Mainman, 1975). It argues that the extent to which a person complies depends upon perceived disease severity, susceptibility to the disease, benefits of the treatment recommended and barriers to following the treatment.

Varying degrees of support have been found for this model. For example, it has been found that the more the patients perceive their condition to be serious, the more likely they will be to comply with the recommended treatment. However, Glasgow et al. (1997) found that perceived seriousness of diabetes was not predictive of adherence. In a study of drug therapy defaulting, Fincham and Wertheimer (1985) found that belief in the benefits of medical care and low barriers to care predicted high adherence. Glasgow et al. (1997) found that the perceived effectiveness of the treatment was a better predictor of adherence in diabetes than the perceived barriers.

Social learning theory has also been used with varying degrees of success to explain non-adherence. Research showed that although internal locus of control predicts adherence to a weight-control programme for patients with diabetes, its importance is small and depends on the degree of social support. In a study of patients with rheumatoid arthritis, it was found that patients' predictions concerning their adherence (self-efficacy expectations) with treatment predicted actual adherence.

These social cognitive models of adherence describe the beliefs that are associated with or predict adherence. These models can be criticized on both empirical and theoretical grounds. On empirical grounds the major problem is that the beliefs have been found to predict only a small proportion of the variance of adherence behaviour. Theoretically, the major problem is that these models reify the phenomenon. As such it characterizes the behaviour as fixed and abstracted from the changing social relations and the broader

Table 15.2   *Treatment factors associated with non-adherence (Meichenbaum and Turk, 1987: 43)*

Preparation for treatment	Immediate character of treatment	Administration of treatment	Consequences of treatment
Characteristics of treatment setting	Characteristics of treatment recommendations	Inadequate supervision by professionals	Medication side effects
Long waiting time	Complexity of treatment regimen	Absence of continuity of care	Social side effects
Long time elapsed between referral and appointment	Duration of treatment regimen	Failure of parents to supervise drug administration	
Timing of referral	Degree of behavioural change		
Absence of individual appointment times	Inconvenience Expense		
Lack of cohesiveness of treatment delivery systems	Characteristics of medicine		
Inconvenience associated with operation of clinics	Inadequate labels		
Poor reputation of treatment facility	Awkward container design		

social context within which adherence occurs. Treatment is not usually a one-off event but extends over a period of time. In the case of chronic illness this period can be a lifetime. To understand adherence fully therefore requires an understanding of the social context and how the patient integrates the treatment into his/her everyday life.

Disease characteristics

Certain disease characteristics have been found to be associated with adherence. Perhaps the most frequently mentioned disease characteristics are the severity of the disease and visibility of the symptoms. The relationship with disease severity would appear not to be linear. A number of studies have found that patients with asymptomatic chronic diseases frequently do not comply with treatment. When the symptoms are obvious and unwanted, the person is more likely to comply with treatment that offers a promise of removing them. However, when the prognosis is poor there is evidence that the rate of adherence is reduced. For example, adherence is lower in those cancer patients whose survival prospects are poor.

Treatment factors

There are a large number of treatment factors associated with adherence. These are summarized in Table 15.2 under four broad temporal headings. Before the patient is actually prescribed a treatment, s/he has to obtain an appointment with the physician. The character of this process prepares or sets the scene for the physician's recommendations. Lengthy or inconvenient waiting times can lead to considerable frustration and an unwillingness to comply.

The more complicated the treatment prescribed, the less likely the patient is to comply fully. Admittedly, there have been attempts to simplify treatment regimens by providing patients with detailed information. However, the evidence suggests that adherence is still poor. One reason is information overload (Meichenbaum and Turk, 1987). In an attempt to cope with a very complicated treatment regimen the patient simply gets confused or ignores much of the information. Although physicians may explain the treatment, patients frequently do not understand or forget the instructions provided. Ley (1979) found that patients forget at least one-third of the information given by their physician. A variety of factors influences understanding. Basically, the more extensive and complex the instructions given, the less likely the patient is to recall it subsequently.

Besides complexity, an important treatment characteristic is the actual length of the treatment regimen. Adherence declines with an increase in the number of medications or doses and with the length of recommended treatment (Hulka et al., 1976a, b). It is estimated that adherence with long-term therapy declines to approximately 50%, irrespective of illness or setting. Masur (1981) suggests that it is not the length of treatment that is the reason for this decline in adherence but rather the absence of symptoms. Long-term therapy is often recommended for chronic medical conditions which have few symptoms or for which there is no definite improvement in symptoms as a result of medication. In these cases the patient has no feedback on the benefits of medication. This lack of feedback undermines any motivation to comply with the medication. When patients with hypertension are able to identify symptoms of their disease that are controlled by medication they are more likely to comply with it.

The actual character of the treatment is also important. For example, some people with asthma do not like taking inhaled medication while others do not follow the correct inhalation procedure, thus reducing overall adherence. Understanding how the patient feels about a particular procedure or treatment is a necessary step in improving adherence.

It would perhaps be expected that those drugs with few **physical side effects** would be associated with higher adherence. It would seem that the social side effects, in terms of stigma, are just as important (see section on empowerment). A related factor is the extent to which the treatment disrupts the patient's everyday life.

KT

Interpersonal factors

The character of the physician–patient relationship is at the centre of research into adherence. Physician styles in physician–patient communication have been classified as either 'patient-centred' or 'authoritarian' (see Chapter 14). The patient-centred or affiliative style is designed to promote a positive relationship and includes behaviours such as interest, friendliness and empathy. The authoritarian or control-oriented style is designed to maintain the physician's control in the interaction. Not surprisingly, patients prefer those physicians who adopt the more affiliative style (Buller and Buller, 1987). Various related styles of physician interaction have been associated with adherence.

In behavioural terms the physician keeps good eye contact, smiles a lot and leans in towards the patient – all behaviours which are interpreted as demonstrating interest and consideration. Hall et al. (1988) found in their meta-analysis of 41 studies that patient satisfaction was associated with perceived interpersonal competence, social conversation and better communication as well as more information and technical competence.

Several studies have found an association between physician job satisfaction and aspects of adherence. For example, patients were found to be more satisfied with those physicians who had high job satisfaction. A related factor is the physician's sense of security. Since many conditions are resistant to standard medical interventions many physicians can experience a sense of inadequacy. This, in turn, could lead to reduced job satisfaction and more conflict with patients. Indeed, when general practitioners receive complaints from their patients, they initially feel out of control, and may experience feelings of shock, panic and indignation.

Physicians and patients have a different view of health and illness. For example, a study comparing the definitions of health by family physicians and patients with asthma found that the former defines health in terms of absence of disease, whereas the latter refers to it as 'being able', 'taking action' and 'physical well-being'. The more understanding the physician has of the patient's belief system, the more compliant the patient is. For example, Hispanic patients tend to comply more when their physician is more understanding of their cultural norms and practices.

An important although less explored factor is the physician's view of the patient. This factor overlaps with the physician's understanding of the patient's health beliefs and suggests that when the physician has a positive view of the patient then s/he will adopt a much more affiliative style of communication. This helps to explain the well-established social class effect that upper- and middle-class patients receive more information and attention from physicians. For example, a large survey of state employees in Massachusetts showed that physicians are more likely to discuss healthy lifestyle issues such as diet and exercise with high-income patients but they discuss smoking more with low-income patients. Physicians frequently report more frustration with and less interest in lower- and working-class patients.

Social and organizational setting

The medical consultation takes place in a social setting. Meichenbaum and Turk (1987) identified 10 setting characteristics potentially associated with non-adherence. Adherence is greater when the referral to a specialist is seen as part of the assessment rather than as a last resort, when care involves follow-up and is personalized, when appointments are individualized and waiting times are reduced, when treatment is available on site, when treatment is carefully supervised through home visits, special nursing care, etc., when there are good links between inpatient and outpatient services and when staff have a very positive attitude towards the treatment. In particular with long-term therapy, there is evidence that regular follow-up by the physician increases adherence.

It is not just the immediate medical context but also the local social context, in terms of family and friends, which is important. If family members remind and assist the patient concerning their medication it would only be expected that the patient would be more compliant. Indeed, it has been suggested that the patient's partner's views of the medication prescribed is the most important factor in explaining adherence. In a meta-analysis of 122 studies on the impact of social support DiMatteo (2004) found that practical support had a high correlation with adherence. He also found that adherence was higher in cohesive families and lower in families in conflict. This concern with social context requires consideration of the broader socio-political context that conditions the character of health care and of adherence.

Alternatives to Adherence

While the extensive literature on non-adherence has provided some insight into the character of the phenomenon, it has not contributed to its reduction. One of the main reasons for this lack of progress is that the majority of adherence research has been based upon a static model of the phenomenon that ignores the broader social context of health care and the dynamic nature of health and illness behaviour. An alternative more social and psychological approach requires an understanding of the role of medicine in our society and of the actual lived experience of illness and of managing illness.

The role of medicine

In western society medicine has been based upon power and authority. Since it is founded on the assumption that it has the monopoly on truth, it follows that patient non-adherence is a result of ignorance and/or deviance. Thus it is not surprising that Trostle describes the literature on compliance as 'a literature about power and control' (1998: 1299). He argues that the increasing research interest in medical compliance is a reflection of 'a concern for market control combined with a concern for therapeutic power' (1998: 1301). However, this very concern with maintaining power may carry with it an equal and opposite reaction evidenced by a reluctance of patients to comply.

According to reactance theory (Brehm, 1966), individuals believe they have the right to control their own behaviour. When this right is threatened they react and attempt to regain control over that behaviour and to prevent the loss of other freedoms. Basically, people do not like being pushed around and will attempt to subvert attempts to do so. In a revision of the original theory, the concept of freedom was defined as equivalent to that of control. People like to feel in control of their lives. Any attempt to reduce the sense of control over specific areas of our lives is a threat to the sense of freedom and is generally resisted.

The theory of psychological reactance has been used as an explanatory framework for non-compliance. The more extensive and complex the treatment prescribed, the greater the threat to perceived freedom (Fogarty, 1997). Admittedly, this threat would be accepted if there was an indication that it was worthwhile. However, the very complexity of some regimens may sensitize the patient to additional threats to their freedom such that patients may become resistant to additional demands. Non-compliance can thus be interpreted as a means of resisting medical dominance.

Admittedly, not all patients are critical of the traditional authoritarian stance of the physician or feel the need to resist or not comply. Some people are more accepting of authority than others. In the late twentieth century, however, there was considerable public opposition to the idea of the all-powerful doctor and there were vocal demands for greater control over health care. Despite this apparent change in public attitudes, several researchers found that many people were still reluctant to adopt a more resisting, consumerist attitude. Haug and Lavin (1983) found that while younger and more educated patients were more consumerist in their attitude regarding their role in the doctor–patient encounter, older patients were more accepting and accommodating.

Lupton (1997) investigated the impact of the supposed cultural shift on the attitudes of patients in Australia. She argued that contemporary popular advice is that the patient should adopt an active consumerist attitude to health care. In her interviews with a sample of patients, Lupton found a more mixed picture. Many of the patients, especially the older ones, still preferred the passive patient role. Admittedly, they accepted that the traditional authoritarian image of the doctor had been challenged over the past generation as a result of publicity about medical negligence and sexual harassment. This resulted in a certain ambivalence about the doctor and a tension between adopting the consumerist or passive patient role. Thus while some patients would demand a more active role in their treatment and would be frustrated if they were denied it, many patients still preferred to adopt the traditional passive patient role.

The more consumerist stance of certain patients is not always welcomed by physicians. Although several studies have shown that patients generally express a desire for information about their condition, many physicians are reluctant to disclose much information. One study found that physicians often ignore patients' requests for information. Indeed it was found this was often met by challenges to their intelligence.

Trostle suggested that 'the last decade's preoccupation with adherence is a consequence of the declining authority of the [medical] profession' (1998: 1303). In traditional non-western societies the physician maintains the dominant role and the patient is more inclined to adopt a compliant stance. For example, first generation Japanese-Americans are much more likely to report a willingness to comply than their second-generation peers. Conversely, in western society the demand for greater control over one's life conflicts with the traditional passive role and leads to greater resistance to medical advice.

Another feature of medical dominance is the power of the physician to define what is sickness. It is often assumed that the doctor typically makes the correct diagnosis and prescribes appropriate treatment. This is the ideal medical model. Thus non-adherence is the patient's fault. However, the evidence suggests that there are many sources of error on the part of the physician. For example, patients frequently attend with a variety of psychosocial problems, but the physician often ignores these. Bertakis et al. (1991) estimated that as many as 85% of patients who come to see their family doctor have some degree of psychological distress. Scientific medical discourse does not contain language to handle these issues so the physician prefers to focus concern on biomedical matters which may be of limited concern to the patient.

In a large study conducted over 11 sites in the USA, Bertakis et al. (1991) content analysed 550 physician–patient interviews. They found that physician questions about biomedical topics were negatively related to patient satisfaction while physician questions about psychosocial topics were positively associated with patient satisfaction. In addition, those patients whose physician dominated the interview reported less satisfaction. Bertakis et al. concluded that 'patients are most satisfied by interviews that encourage them to talk about psychosocial issues in an atmosphere that is characterized by the absence of physician domination' (1989: 80).

However, Waitzkin argues that the exclusion of discussion of the social context of health complaints is a 'fundamental feature of medical language ... a basic part of what medicine is in our society' (1989: 232). Not only does medical language ignore these social issues but also medical treatment does not address these social issues. He suggests a redirection for medicine: 'by suggesting collective action as a meaningful option, medical professionals might begin to overcome the impact that its exclusion exerts'. To do this it needs to recognize the 'limits of medicine's role and the importance of building links to other forms of praxis that seek to change the social context of medical encounters' (1989: 237).

The movement towards patient-centred models of medical treatment indicates that the medical profession is well aware of the growing criticism. So too are pharmacists who play a central role in dispensing medication. A recent report by the Royal Pharmaceutical Society of Great Britain (1997) called for a new approach to patient care. In a commentary on the report, Marinker noted that 'compliance may have been appropriate within a welfare state rooted in the values and thinking of society in the 1930s, when services were driven by benign paternalism and the practice of patients trusting their doctors' (1997: 747). The alternative that the report proposed was 'concordance' which is a model of the doctor–patient relationship based upon mutual respect. Marinker (1997: 747) concluded: 'The price of compliance was dependency – it belongs to an older world. The price of concordance will be greater responsibility' for both the doctor and the patient. While this vision of shared responsibility seems commendable, as we shall discuss subsequently, it also holds the potential of medical neglect.

Overall, there is much evidence to suggest that non-adherence is an implicit structural component of the contemporary medical-dominated health-care system. To reduce non-adherence thus requires a reassessment of this system. It also needs an understanding of what it means to the patient to be ill.

Lived Experience of Chronic Illness

The extent to which people, especially those with chronic illness, comply with recommended treatment is enmeshed in their experience of living with illness. Adherence is not a fixed event but a changing process. A series of qualitative studies of illness have identified a number of processes that help us to understand the extent to which people accept the prescribed treatment regimens. Three of these processes are considered here.

Self-regulation

Individuals with chronic illness actively monitor and adjust their medication on an ongoing basis, i.e. self-regulation. It is not that they are recklessly ignoring professional

Table 15.3   *Reasons for self-regulation of medication (Conrad, 1985: 34–5)*

- *Testing*: the way patients test the impact of varying dosages.
- *Controlling dependence*: the way patients assert to themselves and others that they are not dependent on the prescribed medication.
- *Destigmatization*: an attempt to reject the illness label and to be 'normal'.
- *Practical practice*: the way patients modified their dosage so as to reduce the risk of seizures, e.g. increasing the dosage in high stress situations.

advice but rather they are carefully regulating it according to a variety of factors. This is illustrated in the study conducted by Conrad (1985). Over a three-year period he conducted interviews with 80 individuals who had epilepsy about their life experiences with the disease. He noted that the individuals developed a personal 'medication practice' which best fitted with their self-image and their lifestyle. The patients realized the benefits of medication for seizure control and frequently stated that the medication helped them be more 'normal'. However, simultaneously the medication was seen as a daily reminder that they had epilepsy. They felt that reducing the medication was evidence that they were 'getting better'. Side effects were a frequently given justification for not complying with the recommended treatment. However, although side effects were mentioned they rarely referred to bodily side effects. Rather, they referred to social side effects. If the people with epilepsy felt that the medication was impairing their ability to handle routine social activities, they modified the medication to reduce this impact.

Table 15.3 summarizes four reasons that Conrad suggested underlie individuals' preference to self-regulate the treatment rather than comply fully with the recommended regimen. These illustrate how non-adherence is a rational process whereby the individual carefully adjusts the medication to maximize its impact.

People carefully monitor the impact of prescribed medication and adjust the dosage accordingly. They do not simply follow the standardized instructions provided by the physician but rather adjust them to suit their own personal needs. This is illustrated in a study by Hunter et al. (1997) who looked at middle-aged women's usage of hormone replacement therapy (HRT). They interviewed 45 women and identified three broad themes within which the women talked about HRT:

1   *Hot flushes and night sweats*: the women would not take the medication when there were no symptoms, e.g. one woman said: 'I have no extraordinary symptoms, therefore I have no need of HRT' (p. 1544).
2   *Doctors' opinions and behaviour*: the women listened carefully to their doctor's advice and decided whether or not to take HRT, e.g. one woman said: 'I came to the doctor and had a discussion. I felt that I weighed up the advantages and disadvantages' (p. 1544).
3   *Taking hormones or medication for a 'natural' process*: the women were reluctant to take medication for something that they felt was natural. They sometimes referred to a similar concern with taking the contraceptive pill, e.g. 'I might consider it if I was suffering from symptoms which I felt I could not put up with. I'm a bit wary. I never really wanted to go on the pill because I'm always a bit wary of interfering with nature' (p. 1545).

This study illustrates that the patient's attitude to the recommended treatment is interwoven with their attitude to the illness and their attitude to their physician.

The Self-Regulatory Model of Illness developed by Leventhal and Cameron (1987) provides a framework to explore patients' medication beliefs. This model considers health-related decisions as dynamic rather than static. According to the model whether a person adopts a certain coping procedure (e.g. adherence with medication) depends upon perception of illness threat and the perceived efficacy of the coping strategy. According to the model, concrete symptom experience is important in formulating both representations of the disease and in monitoring medication efficacy. Thus, a perceived lack of evidence of the disease or of the efficacy of the medication would encourage non-adherence. For Leventhal, the patient can best be considered as an active problem-solver.

An extension of this approach was developed by Horne and Weinman (1999). They developed a measure of medication beliefs that distinguished between the perceived benefits and harms of the medication. They found that patients' beliefs about the efficacy and necessity of medication were tempered by concerns about the potential for harm. A study of patients with chronic illness found that there was a strong relationship between perceived necessity of the medication and reported adherence to the treatment (Horne and Weinman, 1999). In a recent extension of this work with individuals who had asthma it was found that there was a relationship between illness perceptions (see Chapter 11), medication beliefs and adherence (Horne and Weinman, 2002). Those individuals with strong medication necessity beliefs also perceived asthma as having a lengthy timeline and that its consequences were serious. A statistical model found that treatment concerns and necessity and illness consequences were significant predictors of reported medication adherence.

A recent study using the Beliefs about Medicines Questionnaire (BMQ) found further supporting evidence of the importance of the patients' medication beliefs. The study considered medication adherence among individuals suffering from chronic arthritis (Treharne et al., 2004). It found that those who perceived their medications as being more necessary and those who perceived medications as not being overused were more adherent to the prescribed medication.

Similar findings were found in a study of non-pharmacological treatment for dizziness (Yardley et al., 2001). In this study patients were interviewed about the treatment. It was found that those patients who did not adhere to the recommended treatment attributed their symptoms to causes inconsistent with the rationale for the therapy. However, some other patients who did adhere also attributed inconsistent causes but emphasized trust in their physician or a willingness to try anything that might help. These patients reported an improvement in symptoms during the treatment period although they were hesitant about attributing the cause of this to the treatment. Yardley et al. concluded that while this study provided some evidence for Leventhal's illness regulation model there were also inconsistencies. It was suggested that these might be explained by considering the role of the therapist. They concluded that their findings 'highlight the reciprocal interactions between subjective experiences of bodily symptoms, abstract images of illness and treatment and social interactions between patient and therapist – in other words between the "material" (i.e. concrete, embodied) and the discursive (i.e. symbolic, socio-culturally mediated) aspects of healthcare'. Together these findings would extend the illness regulation model to include the discursive and social context within which the illness and the treatment are situated.

Fear of medication

From the physician's perspective, non-adherence can seem a foolhardy process. However, to the lay person non-adherence can be perceived as a means of reducing a variety of fears. This is illustrated in the findings of a study conducted by Donovan and Blake (1992). They investigated the extent to which a sample of people with various forms of arthritis complied with the recommended treatment. The study involved interviews and observations of 44 patients over a period of several years. They found that about half the patients did not follow the prescribed treatment. Detailed questioning of these patients revealed that they were carefully considering the implications of this non-adherence. It was not just a matter of obeying instructions or not – they were experimenting with dosages and timing. They were reluctant to follow the prescribed treatment for these reasons:

- fear of side effects;
- fear of dependency;
- fear of reduced effectiveness;
- did not fit with lifestyle;
- drugs are a sign of weakness;
- drugs do not fit with health beliefs.

Similarly, in a study of lay people's perceptions of medicines, it was found that many people have a range of fears and anxieties about medication. This was especially the case among those people who reported that they often did not comply with prescribed medication. It has been suggested that physicians should consider other options than medication.

In the development of the Beliefs about Medicines Questionnaire, Horne (1997) distinguished between *general overuse* (beliefs that medicines in general are over-used by doctors) and *general harm* (beliefs that medicines in general are harmful addictive poisons). These two beliefs were found to be closely related. Subsequent work in a sample of male British students found that those with less experience of medication and those from an Asian background had a stronger belief in the general harm of medicines (Horne et al., 2004). This would indicate that medication beliefs are closely intertwined with gender and cultural identity and with experience of medication.

Identity control

Medication adherence is also tied to the extent to which the patient accepts that s/he has an illness and wishes to control it, i.e. **identity control**. This is illustrated in the study by Adams et al. (1997). They conducted detailed interviews with a sample of asthma sufferers registered with a general practice in South Wales. Analysis of these interviews revealed that the extent to which the individuals complied with the recommended treatment (daily use of a curative and a prophylactic inhaler) was intimately bound up with how they defined themselves and their attitude to the illness. Three groups of patients, each with a particular pattern of medication, were identified:

1 *Deniers/distancers*: these were the individuals who argued that despite the medical diagnosis they did not have asthma but rather just 'bad chests'. They would fall into Goffman's (1963) 'discreditable' category and took steps to ensure that others were not aware of their diagnosis. They generally had a negative view of people with asthma (e.g. 'weakling' or 'wimp') and wished to avoid such a label. Although they took reliever medication when necessary, they were reluctant to take prophylactic medication regularly. While the former helped their 'bad chest', the latter was a symbol that they were 'asthmatic'.

2 *Accepters*: these individuals reluctantly accepted that they had asthma. They also held a variety of negative associations of people with asthma. They emphasized that they were not stereotypical asthmatic people but rather more like certain individuals who were able to achieve despite having asthma, e.g. certain athletes. They defined asthma as a 'condition' that needed to be controlled. As such they not only took the reliever medication but also the prophylactic medication. However, these individuals emphasized that although they took their medication regularly they were not dependent on their doctor. Rather, they were proud that they controlled their asthma themselves, using the drugs, with limited contact with their physician.

3 *Pragmatists*: these individuals did not fall neatly into the previous two categories although they were closer to the accepters. All of them accepted that they had asthma but their notions of asthma and medication usage were somewhat idiosyncratic. Unlike the secrecy of the deniers and the public stance of the accepters this group adopted a more pragmatic attitude and practised what Adams et al. described as a strategic policy of disclosure. This was related to their self-medication practices to which they adopted a pragmatic stance.

These studies illustrate that the extent of adherence with the recommended treatment is intertwined not only with the character of the disease but also with the patient's self-definition. Adherence or non-adherence is not only a means of managing symptoms but also of managing self-identity.

Medical Error

In assessing the benefits of adherence the positive effects need to be weighed against the potential negative effects. The term **iatrogenesis** was developed by Ivan Illich (1976) to describe health problems that are caused by medicine. Over the past ten years there has been increasing concern at the extent of **medical error**. In 2000 the US Institute of Medicine (IOM, 2000) published a report summarizing the growing evidence on the risk to the health of patients due to medical error. This report highlighted two studies – one in Colorado and Utah and the other one in New York (Brennan et al., 1991) – that found that adverse events occurred in 2.9% and 3.7% of hospitalizations, respectively. Extrapolating to the whole of the USA the report estimated that 44,000 to 98,000 Americans die each year as a result of medical error. That is more than die each year from motor-vehicle accidents, breast cancer or AIDS.

Since the publication of the IOM report, other countries have produced similar reports. For example, in 2001 the UK Chief Medical Officer produced a report entitled *An Organisation with a Memory* (Department of Health, 2000) and a subsequent action report detailing specific recommendations. This was followed by a report by the UK Chief Pharmaceutical Officer (Smith, 2004). These reports also referred to the high rate of adverse medical events. They highlighted one British study that found that 10% of patients admitted to two London teaching hospitals had experienced an adverse event, of which half were preventable. It was estimated that such adverse events generated up to £2 billion in additional costs to the NHS (DOH, 2000). A recent survey conducted by the Health Foundation (2004) in the UK estimated that as many as 40,000 deaths a year were due to medical error.

Smith (2004) estimated that 10–20% of adverse medical events are due to medication errors. In a study of 550,000 prescriptions written by GPs in Britain pharmacists identified and averted 54 potentially harmful cases (0.01%). However, a large proportion of errors go undetected or unreported. For this reason Smith proposed a medication error iceberg to describe the situation. At the tip were those errors that cause actual damage and are reported. But then there are the unreported errors that include errors identified with potential to cause harm (near-misses), errors identified but considered insignificant, potential errors and unnoticed actual errors. Together, this indicates the extent of the problem is much greater than appears from initial figures.

Explanations for medical error

Explanations of medical error frequently distinguish between the person and systems approaches. The person approach focuses on the individual and leads to the so-called 'name, blame and shame' approach to error management. The alternative systems approach considers the broader context within which errors occur. It emphasizes the importance of organizational change in order to reduce the risk of error. A summary of the person and system explanations of medical error is provided in Figure 15.1.

It should be noted that in hospitals it is junior physicians who do most of the prescribing. They are the ones with least knowledge and also the ones who make the most prescribing errors. In a survey of junior hospital physicians in internal medicine training programmes, it has been found that 45% reported making at least one error, 31% of which resulted in a patient's death.

Weingart et al. (2000) in their review of medical error identified a series of potential risk factors. These included:

- age of patient: older patients are more at risk;
- type of intervention: certain types of surgery are particularly risky;
- emergency room usage;
- lengthy medical care;
- intensive medical care.

They concluded 'unless we make substantial changes to the organisation and delivery of medical care, all patients – particularly the most vulnerable – will continue to bear the burden of medical error' (Weingart et al., 2000: 776).

	THE PERSON APPROACH	
Forgetfulness		Poster campaigns
Inattention		Procedure review
Poor motivation		Disciplinary action
Carelessness		Threat of litigation
Negligence		Retraining
Recklessness	Nurses	Naming, blaming and shaming
Distraction	Physicians	
	Surgeons	
CAUSES OF	Anaesthetists	REACTION TO
ERROR	Pharmacists	ERROR
	Other health-care workers	
Error-provoking conditions		Error is generalized rather
within the workplace,		than isolated
e.g. time pressure,		
understaffing inadequate		System is reviewed to limit
equipment, fatigue,		the incidence of error
inexperience		
	THE SYSTEMS	
Weaknesses in defences,	APPROACH	System is reviewed so that
e.g. unworkable		if an error occurs its
procedure, design		damaging effects are
deficiencies, equipment		minimized
failure		

Figure 15.1   Person and system approaches to medication error (based on Smith, 2004)

An important factor overall is the character of the physician–patient relationship. A survey of American physicians and members of the general public found that they agreed on two possible causes of medical error: shortage of nurses (53% physicians versus 65% of the public) and overwork, stress and fatigue of health providers (50% versus 70%). In addition, 72% of the public referred to too little time with their physician and 67% referred to health-care professionals not working as a team or not communicating.

Medical silence

One common problem raised by all of the recent reports has been that of medical silence: the reluctance of health professionals, in particular physicians, to report errors. In a survey of physicians conducted in five countries (Australia, New Zealand, Canada, USA and UK) a large proportion reported that they felt discouraged from reporting or that they were not encouraged to report (Blendon et al., 2001). The proportion was over 60% in Australia and about 30% in the UK. This contrasts with the large proportion of patients and the general public who would prefer reporting of medical errors (Gallagher et al., 2003).

The DOH (2000) identified several reasons for this reluctance to report on the part of medical personnel. These included:

- lack of awareness that an error has occurred;
- lack of awareness of the need to report, what to report and why;

- perception that the patient is unharmed by the error;
- fear of disciplinary action or litigation, for self or colleagues;
- lack of familiarity with reporting mechanisms;
- loss of self-esteem;
- staff feeling they are too busy to report;
- lack of feedback when errors are reported.

The IOM (2000) report expressed alarm that despite the high rate of error 'silence surrounds this issue. For the most part, consumers believe they are protected' (2000: 3). It continued: 'The goal of this report is to break this cycle of inaction. The status quo is not acceptable and cannot be tolerated any longer. Despite the cost pressures, liability constraints, resistance to change and other seemingly insurmountable barriers, it is simply not acceptable for patients to be harmed by the same health care system that is supposed to offer healing and comfort' (IOM, 2000: 3). This reluctance on the part of physicians to report has led to the establishment of mandatory reporting systems in many countries.

However, the reluctance of physicians to report also reflects their power and status in society and the reticence of the public and the patient to question medical authority. Thus implicit within any model to reduce medical error and to improve patient safety is the challenge of increasing public and patient involvement and control of health care.

Patient Empowerment

Rather than attempting to control the patient, an approach that is implicit within models of compliance, empowerment attempts to increase patient autonomy and self-control. The empowerment approach is derived from the work of community educators and psychologists and is defined as the process whereby 'people gain mastery over their lives' (Rappaport, 1987). Instead of imposing the views of the expert health professional, empowerment seeks to enhance the patients' self-understanding and the potential of self-care (Feste and Anderson, 1995).

The focus of this approach is the enhancement of the strengths and potential of the patient. Through dialogue the health professional seeks to understand the needs of the patient. It has been suggested that the aim of patient education within this model is to 'blur' the boundaries between professional-as-teacher and patient-as-learner. Instead of the professional's health knowledge being considered paramount, the patient's lay health beliefs and knowledge is considered of equal or greater value. A central component of this understanding is the opportunity for patients to tell their stories. In describing this process Hunter notes that 'medicine has the power not only to rewrite the patient's story of illness but also to replot its course' (1991: 139). Dependent upon the story that is handed back the patient will assess its relevance to their lives. As Hunter continues: 'if the two are widely disparate and the physician fails to recognize the distance between them, the interaction founders. The medicine will go untaken, the consultation unsought, the prescription unfilled' (1991: 142).

Desire for control

Patient empowerment can aim to involve the patient more in health care through attention to patient needs or it can increase the patients' awareness of the broader social and political factors that adversely affect their health status. Admittedly, as Lupton (1997) found, not all patients wish to be actively involved in their personal health care or in taking broader collective action.

Desire for control can be conceptualized along three dimensions (Auerbach, 2001):

- Cognitive/informational control is concerned with processing relevant information and thereby reducing ambiguity and leading to an enhanced sense of control over the particular situation. In the case of health care this involves obtaining and reviewing information about the health problem and the proposed treatment.
- Decisional control refers to the opportunity for reviewing and selecting preferences for treatment.
- Behavioural control involves direct action whereby the individual is involved in changing the situation. It implies that the patient has the opportunity to select and guide the actual treatment.

There is substantial evidence that patients desire information about their health. Younger more educated patients have a greater desire for such information. In the case of decisional control, the evidence is more equivocal with many patients indicating that they would prefer physician control or at best some form of joint or collaborative control. A variety of factors influence this preference: (1) less desire for control when the disease is serious; (2) less desire for control among older patients; (3) less desire for control among patients with lower education. In concluding his review, Auerbach stated: 'if there is a predisposition on the part of patients to want to assume control, it is strongly influenced by their appraisal of whether they think involvement on their part will positively influence the outcome of their situation' (2001: 197).

Critical approach to empowerment

Many health-care providers have enthusiastically endorsed the idea of empowerment. However, there is a need for some caution as regards its implications for patient care. Although most physicians prefer to adopt the dominant role in patient care, there is increasing evidence that many are promoting greater control by the patient. Indeed, this orientation connects with the identification of the patient as responsible in some way for both their illness and their treatment. This is particularly the case in those illnesses associated with lifestyle practices such as smoking, diet and exercise, but also with chronic diseases.

This critical approach to patient empowerment considers it part of the extended biopsychosocial model (Salmon and Hall, 2003). This model extends the traditional dualistic approach to the body by identifying psychosocial factors as aetologic agents of disease. This in turn leads to concern with promoting increased control and various coping strategies as ways of patient empowerment. Implicit in this discourse is the transformation of the patient from a passive sufferer to an active manager of their own suffering 'from which it is a small step to locating with the patient the moral responsibility to become well' (Salmon and Hall, 2003: 1973). This provides the physician with the opportunity to evade responsibility for treatment of those problems for which they have limited insight (e.g. chronic illness and mental illness). Thus the language of empowerment can serve the physician's interests rather than those of the patient. It can also absolve the physician of responsibility for certain medical errors.

A graphic illustration of the negative impact of empowerment is the enthusiasm of many physicians to promote the so-called 'fighting spirit' attitude among cancer patients. Initial research by Greer et al. (1979) had suggested that patients with this attitude had better survival prospects. Many patients report that their clinicians encourage them to be positive and to fight. Unfortunately, such encouragement can be disempowering as the patient feels depressed because s/he cannot control the disease.

Another example of this disempowering advice is the case of 'patient-controlled analgesia' (PCA) which is a strategy designed to provide post-operative patients with control over their analgesia. However, in interviews with the patients it was found that PCA did not give them control over their pain. Rather, they liked PCA because it freed them of the need to exercise control by 'bothering' nurses with requests for analgesia. In a comparison study that involved teaching post-operative patients to feel in control of their recovery it was found that patients interpreted the programme as a request not to annoy the staff. Together these studies question the practice of strategies designed to empower patients.

Kugelmann (1997) develops a similar critique in his review of the growth of the gate control model of pain. He notes that an important component of this and other biopsychosocial models is the insistence on personal responsibility for pain management. The alternative to assuming responsibility is learned helplessness and passivity. While the patient is expected to assume responsibility 'they should not expect, however, that the professionals should relinquish their salaries or expertise' (1997: 61). Kugelmann also connects his critique with the ignorance of social problems. 'If pain is truly epidemic today, then something is terribly wrong, not only with patients, or inadequate pain technologies, but with the social matrix that produces suffering. To tempt people to be co-managers in such a social world only deepens our true helplessness' (1997: 62).

Other researchers have questioned the whole movement towards promoting empowerment. As Lord and McKillop Farlow note: 'people mistakenly talk about "empowering families" or "empowering professionals" as if empowerment is something one person does to another' (1990: 2). Powers argues that rather than challenging the traditional medical paternalism, 'empowerment equals paternalism' (2003: 229). Within a capitalist state this promotion of empowerment has a hidden agenda:

1 It allows health care disciplines to reframe questions regarding oppression to questions regarding free individual choices among predetermined alternatives in the context of a belief in natural rights.
2 It allows the health care provider to assign blame when the strategy fails, i.e. when the patient chooses the 'wrong' option.
3 It makes health education a technology of the self, a way to get people to think they are taking charge of their own health and exercising their rights instead of being dependent.

The move towards empowerment is especially directed at those people who do not conform to mainstream values and practices rather than attempting to promote broader changes in social structures. The physician and other health professionals can now continue to disparage the most deprived and marginalized not for their non-compliance but rather for their refusal to accept responsibility for self-management.

These criticisms are a challenge and highlight the need for health psychology to adopt a broad critical perspective such that it does not simply continue to be agents of health-care oppression although in the guise of a more critical language.

Future Research

1 New medical procedures and drugs are constantly being developed. While these can be efficacious in the controlled clinical trial setting, there is an ongoing need to assess the problems involved in their adoption in the community.
2 Different health problems require different forms of treatment. Research needs to consider the appropriateness of different interventions.
3 Similarly, not everyone will accept certain procedures. Further research is needed to explore the meaning of different treatments to different populations.
4 As attitudes to health care change, research needs to address the changing needs of different client groups and how these can best be addressed.
5 Research needs to address how best to involve people more directly in all aspects of their health care.

Summary

1 Adherence refers to the extent to which the patient follows the prescribed treatment regimen.
2 A wide range of social and psychological factors has been found to be associated with non-adherence. These factors are associated with the characteristics of the patients, the disorders they have, the treatments they are given, and the relationships they have with their physicians and organizational factors.
3 Social characteristics associated with non-adherence include: characteristics of individual's social situation; lack of social support; family instability or disharmony; parent's expectations and attitudes towards treatment; residential instability; an environment that supports non-adherent behaviour; competing or conflicting demands; lack of resources.
4 Personal characteristics associated with non-adherence include: demographics; sensory disabilities; type and severity of psychiatric disorder; forgetfulness; lack of understanding.
5 Health beliefs associated with non-adherence include: inappropriate or conflicting health beliefs; competing socio-cultural and ethnic folk concepts of disease and treatment; an implicit model of illness.
6 An alternative approach is to consider the impact on patient behaviour of the socio-political role of the physician and the meaning of the health problem and of the prescribed medication for the patient.

7 Medical error leads to a wide range of health problems. Explanations of medical error include both person and system factors. Medical silence has traditionally concealed the extent of medical error.

8 Patient empowerment aims to involve patients in health care through listening to their needs not as recipients but as active partners in the process of health care.

9 Patient empowerment conversely can centre responsibility for illness management on the patient and absolve the physician and health professional from responsibilities.

 # Key Terms

empowerment

medical error

iatrogenesis

physical side effects

identity control

16 Pain

Pain comes unsharably into our midst as at once that which cannot be denied and that which cannot be confirmed. (Scarry, 1985: 4)

Prolonged pain, even if not particularly severe, tends to take the joy out of life. (Finkelstein and French, 1993: 36)

Outline

This chapter discusses the nature of pain and the distinction between acute and chronic pain. The focus is chronic pain. We discuss the major theories, including direct line of transmission theories and multidimensional gate control theory, which acknowledges psychological influences. A range of psychosocial factors implicated in the mediation of the pain experience are considered. We summarize pain assessment methods. Finally, we explore the issue of pain management using psychological techniques.

What is Pain?

Pain evolved as a biological safety mechanism to warn us when something is physically wrong, allowing us to take appropriate action to alleviate the problem. It is a highly adaptive phenomenon. The importance of this mechanism can be seen when cases of congenital universal insensitivity to pain (CUIP) are considered. One such case was a young Canadian woman, Miss C, who never experienced pain. She suffered repeated injuries (e.g. third degree burns) and severe medical problems from not making positional adjustments normally evoked by discomfort or pain (e.g. pathological abnormalities in knees, hips and spine). Consequently, Miss C died aged just 29 (see Melzack and Wall, 1982). Most cases of CUIP involve premature death.

Pain is a uniquely personal human experience, which has been defined in many ways, including:

- An aversive, personal, subjective experience, influenced by cultural learning, the meaning of the situation, attention and other psychological variables, which disrupts ongoing behaviour and motivates the individual to attempt to stop the pain (Melzack and Wall, 1988).

- Whatever the person experiencing it says it is, existing whenever the experiencing person says it does (McCaffery and Thorpe, 1988).
- It is an unpleasant sensory and emotional experience associated with actual or potential tissue damage, or described in terms of such damage (Merskey, 1996).

Such definitions highlight the subjective, emotional and multidimensional nature of pain experience. Pain has been further classified as either acute or chronic, differentiated only by duration (acute being under and chronic over six months). The six-month cut-off is relatively arbitrary and recently a three-month threshold has been suggested.

Acute pain is a useful biological response provoked by injury or disease (e.g. broken leg, appendicitis), which is of limited duration (International Association for the Study of Pain, 1992). It tends to be amenable to pharmacological treatment. **Chronic** pain is described as pain persisting for six months or more and tends not to respond to pharmacological treatment.

Further definitional distinctions include:

- malignant (associated with progressive illness e.g. cancer);
- benign (not associated with progressive illness e.g. lower back pain);
- progressive (becomes worse overtime e.g. arthritis);
- intractable (resistant to treatment e.g. lower back pain);
- intermittent (pain that fluctuates over time and in intensity e.g. fibromyalgia);
- recurrent (acute pain occuring periodically e.g. migraine);
- organic (involving observable tissue damage e.g. arthritis);
- psychogenic (absence of demonstrable pathology e.g. fibromyalgia);
- referred (pain originating in one body area which is perceived as originating from another e.g. perceiving an earache that in fact originates from a bad tooth).

Responses to acute pain that are adaptive will often be maladaptive in response to chronic pain.

Pain is a complex, multidimensional phenomenon with physiological (aetiology), sensory (intensity, quality), affective (emotional response), cognitive (thoughts about the experience) and behavioural (e.g. grimacing, avoidance) components. It can affect anyone at any time, often involving all aspects of a person's life including physical, psychological and emotional states, disrupting daily activities, work, finances, social, marital and family life and relationships (e.g. Marcus, 2000). In addition to the association between many chronic illnesses and pain (e.g. cancer, HIV/AIDS, sickle-cell anaemia), particular groups appear more likely to experience chronic pain, especially the elderly and many disabled people even in the absence of illness (e.g. pain from braces or harnesses).

The cost of pain

Pain inflicts significant costs on individuals, their families, the health services and society in general. It is the most commonly cited reason for which patients seek medical help. It is estimated that 80% of all doctor consultations in the USA and around 40% in the UK relate to pain. Pain is associated with extended hospital stays, lost working days and increased take-up of benefits. The resultant economic costs are very high. Back pain is the most common chronic pain condition. In 1998, it was estimated that in the UK back pain had a prevalence rate of 37% (or 17.5 million individuals), equating to direct costs for care and treatment of £1.63 billion and indirect costs as lost production and informal care of £10.67 billion (Maniadakis and Gray, 2000).

The cost of pain in terms of human suffering is also high. Pain statistics are likely to under-represent the problem as many people endure significant levels of pain without seeking help. Pain is often the most distressing and debilitating aspect of chronic illness. Its effects on quality of life can be devastating to the individual and their significant others, including distress, loss of function, relationship problems, social, financial and employment difficulties and stigma. The emotional toll of severe chronic pain should not be underestimated. It is estimated that around 50% of severe chronic pain patients consider suicide. Similarly, the experience of unremitting pain in cancer patients has been reported as the most common reason underlying requests for physician-assisted dying.

Theories of Pain

The specific mechanisms for the transmission and perception of pain are not well understood, although our knowledge is expanding. Several prominent theories of pain have been proposed including specificity theory, pattern theory and gate control theory. Both specificity theory and pattern theory view pain as a sensory experience.

Specificity theory

Specificity theory suggested by Von Frey in 1894 describes a direct causal relationship between pain stimulus and pain experience. Stimulation of specific pain receptors (nociceptors) throughout the body sends impulses along specific pain pathways (A-delta fibres and C-fibres) through the spinal cord to specific areas of the sensory cortex of the brain. Stimulus intensity correlates with pain intensity, with higher stimulus intensity and pain pathway activation resulting in a more intense pain experience. Failure to identify a specific cortical location for pain, realization that pain fibres do not respond exclusively to pain but also to pressure and temperature, and the disproportional relationship between stimulus intensity and reported pain intensity (e.g. injured soldiers reporting little pain while similarly injured civilians requiring substantial medication) led to specificity theory losing favour.

Pattern theory

Pattern theorists proposed that stimulation of nociceptors produces a pattern of impulses that are summated in the dorsal horn of the spinal cord. Only if the level of the summated output exceeds a certain threshold is pain information transmitted onwards to the cortex resulting in pain perception. Evidence of deferred pain perception (e.g. soldiers not perceiving pain until the battle is over), intact pain transmission

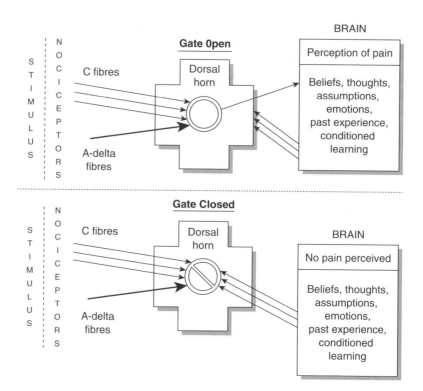

Figure 16.1   Illustration of gate control theory of pain

systems where pain is perceived without (ongoing) injury (e.g. phantom limb) and injury without pain perception (e.g. CUIP) raised questions concerning the comprehensiveness of pattern theories. In addition, there was growing evidence for a mediating role for psychosocial factors in the experience of pain, including cross-cultural differences in pain perception and expression.

Gate control theory

The growing body of evidence contradicting direct line of transmission theories culminated in the development of the **gate control theory** (GCT; Melzack and Wall, 1982). GCT views pain as a multidimensional and perceptual experience, in which ascending physiological inputs and descending psychological inputs are equally involved. GCT posits that there is a gating mechanism in the dorsal horn of the spinal cord that permits or inhibits the transmission of pain impulses (see Figure 16.1).

The dorsal horn receives inputs from nociceptors which it transmits to the brain via a neural gate. The dorsal horn also receives information from the brain about the psychological and emotional state of the individual. This information can act as an inhibitory control that closes the neural gate preventing the transmission of the nociceptive impulses and thus modifying the perception of pain. The mechanism operates based on the relative activity of the peripheral nociceptor fibres and the descending cortical fibres. Pain impulses must reach conscious awareness before pain is experienced. If awareness can be prevented, the experience of pain is decreased, eliminated or deferred.

GCT is the most influential theory of pain and continues to inform theoretical and empirical work. GCT offered substantial explanatory power, acknowledging a role for descending control and psychological, social and behavioural factors. However, the theory has received criticism, the most significant being the absence of direct evidence of a 'gate' in the spinal cord. More recently Melzack (1999) has updated the theory describing a neuromatrix, in place of the gate. Pain is the result of the output from this neural network programme, which is determined by sensory, cognitive, affective, experiential and genetic influences. Mapping the neural networks proposed by Melzack, and development of treatment approaches based on the theory, will determine the theory's potential to further our understanding of pain.

Psychological Aspects of Pain

Many psychosocial factors have been investigated in relation to pain and these appear to exert independent effects on the experience of pain. However, these factors are interconnected and interacting and often the difference identified in one factor (e.g. low self-efficacy) may be mirrored in another (e.g. low internal locus of control). The relative degrees of influence within the network of contributing factors need further elucidation. The most significant determinant of pain chronicity appears to be the level of impact on activities of daily living, the functional disability associated with the pain.

While the role of psychological factors in the experience of pain is now generally accepted, discussion of psychological inputs to pain is likely to provoke passionate responses and/or denials from sufferers, who fear invalidation of their very real experiences as 'all in the mind'. Health professionals need to be sensitive to this fear and present psychological issues skilfully, in ways that do not invalidate the experience of the individual.

Cognitions

Cognitions influence and interact with our emotions and behaviour. An individual's cognitions influence the experience of pain, particularly the appraisal of situations for their significance and meaning (e.g. association of pain and sexual pleasure for masochists). Three aspects of cognition that have received attention in relation to pain are attention, dysfunctional thinking and coping styles.

Increased attention to pain has been associated with increased pain perception. Pain may demand attention, reducing the ability to focus on other competing activities and therefore increasing pain perception. This may explain why distraction techniques are useful in combating pain. However, the role of attention may differ for acute and chronic pain. In acute pain, taking attention away from pain (e.g. via distraction) appears to be associated with reduced anxiety and depression whereas it has an opposite effect

KT

for chronic pain patients, for whom attending to rather than avoiding the pain may be more adaptive.

Dysfunctional thoughts, attitudes and beliefs about pain are automatic patterns of thinking that block the attainment of an individual's goals (e.g. participating in work or social activity). A major form of dysfunctional thinking that influences the pain experience is **catastrophizing** (e.g. it's hopeless, pain has ruined my life, I can't cope, it will never get better). Catastrophic thinking has been found to increase likelihood of chronicity, level of perceived intensity and disability and even to have a small association with pain onset (e.g. Crombez et al., 2003). Other dysfunctional thoughts include negative mental bias, discounting the positive, fortune telling and magnification.

Cognitive coping styles are strategies an individual uses to attempt to deal with their pain. They can be divided into active and passive coping. Both can be functional or dysfunctional. Active coping might include keeping oneself busy or taking recreational drugs, which could easily become dysfunctional. Passive coping might include resting, which would be useful in the early stages of pain but could become dysfunctional if continued for too long. In general, active coping styles have been found to be associated with improved coping, reduced pain intensity and improved recovery rates. However, McCracken and Eccleston (2003) suggest that acceptance of pain and its incorporation into one's sense of self appears to be an adaptive cognitive technique for chronic pain. Specific coping techniques are detailed below under pain management.

Self-efficacy

Self-efficacy beliefs (Bandura, 1977) have been identified as a significant component of cognition and refer to an individual's beliefs about how well they can handle a given situation. A relationship between an individual's self-efficacy beliefs about their ability to manage pain, whether acute, chronic or experimentally induced, has been found (e.g. Brekke et al., 2003). Low self-efficacy beliefs have been associated with higher chronic pain-related disability levels, as well as with depression, although the associations are insufficient to eliminate the strong influence of pain intensity. Self-efficacy beliefs may also relate to a second cognitive component that has been associated with pain, **perceived control.**

Perceived control

Both cognitive control (e.g. ability to distract thoughts from the pain) and behavioural control (e.g. being able to remove pain inducing stimuli) have been found to influence pain experience. Bowers (1968) showed that individuals endure more pain when they control the pain-stimulus on/off switch than when it is controlled by someone else. This concept relates to the development of patient controlled (PCA) (or self-administered) analgesia, in the management of post-operative pain and in palliative care. PCA resulted in patients administering less analgesic morphine than when it was controlled and administered by nurses or through continuous infusion. PCA appears to result in better pain management, less opiate use and earlier discharge from hospital than intramuscular therapy (Royal College of Surgeons and Anaesthetists, 1990).

Rotter's (1966) theory of locus of control (LOC) has also been applied to the concept of pain. Individuals with an internal locus of control believe that what happens to them is under their own control, while those with an external LOC believe that what happens is due to chance, fate or powerful others. This theory has been applied to pain.

Previous experience and conditioning

Previous experience of pain is a significant factor in current pain experience. Both classical and operant **conditioning** have been implicated in the etiology of chronic pain via the association of behaviour and pain. In classical conditioning theory a particular situation or environment may become associated with pain (e.g. the dentist) and therefore provoke increased anxiety and pain perception. Jamner and Tursky (1987) report that even the words used by migraine sufferers to describe their pain appear to reinforce the experience by provoking stronger physiological responses than non-pain words. In operant conditioning theory, pain stimuli are perceived as a sensation and an unpleasant affect that generally evokes responses like grimacing or limping demonstrating the person is in pain. Pain behaviours become conditioned responses through positive (e.g. attention, medication, time off work) and negative (e.g. disapproval of others, loss of earnings) reinforcements. Pain behaviours may be functional and appropriate (e.g. removing hand from a burning source of heat), or they may be less functional and therefore pain maintaining (e.g. avoidance, alcohol).

KT

Secondary gains

The role of secondary gains in the development and maintenance of pain and illness behaviours has been described. Secondary gain relates to social rewards accruing from the demonstration of pain behaviours (e.g. receiving attention, financial benefits, time off work). These secondary gains are thought to reinforce pain behaviours and thus maintain the condition. For example, receipt of financial disability compensations has been associated with slower return to work and increased pain. However, this may actually reflect that those in receipt of compensation can allow themselves appropriate time to recover and says nothing about the quality of life of those who returned to work earlier. For many individuals, pain results in the loss of jobs, social contact, leisure activities, valued identities, reduced incomes and concomitant reduced standard of living. Such losses are very real and distressing and are often associated with substantial hardships, lowered mood and loss of self-esteem, unlikely to be outweighed by incidental benefits.

Personality

It has been suggested that there is a 'pain-prone personality' (Engel, 1959) and that psychological factors are the primary contributor to the pain experience for pain-prone individuals. Features of the pain-prone personality include continual episodes of varying chronic pain, high neurotic symptoms (guilt feelings, anxiety, depression and hypochondria). Generally, empirical support for the pain-prone personality has not been forthcoming and it has been suggested that the higher scores for particular personality factors (i.e. neurotic triad) may be a consequence rather than a cause of long-term pain.

Mood

The most common moods that have been associated with pain are anxiety and depression. Where these moods are present pain appears to be increased. It has been reported that acute pain increases anxiety but once pain is decreased through treatment the anxiety also decreases, which can cause further decreases in the pain, a cycle of pain reduction. Alternatively, chronic pain remains unalleviated by treatment and therefore anxiety increases which can further increase the pain, creating a cycle of pain increase. Research has shown that anxiety increases pain perception in children with migraine and people with back pain and pelvic pain (McGowan et al., 1998).

Anxiety is normally a result of fear. Pain-related fear can be specific or general (e.g. the pain is going to get worse or what will the future be like). The fear-avoidance model of pain suggests that fear of pain amplifies perception and leads to pain avoidance behaviours in some people, especially those with a propensity to catastrophic thinking (Vlaeyen and Linton, 2000). This cycle results in pain experience and behaviours becoming separated from pain sensation through exaggerated pain perception. A prospective study by Klenerman et al. (1995) found fear-avoidance variables correctly predicted future outcome in 66% of patients. A more recent prospective study (Linton et al., 2000) also found that higher baseline scores for fear avoidance in a non-pain population were associated with double the likelihood of reporting back pain in the following year and a significantly increased risk of reduced physical functioning.

People who experience severe and persistent pain often have feelings of hopelessness, helplessness and despair. Depression is commonly associated with pain and may even have a causal role in the development of chronic pain. Others have argued that depression is most likely the consequence of experiencing protracted pain, supported by the fact that any effective treatment leads to mood improvements. One prospective study on depression and chronic pain suggests that the relationship between the two may not be unidirectional (Magni et al., 1994). There are many overlaps between depression and pain including the central involvement of the same neurotransmitters, serotonin, norepinephrine, subtance P and corticotrophin-releasing factor (Campbell et al., 2003).

While correlations between mood states and pain have been found, the causal direction and the nature of the relationships remains unclear. Most recent work appears to indicate that negative mood states are an outcome of chronic pain rather than a cause.

Stress

Chronic pain both exacerbates and is exacerbated by stress. Although closely related to anxiety, stress appears to influence pain directly but in different contexts may increase or decrease the perception of pain and its intensity. Acute pain can produce stress-induced analgesia in which the body's internal pain relief systems (e.g. endogenous opioids) are activated, at least temporarily blocking perception of pain (e.g. at the time of a car crash). Alternatively, experimental studies have shown that experiencing stress (e.g. arithmetic test with ongoing negative performance feedback) appears to increase the likelihood of experiencing pain and effect the perception of pain intensity (e.g. Gannon et al., 1987).

Experiencing persistent high levels of pain can itself be a substantial stressor, possibly even the most significant stressor in the lives of many individuals. It is also often the source of additional life stresses, like loss of employment, relationship difficulties and financial hardship. Individual, stereotypical physiological responses to stress (e.g. clenching jaws, migraine headaches) can be a direct source of pain and the physiological arousal associated with stress may lead to increased pain and inhibit effective adaptation. Stress is such a frequent concomitant of pain that stress management techniques are routinely included as an integral part of pain management programmes.

Socio-Cultural Influences on Pain

Socio-cultural factors that influence the experience of pain include culture, gender, and significant others. One problem with this approach is a tendency to treat the group of interest as relatively homogeneous, whether the grouping is based on a particular pain condition or a particular socio-cultural variable. However, most groups are likely to be fairly heterogeneous. For example, in the UK, the ethnic category African-Caribbean might include both individuals recently arrived from the Caribbean and third or fourth generation African-Caribbeans born in Britain. Similar sub-groups of patients can be identified on the basis of psychosocial and behavioural characteristics.

Culture

The pain experience is expressed differently across cultural groups. Pain tolerance levels, communication about pain, pain behaviours and the meaning of pain are all influenced by culture via social learning. Melzack and Wall (1982) cite the Indian hook-swinging religious ceremony in which a man is suspended by hooks under his skin and muscles and swings freely without appearing to feel any pain. Cultural influences may encourage avoidance or acceptance of pain, demonstrable pain behaviours or stoic concealment. Culture may also affect the treatment received within health-care systems in terms of cultural expectations (e.g. appropriateness of medication demands) and communication traditions (e.g. non-verbal expression). There is also growing acknowledgement that cultural groups differ biologically in their pain tolerance thresholds as well as their physiological responses to pain medications (Giger and Davidhizar, 2004). The influence of social factors and discrimination and how these affect the experience of pain treatment for minority groups need further research.

Gender

There is much evidence to suggests that women are better at dealing with pain than men. Many factors including biology, sex hormones, culture, socialization and role expectations, psychology, and past experience have been offered as explanatory variables. However, the relationship between pain and gender is complex. In addition the particular type of pain (e.g. experimentally induced versus labour-pain), when it occurs (e.g. when in the menstrual cycle and in relation to childbirth) and researcher's gender are all implicated in pain reporting. Skevington (1995) argues gender differences may have been overemphasized and significant similarities exist between the sexes regarding pain experiences and actual differences may relate to treatment behaviour (e.g. help-seeking, self-treatment) and pain severity. Further research is needed to unpack the relationship between gender and pain.

Age

The experience of pain has been found to vary across the lifespan. Less is known about pain in children than in adults. Previously, infants (< 3 months) would not be given analgesia during minor surgery (e.g. circumcision) as it was thought they were unable to feel pain. Subsequently this has been refuted, with facial pain expressions and differences in crying intensity and pitch having been identified. Chronic pain in children appears to be under-represented in the pain literature, despite the reporting of both persistent and recurring chronic pain (mainly in the head, limbs and gut) by children, and increased pain reporting with age. For older adults, pain may be a pervasive aspect of their lives differing qualitatively from that experienced by younger age groups. Older adults may experience more intense and persistent pain, a greater number of pain sites and conditions, reduced endogenous analgesic responses and increased levels of disability. Some reviewers however report decreases in prevalence, intensity and pain reporting with growing age.

Whether such findings reflect an actual decrease in pain or an acceptance of pain as part of life is unclear. However, older adults are certainly likely to have a greater number of disorders that can cause pain and while their experience of pain may not vary in some dimensions from those of younger adults, its impact on their quality of life is likely to be greater. The elderly are consistently under-represented in the pain literature and pain in this group is substantially under-diagnosed and under-treated. Health psychologists should work to improve diagnostic techniques and understanding of the pain across the life span, especially among children, older adults and the way it interacts with other aspects of their lives.

Significant others and the family

A common concept in chronic pain research is that subjective pain and pain-related behaviour (e.g. limping) may be affected by significant others who are perhaps one of the major reinforcers for pain-related behaviours and chronicity. Spousal solicitousness may inadvertently maintain or increase the experience of pain and disability. Pain may have substantial effects on an individual's partner as well as themselves, including changes to lifestyle, marital and sexual problems and effects on mood.

Partners may have to go through similar adjustment and coping processes as the individual in pain. Skevington (1995) suggests that due to their involvement as primary carers, 'women are major agents in the shaping of other people's perceptions, attitudes and behaviour related to pain and suffering' (1995: 276).

Parents are the most significant influence on a child's pain perception, modelling behaviours as well as reinforcing them. Parents' reactions to their children's pain may affect pain perception and related behaviours, like attention to the scratching behaviour of children with a skin condition reinforcing that behaviour. Pain within the family is likely to affect all family members and the family will affect how they all cope. The family represents the main environment in which pain is manifested and should be taken into consideration in the development of interventions.

Further research is required with measurement instruments specifically developed to assess the relevant variables in pain populations and needs to be extended to include families and significant others.

Assessment

Pain **assessment** is not a simple process. Part of the problem is the inherent difficulty in trying to describe a uniquely individual experience to another person. Assessment is crucial to the understanding and treatment of pain including its underlying mechanisms and mediating factors, as well as the development of effective treatment programmes.

KT

Assessments are mostly undertaken for medical, research or compensation claim purposes and the purpose will influence the type of assessment used. Assessment measures may include intensity, psychological and functional effects and pain behaviours. Assessment methods can generally be grouped under one of four categories: physiological measures, pain questionnaires, mood assessment questionnaires and observations (direct observations or self-observations). Table 16.1 summarizes some of the common measures that have been described in the literature. Medical examinations form the backbone of clinical pain assessments and include joint mobility and heart rate. Other physiological measures attempt to measure objective physical responses to pain. For example, EEGs measure electrical activity in the brain and EEG spikes have been shown to correlate with intensity of pain stimuli, presence of analgesics and subjective reports of pain (Chapman et al., 1985). Much of the work using physiological measures comes from the experimental rather than clinical paradigm and results have been inconsistent across differing levels of reported pain. It has been suggested that such measures are more useful for assessing emotional responses to pain than pain itself (Chapman et al., 1985).

Pain questionnaires typically present commonly used descriptive words (for aspects of pain or mood) that the individual uses to rate their current experience. The words may be presented in rating scales or descriptive lists. The McGill Pain questionnaire – MPQ (Melzack, 1975) is possibly the best known and most frequently used questionnaire although some of the newer instruments are showing promise. The MPQ utilizes verbal descriptive scales.

Table 16.1   *Summary of common pain assessment measures*

Physiological measures	Questionnaires assessing pain	Questionnaires assessing mood	Observations – direct or self
Medical examination including pain sites, joint mobility, history etc.	Minnesota Multiphasic Personality Inventory (MMPI) (Dahlstrom & Welsh, 1960)	Beck's depression inventory (Beck, 1977)	Activity levels
Muscle tension–electromyography (EMG)	McGill Pain Questionnaire (MPQ) (Melzack, 1975)	Hospital Anxiety and Depression Scale (Zigmond and Snaith, 1983)	Standing and sitting time (uptime and downtime)
Heart rate	Multi-dimensional pain inventory (MPI) (Kearns, Turk, and Rudy, 1985)	Well-being Questionnaire (Pincus, Griffith, Isenberg and Pearce, 1997)	Sleep patterns
Hyperventilation	Sickness Impact Profile (SIP) (Follick, Smith and Ahern, 1985)		Sexual activity
Galvanic skin response	Survey of Pain Attitudes (Jensen, Karoly and Huger, 1987)		Medication requests and usage
Electroencephalograph	Pain Information and Beliefs Questionnaire (Shutty, DeGood, and Tuttle, 1990)		Appetite and eating
Pedometer	Bio-behavioural Pain Profile (Dalton, Feuerstein, Carlson and Roghman, 1994)		Normal household activities
Electroencephalograph (EEG)			Leisure activities

Examples from MPQ	1 Flickering Quivering Pulsing Throbbing Beating Pounding	13 Fearful Frightful Terrifying	PPI (Intensity) 0 No pain 1 Mild 2 Discomforting 3 Distressing 4 Horrible 5 Excruciating

Tick one word in each list that best describes your pain

Other questionnaire scales including verbal rating, box and visual analog scales are shown below. Questionnaires may use a number of scales along with body outlines (mark the body matching where you experience pain) and other techniques.

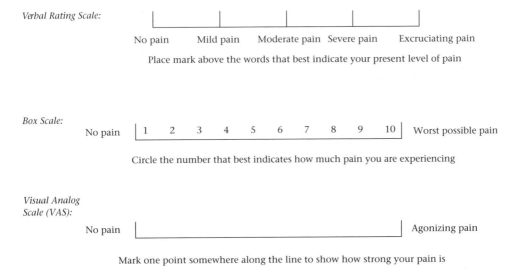

Visual analog scales may be the most appropriate for use with diverse cultural groups, children, the elderly and people with communication difficulties. They are easy to use and therefore frequent ratings can be made then averaged, or peak times and triggers identified. Most pain questionnaires attempt to assess sensory, affective and evaluative dimensions of pain. They can be completed by the individual or as part of an interview. Specific types of pain seem to be described using similar words and questionnaires have been found to discriminate between different pain populations. However, the subjective nature of self-report data and the use of complex and culture specific words represent weaknesses in the use of questionnaires.

Observations of individual pain behaviours and functional levels are also used in assessments, either direct observations by another person (e.g. a nurse on a hospital ward), or self-observations (e.g. in diaries or logs). However, direct and self-observations have drawbacks. Direct observations can never elicit unbiased data, being influenced by the setting in which they occur (e.g. clinical setting, home), the purpose of the assessment (e.g. benefit claim versus treatment assessment) and assessor characteristics (e.g. gender, ethnicity). Similarly, self-observations (e.g. pain diaries) may be inaccurate or overly subjective. An alternate approach is to use interviews that attempt to assess all aspects of the pain experience including a full pain history, assessing emotional adjustment and pre- and post-pain lifestyle. Effective pain assessment must be multidimensional including physiological, medical, sensory, behavioural, affective and evaluative information.

Issues in assessment

Many assessment instruments are insensitive to age, disability and culture. For groups who have communication difficulties, due to age, language problems, sensory or cognitive deficits, assessment may require extended assessment time to enable rapport building. However, time is often at a premium. It may be necessary to rely on the reports of significant others (e.g. carer, interpreter) rather than the individual, which produces additional challenges. Research that focuses on pain assessment among under-represented groups is needed. Similarly, more work is required to address issues around the impact of situational context and assessor characteristics on the assessment process. Further investigation is needed of the influence of assessment, including the impact of compensation claim assessments and of the need to prove the existence of pain and how it restricts the sufferer's daily activities.

Management

Before the complex and multidimensional nature of pain had been accepted, pain was treated through the administration of analgesic drugs, surgery and rest. Today pain management programmes seek to address the pain experience utilizing pharmacological, psychological and physical interventions, with considerable emphasis on psychology. The historical aim of pain management was to eliminate pain. More recently the aims have shifted to reducing pain perception, improving coping ability, increasing functional ability, decreasing drug reliance and distress. Many commonly used pain management strategies are listed in Table 16.2.

Whether prescribed by health professionals or independently adopted by the individual, any pain management strategy has the potential to improve the situation (e.g. numbing pain sensations with drugs or improving mood with aromatherapy). Equally any strategy can worsen the situation, as with medication side effects or lowered mood induced by substance abuse. It is important that an individual's own attempts at self-management are respected and that health professionals work in partnership with the individual to identify the optimum programme for that individual.

Behavioural strategies

Most behavioural strategies are based upon operant learning processes, like using operant conditioning in which pain behaviours are ignored (negative reinforcement) and improved activity is praised (positive reinforcement). Conditioning was integral to contingency management. This was a 2–6 week inpatient programme during which nursing staff would ignore medication requests, reinforce targeted 'well' behaviours, introduce increasing exercise quotas, and employ a fixed-schedule 'pain cocktail'. The pain cocktail delivered medication within a strong tasting masking fluid that allowed medication dosages to be reduced without the patient noticing. While such programmes have had good (even dramatic) short-term results, they have been less successful in maintaining such gains, possibly due to non-generalization outside the hospital environment. It is rare for programmes today to focus solely on conditioning methods.

Graded exercise strategies involve setting a starting level of activity that the person can manage and then developing a schedule to gradually increase the length of time and intensity of the exercise. The schedule allows the person to gain the confidence to handle each new level before the next increment.

Table 16.2   *Common Pain Management Strategies*

Multidisciplinary Pain Management Centres/Programmes				
Cognitive Behavioural Therapy (CBT)				
Behavioural	Cognitive	Pharmacological	Physical	Other
Operant conditioning	Cognitive restructuring	Non-opioid analgesics:	Surgical	Hypnosis
Contingency management	Cognitive coping skills training e.g. distraction	Paracetamol NSAIDS (e.g. ibuprofen, aspirin)	Transcuta-neous electrical nerve stimulation (TENS)	Other alternative therapies e.g. REIKI, Chinese medicine, music therapy
Graded exercise	Acceptance	Opioid analgesics: Morphine & derivatives (e.g. codeine)	Acupuncture Physiotherapy Heat and Cold	Support groups
Biofeedback	Imagery	Local anaesthetics	Vibration Massage Aromatherapy	Internet advice
Autogenic training	Meditation & prayer	Indirect action drugs (e.g. sedatives, antidepressants, tranquillizers)	Spinal cord stimulation	Self-help books
Relaxation	Information	Placebos	Reflexology	Spiritual including prayer
Progressive muscle relaxation	Stress management	Selfmedications: (e.g. cannabis, alcohol, heroine)	Mobility enhancing exercise	

Biofeedback and autogenic training teach the individual to control aspects of their physiology. A machine is used to monitor some aspect of physiology (e.g. heart rate, muscle tension) and the individual receives continuous feedback through visual and audio signals, through which they learn to control their response. Individuals may also be taught stress management techniques (e.g. relaxation, guided imagery, deep breathing). However, primarily the patient uses the feedback to experiment and discover the technique(s) that works best for them. Eventually the technique is learned well enough that the machine is no longer required. The support concerning biofeedback and pain reduction is modest and other techniques are likely to work as well if not better. It is also likely that any positive effects may be artefacts of relaxation processes.

Relaxation has a convincing history as a treatment for anxiety and stress, and has had some success as an adjunctive therapy for the treatment of acute and chronic pain. Relaxation probably affects pain perception both directly and indirectly (through its positive effects on stress and anxiety). Relaxation may involve progressive muscle relaxation (tensing and relaxing different muscle groups in succession from the feet to the head) or more simply deep rhythmic breathing, and is often used in conjunction with meditation or imagery techniques.

Cognitive strategies

Cognitive strategies work on the principle that our cognitions (thoughts, beliefs, etc.) are responsible for the consequences of events, not the event itself, and if these cognitions can be changed the consequence(s) will also change. In relation to pain management, cognitive strategies aim to help the individual identify and understand their cognitions and their connection with their experience of pain and then change negative cognitions to improve it. This includes teaching individuals to identify and challenge distorted thinking (e.g. catastrophizing), a process known as cognitive restructuring, an active coping technique that promotes the internal attribution of positive changes.

Training in cognitive coping skills has generally been found to be beneficial to pain patients. For example, Gil et al. (2000) found enhanced pain coping in patients with sickle-cell disease following brief coping skills training. Distraction and positive self-talk are just two examples from the repertoire of coping skills. Distraction techniques involve deliberately shifting attention away from pain to non-painful stimuli in the immediate environment or to some stimuli of interest (e.g. watching television). Redirecting attention may be more effective in relation to acute pain as it appears to reduce the perception of pain at least only for as long as the person remains distracted. Positive self-talk teaches the individual to use positive self-statements when thinking about their pain (e.g. I cope well with my pain). The beneficial effect of positive self-talk may relate to resultant boosts in self-esteem and self-efficacy.

While coping strategies can be helpful, there is growing evidence that pain control efforts directed at uncontrollable pain can come to dominate an individual's life and distance them from important and valued aspects of their lives like family, friends and work. McCracken et al. (2004) describe acceptance as an acknowledgement of reality (i.e. pain is present, persistent and not easily controlled) and a willingness to persist in valued activities in spite of pain-related sensations, thoughts and related feelings. They found pain acceptance was associated with better work status, lower reports of pain and lower pain-related anxiety, avoidance behaviour, depression and disability, independent of pain intensity. Treatment approaches that incorporate acceptance have shown positive results (e.g. mindfulness meditation). However, further studies are needed to confirm these results and to identify when and for whom they are most likely to be of benefit.

Imagery involves forming and maintaining a pleasant, calming or coping image in the mind. In guided imagery attention is guided away from an undesirable sensation or mood (e.g. pain) by another person who verbally describes the image while the patient relaxes. Most imagery involves relaxation and employs images of a peaceful, safe, pain-free place, which the individual focuses upon while relaxing. The person may also be guided to visualize energy flowing into their body and pain flowing out. The benefits derived from this type of imagery are probably due to relaxation and distraction effects. Alternatively, confrontational imagery may be employed, for example visualizing white blood cells as an army attacking the source of pain (e.g. a tumour). Imagery has been found to be effective for the treatment of pain. The benefits of imagery may relate to relaxation, distraction effects and an active stance increasing feelings of self-efficacy. As imagery generally involves elements of relaxation it is unclear what unique and independent effects it has.

Meditation also frequently forms part of relaxation training and involves the individual focusing their attention on a simple stimulus, like a monosyllable word repeated slowly and continuously (aloud or in their head), to the exclusion of all other stimuli. Mindfulness-meditation involves focusing attention on the moment-to-moment reality, including the self in each moment, in a non-reactive, non-judgemental way, attending to and accepting all aspects of the current experience. Early work on mindfulness-meditation looked at chronic pain and found positive benefits including lower back pain reports and less medication usage. However, more recent work has not looked at pain, so further studies are needed. Prayer is another common coping strategy patients have reported to be helpful in response to pain, including headaches, neck-pain and back pain (McCaffery et al., 2004). Both meditation and prayer inherently involve some distraction and possibly aspects of relaxation, although this is far from consistent.

Information provision has been shown to reduce pain reports and intensity, possibly by alleviating the fear and anxiety of not knowing what to expect for acute and postoperative pain (Williams et al., 2004). The widespread interest in self-help literature, Internet information and support groups may be indicative of the desire of people in pain to understand their experience, what to expect and potential treatment options.

Cognitive-behavioural therapy

Cognitive-behavioural therapy (CBT) utilizes the full range of cognitive and behavioural techniques already described in individualized programmes that emphasize relapse prevention strategies. Stress management training is often included due to the significant levels of stress implicated in the generation and exacerbation of pain. The literature on CBT and pain suggests it shows considerable promise as an effective treatment for pain in adults (Eccleston et al., 2002). It forms the major component of most current pain management programmes. Improved mood, affect, function and coping have been associated with CBT in up to 85% of pain patients. While there is some support for the efficacy of CBT for the control of headache pain in children, there is a paucity of research relating to other pain conditions in children, as well as CBT for pain in the elderly and people with intellectual or communication difficulties, probably as it may be assumed not to be an appropriate treatment option for these groups.

KT

Pharmacological strategies

Various analgesics and anaesthetics are prescribed for the treatment of pain. Anaesthetics (local or central) are used to numb the sensation of pain. The identification of endogenous opioid mechanisms have confirmed the status of opioid analgesics as an effective pain treatment. However, the associated perceived high risk of addiction has resulted in their use being restricted to severe pain cases like cancer, a perception challenged by the findings from studies of patient-controlled analgesia and low dose opioid treatment that suggest the risk of addiction may not be very high (e.g. Urban et al., 1986). Non-opioid analgesics, NSAIDs (non-steroidal anti-inflamatory drugs) and drugs that control pain indirectly (e.g. antidepressants, sedatives) are commonly used. Drugs with indirect effects may be beneficial due to their action on higher brain regions, modulating the downward transmission of pain, or due to their modulating effects on negative mood states.

Another aspect relating to drugs is the placebo effect. It has been shown that substantial pain relief occurs in about 50% of patients when they are treated with an inert compound rather than the drug they are expecting, often equalling the relief felt by those receiving the actual medication (Melzack and Wall, 1982). The effect is strongest with high doses, when it is injected and depends upon the individual believing they are receiving a pain-relieving substance. The effect rapidly declines with repeated use.

In addition to prescribed drug treatments many individuals self-medicate with recreational drugs like alcohol and cannabis to alleviate their pain. However, there is considerable anecdotal evidence for cannabis as an effective pain control treatment, and an endogenous cannabinoid pain control system has now been identified. This system functions as a parallel but distinct mechanism from the opioid system in modulating pain (Iverson and Chapman, 2002). Cannabinoids have now been authorized for the treatment of pain and other conditions in a number of countries, including the Netherlands and the UK. While current research may result in new cannabinoid-based NSAID-like treatments in the future, problems with the restricted range of dosages that allow pain control before producing psychotropic effects and concerns about the incidental condoning of recreational cannabis use mean this is far from being certain. The informal use of cannabis for pain control and its interaction with other pain control strategies warrants further investigation.

Physical strategies

Surgical control of pain mainly involved cutting the pain fibres to stop pain signal transmission. However, it provided only short-term results and the risks associated with surgery mean it is no longer viewed as a viable treatment option (Melzack and Wall, 1982).

Physiotherapy may be used to increase mobility and correct maladjusted posture, encourage exercise and movement (often despite pain), and education. In addition individuals may be taught safe ways to function (e.g. stand up, sit down, lift objects). Physiotherapy is about maintaining mobility, increasing function and helping the individual manage their lives (e.g. Eccleston and Eccleston, 2004).

Many physical strategies involve some form of sensory control employing variations of counter-stimulation. Counter-stimulation is a frequently used natural response to pain (e.g. squeezing hard on an area of pain), that provides temporary pain relief. Sensory techniques work on the same basis, like the stimulation of nerves under the skin in TENS treatment (e.g. Chesterton et al., 2003). Such techniques appear more beneficial for acute pain but show less consistent results for chronic pain (e.g. Köke et al., 2004).

A recent additional strategy is the promotion of mobility enhancing exercise to help retain and improve physical function and prevent lack of mobility from exacerbating pain problems. General practitioners can now refer pain patients to specialist rehabilitation classes at local fitness centres, which has shown some success for older people with musculo-skeletal disorders (Avlund et al., 2000).

Other strategies and approaches

There are many other strategies and alternative therapies that individuals use in their efforts to deal with their pain. Acupuncture has been around for centuries and while the mechanisms by which it produces beneficial effects are not well understood it does appear to exert substantial analgesic effects (World Health Organization, 2003). This may derive from the incidental involvement of counter-stimulation, placebo effects, distraction and relaxation, as well as the release of natural pain relieving endorphins.

There is substantial, reliable evidence that hypnosis has beneficial effects for the treatment of acute (e.g. childbirth) and chronic pain (e.g. cancer-related) conditions. Hypnosis involves relaxation, assurances of pain reduction, distraction, and cognitive restructuring (via guided imagery), and may include an altered state of consciousness (Marks et al., 1988).

Individuals frequently use complementary or alternative therapies (e.g. aromatherapy, Chinese medicine) to combat pain and there is growing support for the belief that they help chronic pain control (e.g. National Institutes of Health, 1997). Again the mechanisms are not well understood and may derive from placebo effects, relaxation, distraction or improved self-efficacy from active coping. Further research concerning the efficacy of different therapies and their interactions with more traditional approaches is needed. Similarly self-help information, support groups and Internet use for information and advice may be of value in pain management, but need further investigation.

The widespread use of alternative strategies may reflect dissatisfaction with mainstream approaches. It is important that such strategies are evaluated independently and in conjunction with traditional approaches.

Palliative care

Palliative care refers to the alleviation of symptoms of illness when there is no cure available, particularly concerning terminal illness. Its aims are to reduce suffering, fear and distress, normalize the dying process, maintain active participation in life, increase quality of life and maintain dignity until death for the patient. Pain constitutes a major part of the experience of 50–90% of terminally ill patients. It may result from the disease, treatment side effects (e.g. radiotherapy), concurrent illness, nervous system hyperactivity or lack of mobility. A quarter of terminally ill patients are thought to die with insufficient pain relief, possibly due to assessment difficulties or patients' fears (around addiction, disease progression, distracting medical staff from treatment focus, or looking weak) preventing medication seeking or taking. Terminally ill patients are often asked to take part in drug trials, even without any expectation of the drugs helping them. Despite this, effective pain management underpins palliative care, including medication, CBT and alternative therapies.

Multidisciplinary pain management centres/programmes

Originally run as inpatient programmes, today pain management programmes tend to be run on an outpatient basis in specialist pain management centres.

Multidisciplinary teams may include doctors, nurses, physiotherapists, psychologists, psychiatrists, occupational therapists and counsellors, and provide a range of management techniques underpinned by CBT. Individual programmes are developed that aim to improve the individual's quality of life by reducing pain (as far as possible), increasing activity and coping, restoring function, promoting self-efficacy and self-management. The patient receives a full assessment, education, skills training, exercise schedules, relapse prevention and family work. Multidisciplinary rehabilitation programmes represent the most comprehensive approach to date, by targeting the individual's specific pain experience and tailoring appropriate treatment combinations.

Treatment issues

Pain management can be a particularly controversial issue. Evidence suggests that in many circumstances pain is under-treated. Some of the reasons for this include inadequate assessment, focus on underlying pathologies, negative stereotypes and erroneous assumptions about certain population groups, addiction fears, the inappropriateness of non-pharmacological treatments and patients' inability to verbalize pain information or requests for medication (e.g. Greenwald et al., 1999). Many medical professionals have their own benchmarks concerning acceptable pain behaviour and medication levels for different conditions. It has also been shown that many prejudices and misconceptions operate in the treatment of pain patients, with various populations (e.g. children, people with communication difficulties and the elderly) being under-treated for pain (Todd et al., 2000). For example, sickle-cell patients are often assumed to be drug addicts and their pain outcries to be drug-seeking behaviour, resulting in inadequate medication being administered. Similarly, pain has only recently been recognized as part of the symptom repertoire of HIV/AIDs and therefore up to 85% of people with HIV/AIDs receive inadequate pain management (Marcus et al., 2000).

Pain is sometimes deemed to be psychogenic, resulting from emotional, motivational or personality problems. However, the distinction between organic and psychogenic pain may have little practical value. A number of diseases where historically pain was not thought to be a valid symptom have subsequently had a physiological basis for pain identified including multiple sclerosis and HIV/AIDs (e.g. Marcus et al., 2000), so some pain designated psychogenic may relate to as yet undetected or unidentified organic pathology. In addition, long-term chronic pain is associated with decreased natural endorphin production, meaning that over time, the same level of pain stimuli is likely to result in higher perceived pain intensity. While psychogenic pain may represent a convenient label for cases where underlying pathology has not been found, it has a tendency to inherently ascribe the problem to the patient and thus promote prejudice and injustice. Health psychologists must endeavour to promote the sensitive and respectful treatment of individuals reporting pain, both within the discipline and externally, in terms of research, intervention development, and treatment.

Future Research

1 Further work to verify and map the neuromatrix proposed by Melzack is required, along with the development of treatment approaches based on this mapping.
2 Long-term, prospective studies are required to further elucidate the relationships between various psychosocial factors and pain, particularly the relative weights of their influence and the identification of relatively homogeneous sub-groups within the chronic pain patient population.
3 Additional research regarding the pain experience of under-represented groups (e.g. babies, the elderly, people with disabilities) is needed, including development of improved measurement instruments and assessing the efficacy of CBT in these groups. The use of qualitative methods might provide valuable new insights in this area.
4 The influence of various social factors (e.g. SES, poverty, discrimination) on the treatment of pain should be a significant research focus, particularly for groups who disproportionately experience inadequate pain treatment (e.g. elderly, children, minority groups).
5 Further research is needed to unpack the relationship between gender and the pain experience, particularly to look at the similarities between the sexes in the experience of common types of pain.
6 The impact of context and assessor characteristics on the assessment process needs further investigation, including assessment for claim purposes.
7 The continued investigation of the use of cannabinoids and other herbal treatments in pain control is required, including the extent and efficacy of its informal use and interactions with other pain control strategies.
8 Alternative therapies and treatment strategies need further evaluation, independently and in conjunction with traditional approaches.

Summary

1 Early pain theories proposed that pain was a sensation that involved a direct line of transmission from the pain stimulus to the brain. However, the growing body of evidence for the psychological mediation of pain saw the development of the multidimensional gate control theory, which acknowledged psychosocial influences.
2 Many psychological variables that influence the pain experience have been examined including cognitions, self-efficacy, perceived control, prior experience, conditioning, secondary gains, personality, mood and stress.
3 Similarly socio-cultural factors such as culture, gender, age, the role of significant others and the family have been implicated.
4 Particular groups appear to be under-represented in the pain literature including ethnic minorities, children, the elderly, some disabled people and people with certain medical conditions (e.g. HIV, CFS).
5 Assessment of pain is difficult and various techniques are used singly or in combination (e.g. medical examinations, observations, questionnaires, diaries and logs, and interviews).
6 A wide variety of pain management strategies exist. Currently, the most successful approach appears to be programmes that combine cognitive behaviour therapies and traditional medical therapies.

7 The assessment and treatment of pain, particularly chronic pain, can be influenced by misconceptions about specific patient groups including ethnic minorities, children, the elderly, some disabled people, and people with certain medical conditions (e.g. sickle-cell disease sufferers assumed to be drug users).

8 The body of research suggests that pain is a complex and multidimensional phenomenon that includes biological, psychological and behavioural components. Health psychologists can make a significant contribution in promoting sensitive and respectful research and treatment for people experiencing long-standing painful conditions.

 Key Terms

acute	cognitions
assessment	gate control theory (GCT)
catastrophizing	perceived control
chronic	

17

Cancer and Chronic Diseases

Chronic diseases – such as heart disease, cancer, and diabetes – are the leading causes of death and disability … Adopting healthy behaviors such as eating nutritious foods, being physically active, and avoiding tobacco use can prevent or control the devastating effects of these diseases. (US Centers for Disease Control and Prevention, 2005)

Outline

In this chapter we consider three life-threatening and disabling diseases: cancer, coronary heart disease and HIV/AIDS. In each case we consider five issues: 'What is …?'; 'Interventions for …'; 'Living with …'; 'Adaptation to …'; and 'Caring for someone with …'. The contribution of psychosocial interventions for patients suffering from these conditions has been evaluated in systematic reviews. The evidence suggests that psychosocial interventions have not yet demonstrated their full potential. The quality of evaluation research with psychosocial interventions has generally been rather poor and the findings inconclusive. We suggest further research to consolidate psychological knowledge and understanding of treatment and health care for these conditions.

General Issues

Chronic illness and cancer have replaced acute illness as the predominant disease pattern in developed countries over the past 50 years. Greatly improved longevity has meant an increased **burden of disease** caused by cancer and chronic conditions such as heart disease, stroke, AIDS, back pain, diabetes and dementia. As life expectancy of the human population increases, so does the prevalence of diseases of older age. A large proportion of the global burden of disease is caused by a **toxic environment** that encourages health-aversive behaviours and choices. As we saw in Chapter 1, the major risks of underweight (developing countries), overweight and obesity (developed countries), unsafe sex, high blood pressure, alcohol and tobacco (everywhere) account for 30% of the global disease burden. All are consequences of the toxic environment, which is creating a significant proportion of ill-health and suffering in the world.

Over 60% of people in developed countries live to at least 70 years of age, compared with only about 30% in developing countries. Of the 45 million deaths among adults worldwide in 2002, 32 million were caused by non-communicable diseases. HIV/AIDS has become the leading cause of mortality among adults aged 15–59 years. Unipolar depressive disorders are the leading cause of disability for females.

Chronic illnesses most often strike in middle and older age and, while they can be fatal, most people with a chronic illness live for many years with the condition. As a consequence cardiovascular and coronary heart disease and HIV/AIDS are significant causes of disability (see Chapter 1 for figures).

The evidence suggests that personality is a poor predictor of the development of disease (Chapter 12). Health-aversive behaviours, and genetic factors, are the primary determinants of many chronic illnesses. The focus of this chapter will be on the psychological aspects of disease management. Management of fatal or chronic diseases is a principal feature in the lives of 10–15% of the population. This informal care occurs almost invisibly with little recognition or financial support from society at large.

People with different serious chronic illnesses have similar concerns and needs (World Health Organization, 2004). Chronic illness typically involves restrictions on activities of daily living, increases in pain, fatigue, depression and anxiety. Patients must cope with ongoing symptoms, their ambiguity, the life threat involved, and the requirements of treatment. Maintaining effective relationships with health-service personnel and family and friends requires many adaptations (Stanton and Revenson, 2005) and adjustments in lifestyle. Uncertainties over prognosis can cause a great deal of worry and fear. In cancer prognosis can often be predicted, as there is a short period of evident decline, but in CHD people tend to live with greater disability for longer time, but die suddenly with little warning after a rapid deterioration (World Health Organization, 2004). In all life-threatening conditions, family members can experience emotional, economic and social challenges.

Sontag (1978) pointed out that illnesses are often constructed metaphorically, a tendency that needs to be guarded against for the unwanted surplus meanings such metaphors often carry. Sontag stated: 'The most truthful way of regarding illness – and the healthiest way of being ill – is one most purified of, most resistant to, metaphoric thinking' (p. 25). For example, cancer is viewed as a disease of repression, of inhibited passion. The sufferer is a suppressor of emotion, which after many years emerges from the unconscious self as malignant growth. In Chapter 12 we concluded that empirical support for the psychosomatic position does not exist. Sontag believed that when the aetiology and treatment of a disease is more fully understood, the metaphorical connotations will fade. However, metaphorical thinking can be useful in coping but it carries the danger that victims and families may blame themselves which may engender hopelessness, and increase feelings of stigmatization.

Petrie and Revenson (2005) identified three developments in psychological interventions for chronic illness:

1   Psychological interventions are becoming more theory-based and sophisticated in the behavioural targets they are seeking to alter. Successful interventions are typically based on a model of behaviour change and analyse the key issues that the intervention is aimed to resolve.
2   An increased awareness of sub-populations for whom the intervention may be more efficacious.
3   An increasingly sharp focus on possible biobehavioral and psychosocial mechanisms.

Table 17.1   *Comparison of three life-threatening conditions*

Feature	Cancer	CHD	HIV/AIDS
Preventable	Yes, in part	Yes, in part	Yes, totally
Behavioural risk factors	Yes, smoking, diet, drinking	Yes, diet, smoking, drinking	Yes, unsafe sex (often after drinking)
Stigma	Strong	Some	Severe
Onset	Mixed	Slow	Slow
Treatable	Mixed	Yes	Yes, with HAART, but expensive and so not universally available
Prognosis	Mixed	Good	Good, with HAART, not otherwise

In the next three sections we review psychosocial aspects and interventions for people diagnosed with cancer, CHD and HIV/AIDS respectively. Table 17.1 compares and contrasts these three conditions in terms of key features of such life-threatening conditions.

Cancer

The study of the psychological aspects of cancer care and treatment is referred to as '**psycho-oncology**'. Psycho-oncology is concerned with (1) the psychological responses of patients, families and caregivers to cancer at all stages of the disease, and (2) the psychosocial factors that may influence the disease process. Unfortunately many cancer patients remain untreated owing to **stigmatization** and lack of resources to diagnose, treat and support. Cancer causes anxiety and depression in more than one-third of patients and often affects the sufferer's family emotionally, socially and economically. Inequalities in cancer treatment and care occur across different regions and social groups.

What is cancer?

'Cancer' is an umbrella term for more than 100 different but related diseases. Cancer occurs when cells become abnormal and keep dividing and forming more cells without any internal control or order. Normally, cells divide to produce more when the body needs them to remain healthy. However if cells keep dividing when new cells are not needed, a mass of extra tissue known as a **tumour** or neoplasm forms, which can be benign or malignant. Benign tumors are not cancerous and, usually, can be removed and when removed, in most cases, do not re-form. Cells from benign tumours also do not spread to other parts of the body and so benign tumors are rarely life-threatening. In the case of malignant tumours, cancer cells can invade and damage nearby tissues and organs. They can also break away from a malignant tumor and enter the bloodstream or the lymphatic system forming new tumors or **metastasis** in other parts of the body.

Traditionally the diagnosis and prognosis of cancer was withheld from patients, due to stigma and fear. The custom of 'never telling' precluded talking with patients about their feelings and how they were coping with illness and the threat of death (Holland, 2004). Over the last 30 years, patients' improved rights to information and the reduced stigma of cancer have enabled a more open dialogue between patients and doctors. In the majority of countries today, patients learn their diagnosis and treatment options. Not all cultures yet fully use the patient empowerment model, however. For example, in Greece it is still usual practice to not inform the patients of their diagnosis as doctors prefer to inform the next of kin (Mystakidou et al., 2004).

Holland (2004) points out that a second stigma, the fear of mental disorders, also persists and acts as a barrier to the integration of the psychosocial expertise fully into cancer care, the identification of patients who are distressed, and patients' acceptance of psychological help. Chapple et al. (2004) studied the stigma, shame and blame experienced by 45 patients with lung cancer using narrative interviews. The participants experienced stigma because the disease is strongly associated with smoking. This experience occurred whether or not they actually were smokers. Interactions with family, friends and doctors were affected and many felt unjustly blamed for their illness. Some patients concealed their illness, which sometimes had adverse financial consequences or made it hard for them to gain support from other people. Some indicated that newspaper and television reports may have added to the stigma: television advertisements aim to put young people off tobacco, but they usually portray a dreadful death, which may exacerbate fear and anxiety.

Interventions for cancer

The purpose of treatment can be to cure the cancer, control it, or treat its symptoms. The type of treatment depends on the type of cancer, the stage of the cancer, and individual factors such as age, health status and the personal preferences of the patient and his/her family. The patient needs to be empowered to discuss with the professional care team which treatment choices are most suitable. The four major treatments for cancer are surgery, radiation, chemotherapy and biological therapies such as hormone therapies (e.g. tamoxifen) and transplant options (e.g. with stem cell therapy or bone marrow).

Psychosocial interventions for cancer include:

- counselling;
- psychotherapy;
- behaviour therapy (e.g. systematic desensitization);
- cognitive behavioural therapy;
- pain control techniques (see Chapter 16);
- biofeedback;
- relaxation;
- hypnosis;
- guided imagery;
- music therapy;
- art therapy;
- group support;
- complementary therapies;
- yoga and meditation.

Objective evidence of efficacy has not generally been very strong. Reviews in the 1990s focusing on the four main psychosocial interventions – behavioural therapy (including relaxation, biofeedback and hypnosis); educational therapy (including training in coping skills and providing information to enhance a patient's sense of control); psychotherapy (including counselling); and support groups (which help patients to express their emotions) indicated some limited evidence of efficacy. One encouraging line was a reduction in the side effects of chemotherapy after biofeedback and relaxation therapy and a reduction in pain, less mood disturbance, and fewer maladaptive coping responses after supportive group therapy. Some researchers even claimed that their interventions extended their patients' survival.

Meyer and Mark (1995) carried out a meta-analysis of 62 studies that had compared treatment and control groups for different kinds of psychosocial, behavioural and psycho-educational interventions. They found significant beneficial effect sizes ranging from 0.19 to 0.28.

Ten years after this review, the position is by no means clear as there have been conflicting results from systematic reviews and the picture does not look as encouraging as it did back then. The results from the most recent systematic reviews often do not match the enthusiasm and good intentions of therapists and psycho-oncologists. Unfortunately the quality of evaluation research has been rather poor with small samples, poor designs and weak effects. This situation must be corrected.

Edwards et al. (2004) reported a systematic review of psychological interventions for women with metastatic breast cancer. This study assessed the effects of psychological interventions (educational, individual cognitive behavioural or psychotherapeutic, or group support) on psychological and survival outcomes for women with metastatic breast cancer. Five studies showed very limited evidence of short-term benefit arising from these interventions which was not sustained at long-term follow-up. The effects of the interventions on survival were not statistically significant.

Chow et al. (2004) carried out a meta-analysis to investigate whether psychosocial intervention improves survival in cancer. Eight randomized trials with 1,062 patients published between 1966 and June 2002 were identified. One- and four-year survival rates were evaluated but these showed no statistically significant difference in the overall survival rates, suggesting again that psychosocial intervention does not lengthen survival.

Fellowes et al. (2004) carried out a systematic review of aromatherapy and massage with patients with cancer. The reviewers investigated whether these therapies decrease anxiety and depression, lessen symptom distress and/or improve patients' quality of life. Four trials (207 patients) measuring anxiety detected a reduction in anxiety of 19–32%. The evidence for any impact on depression was variable with only one trial finding any significant difference in this symptom. However, three studies (117 patients) found a reduction in pain following intervention, and two (71 patients) found a reduction in nausea.

It is clear from the above review that the quality of research in this field is poor. Unless this situation is corrected, it is unlikely that psycho-oncology will reach its full potential in cancer care. Larger-scale evaluations with longer-term follow-up are needed.

Living with cancer

In spite of the negative results concerning long-term benefits, there are several aspects of cancer experience that psychological expertise can help to understand, e.g. pain, fatigue, depression and anxiety. Incidence estimates for pain range from 14% to 100%, for depression, from 1% to 42%, and for fatigue, from 4% to 91%. The lack of consistency across studies suggests that measurement, conceptual and methodological issues remain unsolved.

Most clinical assessments of pain, depression and fatigue rely on self-report. A variety of assessment tools is available. The Hospital Anxiety and Depression Scale (HADS) and the EORTC OLQ-C30 have both shown promise for screening treatable unmet needs in patients attending routinely for radiotherapy. However, few instruments exist for children and adolescents, older adults, individuals with cognitive impairments, and individuals from different ethnic and cultural groups. There is also relatively little research on the role played by informal carers in the management of symptoms. The most commonly described strategy for improving symptom management involves regular assessment using visual analogue or numerical scales, followed by quality of life (QoL) improvement interventions. Studies on efficacy of interventions on QoL have found positive results.

Rehse and Pukrop (2003) meta-analysed controlled studies of psychosocial interventions on QoL. The overall effect size was 0.31. The most important moderating variable was duration of psychosocial intervention with treatments lasting more than 12 weeks being more effective than shorter interventions. Uitterhoeve et al. (2004) also reviewed psychosocial interventions for improving QoL of advanced cancer patients. Twelve trials evaluating behaviour therapy found positive effects on one or more indicators of QoL, for example, depression. These two systematic reviews are consistent in showing significant benefits from behavioural and psychosocial interventions for cancer patients' QoL.

Eysenbach (2003) explored the impact of the Internet on cancer outcomes. Eysenbach distinguished four areas of Internet use: communication (electronic mail), community (virtual support groups), content (health information on the World Wide Web), and e-commerce. He claimed that over 12.5 million health-related computer searches were being conducted each day on the World Wide Web. Eysenbach estimated that, in the developed world, 39% of cancer patients were using the Internet, and approximately 2.3 million persons living with cancer worldwide were online. For more discussion of the Internet and health communication, see Kreps (2003).

Adaptation to cancer

A variety of factors have been associated with adaptation to cancer patients, partners and families, and the interactions between the patients and their families. A large amount of research has studied coping styles such as fighting spirit, helplessness/hopelessness, denial and avoidance. This topic has led to mixed and inconsistent findings. Watson et al. (1999) studied the influence of psychological responses on survival in women with early-stage breast cancer. Psychological response was measured by the mental adjustment to cancer (MAC) scale, the Courtauld emotional control (CEC) scale, and the HAD scale 4–12 weeks and 12 months after diagnosis. The women were followed up for at least 5 years. There was a significantly increased risk of death from all causes by 5 years in women with high scores on depression, helplessness and hopelessness. No significant results were found for 'fighting spirit'.

Petticrew et al. (2002) reviewed evidence on psychological coping in relation to survival and recurrence in people with cancer. However, the results from Watson et al.

(1999) were excluded. The majority of studies that had investigated fighting spirit (10 studies) or helplessness/hopelessness (12 studies) found no significant associations with survival or recurrence. Positive findings were confined to small studies, indicating a potential publication bias. Little consistent evidence was available that coping styles play a part in survival or recurrence. Watson et al. (2003) contested the fairness of this review.

Laubmeier et al. (2004) studied the role of 'spirituality' which may well be related to emotional well-being and QoL. Spirituality, particularly the existential component, was associated with less distress and better quality of life, regardless of life threat.

Cunningham and Watson (2004) carried out an interview study on how psychological therapy may prolong survival in metastatic cancer patients. They interviewed 10 medically incurable cancer patients who had outlived their prognoses from 2.2 to 12.5 years. Common themes were:

- 'authenticity', a clear understanding of what was important in one's life;
- 'autonomy', the perceived freedom to shape life around what was valued;
- 'acceptance', a perceived change towards enhanced self-esteem, greater tolerance for and emotional closeness to others, and a more peaceful and joyous affective experience.

Cunningham and Watson (2004) stated 'survivors' displayed a higher degree of early involvement in their psychological self-help than did their non-surviving peers, suggesting that healing may be assisted by a 'greater authenticity of thought and action'.

Vance and Eiser (2004) systematically reviewed studies of the effects of parents' behaviour on children's cancer coping. Parents who criticized, or apologized, had more distressed children. Parents who were permissive had more problems with adherence. Longitudinal studies to determine how parenting behaviours affect longer-term child adjustment are recommended.

Labay and Walco (2004) studied empathy in the psychological adjustment in siblings. Participants were 29 siblings and 14 children with acute lymphoblastic leukaemia, myelocytic leukaemia, or non-Hodgkin's lymphoma. Siblings did not exhibit increased rates of behaviour problems, but displayed more social and academic difficulties. However empathy was found to be a significant predictor of externalizing and total problems. Cancer knowledge was not related to adjustment, but was associated with empathy. Empathy may play an important role in sibling adjustment following diagnosis.

Manne et al. (2004) studied couples' support-related communication, psychological distress, and relationship satisfaction among women with early stage breast cancer. For the study, 148 completed a videotaped discussion of a cancer-related issue and a general issue and measures of psychological distress and relationship satisfaction. During cancer-issue discussions, patients reported less distress when partners responded to disclosures with reciprocal self-disclosure and humour and when partners were less likely to propose solutions. Results suggest partner responses play a role in women's adaptation to breast cancer

Caring for someone with cancer

The stress experienced by the family members can often be high. The condition can create emotional turmoil with fear, anxiety, stigma, depression, hopelessness, fatigue, pain and insomnia all entering the relationship at various stages. The social support provided by the immediate family and friends can be a key factor in promoting the patient's adaptation and QoL. The so-called 'carer burden' can be high, and interventions are available to support the informal carer.

The problems are likely to become particularly challenging if the patient moves into palliative care. It is understandable that most patients want to be at home during their final illness. Informal carers are vital to the support of patients at home but often have unmet needs. Anxiety, depression and feelings of isolation are common, particularly after the patient's death. Ramirez et al. (1998) report that approximately one-third of cancer patients in the UK receive care from one close relative only, while about half are cared for by two or three relatives, typically a spouse and an adult child. Approximately two-thirds of cancer patients and a third of non-cancer patients typically receive some kind of formal home nursing.

Harding and Higginson (2003) reviewed interventions to support carers in cancer and palliative care. Poor designs and methodology, a lack of outcome evaluation, small sample sizes and a reliance on intervention descriptions and formative evaluations characterized the literature. They suggested that alternatives to 'pure' RCTs would need to be considered in carrying out evaluation research in this domain. As was the case in reviewing interventions for obesity, smoking and drinking (Chapters 6–8) it is apparent that larger-scale studies of higher quality are needed.

Coronary Heart Disease

What is coronary heart disease?

Coronary heart disease (CHD) or coronary artery disease (CAD) occurs when the walls of the coronary arteries become narrowed by a gradual build-up of fatty material called atheroma. The two main forms of CHD are myocardial infarction (heart attack) and angina.

KT

Myocardial infarction (MI) occurs when one of the coronary arteries becomes blocked by a blood clot and part of the heart is starved of oxygen. It usually causes severe chest pain. A person having a heart attack may also experience sweating, light-headedness, nausea or shortness of breath. A heart attack may be the first sign of CHD in many people.

KT

Angina is the most common form of CHD. It is characterized by a heavy or tight pain in the centre of the chest that may spread to the arms, necks, jaw, face, back or stomach. Angina symptoms occur when the arteries become so narrow from the atheroma that insufficient oxygen-containing blood can be supplied to the heart muscle when its demands are high, such as during exercise.

There are two categories of angina, stable or unstable angina. Stable angina is characterized by chest pain relieved by rest, resulting from the partial obstruction of a coronary artery by atheroma. Unstable angina occurs with lesser degrees of exertion or while at rest. This type increases in frequency and duration and worsens in severity. Unstable angina is an acute coronary syndrome (ACS) that requires immediate medical attention. This is usually caused by the formation of a blood clot at the site of a ruptured plaque in a coronary artery. If left untreated, it can result in heart attack and irreversible damage to the heart.

Interventions for CHD

People with suspected CHD usually undergo several different tests for absolute diagnosis and to determine the best treatment to relieve symptoms. These include stress **exercise tolerance test (ETT)**, **electrocardiogram (ECG)** and **coronary angiogram**. Seeking a diagnosis can be a stressful time for people with suspected CHD and their family and friends. Patients commonly feel apprehension about the procedure and find some parts of the procedure unexpected with doctors' technical language being an obstacle to understanding. `KT`

Many people with CHD have to make lifestyle changes and take a regime of medication such as **ACE inhibitors, statins, anticoagulant drugs** and **betablockers**. Clinical guidelines are not always implemented because lack of time among physicians who spend an average of about 15 minutes discussing risk factor, lifestyle changes or treatment. This may not be an appropriate time to discuss such issues with a patient who may well feel shocked by the diagnosis of being at risk of CHD and show low levels of compliance with physician advice. `KT`

Riesen et al. (2004) acknowledged that, although high rates of compliance with lifestyle changes and lipid lowering agents are reported in clinical trials, rarely are the findings reproduced in regular practice. They recommended the use of educational materials as well as regular telephone contact to improve compliance. However, further research is needed into the causes of poor compliance and methods of improving adherence with lipid-lowering agents.

People living with angina have increased risk of anxiety and depression. Lewin et al. (2002) evaluated the efficacy of a CBT disease management programme, the **Angina Plan** (Box 17.1), to aid the psychological adjustment of patients with newly diagnosed angina. At six-month follow-up, Angina Plan patients showed a significantly greater reduction in anxiety, depression, frequency of angina, use of *glyceryl trinitrate* and physical limitations. They were also more likely to report a change in diet and increased their daily walking. `KT`

BOX 17.1

THE ANGINA PLAN – A PSYCHOLOGICAL DISEASE MANAGEMENT PROGRAMME FOR PEOPLE WITH ANGINA (LEWIN ET AL., 2002)

The Angina Plan consists of a patient-held booklet and audio-taped relaxation programme. Before commencing the 30–40 minute Angina Plan session, the patient is sent a questionnaire designed to establish if s/he holds any of the common misconceptions about angina (for example, each episode is a mini heart attack or angina is caused because your heart is worn out). The patient's partner or a friend is invited to the session.

(Continued)

BOX 17.1   (Continued)

After blood pressure has been taken and body mass index has been recorded, the Angina Plan facilitator discusses any misconception that were revealed in the questionnaire with the patient and, if possible, his or her partner in an effort to correct their understanding. Personal risk factors are then identified. Personal goals to reduce the risk factors are then set. They are provided with a relaxation tape and encouraged to use it. The Plan also contains written information such as the role of frightening thoughts and misconceptions in triggering adrenaline release and anxiety and how this can result in poor coping strategies.

The patient is contacted by the facilitator at the end of weeks 1, 4, 8 and 12. During these phone calls, the patient is praised for any success. They are also asked if they want to extend successful goals. Unsuccessful goals can be revisited. Adding procedures that encourage specific implementation intentions (see Chapter 8) to this programme could well improve the success of the Angina Plan.

Other forms of invasive treatment may be necessary when medication alone does not relieve angina. Referral to a cardiologist or a heart surgeon may be required for further treatment to gain effective control of angina symptoms and for some people to prolong life. Invasive **revascularization** treatment may include either a **percutaneous coronary intervention (PCI)** or **coronary artery bypass graft (CABG)** surgery.

Living with CHD

Waiting for invasive treatment to improve or prolong life can be very stressful and have deleterious effects on the quality of daily life. Pre-surgical depression predicts cardiac hospitalization, continued surgical pain, failure to return to previous activity and depression at 6 months (Burg et al., 2003). Jónsdóttir and Baldursdóttir (1998) surveyed people on a waiting list for CABG in Iceland. They found that waiting for surgery had negative effects on the work and daily life of the majority of respondents. Prominent symptoms reported included fatigue, shortness of breath, chest pain, anxiety and depression. Eighty-seven percent reported experiencing stress. The majority reported negative influences of their illness on their spouses and family, with 80% reporting emotional effects. They concluded that pre-operative psychological assessment that focuses on level of stress and anxiety as well as coping skills and social support are needed. Fitzsimons et al. (2000) conducted a qualitative analysis into the experience of waiting for a CABG in Northern Ireland. They identified three central themes in this experience – uncertainty, chest pain and anxiety – with six secondary themes: powerless, dissatisfaction with treatment, anger/frustration, physical incapacity, reduced self-esteem and altered family and social relationships, again pointed to a need for psychological intervention during this period.

Arthur et al. (2000) conducted a randomized controlled trial (RCT) of a multi-dimensional pre-operative intervention on pre-surgery and post-surgery outcomes in low-risk patients awaiting elective CABG. The intervention consisted of individualized, prescribed exercise training twice per week in a supervised environment, education and reinforcement and monthly nurse-initiated telephone calls to answer questions and provide reassurance. Patients who received the intervention spent one day less in the hospital and less time in the intensive care unit. Patients in the intervention group reported a better quality of life during the waiting period than the control group. The improved quality of life continued up to 6 months after surgery. Using outcome measures such as length of hospital stay as well as quality of life measures provides evidence of cost-effectiveness, helpful information for budget holders wondering whether to invest in such interventions.

Mookadam and Arthur (2004) systematically reviewed social support and its relationship to morbidity and mortality after acute myocardial infarction. The authors were interested in the socio-economic determinants of health, including social change, disorganization and poverty that have been associated with an increased risk of morbidity and mortality. Social support is a possible mediator linking these factors to health and illness. Having low social support networks was a predictor of one-year mortality following acute myocardial infarction. Low social support is equivalent to many 'classic' risk factors, such as elevated cholesterol level, tobacco use and hypertension.

Adaptation to CHD

Cognitive adaptation has been shown to predict psychological adjustment to diseases such as arthritis, cancer, AIDS and heart disease. According to the cognitive adaptation theory, some people who are faced with a chronic illness maintain or develop an optimistic outlook, attempt to regain control or mastery over the event and find ways to restore or enhance their self-esteem (Taylor, 1983). Helgeson and Fritz (1999) tested whether people with high cognitive adaptation scores would be less vulnerable to a new coronary event due to **restenosis** within six months of initial PCI. Three components of cognitive adaptation were measured, self-esteem, optimism and control. Patients with a low cognitive adaptation score were more likely to have a new cardiac event even when demographic variable and medical variables thought to predict restenosis were statistically controlled.

KT

A large number of MI patients do not return to work or regain normal functioning despite being physically well. There is evidence that cardiac rehabilitation programmes can reduce distress and disability, increase confidence and improve modifiable risk factors. However, many patients do not attend rehabilitation programmes after their MI. Patients' beliefs and perception about their illness are key determinants of recovery after a MI. Petrie et al. (2002) evaluated a brief hospital intervention designed to alter patients' perceptions about their MI. The content of the intervention was individualized according to the patients' responses on the Illness Perception Questionnaire (Weinman et al., 1996). The intervention caused significant positive changes in patients' views of their MI. The intervention group reported being better prepared for leaving hospital and subsequently returned to work at a significantly faster rate than the control group. At the three-month follow-up, the intervention group reported a significantly lower rate of angina symptoms.

Cooper et al. (1999) investigated whether the illness beliefs held during their hospital stay by patients who had a MI or who had undergone CABG could predict cardiac rehabilitation attendance. As well as being older, less aware of their cholesterol values and less likely to be employed, non-attenders were less likely to believe their condition was controllable and that their lifestyle may have contributed to their illness. Stewart et al. (2004) found a difference in the health information needs between men and women recovering from an acute coronary event. Men that had received significantly more information reported a greater satisfaction with health-care professionals meeting their information needs. Women reported wanting more information than men concerning angina and hypertension. Men wanted more information about sexual function. Patients who reported receiving more information reported less depressive symptomatology. Most patients of both sexes preferred a shared decision-making role with their doctor. The majority felt their doctor had made the main decisions. Cardiac rehabilitation that is individualized to patients' needs may be more attractive and effective than current practice of thinking of cardiac rehabilitation as a place to do exercise and be informed about lifestyle changes.

Caring for someone with CHD

Concordance occurs between men with CHD and their spouses for body mass index, history of smoking, current smoking status, frequency of exercise, miles per exercise session and the amount of fat and fibre in the diet. Behavioural risk factors are correlated among marital partners. Involving partners in lifestyle interventions may be more efficacious than individual patient education strategies.

Moser and Dracup (2004) compared the emotional responses and perception of control of MI and revascularization patients and their spouses and examined the relationship between spouses' emotional distress and patients' emotional distress and psychosocial adjustment to their cardiac event. They found that spouses had higher levels of anxiety and depression than the patients. There were no differences in level of hostility. The patients also had a higher level of perceived control than did the spouses. Spouse anxiety, depression and perceived control were correlated with patient psychosocial adjustment to illness even when patient anxiety and depression were kept constant. The patients' psychosocial adjustment to illness was worse when spouses were more anxious or depressed than patients. Attention should be given to the psychological needs of spouses of patients who have suffered a cardiac event. Moser and Dracup also found that patients' psychosocial adjustment was best when patients were more anxious or depressed than spouses. This finding suggests that interventions that address the psychological distress of spouses may well improve patient outcomes.

Johnston et al. (1999) evaluated the effectiveness of a cardiac counselling rehabilitation programme for MI patients and their partners. They found that the programme resulted in more knowledge, less anxiety, less depression and greater satisfaction with care for both patients and their partners and less disability in patients. This study was published five years earlier than the Moser and Dracup (2004) study in the same journal, thus highlighting that it can take a long time for research findings to be disseminated, synthesized and put into practice. Conducting research to influence practice is very time consuming and there are usually many barriers to overcome. In order for research to have an impact, health psychologists must have an awareness of promotional techniques, the politics of the context in which they practise and the power of economical factors.

One problem for evaluation of cardiac patients' experience of QoL is identifying an instrument that is not only reliable and valid but also responsive to change. Instruments that are not very responsive will tend to under-represent the benefits of programme attendance. Research indicates that the most responsive instruments are: Beck Depression Inventory, Global Mood Scale, Health Complaints Checklist, Heart Patients' Psychological Questionnaire and Speilberger State Anxiety Inventory.

Rees et al. (2004) reviewed psychological interventions for coronary heart disease, typically, stress management interventions. They included RCTs, either single modality interventions or a part of cardiac rehabilitation with a minimum follow-up of six months. Stress management (SM) trials were identified and reported in combination with other psychological interventions and separately. The quality of many trials was poor, making the findings unreliable. The authors concluded that psychological interventions showed no evidence of effect on total or cardiac mortality, but small reductions in anxiety and depression in patients with CHD. Similar results were seen for SM interventions when considered separately.

Cardiac rehabilitation services are offered to patients but many invited patients fail to attend the sessions. Cooper et al. (2002) reviewed the literature. The results showed that non-attenders are more likely to be older, to have lower income/greater deprivation, to deny the severity of their illness, are less likely to believe they can influence its outcome or to perceive that their physician recommends cardiac rehabilitation. They also found that job status, gender and health concerns play an indirect role in attendance behaviour.

HIV/AIDS

What is HIV/AIDS?

HIV (human immunodeficiency virus) is a retrovirus that infects and colonizes cells in the immune system and the central nervous system (T-helper and monocyte macrophage cells). Initial flu-like symptoms are followed by a quiescent, asymptomatic period (lasting years) during which the immune system battles the virus. Eventually the virus compromises the immune system and the individual becomes symptomatic. Finally the immune system is overwhelmed and the individual becomes vulnerable to opportunistic diseases, signifying development of full-blown **AIDS (acquired immune deficiency syndrome)** and eventually resulting in death.

KT

KT

In 1996, the introduction of highly active antiretroviral therapy (HAART) redefined the illness and improved the outlook for infected individuals. However, antiretrovirals do not eliminate the virus, but only suppress it and, currently, only one in ten who need the treatment actually receive it. HIV persistence eventually causes disease in all infected persons (Sleasman and Goodenow, 2003).

Interventions for HIV/AIDS

The HIV virus has a short half-life allowing rapid replication and mutation, which makes vaccine development problematic and increases the likelihood of drug resistance. Absence of a workable vaccine means antiviral medications are the primary treatment for HIV. Combination therapies (HAART) have been shown to decrease an individual's HIV viral load to undetectable levels, reducing associated morbidity and mortality. However, 95–100% adherence is required to produce and maintain successful virologic suppression, with even 80–90% adherence rates showing no viral suppression in some patients. Non-adherence promotes viral drug resistance and cross-resistance, and drug resistant strains can be transmitted to uninfected patients leaving them without effective treatment options. HIV combination drug therapies involve complex, disrupting and challenging medication regimens involving numerous drugs taken several times a day with specific food instructions. In addition, treatment often commences during the asymptomatic phase, drug toxicity commonly results in severe, unpleasant side effects (e.g. vomiting, lipodystrophy) and treatment must continue for the rest of the person's life. Moreover, the long-term treatment stability and maintenance of viral suppression are not certain.

Adherence rates for HAART tend to be sub-optimal. Fogarty et al.'s (2002) review yielded 200 variables associated with adherence to HIV medication regimens falling into four broad categories: regimen characteristics; psychosocial factors; institutional resources; and personal attributes. Of the psychosocial factors reported, positive disease and treatment attitudes, good mental health and adjustment to HIV were positively associated with adherence while perceived negative social climate was negatively associated. Lack of access to institutional resources (financial, institutional, medical) was negatively associated with adherence. Finally, non-adherence was linked to personal attributes of younger age, minority status and history of substance use. Patients' active involvement in their medical care and treatment decision-making also promotes adherence while low health literacy is associated with poor adherence.

The chronic status of HIV/AIDS and the limited accessibility to HAART for many people living with HIV/AIDS (PLWHA) means that psychosocial support interventions are increasingly important. Programmes of pain management, stress management, coping effectiveness training, sleep disorders and exercise promotion have been found to enhance immune system function, medication adherence and adaptive coping and to decrease anxiety, stress and depression (Chesney et al., 2003). Supportive interventions, especially those that improve function and self-management and maximize independence, represent an essential part of HIV/AIDS treatment.

Living with HIV/AIDS

People living with HIV/AIDS face the general stressors of the chronically ill and may face additional stresses unique to HIV/AIDS, e.g. additional uncertainty and decision-making due to rapidly changing treatment developments/outlook, infectivity persistence, the imperative for major behaviour change (e.g. sexual behaviour), anticipatory grief and the excessive stigma associated with the condition. The quality of life of PLWHA is severely compromised, particularly in the later stages of the disease, due to pain (experienced by 30–90% PLWHA), discomfort, and mobility difficulties (e.g. Hughes et al., 2004).

The major stressors encountered by PLWHA are summarized in Box 17.2. Different stressors may be experienced at different stages of the illness, with stress peaks at initial diagnosis, onset of symptomology, sudden immune system cell (CD4) count decline, onset of opportunistic infections and diagnosis of AIDS.

BOX 17.2

HIV/AIDS RELATED STRESSORS

Disease-related stressors

- Being tested and receiving test results;
- diagnoses – seropositivity, symptomatic phase and AIDS;
- treatment commencement;
- intermittent symptoms and opportunistic disease;
- emergence of new symptoms;
- for children, neurocognitive and emotional developmental problems;
- developing drug resistance and treatment failures;
- co-infections (e.g. hepatitis);
- further exposure to the virus;
- medication side effects;
- pain, discomfort, sexual difficulties, mobility restrictions and progressive physical deterioration;
- complications from ongoing substance use;
- drug trials and drug holidays.

External life-stressors

- Enacted stigma (e.g. ostracism and discrimination);
- disclosure reactions;
- bereavement;
- substance use;
- employment changes;
- reduced income;
- loss/lack of health insurance;
- access to treatment;
- rejection and loss of social support;
- uncertainty.

Emotional/psychological stressors

- Felt stigma (internalization, fear, shame, guilt);
- disclosure decisions;
- reproductive decision-making;
- grief;
- risk behaviour and decision-making;
- anger;
- rejection and isolation;
- changing expectations;
- preparing for death;
- guilt.

Stress has been associated with psychological problems (e.g. anxiety, hopelessness, helplessness, suicidal ideation), psychiatric disorders (e.g. depression, anxiety), negative health behaviours (e.g. drug use) and disease progression. Sub-clinical distress symptoms, including depression and anxiety, are common in PLWHA though some studies show little difference to comparison HIV-negative populations. Women are increasingly affected by HIV/AIDS and may face 'triple jeopardy', in relation to their individual, reproductive and caregiving roles (Murphy, 2003) and therefore may experience higher levels of psychiatric morbidity (Tostes et al., 2004).

Few conditions have provoked such unprecedented levels of stigma, fear and uncertainty as HIV/AIDS, even in the well informed. These fears are layered on top of pre-existing stigmas and moral judgements associated with particular groups, including gay men, sex workers, drug users and people with mental illnesses, reinforcing existing social inequalities. PLWHA have been treated as pariahs, discriminated against, abandoned and ostracized. HIV/AIDS has even evoked appeals for mandatory testing and elimination of infected individuals. Stigma can intensify all the stressors and problems of living with the disease and is an obstacle to PLWHA fulfilling their human rights and to HIV/AIDS prevention.

The decision to disclose HIV-positive status is a daunting and multifaceted issue that recurs throughout the course of the disease. Non-disclosure increases the likelihood of infecting others and denies knowledge to previous sexual partners, so represents a major barrier to controlling the epidemic. Non-disclosure also decreases social support and access to services. Disclosure decisions are often conflated with simultaneous disclosure of lifestyle choices (e.g. sexuality, drug use) to family and friends. Disclosure decisions may revert to someone other than the PLWHA, particularly regarding children, when family members make decisions, including whether to tell the child their own serostatus (DeMatteo et al., 2002).

AIDS-related deaths may generate atypical bereavement complicated by a host of factors including survivor guilt, the effects of stigma and inadequate social support. AIDS-related deaths tend to be among relatively younger people. Many people who are affected by HIV/AIDS experience multiple bereavements, increasing distress and psychological problems (e.g. guilt, depression, suicidality, disenfranchised grief, numbing).

Adaptation to HIV/AIDS

Post-HAART, HIV/AIDS has been defined as an incurable, chronic and life-threatening illness. Coping with HIV/AIDS is a complex, multidimensional phenomenon that is influenced by personality, contextual and cultural factors. It involves a process of continual adjustment in response to stress, challenging life events, and personal and interpersonal issues. Multiple stressors and negative psychological outcomes are deterrents to successful adjustment. Adaptation is also influenced by health behaviours, which have a bi-directional influence on mood states (e.g. depressed people drink more, which increases depression resulting in increased alcohol consumption, as well as increased risky sex behaviours). An increased number of symptoms and onset of the symptomatic stage are key predictors of adjustment. Factors associated with good psychosocial adjustment to HIV/AIDS include healthy self-care behaviours (medical care, healthy lifestyle, awareness and ability to take action to meet personal needs); a sense of connectedness (one close confidante, openness, disclosure); a sense of meaning and purpose (cognitive appraisal that there is something to live for, optimistic attitude); and maintaining perspective (realistic acceptance e.g. not viewing condition as imminently fatal). Adaptive coping skills have consistently been associated with increased self-esteem, increased self-efficacy and perceived control. They include active behavioural (planning, help and information seeking, relaxation exercises) and cognitive (cognitive reframing, finding meaning, emotion work, problem solving) strategies. Problem-focused coping appears more appropriate for situations that cannot be changed, whereas emotion-focused coping is more suitable where change is not possible (Park et al., 2001).

Adaptive coping strategies along with good social support can mediate the negative effects of stress. Adaptive coping strategies have also been associated with health-related benefits. Finding meaning in the experience of HIV/AIDS has been associated with maintaining immune system cell (CD4) levels, optimism with higher CD4 counts, medication adherence and lower distress, and perceived control, problem-focused coping and social support associated with longer survival. Adaptive and maladaptive coping strategies are not mutually exclusive, co-occuring or changing depending on context. Maladaptive coping strategies have been associated with poor adjustment including lower fighting spirit, higher hopelessness, anxious preoccupation and a fatalistic attitude. Passive and avoidant coping, psychological inhibition and withdrawal have been associated with increased risk behaviours, distress and more rapid disease progression (Stein and Rotheram-Borus, 2004).

Another factor associated with successful adaptation is social support. Zuckerman and Antoni (1995) reported that seven social support criteria were especially related to optimal adjustment to HIV/AIDS: feeling supported, satisfaction with support received, perceived helpfulness of peers, total perceived availability and individual dimensions of support, absence of social conflict, greater involvement of AIDS-related community activities and greater number of close friends. These criteria were related to adaptive coping strategies, increased self-esteem and sense of well-being and decreased depression, hopelessness, anxiety, mood disturbances, dysphoria and risk behaviour. Parental adaptation and support may be the most important influences on the adaptation of children and adolescent PLWHA.

Caring for someone with HIV/AIDS

The burden of care for people with HIV/AIDS, both formal and informal, is being borne primarily by lay carers within the family or the community, the majority of whom are women and girls (UNAIDS, 2004). There is some evidence, especially in Africa and Asia, that the least acknowledged carers are children (caring for a lone or surviving parent) and that older women, already vulnerable through higher levels of chronic poverty, lack of resources and their own substantial health problems, are disproportionately affected.

Caring involves a broad spectrum of psychological, spiritual, emotional and practical work throughout the course of the illness. It can be a rewarding undertaking from which caregivers derive a sense of purpose and self-esteem. However, the caring literature consistently reports the inherently stressful nature of caring for someone with a chronic illness (e.g. Chesler and Parry, 2001). Many of the stressors and negative psychological outcomes experienced by PLWHA equally affect their carers. Caring is associated with anxiety, depression, overwork, fatigue, fear of death, decreased libido, helplessness, frustration and grief. While other care domains may be similar (e.g. cancer), the greater dependence of PLWHA, and involvement and identification with them, results in increased patient contact and higher intensity of emotional work increasing the negative consequences. Neurological and/or cognitive symptoms associated with HIV/AIDS (from direct effects, opportunistic diseases or other causes) can make the burden of care especially arduous. The effects of multiple bereavements and the carers' own health problems (including own HIV-positive status) also increase mental health problems. The circumscribing effects of stigma create barriers to accessing social support and resources for carers.

The needs of carers are rarely prioritized and 'burnout' is a common problem. Burnout is defined as emotional exhaustion, depersonalization and a damaged sense of personal accomplishment (e.g. Maslach and Jackson, 1981). Emotional support and stress management programmes can help prevent stress, depression and burnout in carers.

Future Research

1 Adherence – research into the optimum time to give information about treatment and how to tailor the content of information for different patients.
2 Research designed to understand the experience of waiting for PCI and other procedures, and how interventions can improve outcomes.
3 We need a better understanding about why some people do not attend cardiac rehabilitation. The focus of the research should be on the content of the programme and why it is only attractive to some people.
4 More research is needed into the psychological impact of being told your spouse has a serious illness in order to cater for the needs of family members.
5 More longitiudinal studies are needed with HAART. The literature spans a very short timeframe (post-HAART only eight years), and is based on specific populations (e.g. gay men) from developed countries, unrepresentative of the developing world, where the epidemic is at its highest.
6 A variety of psychosocial interventions have been developed for patients with cancer and other life-threatening conditions. Although these studies have shown short-term benefits, in regard to long-term QoL and survival, the evidence to date is disappointing. Large-scale, better-designed evaluation studies are required.

Summary

General points

1 Chronic illnesses can strike at any age but more often in middle and older age groups and, while they can be fatal, most people diagnosed with a chronic illness live for many years with the condition.

2   Management of fatal or chronic diseases is a principal feature in the lives of 10–15% of the population. This huge amount of informal care occurs almost invisibly to outsiders with little recognition or financial support from society at large.

3   Chronic illness involves restrictions on activities of daily living, increases in pain and fatigue. 'Juggling' relationships with health professionals, family and friends requires many adaptations and adjustments. Patients may have views about their care and treatment that differ from those of the professionals.

4   Life-threatening diseases are associated with a great variety of metaphors and meanings. Metaphor can be a useful way of coping but may lead to guilt, self-blame and feelings of hopelessness.

5   Stigmatization adheres to people with cancer and chronic diseases. This can be a heavy extra burden for victims to carry.

6   It is important to consider the needs of the family members of people with cancer and chronic diseases.

Cancer

1   Approximately one out of every two men and one out of every three women will have cancer during their lifetime.

2   Cancer occurs when cells keep dividing and forming more cells without internal control or order. This cell growth is known as a tumour or neoplasm and can be benign or malignant.

3   Treatment can aim to cure the cancer, control it, or treat its symptoms. The type of treatment depends on the type of cancer, the stage of the cancer, and individual factors such as age, health status, and the personal preferences of the patient and his/her family. The patient ideally is empowered to discuss with the professionals the treatment choices.

4   The four major treatments for cancer are surgery, radiation, chemotherapy, and biological therapies such as hormone therapies (e.g. tamoxifen) and transplant options (e.g. with bone marrow or stem cell therapy).

5   Interview and diary studies suggest common themes among long-term survivors: 'authenticity', 'autonomy' and 'acceptance'.

Coronary heart disease

1   CHD is a leading cause of death in western countries.

2   The two main forms of CHD are myocardial infarction and angina.

3   Decreases in the CHD death rates are mainly due to a reduction in major risk factors, principally smoking. Spending on primary prevention does not reflect this finding.

4   Seeking treatment for CHD can be stressful for both people with CHD and their family members. It is important to tailor the information about CHD to the needs of individual patients.

5   Psychological disease management can help angina patients to adjust but psychological services are currently patchy and inadequate.

HIV/AIDS

1   HIV/AIDS has become a worldwide pandemic that has infected around 60 million people, and become the fourth largest killer in the world. There are around 5 million new cases each year.

2   HIV (human immunodeficiency virus) is a retrovirus that infects and colonizes cells in the immune system and the central nervous system (T-helper and monocyte macrophage

cells). Initial flu-like symptoms are followed by a quiescent, asymptomatic period (lasting years) during which the immune system battles the virus.

3   The most effective treatment consists of combination therapies (HAART), which have been shown to decrease an individual's HIV viral load to undetectable levels, reducing associated morbidity and mortality.

4   Adaptive coping strategies along with good social support can moderate the negative effects of stress. Finding meaning in the experience of HIV/AIDS has been associated with medication adherence, lower distress and perceived control.

5   Interventions that target adaptive coping skills, emotion work and increasing social support appear to be most effective in helping patients to adapt to living with their illness.

KT   Key Terms

ACE (Angiotensin Converting Enzyme) inhibitors

AIDS (acquired immune deficiency syndrome)

Angina

Angina Plan

anticoagulant drugs

atheroma

betablockers

burden of disease

coronary angiogram

coronary artery bypass graft (CABG)

electrocardiogram (ECG)

exercise tolerence test (ETT)

HIV (human immunodeficiency virus)

metastasis

myocardial infarction (MI)

percutaneous coronary intervention (PCI)

psycho-oncology

restenosis

revascularization

statins

stigmatization

toxic environment

tumour (benign or malignant)

Part Four

Health Promotion and Disease Prevention

Part 4 is concerned with some of the major settings and processes involved in health promotion and disease prevention. We give emphasis to theoretical and methodological issues that fall squarely within the interface between research and practice. Whenever possible we indicate the practical implications of research for the improvement of healthcare delivery.

Chapter 18 discusses immunization and screening, two main mechanisms for disease prevention available to healthcare. Although immunization programmes for infectious childhood diseases have advanced well in most industrialized countries, there is considerable variation over time and place. Most industrialized countries have introduced screening programmes for breast and cervical cancer yet many women are reluctant to participate. Women's perceptions of these different programmes are considered. Finally, recent genetic advances have held out the prospect of genetic screening programmes. Ethical and psychological factors associated with these programmes are reviewed.

Chapter 19 reviews the extent to which work experience impacts upon the health of employees, and examines the implications of this impact. The key theories and research findings that support or refute these theories are discussed. The key factors that contribute to employee satisfaction and well-being are highlighted, along with workplace characteristics that may be detrimental to employee health, well-being and satisfaction. References are made to occupational stress, with suggested interventions to reduce high levels of workplace stress. The impact of redundancy and unemployment are discussed, as are health behaviours of alcohol consumption and exercise. Finally, we consider anticipated changes in the workplace over coming years, and their potential impact on employee health.

Chapter 20 focuses upon the psychological dimensions of health promotion. Three major health promotion approaches are described: the behaviour change approach, the self-empowerment approach and the 'collective action' or community development approach. Health promotion interventions informed by each approach are described and critically evaluated. Critiques of the contemporary 'ideology of health promotion' are presented.

18

Immunization and Screening

An ounce of prevention is worth a pound of cure. (Anon)

Outline

In this chapter we consider two main forms of disease prevention available within health-care systems: immunization and screening. Although immunization for infectious childhood diseases is generally high in most industrialized countries, there is considerable variation over time and place. The various social and psychological factors that have been found to be associated with its uptake are reviewed. Most industrialized countries have introduced screening programmes for breast and cervical cancer yet many women are reluctant to participate. This chapter considers women's perceptions of these different programmes. Finally, recent genetic advances have held out the prospect of genetic screening programmes. Ethical and psychological factors associated with these programmes are reviewed. Some critical issues regarding the introduction of these programmes are considered.

Immunization

Immunization has been described as one of the most successful examples of the primary prevention of disease. Infectious diseases that were once the major causes of death and disability in both the industrialized and the developing world have now largely been eradicated. According to medical science this has been due largely to a range of vaccination programmes (but see below). These vaccination programmes are generally targeted at specific sub-groups of the population such as children, travellers and seniors. The most extensive programmes have been targeted at children. Despite the apparent success of mass immunization programmes, a large proportion of at-risk individuals in western societies are not immunized against certain diseases.

Uptake of immunization among children

There has been substantial public debate about the safety of the measles/mumps/rubella (MMR) vaccine. The proportion of children immunized against MMR by their second

Table 18.1   *Parental reasons for non-immunization (Meszaros et al., 1996: 698)*

- *Risk/benefit ratio*: perception that the risks of contracting the disease outweigh the benefits of being immunized.
- *Individual risk*: belief that the societal statistics which public health planners use do not apply to their child. Further, the parents believe that they can protect the child from exposure.
- *Ambiguity aversion*: aversity to options with ambiguous outcomes such that parents will prefer a straightforward Yes/No assessment of the likelihood of their child contracting a disease. When there is disagreement about potential risk they will err on the side of caution. Further, some parents may already be sceptical of medical information.
- *Omission bias*: preference for acts of omission over acts of commission.
- *'Free riding'*: assumption that since most of their children's peers have been vaccinated they are protected.

birthday has fallen steadily in the UK over the past decade from 91% in 1991/92 to 82% in 2002/03 (National Statistics, 2004).

The rates of immunization are generally lower among children from low-income families. A study of the uptake of the MMR vaccine in 10 health districts in north London in 1993 found that the rate ranged from 69% in one inner city district to 91% in one suburban or rural district where social conditions would be expected to be better. It was suggested that the low rate of uptake in the deprived inner city area might be due to the higher mobility of families living there leading to difficulties for the health authorities in tracing them and in arranging appointments. This study also found that immunization was lower in larger and one-parent families – further indicators of social position.

A study of mothers from North West England found that those with lower educational qualifications, living alone, with large families and having a sick child were less likely to immunize their child (New and Senior, 1991).

Parental reasons for non-immunization of children

Several studies have identified a variety of reasons expressed by parents for not having their children immunized. These reasons have been summarized by Meszaros et al. (1996) (Table 18.1).

In their study, Meszaros et al. (1996) attempted to assess the relative importance of each of these explanations in a questionnaire survey of readers of *Mothering*, a popular magazine read by mothers in the USA. They found that the most important predictors of parents having their child immunized were the perceived dangers of the vaccine, doubts about medical claims that vaccines are effective, omission bias, belief that physicians overestimate the dangerousness of the disease, perceived ability to protect their child and perceived assessment of the likelihood of their child contracting the disease.

This fear of the adverse effect of immunization may be exaggerated in certain communities. A study in England in 1996 found that the uptake of childhood immunization was particularly low among orthodox Jews. Mothers suggested that the main reason for their low uptake was their fear of a negative reaction, logistical difficulties and unsympathetic treatment by health staff. According to the health professionals, the mothers' fears were exaggerated because they lived in a close-knit community that perpetuated tales of bad reactions. The perceived dangers of immunization has also been identified as a major cause of reduced uptake of influenza vaccination among seniors (Armstrong et al., 2001).

Besides these factors, an additional factor is the perceived relative risk. In a qualitative investigation of the views of a sample of inner-city parents in Baltimore, it was found that although some parents accepted that they or their children might be vulnerable to infectious diseases, other threats such as drugs, street violence and 'the wrong crowd' were considered more severe. Further, vaccines were viewed as only partly successful. The continued occurrence of chickenpox was frequently cited as evidence of vaccine failure. Fears can even be stimulated by medical opinions that immunization may itself increase risk, i.e. the MMR scare in the UK.

A frequent explanation given by mothers in several studies is the natural/unnatural distinction. New and Senior (1991) found that whereas vaccination was perceived by some mothers as unnatural, by implication whooping cough was natural and therefore acceptable. Admittedly, some other women had weighed up the benefits and risks of immunization and decided in favour of immunization. It would be expected that these were the women who were more accepting of the medical viewpoint, with all its doubts and confusions.

This natural/unnatural distinction was also alluded to in a large German study. The most significant predictors of measles immunization were parental natural health orientation, advice of paediatrician, birth order position, dangerousness of measles, marital status, reliability of vaccination and smoking. A natural health orientation and advice of paediatricians may be interactive since individuals with a natural health orientation may select like-minded physicians. A more detailed analysis of the subjective relevance of measles found that those who assessed the likelihood of contracting measles as high and the latency as low were more likely to have their children immunized.

Parental concern about the possible risks of vaccination is also expressed in homeopathic beliefs. In a survey of parents of children in South West England, it was found that the commonest reasons given for non-immunization of their children were homeopathy and religious beliefs.

Other studies (e.g. Smailbegovic et al., 2003) have found less evidence of the use of complementary medicine as an alternative to conventional immunization although this may be the case among some sub-groups. A study in Alberta, Canada found that among some religious sub-groups there was evidence that not only did they refuse to have their child immunized on the basis of their religious beliefs but also because of their preference for alternative healthcare (Kulig et al., 2002).

Immunization programmes and the role of health professionals

Health professionals play an important role in encouraging or discouraging immunization among their patients. There is evidence that some family doctors have concerns about the safety of vaccines. A report in Britain (Peckham et al., 1989) concluded that the main obstacle to parents having their child immunized was misconceptions by the family doctor concerning contraindications. New and Senior (1991) in their study of mothers in North West England found that most who had not had their children fully immunized claimed that either their child was contraindicated to pertussis vaccine or their doctor had advised them against it. Further, many of the mothers said they had received conflicting advice from different health professionals that led to confusion and loss of confidence in such advice. Indeed, some mothers said it was the actual attempt by the health professionals to convince them of the minimal risk that deterred them. As one mother said: 'Until they find a safe vaccine, one in 300,000 is still too large; I wouldn't play Russian roulette with my child.'

A study of parents in Utah in the late 1980s found similar concerns. The most common reason given for non-immunization was that the child was ill at the time they were to be vaccinated. The authors noted that it is unlikely that these children were seriously ill but 'it is possible that, because of adverse media, parental worries, and concern about possible litigation, physicians and public health officials have been affected and failed to emphasize the importance of a young child receiving the complete immunization series and of not unnecessarily delaying immunization' (Smailbegovic et al., 2003: 286).

Taken together these findings would suggest that while parents may be hesitant about having their child immunized because of their anxiety about the potential risk, this image is compounded by media speculation and by the advice they receive from health professionals.

Critical perspective on immunization

These explanations of non-immunization tend to portray the non-compliers as deviant and to be based upon uncritical support for the public health message on immunization. A more critical perspective would begin by questioning the validity of the public health message. For example, the argument developed by McKeown (1979) suggests that it has been widespread improvements in social conditions rather than immunization that have led to the rapid decline in infectious diseases in the past century. Indeed, it has been estimated that at most 3.5% of the decline in infectious disease mortality in the US during the past century can be attributed to medical measures.

There is also the argument over the frequency of side effects of vaccines. Public health authorities would tend to adopt a war analogy and talk about acceptable levels of collateral damage and to argue that these are minimal and that even their low frequency has to be compared with the benefit to society due to the overall control of infectious diseases. Recently the public debate about the safety of the triple vaccine and the autism–vaccine link have re-opened this concern just at the time when the public health authorities were congratulating themselves over the control of polio. Dew (1999) has also raised the issue of the power of the pharmaceutical companies in promoting the value of immunization and downplaying the debate about side effects although the evidence is that the large drug companies do not consider vaccines a particularly lucrative product (Rappuoli et al., 2002). There is obviously a need for some caution.

From a more critical perspective vaccination can be considered as the adoption by the state of a particular view of health. As Martin (1994) has stressed: 'accepting vaccination means accepting the state's power to impose a particular view about the body and the immune system – the vision developed by medical science' (1994: 194). This vision places the germ theory of disease at the centre of our understanding and downplays the importance of social conditions and lifestyle factors. An alternative approach would be to consider the importance of social inequalities in the distribution of infectious diseases (Dew, 1999). Previously, we highlighted how low uptake of immunization was higher in deprived neighbourhoods. Vaccination tends to focus on boosting the resistance of the host organism while ignoring those social conditions that make the host more vulnerable in general. A study of mothers of non-immunized children in a deprived area of London found that they had a very sceptical attitude on government advice (Smailbegovic et al., 2003). For example, one mother said: 'I have a lack of faith in the government line on the subject of immunization, there is a lot more involved than the safety of individual children' (2003: 307).

The parents in this and other studies (e.g. Evans et al., 2001) often believed that the advice given by health professionals was biased. The parents' reluctance to participate in immunization programmes could be considered part of a more resistant stance to the doctrinaire approach of some government officials and to perceived state control in general. This would suggest that programmes designed to increase immunization need to separate its promotion more from the institutions of state control in general and to involve the parents, recipients and lay health workers more in the process of implementation (Whittaker, 2002).

Screening

Screening is the procedure whereby those sections of the population who are most at risk of developing a particular disease are examined to see whether they have any early indications of that disease. The rationale behind this strategy is that the earlier the disease is identified and treated, the less likely it is to develop into its full-blown form. Within public health circles there has been sustained debate as regards the value of this strategy.

Wilson and Junger (1968) identified ten prerequisites for a successful screening programme (Table 18.2).

In western countries there have been several attempts to introduce mass screening for a limited number of conditions that satisfy all or most of these criteria. However, despite the supposed benefits of these programmes there have been various problems in their implementation. It was generally assumed by their proponents that the major problem would be the introduction of the programmes. However, the problem has centred on the reluctance of at least a proportion of the targeted population to make use of these programmes and the unexpected negative side effects of participation.

Screening for breast and cervical cancer

Over the past decade there has been a concerted effort in most industrialized societies to introduce screening programmes for breast cancer. The reason for this is that it seemed to satisfy most of the criteria for screening previously outlined. It is currently the most prevalent or the second most prevalent form of female cancer in western

Table 18.2   *Prerequisites of screening (Wilson and Junger, 1968, p. 26j; reproduced with permission)*

- Condition sought should be an important health problem.
- Accepted treatment for patients with the disease.
- Facilities for treatment and diagnosis should be available.
- Recognizable latent or early symptomatic stage.
- Suitable test or examination.
- Test should be acceptable to the population.
- Natural history of the condition should be adequately understood.
- Agreed policy on whom to treat as patient.
- Cost should be economically balanced in relation to possible expenditure on medical care as a whole.
- Case finding should be a continuing process and not a once-and-for-all project.

society. In the UK it is estimated that approximately 38,000 women are diagnosed with breast cancer each year and about 13,000 die from the disease. It is estimated that the lifetime risk of breast cancer for women is now one in eight. Not only is it widely prevalent but its incidence is also increasing by 1% to 2% per annum. The reason for this is unclear.

Partly in response to the epidemiological and medical evidence about the widespread prevalence of the disease and the association between stage of identification and success of treatment, there has been a demand not only from health authorities but also from women's organizations for the introduction of breast cancer screening programmes. Initially, the method favoured was breast self-examination, but due to queries about the accuracy of this procedure the favoured method is now mammography coupled with clinical breast examination by a health professional. In most countries mammography programmes have been targeted at all women aged 50 to 69 years, although some countries also attempt to cover younger and older women. The reason for the focus on the limited age band is because evidence suggests it is the most cost effective in terms of case finding although there continues to be debate about the most appropriate age range.

Cervical cancer is a much less prevalent condition. It is the eighth most prevalent form of cancer among women but the most common in women under 35 years of age. In the UK the disease accounts for about 1,850 deaths per annum. The cause of the disease remains unknown although it is thought that a viral infection spread by sexual intercourse may be an important factor.

There is evidence that the pre-cancerous stage of the disease can be detected at an early stage using a simple cervical smear test (**pap test**). Most western countries have introduced campaigns to encourage women to attend for regular smear tests, usually at least once every three to five years.

Who participates in cancer screening programmes?

With the introduction of mammography screening programmes in various countries over the past decade the proportion of women participating in such programmes has increased. In the UK women aged 50–64 years are invited every three years for a mammogram. It is estimated that approximately 1.5 million women attend every year. The smear test for cervical cancer has been around for a longer period and its uptake is generally higher. In the UK almost 4 million women participate in the cervical screening programme each year.

Several studies have shown that use of cancer screening programmes is lower among women from low socio-economic status (SES) backgrounds (e.g. Frazier et al., 1996) and, to a lesser extent, among those from ethnic minorities. Admittedly, some studies have found less evidence of this trend. The US Center for Disease Control and Prevention (1995) claimed to have found few ethnic differences. It found that between 1987 and 1992 there had been substantial increases in uptake of mammography among black and hispanic women such that now their screening rates differ little from those of white women.

Health service organization for cancer screening

Several studies have found that the most important factor in explaining variation in participation is the extent to which the woman's doctor recommends participation. Women are more likely to undergo cancer screening if they see female rather than male physicians. Some physicians are reluctant to advise mammography for a variety of reasons including scepticism about its effectiveness in general or for certain groups of women and fear of the effect of radiation. Physicians are especially less likely to refer older women for screening. Further, Frazier et al. (1996) found that black women were more likely to report that their physician had not recommended participation.

More countries and regions are now establishing dedicated cancer screening programmes with postal invitations to women to attend on a regular basis. Despite these moves a proportion of women are still reluctant to participate in these programmes. Similarly, some women do not participate even when they are personally encouraged to attend by their physician. A personal invitation by a woman's family doctor is as effective as a home visit from a nurse conveying the same message. However, despite the best intentions of family doctors many women fail to receive such personal invites because of inaccurate registers.

Health beliefs and cancer screening

This reluctance of many women to participate in screening programmes has contributed to a large number of studies that have investigated what women think about these services. Many studies of health beliefs have been based upon various social cognition models of health behaviour especially the Health Belief Model (HBM) and the Theory of Reasoned Action. These models argue that it is possible to identify a certain typical belief pattern that will predict use of health services such as screening. Although the models have not been statistically predictive, examination of individual components gives some insight into the reluctance of many women to participate in screening programmes.

In the case of breast cancer screening, the most frequently cited predictors are perceived susceptibility and perceived barriers. A meta-analysis of a large number of US studies (McCaul et al., 1996) found a strong relationship between family history (actual risk) and **mammography** utilization but also a moderate relationship between

KT

perceived vulnerability (perceived risk) and use of mammography. In a UK study, Sutton et al. (1994) also found a relationship between perceived risk and attendance. Perceived susceptibility to breast cancer is the best predictor of future intention to participate in mammography. However, they add that 'it is questionable ... whether heightened feelings of susceptibility alone will sufficiently motivate women to obtain mammograms in the absence of a physician's recommendation' (1994: 68).

Various barriers to attendance for mammography, both physical and psychological, have been reported. In a survey of women in the USA those who did not attend for mammography had a stronger belief that screening was not necessary in the absence of symptoms, a preference not to think about it and a worry about the effect of radiation. Perceived barriers are the most important predictor of non-attendance for a smear test. The barriers they considered included dislike of the health service, fear of the examination, and fear of the result. McCaul et al. (1996) found that women who worry about breast cancer are more likely to engage in various self-protective actions such as breast self-examination and attendance for mammography. A non-linear relationship has been found with the highest attendance among women who were 'a bit worried', while those at the two extremes of worry were less likely to attend. Health promotion campaigns must balance advice to women on perceived risk with the negative impact of excessive worry. Other barriers reported include belief that a mammogram is appropriate only when there are symptoms, concern about radiation exposure, cost and access-related factors.

A related model is the Attitudes to Illness Model developed by Kellner (1986). According to this model people with hypochondriacal symptoms are less likely to seek health care. A study of Spanish women found that those with high fear of illness were less likely to participate in a cancer screening programme (Lostao et al., 2001).

With respect to benefits, several studies have indicated that the most frequently given reason for non-participation in cancer screening is that the women do not feel it necessary as they were healthy. It is thought that it is only necessary to have mammograms when one is sick. In a survey of rural women in Alberta in 1992, it was found that the two most frequently given reasons for non-utilization of mammography was that the women had not been encouraged to do so by a doctor and that they felt they were healthy and did not need to use it. Perceiving one's health as good is inversely associated with recent mammography. Harlan et al. (1991) found that the most frequently given reason for not having a cervical smear was not believing it necessary.

Although the Health Belief Model (HBM) has been widely used in studies designed to predict attendance for breast cancer screening, the results have not always been consistent. Women who never schedule a mammogram are more likely to perceive both fewer benefits of and barriers to mammography. They did not find any relationship between perceived susceptibility and mammography usage. They suggested that possibly other variables such as knowledge was a more important overriding factor. Many women are either unaware of the availability of the services or do not understand the character of the investigation. Many women do not understand that the early stages of cervical carcinoma are not accompanied by any symptoms. Similarly, Harlan et al. (1991) found that the main reason for non-participation in cervical screening was that women did not think it necessary because they did not have any symptoms. Since mammography occurs when there are no symptoms of breast cancer women are required to trust the screening advice they are given by their doctor in order to participate.

The Theory of Reasoned Action has met with some success in predicting cancer screening behaviour. In a large survey of women in Seattle, attitude and subjective norm both predicted participation in mammography as did affect, which was a measure of the emotions associated with having a mammogram. It has also been found that facilitating conditions a measure of logistics, and habit, a measure of previous use of mammography, also independently predicted usage.

Several researchers have used the Transtheoretical Model of Change (Prochaska and DiClemente, 1983) to explore the extent of participation in screening programmes. Women who are classified as pre-contemplators (i.e. those who never had a mammogram and did not plan to have one) score higher on a measure of negative beliefs including the beliefs that mammograms lead to unnecessary surgery and that they are only advisable if you have some breast symptoms. Knowledge of the recommended screening interval and having no anticipated barriers to screening are associated with higher decisional balance scores in the stages of change classification of a sample of women. Action/maintainers are less likely to agree with the various psychological and physical barriers to screening.

There is a tendency in these health belief studies to adopt once again a **deficit model** to explain non-participation in screening. The women who do not use the service tend to be characterized as lacking in knowledge and concern about their health. This is especially the case when there are attempts to explain the lower utilization by women from low SES and from ethnic minorities. An alternative perspective is to view this non-attendance as a form of resistance to what is perceived as an unnecessary interference in their lives or even of something that could increase the likelihood of cancer (see Chapter 15). Several studies have explored this alternative perspective.

KT

Critical view of cancer screening programmes

Despite the widespread support for breast cancer screening and the estimates that it can lead to a reduction of up to 35% in mortality from that disease (IARC, 2002), a few critics have raised some cautions. For example, Skrabanek (1985) questioned the sensitivity and specificity of mammography and also queried the claimed value of early intervention. A review of British data found that the introduction of breast cancer screening programmes has led to greater detection but not to a reduced mortality rate. There has also been a renewed interest in the value of breast self-examination (BSE) as a technique for early detection of breast cancer. It is argued that BSE alone may reduce breast cancer mortality by up to 18% and should be used as a complement if not a substitute for mammography screening.

Although cervical screening has been widely promoted there is also debate about its value. A review of British figures in 1997 indicated that the decline in deaths from cervical cancer preceded the establishment of screening programmes. It could be argued that the overall costs to the nation in terms of expenditure and to the woman in terms of psychological distress outweigh the benefits in terms of increased life expectancy. There is obviously a need for continued surveillance.

A particular concern is how women perceive the development of these various cancer screening strategies. Despite the advances in the treatment of cancer, or indeed partly due to the character of these advances, cancer remains the most feared disease in western society. A survey of a random sample of adults resident in Northern Ireland found that cancer was the most feared disease, especially among women. The reason for this fear was because cancer was perceived as incurable and as leading to a painful death.

Several qualitative studies have explored women's fear of cancer and their reluctance to use the various screening services. Blaxter (1983) conducted interviews with women from Glasgow about their views on health and illness. She found that the women were reluctant to talk about cancer. Blaxter suggested that this lack of reference to cancer was a coping strategy used by the women to protect themselves from cancer: 'to talk about it was to invoke it, to speak briefly or in a lowered voice was to leave it sleeping' (1983: 125). Participation in screening would threaten this form of psychological defence.

An interview study with a sample of working-class women in Northern Ireland found evidence of a fear of cancer and a reluctance to interfere. One woman explained why she had not had a smear test taken:

> I think you have the fear, you see, of it. But they say they can get it in time ... but sure how do they know they've got it in time. They don't know until they start opening you up and if they open you up, it would spread. So I would say, leave well enough alone. (Murray and McMillan, 1988: 42)

Similarly, Russell et al. (2003) found in their study of African-American women that they thought that many of their peers preferred not to look for cancer: 'For instance, like a car, if there's nothing wrong with it, you don't fix it; you don't go looking for anything' (2003: 33). A fatalistic attitude to cancer among some women tends to lead them to question the value of cancer screening. A study of African-American low income women (Gregg and Curry, 1994) found that they had a very negative image of the disease. They not only believed that cancer was deadly but they felt that if the cancer could be detected by mammography then it was already beyond cure.

Balshem (1991) linked these negative beliefs about cancer with the life experiences of the women. She conducted an ethnographic study of a working-class community in Philadelphia that seemed very resistant to a health promotion campaign aimed at encouraging healthier lifestyles including attendance for breast cancer screening. When she interviewed these women, Balshem found that the health promotion message was counter to their experience. They believed that fate determined who got cancer and who survived. To look for cancer was to tempt fate; it was 'looking for trouble'. To quote Balshem: 'Challenging fate is a risky business. Cancer inspires not challenge but taboo' (1991: 166). Thus the women preferred not to think about cancer.

Other qualitative work would suggest that some women would prefer to conduct self-examination rather than attend a medical centre for investigation. For example, a study of older African-American women found that they did not think it necessary to use the health service since after self-examination they had found no lumps. Other women felt that they accepted lumps and bumps as part of life and were more concerned about other people's health rather than their own.

Another important issue to consider is the sexual connotations of both breast and cervical cancer. Breasts are at the centre of a woman's sexual identity. Women fear breast cancer partly because of the threat to this identity. Also, the evidence that a sexually transmitted virus may contribute to cervical cancer has been widely discussed. This has contributed to some women's reluctance to have a smear test. McKie (1993, 1995) considered the views of a sample of English working-class women. She found that in the minds of some of the women the test was associated with sexual promiscuity, a label that they did not want to have. By avoiding the test they sought to avoid the label.

Willingness to participate in breast cancer screening programmes depends upon its congruence with broader cultural beliefs and norms, especially those concerned with the body. For example, in a study of women of Mexican descent resident in Texas, Borrayo and Jenkins (2001a) found that they felt that participation in breast cancer screening conflicted with a strongly held cultural norm of female modesty. Borrayo and Jenkins argued that the women's behaviour revolved around a basic social-psychological problem (BSPP) that cancer screening was insensitive since it violated strongly held cultural beliefs. Participation in screening required the women to break these norms and to behave in a manner they considered to be indecent. The women believed that it was indecent for others to touch or see their bodies. Borrayo and Jenkins concluded that these norms were more important than such factors as socio-economic status and must be taken into consideration in the development of screening programmes. The women in this study also felt that they should not participate in screening since they were healthy. Indeed, the very participation in a medical procedure held out the prospect of them losing their sense of feeling healthy (Borrayo and Jenkins, 2001b).

Together these findings suggest that women are anxious about the prospect of cancer but are also anxious about the whole medicalization of the disease. The technology that surrounds mammography acts to disempower women and to alienate them from their bodies. Alternative approaches that seek to challenge this medicalization of cancer screening are still being developed. One strategy would be to work with the community to connect cancer screening with a broader programme of community empowerment (e.g. Baillie et al., 2004). Such a strategy would work to challenge the power of the medical establishment and to humanize the tools of technology.

Anxiety about medicalization and the medical system may act as a disincentive to screening for other cancers. Recently the British government introduced a colorectal cancer screening programme. It was found that people from deprived backgrounds were less likely to make use of this programme. Interviews and surveys identified people from lower SES as perceiving fewer benefits and more barriers to participation. These individuals tended to view the procedure with suspicion and it was suggested that this might reflect a lower level of trust in the medical system since they more frequently had negative experiences with the system (Wardle et al., 2004).

Experience of cancer screening

Most of the research on cancer screening has concentrated on describing those factors associated with initial attendance. However, according to current guidelines women are expected to attend not once but on a regular basis. Few studies have examined this process of reattendance although the evidence does suggest that rate of attendance for follow-up is lower than for initial examination (Sutton et al., 1994). One important factor in reattendance is the woman's reaction to the initial test. Evidence suggests that this is not always positive.

Women will often find mammography screening painful. Keefe et al. (1994) reviewed several studies on the experience of pain during mammography and found that the percentage of women reporting pain varied widely across studies with a range of

1–62%. Admittedly, four of the eight studies reviewed by Keefe et al. (1994) found that at least one-third of the women reported some degree of pain during mammography. A Canadian study in 1994 reported that 40% out of a sample of women undergoing screening mammography agreed that it hurt. Admittedly, it would seem that many women accept the pain and discomfort since it is short-term but has long-term benefits. However, some are less accepting and indeed feel that the pain may actually increase their risk of cancer. For example, one woman commented in Eardley and Elkind's (1990: 696) study: 'The straight answer is – if I don't have cancer now, I'll have it after this [the pressure of the machine].' Such a viewpoint may act as a disincentive for repeat mammography.

More recent research would suggest that with improved training of staff there is less evidence of the procedure being painful. For example, a study of women who participated in a mammography programme in the English Midlands (Hamilton et al., 2003) found that although all of the women reported some discomfort they also were very positive in their view of the staff. It would seem that satisfaction with staff reduced both pain and embarrassment. An important factor is perceived control. When people believe that they have control over an aversive stimulus they experience less stress and have greater tolerance for the unpleasantness (Staub et al., 1971). Providing women with a greater sense of control over the mammography procedure could be an important aid to reducing their discomfort.

There is also evidence that cervical screening can be uncomfortable for some women. In a survey of women in the East End of London, 54% rated having a smear test as painful or uncomfortable and 46% found it embarrassing. Again, such experiences would not be expected to encourage reattendance.

Psychological consequences of cancer screening

In the initial haste to establish screening programmes, the psychological costs in terms of increased anxiety were overlooked. Recently, with the publication of a series of more critical reports there has begun a reassessment. Wardle and Pope (1992) in reviewing the research organized it into five groups:

1 *Impact of screening publicity*: although Skrabanek (1985) warned of the creation of a cancerphobia as a result of publicity campaigns for screening, the evidence for this is limited. Admittedly, several studies (e.g. Eardley and Elkind, 1990) have found that women were alarmed when they received an invitation to attend. However, bearing in mind the evidence by McCaul et al. (1996), it would seem that a certain rise in anxiety increases participation. Lower levels of anxiety about breast cancer occur among those who do not attend a mammography screening programme. However, excessive anxiety may also act as a disincentive.

2 *Psychological costs of participation*: participation in screening programmes is not always positive (Eardley and Elkind, 1990). The psychological effects may be disguised because of a selection effect such that the more anxious women avoid screening. Middle-class women who tend to attend are more comfortable with the whole medical/scientific approach, whereas women from other social groups and cultures may be much more uncomfortable.

3 *Psychological costs of diagnosis of cancer*: not surprisingly the evidence suggests that a diagnosis of cancer is met by alarm and despair. An increased rate of suicide among women positively screened in Scandinavia has been found. Also of concern is the finding that the increased rate of cardiovascular mortality following cancer screening offset the cancer mortality reduction.

4 *Psychological response to diagnosis of abnormality*: although the screening test does not definitively identify cancer, evidence would suggest that any indication of abnormality is usually interpreted by the woman as such. Evidence suggest that around 95% of women who are told by mail that they had to return for further tests reported that they are upset or anxious. Heckman et al. (2004) found similar findings. Until the possibility of cancer is ruled out these women will experience distress similar to being diagnosed with cancer. This distress can continue after cancer has been ruled out. The extensive nature of this distress has led some to conclude that the life years of mood impairment outweigh the benefits of cancer screening in terms of additional life years.

5 *Psychological costs of false positive diagnosis*: a large proportion of women with an initial positive diagnosis from the mammogram will later be declared negative on further examination. These are known as **false positive** cases. Not surprisingly, women will be extremely alarmed at being informed that there may be something wrong. Schwartz et al. (2004) found in a telephone survey of American adults that 40% of those who had received a false positive result characterized the experience as 'very scary' or the 'scariest time of my life'. However, 98% of the participants were glad that they had participated in the screening.

KT

The false positive result is followed by further anxiety provoking investigation that will include clinical examination and possibly surgery. In a 10-year follow-up, Elmore et al. (1998) found that one-third of the women who obtained some positive results were required to undergo additional investigations, including *biopsies*, even though it turned out that they did not have breast cancer. It seems that approximately half of those women recalled for a breast biopsy overestimate their risk of cancer (Lebel et al., 2003).

Men and cancer screening

Most of the research on screening for cancer has focused on breast and cervical cancer. These are women's diseases. There are also cancers specific to men – testicular and prostate – yet these have received much less clinical and research interest. Prostate cancer is the most common male cancer and its incidence is expected to reach epidemic proportions in the coming years. There is a need for greater research into male screening practices.

It is well known that men are much less likely to engage in preventive health practices such as screening (e.g. Courtney et al., 2002). Male socialization encourages such qualities as independence, self-reliance, toughness and risk-taking. Thus it is not surprising that men are more likely than women to engage in risky health practices and to make less use of all forms of health care (Courtney, 2000). Even when they do engage with health services they receive less physician time and fewer medical services than women. As Gray (2003) commented in his book about the experience of prostate cancer: 'Real men, after all, are supposed to be unconcerned about health matters. Real men don't fuss about their bodies. Real men don't need help' (2003: 24).

A major component of hegemonic models of male masculinity is self-sufficiency that discourages use of health services (Lee and Owens, 2002). Gray (2003) noted how reluctant men are to disclose their weaknesses to others. Even in prostate support groups they sought information about the disease rather than emotional support. However, with involvement in the support groups this attitude changed and the men were pleasantly surprised with the connections they made with other men. Thus screening for male cancers needs to emphasize its potential for enhancing male strength.

Genetic Screening

The recent rapid advances in genetic research now hold out the prospect of genetic screening for different diseases. This can take various forms (see Lerman, 1997):

- *Carrier* testing investigates people who are likely to be carriers of the genes for such diseases as *cystic fibrosis* or *Tay-Sachs disease*. This form of testing is usually conducted in the context of reproductive decision-making.
- *Pre-symptomatic* testing allows the identification of a disease before the symptoms actually develop. This form of testing is used to determine the person's risk of developing such late-onset diseases as Huntington's disease.
- *Susceptibility* testing is designed to test for a person's susceptibility to develop a disease, although whether or not that disease develops depends upon a variety of environmental and nutritional factors partly outside the person's control.

Although the general principles underlying genetic screening are similar to those of other forms of screening there are certain unique features. Lerman (1997) described several distinguishing features that need to be taken into consideration when investigating the psychological aspects (Table 18.3). These factors need to be accounted for in exploring the development of these services.

Attitudes towards genetic testing

There have been several studies of public attitudes to genetic screening. These indicate that while the public generally has a positive attitude towards the procedure this is mixed with concern and anxiety regarding the use to which such information could be put by certain individuals or groups. For example, Shaw and Bassi (2001) conducted a survey of over 200 adults in Pennsylvania. They found that overall the participants were very optimistic about the potential benefits of genetic screening. However, they also expressed concern at the prospects of genetic testing being 'conducted by the wrong people'.

Attitudes towards genetic testing depend upon a variety of factors. These include family history of the disease and potential benefit of the test in terms of the treatability of the disease. There seems to be a very strong interest in genetic testing for breast cancer. In an interview study of women in the UK with a family history of the disease

Table 18.3 *Features of genetic screening (Lerman, 1997: 4)*

- *Type of information*: genetic information is probabilistic and uncertain. In some cases you can say with certainty that a person will develop a disease but when is less clear (e.g. Huntington's disease). In other cases it is unclear whether the person will develop the disease at all (e.g. cancer).
- *Medical value*: control over disease onset is limited for certain diseases (e.g. cancer) and non-existent for others (e.g. Huntington's disease).
- *Timescale*: the timescale is variable in that the results of genetic testing concern events which may occur far in the future.
- *Impact of results*: the results not only affect the individual but the family since genetic susceptibility is transmitted within families.

Foster et al. (2002) found that most of the women felt an obligation to get tested for two reasons – to improve their own health prospects and that of their children. They found that for some of the women there was no real choice – it had to be done. One woman said: 'I don't feel that I have got decision to make. I mean I see this as, as being the next, the next step forward, I don't want to be seen to be making the decision anyway I think it's a case of got to know, not will I want to know.'

Psychological consequences of genetic screening

Unlike cancer screening, genetic testing is often initiated by individuals when they suspect that because of family history they may be carriers. Thus they would be expected to be in a heightened state of anxiety. Several studies have found a reduction in such anxiety following testing. However, in some cases there was evidence of subsequent psychological distress. Lawson et al. (1996) found that of 95 individuals receiving the results of a test for Huntington's disease, two made plans for suicide and seven had clinical depression. Interestingly, there was no difference between those tested positive and those tested negative. Tibben et al. (1993) found that carriers tended to minimize the impact of the test results on their futures.

There is evidence that the positive effect of screening is only short term. At six-month follow-up Tibben et al. (1993) found that one-quarter of the carriers exhibited signs of psychopathology. They continued to follow the group for three years and found that for the first six months there was a rise in avoidant thoughts and a decrease in intrusive feelings. This was followed by a reversal of this pattern. It was suggested that this was evidence of a coping strategy whereby the carriers 'dose themselves' with tolerable levels of intrusive thoughts as they begin to process and accept the test results.

Genetic screening can also have a dramatic impact on the family of the carrier. Hans and Koeppen (1989) found that partners often reacted with disbelief and denial. However, this turned to resentment and hostility as they became aware of the threat of transmission to their children. The partners can play an important role in helping the carrier cope with the diagnosis (Tibben et al., 1993).

The evidence of psychological impact of genetic screening has been followed by calls for greater provision of psychological support services. It has been suggested that such services be made available prior to testing such that the testees are fully aware of the issues and also afterwards so that they and their families can begin to come to terms with the findings.

Table 18.4   *Possible advantages and disadvantages of childhood genetic testing (Michie and Marteau, 1996: 9)*

	Advantages	Disadvantages
Those with a faulty gene	Time to adjust and avoid emotional problems. Enables parents to help child prepare. Enables child and parents to prepare practically for the future. Allows child to take informed choices. Avoids problem of 'family secrets'. Child doesn't miss opportunity for testing. Relieves child's anxiety about future. Relieves parental anxiety.	Child's self-esteem and long-term adjustment may be impaired. Family's perception and treatment of child may be adversely affected. May lead to discrimination from others. May adversely affect marriage opportunities. May not have wanted to be tested if asked when older. May generate unwarranted anxiety before possible early signs.
Those without a faulty gene	Emotional relief. Able to plan life. Avoids adverse effects of later disclosure. Avoids pre-selection of the 'sick' individual inheriting the gene. Relieves anxiety about possible early signs.	Rejection by family for being unaffected. False reassurance about health status.

This is then followed by further anxiety provoking investigation that will include clinical examination and possibly surgery. Predictive genetic testing can be applied to children. This has a variety of implications that have yet to be researched. Michie and Marteau (1996) summarized the possible advantages and disadvantages (Table 18.4).

Some ethical issues

The prospect of widespread genetic screening has provoked sustained debate about the ethical issues. There is a concern that the needs of individuals and families are being made subservient to broader eugenic goals. The advocates of genetic screening often claim that their programmes are based on the public's right to know. Yet there is little evidence that the public wants to know. Genetic screening raises a number of other issues such as the ability of lay people to interpret genetic information, the competence of health personnel in explaining aspects of genetic screening and the use made of genetic information. Future programme development needs to consider these and other ethical issues.

In a review of the social impact and ethical implications of genetic testing, Davison et al. (1994) identified three areas of popular perception that have implications for predictive testing for Huntington's disease:

1 Both positive and negative results can lead to personal and family anguish. While the former is expected there is also evidence that those who are cleared suffer from survivor guilt and a feeling they do not belong to their family.
2 Some families who inherit the gene have developed ways of deciding who in the family will be sufferers. This lay procedure is undermined by medical investigation.
3 Knowing about possible futures may decrease the quality of a person's life. They note that this finding 'is not easily accommodated within the essentially rationalist or utilitarian philosophy underlying the idea of screening' (1984: 354).

One particular aspect of remaining ignorant is that it allows the maintenance of hope. Many lay people are happy to tolerate uncertainty because of the hope that they will survive.

The premise of much genetic testing is that people understand the basic principles of inheritance. However, there is evidence that this is not always the case. In a qualitative study of people at risk of familial adenomatous polyposis (FAP), which geneticists consider almost 100% hereditary, many participants referred to what they considered to be the vital role of the environment. Many of the family members also minimized the threat posed by the disease. While advising these people that they are at risk may be formally correct, it has immense implications for the future quality of their lives.

Conclusions About Disease Prevention

The development of immunization and screening programmes designed to prevent the onset of specific diseases is premised within a medical model of disease causation and control. Despite such limitations they still offer the promise of contributing to the health of society. However, in their design specific attention must be given to the human side of these interventions. Eardley et al. (1985: 960) concluded their review of the reluctance of women to participate in cervical screening with the comment: 'When a programme of screening fails to take account of women's needs, expects women to take the initiative in making an appointment, and is organized in a way to suit the convenience of the provider rather than the user, then it is less likely that women will make use of the service.' Such comments are supported by the evidence on the difficulties of implementing disease prevention services.

Future Research

1 There are secular trends in immunization rates that are connected to media reports of adverse effects. There is a need further to understand how lay people interpret these reports.
2 Focus of research into non-immunization tends to focus on the individual and/or family to the neglect of the broader social context. Future research needs to consider both social and psychological factors.

3 Participation in cancer screening is related to age, social and ethnic factors. While there has been much quantitative research, there is a need for more qualitative research into the meaning of cancer and cancer screening within certain sub-groups.
4 Cancer screening programmes are usually medically defined and controlled. There is a need to explore more participatory forms of screening that women themselves can manage.
5 There is limited research on men's health in general and specifically on men's screening practices. Such research needs to connect an understanding of men's health within the broader study of men's social identity.
6 Genetic research premises a host of social, psychological and ethical issues. There is a need for an expanded programme of research to investigate both professional and public perceptions of genetic screening and the impact on different populations.

Summary

1 Participation in immunization programmes is related to the social character of children's families.
2 The health professional plays a central role in deciding whether parents have their children immunized.
3 Parents have a range of fears and anxieties about immunization.
4 Many countries have implemented screening programmes for breast and cervical cancer.
5 Besides organizational details, the health professional, especially the family doctor, is central to explaining participation in these programmes.
6 Women have a variety of beliefs and fears about these programmes.
7 Men have particular fears and concerns about disease prevention programmes.
8 The so-called genetic revolution has many implications for screening.
9 Both the general public and people who are at risk of certain diseases have a variety of concerns about genetic screening.

 ## Key Terms

deficit model	mammography
false positive	pap test
immunization	screening

19 Work and Health

Anna Kenyon

No other technique for the conduct of life attaches the individual so firmly to reality as laying emphasis on work; for his work at least gives him a secure place in a portion of reality, in the human community. (Sigmund Freud, 1961: 27)

Outline

This chapter reviews the extent to which work experience can impact upon the health of employees, and examines the implications of this impact. We draw upon the key theories and the research findings that support or refute these theories. The key factors that appear to contribute to employee satisfaction and well-being are highlighted, along with workplace characteristics that may be detrimental to employee health, well-being and satisfaction. Reference is made to occupational stress, with suggested interventions to reduce high levels of workplace stress. The impacts of redundancy and unemployment are discussed, as are health behaviours relevant to the workplace such as alcohol consumption and exercise. Finally, we consider anticipated changes in the workplace over coming years, and how such changes are likely to impact upon employees' health.

Health and Work

The impact of working life on health has received increasing attention over recent years, with governmental bodies, employers, unions, occupational health experts and employees becoming increasingly aware of the consequences of a working environment that does not support good health. The sources of potentially detrimental workplace characteristics are varied. For example, recent literature has documented the adverse consequences associated with high levels of occupational stress, excessive role demands, low levels of role control, and insufficient social support upon employee health (Head et al., 2002). Research has also explored the relationship between health behaviours and work experience, such as alcohol consumption (Head et al., 2002) and exercise and tobacco use (Johansson et al., 1991). In addition to these elements, there have been attempts to establish the key features that contribute to a healthy working environment, and it has been suggested that the workplace may also provide an effective setting for interventions designed to improve health and reduce health inequalities (Department of Health, 1999).

A variety of working environments and roles have been assessed and analysed with the intention of clarifying optimal employment criteria, whether this be with the aim of raising productivity and workplace satisfaction, reducing absence and staff turnover, or to safeguard the health of employees.

Demographics and Characteristics of the Workforce

In 2004, the UK workforce comprised of 12,338,000 women and 14,230,000 men. This represents 67% of women and 79% of men that are in employment (ONS, 2004). Of the economically active (i.e. individuals that are over 16 years of age and are either in employment or seeking employment) 10% were unemployed. There would appear to be a clear distinction between the working patterns of women and men in the UK, with 44% of women working part-time, compared with only 10% of men. So too are the roles of men and women distinct, with the majority of administrative and secretarial roles (80%) and personal service jobs (84%) occupied by women; while men dominate the skilled trades (92%), and the process, plant and machine operative roles (85%) (Equal Opportunities Commission, 2004).

With regard to positions of authority, men still dominate the upper stratum within the UK. Only 18% of MPs are women (House of Commons, 2004), and managerial and senior official posts are predominantly occupied by men (2,656,000 men compared with 1,277,000 women). In 2003, the average earnings of men and women within the UK reveal a 25% pay difference, with weekly earnings for women working full-time averaging £396.00, compared with £525.00 for men. A discrepancy is also apparent between white employees and employees from ethnic minorities with regard to both unemployment rates and earning levels. Whites experience lower levels of unemployment (Carmichael and Woods, 2000) and higher average weekly earnings (Berthoud, 2000).

The picture across Europe is not dissimilar, although differences clearly exist among the different countries within Europe. In 2004, Europe underwent expansion, with ten additional countries becoming full members of the European Union (EU). Prior to expansion, the EU comprised 15 countries (EU15). The transition for the countries joining the EU has presented distinct challenges for the different countries, based upon the existing economy, culture and health characteristics of each country. It is therefore difficult to refer to 'Europe' as a single entity because significant differences exist between the EU15 and the ten accession countries. In 2002 the overall employment rate across the EU15 was 64.3% (European Commission, 2002). This research revealed marked changes in the growth across different sectors, with expansion occurring within industrial and service sectors and depletion of employment apparent within agricultural sectors. The average unemployment rate across the EU15 countries in 2003 was 8%. The gender difference in unemployment rates across the EU15 is 1.6%, with women experiencing higher levels of unemployment than men (Bishop, 2004). Earning inequality is not

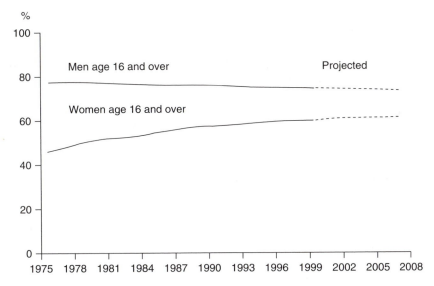

Figure 19.1   Labor force participation rates, 1975–2008
(Source: US Department of Labor, 2005)

confined to the UK, and European women earn approximately 25% less than European men (European Commission, 2000). The European average weekly working hours in 2002 were 40.0 hours per week, ranging from 43.3 hours in the UK to 37.7 hours in France. Thus people in the UK are working longer hours than their continental counterparts. In the United States, average weekly working hours in 2002 were 42.8 hours. The precise impact of such discrepancies in working hours upon productivity is a moot point. Certainly the health outcomes are unlikely to be beneficial.

The US Department of Labor (2005) report that about 60 percent of all women are in the US labour force compared with nearly 75 percent of all men (see Figure 19.1). The participation rate is the share of the population 16 years and older, working or seeking work. In 2005 women accounted for 47 percent of the labour force, up from 40 percent in 1975. The Department states that the long-term increase in the female labour force mainly reflects the greater frequency of paid work among mothers. In contrast, slow long-term decline in work activity among men reflects the trend to earlier retirement. Among married-couple families where both the wife and the husband work, about one-fifth of the wives earn more than their hubands.

The US Department of Labor (2005) also reports that among married couples, the combined weekly working hours of husbands and wives are rising. In 1969, couples aged 25–54 worked an average of 56 hours a week. By 2000, this had increased to 67 hours. Average combined hours have increased by almost 20 percent over the past 3 decades for both groups. The increase mostly reflects the fact that more and more women are working, with those who work increasingly likely to be employed year round.

There are clear differences apparent between the USA, Europe and Japan with regard to annual leave allowance. Europe fares well, with an average of 25.9 days of paid annual leave allowance. This is in contrast to 18.1 days in Japan. However, many employees in Japan do not take the full allowance offered, and although the allowance has undergone slight increases over the past decade, the take-up rate has decreased over this period. In 2002, only 48.4% of annual leave was taken in Japan (8.8 days). No such patterns in holiday use are apparent in Europe or the USA. In the USA, annual leave is accumulated according to service and ranges from 9.6 days for one year's service to 20.3 days for 20 years service (European Foundation, 2002).

In 2004, employment in the USA was 62.3%, with unemployment at 5.6%. The percentage for employed men was 69.2%, but somewhat lower for women at 55.9%. Women's earnings were approximately 76.5% that of men's. Ethnic differences reveal employment rates of 63.5% for white employees, 57.3% for black or African-American, and 62.2% among the Asian population (US Census Bureau of Labor Statistics, 2004).

With the advances in communication systems and the technological developments within the workplace, flexible working practices are increasingly apparent. Remote or 'teleworking' is an area that is likely to increase in prominence over future years. This is in part due to the necessity to accommodate an increasingly diverse workforce. For example, women are increasingly returning to work following starting a family, presenting a need for flexible working patterns to accommodate childcare responsibilities. Remote working enables employees to be productive when away from the usual work location. The European Commission estimates there to be 4.5 million teleworkers employed within the EU, and 10 million teleworkers in total. Across Europe, part-time workers constitute 18% of the overall workforce, and employees on fixed-term contracts constitute 13.4%, demonstrating a fairly high proportion of flexible working arrangements. In the UK, part-time employees constitute 24.8% of the workforce, and fixed-term contracts constitute 6.7% (European Foundation, 2002).

Health and Well-Being within the Workplace

KT

Job satisfaction and contentment within the workplace have consistently been linked with improved health (Karasek and Theorell, 1990; Stokols, 1992; Warr, 1994). There is much research to suggest that satisfied and healthy employees are likely to be more productive than less satisfied and less healthy counterparts. It is therefore in the interest of employers to ensure that the working environment is one in which employee satisfaction and health are optimized. The barriers to a satisfying and healthy environment may relate to the role or to individual reactions to certain elements of the working environment. Although there is unlikely to be one 'ideal' workplace that will suit all individuals, there are certain common elements that would appear to suit the majority.

KT

Jahoda (1982) suggested that employment provides both **manifest benefits** (e.g. benefits associated with income) and **latent benefits** (e.g. benefits associated with meeting psychological needs). Jahoda identified five latent benefits of employment: time structure, social contact, common goals, status and activity. Research has largely supported the idea that such latent benefits are associated with well-being (Evans and Haworth, 1991). In attempting to assess the respective impact of the various latent benefits identified, Jahoda argued the most important latent benefit to be that of structured time. A lack of purpose and lack of time structure has been found to be associated with higher psychological distress and depression, and lower self-esteem (Evans and Haworth, 1991).

Research on work and health can generally be classified according to three broad categories. Each area has examined the impact of three distinct factors in relation to employee health:

1 *Physical* aspects of the working environment.
2 *Sociological* considerations defined by objective measures (e.g. shift work or weekly working hours) and *social* aspects (e.g. social status, economic security/adequacy).
3 *Psychological* (e.g. perceived control and decision latitude) and *psychosocial* aspects (e.g. relationships with colleagues/line manager, integration within the workplace).

The majority of research has been within the above categories, with relatively little cross-over between the disciplines. A more multidisciplinary approach would be helpful. Although past research has tended to focus primarily upon physical working conditions, more recent research has looked at psychosocial factors and the impact of such factors upon health (Health and Safety Executive, 1998). Psychosocial factors have been associated with alcohol dependence, self-reported physical functioning, sickness absence and mental health (Stansfeld et al., 2000).

Role Demand and Control: A Theoretical Starting Point

Perhaps one of the most influential theories within the research examining the relationship between work and health is that proposed by Karasek (1979). Karasek's **job strain or demand–control model** suggested that role demand and control were two key elements that will interact to determine an employee's well-being, with a highly demanding role having a detrimental impact upon health only when accompanied by low control. Indeed, high demand and low control were believed to be the least favoured combination with regard to health outcomes. Other combinations of these variables were not thought to be detrimental or otherwise to an individual's health, although each had a specified outcome. Low demand and high control were believed to result in a low-strain job; low demand coupled with low control was suggested to represent a passive job; and high demand coupled with high control was thought to manifest in an active job.

The aspects deemed to influence the degree of role demand included criteria such as the necessity to work at a fast pace or very intensively, or working with conflicting demands that are difficult to combine. Control is also referred to as decision latitude, which in turn has two key components: decision authority and skill discretion. Decision authority is gauged by the degree to which an employee can decide the methods, pace and order in which they conduct their role, the capacity to decide when to break and who to work with, and having involvement in decisions that impact upon their work. Skill discretion assesses the extent to which an individual finds the role interesting, the

KT

scope to learn new skills, having a variety of tasks to conduct and utilizing a broad range of skills at an appropriate level of expertise. The demand–control model was subsequently extended to incorporate the concepts of physical exertion, job insecurity, and social support from supervisors and colleagues (Karasek and Theorell, 1990).

The interaction between high role demands and low control has been found to have deleterious effects upon mental health (Mausner-Dorsch and Eaton, 2000), immune functioning (Meijman et al., 1995), and has been found to increase incidence of coronary heart disease (Sacker et al., 2001). Despite the significant support for Karasek's suggested interaction between demand and control, there is also a substantial body of research that has failed to establish the hypothesized interaction between these two variables (Friedman et al., 2001). Indeed, adverse health effects have been independently associated with both job demands and decision latitude (Stansfeld et al., 2000). High job demands have been linked to increased incidence of coronary heart disease (CHD) under conditions of both high and low decision latitude, even when health behaviours and conventional risk factors are controlled for. High job demands have also been independently associated with poor mental health and obesity (Head et al., 2002). There would appear to be a U-shaped relationship between role demands and the subsequent degree of strain experienced, with both excessively low demands and excessively high demands manifesting in high levels of strain (French et al., 1982). (See Figure 19.2.)

Equally, low control/decision latitude has been found to influence health outcomes when analysed independently from role demands. For example, although low decision latitude was not found to be associated with diabetes, fatal CHD or non-fatal myocardial infarction (MI), it was found to be linked with increased incidence of angina, obesity, alcohol dependence, poor mental health, and increased sickness absence (Head et al., 2002). Low control has fairly consistently been associated with job-related strain (O'Driscoll and Cooper, 1996).

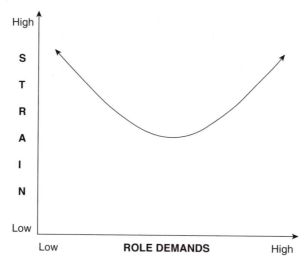

Figure 19.2   The relationship between role demands and strain (French et al., 1982)

Foundations for Health at Work

In recognition of the tendency of research to confine itself to the discipline within which it operates, Warr (1994) attempted to identify a set of core multidisciplinary workplace characteristics that he believed to be central to employee health and well-being. These are listed in Box 19.1, and provide a broad synopsis of the key areas pertinent to the study of work and health. Clearly some of these criteria reflect the elements incorporated within Karasek's demand–control model; however, there are additional elements that contribute to greater depth, and arguably, to greater applicability.

BOX 19.1

'ENVIRONMENTAL FOUNDATIONS' OF HEALTH AT WORK (WARR, 1994)

- Opportunity for control
- Opportunity for skill use
- Externally generated goals
- Variety
- Environmental clarity
- Availability of money
- Physical security
- Opportunity for interpersonal contact
- Valued social position

The research examining the influence of Warr's **environmental foundations** upon employee well-being is fairly extensive. A brief overview will be provided to place these elements within an empirical context, incorporating other relevant considerations where appropriate. The areas discussed will be broadly based around, although not restricted to, the environmental foundations identified by Warr. As the variables impacting upon work experience are unlikely to operate in isolation, there will be significant cross-over of the areas discussed.

`KT`

Opportunity for control/decision latitude

There is increasing agreement that appropriate levels of control over the environment are important to the well-being and physical health of employees, irrespective of **role demand** (Jones and Fletcher, 1996). However, there has been criticism of Karasek's conceptualization of decision latitude, with suggestion that some of the elements measured are in fact more closely related to job opportunity and scope rather than control. For example, experiencing variety and learning new skills could arguably reveal little of the decision latitude within a role, but rather be a reflection of the breadth of role requirements and the opportunity for development. This led Wall et al. (1996) to formulate a more focused measure of control. Interestingly, it was found that with clearly defined role demands and a tighter measure of control, the interaction between the two variables, as predicted by Karasek, was in fact increased, albeit to

`KT`

a fairly moderate degree. This finding demonstrates the importance of conceptual definitions upon research findings, and highlights the need for clarity in the concepts and measures utilized.

Despite definition disparities, there remains strong support for the supposition that high control and decision latitude is the favourable working condition. However, it has also been suggested that control may operate in a similar way to strain, insofar as too little control may be detrimental, as may too much control, with an optimal level of control somewhere in between (see Figure 19.3). This idea was proposed by Warr (1987) in his 'Vitamin Model' of stress. An optimal degree of control was believed to enable a person to make appropriate adjustments in order to moderate the strain imposed upon them, whereas either too little or too much control would not serve this function. Too little control would possibly not permit the individual to make the necessary adjustments; too much control may place greater responsibility for the outcome upon the individual, manifesting in greater strain (Spector, 1998).

Opportunity for skill use

Skill use or utilization has been defined as the extent to which employees perceive that their job provides the opportunity for skill use and skill development (Morrison et al., 1999). Skill utilization at work has been strongly associated with job satisfaction (Morrison et al., 1999). If then, as much of the research suggests, job satisfaction contributes to employee well-being and health, it is possible to see how skill utilization may impact upon employee health, be this directly, or indirectly through job satisfaction. Aptly illustrating the cross-over among the concepts discussed, much of the research that has examined the methods in which skill use and skill efficacy may be optimized have implicated role demand and control as key determinants. Despite this, much of the research has examined demand and control independently of skill utilization and efficacy. Skill use and efficacy can be regarded as an outcome measure of learning, and therefore attempts to increase employee effectiveness by ensuring optimal learning conditions also ensure effective skill utilization and efficacy. Strain resulting from excessive role demands has also been found to hinder learning, and hence also skill utilization and efficacy as outcome measures. Attending to the demand–control workplace conditions may therefore ensure that employees develop skills at an optimal rate.

Two key dimensions of strain are depression and anxiety (O'Driscoll and Cooper, 1996), both of which have been found to impede skill acquisition and skill use. Depression has been associated with reduced motivation to overcome challenges and with the avoidance of challenges (Frese and Stewart, 1984), and reduced self-efficacy (Bandura, 1997). Anxiety has been found to inhibit understanding and experimentation with new ideas (Warr and Downing, 2000) and skill acquisition (Colquitt et al., 2000). Such findings suggest a clear negative impact of both depression and anxiety upon the performance of employees within the workplace. However, Eysenck and Calvo (1992) suggested that anxiety might serve to either increase or decrease employee productivity, depending upon the response of the individual. High levels of anxiety may drain the cognitive resources available to the individual, resulting in a reduction in working memory resources, and a subsequent reduction in productivity. Alternatively, anxiety may prompt an increase in cognitive arousal, and therefore play a motivational role that serves to raise productivity. Clearly the individual response may be determined in part by the duration and/or complexity of the task undertaken. This theory works on the assumption that employees have a limited pool of cognitive resources from which they may draw, a viewpoint that not all theorists have shared.

It would appear that through employers' consideration of the psychological health and well-being of employees (e.g. by ensuring an appropriate balance of demand and control), the rate at which new skills are learnt will be improved, manifesting in higher skill utilization and efficacy. In turn, this is likely to result in higher job satisfaction, which in itself will contribute to a more productive and healthy employee.

Role criteria: clarity, goals and reward

Although role overload has been identified as the major contributor with regard to role strain, role ambiguity and conflicting role demands also appear to manifest in elevated ratings of role strain (O'Driscoll and Beehr, 1994). **Role ambiguity** refers to a lack of available information necessary to conduct the role. Unpredictable consequences of one's role performance and information deficiency regarding expected role behaviours serve as the typical measures for role ambiguity. In order to reduce role ambiguity, and therefore also moderate the negative impact associated with it, the effective communication of role expectations and requirements is paramount. Clarity in role boundaries, working procedures and practice, and the expected time frame and outcome of task completion may all help to avoid role ambiguity.

Kanfer and Ackerman (1989) suggest that the varied tasks that an individual is required to undertake places a 'drain' upon the cognitive resources available, according to whether the demands are on-task, off-task or self-regulatory activities. On-task activities relate to any behaviour directly involved in the work task, such as production, quality and conduct of work-related communications. Off-task activities relate to additional behaviours that do not directly contribute to the work-task, such as chatting with colleagues or planning leisure activities. Self-regulatory activities involve monitoring the environment, such as attending to physical comfort, emotional well-being, or circumstantial consistency. Kanfer and Ackerman suggest that when self-regulatory activities can be disengaged, for example when the physical environment is comfortable, and there is an absence of emotional disturbance or threat to circumstantial consistency, then more cognitive resources can be allocated to on-task activities directly related to productivity. Once again, a parallel can be drawn to Warr's environmental foundations, in which physical security was highlighted as an important component of occupational health, as was the availability of money, thereby alleviating concerns of financial security. By minimizing sources of work-related anxiety, productivity of employees may also therefore be optimized.

Although within most roles a degree of prioritization will be necessary, it is helpful to ensure that the demands placed upon the individual do not manifest in high levels of conflict. Role conflict may be defined as the incompatible demands that are placed upon an individual and has been classified as four distinct forms:

1 *Intrasender*: the communication of mutually incompatible expectations from one supervisor/manager/client.

2 *Intersender*: the communication of mutually incompatible expectations from two or more people.

3 *Person–role conflict*: an individual's perception of conflict between own expectations/ values and those of the organization/managers/colleagues.

4 *Inter-role conflict*: occupation of two or more roles that have conflicting priorities and requirements. (Quick and Quick, 1984)

KT

Role conflict has been found to impede successful goal attainment (Cantor and Blanton, 1996) and there would appear to be a clear relationship between goal progress/ attainment and psychological well-being. Goal attainment can be regarded as one of the 'rewards' received in return for the efforts expended in the role, for although the achievement of an isolated task may not inflate an employee's wage at the end of the working week, the sense of satisfaction and accomplishment may nevertheless be a rewarding element of the role. Through improved understanding among employers regarding the significance of role accomplishment and through greater recognition of the need to ensure low levels of role conflict, organizational strategies may be developed and implemented to manipulate these workplace characteristics appropriately (e.g. through considered role design and effective paths of communication). Such strategies are likely to ensure that employees are satisfied and adequately rewarded in their work, and therefore assist the staff retention and productivity within an organization.

KT

The perception of reward is an important consideration, whether this relates to earnings, role satisfaction or career progression. The **equity theory** (Adams, 1965; Mowday, 1996) suggests that there is a tendency among employees to balance the input of a situation with the outcome of a situation. Input in this context may refer to effort expended, skills utilized or time invested; output may refer to financial reward, promotion, job satisfaction or job security. According to this theory, tension results when an individual perceives there to be an imbalance between the input and the output of a situation.

Equity theory received partial empirical support from a study conducted by Probst (2002). This research consisted of a simulated working environment, whereby students were required to produce paintings over a specific period of time while adhering to certain safety procedures. There was the potential for financial gain in return for high levels of productivity, and an experimental group was threatened with exclusion from the study should productivity be inadequate, thereby also foregoing the potential for financial gain. The experimental group was attempting to simulate employees threatened with redundancy. Overall, higher levels of productivity resulted in compromised quality of work and reduced adherence to safety procedures. Participants threatened with exclusion were found to have higher levels of productivity, but produced work of poorer quality and were more likely to violate the safety procedures than their secure counterparts.

This study does indicate that imbalances in input and output may lead to compromised work quality. However, the theory is less consistent with regard to productivity, which appears to increase despite the low output apparent in the simulated threatened redundancy. Probst maintains that the results are consistent with the notion that an individual's cognitive resource pool is finite, and in this example productivity, quality of work and safety adherence compete for employee resources.

It is necessary to question the extent to which a simulated working environment accurately reflects the workplace and work experience. Students participating in a two-hour study are unlikely to experience the same pressures that are faced within the workplace. Threat of exclusion from the study is unlikely to be comparable to the threat of redundancy, with the subsequent changes in income and security that may result from losing regular employment. Research relying upon simulated conditions in this way may help to direct subsequent research. However extreme caution should be taken prior to applying the findings within a work setting.

Workplace social support

Social support has received a great deal of attention within the literature. It has been suggested that high levels of social support within the workplace contribute to enhanced physical health (Niedhammer and Chea, 2003) and higher ratings of job satisfaction (De Jonge et al., 2001). Workplace social support has also been found to moderate the negative impact of occupational stress upon health outcomes (Frese, 1999). The effects of workplace support may also extend beyond the parameters of the workplace. In a study assessing the impact of workplace social support upon heart rate, an inverse relationship was found to exist, with low support correlating with measures of elevated heart rate. The effects spanned a 24-hour period, encompassing work time, leisure time and sleep (Unden et al., 1991). This relationship was apparent among both men and women, across a range of occupational groups, and was independent of physical strain.

More recent research has been consistent with these findings. Evans and Steptoe (2001) conducted a study in which the impact of workplace social support upon heart rate was examined. The study took place over a period involving three work days and two leisure days. A clear relationship was apparent on work days, with low levels of workplace social support associated with elevated heart rate during both the day time and evening of work days. The effect was not apparent for leisure days, highlighting the value and potential health-benefits associated with full day breaks from work.

Some research has indicated the possibility of gender differences in responses to workplace social support. For example, social support has been negatively associated with burnout in women, but not in men (Greenglass and Burke, 1988). Greenglass and Burke suggest that such a gender distinction may reflect the tendency of women to utilize social support more effectively than men due to the congruence between traditional female gender roles and requesting help, and the incongruence between traditional male gender roles and requesting help.

The influence of workplace social support is by no means straightforward, with significant disparity apparent in the research that has attempted to establish the effects of workplace social support, and the processes by which workplace social support may exert an influence. Some studies have found no such moderating effect of workplace social support upon the health outcomes of role strain. Beehr et al. (2003) suggest that such inconsistencies may be due to the methods used to study social support and the context in which it is studied. Indeed this is a recurring difficulty within the field of occupational health, with objective measures being somewhat elusive for certain areas under study. For example, methods assessing the level of workplace social support have largely relied upon subjective self-reports. It is highly plausible that individuals rating the support received from their management will be dependent upon the quality of the relationship between the individuals involved, which in turn may be heavily influenced by the performance and competency of the employee (i.e. the manager may show more positive support to an employee performing well compared with an employee that is underperforming). In continuation of this example, the competent employee enjoying a positive relationship with his or her manager may experience lower levels of occupational stress than the comparative employee struggling to perform, and a moderating effect of social support may therefore be deduced. This example demonstrates the various factors that may contribute to a self-rated evaluation of workplace social support, and illustrates how subjective measures may create inconsistencies within the research.

Career progression and opportunity

The opportunity for career progression is also likely to have bearing upon individual well-being. It is an aspect likely to be accompanied by other variables identified in Warr's environmental foundations, such as increased financial reward, a more valued social position, and greater control and autonomy. A perceived lack of promotion opportunity and lack of career progression has been identified as a primary source of job dissatisfaction (Rabinowitz et al., 1983).

In addition to the opportunity for career progression, the degree of role stability may also be an important element, again broadly linking to Warr's environmental foundations. For example, role stability may be accompanied by availability of money through continued stable employment, opportunity for interpersonal contact with colleagues with whom relationships have been established, and the opportunity for control in terms of making one's own decisions regarding the continuation of employment with a particular employer. The insecurity associated with an unstable position has indeed been found to be a risk factor for mental and physical health and psychosocial well-being (Isaksson et al., 2000). This is likely to be a key consideration as working practices evolve over coming years, as one consequence of the flexibility introduced in response to the post-industrial workforce is the emergence of roles that do not conform to the traditional patterns of permanent employment. For in addition to the benefits associated with flexible working contracts is the less favourable consequence of role instability.

The remainder of this chapter focuses upon specific areas of occupational health, each of which will incorporate to a greater or lesser degree some of the workplace characteristics discussed above.

Key Topics in Occupational Health Psychology

Occupational stress and interventions to reduce it

The definition of stress has been an area of substantial debate. Stress has been defined as an independent variable, a dependent variable and as a process. It has been examined from medical, behavioural and social science perspectives, each of which will conceptualize stress according to the understanding pertaining to the respective discipline. The ambiguity of the term 'stress' means that it can be equally used to define a stimulus (e.g. a stressful situation), a response (e.g. a behavioural reaction), or an interaction between the two. Contemporary views point to a relational definition of stress, with the idea that stress is the result of a transaction between the environment and the individual. The transactional viewpoint acknowledges the processes involved in the experience of stress, with 'stress' neither residing solely within the environment or within the individual, but rather emerging as a result of the relationship between the two. Despite the inconsistencies in definition, stress is a term frequently used to describe individual feelings and reactions to events or demanding situations. Chapter 13 provides a more detailed discussion of theories of stress. This section will refer specifically to stress within the workplace.

The prevalence of workplace stress within the United Kingdom is believed to result in an average of thirteen-and-a-half lost working days each year, with one in five employees believing their job to be very or extremely stressful (Smith et al., 2000). Recent media reports in the UK have documented Health and Safety Executive recommendations advising employers to treat mental strain as seriously as physical injuries. Depression and anxiety are the most frequent stress-related complaints presented to general practitioners, and are estimated to affect one in six of the American working population, and approximately 20% of the working population in the UK (Quick et al., 2001). Stress is the second highest cause of absenteeism among non-manual staff (CBI/PPP, 2000).

Two influential theoretical frameworks that have attempted to conceptualize the relationship between work and health are the demand–control model (Karasek, 1979) and the person–environment fit framework (Edwards and Cooper, 1990). The demand–control model has already been discussed above with the suggestion that stress is the result of high role demands coupled with low control. The latter model purports that stress is a result of the poor 'fit' or compatibility of the person (e.g. values, ability) and the environment (e.g. demands, role criteria, working environment). Consistent with equity theory (Adams, 1965; Mowday, 1996) in which it is suggested employees balance their input (e.g. effort) with their output (e.g. reward), stress within the workplace has also been conceptualized in terms of an imbalance between the rewards attained from the role and the effort expended in conducting the role.

Workplace stress management intervention programmes have varied widely, with the objectives, strategies and occupational group often warranting an individually tailored intervention. There are key areas that have tended to form the basis of such interventions and strategies:

- *Appropriate selection and placement of staff*: this is likely to ensure that recruited employees are able to meet the role demands. By providing a realistic job outline at selection stage, reasonable expectations may be encouraged on the part of the employee and may assist the transition into the new working environment.
- *Job redesign*: this may be necessary to incorporate adequate control/decision latitude and ensure a manageable workload. Tasks should ideally have some significance to employees while providing adequate stimulation and opportunity for skill use. Any areas of role ambiguity or role conflict should be addressed.

- *Communication*: high quality communication will reduce uncertainty among employees, particularly important during times of organizational change.
- *Training programmes*: effective training in working methods and schedules may reduce strain through enhanced competency.
- *Environmental risk assessment*: a risk assessment enables employers to identify any potentially hazardous environmental threats, thereby preventing such threats manifesting in additional strain upon employees.

Much of the research on health at work points to the detrimental impact of high levels of stress, manifesting in decreased job satisfaction (Fox et al., 1993), poor mental health (Mausner-Dorsch and Eaton, 2000) and compromised immune function (Meijman et al., 1995). However, some research has suggested that there may be positive outcomes following a stressful period (Holahan and Moos, 1994), such as the development of new coping skills, enhanced personal resources (e.g. self-reliance and empathy), and enhanced social resources (e.g. through utilizing the available social support network). It is likely that individual perception and assessment of a stressful situation will influence the response. The way in which a stressful event is perceived may determine whether it serves a positive function, perhaps by prompting individual development and resource utilization, or whether it results in a negative outcome, perhaps resulting in negative affect. It has been suggested that the differences in response may be due to dispositional factors. For example, a hardy personality has been linked with a reduced tendency to exhibit physical symptomatology in response to high levels of stress. This is believed to be due to the interpretation of the stressful event as a challenge that may be mastered and overcome (Kobasa, 1979).

There is still relatively little known about how individuals cope with occupational stress. There are two broad categories of coping strategies within the workplace: (1) problem focused (i.e. attempting to deal with the demands of the situation; and (2) emotion focused (i.e. attempting to deal with the emotional disturbance resulting from those demands) (Lazarus and Folkman, 1984). The past decade has seen the emergence of various coping questionnaires designed specifically for the workplace, and these have been used to assess the prevalence of certain strategies and their efficacy in alleviating stress. However, there is as yet no consensus as to how best to measure coping, and indeed many measures have been developed that have little basis in theory and lack consensus for a standardized set of measures.

Antisocial behaviour in the workplace

Antisocial behaviour in the workplace can be highly detrimental to an organization. Between 1992 and 1996 there were over 2 million violent incidents documented within the workplace in the United States. This involved 1.5 million assaults, 396,000 aggravated assaults, 84,000 robberies, and 51,000 rapes and sexual assaults (Warchol, 1998). Such incidents result in costs to both the employer and the employee. It has been estimated that between 1987 to 1992, workplace aggression within the USA resulted in over 500,000 employees missing 1.7 million work days, with over $55 million in lost wages (Bachman, 1994). Workplace harassment, verbal abuse and aggressive workplace behaviour have been associated with reduced job satisfaction and heightened turnover intentions (Donovan et al., 1998) and poorer psychological well-being (Einarsen and Raknes, 1997).

Unemployment and redundancy

The then editor of the *British Medical Journal*, Richard Smith, stated:

> Unemployment raises the chance that a man will die in the next decade by about a third, and for those in middle age – with the biggest commitments – the chance doubles. (Smith, 1992: 972)

With the substantial volume of literature highlighting workplace characteristics that are potentially detrimental to health, it is easy to overlook the many health-enhancing qualities that satisfying and rewarding employment may bring. Warr (1987) argues that work provides an opportunity for skill utilization, interpersonal contact, additional financial resources, and gives individuals opportunities for control, all of which are factors believed to contribute to psychological well-being. When these aspects are not available or present within the workplace, or when unemployment results in a loss of these aspects, physical and mental health and psychosocial functioning have been found to deteriorate (Dew et al., 1992).

Despite the relative shortage of research papers exploring the positive benefits of employment, the research that has compared unemployed and employed participants points clearly to the adverse impact of unemployment upon psychological well-being. Unemployment has been found to result in lower self-esteem (Muller et al., 1993), and greater incidence of depression (Feather and O'Brien, 1986). From such research it is possible to tentatively deduce that employment reduces psychological distress, promotes higher self-esteem, and reduces incidence of depression. Clearly these are tentative inferences because it is possible that other elements are in some way confounding the relationship between employment and well-being. Equally, low self-esteem, depression or psychological distress may contribute in some way to unemployment.

Jahoda argued that unemployment produces profound life changes, including a loss of structured time, a loss of valued working relationships, the loss of purpose and meaningful life goals, and a loss of status and identity (Jahoda, 1982). It is therefore possibly unsurprising that depression emerges as the prominent mental health outcome in response to job loss (Dew et al., 1992). Recent research has identified financial strain as the primary element mediating the correlation between unemployment and depression (Vinokur and Schul, 1997). The mental health consequences appear to be more apparent among middle-aged people, rather than the younger or older unemployed, among men and single women, rather than married women, and among long-term unemployed (i.e. over four months) rather than those that experience a short period of unemployment (Bartley, 1994). Physical health also would appear to suffer as a result of unemployment or redundancy. Morris et al. (1994) found a strong causal relationship between unemployment and mortality even when tobacco and alcohol use was controlled for.

Job insecurity has been suggested to have similar consequences to that of actual redundancy and unemployment. Indeed within the stress literature it has been documented that the anticipation of a stressful event can present an equally significant source of anxiety as the actual event (Lazarus and Folkman, 1984). As with other sources of excessive strain, job insecurity has been found to result in a deterioration in well-being (Barling and Kelloway, 1996). Lazarus and Folkman suggest that the uncertainty accompanying job insecurity may contribute significant strain, as until the anticipated redundancy has occurred, the necessary coping strategies will not be implemented. Job insecurity has also been associated with a reduction in job satisfaction, although the findings are somewhat mixed. Aspects that have been found to moderate the negative impact of job insecurity include such factors as social support (Lim, 1996) and perceived control (Barling and Kelloway, 1996).

There is a need for further research to explore the contributory factors leading to job insecurity, the impact of long-term job insecurity, and establish the point at which the negative outcomes manifest during the development of job insecurity. Finally, there remains a clear need for an agreed measure of job insecurity. With the current rate of change across many organizations, and the resulting decline in job security, redundancy and unemployment are topical areas of the modern workplace.

The workplace and alcohol consumption

In addition to the well-documented health and anti-social behavioural outcomes associated with alcohol misuse, heavy alcohol consumption has been associated with poor work performance (Kenyon and Marks, 2005) and absenteeism (Upmark et al., 1999). Alcohol misuse within the UK is estimated to cost employers £6.4 billion annually, a result of increased absenteeism, early retirement and premature deaths associated with alcohol use (Alcohol Concern, 2003). Sixty percent of UK firms have been reported to experience problems due to employee alcohol misuse. Broad (2001) found the primary consequences of alcohol use identified by employers to include absenteeism (identified by 75% of employers), poor performance (identified by 61% of employers), disciplinary procedures (identified by 42% of employers) and permanent loss of staff (identified by 30% of employers).

In the United States alcohol consumption has been estimated to cost businesses $132.4 billion annually as a result of reduced productivity (Harwood, 2000). Over recent years attention has turned to the phenomenon of binge drinking, defined as the consumption of eight or more units of alcohol on a single occasion for men, and six or more units of alcohol on a single occasion for women (ONS, 1999). In particular, alcohol consumption among young women has increased dramatically over recent years, with one contributory factor possibly being the changes in working patterns among women (e.g. the increasing number of women remaining within the workforce longer before starting a family). Twenty-seven percent of women regularly binge drink, an increase of 17% over the past year alone. The percentage of women drinking above safe levels has increased by 70% since 1988 (ONS, 2001).

Much of the research examining the relationship between employment and alcohol consumption has focused upon stress and alcohol use, although the findings do appear to be somewhat mixed. The majority of work within this area has found a positive correlation between stress and alcohol consumption, with higher levels of reported stress indicating more frequent and excessive consumption of alcohol. It is necessary to consider the variables impacting upon drinking behaviour, acknowledging possible variation among different occupational groups, the impact of different sources of stress and of broader constructs of occupational health.

The assumption that alcohol consumption is solely associated with negative outcomes in relation to work and productivity should also be questioned. For although the research strongly supports the assumption that excessive alcohol consumption is associated with negative consequences, moderate alcohol use may help to relieve negative responses to stress, or result in other beneficial outcomes that may in fact facilitate improved productivity. Cappell and Greeley (1987) proposed a **tension reduction hypothesis**, whereby the negative physiological and emotional effects of anxiety may be reduced following the consumption of alcohol. Arguably, where moderate alcohol consumption serves to facilitate relaxation, it could be regarded as a health-enhancing behaviour. Furthermore, where consumption of moderate alcohol involves social interaction, there may be potential benefits similar to those documented within the research examining the relevance of social support upon occupational health and productivity. This may be particularly applicable in cases where there is interaction with colleagues as integration within the workplace, feeling part of the team, enjoying the working environment and socializing with colleagues appear to be aspects relevant to occupational health (Kenyon and Marks, 2005).

Despite the possible benefits associated with moderate alcohol consumption, the overwhelming majority of data suggest that alcohol use is a significant cost to individual health, organizations, and indeed the economic health of countries in which alcohol consumption is highly prevalent. There is a great need for employers to play their role in advocating sensible drinking patterns, perhaps through organization of workplace social events that do not solely consist of drinking alcohol. Changing the drinking culture will be no easy feat. However, the increasing emergence of excessive drinking behaviours points to a very real need for interventions at governmental and organizational levels. Further discussion of the evidence linking alcohol consumption with ill-health can be found in Chapter 7.

Health-promoting behaviours

Research indicates that health-promoting behaviours are influenced by work demands and experiences. It has been suggested that high strain jobs may have an impact upon individuals' willingness or ability to engage in health-enhancing behaviours (Hellerstedt and Jeffery, 1997). Work-related stress has been associated with increased alcohol, tobacco and drug use, inadequate sleep or exercise, and consumption of a poor diet (Cohen and Williamson, 1988). A recent study in which Karasek's job strain model was used as a predictor of exercise found that employees in high strain jobs did significantly less exercise than employees in low strain jobs, despite no disparity in each group's intention to exercise (Payne et al., 2002). The authors concluded that work demands may prevent an individual's implementation of their intentions to engage in health-enhancing behaviour. If a relationship between physical health and productivity is established, as would be expected according to current theoretical understanding, it will be necessary for research to guide working practice in order to facilitate employees' engagement in health-enhancing behaviours.

The changing workforce

Technological developments over recent years have transformed many workplaces. The new working arrangements have been accompanied by increased mobility and flexibility, and have opened opportunities for remote working and 'telework'. Remote working or 'telework' can be broadly defined as working outside of a traditional work-place, and using information technology and telecommunication systems (Johnston and Nolan, 2000). It is generally agreed that remote working has both advantages and disadvantages. The most frequently documented benefits include increased autonomy and flexibility, whereas the negative outcomes may include job insecurity and stagnation of career prospects and difficulties with motivation and self-management (Standen et al., 1999).

The scope for controlling one's workload has been consistently linked with beneficial outcomes upon health and well-being, and remote working methods are likely to score highly in this respect. If, however, as has been suggested by Warr (1987), control operates in a curvilinear fashion, with either excessively low or high levels of control failing to show the benefits associated with moderate levels of control (see Figure 19.3), there could be a danger that some patterns of remote working fall beyond the range in which control is beneficial. There are further psychosocial factors relevant to remote working that may impact upon health. For example, remote workers are likely to have less frequent face-to-face contact with employees, and may receive less overall social support as a result. They may also receive less assistance with particularly demanding tasks, manifesting in longer working hours (Standen et al., 1999). It has been shown that remote workers have greater difficulty in delineating between non-work and work domains (Standen et al., 1999), potentially making it more difficult to relax after a day's work.

Over the coming years it is likely that remote working will become ever more prevalent. The ongoing technological developments and the increasingly global economic market are likely to prompt ongoing changes in working practice. The issues currently facing remote workers need to be researched more fully to ensure that any disadvantages associated with remote working may be addressed. Some of these disadvantages may be relatively easy to overcome. For example, solutions may include training programmes to help remote workers discipline their working methods in order to ensure clear delineation of work and leisure time; the establishment of a remote working team to provide a support network; and consideration of the ongoing training needs and career progression opportunities for remote workers.

It is clear that employment plays a key role upon individual health and well-being. With further knowledge of the precise processes involved in the health–work relationship, and the methods by which occupational hazards may be reduced and occupational benefits may be optimized, the workplace may be designed in a way to better meet the needs of both employers and employees. Employers can no longer afford to neglect their role in promoting healthier employees, and the increased levels of job satisfaction, organizational commitment and motivation are likely to manifest in both reduced staff turnover and absenteeism, and higher levels of employee productivity. In this sense, the message is clear: through attending to the occupational health and well-being of employees, everybody wins.

Future Research

1   Further work needs to be conducted to explore the processes involved in the health–work relationship, including the following:
2   The methods by which occupational hazards may be reduced and occupational benefits optimized.
3   Optimal workplace design to meet the dual needs of employer and employees.
4   The scope for the working environment to impact positively upon health outcomes of employees.
5   The impact of teleworking and other emergent working patterns upon employee occupational health.
6   The processes and nature of coping behaviours relating to workplace stress.
7   Methods by which demand and control may be balanced, and clear criteria by which these variables may be measured.
8   Measurement of key occupational health criteria, and identification of practical strategies to optimize each.

Summary

1   The occupational health and well-being of employees has an impact upon employee satisfaction, productivity, attendance and retention.
2   Role demand, control and workplace social support are critical elements of employee occupational health.
3   Role design (e.g. clarity, reward, skill use) is likely to influence workplace satisfaction and productivity.
4   Warr (1994) compiled a multidisciplinary list of elements that may contribute to occupational health.
5   Occupational stress results in significant absence, with depression and anxiety being the most frequent stress-related complaints.
6   Unemployment has been found to be detrimental to health and well-being, with financial strain, loss of working relationships, status, meaningful life goals and time structure contributing to increased incidence of depression, psychological distress and reduced self-esteem.
7   Alcohol consumption has been associated with increased absenteeism and poor work performance.
8   High strain jobs have been found to impact upon engagement in health-enhancing behaviours.
9   The workforce is becoming increasingly diverse necessitating greater flexibility in working patterns.
10   Technological advances have enabled working methods to become more flexible, with the prevalence of remote working patterns increasing.

Key Terms

environmental foundations

equity theory

job satisfaction

job strain (or demand–control) model

latent benefits

manifest benefits

role ambiguity

role conflict

role demand

tension reduction hypothesis

Health Promotion

It is now quite obvious that for many people their network of friends, neighbours, church relationships, and so on, provide not only support, but genuine niches and opportunities for personal development. (Julian Rappaport, 1981: 19)

Outline

This chapter focuses upon the psychological dimensions of health promotion. Three major health promotion approaches are described: the behaviour change approach, the self-empowerment approach and the 'collective action' or community development approach. Health promotion interventions informed by each approach are described and critically evaluated. Two critiques of the western contemporary 'ideology of health promotion' are presented.

What is Health Promotion?

Health promotion is any event, process or activity that facilitates the protection or improvement of the health status of individuals, groups, communities or populations. The objective is to prolong life and to improve quality of life, that is to prevent or reduce the effects of impaired physical and/or mental health in those individuals who are directly (e.g. patients) or indirectly (e.g. carers) affected. Health promotion includes both *environmental* and *behavioural* **interventions**.

Environmental interventions target the built environment (e.g. fencing around dangerous sites) and involve legislation to safeguard the natural environment (e.g. maximum water pollution targets) as well as the production of goods (e.g. a ban on certain beef products). These measures are not usually influenced by those who are affected by them, although this can happen through collective action such as campaigns, boycotts or elections. They do not necessarily require co-operation from those who benefit from them, and they do not typically involve communication with those targeted by them. This is to say, the effectiveness of environmental measures does not depend upon people's awareness of their existence.

Behavioural interventions are primarily concerned with the consequences of individuals' actions. In recent years, this type of health promotion has focused upon the

KT

KT

KT

concept of **empowerment**. Empowerment is the process by which people increase their control over their physical, social and internal environments. Behavioural interventions include raising awareness and knowledge about health hazards, teaching technical (e.g. how to floss one's teeth; how to use a condom) and social skills (e.g. how to say no to drugs; how to negotiate condom use), as well as cognitive-behavioural techniques (e.g. how to practise progressive muscle relaxation; how to re-focus one's thoughts). All of these measures require the active co-operation of those who benefit from them and the use of persuasive and effective communication. The involvement

KT

of health psychologists is substantial. It includes social skills training, **preventive health behaviour** counselling, cognitive-behaviour therapy, education and advertising. This chapter focuses on behavioural interventions.

KT

It is possible to identify three approaches that can inform health promotion interventions. These three approaches pursue different goals, utilize different means to achieve their goals and propose different criteria for their **evaluation**. However, they all aim to promote good health and to prevent or reduce the effects of ill-health (French and Adams, 1986). These three approaches are considered in turn. [See also Reading 19 in Marks (2002a).]

Behaviour Change Approach

The goal of this approach is to bring about changes in individual behaviour through changes in the individual's cognitions. The approach is based upon the assumption that humans are rational decision-makers and therefore relies heavily upon the provision of information about risks and health hazards through the mass media as well as

KT

leaflets and posters. Information is presented as factual and attributed to an expert source. Here, health promotion is really synonymous with **health education** that aims to increase individuals' knowledge about the causes of health and illness.

As we saw in earlier chapters, psychologists have been developing theories about the relationship between knowledge, attitudes and behaviour for some time, known as social cognition models (SCMs). These have been researched in a wide range of preventive health behaviours such as vaccination uptake, breast self-examination and contraceptive use. SCMs aim to predict the performance of behaviours and, by implication, to provide guidance as to how to facilitate their uptake by manipulating relevant variables (such as beliefs, attitudes and perceptions). It is suggested that there is a close relationship between people's beliefs, attitudes and intentions to act in particular ways. Consequently, by bringing about changes in beliefs it is hoped to bring about changes in behaviour.

For example, consider how the issue of smoking is dealt with by the Health Belief Model (HBM; Becker, 1974). Smokers deciding whether or not to give up smoking would be expected to consider:

- how susceptible they are to lung cancer and other smoking-related conditions;
- how serious these conditions are;
- the extent and value of the benefits of giving up smoking;
- the potential negative consequences of giving up smoking.

In addition, the HBM acknowledges the role of cues to action, internal (e.g. a symptom such as a smoker's cough) and external (e.g. information, advice or meeting someone with lung cancer), as well as health motivation, i.e. the importance of health to the individual.

The HBM has been applied to a wide range of health behaviours. Overall, the HBM is marginally successful in predicting health behaviours (see Janz and Becker, 1984; Sheeran and Abraham, 1995). Each key variable of the HBM tends to be significantly correlated with the behaviour under study. This suggests that the variables identified by the HBM are relevant ingredients and contribute to the process that generates health behaviour. However, the variables of the HBM only *control* a relatively small amount of the *variance* in individuals' health behaviour (around 10% when combined). In other words, our ability to accurately predict health behaviour on the basis of the HBM is severely limited.

The theory of reasoned action (TRA; Fishbein and Ajzen, 1975) and its revised version, the theory of planned behaviour (TPB; Ajzen, 1985, 2002a, 2002b), propose that behaviour is informed by attitudes towards the behaviour as well as subjective norms about the behaviour, that is what significant others think one should do. These variables (and in the case of the TPB an additional variable: perceived control over the behaviour) combine to generate an intention to behave in a particular way, which is then used to predict actual behaviour. Attitudes and subjective norms are based upon beliefs held by the individual. So, for example, a woman's belief that birth control pills are a potential health risk and her belief that her friends and relatives would not approve of her taking such a risk are thought to generate a negative attitude towards taking birth control pills, as well as social pressure not to take them, thus giving rise to the intention to refrain from the use of birth control pills and, hopefully, to consider other forms of contraception.

Implications for health promotion practice

The TRA and TPB have been used to predict numerous health relevant behaviours, including smoking, alcohol consumption, contraceptive use/safer sex, health screening attendance, exercise, food choice, riding a bus instead of using a car, and breast/testicle self-examination (see Ajzen, 1991; Armitage and Conner, 2002; Conner and Sparks, 2005; Fishbein and Ajzen, 2005). Overall, the evidence suggests that TRA and TPB do contribute to our understanding of the antecedents of health relevant behaviours.

Across studies TRA variables control a total of between 43% and 46% of the variance and TPB variables control 50% of the variance in intentions to behave (Conner and Sparks, 2005).

Thus, TRA and TPB variables control around 50% of the variance in people's expressed intentions to behave. However, it is important to bear in mind that the TRA and TPB generally do not predict behaviour but only the intention to behave. Unfortunately, the association between intention to behave and actual behaviour is far from perfect. Sheeran (2002) carried out a meta-analysis of meta-analyses of prospective tests of the intention–behaviour relationship and, across 422 studies with 82,107 participants, found that intentions controlled only 28% of the variance in behaviour. This means that the large majority of 72% of the variance in behaviour remains unaccounted for by a knowledge of people's stated intentions. Either this leaves plenty of scope for theoretical constructs over and above intentions, or the studies are methodologically flawed because a real intention would necessarily translate into an action (Smedslund, 2000).

Conducting a meta-analysis of studies looking at the theory of planned behaviour should provide a better understanding of its efficacy. Armitage and Conner (2002) reviewed 185 TPB studies published up to the end of 1997. They found that the TPB accounted for 27% and 39% of the variance in behaviour and intention, respectively, thus highlighting that currently TPB has limited applied use in changing health behaviours.

Hobbis and Sutton (2005) discuss the idea that because the TPB offers little guidance on how to promote behaviour change it might be fruitful to fuse the techniques of cognitive-behavioural therapy (CBT) with interventions based on TPB. We have already discussed CBT in Chapter 8. CBT aims to enlighten a person about how their beliefs, automatic thoughts and assumptions influence feelings and behaviour. Baranowski (2005) points out that TPB and CBT may be difficult to integrate because CBT is directed at people who are already seeking change while TPB is directed at population groups the majority of whom have not expressed any interest in making changes. Fishbein and Ajzen (2005) also thought that applying CBT methods to people who have no intention to change might encounter resistance. One could add that it would also be unethical. As pointed out by Fishbein and Ajzen (2005), one can consider behaviour change as requiring at least two kinds of intervention: one for changing intentions (TBP) and one for implementing intentions (CBT). Fishbein and Ajzen (2005) argue that many community interventions already do combine multiple techniques drawn from the TPB, the transtheoretical stages of change model (Prochaska and DiClemente, 1983) and CBT.

KT

The crucial significance of **implementation intentions** was described by Gollwitzer (1999). Implementation intentions requires the participant to specify when, where, and how the plan to perform the intended behaviour will be carried out. Sheeran et al. (in press) suggest three processes underlie intention–behaviour discrepancies: intention viability, intention activation and intention elaboration. They describe implementation intentions as 'if–then plans that connect good opportunities to act with cognitive or behavioural activities that will be effective in accomplishing one's goals'. These if–then plans are of the form: 'if situation X occurs, then I will carry out behaviour Y'. Higgins and Conner (2003) carried out a study combining TPB with the strategy of implementing intentions on adolescent smoking. CBT is a perfect example of a technology designed to facilitate implementation intention because its principal aim is to guide the participant to use techniques and skills designed to implement a specific intention to carry out a preventive behaviour, e.g. to quit smoking, reduce drinking, manage anger or use condoms.

There are a growing number of social cognition models being used to predict health-relevant behaviours (Conner and Norman, 2005). Theoretical developments in this area have been pursued in two directions: (1) the development of process or stages models of behaviour change, and (2) extensions of the TPB through incorporating additional variables. Process or stages models attempt to provide a more dynamic understanding of health behaviour. For example, Weinstein (1988) proposes that individuals move through qualitatively different stages that characterize the precaution adoption process. Different variables become instrumental at different stages. Prochaska and DiClemente's (1983, 1992) Transtheoretical Model of Change and Schwarzer's (1999) Health Action

Process Approach also take a more dynamic and process-orientated approach to health behaviour.

Extensions of the TPB have been based on the addition of predictor variables and moderator variables to the theory. While predictor variables broaden the theory by adding further ingredients to it, moderator variables deepen it by taking into account those factors that may affect the direction and/or strength of the relationship between the predictor variables and the outcome measure (see Perugini and Bagozzi, 2001). Predictor variables that have been added to the TPB include moral norms, anticipated feelings and self-identity (Evans and Norman, 2003). Moderator variables used to improve predictive power of the theory include implementation intentions (Orbell and Sheeran, 2002) and attitudinal ambivalence (Conner et al., 2003). Increases in the predictive power of the theory as a result of these additions and developments have been noted but they do not constitute a marked improvement in our ability to predict health-related behaviour and there is little use of them outside a research context.

Efforts are ongoing to improve and understand the applicability of the models in practice. For example, Abraham et al. (2002) categorized and quantified messages in publicly-available safer sex promotion leaflets in the UK and Germany to find out the extent to which the content targeted cognitive correlates of condom use identified in a meta-analysis by Sheeran et al. (1999). Twenty coding categories based on the strongest correlates of heterosexual condom use identified by Sheeran et al. (1999) were used. A score of 1 was allocated to leaflets for each message that corresponded to one of the 20 categories. Sixty-nine percent of UK leaflets and 94% of the German leaflets did not score more than 10 out of 20. One German leaflet scored 18 out of 20. The efficacy of this evidence-based leaflet in changing antecedent cognitions of condom use was tested (Kraché et al., in press) under three conditions: (1) presentation of the leaflet; (2) presentation of the leaflet plus incentive for systematic message processing and (3) no-leaflet control. Presentation of the leaflet alone did not produce significant changes in the cognitive antecedents of condom use. At four weeks follow-up, the leaflet plus motivational incentive condition had significantly higher scores on two measures, attitude towards condom use with new partners and pregnancy motivation. Although a higher score than the control, normative beliefs regarding preparatory actions did not reach significance. The authors concluded that the way in which people read leaflets may be as important as leaflet contents to persuasiveness. In this experiment the motivation incentive was a quiz enabling participants to win attractive prizes. The authors suggested investigating using prize draws without quizzes. Using incentives that are meaningful to the participants and involving participants in the choice of incentive may also prove to be more successful. This would involve shifting from the top-down approach to health promotion.

Despite the increasing range and complexity of social cognition models, it is possible to identify a number of shared characteristics on which to base a critique of the genre.

First, all SCMs conceptualize the individual as a rational decision-maker. Variables of relevance in SCMs are cognitions such as beliefs, attitudes and perceptions. This means that SCMs are only concerned with conscious, cognitively mediated health behaviours (e.g. the decision to buy a smoke alarm). However, it has been pointed out that many **health habits** occur routinely (Bennett et al., 1995) (e.g. brushing one's teeth in the morning) and do not involve conscious decision-making.

KT

Furthermore, SCMs do not take into account the role of impulse and/or emotion. Even where models do include the variable 'volitional control' (e.g. TPB, Ajzen, 1985), it is conceptualized as a conscious belief (in one's own efficacy) that the individual includes in his/her rational appraisal. However, situational pressure such as physical and emotional 'urges' as well as power relations can have a strong and direct influence on health-relevant behaviours.

Another assumption of SCMs is that a predictive model can be designed that is applicable to a wide range of health behaviours. In other words, it is assumed that the same variables (e.g. attitudes and subjective norm) inform different behaviours (e.g. attendance at dental check-ups as well as condom use). However, the predictive power of any one SCM varies depending on its context of application. There is rarely full confirmation for the Health Belief Model in the literature; rather, different variables appear to be important for different health behaviours.

Similarly, SCMs assume that the same variables are relevant to diverse groups of people. However, there is evidence to the contrary from studies that have identified different psychological antecedents of HIV preventive behaviour for men and women, people of different ages, as well as people with different amounts of sexual experience (Abraham and Sheeran, 1994).

Another problem is that SCMs focus exclusively upon mental representations of the social world and their effects upon behaviour. They do not take into account the direct effects of material, physical and social factors. Thus, something like lack of access to health resources (e.g. healthy food, condoms, the local gym), can only feature as lack of volitional control (i.e. the belief that 'I cannot put the health behaviour into practice'), thus maintaining a focus upon the individual as opposed to his/her social and material location. As we have seen in Chapters 1 and 2, material, physical and social factors can place severe constraints on the individual's ability to act upon information. For this reason, health promotion programmes may instill a greater sense of frustration, hopelessness and lack of control, possibly even causing *decrements* in well-being.

In addition, decisions about health-relevant behaviours are conceptualized in SCMs as individual decisions. Yet many health behaviours arise out of an interaction between two or more people (e.g. condom use), suggesting that the individual level of analysis is too narrow a focus for a theory of behaviour change.

Finally, SCMs rely upon a conceptualization of behaviour as an isolated, narrowly defined piece of action. However, the same behaviour (e.g. smoking a cigarette) could be seen to form a part of a number of different social practices (e.g. going to the pub, dieting, rebelling) and its meanings would, therefore, differ within each context. From this perspective, the attempt to predict a behaviour such as smoking without specifying the context within which it takes place and without identifying the practice of which it forms a meaningful part makes little sense.

Implications for health promotion practice

Even though social cognition models are concerned with behaviour change, there is little explicit discussion of exactly how their insights could inform the design of health promotion interventions (for exceptions, see Tones, 1987; Abraham and Sheeran, 1994; Conner et al., 1994). This may be due to the assumption that once we have accurately and reliably identified the cognitive precursors of health-relevant behaviours, they will be amenable to easy manipulation. Alternatively, a reluctance to formulate concrete recommendations for practice may be a reflection of the pervasive and unfortunate divide that exists between academics and practitioners.

Whatever the reason, the preoccupation of SCM researchers with the prediction of behavioural intentions on the basis of social cognitions has prevented them from addressing the crucial question of how social cognitions are formed and how they can be changed. In other words, even if we could predict someone's behaviour on the basis of knowing their relevant beliefs, attitudes and/or perceptions, this would not tell us anything about if and how these could be modified.

One result of this reluctance to shift the focus from content (of beliefs or percep-tions) to process (of belief formation or change) is that it creates the impression that the provision of relevant information is sufficient to induce changes in social cogni-tions. For example, accurate information about the spread and method of transmis-sion of a disease, as well as the nature of its symptoms, could have a direct effect upon perceived susceptibility and severity, as defined by the HBM. Similarly, information about other people's opinions of those who do or do not engage in particular health-relevant behaviours could be expected to directly inform subjective norms, as concep-tualized by the TRA. Even perceived behavioural control could be manipulated through the provision of information about the extent to which other people similar to oneself have succeeded in taking up a particular preventive health behaviour.

Thus, even though SCM theorists stress that information about a disease does not by itself generate behaviour change and that changes in attitudes and beliefs are required (e.g. Tones, 1987; Ross and Rosser, 1989), they are actually talking about a particular kind of information, namely biomedical, rather than information as such. In fact, it is sug-gested that other types of information are instrumental in bringing about changes in belief structure and consequently attitudes. For example, Tones suggests that 'teaching young people about the effects of various substances on the body might convince them of the damage which might be done' (1987: 315); Abraham and Sheeran draw attention to the positive effects of 'providing heterosexual couples with instructions for condom use which included suggestions on how to eroticize them' (1994: 176). Thus, it can be argued that SCMs share both the aim (i.e. to bring about individual behaviour change) and method (i.e. provision of information) of the behaviour change paradigm.

Returning to the practice of health promotion, the work of some SCM theorists who explored different methods of modifying social cognitions (e.g. Abraham and Sheeran, 1994) will be discussed in the next section (self-empowerment approach).

Critique of the behaviour change approach

The behaviour change approach attracts a number of criticisms (see Box 20.1). First, it is unable to target the major causes of ill-health. Individual behaviour change, even when successfully implemented, cannot address socio-economic factors such as poverty, unemployment or environmental pollution. Its objective is change within the individual rather than change in the individual's environment. Second, the choice of what type of preventive behaviours to adopt lies with the 'experts' whose task it is to communicate this information to the public. As a result, recommendations and advice provided 'from above' can easily be seen to be incompatible with community norms, values and practices. In addition, receiving health advice in a top-down fashion can be a disempowering experience (Homans and Aggleton, 1988). Third, there is no direct link between knowledge, attitudes and behaviour. The behaviour change paradigm does not address the many variables other than cognitions about disease that inform human actions. Fourth, in its application the behaviour change paradigm tends to assume homogeneity among the receivers of its health messages. However, information is not received or processed uniformly by those to whom it is directed: mood, motivation, past experience, interest, perceived relevance, lay beliefs, group membership and many other factors mediate the way in which a message is 'heard' and interpreted.

BOX 20.1

CRITICISMS OF THE THREE APPROACHES TO HEALTH PROMOTION

Criticisms of the behaviour change approach

- is unable to target the major socio-economic causes of ill health;
- operates 'top-down';
- assumes that there is a direct link between knowledge, attitudes and behaviour;
- assumes homogeneity among the receivers of health promotion messages.

Criticisms of the self-empowerment approach

- is assumed that rational choices are healthy choices;
- strong reliance upon simulation;
- inadequate concept of power.

Problems associated with the collective action approach

- vulnerable to lack of funding and to official oppositions;
- danger of creeping professionalization;
- problematic concept of 'community'.

In the light of these issues it is perhaps not surprising that the behaviour change approach has generally yielded relatively small effects on actual health behaviour when implemented in real-world interventions.

Self-Empowerment Approach

The goal of this approach to health promotion is to empower individual people to make healthy choices. Self-empowerment can be defined as the process by which groups and individuals increase their control over their physical, social and internal environments. In order to facilitate self-empowerment, **participatory learning** techniques allow people to examine their own values and beliefs and explore the extent to which factors such as

KT

past socialization as well as social location affect the choices they make (Homans and Aggleton, 1988). Group work, problem-solving techniques, client-centred counselling, assertiveness training and social skills training as well as educational drama are forms of participatory learning. The self-empowerment paradigm, with its emphasis upon self-awareness and skills, resonates with what Stroebe and Stroebe (1995) refer to as the 'therapy model' of health promotion that deploys a wide range of psychological techniques such as cognitive restructuring, skills training and self-conditioning in order to help individuals act upon their intentions to adopt health behaviours.

Examples of therapeutic approaches using the techniques of cognitive-behavioural therapy and motivation enhancement are described in Chapters 8, 9 and 10. However, the self-empowerment approach relies upon the individual person's inherent capacity to act rationally more than the therapy model does.

Empowerment is the principle value of community psychology (Rappaport, 1987) with which the work described in this chapter has much in common.

Self-empowerment is particularly popular within health education for young people. For example, peer pressure has been identified as a powerful obstacle to the adoption of healthy practices by young people. Here, self-empowerment techniques encourage young people to make independent decisions by developing their psycho-logical resources to resist peer pressure, the so-called 'say no' technique. This has been attempted through assertiveness training, social skills training, inoculation to persuasive appeals and life skills training, with limited success (Hopkins, 1994: 335).

A range of HIV-preventive interventions for young people are informed by a self-empowerment rationale (Abraham and Sheeran, 1994). These include rehearsal of communication and interaction sequences that might be involved in condom purchase or sexual negotiation, questioning and challenging sexual scripts that do not allow space for negotiation of contraceptive use, peer education programmes, as well as group-based cognitive-behavioural programmes aiming to identify and then modify personal obstacles to HIV prevention. All of these involve reflexive self-appraisal as well as the acquisition of new skills. Abraham and Sheeran (1994) argue that such empowerment-based interventions can be effective in increasing perceived **self-efficacy** that has been shown to be a powerful predictor of intention formation and behaviour (e.g. Bandura, 1992). Thus, Abraham and Sheeran (1994) move beyond the more simplistic behaviour change/information giving approach, to manipulate SCM variables through empowerment techniques. Indeed, these authors also acknowledge the importance of power relations and cultural resources that require change at a community level.

KT

An example of an empowerment-based intervention (Lugo, 1996)

The Resource Sisters/Compañeras Program was an empowerment education project for pregnant women in Orange County, Florida (Lugo, 1996). The programme focused on areas that had high rates of low birth weight babies, infant mortality, substance-exposed newborns and poverty. It was implemented in an inner city area, a rural section of the county and a quasi-suburban area. The programme was designed to: (a) employ and enhance the natural skills of women from the community (peer counsellors) to assist other women and foster collective problem-solving; (b) provide outreach and case management through home visits; (c) develop ongoing peer support groups.

Local women were recruited and trained to become peer educators. The intensive three-week group training covered empowerment, resources, needs assessment, case management, women's issues, problem posing, prenatal health, labour and delivery and group facilitation. Trained peer counsellors visited women in their homes who had been identified as high risk (medically, demographically and/or psychosocially) by the state screening programme. These visits provided an opportunity for individual needs assessment and case management, as well as to encourage the women to attend support group meetings. These meetings took place in clients' neighbourhoods and their purpose was to be a forum where women could define their own health issues.

The evaluation showed that around 20% of women who had been contacted came to at least one support group meeting. Participation was greatest in the rural community and was lowest among white women. Over 40% of women who had come to one group meeting returned several times. Thus, obtaining a high level of initial participation seemed to be a challenge.

Issues raised and discussed by the women in the groups commonly included domestic violence, stress, relationships, parenting, physiological and emotional changes during pregnancy and concerns with basic survival (food, housing, etc.). The groups were a forum for discussion of individual choices, decision-making and self-care, as well as collective problem-solving. The groups developed social cohesion that was demonstrated by contact among participants outside the group meetings. Peer counsellors reported an increased sense of empowerment and options since working with the programme. However, after the first year of the programme there were no significant differences between clients' and non-clients' low birth weight rates. Thus, the programme had not contributed to improved pregnancy outcomes.

Lugo (1996) draws attention to the fact that the programme was externally imposed, as an alternative model for providing state-mandated case management for at-risk pregnant women. This raises the question of whether empowerment can occur within the context of a programme and a circumscribed source of funding whose major purpose is individual medical case management. Lugo (1996) proposes that the best promise for success lies in efforts that hold empowerment and community development as core functions.

Implications for health promotion practice

The self-empowerment approach assumes that healthy choices are facilitated by increased personal control. We saw in Chapter 2 that one explanation of health gradients has been linked to the concept of personal control. Interventions designed to increase feelings of personal control therefore carry the potential to improve health. Self-empowerment interventions aim to provide a space in which individuals are able to understand themselves and make new choices as active agents of change in their own lives and on their own terms. Such interventions confront the challenge of enabling those who feel, and arguably also are, the most powerless in society to take control of their health. Self-empowerment also involves critical appraisal of the social and cultural factors that shape participants' health behaviours. As a result, participants may have to confront the reality of their social and economic powerlessness. This may be difficult to address within a personal empowerment group setting. Finally, self-empowerment workers need to negotiate the tensions between their roles as 'educator' and 'facilitator'. They need to be aware that the support they give may disempower clients.

Critique of the self-empowerment approach

There are a number of criticisms that can be made of the self-empowerment approach. First, there is an assumption that rational choices are healthy choices. However, there is evidence that people may engage in unhealthy or risky behaviours for perfectly rational reasons, e.g. mothers who refuse infant immunization because they consider it to be too risky or alternatively ineffectual (New and Senior, 1991). Second, self-empowerment techniques rely upon simulation: skills are practised in safe environments and artificial settings such as assertiveness training groups. It is assumed that skills acquired in this way can be transferred to real-life situations. However, it could be argued that powerful influences such as the fear of losing face, social reputations or loyalties that characterize real-life social situations are likely to interfere with such transference of skills. Third, the paradigm does not have an adequate concept of power (Homans and Aggleton, 1988). It is assumed that power is a potential resource that resides within the individual and can be mobilized through empowerment techniques. However, systematic inequalities with regard to access to material, social and psychological resources in society mean that people are not equal in their ability to put healthy choices into practice (see Chapter 2). In other words, the self-empowerment paradigm maintains a focus upon the individual as the locus of change and is therefore unable to address structural inequalities of power in society. Sykes et al. (2004) found that despite the endorsement of the concept of empowerment, the European Commission's 1996–2000 Health Promotion Programme was in actuality disempowering. Through its vagueness, discourse containing clear hierarchies of power and an emphasis on scientific methods of evaluation, the public were positioned as passive recipients of health promotion.

Collective Action or Community Development Approach

The aim of collective action is to improve health by addressing socio-economic and environmental causes of ill-health within the community. Thus, this approach recognizes the close relationship between individual health and its social and material contexts, which consequently become the target for change. Individuals act collectively in order to change their environment rather than themselves. Therefore, the collective action approach constitutes the interface between the environmental and the behavioural approaches to health promotion in that it is concerned with the ways in which collectivities can actively intervene to change their physical and social environment. The psychologist serves as an agent of change.

It could be argued that self-empowerment is part of a social action process that culminates in the ability to take collective action. Therefore, a separation of the self-empowerment and collective action approaches may seem somewhat artificial. However, self-empowerment interventions typically limit themselves to the development of interpersonal skills in narrow settings and are therefore unlikely to constitute more than simply a first stage in a community empowerment process. Furthermore, self-empowerment can be a consequence rather than a precondition of collective action.

The collective action approach has been influenced by Freire's (1973) idea of **critical consciousness** in which the community comes to recognize the way in which social and economic conditions help to restrict health and wellness and how these conditions can be transgressed by political action. Another concept relevant to this approach is

that of **social capital**, referring to the community's ability to support empowerment through participation of local organizations and networks. Putnam (2000) discusses two kinds of social capital, bonding social capital which refers to within-group social capital and bridging social capital which is concerned with linking with outside bodies with the power and resources to enable mutually interesting benefits to accrue.

We can give two examples of collective health promotion. First, 'People-Centred Health Promotion' (PCHP) is described by Raeburn and Rootman (1998). They use the mnemonic 'PEOPLE' to define their approach:

- People-centredness
- Empowerment
- Organizational and community development
- Participation
- Life quality
- Evaluation

PCHP starts with people's everyday experience considered in a collective or community. The members of any community know best what their needs are and the role of the professional is seen as that of a *facilitator*. As described above, empowerment refers to people taking more control, building up 'strength', 'capacity' or 'resources' as a person, group or community. The concept of *personal control* refers to self-efficacy, sense of coherence, competence, effectiveness, and coping (discussed in more detail in Chapters 12 and 13). *Strength building* is concerned with the enhancement of skills, knowledge and competence, increasing assets and resources (Rappaport, 1987). PCHP considers people rather than individuals, i.e. 'people in their collectivity, rather than as isolated persons' (Raeburn and Rootman, 1998: 26). The PCPH approach advocates organization development, a change process or progression of changes as an organization is transformed to deal more effectively with the needs of the community.

According to Raeburn and Rootman (1998), the process of *community development* contains seven steps:

1 Participatory formulation of a philosophy of action and overall objectives.
2 Participatory planning of action through community needs assessment.
3 Consensual setting of time-limited goals.
4 Consensually agreed resource plans.
5 Allocation of tasks and actions to as many participants as possible.
6 Regular review of all major project goals and processes in a public forum.
7 Periodic assessment of outcomes.

Raeburn and Rootman (1998) describe several interesting case studies of health promotion projects involving empowerment and community development using the PCHP approach. These include the Superhealth Lifestyle Programmes, low-cost community approaches to weight control, healthy eating and stress management.

A second example of the community development approach to health promotion is the concept of the **healthy living centres (HLCs)**. In the UK the government allocated £300 million from the National Lottery 'New Opportunities Fund' to the development of **healthy living centres** over the period 1999–2003. A total of 349 projects were funded across the UK focusing on the health of the most vulnerable 20% of the UK population. The HLCs work with local priorities for improving public health and tackling social exclusion as well as supporting government health policies.

The HLC initiative is being evaluated. Results are expected in August 2005. An interim evaluation report stated that HLCs are successfully targeting disadvantaged sectors of the society. Data collected from 96 HLCs in 2003 showed that the majority of users were women (72%); 44% were over the age of 55; 12% were from ethnic minorities, 23% were employed and 10% were ill or disabled. Approximately one-third of the 3,399 respondents said that their health was only fair or poor. Most HLCs users (88%) had a good opinion of the services/facilities offered. However, users from ethnic minority groups and those with poorer general health held less favourable opinions than other groups (Bridge Consortium Team, 2003).

Collective action as community empowerment

Campbell (2000, 2003) developed a peer-education programme among sex workers in an isolated 400-person shack settlement in a southern African gold mining community where more than six out of every ten women were HIV positive. The programme aimed to increase knowledge about sexual health risks and personal vulnerability to HIV infection, to encourage people to seek out early diagnosis and treatment, and to encourage the use of condoms. The programme was based on the ideas of critical consciousness of Freire and of bonding and bridging social capital as suggested by Putnam. Implementing these ideas in everyday practice was a far from easy task. Obtaining permission from a gang of armed men who 'policed' the camp, collective working among women who were used to competing for work against each other, alcoholism, fighting and overall mistrust and suspicion throughout the everyday workings of the camp made the aims and ideals of the project excessively difficult to achieve. The peer-educator team worked against these setbacks and achieved respect, strength as a team, and self-confidence using participatory methods and achieved some recognition of the gender-related oppression and stigmatization of the sex workers in the camp.

Unfortunately, the concrete results in condom use and reducing the spread of HIV were not very successful. The evaluators pinpointed poverty as one primary reason for people being unable to change their life circumstances. Lack of collaboration by powerful community stakeholders (mining industry, mine medical doctors) was viewed as the greatest obstacle to the success of the programme (Campbell, 2004).

Implications for health promotion practice

The aim of community **outreach programmes** and development is to make contact with 'hard-to-reach' or marginalized members of the population and involve them as fully active participants in health promotion actions. Those who are easily located by the outreach workers are less likely to be in need of their services (the **inverse care law**).

Making contact repeatedly with members of a large, transient population such as homeless young people in large cities constitutes a major challenge to outreach workers. Also, it is important to distinguish between individual outreach, which aims to facilitate individual behaviour change through the provision of information and personal development, and community outreach, which aims to change community norms and behaviours. The former is associated with the self-empowerment approach.

Community development, with its emphasis upon collective ownership and control over health choices and health status, is much more likely to come into conflict with statutory health promotion agencies. This is particularly the case when marginalized communities such as drug users make choices that more dominant communities consider a threat to public health.

Community health promotion strategies may not be successful in all types of community. For example, drug users' networks are primarily sustained because of functional needs such as dealing and scoring (Rhodes, 1994) rather than for political or social reasons. They do not share ritual celebrations of social identity as does the gay community in both the UK and USA. This, together with the absence of infrastructures for action, makes it more difficult to mobilize outreach strategies within such communities.

Critique of the collective action approach

It is clear that the collective action approach is deeply political. It involves the collective organization of those who are traditionally excluded from decision-making processes and a direct and active challenge to power relations associated with health and illness. As a result, health promotion initiatives using this approach have the potential to come into conflict with those whose interests lie with the status quo such as industry, employers, government departments and local councils that aim to make financial savings. Consequently, community action as a form of health promotion is vulnerable to lack of public funding and official opposition. In addition, there is a danger of creeping professionalization (Homans and Aggleton, 1988) whereby those involved in the initiative become removed from the grass-roots concerns of those they set out to represent. Alternatively, because of the effort needed to make this type of project work, professionals may become emotionally involved that may lead to feelings of 'burn-out'.

Finally, the notion of community, upon which the collective action paradigm depends, is itself problematic. For example, people who live in the same geographical space (or those who share a sexual preference, language, ethnic background, age group or social class) do not constitute homogeneous groups. The concept of community obscures the diversity of lifestyles that exists within such groups, and can therefore fail to address the diverse needs of people within a community. Furthermore, self-appointed community leaders or representatives can emerge who claim to speak for all members of the community but in reality represent the dominant group (see Box 20.1 for a summary).

Homans and Aggleton (1988) recognize the limitations that often prevent community initiatives from actually achieving social change, most crucially lack of resources, and they propose an additional, social transformatory model that aims to bring about far-reaching change throughout society. The principles described in Chapter 2 at a global level apply equally well at a local level: unless the powerful members of a community are willing to collaborate to help the oppressed members, the power differentials and inequalities will always remain.

Health Promotion and Disability

A major limitation of health promotion activities is that people with disabilities are largely omitted from health promotion literature, campaigns and interventions. This omission occurs in spite of the fact that there is a wealth of data that indicates that people with disabilities are at increased risk of morbidity and mortality from various health risks and secondary conditions including cardiovascular disease, cancer and HIV (Turner and Moss, 1996). People with Downs Syndrome are at increased risk from obesity, cardiovascular disease and leukaemia (Johnstone, 1998). People with learning disabilities are at higher risk than the general population for obesity and cardiovascular disease (Bell and Bhate, 1992). Similarly, people with severe mental illnesses are at an increasingly high risk of HIV infection. Some of these findings may be related to health risk behaviours. In addition, many people with disabilities are likely to have more sedentary lifestyles (Flynn and Hirst, 1992).

The ideology of normalcy and the prevalence of the medical model in health services and health promotion mean that the special needs of disabled populations are unlikely to be met. An example is the predominantly visual and written format of many health promotion campaigns, which are unlikely to reach individuals with visual impairments or learning disabilities. Areas such as smoking education, fitness and sexual health interventions are given little consideration concerning people with disabilities. In addition, the health deficits of people with disabilities may fall outside of national targets, as is the case for people with learning disabilities (Turner and Moss, 1996). Studies of health promotion interventions rarely focus on these at risk populations.

Health beliefs, attitudes and subjective norms underlie behaviour change approaches to health promotion interventions, yet it is not clear if disabled people, collectively or individually, differ from non-disabled people along these dimensions. Self-empowerment may be particularly desirable for people with disabilities who may have more difficulty asserting themselves. Finally, people with disabilities-led organizations and centres for independent/integrated living represent a clear example of collective action and empowerment yet have not been utilized as potential sites for health promotion for people with disabilities, despite having the potential to be the most appropriate and accessible locations for such efforts. There is a need to include people with disabilities in health promotion research and interventions. Seeing disability as a state of being rather than as a problematic, personal tragedy, and accepting that people with disabilities can be healthy (Lollar, 2001), and/or are able to take appropriate action to improve their own health, are essential steps in addressing the health needs of people with disabilities.

Health Risk Communication

In 1995 there was widespread reporting that the third generation of oral contraceptive pill doubled the risk of thromboembellism, resulting in women ceasing to take the pill, an increased number of unwanted pregnancies and termination requests (Shickle, 2000). Health risk refers to the likelihood that an individual or group (e.g. pill takers) will experience a particular undesirable health outcome (thromboembellism) in response to their own characteristics/behaviour (taking the pill) or a specific causal agent (third-generation pill). Health risk information about causation and risk is often imprecise, incomplete, abstract and yet ever changing. Translating and communicating such information in a meaningful way is a complex undertaking affected by a multiplicity of factors including health illiteracy and innumeracy, the media and the ubiquity of health information. Health risk information is a fundamental aspect of health promotion work and improving the public's understanding of such information is essential and was a target of the government's white paper *Saving Lives: Our Healthier Nation* (Department of Health, 1999).

Risk information is commonly cited in imprecise numerical terms, often using probabilities and percentages (e.g. 200% increase in risk of thromboembellism from pill). There is substantial evidence that both the general public and professionals have difficulty understanding even simple probabilistic data. Gigerenzer (2002) reports that in a sample of 1,000 individuals over a third were unable to correctly identify that 40% meant 4 out of every 10 people (rather than 1 in 4 or every 40th person). Similar interpretative problems among medical students and professionals have been reported (Hoffrage and Gigerenzer, 1998).

The mass media are a key source of information about health issues yet they have a paradoxical 'love/hate' relationship to health promotion activities. On the one hand mass media are viewed as an essential tool for the delivery of health messages and, on the other, as a highly suspect deliverer of low-quality health information (Lupton, 1995). The mass media rarely spark concerns that do not already exist but rather they tend to exaggerate them. This 'scaremongering' effect can be seen in many of the health controversies that have occurred over the last few decades including pill–thromboembellism, pill–cancer, HRT–cancer and the MMR–autism scares.

Health information is necessarily interpreted, filtered and compressed before being released, whether through the mass media or professional sources. Often this process results in ethical dilemmas and, as in many of the controversies mentioned, information that is fragmentary, sensationalized and error-prone (Resnik, 2001). Information released within news or documentary programmes influences how health information is received. For example, in January 1991 in the UK, an *Eastenders* soap character being diagnosed as HIV-positive resulted in the largest ever observed peak in requests for HIV testing. Health-related information is communicated within a social context, and much of the information people receive (from media, advertisements, Internet, professionals) is disseminated and filtered through discussion and behaviour within social networks. The pervasiveness and immediacy of health-related information in the media, advertisements, the Internet and social interactions influence how risk information is understood.

A tension exists between the desire for sufficient information to enable informed decision-making and the possibility of information/advice overload or fatigue. U-turns in the content and advice of information delivered are likely to exacerbate such fatigue, increasing confusion and decreasing confidence in new information (e.g. soya products reported as cancer protective then later being causally linked to cancer).

While information provision is a necessary aspect of informed decision-making, it is not sufficient, as the information must also be understood. The effects of new sources of health information (e.g. the Internet) have yet to be adequately assessed (see Kreps, 2003). Those designing health promotion interventions must forge links with the discipline of risk communication. Concerted efforts are needed to increase the quality and accessibility of health risk information.

Is Health Promotion Effective?

Having considered the theoretical bases and given examples of different approaches to health promotion, it is time to address the question of evaluation. Evaluation of the effectiveness of health promotion initiatives is an extremely difficult undertaking. First of all, we need to differentiate between *outcome evaluation*, i.e. an assessment of changes brought about by the intervention, and *process evaluation*, i.e. an understanding of how and why the intervention worked. In addition, outcome evaluation can focus on a range of different criteria, such as behavioural (e.g. how many people have stopped smoking) or cognitive (e.g. the extent to which people's knowledge about the health risks of smoking has increased) or health status (mental or physical). Furthermore, there may be unintended consequences of an intervention, such as increases in anxiety that may be generated by provision of information about particular risks.

French and Adams (1986) specified evaluation criteria that are appropriate for different types of health promotion interventions. For example, a mass media campaign based on the principles of the behaviour change model would be best evaluated by measuring changes in compliance, morbidity and mortality rates, as well as knowledge increases, attitude and behaviour change, whereas self-empowerment would be assessed through self-reports of changes in self-esteem, lifeskills and independent decision-making. However, it is important to bear in mind that a health promotion evaluation should only assess the extent to which a campaign has achieved its objectives and that these can be limited. For example, a campaign whose purpose it is to warn people about potential risks should not be evaluated by measuring behaviour change. In other words, campaign objectives and evaluation criteria need to be carefully matched.

In recent years, increasing emphasis has been placed upon evaluation and the need for evidence-based health promotion. Within a climate of financial pressures and budget cuts, public service expenditure needs to be cost effective. Governments and funding bodies are more likely to invest in health promotion projects that can be shown to work. In addition, there are ethical reasons for systematic evaluations: ineffective or counterproductive interventions should not be repeated, while effective interventions should be made available as widely as possible.

Everitt and Hardiker (1997) stated that health promotion evaluations should look at multiple perspectives. Nutbeam (1999) gave examples of the different perspectives and emphasis on what represents 'success' for a health promotion programme. For policy-makers and budget managers, success is often defined in terms of the relationship between investment and the achievement of health outcomes in the short term. Shannon (2004) reported the inherent difficulties in demonstrating a cause and effect link between public health interventions and clinical outcomes highlighted by

Ian Kennedy, the chairman of the NHS Healthcare Commission. He stated: 'You will have to persuade the least readily persuadable people in the land – (the Treasury) – that this money (for public health programmes) is well spent' (2004: 1, 222). For health promotion practitioners, Nutbeam (1999) suggested success may be defined in terms of the practicality of implementation of a programme and the possibilities of engaging people and organizations in action for health. For the population who are to benefit from health promotion action, relevance to perceived needs and opportunities for community participation may define success. For academic researchers, success is likely to be defined in terms of the methodological rigour, maintenance of programme integrity and achievement of predetermined outcomes. Marks and Sykes (2002b) report an example of a multiple perspective health promotion evaluation.

As well as adopting a pluralistic approach to evaluation, evaluators must be pragmatic by using data that can be realistically obtained yet remains meaningful and useful to the many key players involved in implementing the learning from evaluations. Often, this is not an easy task.

The 'Ideology of Health Promotion'

Health promotion is concerned with strategies for promoting health. It is assumed that (a) good health is a universally shared objective; (b) there is agreement on what being healthy means; (c) there is a scientific consensus about which behaviours facilitate good health. From this perspective, the real (and only) challenge for health experts and educators is to find effective ways of helping people to maximize their health.

However, there have been criticisms of this contemporary 'ideology of health promotion'. Evans (1988) was concerned that such an ideology can begin to drive health promotion interventions that instead ought to be informed by scientific evidence (both biomedical and psychosocial). Evans drew attention to programmes directed at lifestyle changes that are not unequivocally justified by biomedical research evidence, such as the recommendation to reduce cholesterol levels in the blood to prevent heart disease. Evans worried that 'by increasingly promoting presumably non-risky behaviours, we may be contributing to a type of mass hypochondriasis resulting in an increasingly diminished freedom in human lifestyle and quality of life' (1988: 207). This, he suggested, can result in an unhealthy obsession with exercise, an inability to enjoy a meal, as well as a reduction in spontaneity of lifestyle.

Lupton (1995) developed a critique of the **discourse of risk** prevalent in contemporary health promotion. She proposed that 'risk, in contemporary societies, has come to replace the old-fashioned (and in modern secular societies now largely discredited) notion of sin' (1995: 89). This is achieved through the practice of health risk appraisals and screening programmes. Lupton likens these practices to religious confessions where sins are confessed, judgement is passed and penance is expected. Lupton points out that risk discourse attributes ill-health to personal characteristics such as lack of will-power, laziness or moral weakness. In this way those 'at risk' become 'risk takers' who are responsible for their own ill-health as well as its effects upon others and society as a whole.

Lupton argues that risk discourse can have detrimental consequences for those positioned within it: being labelled at risk can become a self-fulfilling prophecy since people may feel reluctant to seek medical advice for fear of being reprimanded. Also, it can give rise to fatalism, as well as anxiety, uncertainty and fear, as, for example, for women 'at risk' of breast cancer who can experience their 'at risk' status as a half-way house between health and illness (Gifford, 1986).

The 'ideology of health promotion' has not gone unchallenged, however. Recent publications have explored the function and position of contemporary health promotion in an attempt to formulate alternatives to individualistic risk-based approaches (e.g. De La Cancela et al., 1998; MacDonald, 1998) [A useful paper by MacDonald (2000), on 'A new evidence framework for health promotion' is Reading 20 in Marks (2002a).]

Future Research

1   More studies that carry out systematic evaluations of health promotion interventions are needed. In order to be of use in informing the design of future interventions, such studies should specify whether they evaluate process or outcome or both. In addition, researchers must ensure that intervention objectives and evaluation criteria are carefully matched and that unintended effects of the intervention are detected. This can be done through the use of qualitative research methods such as semi-structured interviewing of participants or participant observation. Evaluation studies must aim to find realistic ways to consider multiple perspectives.
2   There is a role for psychological studies of the processes involved in community action. Health psychologists need to extend their focus from the individual towards group processes in order to make full use of the collective action paradigm.
3   SCM researchers are concerned with the prediction of behaviour on the basis of social cognitions. However, there is little research into how exactly health-relevant social cognitions may be successfully changed. Abraham and Sheeran (1994) proposed that self-empowerment techniques can be used in order to modify social cognitions. This hypothesis merits further investigation.
4   SCMs and the behaviour change approach do not address variables other than social cognitions that may have a direct effect upon health-relevant behaviours. In recent years, health psychologists have begun to draw on insights from social constructionism in order to explore the meanings and significations associated with health-relevant practices. Social constructionist work has explored the implications of discourse analytic research for applied psychology including health promotion (Yardley, 1997; Willig, 1999).

Summary

1   Behavioural health promotion interventions require the active co-operation of those who benefit from them and the use of persuasive and effective communication. Behavioural interventions include information provision and the teaching of behavioural, social and cognitive skills.
2   Three major approaches to health promotion are the behaviour change approach, the self-empowerment approach and the collective action approach. Each pursues different goals, utilizes different means to achieve its goals and proposes different criteria for intervention evaluation.

3 The behaviour change approach aims to bring about changes in individual behaviour through changes in the individual's cognitions. Social cognition models are utilized in order to make the link between knowledge, attitudes and behaviour. However, attempts by SCMs to predict behaviour on the basis of cognitions has led to disappointing results.

4 Criticisms of the behaviour change approach include its inability to target socio-economic causes of ill-health, its top-down approach to education, its exclusive focus upon cognitions, its assumption of homogeneity among receivers of health messages and its individualism.

5 The self-empowerment approach aims to empower people to make healthy choices. Participatory learning techniques are used in order to increase participants' control over their physical, social and internal environments.

6 Criticisms of the self-empowerment approach include its assumption that rational choices are healthy choices, its reliance upon simulation in safe environments, its inadequate conceptualization of power and its consequent focus upon the individual as the target for change.

7 The collective action approach recognizes the close relationship between individual health and socio-economic factors. It aims to remove the socio-economic and environmental causes of ill-health through the collective organization of members of the community.

8 Health promotion interventions that use the collective action approach can encounter a number of difficulties. They can come into conflict with powerful bodies and they are vulnerable to lack of public funding and official opposition. Other problems include creeping professionalization and difficulties associated with defining and identifying communities.

9 The 'ideology of health promotion' can threaten the scientific basis of health promotion interventions. It can give rise to an unhealthy social obsession with exercise and diet and lead to the blaming of the victims of ill-health.

10 Continuous psychological research is needed to understand the dynamic and ever changing discipline of health promotion.

 # Key Terms

critical consciousness
(conscientizacao)

discourse of risk

empowerment

evaluation

health education

health habits

health promotion

healthy living centres

implementation intentions

intervention

inverse care law

outreach programmes

participatory learning

preventive health behaviour

social capital

Glossary

ACE (Angiotensin Converting Enzyme) Inhibitor: a drug that is important in the regulation of blood pressure.

Acquisition: the process of learning a response or taking up a specific behaviour through association or conditioning.

Action research: a type of research concerned with the process of change and what else happens when change occurs. Action research is particularly suitable for organizations or systems requiring improvement or change.

Action stage: one of the stages proposed by the *transtheoretical model of change* in which a person takes specific actions with the aim of changing unwanted behaviour, bringing positive benefits to well-being.

Acute: the early stages of a condition; a condition that lasts for less than six months.

Addiction: a term used to describe a person's physical and psychological dependency on an activity, drink or drug, seemingly beyond conscious control. Addiction is said to occur when there is: a strong desire to engage in the particular behaviour (especially when the opportunity to engage in such behaviour is not available); an impaired capacity to control the behaviour; discomfort and/or distress when the behaviour is prevented or ceased; persistence of the behaviour despite clear evidence that it is leading to problems.

Addiction theories: theories based on the construct of addiction used to explain alcoholism and other excessive behaviours (e.g. gambling, shopping, drug use, over-eating).

Adipose tissue: tissue in the body in which fat is stored as an energy reserve and which in excess leads to obesity.

AIDS (acquired immune deficiency syndrome): an advanced HIV infection which generally occurs when the CD4 count is below 200/ml. It is characterized by the appearance of opportunistic infections which take advantage of the weakened immune system and include: pneumocystis carinii pneumonia; toxoplasmosis; tuberculosis; extreme weight loss and wasting; exacerbated by diarrhoea; meningitis and other brain infections; fungal infections; syphilis; malignancies such as lymphoma, cervical cancer and Kaposi's sarcoma.

Alcohol dependence syndrome: a psychophysiological disorder characterized by increased tolerance, withdrawal symptoms following reduced consumption, a persistent desire, or unsuccessful efforts to reduce or control drinking.

Alternative (or complementary) medicine: forms of health care that are not controlled by professional medicine and are based on non-orthodox systems of healing.

Anchoring: the process whereby unfamiliar concepts are given meaning by connecting them with more familiar concepts.

Angina: the most common form of coronary heart disease. It is characterized by a heavy or tight pain in the centre of the chest that may spread to the arms, necks, jaw, face, back or stomach. Angina symptoms occur when the arteries become so narrow from the *atheroma* that insufficient oxygen-containing blood can be supplied to the heart muscle when its demands are high, such as during exercise.

Angina Plan: the Angina Plan is a psychological intervention for angina patients. It consists of a patient-held booklet and audio-taped relaxation programme.

Anticoagulant drugs: drugs that prevent the clotting of blood.

Anti-essentialist view of human sexuality: the view of human sexuality as a set of potentialities which may or may not be realized within differing social, cultural and historical contexts.

Artefact: an uncontrolled and possibly unknown variable or factor causing a misleading, spurious finding in a study.

Assessment: a procedure through which a patient, client, participant or situation can be evaluated against a benchmark or criterion enabling further actions or interventions to be administered, interpreted or understood.

Atheroma: Furring-up of an artery by deposits, mainly of cholesterol, within its walls. Associated with atherosclerosis, atheroma has the effect of narrowing the lumen (channel) of the artery, thus restricting blood flow. This predisposes a person to a number of conditions, including thrombosis, angina, and stroke.

Attribution bias: the tendency to attribute positive things to oneself and negative things to others.

Attribution theory: theory of lay causal explanations of events and behaviours.

Attributions: perceived or reported causes of actions, feelings or events.

Authoritarian doctor: a personality type or leadership style favouring obedience rather than freedom of expression.

Benign tumour: a growth which is not cancerous.

Betablockers: drugs that block the actions of the hormone adrenaline that makes the heart beat faster and more vigorously.

Between groups design: a research design involving two or more matched groups of participants that receive different conditions, for example, an intervention versus a control condition.

Biological reductionism: the assumption that all human experience can be directly traced to and explained with reference to its biological basis.

Biomedicine: a health system which identifies the cause of agreed diseases and symptoms as lying in certain physiological processes.

Biopsychosocial model: the view that health and illness are produced by a combination of physical, psychological and cultural factors (Engel, 1977).

Black Report: a report on health inequalities published in the UK in 1980 named after the chairman of the committee who produced the report, Sir Douglas Black.

Body mass index (BMI): the body weight in kilograms divided by the square of the height in metres; has a normal range of 20 to 25.

Burden of disease: a concept referring to the overall costs associated with a disease measured by the economic, social and psychological resources that are expended during care, treatment and rehabilitation.

Case studies: retrospective written reports on individuals, groups or systems.

Case-control study: an epidemiological study in which exposure of patients to factors that may cause their disease (cases) is compared to the exposure to the same factors of participants who do not have the disease (controls).

Catastrophizing: the tendency to become emotional and pessimistic about symptoms, illness or difficulties.

Causal ontologies of suffering: causal frameworks for explaining illness and suffering.

Cessation: the process of stopping (ceasing) a specific behaviour, habit or activity; one possible outcome of the *action stage* in the *transtheoretical model of change.*

Cholesterol: a lipid produced in the body from acetyl-CoA and present in the diet.

Chronic: any condition that continues for at least six months.

Chronic fatigue syndrome (CFS):   a syndrome identified in Nevada, USA, in 1984, characterized by severe fatigue and other symptoms suggesting a viral infection and persisting over long periods of time. There is much current controversy as to whether it is a *psychosomatic disorder* or caused by an as-yet-unidentified virus. CFS is thought to be identical to *myalgic encephalomyelitis* (ME).

Classical conditioning: a learning process whereby a previously neutral stimulus (*conditioned stimulus, CS*) comes to evoke a certain response (unconditioned response, UCR) as a result of repeated previous pairings with a stimulus (*unconditioned stimulus, UCS*) which naturally evokes the response.

Clinical health psychology: the application of psychological theory and research to the prevention and treatment of illness, the identification of etiologic and diagnostic correlates of health and illness and related dysfunctions.

Cognitions: thoughts, beliefs and images forming the elements of a person's knowledge concerning the physical and psychosocial environment.

Cognitive-behavioural therapy (CBT):   modification of thoughts, images, feelings and behaviour using the principles of *classical* and *operant conditioning* combined with cognitive techniques concerned with the control of mental states.

Communication styles: different approaches to verbal interaction which are characterized by particular linguistic and rhetorical techniques and strategies such as listening or question asking.

Communicative event: a joint achievement that is the product of participants' strategic deployment of culturally available discursive resources.

Community health psychology: advancing theory, research and social action to promote positive well-being, increase empowerment, and prevent the development of problems of communities, groups and individuals.

Compensatory conditioned response model: influential model put forward by Siegel (1975) to account for the phenomena of addiction, such as tolerance, dependence and withdrawal, using the principles of *classical conditioning.*

Compliance (or adherence):   the extent to which a person's behaviour changes as a direct consequence of specific social influence: e.g. a measure of the extent to which patients (or doctors) follow a prescribed treatment plan.

Concordance: model of physician-patient relationship based upon mutual respect and involvement in treatment.

Conditioning: processes of associating stimuli and responses (see classical conditioning and operant conditioning) producing learning and experience.

Conditioned stimulus (CS):   a stimulus that, because of pairing with another stimulus (*unconditioned stimulus, UCS*) which naturally evokes a reflex response, is eventually able to evoke that response (see *classical conditioning*). The acquisition is believed to occur when there is a positive contingency between two events such that event A is more likely in the presence of event B than in the absence of B.

Consumerist: style of healthcare that emphasizes opportunities for patient choice.

Contemplation stage: the stage of intending to change at some, as yet unspecified time in the future; one of the stages of the *transtheoretical model of change.*

Control group: a group of participants assigned to a condition that does not include the specific treatment being evaluated; used for comparative purposes.

COPE: questionnare devised by Carver et al. (1989) to assess the individual's predominant coping strategies in response to stress (see Box 13.3).

Coronary angiogram: an X-ray of the arteries to help to see if any of the arteries are blocked by atheroma.

Coronary artery bypass graft (CABG): an operation that enables a blocked area of the coronary artery to be bypassed so that blood flow can be restored to heart tissue that has been deprived of blood because of coronary heart disease (CHD). During CABG, a healthy artery or vein is taken from the leg, arm, or chest and transferred to the outside of the heart. The new healthy artery or vein then carries the oxygenated blood around the blockage in the coronary artery.

Coronary heart disease (CHD): restriction of the blood flow to the coronary arteries often evidenced by chest pains (angina) and which may result in a heart attack.

Cost effectiveness: method of economic analysis that takes account of both the effectiveness and the cost of an intervention.

Critical health psychology: analyses how power and macro-social processes influence health, health care and social issues, and studies the implications for the theory and practice of health psychology.

Critical consciousness (*conscientizacao*): a concept developed by Paulo Freire referring to the ability to perceive social, political and economic oppression and to take action against oppressive elements of society.

Cross-over or within-participants design: a research design in which participants are placed in two or more conditions; in theory, participants 'act as their own controls'. However, there are sequence effects, practice effects, and other issues that make this design more complicated.

Cross-sectional studies: involve obtaining responses from a sample of respondents on one occasion only. With appropriate randomized sampling methods, the sample can be assumed to be a representative cross-section of the population(s) under study and it will be possible to make comparisons between different sub-groups, e.g. males vs. females, older vs. younger, etc.

Culture: a system of meanings and symbols that defines a worldview that frames the way people locate themselves within the world, perceive the world, and find meaning within it.

Deficit model: an explanation used by health-care professionals to account for low compliance, e.g. women who do not use a screening service may be characterized as lacking in knowledge and concern about their health.

Deviant patient: a perspective on doctor-patient communication focusing on the characteristics of the patient as creating problems for the doctor.

Diary techniques: any data collection method in which the data are linked to the passage of time. They often involve self-report but may also contain information about observations of others.

Direct observation: directly observing behaviour in a relevant setting, e.g. patients waiting for treatment in a doctor's surgery or clinic. The observation may be accompanied by recordings in written, oral, auditory or visual form. Includes casual observation, formal observation and participant observation.

Disability: (1) 'A physical or mental impairment that substantially limits one or more major life activities, a record of such impairment, or a perception of such impairment'. (2) 'Any physical and/or mental impairment that substantially limits one or more of the major life activities (caring for one's self, walking, seeing, hearing, and the like)' (The Americans with Disabilities Act, 1990).

Disability culture: a group identity, a common history of oppression and a common bond of resilience held with pride and consisting of art, music, literature, and other expressions of the experience of disability.

Disability-adjusted life year (DALY): the total amount of healthy life lost, to all causes, whether from premature mortality or from some degree of disability during a period of time. The DALY is the sum of years of life lost from premature mortality plus years of life with disability, adjusted for severity of disability from all causes, both physical and mental (Murray and Lopez, 1997).

Discourse: talk or text embedded in social interaction presenting an account of the constitution of subjects and objects; an opinion or position concerning a particular subject.

Discourse analysis: a set of procedures for analysing language as used in speech or texts. It has links with ethnomethodology, conversation analysis and the study of meaning (semiology).

Discourse of risk: ways of talking and practices that attribute ill health to personal characteristics and construct an 'at-risk' status as a state in between health and illness.

Disease prototype: cognitive construct or model of a representative case of a specific disease.

Disease theories: the idea that the loss of control of behaviour such as alcohol consumption or eating is a disease based on personal or inherited characteristics that predispose particular individuals to the condition (e.g. alcoholism or obesity).

Doctor-centred communication style: a communication style which primarily makes use of the doctor's expertise by keeping control of the interview agenda.

Dual processing model: the idea that cognitive representations of danger (e.g. illness threat) are processed independently of the emotional processing.

Ecological approach: a model or theory about health and behaviour that emphasizes environmental influences.

Ecological validity: the extent to which the environment within which behaviour or experience is studied captures the relevant features of the real-world environment.

Electrocardiogram (ECG): a physiological measure used to examine the electrical activity of the heart.

Emotional liability: a personal characteristic referring to an unstable, variable pattern in a person's responses to events.

Empowerment: any process by which people, groups or communities can exercise increased control or sense of control over aspects of their everyday lives, including their physical and social environments.

Energy expenditure: use by the body of chemical energy from food and drink or body stores during the processes of metabolism that is dissipated as heat, including heat generated by muscular activity; the day's total energy expenditure is measured in calories of heat lost.

Energy intake: the chemical energy in food and drink that can be metabolized to produce energy in the body; the day's total energy intake is measured in calories supplied by all food and drink consumed.

Environmental foundations: key elements of the working environment relevant to the occupational health and well-being of employees.

Epidemiology: the study of associations between patterns of disease in populations and environmental, lifestyle and genetic factors.

Equity theory: the tendency of individuals to balance the effort invested in a role with the rewards obtained from the role in return.

Ethnicity: pertaining to ethnic group or race.

Ethnocentrism: a bias in perception, thinking or principles stemming from membership of a particular ethnic or cultural group.

Ethnographic methods: seek to build a systematic understanding of a culture from the viewpoint of the insider. Ethnographic methods are multiple attempts to describe the shared beliefs, practices, artefacts, knowledge and behaviours of an intact cultural group. They attempt to represent the totality of a phenomenon in its complete context and naturalistic setting.

Evaluation: the assessment of the efficacy or effectiveness of an intervention, project or programme in terms of processes and/or outcomes.

Exercise tolerence test (ETT): the recording of the heart's electrical activity while it is under the stress of increased physical demand.

Extrinsic motives: motives based on external factors such as appearance, conformity or norms.

False positive: a result of a medical test that incorrectly identifies the person as having a certain condition.

Fat: *triglycerides* that are either solid (e.g. butter, lard) or liquid (e.g. vegetable or fish oil) at room temperature.

Fat balance equation: states that the rate of change of fat stores equals the rate of fat intake minus the rate of fat oxidation.

Fetal alcohol syndrome: abnormality found in children whose mothers drink heavily during pregnancy, characterized by facial abnormalities, mental impairment and stunted growth.

Flowchart model: a diagrammatic representation of the relationships between processes and/or variables which are believed to be related to each other.

Focus groups: one or more group discussions in which participants focus collectively upon a topic or issue usually presented to them as a group of questions (or other stimuli) leading to the generation of interactive data.

Framework: a general representation for conceptualizing a research field or question.

Galenic medicine: health system derived from Greek and Arabic health beliefs.

Gate control theory (GCT): a theory that views pain as a perceptual experience, in which ascending physiological inputs and descending psychological inputs are equally involved. It posits a gating mechanism in the dorsal horn of the spinal cord that permits or inhibits the transmission of pain impulses to the brain.

General adaptation syndrome (GAS): influential three-stage model of the physiological response to stress put forward by Hans Selye but no longer thought to be valid.

Germ theory: theory of disease that focuses on identifying specific germs or pathogens as the primary cause of disease.

Global burden of disease (GBD): the universal totality of economic, social and psychological costs of a disease attributable to both morbidity and mortality over a fixed interval of time.

Gradient of reinforcement: principle applied mainly to *operant conditioning* whereby the acquisition of a learned response occurs more quickly, the more rapidly reward follows the occurrence of the response.

Gross national income (GNI):   the total net value of all goods and services produced within a nation over a specified period of time, representing the sum of wages, profits, rents, interest and pension payments to residents of the nation.

Grounded theory analysis: an analysis of transcripts involving coding followed by the generation of categories, using constant comparative analysis within and between interview transcripts. This is followed by memo-writing which requires the researcher to expand upon the meaning of the broader conceptual categories. This in turn can lead to further data generation through theoretical sampling.

Hardiness: personality trait first proposed by Kobasa and consisting of a high level of commitment, sense of control and willingness to confront challenges. Hardiness may protect the individual against the effects of stress.

Hassles scale: life events stress scale designed by Kanner and associates and focusing on everyday events that cause annoyance or frustration. See also *uplifts scale* and *social readjustment rating scale (SRRS)*.

Health Belief Model (HBM):   psychological model which posits that health behaviour is a function of a combination of factors including the perceived benefits of and barriers to treatment and the perceived susceptibility to and seriousness of the health problem.

Health communication: the field of study concerned with the ways in which communication can contribute to the promotion of health.

Health education: the process by which individuals' knowledge about the causes of health and illness is increased.

Health gradient: the relationship between *socio-economic status (SES)* and mortality or morbidity that normally shows a monotonic increase as SES changes from low to high.

Health habits: routine behaviours acquired by learning or conditioning that protect health or put health at risk.

Health promotion: any event, process or activity which facilitates the protection or improvement of the health of individuals, groups, communities or populations.

Healthy living centres: local organizations designed to promote health and reduce health inequalities.

Hermeneutic phenomenology: study of personal meanings underpinning everyday reality.

Historical analysis: the use of data produced from memory, historical sources or artefacts.

HIV (human immunodeficiency virus):   the virus that causes acquired immune deficiency syndrome (AIDS); it replicates in and kills the helper T cells.

Human sexual response cycle: a sequence of stages of sexual arousal taking the individual from initial excitement to a plateau phase, through orgasm, to resolution of sexual tension.

Humours (doctrine of the four humours):   dating back to the physicians of ancient Greece, the belief that the body is essentially composed of four constituents or humours, blood, phlegm, black and yellow bile, and that diseases and psychological characteristics are attributable to an excess or shortage of one or more of the four.

Hysteria (conversion hysteria):   physical symptoms which appear to indicate organic disease but where there is no clinical evidence of disease. Believed by some practitioners to be psychologically caused although this is normally denied vehemently by sufferers.

Iatrogenesis: health problems caused by medical or healthcare interventions including accidents, inappropriate treatments, incorrect diagnoses, drug side effects and other problems.

Identity control: term used to describe the process by which a person deliberately attempts to control the image they present to others.

Illness perceptions: beliefs about illness.

Illness representations: organized mental model of character of illness.

Immunization: medical procedure designed to protect susceptible individuals from communicable diseases by the administration of a vaccine. This procedure is aimed at both immediate protection of individuals and also immunity across the whole community where the uptake rate is high.

Implementation intentions: specific plans about how intentions to change a piece of behaviour will actually be successfully implemented.

Income distribution: the distribution of income across the population. It can be measured in terms of the percentage share of national income earned by the best off or worst off proportions of the population; e.g. in the USA in 1991 the highest 20% of the population received 41.9% of the total national income while the worst off 20% received 4.7%.

Indigenous: belonging to a particular culture, race, or tribal group.

Individualism: a cultural value that enshrines the personal control and responsibility of the individual.

Inequalities: a difference in life opportunities that is correlated with social position or status, ethnicity, gender, age or any other way of grouping people (see also *social inequality*).

Interaction analysis system (IAS):   an observation instrument which identifies, categorizes and quantifies features of the doctor–patient encounter.

Interactive dyad: focusing on communication between two people.

Internal validity: the degree to which the results of a study can be attributed to the manipulations of the researchers and are likely to be free of bias.

Interpretative phenomenological analysis (IPA):   a technique for analysing qualitative data which seeks the meaning of experience.

Interpretative repertoire: linguistic devices that people draw upon in constructing their accounts of events.

Intervention: the intentional and systematic manipulation of variables with the aim of improving health outcomes.

Interviews (structured or semi-structured):   a structured interview schedule is a prepared standard set of questions which are asked in person, or perhaps by telephone, of a person or group of persons concerning a particular research issue or question. A semi-structured interview is much more open ended and allows the interviewee scope to address the issues which he/she feels to be relevant to the topics being raised by the investigator.

Inverse care law: the observation that the highest access to care is available to those who need it least (e.g. the more educated, articulate, affluent members of society) while the lowest access to care is available to those who need it most.

Intrinsic motives: motives based on feelings of pleasure, pride or enjoyment brought about by participating in an activity.

Job satisfaction: a positive emotional state resulting from work experience.

Job strain or demand control model: the idea that employee well-being depends upon the interaction of role demand and control as proposed by Karasek.

(To) legitimate: to justify one's position in the face of stigma, illness or invalidity.

Latent benefits: the less tangible benefits of employment, e.g. satisfaction of psychological needs.

Liver cirrhosis: frequently fatal form of liver damage usually found among long-term heavy drinkers. Initially fat accumulates on the liver, enlarging it; this restricts blood flow, causing damage to cells, and scar tissue develops, preventing the liver from functioning normally.

Locus of control: personality traits first proposed by social psychologists and then adapted by health psychologists to distinguish between those who attribute their state of health to themselves, powerful others or chance.

Longitudinal designs: involves measuring responses of a single sample on more than one occasion. These measurements may be prospective or retrospective, but prospective longitudinal designs allow greater control over the sample, the variables measured and the times when the measurements take place.

Maintenance stage: the continued practice of or adherence to a specific health-promoting behaviour, e.g. abstinence from smoking; one of the stages in the *transtheoretical model of change.*

Mammography: a method for imaging breast tissue of women using radiography for detecting early signs of breast cancer.

Manifest benefits: the concrete benefits of employment, e.g. income.

Medical error: errors in medical diagnosis and treatment.

Medical model: a way of thinking about health and illness that assumes all health and illness phenomena are physiological in nature. According to this model, health, illness and treatments have a purely biological or biochemical basis.

Medical silence: reluctance of the medical profession to publicly acknowledge or report errors.

Medicalization: the process by which experiences and practices which do not match those defined as 'natural' and 'healthy' are pathologized and treated as dysfunctional.

Meta-analysis: a quantitative literature review that combines the evidence from relevant previous studies, taking account of criteria for quality, allowing high statistical power.

Metastasis: the spread of cancer cells to secondary sites in the body.

Model: an abstract representation of relationships between processes believed to influence each other.

Moral discourses of suffering: language derived from moral principles used to describe and explain health and illness.

Motivation enhancement therapy: brief intervention developed by W.R. Miller for the treatment of alcohol and drug problems, that aims to boost the clients' self-esteem and motivation to change, in contrast to traditional, more confrontational approaches.

Multidimensional Health Locus of Control (MHLC) scale: a popular scale for assessing a person's attributions of experience as internally/externally controlled, controlled by powerful others, or by chance.

Multiple regression: a statistical technique based on correlations between variables enabling predictions to be made about dependent variables using a combination of two or more independent variables.

Myalgic encephalomyelitis (ME): syndrome first observed in an epidemic at the Royal Free Hospital, London, in 1955, now usually thought to be identical to *chronic fatigue syndrome* and controversial for the same reasons.

Myocardial infarction (MI): a form of *coronary heart disease* (CHD) or 'heart attack' that occurs when one of the coronary arteries becomes blocked by a blood clot and part of the heart is starved of oxygen. It usually causes severe chest pain. MI is often the first sign of CHD in many people.

Narrative: structured discourse which connects agents and events over time in the form of a story.

Narrative approaches: seek insight and meaning through the acquisition of data in the form of stories concerning personal experiences (Murray, 1997a). These approaches assume that human beings are natural storytellers and that the principal task of the psychologist is to explore the different stories being told.

Nicotine paradox: nicotine is a stimulant yet smokers experience relaxation when they smoke.

Obesity: an excessive accumulation of body fat, usually defined as a body mass index (BMI) greater than 30.

Obesogenic: referring to an environment that exposes the population to a large number of foods and drinks that have a high percentage of fats.

Objectification: the process whereby a more abstract concept acquires meaning through association with everyday phenomena. The process transforms an abstract concept into a concrete image.

Occupational stress: psychological, emotional or physical strain resulting from workplace demands and environment.

Operant conditioning: a learning process whereby a normally voluntary form of behaviour comes to occur with increasing frequency in a particular situation, or in the presence of a particular stimulus, as a result of previously and repeatedly having been rewarded in similar circumstances.

Opportunistic intervention: an attempt to modify health hazardous behaviour, such as smoking or heavy drinking, by a health professional, frequently a doctor, who has been consulted for other reasons.

Outreach programme: an intervention which aims to achieve subcultural change among hard-to-reach target constituencies in order to improve health outcomes.

Pap test: a medical procedure for conducting cervical screening examinations.

Participatory learning: the full participation of people in the processes of learning about their needs and opportunities, and in the action required to address them.

Patient-centred communication style: a doctor's communication style which mobilizes the patient's knowledge, experience and involvement through techniques such as silence, listening and reflection.

Patient satisfaction: a measure of the extent to which patients' expectations of what a medical encounter ought to provide have been met (as judged by the patients).

Perceived control: the feeling of having control over one's actions in response to others and the environment.

Percutaneous coronary intervention (PCI): a procedure that unblocks narrowed coronary arteries without performing surgery. This may be done with either a balloon catheter to push the atheroma to the side of the artery or a stent inserted to keep the artery open.

Pessimistic explanatory style: tendency of some individuals to blame themselves for everything that goes wrong in their lives, believed to be associated with poor physical health.

Phenomenology: study of the participant's perspective of the world.

Physical dependency: evidenced when a person experiences unpleasant physical symptoms when he/she stops using or reduces consumption of a drug, tobacco or alcohol.

Physical side effects: unwanted physiological effects that accompany medication.

Placebo control: a control condition that appears similar to a treatment when in fact it is completely general.

Post-traumatic stress disorder (PTSD): long-term psychological and physiological effects of exposure to traumatic stress, including insomnia, nightmares, flashbacks, problems of memory and concentration, acting or feeling as if the event is recurring and a greatly increased sensitivity to new stressful events.

Poverty: the level of income below which people cannot afford a minimum, nutritionally adequate diet and essential non-food requirements.

Precontemplation stage: the stage of knowing that a habit or behaviour is hazardous but without any intention to change it in the foreseeable future; one of the stages in the *transtheoretical model of change*.

Preparation stage: intending to take action in the immediate future, having developed a specific plan of action; one of the stages in the *transtheoretical model of change*.

Prevalence: the number of people with a disease or behaviour as a proportion of the population or sub-population at any point in time.

Preventive health behaviours: behaviours people choose to engage in with the aim of protecting and/or improving their health status.

Psychological dependency: a state associated with repeated activity or consumption of a drug or drink which leads to negative affect following reduced consumption or abstinence and a persistent desire or unsuccessful efforts to cut down or control the activity.

Psychoneuroimmunology (PNI): the study of the effects of psychological variables and especially stress on the immune system.

Psycho-oncology: the psychological aspects of cancer care and treatment.

Psychosocial explanations: accounts of events and experiences based on theories and research from psychology and the social sciences.

Psychosomatic (or somatoform) disorders: physical ailments believed to be psychologically caused including *hysteria* and some conditions which have organic features such as ulcers and asthma.

Psychosomatic medicine: a precursor of modern health psychology which flourished from the 1930s to the 1950s, its proponents, including Alexander and Dunbar, believed that psychoanalytic theories about unconscious conflicts could be extended to explain susceptibility to various organic diseases.

Public health psychology: the application of psychological theory, research and technologies towards the improvement of the health of the population.

Quasi-experimental design: comparison of two or more treatments in as controlled a manner as possible but without the possibility of manipulating an independent variable or randomly allocating participants.

Questionnaires: many constructs in health psychology are measured using questionnaires consisting of a standard set of items with accompanying instructions. Ideally a questionnare will have been demonstrated to be both a reliable and valid measure of the construct(s) it purports to measure.

QUIT FOR LIFE (QFL) Programme: a psychological therapy using cognitive behavioural principles enabling smokers to quit (Marks, 1993, 2005).

Racism: discrimination on the basis of race or skin colour.

Randomized controlled trials (RCTs): these involve the systematic comparison of interventions employing a fully controlled application of one or more interventions or 'treatments' using a random allocation of participants to the different treatment groups.

Reactance theory: a theory concerning the tendency to resist attempts by others to control one's behaviour.

Relapse: going back to consumption of tobacco, alcohol or a drug after a period of voluntary abstinence.

Relapse prevention therapy: strategies and procedures for reducing the likelihood of *relapse*.

Restenosis: coronary artery blockage that occurs following *percutaneous coronary intervention (PCI)*.

Revascularization: a term that describes surgical and catheter procedures that are used to restore blood flow to the heart.

Role ambiguity: lack of information necessary to conduct the role and information deficiency regarding expected role behaviours, role objectives and responsibilities.

Role conflict: incompatible role demands placed upon an individual.

Role demand: the expectations placed upon a person within a role.

Safer sex practices: those sexual practices that do not involve the exchange of bodily fluids which may contain the human immunodeficiency virus. Such bodily fluids are blood, semen and vaginal fluids.

Screening: procedure for the identification of the presence of certain diseases, conditions or behaviours in a community. Those sections of the population who are most at risk of developing a particular disease are examined to see whether they have any early indications. The rationale behind this strategy is that the earlier the disease is identified and treated, the less likely it is to develop into a fatal condition.

Self-determination: engaging in activities for their enjoyment or intrinsic motivation.

Self-efficacy: belief that one will be able to carry out one's plans successfully; a term proposed by Bandura (1977) and thought to be associated with positive health behaviours.

Self-regulation: process by which individuals monitor and adjust their medication on an ongoing basis.

Self-regulatory model: this model suggests that health-related practices or coping responses are influenced by patients' beliefs or representations of the illness. These illness representations have a certain structure.

Sensation seeking: a personality trait or type that is characterized by a strong desire for new sensations.

Sense of coherence: a personality trait originally proposed by Antonovsky to characterize people who see their world as essentially meaningful and manageable; associated with coping with stress.

Sense of community: a feeling that one belongs to a group located in space and time with a common identity, history and culture.

Sex survey: a large-scale, questionnaire-based instrument which aims to provide quantifiable, descriptive data about a population's sexual habits.

Sexology: the scientific study of human sexual behaviour.

Sexual meanings: the significance which is attributed to sexual practices as a result of the application of socio-historically and culturally variable and changing interpretative frames.

Sexuality: those aspects of human experience which are influenced by and/or expressive of sexual desire and/or practice.

Single case experimental designs: investigations of a series of experimental manipulations on a single research participant.

Social capital: the institutions, relationships, and norms that shape the quality and quantity of a society's social interactions. Social capital is not just the sum of the institutions which underpin a society – it is the glue that holds them together.

Social cognition: a cognitive model of social knowledge.

Social cognition models (SCMs): theories about the relationship between social cognitions, such as beliefs and attitudes, and behaviour, which aim accurately to predict behaviour or behavioural intentions.

Social constructionism: (1) the philosophical belief that there is no single, fixed 'reality' but a multiplicity of descriptions, each with its own unique pattern of meanings; (2) 'many potential worlds of meaning that can be imaginatively entered and celebrated, in ways which are constantly changing to give richness and value to human experience' (Mulkay, 1991: 27–8).

Social inequality: being treated differently as a consequence of age, race, gender, disability, sexual preference or other attribute (see also *inequality*).

Social justice: the process of treating a person, group or community fairly and equally.

Social readjustment rating scale (SRRS): measurement scale for life events stress developed by Holmes and Rahe and widely used in research on life events stress and illness. See also *hassles scale* and *uplifts scale*.

Social representations (SRs): system of ideas, values and practices specific to a particular community which enables individuals to orient themselves in the world and communicate with each other.

Social support: informal and formal supportive relationships.

Socio-economic status (SES): position or class based on occupation, education or income.

Stages of change: the stages of precontemplation, contemplation, preparation, action, maintenance, and termination in the *transtheoretical model of change*.

Statins: drugs used to reduce cholesterol levels.

Stigmatization: being treated as an object of derision and shame purely as a consequence of others' ignorance and prejudice.

Stress: strain resulting from demands that exceed the resources that a person has to deal with the demands.

Stress inoculation training: a self-instructional *cognitive-behavioural* method for stress management developed by Meichenbaum (1985), in which positive and useful responses to possible stressors are rehearsed.

Stress management workshops: training programmes in stress management usually delivered to groups, frequently lasting for a whole day or a weekend, and focusing on changing the way in which participants appraise situations as stressful and cope with stressful events.

Surveys: systematic methods for determining how a defined sample of participants respond to a set of standard questions attempting to assess their feelings, attitudes, beliefs or knowledge at one or more particular times.

Symmetry rule: tendency to search for a label for bodily symptoms and to expect symptoms if we have an illness label.

Systematic review: review of the empirical literature concerning the efficacy or effectiveness of an intervention that considers all of the relevant studies taking account of quality criteria.

Systems theory approach: a theory concerned with the contextual structures, processes or relationships within communities, groups or families.

Teleworking: working outside of the traditional workplace and using information technology and telecommunication systems.

Temperance societies: originating in the USA in the nineteenth century, these societies, of which Alcoholics Anonymous is an example, are dedicated to counteracting the harmful effects of drinking, usually advocating teetotalism.

Tension reduction hypothesis: the hypothesis that people enjoy alcohol primarily because it reduces tension (anxiety, stress), rather than as a drug which directly produces positive moods.

Theory: a general account of relationships between processes believed to influence, cause changes in, or control a phenomenon.

Theory of planned behaviour (TPB): theoretical model which argues that behavioural intention is controlled by attitudes, subjective norms and perceived control.

Theory of reasoned action (TRA): theoretical model which argues that behavioural intention is controlled by attitudes and subjective norms.

Toxic environment: a term referring to environmental and social conditions that promote disease, disorder and death.

Transtheoretical model of change (TTM): a model of behaviour change developed by DiClementi, Prochaska and others which attempts to identify universal processes or stages of change specified as *precontemplation, contemplation, preparation, action, maintenance* and termination.

Triangulation: collecting evidence using different methods to provide complementary perspectives.

Triglyceride: the main component of dietary fats and oils and the principal form in which fat is stored in the body; composed of three fatty acids attached to a glycerol molecule which are saturated, monounsaturated and polyunsaturated.

Tumour (benign or malignant): an abnormal new mass of tissue that serves no purpose. A tumour may be malignant or non-malignant depending on whether it is life-threatening or not.

Type A/B personality: the Type A personality, in contrast to the Type B personality, is characterized by intense achievement motivation, time urgency and hostility.

Twelve-step facilitation programme: a theraputic regime which attempts to change thinking and behaviour in a series of 12 steps, as advocated by Alcoholics Anonymous.

Unconditioned stimulus (UCS): stimulus that evokes a response or reflex without training, e.g. a loud sound will naturally evoke a startle response.

Uplifts scale: life events scale designed by Kanner and associates (1981) to assess desirable events in contrast to their *hassles scale*.

Viral challenge studies: method of studying the relationship between stress and susceptibility to infectious disease in which volunteers are deliberately exposed to minor viruses, usually colds or flu, to determine whether those who have experienced higher levels of stress prior to exposure are more likely to contract the infection.

Well-being: the state of 'wellness'; the general state of health of an individual.

Wernicke–Korsakoff syndrome: a form of irreversible brain damage sometimes found among long-term heavy drinkers, its symptoms include extremely impaired short-term memory, confusion and visual disorders.

Bibliography

Abbott, A. (2004) 'Ageing: growing old gracefully', *Nature, 428*: 116–18.

Abraham, C., Kraché, B., Dominic, R. and Fritsche, I. (2002) 'Do health promotion messages target cognitive and behavioural correlates of condom use? A content analysis of safter sex promotion leaflets in two countries', *British Journal of Health Psychology*, 227–46.

Abraham, C. and Sheeran, P. (1994) 'Modelling and modifying young heterosexuals' HIV-preventive behaviour: a review of theories, findings and educational implications', *Patient Education and Counselling, 23*: 173–86.

Abraham, C. and Sheeran, P. (2004) 'Deciding to exercise: the role of anticipated regret', *British Journal of Health Psychology, 9*: 269–78.

Abraham, C., Sheeran, P., Spears, R. and Abrams, D. (1992) 'Health beliefs and promotion of HIV-preventive intentions among teenagers: a Scottish perspective', *Health Psychology, 11*: 363–70.

Academy of Medical Sciences (2004) *Calling Time: The Nation's Drinking as a Major Health Issue.* London: The Academy of Medical Sciences.

Adams, J.S. (1965) 'Inequity in social exchange'. In K. Berkowitz (ed.), *Advances in experimental social psychology* (Vol. 2, pp. 267–99). New York: Academic Press.

Adams, J.S. and Jacobsen, P.R. (1964) 'Effects of wage inequities on work quality'. *Journal of Abnormal and Social Psychology, 69*: 19–25.

Adams, S., Pill, R. and Jones, A. (1997) 'Medication, chronic illness and identity: the perspective of people with asthma', *Social Science and Medicine, 45*: 189–201.

Adler, N.E. and Matthews K.A. (1994) 'Health psychology: why do some people get sick and some stay well', *Annual Review of Psychology, 45*: 229–59.

Adler, N.E., Boyce, T., Chesney, M.A., Cohen, S., Folkman, S., Kahn, R.L. and Syme, S.L. (1994) 'Socioeconomic status and health', *American Psychologist, 49*: 15–24.

Aggleton, P., Davies, P. and Hart, G. (1994) *AIDS: Foundations for the Future.* London: Taylor & Francis.

Agnostinelli, G. and Grube, I.W. (2002) 'Alcohol counter-advertising and the media: A review of recent research', *Alcohol Research and Health, 26*: 15–21.

Ajzen, I. (1985) 'From intention to actions: a theory of planned behavior', in J. Kuhl and J. Beckmann (eds), *Action-control: From Cognition to Behavior.* Heidelberg: Spring. pp. 11–39.

Ajzen, I. (1991) 'The theory of planned behavior', *Organizational Behavior and Human Decision Processes, 50*: 179–211.

Ajzen, I. (2002a) 'Residual effects of past on later behavior: Habituation and reasoned action perspectives', *Personality and Social Psychology Review, 6*: 107–22.

Ajzen, I. (2002b) 'Perceived behavioral control, self-efficacy, locus of control, and the theory of planned behavior', *Journal of Applied Social Psychology, 32*: 665–63.

Ajzen, I. and Fishbein, M. (1980) *Understanding Attitudes and Predicting Social Behavior.* Englewood Cliffs, NJ: Prentice-Hall.

Ajzen, I. and Fishbein, M. (2004) 'Questions raised by a Reasoned Action Approach: Comment on Ogden (2003)', *Health Psychology, 23*: 431–34.

Albrecht, G.L., Seelman, K.D. and Bury, M. (eds) (2001) *Handbook of Disability Studies.* London: Sage.

Alcohol Concern (2003) *Interim Analytical Report.* London: Cabinet Office.

Aldhous, P. (1992) 'French venture where US fear to tread', *Science, 257*: 25.

Aldwin, C.M. and Park, C.L. (2004) 'Coping and physical health outcomes: an overview', *Psychology and Health*, 19: 277–81.

Alexander, F. (1950) *Psychosomatic Medicine*. New York: Norton.

Allied Dunbar, Health Education Authority, Sports Council (1992) *Allied Dunbar National Fitness Survey*. London: HEA and Sports Council.

Amelang, M. and Schmidt-Rathjens, C. (1996) 'Personality, cancer and coronary heart disease: further evidence on a controversial issue', *British Journal of Health Psychology*, 1: 191–205.

American Psychological Association (1992) 'Ethical principles of psychologists and code of conduct', *American Psychologist*, 47: 1597–611.

Andersen, B.L. (2002) 'Biobehavioral outcomes following psychological interventions for cancer patients', *Journal of Consulting and Clinical Psychology*, 70: 590–610.

Andersen, R. and Newman, J.F. (1973) 'Societal and individual determinants of medical care utilization in the United States', *Milbank Memorial Fund Quarterly*, 51: 95–124.

Anderson, K.O. and Masur, F.T. (1990) 'Psychologic preparation for cardiac catheterization', *Heart and Lung*, 18: 154–63.

Anderson, R.J., Clouse, R.E., Freedland, K.E. and Lustman, P.J. (2001) 'The prevalence of comorbid depression in adults with diabetes: A meta-analysis', *Diabetes Care*, 24: 1069–78.

Anselman, R.A. (1996) '"The want of health": an early eighteenth century self-portrait of sickness', *Literature and Medicine*, 15: 225–43.

Antoni, M.H., Cruess, D.G., Cruess, S., Lutgendorf, S., Kumar, M., Ironson, G., Klimas, N., Fletcher, M.A. and Schneiderman, N. (2000) 'Cognitive-behavioral stress management intervention effects on anxiety, 24–hr urinary norephinephrine, and T-cytotoxic/suppressor cells over time among symptomatic HIV-infected gay men', *Journal of Consulting and Clinical Psychology*, 68: 31–45.

Antoni, M.H., Lehman, J.M., Kilbourn, K.M., Boyers, A.E., Culver, J.L., Alferi, S.M. et al. (2001) 'Cognitive-behavioral stress management intervention decreases the prevalence of depression and enhances benefit finding among women under treatment for early-stage breast cancer', *Health Psychology*, 20: 20–32.

Antonovsky, A. (1979) *Health, Stress, and Coping*. San Francisco: Jossey-Bass.

Argyris, C. (1975) 'Dangers in applying results from experimental social psychology', *American Psychologist*, 30: 469–85.

ARIC Investigators (1989) 'The Atherosclerosis Risk in Communities (ARIC) Study: design and objectives', *American Journal of Epidemiology*, 129(4): 687–702.

Armitage, C.J. and Conner, M. (2002) 'Reducing fat intake: interventions based on the Theory of Planned Behaviour', in D. Rutter and L. Quine (eds), *Changing Health Behaviour*. Buckingham: Open University Press.

Armstrong, D. (1987) 'Theoretical tensions in biopsychosocial medicine', *Social Science and Medicine*, 25: 1213–18.

Armstrong, K., Berlin, M., Schwartz, S., Propert, K. and Ubel, P.A. (2001) 'Barriers to influenza immunization in a low-income urban population', *American Journal of Preventive Medicine*, 20: 21–5.

Arnett, J. (2000) 'Optimistic bias in adolescent and adult smokers and non-smokers', *Addictive Behavior*, 25: 625–32.

Arrow, K. (1963) *Social Choice and Individual Values*, 2nd edn. New York: Wiley.

Arthur, H.M., Daniels, C., McKelvie, R., Hirsh, J. and Rush, B. (2000) 'Effect of a preoperative intervention on preoperative and postoperative outcomes in low-risk patients awaiting elective coronary artery bypass graft surgery. A randomized, controlled trial', *Annals of Internal Medicine*, 133: 253–62.

ASH (Action on Smoking and Health) (2004) http://www.ash.org.uk/?quit (consulted 5 March 2005).

Ashton, C.M., Haidet, P., Paterniti, D.A., Collins, T.C., Gordon, H.S., O'Malley, K., Petersen, L.A., Sharf, B.F., Suarez-Almazor, M.E., Wray, N.P. and Street, R.L. (2003) 'Racial and ethnic disparities in the use of health services. Bias, preference, or poor communication?', *Journal of General and Internal Medicine*, 18: 146–52.

Association of Community Health Councils (1989) *Cervical Cytology Screening: Getting it Right*. London: ACHC.

Auerbach, S.M. (2001) 'Do patients want control over their own health care? A review of measures, findings, and research issues', *Journal of Health Psychology*, 6: 191–204.

Austin, S. and Gortmaker, S. (2001) 'Dieting and smoking initiation in early adolescent girls and boys: a prospective study', *American Journal of Public Health, 91*: 446–50.

Avert Organisation (2004) *History of AIDS*. Published by Avert Organisation at www.avert.org/ historyi.htm

Avis, N.E., Brambilla, J., Vass, K. and McKinlay, J.B. (1991) 'The effect of widowhood on health: a prospective analysis from the Massachusetts Women's Health Study', *Social Science and Medicine, 33*: 1063–2070.

Avlund, K., Osler, M., Damsgaard, M.T., Christensen, U. and Schroll, M. (2000) 'The relations between musculoskeletal diseases and mobility among old people: are they influenced by socio-economic, psychosocial and behavioural factors?', *International Journal of Behavioural Medicine, 7*: 322–39.

Babor, T.F. and Grant, M. (eds) (1992) *Project on Identification and Management of Alcohol Related Problems. Report on Phase II: A Randomised Clinical Trial of Brief Interventions in Primary Health Care*. Geneva: World Health Organization.

Babor, T.F., Caetano, R., Casswell, S., Edwards, G. et al. (Alcohol and Public Policy Group) (2003) *Alcohol: No Ordinary Commodity – Research and Public Policy*. Oxford and London: Oxford University Press.

Bachman, R. (1994) 'Violence and theft in the workplace', in *Crime Data Brief: National Crime Victimisation Survey*. Washington, DC: Bureau of Justice Statistics, US Department of Justice.

Backett-Milburn, K., Cunningham-Burley, S. and Davis, J. (2003) 'Contrasting lives, contrasting views? Understandings of health inequalities in differing social circumstances', *Social Science and Medicine, 57*: 613–23.

Bagnardi, V., Blangiardo, M., La Vecchia, C. and Corrao, G. (2001) 'Alcohol consumption and the risk of cancer: a meta-analysis', *Alcohol Research and Health, 25*: 263–70.

Baillie, L., Broughton, S., Bassett-Smith, J., Aasen, W., Oostinde, M., Marino, B.A. and Hewitt, K. (2004) 'Community health, community involvement, and community empowerment: too much to expect?', *Journal of Community Psychology, 32*: 217–28.

Balarajan, R. and Soni Raleigh, V. (1993) *Ethnicity and Health: A Guide for the NHS*. London: Department of Health.

Bales, R.F. (1950) *Interaction Process Analysis: A Method for the Study of Small Groups*. Cambridge, MA: Addison-Wesley.

Balint, M. (1964) *The Doctor, his Patient and the Illness*. New York: International Universities Press.

Balshem, M. (1991) 'Cancer, control, and causality: talking about cancer in a working class community', *American Ethnologist, 18*: 152–71.

Bancroft, A., Wiltshire, S., Parry, O. and Amos, A. (2003) '"It's like an addiction first thing ... afterwards it's like a habit": daily smoking behaviour among people living in areas of deprivation', *Social Science and Medicine, 56*: 1261–7.

Bandura, A. (1977) 'Self efficacy: Towards a unifying theory of behaviour', *Psychological Review, 84*: 191–215.

Bandura, A. (1986) *Social Foundations of Thought and Action: A Social Cognitive Theory*. Englewood Cliffs, NJ: Prentice-Hall.

Bandura, A. (1992) 'Exercise of personal agency through the self-efficacy mechanism', in R. Schwarzer (ed.), *Self-efficacy: Thought Control of Action*. Washington: Hemisphere. pp. 3–38.

Bandura, A. (1997) 'The anatomy of stages of change', *American Journal of Health Promotion, 12*: 8–10.

Baranowski, T. (2005) 'Integration of two models, or dominance of one?', *Journal of Health Psychology, 10*: 19–21.

Barling, J. and Kelloway, E.K. (1996) 'Job insecurity and health: the moderating role of control', *Stress Medicine, 12*: 253–9.

Barnes, C. and Mercer, G. (2001) 'Disability culture: assimilation or inclusion?', in G.L. Albrecht, K.D. Seelman and M. Bury (eds), *Handbook of Disability Studies*. London: Sage.

Barraclough, J., Pinder, P., Cruddas, M., Osmand, C., Taylor, I. and Perry, M. (1992) 'Life events and breast cancer prognosis', *British Medical Journal, 304*: 1078–81.

Bartley, M. (1994) 'Unemployment and ill health: understanding the relationship', *Journal of Epidemiology Community Health, 48*: 333–7.

Bates, M.S. (1996) *Biocultural Dimensions of Chronic Pain: Implications for Treatment of Multiethnic Populations*. Albany, NY: State University of New York Press.

Bates, S. (1997) 'Tobacco sponsorship to end within nine years', *Guardian*, 5 December: 1.

Baum, A. and Spencer, S. (1997) 'Post-traumatic stress disorder', in A. Baum, S. Newman, J. Weinman, R. West and C. McManus (eds), *Cambridge Handbook of Psychology, Health and Medicine*. Cambridge: Cambridge University Press. pp. 550–5.

Baum, F. (2000) 'Social capital, economic capital and power: further issues for a public health agenda', *Journal of Epidemiology and Community Health*, *54*: 409–10.

Baur, C. (2000) 'Limiting factors on the transformative powers of e-mail in patient–physician relationships: a critical analysis', *Health Communication*, *12*: 239–59.

Becker, M.H. (ed.) (1974) 'The health belief model and personal health behavior', *Health Education Monographs*, *2*: 324–508.

Becker, M.H. and Mainman, L.A. (1975) 'Sociobehavioral determinants of compliance with health and medical care recommendations', *Medical Care*, *13*: 10–14.

Becker, M.H. and Rosenstock, I.M. (1984) 'Compliance with medical care', in A. Steptoe and A. Matthews (eds), *Health Care and Human Behaviour*. London: Academic Press.

Beehr, T.A., Farmer, S.J., Glazer, S., Gudanowski, D.M. and Nair, V.N. (2003) 'The enigma of social support and occupational stress: source congruence and gender role effects', *Journal of Occupational Health Psychology*, *8*: 220–31.

Begum, N. (1996) 'General practitioners' role in shaping disabled women's lives', in C. Barnes and G. Mercer (eds), *Exploring the Divide*. Leeds: The Disability Press. pp. 157–72.

Bell, A.J. and Bhate, M.S. (1992) 'Prevalence of overweight and obesity in Down's syndrome and other mentally handicapped adults living in the community', *Journal of Intellectual Disabilities Research*, *36*: 359–64.

Bennett, K.M. (2004) 'Why did he die? The attributions of cause of death among women widowed in later life', *Journal of Health Psychology*, *9*: 345–53.

Bennett, P. and Murphy, S. (1997) *Psychology and Health Promotion*. Buckingham: Open University Press.

Bennett, P., Murphy, S., Carroll, D. and Ground, I. (1995) 'Psychology, health promotion and aesthemiology', *Health Care Analysis*, *3*: 15–26.

Benoist, J. and Cathebras, P. (1993) 'The body: from immateriality to another', *Social Science and Medicine*, *36*: 857–65.

Bensing, J. (1991) 'Doctor–patient communication and the quality of care', *Social Science and Medicine*, *11*: 1301–10.

Bentler, P.M. (1989) *EQS: Structural Equations Program Manual*. Los Angeles: BMDP Statistical Software.

Benveniste, J., Lecouteur, A. and Hepworth, J. (1999) 'Lay theories of anorexia nervosa: a discourse analytic study', *Journal of Health Psychology*, *4*: 59–69.

Benzeval, M., Judge, K. and Whitehead, M. (eds) (1995) *Tackling Inequalities in Health: An Agenda for Action*. London: King's Fund.

Berger, K., Ajani, U.A., Kase, C.S., Gaziano, J.M., Buring, J.E., Glynn, R.J. and Hennekens, C.H. (1999) 'Light to moderate alcohol consumption and risk of stroke among US male physicians', *New England Journal of Medicine*, *341*: 1557–64.

Berger, P. and Luckmann, T. (1966) *The Social Construction of Reality: A Treatise on the Sociology of Knowledge*. New York: Penguin.

Berghom, I., Svensson, C., Berggren, E. and Kamsula, M. (1999) 'Patients' and relatives' opinions and feelings about diaries kept by nurses in an intensive care unit: A pilot study', *Intensive and Critical Care Nursing*, *15*: 185–91.

Bertakis, K.D., Roter, D. and Putnam, S.M. (1991) 'The relationship of physician medical interview style to patient satisfaction', *Journal of Family Practice*, *32*: 175–81.

Berthoud, R. (2000) 'Ethnic employment penalties in Britain', *Journal of Ethnic and Migration Studies*, *26*: 389–416.

Berthoud, R. (2003) *Multiple Disadvantage in Employment: A Quantitaive Analysis*. York: Joseph Rowntree Foundation.

Bibace, R. and Walsh, M.E. (1980) 'Development of children's conceptions of illness', *Pediatrics*, *8*: 533–43.

Bigelow, G.E. (2001) 'An operant behavioural perspective on alcohol abuse and dependence', in N. Heather, T.J. Peters, and T. Stockwell (eds), *International Handbook of Alcohol Dependence and Problems,* London: Wiley.

Bird, J.E. and Podmore, V.N. (1990) 'Children's understanding of health and illness', *Psychology and Health*, *4*: 175–85.

Bishop, G.D. (1987) 'Lay conceptions of physical symptoms', *Journal of Applied Social Psychology*, *17*: 127–46.

Bishop, G.D. and Teng, C.B. (1992) 'Cognitive organization of disease information in young Chinese Singaporeans'. Paper presented at the First Asian Conference in Psychology, Singapore.

Bishop, K. (2004) 'Employment and unemployment in the new EU member countries', *Labour Market Trends, July*: 283–94.

Black, D., Morris, J.N., Smith, C., Townsend, P. and Whitehead, M. (1988) *Inequalities in Health: The Black Report: The Health Divide*. London: Penguin.

Blair, S.N., Kohl, H.W., Gordon, N.F. and Paffenbarger, R.S. (1992) 'How much physical activity is good for health?', *Annual Review of Public Health*, *13*: 99–126.

Blane, D., Bartley, M. and Davey Smith, G. (1997) 'Disease aetiology and materialist explanations of socioeconomic mortality differentials', *European Journal of Public Health*, *7*: 385–91.

Blaxter, M. (1983) 'The causes of disease: women talking', *Social Science and Medicine*, *17*: 59–69.

Blaxter, M. (1990) *Health and Lifestyles*. London: Routledge.

Blaxter, M. (1993) 'Why do victims blame themselves?', in A. Radley (ed.), *Worlds of Illness: Biographical and Cultural Perspectives on Health and Disease*. London: Sage. pp. 124–42.

Blaxter, M. (1997) 'Whose fault is it? People's own conceptions of the reasons for health inequalities', *Social Science and Medicine*, *44*: 747–56.

Block, G., Patterson, B. and Subar, A. (1992) 'Fruit, vegetables and cancer prevention: a review of the epidemiological evidence', *Nutrition and Cancer*, *18*: 1–29.

Blumenthal, J.A., Sherwood, A., Gullette, E.C.D., Georgiades, A. and Tweedy, D. (2002) 'Biobehavioral approaches to the treatment of essential hypertension', *Journal of Consulting and Clinical Psychology*, *70*: 569–89.

Blumhagen, D. (1980) 'Hyper-tension: a folk illness with a medical name', *Culture, Medicine and Psychiatry*, *4*: 197–227.

Bombardieri, D. and Easthorpe, G. (2000) 'Convergence between orthodox and alternative medicine: a theoretical elaboration and empirical test', *Health*, *4*: 479–94.

Bond, M.J. and Feather, N.T. (1988) 'Some correlates of structure and purpose in the use of time', *Journal of Personality and Social Psychology*, *55*: 321–29.

Bondy, S.J., Rehm, J., Ashley, M.J., Walsh, G., Single, E. and Room, R. (1999) 'Low risk drinking guidelines: the scientific evidence', *Canadian Journal of Public Health*, *90*: 264–70.

Borrayo, E.A. and Jenkins, S.R. (2001a) 'Feeling indecent: Breast cancer screening resistance of Mexican-descent women', *Journal of Health Psychology*, *6*: 537–49.

Borrayo, E.A. and Jenkins, S.R. (2001b) 'Feeling healthy: So why should Mexican-descent women screen for breast cancer?', *Qualitative Health Research*, *11*: 812–23.

Borrini-Feyerabend, G. (1995) 'Promoting health as a sustainable state', *Medicine and Global Survival*, Part 1: 2(3): 162–75; Part 2: 2(4): 227–34.

Bostick, R.M., Sprafka, J.M., Virnig, B.A. and Potter, J.D. (1994) 'Predictors of cancer prevention attitudes and participation in cancer screening examinations', *Preventive Medicine*, *23*: 816–26.

Bourdieu, P. (1984) *Distinction: A Social Critique of the Judgement of Taste*. London: Routledge & Kegan Paul.

Boureaudhuij, I.D. (1997) 'Family food rules and healthy eating in adolescents', *Journal of Health Psychology*, *2*: 45–56.

Bowers, K.S. (1968) 'Pain, anxiety and perceived control', *Journal of Consulting and Clinical Psychology*, *32*: 596–602.

Bowling, A. (1991) *Measuring Health: A Review of Quality of Life Measurement Scales*. Buckingham: Open University Press.

Bowling, A. (1995) *Measuring Disease: A Review of Disease-Specific Quality of Life Measurement Scales*. Buckingham: Open University Press.

Boyle, M.A. and Morris, D.H. (1999) *Community Nutrition in Action: An Entrepreneurial Approach*. Belmont, CA: West/Wadsworth.

Bray, S.R., Gyurcsik, N.C., Culos-Reed, S.N., Dawson, K.A. and Martin, K.A. (2001) 'An exploratory investigation of the relationship between proxy efficacy, self-efficacy and exercise attendance', *Journal of Health Psychology*, *6*: 425–34.

Brehm, J.W. (1966) *A Theory of Psychological Reactance*. New York: Academic Press.

Brekke, M., Hjortland, P. and Kvien, T. (2003) 'Changes in self-efficacy and health status over 5 years: a longitudinal observational study of 306 patients with rheumatoid arthritis', *Arthritis Rheumatology*, *49*: 342–8.

Brennan, T.A., Leape, L.L., Laird, N.M. et al. (1991) 'Incidence of adverse events and negligence in hospitalized patients: Results of the Harvard Medical Practice Study', *New England Journal of Medicine*, *324*: 370–6.

Brewin, C.R., Dalgleish, T. and Joseph, S. (1996) 'A dual representation theory of posttraumatic stress disorder', *Psychological Review*, *103*: 670–86.

Bridge Consortium Team (2003) http://www.nof.org.uk/documents/live/3999p__HLC_Evaluation_Year2.pdf.

British Medical Association (1989) *BMA Guide to Alcohol and Accidents*. London: BMA.

Broad, M. (2001) 'Survey shows firms ready to expand drink and drugs tests', *Personnel Today*, 7 August. Available online: www.personneltoday.co.uk/Articles/Article.aspx?liArticleID=8550

Bronfenbrenner, U. (1979) *The Ecology of Human Development*. Cambridge, MA: Harvard University Press.

Broome, A. and Llewellyn, S. (eds) (1995) *Health Psychology: Processes and Applications*, 2nd edn. London: Chapman & Hall.

Brown, M. and Auerback, A. (1981) 'Communication patterns in initiation of marital sex', *Medical Aspects of Human Sexuality*, *15*: 105–17.

Brown, M.S. and Goldstein, J.L. (1984) 'How LDL receptors influence cholesterol and atherosclerosis', *Scientific American*, *251(5)*: 52–60.

Brown, S.D. (1996) 'The textuality of stress: drawing between scientific and everyday accounting', *Journal of Health Psychology*, *1*: 173–93.

Brown, S.E. (2001) 'Disability culture', *Independent Living Institute Newsletter*, *12*. www.independentliving.org/newsletter/12.01.html

Brownell, K. (1991) 'Personal responsibility and control over our bodies: when expectation exceeds reality', *Health Psychology*, *10*: 303–10.

Brydon-Miller, M. (2004) 'Using partipatory action research to address community health issues', in M. Murray (ed.), *Critical Health Psychology*. New York: Palgrave. pp. 187–202.

Buller, M.K. and Buller, D.B. (1987) 'Physicians' communication style and patient satisfaction', *Journal of Health and Social Behavior*, *28*: 375–89.

Bullock, H.E. and Lott, B. (2001) 'Building a research and advocacy agenda on issues of economic justice', *Analyses of Social Issues and Public Policy*, *1*: 147–62.

Burg, M.M., Benedetto, M.C., Rosenberg, R. and Soufer, R. (2003) 'Presurgical depression predicts medical morbidity 6 months after coronary artery bypass graft surgery', *Psychosomatic Medicine*, *65*: 111–8.

Burns, M. and Gavey, N. (2004) '"Healthy weight" at what cost? "Bulimia" and a discourse of weight control', *Journal of Health Psychology*, *9*: 549–66.

Byrne, B.M. (1994) *Structural Equation Modeling with EQS and EQS/Windows*. Thousand Oaks, CA: Sage.

Byrne, P.S. and Long, B.E.L. (1976) *Doctors Talking to Patients*. London: HMSO.

Cabinet Office, Prime Minister's Strategy Unit (2004) *Alcohol Harm Reduction Strategy for England*, London: Cabinet Office.

Calnan, M. (1987) *Health and Illness: The Lay Perspective*. London: Tavistock.

Calnan, M. and Williams, S. (1991) 'Style of life and the salience of health: an exploratory study of health related practices in households from differing socio-economic circumstances', *Sociology of Health and Illness*, *13*: 506–29.

Calnan, M. and Williams, S. (1992) 'Images of scientific medicine', *Sociology of Health and Illness*, *14*: 233–43.

Campbell, C. (2000) 'Selling sex in the time of AIDS: the psycho-social context of condom use by southern African sex workers', *Social Science and Medicine*, *50*: 479–94.

Campbell, C. (2003) *Letting Them Die: Why HIV/AIDS Prevention Programmes Often Fail*. Oxford: James Curry.

Campbell, C. (2004) 'Health psychology and community action', in M. Murray (ed.), *Critical health psychology*. London: Palgrave. pp. 203–21.

Campbell, C. and Murray, M. (2004) 'Community health psychology: promoting analysis and action for social change', *Journal of Health Psychology*, *9*: 187–95.

Campbell, C., Wood, R. and Kelly, M. (1999) *Social Capital and Health*. London: Health Education Authority.

Campbell, K., Waters, E., O'Meara, S., Kelly, S., Summerbell, C. (2002) 'Interventions for preventing obesisty in children (Cochrane Review)', in *The Cochrane Library*, Issue 2. CD001871. Chichester: John Wiley.

Campbell, L.C., Clauw, D.J. and Keefe, F.J. (2003) 'Persistent pain and depression: a biopsychosocial perspective', *Biological Psychiatry*, *54*: 399–409.

Campbell, S.M., Peplau, L.A. and DeBro, S.C. (1992) 'Women, men and condoms. Attitudes and experiences of heterosexual college students', *Psychology of Women Quarterly*, *16*: 273–88.

Cantor, N. and Blanton, H. (1996) 'Effortful pursuit of personal goals in daily life', in J.A. Bargh and P.M. Gollwitzer (eds), *The Psychology of Action: Linking Cognition and Motivation to Behaviour*. New York: Guilford Press. pp. 338–59.

Capaldi, E. (1996) 'Conditioned food preferences', in E.D. Capaldi (ed.), *Why We Eat What We Eat: The Psychology of Eating*. Washington, DC: American Psychological Association. pp. 53–80.

Cappell, H. and Greeley, J. (1987) 'Alcohol and tension reduction: an update on research and theory', in H.T. Blane and K.E. Leonard (eds), *Psychological Theories of Drinking and Alcoholism*. New York: Guildford Press. pp. 15–54.

Carers Online (2003) 'Carers are missing millions: £660m of benefits go unclaimed', 5 December.

Carmichael, F. and Woods, R. (2000) 'Ethnic penalties in unemployment and occupational attainment: evidence for Britain', *International Review of Applied Economics*, *14*: 71–98.

Carroll, D., Davey Smith, G. and Bennett, P. (1996) 'Some observations on health and socio-economic status', *Journal of Health Psychology*, *1*: 23–39.

Cartwright, M., Wardle, J., Steggles, N., Simon, A.E., Croker, H. and Jarvis, M. (2003) 'Stress and dietary practices in adolescents', *Health Psychology*, *22*: 362–9.

Carver, C.S., Scheier, M.F. and Weintraub, J.K. (1989) 'Assessing coping strategies: a theoretically based approach', *Journal of Personality and Social Psychology*, *56*: 267–83.

CBI/PPP (2000) *Focus on Absence: Absence and Labour Turnover Survey*. London: Confederation of British Industry (CBI).

Chalmers, B. (1996) 'Western and African conceptualizations of health', *Psychology and Health*, *12*: 1–10.

Chamberlain, K. (1997) 'Socio-economic health differentials: from structure to experience', *Journal of Health Psychology*, *2*: 399–412.

Chamberlain, K. (2004) 'Food and health: expanding the agenda for health psychology', *Journal of Health Psychology*, *9*: 467–82.

Chamberlain, K. and Zika, S. (1990) 'The minor events approach to stress: support for the use of daily hassles', *British Journal of Psychology*, *81*: 469–81.

Channel 4 (2005) *Jamie's School Dinners*. February–March.

Chapman, C.R., Casey, K.L., Dubner, R., Foley, K.M., Gracely, R.H. and Reading, A.E. (1985) 'Pain measurement: an overview', *Pain*, *22(1)*: 1–31.

Chapple, A., Ziebland, S. and McPherson, A. (2004) 'Stigma, shame, and blame experienced by patients with lung cancer: qualitative study', *British Medical Journal*, *328*: 1470.

Charmaz, K. (1983) 'Loss of self: a fundamental form of suffering in the chronically ill', *Sociology of Health and Illness*, *5*: 168–95.

Charmaz, K. (2003) 'Grounded theory', in J.A. Smith (ed.), *Qualitative Psychology: A Practical Guide to Research Methods*. London: Sage. pp. 81–110.

Chassin, L., Presson, C., Pitts, S. and Sherman, S.J. (2000) 'The natural history of cigarette smoking from adolescence to adulthood in a mid-western community sample: multiple trajectories and their psychosocial correlates', *Health Psychology*, *19*: 223–31.

Chataway, C. (1997) 'An examination of the constraints on mutual inquiry in a Participatory Action Research project', *Journal of Social Issues*, *53(4)*: 747–65.

Cheng, Y.H. (1997) 'Explaining disablement in modern times: hand-injured workers' accounts of their injuries in Hong Kong', *Social Science and Medicine*, *45*: 739–50.

Chesler, M.A. and Parry, C. (2001) 'Gender roles and/or styles in crisis: an integrative analysis of the experiences of fathers of children with cancer', *Qualitative Health Research*, *11*: 363–84.

Chesney, M.A., Chambers, D.B., Taylor, J.M., Johnson, L.M. and Folkman, S. (2003) 'Coping effectiveness training for men living with HIV: results from a randomised clinical trial testing a group-based intervention', *Psychosomatic Medicine*, *65*: 1038–46.

Chesterton, L.S., Foster, N.E., Wright, C.C., Baxter, G.D. and Barlas, P. (2003) 'Effects of TENS frequency, intensity and stimulation site parameter manipulation on pressure pain thresholds in healthy human subjects', *Pain*, *106*: 73–80.

Chopra, M. and Darnton-Hill, I. (2004) 'Tobacco and obesity epidemics: not so different after all?', *British Medical Journal*, *328*: 1558–60.

Chow, E., Tsao, M.N. and Harth, T. (2004) 'Does psychosocial intervention improve survival in cancer? A meta-analysis', *Palliative Medicine, 18(1)*: 25–31.

Clare, L. and Cox, S. (2003) 'Improving service approaches and outcomes for people with complex needs through consultation and involvement', *Disability and Society, 18(7)*: 935–53.

Clark-Carter, D. (1997) *Doing Quantitative Psychological Research: From Design to Report*. Hove: Psychology Press.

Clark-Carter, D. and Marks, D.F. (2004) 'Intervention studies: design and analysis', in D.F. Marks and L. Yardley (eds), *Research Methods for Clinical and Health Psychology*. London: Sage. pp. 166–84.

Clarke, P. and Eves, F. (1997) 'Applying the transtheoretical model to the study of exercise on prescription', *Journal of Health Psychology, 2*: 195–207.

Coakley, J. and White, A. (1992) 'Making decisions: gender and sport participation among British adolescents', *Sociology of Sport Journal, 9*: 20–35.

Coburn, D. (2004) 'Beyond the income inequality hypothesis: class, neo-liberalism and health inequalities', *Social Science and Medicine, 58*: 41–56.

Cohen, A. (1974) *Two-Dimensional Man: An Essay on the Anthropology of Power and Symbolism in Complex Society*. Berkeley: University of California Press.

Cohen, S. and Herbert, T.B. (1996) 'Health psychology: psychological factors and physical disease from the perspective of human psychoneuroimmunology', *Annual Review of Psychology, 47*: 113–42.

Cohen, S. and Miller, G.E. (2001) 'Stress, immunity and susceptibility to upper respiratory infection', in R. Ader, D. Felten and N. Cohen (eds), *Psychoneuroimmunology*, 3rd edn. London: Academic Press. pp. 499–509.

Cohen, S. and Williamson, G.M. (1988) 'Perceived stress in a probability sample of the United States', in S. Spacapan and S. Oskamp (eds), *The Social Psychology of Health*. Newbury Park, CA: Sage. pp. 31–67.

Cohen, S. and Williamson, G.M. (1991) 'Stress and infectious disease in humans', *Psychological Bulletin, 109*: 5–24.

Cohen, S. and Wills, T.A. (1985) 'Stress, social support and the buffering hypothesis', *Psychological Bulletin, 98*: 310–57.

Colby, S., Tiffany, S., Shiffman, S. and Niaura, R. (2000) 'Are adolescent smokers dependent on nicotine? A review of the evidence', *Drug and Alcohol Dependency, 59(Suppl)*: 83–95.

Coleman, E.M., Hoon, P.W. and Hoon, E.F. (1983) 'Arousability and sexual satisfaction in lesbian and heterosexual women', *Journal of Sex Research, 19*: 58–73.

Colette, M., Godin, G., Bradet, R. and Gionet, N.J. (1994) 'Active living in communities: understanding the intention to take up physical activity as an everyday way of life', *Canadian Journal of Public Health, 85*: 418–21.

Colquitt, J.A., LePine, J.A. and Noe, R.A. (2000) 'Toward an integrative theory of training motivation: a meta-analytic path analysis of 20 years of research', *Journal of Applied Psychology, 85*: 678–707.

Conner, M. and Norman, P. (eds) (2005) *Predicting Health Behaviour*, 2nd edn. Buckingham: Open University Press.

Conner, M. and Sparks, P. (2005) 'The theory of planned behaviour and health behaviours', in M. Conner and P. Norman (eds), *Predicting Health Behaviour*, 2nd edn. Buckingham: Open University Press.

Conner, M., Holland, C., Wolinsky, A., Thompson, N. and Gilhespy, M. (1994) 'Changing risky driving behaviour in young adults'. Paper presented to the BPS Social Section Annual Conference, University of Cambridge, 20–22 September.

Conner, M., Povey, R., Sparks, P., James, R. and Shepherd, R. (2003) 'Moderating role of attitudinal ambivalence within the Theory of Planned Behaviour', *British Journal of Social Psychology, 42*: 75–94.

Conrad, K.M., Flay, B.R. and Hill, D. (1992) 'Why children start smoking: predictors of onset', *British Journal of Addiction, 87*: 1711–24.

Conrad, P. (1985) 'The meaning of medications: another look at compliance', *Social Science and Medicine, 20*: 29–37.

Cook, C.C.H. and Gurling, H.M.D. (2001) 'Genetic predisposition to alcohol dependence and problems', in N. Heather, T.J. Peters and T. Stockwell (eds), *International Handbook of Alcohol Dependence and Problems*, London: Wiley. pp. 257–80.

Cooper A., Lloyd G., Weinman J. and Jackson G. (1999) 'Why patients do not attend cardiac rehabilitation: role of intentions and illness beliefs', *Heart, 82*: 234–6.

Cooper, A.F., Jackson, G., Weinman, J. and Horne, R. (2002) 'Factors associated with cardiac rehabilitation attendance: a systematic review of the literature', *Clinical Rehabilitation, 16(5)*: 541–52.

Corin, E. (1995) 'The cultural frame: context and meaning in the construction of health', in B.C. Amick III, S. Levine, A.R. Tarlov and D. Chapman Walsh (eds), *Society and Health*. New York: Oxford University Press. pp. 272–304.

Coulter, A. (1999) 'Paternalism or partnership', *British Medical Journal, 319*: 719–20.

Coupland, J., Robinson, J.D. and Coupland, N. (1994) 'Frame negotiation in doctor–elderly patient consultations', *Discourse and Society, 5*: 89–124.

Courtney, W.H. (2000) 'Constructions of masculinity and their influence on men's well-being', *Social Science and Medicine, 50*: 1385–1401.

Courtney, W.H., McCreary, D.R. and Merighi, J.R. (2002) 'Gender and ethnic differences in health beliefs and behaviors', *Journal of Health Psychology, 7*: 219–31.

Cox, C.L. (1982) 'An interaction model of client health behavior: theoretical prescription for nursing', *Advances in Nursing Science, 5*: 519–27.

Cox, T. (1978) *Stress*. London: Macmillan.

Crawford, R. (1980) 'Healthism and the medicalisation of everyday life', *International Journal of Health Services, 10*: 365–68.

Crombez, G., Bijttebier, P., Eccleston, C., Mascagni, T., Mertens, G., Goubert, L. and Verstraeten, K. (2003) 'The child version of the pain catastrophizing scale (PCS-C): a preliminary validation', *Pain, 104(3)*: 639–46.

Cropley, M., Ayers, S. and Nokes, L. (2003) 'People don't exercise because they can't think of reasons to exercise: an examination of causal reasoning with the Transtheoretical Model', *Psychology, Health and Medicine, 8*: 409–14.

Crossley, M.L. (1999) 'Making sense of HIV infection: discourse and adaptation to life with HIV positive diagnosis', *Health, 3*: 95–119.

Crossley, M.L. (2002) 'The perils of health promotion and the "barebacking" backlash', *Health, 6(1)*: 47–68.

Crossley, M.L. (2003) '"Would you consider yourself a healthy person?" Using focus groups to explore health as a moral phenomenon', *Journal of Health Psychology, 8*: 501–14.

Cummings, J.H. and Bingham, S.A. (1998) 'Diet and the prevention of cancer', *British Medical Journal, 317*: 1636–40.

Cunningham, A.J. and Watson, K. (2004) 'How psychological therapy may prolong survival in cancer patients: new evidence and a simple theory', *Integrative Cancer Therapy, 3(3)*: 214–29.

Curtis, S. and Rees Jones, I. (1998) 'Is there a place for geography in the analysis of health inequalities?', *Sociology of Health and Illness, 20*: 645–72.

Dahlgren, G. and Whitehead, M. (1991) *Policies and Strategies to Promote Equity and Health*. Stockholm: Institute for Future Studies.

Dahlstrom, W.G. and Welsh, G.S. (1960) *An MMPI Handbook: A Guide to Use in Clinical Practice and Research*. Minneapolis: University of Minnesota Press.

Daniels, N., Kennedy, B. and Kawachi, I. (2000) 'Justice is good for our health: How greater economic equality would promote public health', *Boston Review*, Feb/Mar, p. 25.

Dasen, P.R., Berry, J.W. and Sartorius, N. (eds) (1988) *Health and Cross-cultural Psychology: Towards Applications*. Newbury Park, CA: Sage.

Daudpota, I. (2000) 'Water shortage – A way out', *Economist*, 26 May. Available at: http://lists.isb.sdnpk.org/pipermail/econo-list-old/2000-May/001313.html

Davis, L.J. (2002) *Bending Over Backwards: Disability, Dismodernism and Other Different Positions*. London: New York University Press.

Davis, P. (1992) Cited in A. Thomson, 'Let's talk about sex (yes, again)', *The Times,* 3 December.

Davison, C., Macintyre, S. and Davey Smith, G. (1994) 'The potential social impact of predictive genetic testing for susceptibility to common chronic diseases: a review and proposed research agenda', *Sociology of Health and Illness, 16*: 340–71.

Deal, M. (2003) 'Disabled people's attitudes toward other impairment groups: a hierarchy of impairments', *Disability and Society, 18(7)*: 897–910.

Deaton, A. (2001) *Health, Inequality and Economic Development*. WHO Commission on Macroeconomics and Health. CMH Working Papers, No. WG1: 3.

Dejong, G. and Basnett, I. (2001) 'Disability and health policy: the role of markets in the delivery of health services', in G.L. Albrecht, K.D. Seelman and M. Bury (eds), *Handbook of Disability Studies*. London: Sage.

De Jonge, J., Dormann, C., Janssen, P.P.M., Dollard, M.F., Landeweerd, J.A. and Nijhuis, F.J.N. (2001) 'Testing reciprocal relationships between job characteristics and psychological well-being: a cross-lagged structural equation model', *Journal of Occupational and Organizational Psychology, 74*: 29–46.

De La Cancela, V., Chin, J.L. and Jenkins, Y.M. (1998) *Community Health Psychology: Empowerment for Diverse Communities*. London: Routledge.

DelVecchio Good, M.A., Munakata, T., Kobayashi, Y., Mattingly, C. and Good, B.J. (1994) 'Oncology and narrative time', *Social Science and Medicine, 38*: 855–62.

DeMatteo, D., Harrison, C., Arneson, C., Salter Goldie, R., Lefebvre, A., Read, S.E. and King, S.M. (2002) 'Disclosing HIV/AIDS to children: the paths families take to truthtelling', *Psychology, Health and Medicine, 7(3)*: 339–56.

Department of Health (1999) *Saving Lives: Our Healthier Nation*. London: The Stationery Office.

Department of Health (2000) *An Organization with a Memory: Report of an Expert Group on Learning from Adverse Events in the NHS, Chaired by the Chief Medical Officer*. London: The Stationery Office.

Department of Transport (1992) *The Involvement of Alcohol in Fatal Accidents to Adult Pedestrians*. London: Transport Research Laboratory. Report No. 343.

Department of Transport (1996) *Road Accidents, Great Britain, the Casualty Report*. London: Department of Transport.

Dew, K. (1999) 'Epidemics, panic and power: representations of measles and measles vaccine', *Health, 3*: 379–98.

Dew, M., Bromet, E.J. and Penkower, L. (1992) 'Mental health effects of job loss in women', *Psychological Medicine, 22*: 751–64.

DHHS (1996) *Physical activity and health: A report of the Surgeon General*. Atlanta, GA: U.S. Department of Health and Human Services, National Center for Chronic Disease Prevention and Health Promotion.

DHHS (2001) *Healthy People 2010*. Atlanta, GA: U.S. Department of Health and Human Services, Office of Disease Prevention and Health Promotion.

D'Houtaud, A. and Field, M.G. (1984) 'The image of health: variations in perception by social class in a French population', *Sociology of Health and Illness, 6*: 30–60.

Dickerson, S.S. and Kemeny, M.E. (2004) 'Acute stressors and cortisol responses: a theoretical integration and synthesis of laboratory research', *Psychological Bulletin, 130*: 355–91.

DiClemente, C.C. (1993) 'Changing addictive behaviors: a process perspective', *Current Directions in Psychological Science, 2*: 101–6.

DiClemente, C.C. and Prochaska, J.O. (1982) 'Self change and therapy change of smoking behavior: a comparison of processes of change in cessation and maintenance', *Addictive Behavior, 7*: 133–42.

DiClemente, C.C. and Velicer, W.F. (1997) 'The transtheoretical model of health behavior change', *American Journal of Health Promotion, 12*: 38–48.

Diefenbach, M.A. and Leventhal, H. (1996) 'The common-sense model of illness representation: theoretical and practical considerations', *Journal of Social Distress and the Homeless, 5*: 11–38.

Diez Roux, A.V., Stein Merkin, S., Arnett, D. et al. (2001) 'Neighborhood of residence and incidence of coronary heart disease', *New England Journal of Medicine, 345*: 99–106.

Dijkstra, A., Roijackers, J. and De Vries, H. (1998) 'Smokers in four stages of readiness to change', *Addictive Behaviors, 23*: 339–50.

DiMatteo, M.R. (2004) 'Social support and patient adherence to medical treatment: A meta-analysis', *Health Psychology, 23*: 207–18.

Dishman, R.K. (1986) 'Exercise compliance: a new view for public health', *Physician and Sports Medicine, 14*: 127–45.

Dishman, R.K. and Gettman, L.R. (1980) 'Psychobiologic influences on exercise adherence', *Journal of Sport Psychology, 2*: 295–310.

Doise, W. (1986) *Levels of Explanation in Social Psychology*. Cambridge: Cambridge University Press.

Doll, R. and Hill, A.B. (1952) 'A study of the aetiology of carcinoma of the lung', *British Medical Journal, 2*: 1271–86.

Doll, R. and Peto, R. (1981) *The Cause of Human Cancer*. Oxford: Oxford University Press.

Doll, R., Peto, R., Hall, E. and Gray, R. (1994) 'Mortality in relation to consumption of alcohol: 13 years' observation on male British doctors', *British Medical Journal, 309*: 911–18.

Donovan, J.L. and Blake, D.R. (1992) 'Patient non-compliance: deviance or reasoned decision-making?', *Social Science and Medicine, 34*: 507–13.

Donovan, M.A., Drasgow, F. and Muson, L.J. (1998) 'The perceptions of fair interpersonal treatment: development and validation of a measure of interpersonal treatment in the workplace', *Journal of Applied Psychology, 83*: 683–92.

Douglas, M. and Nicod, M. (1974) 'Taking the biscuit: the structure of British meals', *New Society,* 19 December.

Drobes, D.J., Saladin, M.E. and Tiffany, S.T. (2001) 'Classical conditioning mechanisms in alcohol dependence', in N. Heather, T.J. Peters and T. Stockwell (eds), *International Handbook of Alcohol Dependence and Problems*. London: Wiley. pp. 281–97.

Drummond, D.C., Tiffany, S.T., Glautier, S. and Remington, B. (eds) (1995) *Addictive Behaviour: Cue Exposure Theory and Practice*. London: Wiley.

Duijts, S.F., Zeegers, M.P. and Borne, B.V. (2003) 'The association between stressful life events and breast cancer risk: a meta-analysis', *International Journal of Cancer, 107*: 1023–9.

Eaker, E.D., Sullivan, L.M., Kelly-Hayes, M., D'Agostino, Sr. and Benjamin, E.J. (2004) 'Does job strain increase the risk for cornary heart disease or death in men and women?', *American Journal of Epidemiology, 159*: 950–8.

Eardley, A. and Elkind, A. (1990) 'A pilot study of attendance for breast cancer screening', *Social Science and Medicine, 30*: 693–9.

Eardley, A., Knopf Elkind, A., Spencer, B., Hobbs, P., Pendleton, L.L. and Haran, D. (1985) 'Attendance for cervical screening – whose problem?', *Social Science and Medicine, 20*: 955–62.

Eccleston, C., Morley, S., Williams, A., Yorke, L. and Mastroyannopoulou, K. (2002) 'Systematic review of randomised controlled trials of psychological therapy for chronic pain in children and adolescents, with a subset meta-analysis of pain relief', *Pain, 99(1–2)*: 157–65.

Eccleston, Z. and Eccleston, C. (2004) 'Interdisciplinary management of adolescent chronic pain: developing the role of physiotherapy', *Physiotherapy, 90*: 77–81.

Edwards, A.G., Hailey, S. and Maxwell, M. (2004) 'Psychological interventions for women with metastatic breast cancer', *Cochrane Database of Sysematic Reviews, 2*: CD004253.

Edwards, D. (1997) *Discourse and Cognition*. London: Sage.

Edwards, J.R. and Cooper, C.L. (1990) 'The person-environment fit approach to stress: recurring problems and some suggested solutions', *Journal of Organizational Behaviour, 11*: 293–307.

Egger, G. and Swinburn, B. (1997) 'An ecological approach to the obesity pandemic', *British Medical Journal, 315*: 477–80.

Einarsen, S. and Raknes, B.I. (1997) 'Harassment in the workplace and the victimization of men', *Violence and Victims, 12*: 247–63.

Eiser, C., Walsh, S. and Eiser, J.R. (1986) 'Young children's understanding of smoking', *Addictive Behaviors, 11*: 119–23.

Eissa, M.A., Poffenbarger, T. and Portman, R.J. (2001) 'Comparison of the actigraph versus patients' diary information in defining circadian time periods for analysing ambulatory blood pressure monitoring data', *Blood Pressure Monitoring, 6*: 21–5.

Elmone, J.G., Barton, M.B., Moceri, V.M., Polk, S., Arena, P.J. and Fletcher, S.W. (1998) 'Ten year risk of false positive screening mammograms and clinical breast examination', *New England Journal of Medicine, 338*: 1089–96.

Engel, G.L. (1959) 'Psychogenic pain and the pain prone patient', *American Journal of Medicine, 26*: 899–918.

Engel, G.L. (1977) 'The need for a new medical model: a challenge for biomedicine', *Science, 196*: 129–36.

Engel, G.L. (1980) 'The clinical application of the biopsychosocial model', *American Journal of Psychiatry, 137*: 535–44.

Engels, F. (1845/1958) *The Condition of the Working Class in England in 1844*. London: Lawrence & Wishart.

Equal Opportunities Commission (2004) *Facts about Women and Men in Great Britain 2004*. www. eoc.org.uk

Euripides (1954/414BC) *The Bacchae*, trans. P. Vellacott. London: Penguin.

European Commission (1999) *A Pan-EU Survey of Consumer Attitudes to Physical Activity, Body Weight and Health*. Luxembourg: EC. DGV/F.3.

European Commission (2000) *European Employment and Social Policy: A Policy for People*. European Communities.

European Commission (2002) *Employment in Europe: Recent Trends and Prospects, 2002, 2003*. EURES, Employment and European Social Fund.

European Foundation (2002) 'Comparative overview of industrial relations in Europe in 2002', *European industrial relations observatory on-line*.

European Research Information Centre (2004) http://europa.eu.int/com/research/infocentre/article (consulted 5 March 2005).

European Science Foundation (2000) 'Social variations in health expectancy in Europe: an ESF interdisciplinary programme in the social and medical sciences', Strassbourg: IRED (www.uni-duesseldorf.de/health).

Evans, D. and Norman P. (2003) 'Predicting adolescent pedestrians' road-crossing intentions: an application and extension of the Theory of Planned Behaviour', *Health Education Research*, 18: 267–77.

Evans, M., Stoddart, H., Condon, L., Freeman, E., Grizzell, M. and Mullen, R. (2001) 'Parents' perspectives on the MMR immunization: a focus group study', *British Journal of General Practice*, 43: 281–4.

Evans, O. and Steptoe, A. (2001) 'Social support at work, heart rate, and cortisol: A self-monitoring study', *Journal of Occupational Health Psychology*, 6: 361–70.

Evans, P., Hucklebridge, F. and Clow, A. (2000) *Mind, Immunity and Health: The Science of Psychoneuroimmunology*. London: Free Association Books.

Evans, P.D. (1990) 'Type A behaviour and coronary heart disease: when will the jury return?', *British Journal of Psychology*, 81: 147–57.

Evans, R.I. (1988) 'Health promotion – science or ideology?', *Health Psychology*, 7: 203–19.

Evans, S.T. and Haworth, J.T. (1991) 'Variations in personal activity, access to categories of experience and psychological well-being in unemployed young adults', *Leisure Studies*, 10: 249–264.

Everitt, A. and Hardiker, P. (1997) 'Towards a critical approach to evaluation', in M. Sidell, L. Jones, J. Katz and A. Peberdy (eds), *Debates and Dilemmas in Promoting Health: A Reader*. Hampshire: Open University Press.

Eysenbach, G. (2003) 'The impact of the Internet on cancer outcomes', *CA Cancer J Clin*, 53: 356–71.

Eysenck, H.J. (1965) *Fact and Fiction in Psychology*. London: Penguin.

Eysenck, H.J. and Grossarth-Maticek, R. (1991) 'Creative novation behaviour therapy as a prophylactic treatment for cancer and coronary heart disease. Part II: effects of treatment', *Behaviour Research and Therapy*, 29: 17–31.

Eysenck, H.J., Tarrant, M. and Woolf, M. (1960) 'Smoking and personality', *British Medical Journal*, 280: 1456–60.

Eysenck, M.W. and Calvo, M.G. (1992) 'Anxiety and performance: the processing of efficiency theory', *Cognition and Emotion*, 6: 409–34.

Ezzati, M., Lopez, A.D., Rodgers, A., Hoorn, S.V., Murray, C.J.L. and the Comparative Risk Assessment Collaborating Group (2002) 'Selected major risk factors and global and regional burden of disease', *Lancet*, 360: 1347–60.

Farmer, A. (1994) 'AIDS-talk and the constitution of cultural models', *Social Science and Medicine*, 38: 801–10.

Feather, N.T. and O'Brien, G.E. (1986) 'A longitudinal study of the effects of employment and unemployment on school leavers', *Journal of Occupational Psychology*, 59: 121–44.

Fellowes, D., Barnes, K. and Wilkinson, S. (2004) 'Aromatherapy and massage for symptom relief in patients with cancer', *Cochrane Database of Systematic Reviews*, 2: CD002287.

Fenton, K.A., Korovessis, C., Johnson, A.M., McCadden, A., McManus, S., Wellings, K., Mercer, C.H., Carder, C., Copas, A.J., Nanchahal, K., Macdowall, W. and Ridgway, G. (2001) 'Sexual behaviour in Britain: reported sexually transmitted infections and prevalent genital Chlamydia trachomatis infection', *The Lancet*, 358: 1851–4.

Fergus, K.D., Gray, R.E. and Fitch, M.I. (2002) 'Sexual dysfunction and the preservation of manhood: experiences of men with prostate cancer', *Journal of Health Psychology*, 7: 303–16.

Feste, C. and Anderson, R.M. (1995) 'Empowerment: from philosophy to practice', *Patient Education and Counseling*, 26: 139–44.

Fiedler, D.O. (1982) 'Managing medication and compliance: physician–pharmacist–patient interaction', *Journal of the American Geriatrics Society*, 30: S113–S117.

Fieldhouse, P. (1996) *Food and Nutrition: Customs and Culture*, 2nd edn. Cheltenham: Stanley Thornes.

Fillmore, K.M., Golding, J.M., Graves, K.L., Kniep, S., Leino, E.V., Romelsjo, A., Shoemaker, C., Ager, C.R., Allebeck, P. and Ferrer, H.P. (1998a) 'Alcohol consumption and mortality. I. Characteristics of drinking groups', *Addiction*, 93: 183–203.

Fillmore, K.M., Golding, J.M., Graves, K.L., Kniep, S., Leino, E.V., Romelsjo, A., Shoemaker, C., Ager, C.R., Allebeck, P. and Ferrer, H.P. (1998b) 'Alcohol consumption and mortality. III. Studies of female populations', *Addiction*, 93: 219–29.

Fincham, J.E. and Wertheimer, A.I. (1985) 'Using the Health Belief Model to predict initial drug therapy defaulting', *Social Science and Medicine*, 20: 101–5.

Fine, M. and Asch, A. (1982) 'The question of disability: no easy answers for the women's movement', *Reproductive Rights National Network Newsletter*, 4(3): 19–20.

Fine, M. and Barreras, R. (2001) 'To be of us', *Analysis of social Issues and Public Policy*, 1: 175–82.

Finkelstein, V. and French, S. (1993) 'Towards a psychology of disability', in J. Swain, V. Finkelstein, S. French and M. Oliver (eds), *Disabling Barriers – Enabling Environments*. London: Sage and Open University Press.

Fishbein, M. and Ajzen, I. (1975) *Belief Attitude, Intention and Behaviour*. New York: Wiley.

Fishbein, M. and Ajzen, I. (2005) 'Theory-based behavior change interventions: comments on Hobbis and Sutton', *Journal of Health Psychology*, 10: 27–31.

Fitzsimons, D., Parahoo, K. and Stringer, M. (2000) 'Waiting for coronary artery bypass surgery: a qualitative analysis', *Journal of Advanced Nursing*, 32: 1243–52.

Flay, B.R., Hu, F.B., Siddiqui, O., Day, L.E., Hedeker, D., Petratis, J., Richardson, J. and Sussman, S. (1994) 'Differential influence of parental smoking and friends' smoking on adolescent initiation and escalation of smoking', *Journal of Health and Social Behavior*, 35: 248–65.

Fleming, M.F., Barry, K.L., Manwell, L.B., Johnson, K. and London, R. (1997) 'Brief physician advice for problem alcohol drinkers: a randomised controlled trial in community-based primary care practices', *Journal of the American Medical Association*, 277: 1039–45.

Flick, U. (1998) 'The social construction of individual and public health: contributions of social representations theory to a social science of health', *Social Science Information*, 37: 639–62.

Flick, U. (2002) *An Introduction to Qualitative Research*, second edition. London: Sage.

Flynn, M. and Hirst, M. (1992) *This Year, Next Year, Sometime ...? Learning Disability and Adulthood*. London: National Development Team.

Fogarty, J.S. (1997) 'Reactance theory and patient non-compliance', *Social Science and Medicine*, 45: 1277–88.

Fogarty, L., Roter, D., Larson, S., Burke, J.G., Gillespie, J. and Levy, B. (2002) 'Patient adherence to HIV medication regimens: a review of published and abstract reports', *Patient Education and Counseling*, 46: 93–108.

Follick, M.J., Smith, T.W. and Ahern, D.K. (1985) 'The Sickness Impact Profile: a global measure of disability in chronic low back pain', *Pain*, 21(1): 67–76.

Food Standards Agency (2003) *Does Food Promotion Influence Children? A Systematic Review of the Evidence*. London: FSA.

Foster, C., Watson, M., Moynihan, C., Ardern-Jones, A. and Eeles, R. (2002) 'Genetic testing for breast and ovarian cancer predisposition: cancer burden and responsibility', *Journal of Health Psychology*, 7: 469–84.

Foucault, M. (1976) *The Birth of the Clinic*. London: Routledge.

Foucault, M. (1979) *The History of Sexuality*, Vol. 3: *The Care of the Self*. London: Allen Lane.

Fox, B.H. (1988) 'Psychogenic factors in cancer, especially its incidence', in S. Maes, D. Spielberger, P.B. Defares and I.G. Sarason (eds), *Topics in Health Psychology*. New York: Wiley. pp. 37–55.

Fox, M.L., Dwyer, D.J. and Ganster, D.C. (1993) 'Effects of stressful job demands and control on physiological and attitudinal outcomes in a hospital setting', *Academy of Management Journal*, 36: 289–318.

Foxcroft, D.R., Ireland, D., Lister-Sharp, D.J., Lowe, G. and Breen, R. (2003) 'Longer term primary prevention for alcohol misuse in young people: a systematic review', *Addiction*, 98: 397–411.

Francome, C. and Marks, D.F. (1996) *Improving the Health of the Nation*. London: Middlesex University Press.

Frank, A.W. (1993) 'The rhetoric of self-change: illness experience as narrative', *Sociological Quarterly*, 34: 39–52.

Frazier, E.L., Jiles, R.B. and Mayberry, R. (1996) 'Use of screening mammography and clinical breast examination among Black, Hispanic and White women', *Preventive Medicine*, 25: 118–25.

Freire, P. (1970) *Pedagogy of the Oppressed*. New York: Continuum.

Freire, P. (1973) *Education for Political Consciousness*. New York: Continuum.

French, J. and Adams, L. (1986) 'From analysis to sythesis: theories of health education', *Health Education Journal*, 45: 71–4.

French, J., Caplan, R. and Harrison, V. (1982) *The Mechanisms of Job Stress and Strain*. Chichester: Wiley.

French, D.P., Marteau, T.M., Weinman, J. and Senior, V. (2004) 'Explaining differences in causal attributions of patient and non-patient samples', *Psychology, Health and Medicine*, 9: 259–72.

Frese, K. and Stewart, J. (1984) 'Skill learning as a concept in life span developmental psychology: an action theoretic analysis', *Human Development*, 27: 147–62.

Frese, M. (1999) 'Social support as a moderator of the relationship between work stressors and psychological dysfunctioning: a longitudinal study with objective measures', *Journal of Occupational Health Psychology*, 4: 179–92.

Freud, S. (1961) *Civilization and its Discontents*. New York: W.W. Norton.

Frey, L.R., Adelman, M.B. and Query, J.L. (1996) 'Communication practices in the social construction of health in an AIDS residence', *Journal of Health Psychology*, 1: 383–97.

Friedman, H.S., Tucker, J.S., Tomlinson-Keasey, C., Schwartz, J.E., Wingard, D.L. and Criqui, M.H. (1993) 'Does childhood personality predict longevity?', *Journal of Personality and Social Psychology*, 65: 176–85.

Friedman, R., Schwartz, J.E., Schnall, P.L., Landsbergis, P.A., Pieper, C., Gerin, W. and Pickering, T.G. (2001) 'Psychological variables in hypertension: relationship to causal or ambulatory blood pressure in men', *Psychosomatic Medicine*, 42: 393–411.

Friedson, E. (1970) *Profession of Medicine*. New York: Harper and Row.

Furnham, A. and Baguma, P. (1999) 'Cross-cultural differences in explanations for health and illness: a British and Ugandan comparison', *Mental Health, Religion and Culture*, 2: 121–34.

Gallagher, T.H., Waterman, A.D., Ebers, A.G., Fraser, V.J. and Levinson, W. (2003) 'Patients' and physicians' attitudes regarding the disclosure of medical errors', *JAMA*, 2898: 1001–7.

Gallant, S.J., Keita, G.P. and Royak-Schaler, R. (eds) (1997) *Health Care for Women: Psychological, Social and Behavioral Influences*. Washington, DC: American Psychological Association.

Gannon, K., Glover, L., O'Neill, M. and Emberton, M. (2004) 'Men and chronic illness: a qualitative study of LUTS', *Journal of Health Psychology*, 9: 411–20.

Gannon, L.R., Haynes, S.N., Cuevas, J. and Chavez, R. (1987) 'Psychophysiological correlates of induced headaches', *Journal of behavioural Medicine*, 10: 411–23.

Garcia, J., Ervin, R.R. and Koelling, R.A. (1966) 'Learning with prolonged delay of reinforcement', *Psychonomic Science*, 5: 121–2.

Gardner, G. and Halweil, B. (2000) *Underfed and Overfed: The Global Epidemic of Malnutrition Worldwide*. Washington, DC: Worldwide Watch.

Geertz, C. (1973) *The Interpretation of Culture*. New York: Basic Books.

Giddens, A. (1992) *The Transformation of Intimacy*. Cambridge: Polity Press.

Gifford, S. (1986) 'The meaning of lumps: a case study of the ambiguities of risk', in C.R. Janes, R. Stall and S.M. Gifford (eds), *Anthropology and Epidemiology: Interdisciplinary Approaches to the Study of Health and Disease*. Dordrecht: Reidel. pp. 213–46.

Giger, J. and Davidhizar, R. (2004) 'A review of the literature on care of clients in pain who are culturally diverse', *International Nursing Review*, 51: 47–55.

Gigerenzer G. (2002) *Reckoning with Risk: Learning to Live with Uncertainty*. London: Penguin.

Gil, K.M., Carson, J.W., Sedway, J.A., Porter, L.S., Wilson Schaeffer, J.J. and Orringer, E. (2000) 'Follow-up of coping skills training in adults with sickle cell disease: analysis of daily pain and coping practice diaries', *Health Psychology*, 19: 85–90.

Gilbert, R.M. (1984) *Caffeine Consumption*. New York: Alan R. Liss.

Giles-Corti, B. and Donovan, R.J. (2003) 'The relative influence of individual, social and physical environmental determinants of physical activity', *Social Science and Medicine*, 54: 1793–812.

Gill, C.J. (2000) 'Health professionals, disability and assisted suicide: an examination of relevant empirical evidence and reply to Batavia (2000)', *Psychology, Public Policy and Law*, 6(2): 526–45.

Gillies, V. and Willig, C. (1997) '"You get the nicotine and that in your blood": constructions of addiction and control in women's accounts of cigarette smoking', *Journal of Community and Applied Social Psychology*, 7: 285–301.

Glaser, B.G. (1992) *Basics of Grounded Theory Analysis: Emergence Versus Forcing*. Mill Valley, CA: Sociology Press.

Glaser, B. and Strauss, A. (1967) *The Discovery of Grounded Theory: Strategies for Qualitative Research*. Chicago: Aldine.

Glasgow, R.E., Hampson, S.E., Strycker, L.A. and Ruggiero, L. (1997) 'Personal-model beliefs and social-environmental barriers related to diabetes self-management', *Diabetes Care, 20*: 556–61.

Glass, G.V. (1976) 'Primary, secondary and meta-analysis of research', *Educational Research, 5*: 3–8.

Glendinning, A., Shucksmith, J. and Hendry, L. (1997) 'Family life and smoking in adolescence', *Social Science and Medicine, 44*: 93–101.

Godin, G. (1994) 'Theories of reasoned action and planned behavior: usefulness for exercise promotion', *Medicine and Science in Sports and Exercise, 26*: 1391–4.

Goffman, E. (1961) *Asylums. Notes on the Management of Spoiled Identity*. London: Penguin.

Goffman, E. (1963) *Stigma: Notes on the Management of Spoiled Identity*. London: Penguin.

Goldacre, M.J. and Roberts, S.E. (2004) 'Hospital admission for acute pancreatitis in an English population, 1963–98: database study of incidence and mortality', *British Medical Journal, 328*: 1466–9.

Gollwitzer, P.M. (1999) 'Implementation intentions: Strong effects of simple plans', *American Psychologist, 54*: 493–503.

Gordon, B.O. and Rosenblum, K.E. (2001) 'Bringing disability into the sociological frame: a comparison of disability with race, sex, and sexual orientation statuses', *Disability and Society, 16(1)*: 5–19.

Gotay, C.C., Shimizu, H., Muraoka, M., Ishihara, Y., Tsuboi, K. and Ogawa, H. (2004) 'Health attitudes and behaviors: comparison of Japanese and Americans of Japanese and European ancestry', *Health & Place, 10*: 153–61.

Gottlieb, N.H. and Chen, M.S. (1985) 'Socio-cultural correlates of childhood sporting activities: their implications for heart health', *Social Science and Medicine, 21*: 533–9.

Grafstrom, M. (1994) 'The experience of burden in the care of elderly persons with dementia'. Unpublished doctoral dissertation, Karolinska Institute, Stockholm, Sweden.

Graham, H. (1976) 'Smoking in pregnancy: the attitudes of expectant mothers', *Social Science and Medicine, 10*: 399–405.

Graham, H. (1987) 'Women's smoking and family health', *Social Science and Medicine, 25*: 47–56.

Graham, J., Ramirez, A., Love, S., Richards, M. and Burgess, C. (2002) 'Stressful life experiences and risk of relapse of breast cancer: observational cohort study', *British Medical Journal, 324*: 1420–2.

Grant, L. (1995) *Living on Low Income*. Sheffield: Citizens Advice Bureau.

Gray, R. (2003) *Prostate Tales: Men's Experiences with Prostate Cancer*. Harriman, TN: Men's Studies Press.

Gray, R. and Sinding, C. (2002) *Standing Ovation: Performing Social Science Research about Cancer*. Walnut Creek, CA: Altamira Press.

Gray, R.E., Ivonoffski, V. and Sinding, C. (2001) 'Making a mess and spreading it around: Articulation of an approach to research-based theatre', in A. Bochner and C. Ellis (eds), *Ethnographically Speaking*. Walnut Creek, CA: Altamira Press. pp. 57–75.

Greatbatch, D., Heath, C., Campion, P. and Luff, P. (1995) 'How do desk-top computers affect the doctor–patient interaction?', *Family Practice, 12*: 32–6.

Greeley, A.M. (1991) *Faithful Attraction: Discovering Intimacy, Love and Fidelity in American Marriage*. New York: Doherty.

Greenglass, E.R. and Burke, R.J. (1988) 'Work and family precursors of burnout in teachers: sex differences', *Sex Roles, 18*: 215–29.

Greenwald, B.D., Narcessian, E.J. and Pomeranz, B.A. (1999) 'Assessment of psychiatrists' knowledge and perspectives on the use of opiods: review of basic concepts for managing chronic pain', *American Journal of Physical Medicine and Rehabilitation, 78*: 408–15.

Greer, S., Morris, T. and Pettingale, K.W. (1979) 'Psychological response to breast cancer; effect on outcome', *Lancet, 2*: 785–7.

Gregg, J. and Curry, R.H. (1994) 'Explanatory models for cancer among African-American women at two Atlanta neighborhood health centers: the implications for a cancer screening program', *Social Science and Medicine, 39*: 519–26.

Grimm, L.G. and Yarnold, P.R. (eds) (1995) *Reading and Understanding Multivariate Statistics*. Washington, DC: American Psychological Association.

Haines, A.P., Imeson, J.D. and Meade, T.W. (1987) 'Phobic anxiety and ischaemic heart disease', *British Medical Journal (Clinical Research Edition), 295*: 297–99.

Hall, J.A., Roter, D.L. and Katz (1988) 'Meta-analysis of correlates of provider behavior in medical encounters', *Medical Care, 26*: 1–19.

Hall, J.A. and Roter, D.L. (2002) 'Do patients talk differently to male and female physicians? A meta-analytic review', *Patient Education and Counseling, 48*: 217–24.

Hamajima, N., Hirose, K., Rohan, T., Calle, E.E., et al. (Collaborative Group on Hormonal Factors in Breast Cancer) (2002) 'Alcohol, tobacco and breast cancer – collaborative reanalysis of individual data from 53 epidemiological studies, including 58,515 women with breast cancer and 95,067 women without the disease', *British Journal of Cancer, 87*: 1234–45.

Hamilton, E.L., Wallis, M.G., Barlow, J., Cullen, L. and Wright, C. (2003) 'Women's views of a breast cancer service', *Health Care for Women International, 24*: 40–8.

Hans, M.B. and Koeppen, A.H. (1989) 'Huntington's chorea: its impact on the spouse', *Journal of Nervous and Mental Disease, 168*: 209–14.

Harden, A. and Willig, C. (1998) 'An exploration of the discursive constructions used in young adults' memories and accounts of contraception', *Journal of Health Psychology, 3*: 429–45.

Harding, R. and Higginson, I.J. (2003) 'What is the best way to help caregivers in cancer and palliative care? A systematic literature review of interventions and their effectiveness', *Palliative Medicine, 17(1)*: 63–74.

Harlan, L.C., Bernstein, A.M. and Kessler, L.G. (1991) 'Cervical cancer screening: who is not screened and why?', *American Journal of Public Health, 81*: 885–90.

Harré, R. (1979) *Social Being*. Oxford: Blackwell.

Harris, T.O. (1997) 'Life events and health', in A. Baum, S. Newman, J. Weminan, R. West and C. McManus (eds), *Cambridge Handbook of Psychology, Health and Medicine*. Cambridge: Cambridge University Press. pp. 136–8.

Hart, C.L., Davey Smith, G., Hole, D.J. and Hawthorne, V.M. (1999) 'Alcohol consumption and mortality from all causes, coronary disease, and stroke: results from a prospective cohort study of Scottish men with 21-years of follow up', *British Medical Journal, 318*: 1725–9.

Hartley, P. (1998) 'Eating disorders and health education', *Psychology, Health and Medicine, 3*: 133–40.

Hartog M. (2001) 'Overconsumption and health', *Student British Medical Journal, 9*: 408.

Harvey, A.G. and Bryant, R.A. (2002) 'Acute stress disorder: a synthesis and critique', *Psychological Bulletin, 128*: 886–902.

Harwood, H. (2000) *Updating Estimates of the Economic Costs of Alcohol Abuse in the United States: Estimates, Update Methods and Data* (Report prepared by the Lewin Group for the National Institute on Alcohol Abuse and Alcoholism). Bethesda, MD: National Institute on Alcohol Abuse and Alcoholism.

Hastings, G. and MacFadyen, L. (2000) *Keep smiling, no one's going to die. An analysis of internal documents from the tobacco industry's main UK advertising agencies*. Centre for Tobacco Control Research. (Examples of the documents can be viewed at: www.tobaccopapers.com)

Haub, C. (2002) 'How many people have ever lived on earth?', *Population Today, 23*: 4–5.

Haug, M. and Lavin, B. (1983) *Consumerism in Medicine: Challenging Physician Authority*. Beverly Hills, CA: Sage.

Hawkes, J. and Holm, K. (1993) 'Gender differences in exercise determinants', *Nursing Research, 42*: 166–72.

Haynes, R.B (1979) 'Introduction', in R.B. Haynes, D.W. Taylor and D.L. Sackett (eds), *Compliance in Health Care*. Baltimore, MD: Johns Hopkins University Press. pp. 1–7.

Head, J., Martikainen, P., Kumari, M., Kuper, H. and Marmot, M. (2002) *Work Environment, Alcohol Consumption and Ill-health: The Whitehall II Study*, CRR 422/2002, HSE Books.

Health and Safety Executive (1998) *The Changing Nature of Occupational Health*. London: HSE Books.

Health and Safety Executive (2004) 'Work related stress', www.hse.gov.uk/stress

Health Foundation (2004) *The Health Foundation Healthcare Leaders Panel. Survey 1: Patient Safety*. London: Health Foundation.

Heath, A.C. and Madden, P.A.F. (1995) 'Genetic influences on smoking behavior', in J.R. Turner, L.R. Carden and J.K. Hewitt (eds), *Behavior Genetic Approaches in Behavioral Medicine*. New York: Plenum Press. pp. 45–66.

Heath, H. (1998) 'Keeping a reflective practice diary: a practical guide', *Nurse Education Today, 18*: 592–8.

Heath, M., Reader, A. and Beck, M. (2001) 'Effect of penicillin on post-operative pain and swelling in symptomatic necrotic teeth', *Journal of Endodontics, 27*: 117–23.

Heather, N. (2001a) 'Pleasures and pains of our favourite drug', in N. Heather, T.J. Peters and T. Stockwell (eds), *International Handbook of Alcohol Dependence and Problems*. London: Wiley. pp. 5–14.

Heather, N. (2001b) 'Brief interventions', in N. Heather, T.J. Peters and T. Stockwell (eds), *International Handbook of Alcohol Dependence and Problems*. London: Wiley. pp. 605–26.

Heather, N. and Robertson, I. (1997) *Problem Drinking*. Oxford: Oxford University Press.

Heatherton, T.F., Herman, C.P. and Polivy, J. (1991) 'Effects of physical threat and ego threat on eating behavior', *Journal of Personality and Social Psychology*, 60: 138–43.

Heatherton, T.F., Kleck, R.E., Hebl, M.R. and Hull, J.G. (2000) *The Social Psychology of Stigma*. New York: Guilford.

Heckler, M. (1985) *Report of the Secretary's Task Force on Black and Minority Health: Volume 1. Executive Summary*. Washington, DC: US Government Printing Office.

Heckman, B.D., Fisher, E.B., Monsees, B., Merbaum, M., Ristvedt, S. and Bishop, C. (2004) 'Coping and anxiety in women recalled for additional diagnostic procedures following an abnormal screening mammogram', *Health Psychology*, 23: 42–8.

Heelas, P. and Lock, A. (eds) (1981) *Indigenous Psychologies: The Anthropology of the Self*. New York: Academic Press.

Heider, F. (1958) *The Psychology of Interpersonal Relations*. New York: Wiley.

Helgeson, V.S. and Fritz, H.L. (1999) 'Cognitive adaptation as a predictor of new coronary events after percutaneous transluminal coronary angioplasty', *Psychosomatic Medicine, 61(4)*: 488–95.

Hellerstedt, W.L. and Jeffery, R.W. (1997) 'The association of job strain and health behaviours in men and women', *International Journal of Epidemiology*, 26: 575–83.

Hemingway, H. and Marmot, M. (1999) 'Psychosocial factors and the aetiology and prognosis of coronary heart disease: systematic review of prospective cohort studies', *British Medical Journal, 1318*: 1460–7.

Herzlich, C. (1973) *Health and Illness: A Social Psychological Approach*. London: Academic Press.

Herzlich, C. and Pierret, J. (1987) *Illness and Self in Society*. Baltimore, MD: Johns Hopkins University Press.

Heyman-Monnikes, I., Arnold, R., Florin, I., Herda, A., Melfsen, S. and Monnikes, H. (2000) 'The combination of medical treatment plus multicomponent behavioural therapy is superior to medical treatment alone in the therapy of irritable bowel syndrome', *American Journal of Gastroenterology*, 95: 981–94.

Higgins, A. and Conner, M. (2003) 'Understanding adolescent smoking: the role of the Theory of Planned Behaviour and implementation intentions', *Psychology, Health and Medicine*, 8: 173–86.

Hobbis, I.C.A. and Sutton, S. (2005) 'Are techniques used in cognitive behaviour therapy applicable to behaviour change interventions based on the theory of planned behaviour?', *Journal of Health Psychology*, 10: 7–18.

Hoffrage, U. and Gigerenzer, G. (1998) 'Using natural frequencies to improve diagnostic inferences', *Academic Medicine, 73*: 538–40.

Hofrichter, R. (2003) 'The politics of health inequities: contested terrain', in R. Hofrichter (ed.), *Health and Social Justice: Politics, Ideology, and Inequity in the Distribution of Disease*. San Francisco, CA: Jossey-Bass.

Hofstede, G. (1980) *Culture's Consequences: International Differences in Work-related Values*. Beverly Hills, CA: Sage.

Holahan, C.J. and Moos, R.H. (1994) 'Life stressors and mental health', in W.R. Avison and I.H. Gotlib (eds), *Stress and Mental Health: Contemporary Issues and Prospects for the Future*. New York: Plenum. pp. 213–38.

Holbrook, M.L. (1871) *Parturition Without Pain: A Code of Directions for Escaping the Primal Curse*. New York: Wood & Holbrook.

Holland, J., Ramazanoglu, C., Scott, S., Sharpe, S. and Thomson, R. (1991) 'Between embarrassment and trust: young women and the diversity of condom use', in P. Aggleton, G. Hart and P. Davies (eds), *AIDS. Responses, Interventions and Care*. London: Falmer Press. pp. 127–48.

Holland, J.C. (2004) 'IPOS Sutherland Memorial Lecture: an international perspective on the development of psychosocial oncology: overcoming cultural and attitudinal barriers to improve psychosocial care', *Psychooncology, 13(7)*: 445–59.

Holland, J.C., Geary, N., Marchini, A. and Tross, S. (1987) 'An international survey of physician attitudes and practice in regard to revealing the diagnosis of cancer', *Cancer Investigation*, 5: 151.

Hollis, J.F., Connett, J.E., Stevens, V.J. and Greenlick, M.R. (1990) 'Stressful life events, Type A behaviour, and the prediction of cardiovascular and total mortality over six years', *Journal of Behavioural Medicine*, 13: 263–81.

Hollway, W. and Jefferson, T. (2000) *Doing Qualitative Research Differently: Free Association, Narrative and the Interview Method.* London: Sage.

Holmes, T.H. and Rahe, R.H. (1967) 'The social readjustment rating scale', *Journal of Psychosomatic Research*, 11: 213–18.

Holroyd, K.A. and Coyne, J. (1987) 'Personality and health in the 1980s: psychosomatic medicine revisited?', *Journal of Personality*, 55: 359–76.

Homans, H. and Aggleton, P. (1988) 'Health education, HIV infection and AIDS', in P. Aggleton and H. Homans (eds), *Social Aspects of AIDS.* London: Falmer Press. pp. 154–76.

Hopkins, N. (1994) 'Peer group processes and adolescent health-related behaviour: more than "peer group pressure"?', *Journal of Community and Applied Social Psychology*, 4: 329–45.

Horne, R. (1997) 'Representations of medication and treatment: Advances in theory and measurement', in K.J. Petrie and J.A. Weinman (eds), *Perceptions of Health and Illness.* Amsterdam: Harwood Academic. pp. 155–88.

Horne, R. and Weinman, J. (1999) 'Patients' beliefs about prescribed medicines and their role in adherence to treatment in chronic physical illness', *Journal of Psychosomatic Research*, 47: 555–67.

Horne, R. and Weinman, J. (2002) 'Self-regulation and self-management in asthma: exploring the role of illness perceptions and treatment beliefs in explaining non-adherence to preventive medication', *Psychology and Health*, 17: 17–32.

Horne, R., Graupner, L., Frost, S., Weinman, J., Wright, S.M. and Hankins, M. (2004) 'Medicine in a multi-cultural society: the effect of cultural background on beliefs about medications', *Social Science and Medicine*, 59: 1307–13.

Horowitz, D. (1985) *Ethnic Groups in Conflict.* Berkeley: University of California Press.

House of Commons (2004) *Weekly Information Bulletin*, 24 January.

House of Lords Select Committee on Science and Technology (2000) *Complementary and alternative medicine session 1999–2000*, 6th report. London: The Stationery Office.

Hu, F.B. (2003) 'Overweight and obesity in women: health risks and consequences', *Journal of Women's Health*, 12: 163–72.

Hudson, W.W., Harrison, D.F. and Crosscup, P.C. (1981) 'A short-form scale to measure sexual discord in dyodic relationships', *Journal of Sex Research*, 17: 157–74.

Hughes, J., Jelsma, J., Maclean, E., Darder, M. and Tinise, X. (2004) 'The health-related quality of life of people living with HIV/AIDS', *Disability and Rehabilitation*, 26(6): 371–6.

Hulka, B.S. (1979) 'Patient–clinician interactions and compliance', in R.B. Haynes, D.W. Taylor and D.L. Sackett (eds), *Compliance in Health Care.* Baltimore, MD: Johns Hopkins University Press. pp. 63–77.

Hulka, B.S., Cassel, J.C. and Kupper, L.L. (1976a) 'Disparities between medications prescribed and consumed among chronic disease patients', in L. Lasagna (ed.), *Patient Compliance.* Mount Kisco, NY: Futura Publishing. pp. 123–52.

Hulka, B.S., Cassel, J.C., Kupper, L.L. and Burdette, J. (1976b) 'Medication use and misuse: physician–patient discrepancies', *Journal of Chronic Diseases*, 28: 7–14.

Human Development Report (2000) *Human Rights and Human Development.* New York: Oxford University Press.

Human Development Report (2003) *Millennium Development Goals: A Compact among Nations to End Human Poverty.* New York: Oxford University Press.

Hunt, A. and Davis, P. (1991) 'What is a sexual encounter?', in P. Aggleton, G. Hart and P. Davies (eds), *AIDS: Responses, Interventions and Care.* London: Falmer Press. pp. 43–52.

Hunter, K.M. (1991) *Doctors' Stories: The Narrative Structure of Medical Knowledge.* Princeton, NJ: Princeton University Press.

Hunter, M.S., O'Dea, I. and Britten, N. (1997) 'Decision-making and hormone replacement therapy: a qualitative analysis', *Social Science and Medicine*, 45: 1541–8.

IARC (2002) 'Mammography screening can reduce deaths from breast cancer', Press Release No. 139. Available online www.iarc.fr

Ikard, F.F., Green, D. and Horn, D. (1969) 'A scale to differentiate between types of smoking as related to management of affect', *International Journal of the Addictions*, 4: 649–59.

Illich, I. (1976) *Limits to Medicine*. London: Calder and Boyars.

Ingham, R. and Kirkland, D. (1997) 'Discourses and sexual health: providing for young people', in L. Yardley (ed.), *Material Discourses of Health and Illness*. London: Routledge. pp. 150–75.

Ingham, R., Woodcock, A. and Stenner, K. (1992) 'The limitations of rational decision-making models as applied to young people's sexual behaviour', in P. Aggleton, P. Davies and G. Hart (eds), *AIDS: Rights, Risks and Reason*. London: Falmer Press. pp. 163–73.

Ingledew, D.K., Markland, D. and Medley, A.R. (1998) 'Exercise motives and stages of change', *Journal of Health psychology*, 3: 477–89.

Institute of Alcohol Studies (2003) *Crime and Disorder: Binge Drinking and the Licensing Bill*. London: Institute of Alcohol Studies.

International Association for the Study of Pain (1992) *Management of Acute Pain: A Practical Guide*. Seattle, WA: IASP Press.

IOM (2000) *To Err is Human: Building a Safer Health System*. Washington, DC: Institute of Medicine, National Academy of Science.

Irvin, J.E., Bowers, C.A., Dunn, M.E. and Wang, M.C. (1999) 'Efficacy of relapse prevention: a meta-analytic review', *Journal of Consulting and Clinical Psychology*, 67: 563–70.

Isaksson, K., Hogstedt, C., Eriksson, C. and Theorell, T. (eds) (2000) *Health Effects of the New Labour Market*. New York: Kluwer Academic/Plenum.

Iversen, L. and Chapman, V. (2002) 'Cannabinoids: a real prospect for pain relief?', *Current Opinion in Pharmacology*, 2(1): 50–5.

Jahoda, M. (1982) *Employment and Unemployment: A Social-psychological Analysis*. Cambridge: Cambridge University Press.

James, J.E. (1997) *Understanding Caffeine: A Biobehavioral Analysis*. Thousand Oaks, CA: Sage.

Jamner, L.D. and Tursky, B. (1987) 'Syndrome specific descriptor profiling: A psychophysiological and psychophysical approach', *Health Psychology*, 6: 417–30.

Janz, N. and Becker, M.H. (1984) 'The health belief model: a decade later', *Health Education Quarterly*, 11: 1–47.

Jarvis, M.J. (2004) 'Why people smoke', *British Medical Journal*, 328: 277–9.

Jensen, M.P., Karoly, P. and Huger, R. (1987) 'The development and preliminary validation of an instrument to assess patients' attitudes toward pain', *Journal of Psychosomatic Research*, 31(3): 393–400.

Jerram, K.L. and Coleman, P.G. (1999) 'The big five personality traits and reporting of health problems and health behaviour in old age', *British Journal of Health Psychology*, 4: 181–92.

Joffe, H. (1996) 'AIDS research and prevention: a social representational approach', *British Journal of Medical Psychology*, 69: 169–91.

Joffe, H. (2003) 'Social representations and health psychology', *Social Science Information*, 41(4): 559–80.

Joffe, H. and Bettega, N. (2003) 'Social representations of AIDS among Zambian adolescents', *Journal of Health Psychology*, 8: 616–31.

Joffe, H. and Haarhoff, G. (2002) 'Representations of far-flung illnesses: the case of Ebola in Britain', *Social Science and Medicine*, 54: 955–69.

Johansson, G., Johnson, J.V. and Hall, E.M. (1991) 'Smoking and sedentary behaviour as related to work organization', *Social Science and Medicine*, 32: 837–46.

Johnson, A.M. and Wellings, K. (1994) 'Studying sexual lifestyles', in A.M. Johnson, J. Wadsworth, K. Wellings and J. Field (eds), *Sexual Attitudes and Lifestyles*. Oxford: Blackwell. pp. 1–18.

Johnson, A.M., Wadsworth, J., Wellings, K. and Field, J. (eds) (1994) *Sexual Attitudes and Lifestyles*. Oxford: Blackwell.

Johnson, A.M., Mercer, C.H., Erens, B., Copas, A.J., McManus, S., Wellings, K., Fenton, K.A., Korovessis, C., Macdowall, W., Nanchahal, K., Purdon, S. and Field, J. (2001) Sexual behaviour in Britain: partnerships, practices, and HIV risk behaviours, *The Lancet*, 358: 1835–42.

Johnson, J.L., Lovato, C.Y., Maggi, S., Ratner, P.A., Shoveller, J., Baillie, L. and Kalaw, C. (2003) 'Smoking and adolescence: narratives of identity', *Research in Nursing and Health*, 26: 387–97.

Johnston, M. (1995) 'Models of disability: British Psychological Society Presidents' Award Lecture', *Psychologist*, 9(5): 205–10.

Johnston, M., Foulkes, J., Johnston, D.W., Pollard, B. and Gudmundsdottir, H. (1999) 'Impact on patients and partners of inpatient and extended cardiac counseling and rehabilitation: a controlled trial', *Psychosomatic Medicine*, 61: 225–33.

Johnston, P. and Nolan, J. (2000) *eWork 2000: Status-report on New Ways to Work in the Information Society*. Brussels: CEC, DG Information Society.

Johnstone, D. (1998) *An Introduction to Disability Studies*. London: David Fulton Publishers.

Jones, F. and Fletcher, B.C. (1996) 'Job control and health', in M. Schabracq, J. Winnubst and C. Cooper (eds), *Handbook of Work and Health Psychology*. New York: John Wiley. pp. 33–50.

Jónsdóttir, H. and Baldursdóttir, L. (1998) 'The experience of people awaiting coronary artery bypass graft surgery: the Icelandic experience', *Journal of Advanced Nursing*, 27: 68–74.

Jutras, S., Morin, P., Proulx, R., Vinay, M.C., Roy, E. and Routhier, L. (2003) 'Conceptions of wellness in families with diabetic children', *Journal of Health Psychology*, 8: 573–86.

Kamin, L.J. (1977) *The Science and Politics of IQ*. London: Penguin.

Kanfer, R. and Ackerman, P.L. (1989) 'Motivation and cognitive abilities: an integrative/aptitude-treatment interaction approach to skill acquisition', *Journal of Applied Psychology*, 74: 657–90.

Kanner, A.D., Coyne, J.C., Schaefer, C. and Lazarus, R.S. (1981) 'Comparison of two modes of stress measurement: daily hassles and uplifts versus major life events', *Journal of Behavioral Medicine*, 4: 1–39.

Karasek, R.A. (1979) 'Job demands, job decision latitude and mental strain: implications for job redesign', *Administrative Science Quarterly*, 24: 285–306.

Karasek, R. and Theorell, T. (1990) *Healthy Work: Stress, Productivity, and the Reconstruction of Working Life*. New York: Basic Books.

Kawachi, I., Colditz, G.A., Ascherio, A., Rimm, E.B., Giovannucci, E., Stampfer, M.J. and Willett, W.C. (1994) 'Prospective study of phobic anxiety and risk of coronary heart disease in men', *Circulation*, 89: 1992–7.

Kearns, R.D., Turk, D.C. and Rudy, T.E. (1985) 'The West Haven–Yale Multidimensional Pain Inventory', *Pain*, 23: 345–56.

Keefe, R.J., Hauck, E.R., Egert, J., Rimer, B. and Kornguth, P. (1994) 'Mammography pain and discomfort: a cognitive behavioural perspective', *Pain*, 56: 247–60.

Keegan, A., Liao, L.-M. and Boyle, M. (2003) 'Hirsutism: A psychological analysis', *Journal of Health Psychology*, 8: 327–46.

Keehn, R.J. (1980) 'Follow-up studies of World War II and Korean conflict prisoners. III. Mortality to January 1, 1976', *American Journal of Epidemiology*, 111: 194–211.

Kelder, S.H., Perry, C.L. and Klepp, K.I. (1994) 'Longitudinal tracing of adolescent smoking, physical activity and food choice behaviours', *American Journal of Public Health*, 84: 1121–6.

Kellner, R. (1986) *Somatization and Hypochondriasis*. New York: Praeger.

Kelner, M., Wellman, B., Boon, H. and Welsh, S. (2003) 'Responses of established healthcare to the professionalization of complementary and alternative medicine in Ontario', *Social Science and Medicine*, 59: 915–30.

Kendell, R.E., de Roumanie, M. and Ritson, E.B. (1983a) 'The influence of an increase in excise duty on alcohol consumption and its adverse effects', *British Medical Journal*, 287: 809–11.

Kendell, R.E., de Roumanie, M. and Ritson, E.B. (1983b) 'Effects of economic changes on Scottish drinking habits 1978–1982', *British Journal of Addiction*, 78: 365–79.

Kenyon, A.M.P. and Marks, D.F. (2005) 'An exploration of occupational health within a UK organisation', in preparation.

Key, T.J., Fraser, G.E., Thorogood, M., Appleby, P.N., Beral, V., Reeves, G., Burr, M.L., Chang-Claude, J., Frentzel-Beyme, R., Kuzma, J.W., Mann, J. and McPherson, K. (1998) 'Mortality in vegetarians and non-vegetarians: a collaborative analysis of 8,300 deaths among 76,000 men and women in five prospective studies', *Public Health Nutrition*, 1: 33–41.

Keys, A., Anderson, J.T. and Grande, F. (1959) 'Serum cholesterol in man: diet fat and intrinsic responsiveness', *Circulation*, 19: 201–4.

Kiecolt-Glaser, J.K., McGuire, L., Robles, T.F. and Glaser, R. (2002) 'Emotions, morbidity and mortality: new perspectives from psychoneuroimmunology', *Annual Review of Psychology*, 53: 83–107.

King, A.C. (1994) 'Community and public health approaches to the promotion of physical activity', *Medicine and Science in Sports and Exercise*, 26: 1405–12.

Kinsey, A.C., Pomeroy, W.B. and Martin, C.E. (1948) *Sexual Behaviour in the Human Male*. Philadelphia: W.B. Saunders.

Kinsey, A.C., Pomeroy, W.B., Martin, C.E. and Gebhard, P.H. (1953) *Sexual Behaviour in the Human Female*. Philadelphia: W.B. Saunders.

Kivimäki, M., Leino-Arjas, P., Luukkonen, R., Riihimäki, H., Vahtera, J. and Kirjonen, J. (2002) 'Work stress and risk of cardiovascular mortality: prospective cohort study of industrial employees', *British Medical Journal*, *325*: 857–60.

Kleinman, A. (1980) *Patients and Healers in the Context of Culture*. Berkeley, CA: University of California Press.

Klenerman, L., Slade, P.D., Stanley, I.M., Pennie, B., Reilly, J.P., Atchinson, L.E., Troup, J.D.G. and Troup, M.J. (1995) 'The prediction of chronicity in patients with an acute attack of low back pain in a general practice setting', *Spine*, *20*: 478–84.

Kobasa, S.C. (1979) 'Stressful life events and health: an enquiry into hardiness', *Journal of Personality and Social Psychology*, *37*: 1–11.

Köke, A.J.A., Schouten, J.S.A.G., Lamerichs-Geelen, M.J.H., Lipsch, J.S.M., Waltje, E.M.H., van Kleef, M. and Patijn, J. (2004) 'Pain reducing effect of three types of transcutaneous electrical nerve stimulation in patients with chronic pain: a randomised crossover trial', *Pain, 108*: 36–42.

Kraché, B., Abraham, C. and Scheinberger-Olwig, R. (in press) 'Can safer-sex promotion leaflets change cognitive antecedents of condom use? An experimental evaluation', *British Journal of Health Psychology*.

Krantz, D.S. and McCeney, M.K. (2002) 'Effects of psychological and social factors on organic disease: a critical assessment of research on coronary heart disease', *Annual Review of Psychology*, *53*: 341–69.

Kreps, G.L. (1996) 'Promoting a consumer orientation to health care and health promotion', *Journal of Health Psychology*, *1*: 41–8.

Kreps, G.L. (2001) 'Consumer/provider communication research: a personal plea to address issues of ecological vailidity, relational development, message diversity, and situational constraints', *Journal of Health Psychology*, *6*: 597–697.

Kreps, G.L. (2003) 'E-Health: technology-mediated health communication', Special Issue of the *Journal of Health Psychology, 8(1)*: 5–6.

Krieger, N. (1987) 'Shades of difference: theoretical underpinnings of the medical controversy on black/white differences in the United States, 1830–1970', *International Journal of Health Services*, *17*: 259–78.

Krieger, N. and Davey Smith, G. (2004) '"Bodies count", and body counts: social epidemiology and embodying inequality', *Epidemiologic Reviews*, *26*: 92–103.

Kugelmann, R. (1997) 'The psychology and management of pain: Gate control as theory and symbol', *Theory and Psychology*, *7*: 43–66.

Kugelmann, R. (2004) 'Health and illness: a hermeneutical phenomenological approach', in M. Murray (ed.), *Critical Health Psychology*. London: Palgrave.

Kuhn, T.S. (1970) *The Structure of Scientific Revolutions*. Chicago: University of Chicago Press.

Kulig, J.C., Meyer, C.J., Hill, S.A., Handley, C.E., Lichtenberger, S.M. and Myck, S.L. (2002) 'Refusals and delay of immunization within southwest Alberta: Understanding alternative beliefs and religious perspectives', *Canadian Journal of Public Health*, *93*: 109–12.

Kumanyika, S., Jeffrey, R.W., Morabia, A., Ritenbaugh, C. and Antipatis, V.J. (2002) 'Obesity prevention: the case for action', *International Journal of Obesity*, *26*: 425–36.

Kunesh, M.A., Hasbrook, C.A. and Lewthwaite, R. (1992) 'Physical activity socialization: peer interactions and affective responses among a sample of sixth grade girls', *Sociology of Sport Journal*, *9*: 385–96.

Kuper, H. and Marmot, M. (2003) 'Job strain, job demands, decision latitude, and risk of coronary heart disease within the Whitehall II study', *Journal of Epidemiology and Community Health*, *57*: 147–53.

Kurdek, L.A. (1991a) 'The dissolution of gay and lesbian couples', *Journal of Social and Personal Relationships*, *8*: 265–78.

Kurdek, L.A. (1991b) 'Sexuality in homosexual and heterosexual couples', in K. McKinney and S. Sprecher (eds), *Sexuality in Close Relationships*. Hillsdale, NJ: Lawrence Erlbaum.

Kvikstad, A. and Vatten, L. (1996) 'Risk and prognosis of cancer in middle aged women who have experienced the death of a child', *International Journal of Cancer*, *67*: 165–9.

Kvikstad, A., Vatten, L. and Tretli, S. (1995) 'Widowhood and divorce in relation to overall survival among middle-aged Norwegian women with cancer', *British Journal of Cancer*, *71*: 1343–7.

Labay, L.E. and Walco, G.A. (2004) 'Brief report: empathy and psychological adjustment in siblings of children with cancer', *Journal of Pediatric Psychology*, *29(4)*: 309–14.

Lal, D. and Myint, H. (1996) *The Political Economy of Poverty, Equity and Growth: A Comparative Study*. Oxford: Clarendon Press.

Lalonde, M. (1974) *A New Perspective on the Health of Canadians*. Ottawa: Information Canada.

Lamb, S. and Sington, D. (1998) *Earth Story: The Shaping of our World*. London: BBC Books.

Landrine, H. (1997) 'From the back of the bus', *Journal of Health Psychology*, 2: 428–30.

Larsen, K.M. and Smith, C.K. (1981) 'Assessment of non-verbal communication in the patient–physician interview', *Journal of Family Practice*, 12: 283–91.

Lau, R.R. and Hartman, K.A. (1983) 'Common sense representations of common illnesses', *Health Psychology*, 2: 167–86.

Laubmeier, K.K., Zakowski, S.G. and Bair, J.P. (2004) 'The role of spirituality in the psychological adjustment to cancer: a test of the transactional model of stress and coping', *International Journal of Behavioral Medicine*, *11(1)*: 48–55.

Laugesen, M. (1992) 'Tobacco advertising bans cut smoking', *British Journal of Addiction*, 87: 965–6.

Law, M.R., Frost, C.D. and Wald, N.J. (1991) 'By how much does dietary salt lower blood pressure? I – Analysis of observational data among populations', *British Medical Journal*, *302*: 811–15.

Lawson, K., Wiggins, S., Green, T., Adam, S., Bloch, M. and Hayden, M.R. (1996) 'Adverse psychological events occurring in the first year after predictive testing for Huntington's disease', *Journal of Medical Genetics*, 33: 856–62.

Lawson, V.L., Bundy, C., Lyne, P.A. and Harvey, J.N. (2004) 'Using the IPQ and PMDI to predict regular diabetes care-seeking among patients with Type 1 diabetes', *British Journal of Health Psychology*, 9: 241–52.

Lawton, J. (2003) 'Lay experiences of health and illness: past research and future agendas', *Sociology of Health and Illness*, 25: 23–40.

Lazarus, R.S. and Folkman, S. (1984) *Stress, Appraisal and Coping*. New York: Springer.

Lazarus, R.S., Kanner, A.D. and Folkman, S. (1980) 'Emotions: a cognitive-phenomenological analysis', in R. Pluchik and H. Kellerman (eds), *Emotion: Theory, Research and Experience, Vol. 1, Theories of Emotion*. New York: Academic Press. pp. 189–217.

Lebel, S., Jakubovits, G., Rosberger, Z., Loiselle, C., Seguin, C., Cornaz, C., Ingram, J., August, L. and Lisbona, A. (2003) 'Waiting for a breast biopsy: Psychosocial consequences and coping strategies', *Journal of Psychosomatic Research*, 55: 437–43.

Lee, C. and Owens, R.G. (2002) 'Issues for a psychology of men's health', *Journal of Health Psychology*, 7: 209–17.

Leichter, H.M. (1997) 'Lifestyle Correctness and the New Secular Morality', in A. Brandt and P. Rozin (eds), *Morality and Health*. New York: Routledge. pp. 359–78.

Leino, E.V., Romelsjo, A., Shoemaker, C., Ager, C.R., Allebeck, P., Ferrer, H.P. (1998) 'Alcohol consumption and mortality. II. Studies of male populations', *Addiction*, 93: 205–18.

Lerman, C. (1997) 'Psychological aspects of genetic testing: introduction to the special issue', *Health Psychology*, 16: 3–7.

Leserman, J., Petitto, J.M., Golden, R.N., Gaynes, B.N., Gu, H., Perkins, D.O., Silva, S.G., Folds, J.D. and Evans, D.L. (2000) 'Impact of stressful life events, depression, social support, coping and cortisol on progression to AIDS', *American Journal of Psychiatry*, *157*: 1221–8.

Leshan, L.L. and Worthington, R.E. (1956) 'Personality as a factor in the pathogenesis of cancer: a review of the literature', *British Journal of Medical Psychology*, 29: 49–56.

Leslie, C. (1976) *Asian Medical Systems: A Comparative Study*. Los Angeles: University of California Press.

Levav, I., Friedlander, Y., Kark, J.D. and Peritz, E. (1988) 'An epidemiologic study of mortality among bereaved parents', *New England Journal of Medicine*, *319*: 457–61.

Leventhal, H. (1999) Personal communication.

Leventhal, H. and Cameron, L. (1987) 'Behavioral theories and the problem of compliance', *Patient Education and Counseling*, 10: 117–38.

Leventhal, H. and Cleary, P.D. (1980) 'The smoking problem: a review of the research and theory in behavioral risk modification', *Psychological Bulletin*, 88: 370–405.

Leventhal, H., Meyer, D. and Nerenz, D. (1980) 'The commonsense representation of illness changes', in S. Rachman (ed.), *Contributions to Medical Psychology*, vol. 2. Oxford: Pergamon. pp. 7–30.

Leventhal, H., Leventhal, E.A. and Schaefer, P. (1989) *Vigilant Coping and Health Behaviour: A Lifespan Problem*. New Brunswich, NJ: State University of New Jersey, Rutgers.

Lewin, K. (1947) 'Frontiers in group dynamics: II. Channels of group life; social planning and action research', *Human Relations, 1(2)*: 143–53.

Lewin, K. (1948) *Resolving social conflicts: Selected papers in group dynamics*. New York: Harper and Row.

Lewin, R.J., Furze, G., Robinson, J., Griffith, K., Wiseman, S., Pye, M. and Boyle, R. (2002) 'A randomised controlled trial of a self-management plan for patients with newly diagnosed angina', *British Journal of General Practice*, 194–6, 199–201.

Ley, P. (1979) 'Memory for medical information', *British Journal of Social and Clinical Psychology*, 18: 245–56.

Ley, P. (1982) 'Satisfaction, compliance and communication', *British Journal of Social and Clinical Psychology, 21*: 241–56.

Lillard, A. (1998) 'Ethnopsychologies: cultural variations in theories of mind', *Psychological Bulletin, 123*: 3–32.

Lim, V.K.G. (1996) 'Job insecurity and its outcomes: moderating effects of work-based and non-work based social support', *Human Relations, 49*: 171–94.

Linton, S.J., Buer, N., Vlaeyen, J. and Hellsing, A. (2000) 'Are fear-avoidance behaviours related to the inception of one episode of back pain? A prospective study', *Psychology and Health, 14*: 1051–1059.

Litt, I.F. (1993) 'Health issues for women in the 1990s', S. Matteo (ed.), *American Women in the Nineties: Today's Critical Issues*. Boston: Northeastern University Press.

Logie, D.E. and Benatar, S.R. (1997) 'Africa in the 21st century: can despair turn to hope?', *British Medical Journal, 315*: 1444–6.

Lollar D.J. (2001) 'Public health trends in disability: past, present, and future', in G.L. Albrecht, K.D. Seelman and M. Bury (eds), *Handbook of Disability Studies*. London: Sage Publications.

Lord, J. and McKillop Farlow, D. (1990) 'A study of personal empowerment: implications for health promotion', *Health Promotion International, 29*: 2–8.

Lostao, L., Joner, T.E., Pettit, J.W., Chorot, P. and Sandin, B. (2001) 'Health beliefs and illness attitudes as predictors of breast cancer screening attendance', *European Journal of Public Health, 11*: 274–9.

Low Income Project Team (1996) *Low Income, Food, Nutrition and Health: Strategies for Improvement*. London: Department of Health.

Lugo, N.R. (1996) 'Empowerment education: a case study of the Resources Sisters/Compañeras Program', *Health Education Quarterly, 23*: 281–9.

Lupton, D. (1995) *The Imperative of Health: Public Health and the Regulated Body*. London: Sage.

Lupton, D. (1997) 'Consumerism, reflexivity and the medical encounter', *Social Science and Medicine, 45*: 373–81.

Luschen, G., Cockerham, W. and Kunz, G. (1996) 'The socio-cultural context of sport and health: problems of causal relations and structural interdependence', *Sociology of Sport Journal, 13*: 197–213.

Lykes, M.B. (2000) 'Possible contributions of a psychology of liberation: Whither health and human rights?', *Journal of Health Psychology, 5*: 383–98.

Lykes, M.B. (2001) 'Activist participatory research and the arts with rural Mayan women: interculturality and situated meaning making', in D. Tolman and M. Brydon-Miller (eds), *From Subjects to Subjectivities: A Handbook of Interpretive and Participatory Methods*. New York: New York University Press. pp. 183–97.

Lynch, J.W. and Davey Smith, G. (2002) 'Commentary: Income inequality and health: the end of the story?', *Journal of Epidemiology and Community Health, 31*: 549–51.

Lynch, J.W. and Davey Smith, G. (2003) 'Commentary: Income inequality and health: the end of the story?', *International Journal of Epidemiology, 31*: 549–51.

Lynch, J.W. and Kaplan, G.A. (1997) 'Understanding how inequality in the distribution of income affects health', *Journal of Health Psychology, 2*: 297–314.

Lynch, J.W., Davey Smith, G., Kaplan, G.A. and House, J. (2000) 'Income inequality and mortality: importance to health of individual income, psychosocial environment, or material conditions', *British Medical Journal, 320*: 1200–4.

Lynch, J.W., Due, P., Muntaner, C. and Davey Smith, G. (2000) 'Social capital: is it a good investment for public health?', *Journal of Epidemiology and Community Health, 54*: 404–8.

Lynch, J., Davey Smith, G., Harper, S., Hillemeier, M., Ross, N., Kaplan, G.A. and Wolfson, M. (2004) 'Is income inequality a determinant of population health? Part 1. A systematic review', *Milbank Quarterly, 82*: 5–99.

McCaffery, A.M., Eisenberg, D.M., Legedza, A.T.R., Davis, R.B. and Phillips, R.A. (2004) 'Prayer for health concerns: results of a national survey on prevalence and patterns of use', *Archives of Internal Medicine, 164(8)*: 858–62.

McCaffery, M. and Thorpe, D. (1988) 'Differences in perception of pain and development of adversarial relationships among health care providers', *Advances in Pain Research and Therapy, 11*: 113–22.

McCaul, K.D., Dyche Branstetter, A., Schroeder, D.M. and Glasgow, R.M. (1996) 'What is the relationship between breast cancer risk and mammography screening? a meta-analytic review', *Health Psychology, 15*: 423–9.

McCracken, L.M. and Eccleston, C. (2003) 'Coping or acceptance: what to do about chronic pain?', *Pain, 105(1–2)*: 197–204.

McCracken, L.M., Carson, J.W., Eccleston, C. and Keefe, F.J. (2004) 'Acceptance and change in the context of chronic pain', *Pain, 109*: 4–7.

McCrae, R.R. and Costa, P.T. (1985) 'Updating Norman's "adequate taxonomy": intelligence and personality dimensions in natural language and in questionnaires', *Journal of Personality and Social Psychology, 49*: 710–21.

McCreanor, T., Caswell, S. and Hill, L. (2000) 'ICAP and the perils of partnership', *Addiction, 95*: 179–85.

McDermott, M. (2001) 'Redefining health psychology', *Health Psychology Update, 10*: 3–10.

MacDonald, T.H. (1998) *Rethinking Health Promotion: A Global Approach*. London: Routledge.

Macdonald, G. (2000) 'A new evidence framework for health promotion', *Health Education Journal, 59*: 3–11.

McGee, H.M., Hevey, D. and Horgan, J.H. (1999) 'Psychosocial outcome assessments for use in cardiac rehabilitation service evaluation: a 10-year systematic review', *Social Science and Medicine, 48(10)*: 1373–93.

McGee, R. (1999) 'Does stress cause cancer?', *British Medical Journal, 319*: 1015–16.

McGowan, L., Clark-Carter, D. and Pitts, M.K. (1998) 'Chronic pelvic pain: a meta-analysis', *Psychology and Health, 13*: 937–51.

McGue, M. and Christensen, K. (2002) 'The heritability of level and rate-of-change in cognitive functioning in Danish twins', *Experimental Aging Research, 28*: 435–51.

Macinko, J.A., Shi, L., Starfield, B. and Wulu, J.T. (2003) 'Income inequality and health: a critical review of the literature', *Medical Care Research and Reviews, 60*: 407–52.

Macintyre, S. and Hunt, K. (1997) 'Socio-economic position, gender and health', *Journal of Health Psychology, 2*: 315–34.

McKenney, J.W. and Harrison, W.L. (1976) 'Drug-related hospital admissions', *American Journal of Hospital Pharmacy, 33*: 792–5.

McKeown, T. (1979) *The Role of Medicine*. Princeton, NJ: Princeton University Press.

McKie, L. (1993) 'Women's views of the cervical smear test: implications for nursing practice – women who have not had a smear test', *Journal of Advanced Nursing, 18*: 972–9.

McKie, L. (1995) 'The art of surveillance or reasonable prevention? The case of cervical screening', *Sociology of Health and Illness, 17*: 441–57.

MacLachlan, M. (2000) 'Cultivating pluralism in health psychology', *Journal of Health Psychology, 5*: 373–82.

MacLachlan, M. (2004) 'Culture, empowerment and health', in M. Murray (ed.), *Critical Health Psychology*. London: Palgrave. pp. 101–17.

Macleod, J. and Davey Smith, G. (2003) 'Psychosocial factors and public health: a suitable case for treatment?', *Journal of Epidemiology and Community Health, 57*: 565–70.

Macleod, J., Davey Smith, G., Heslop, P., Metcalfe, C., Carroll, D. and Hart, C. (2002) 'Psychological stress and cardiovascular disease: empirical demonstration of bias in a prospective observational study of Scottish men', *British Medical Journal, 324*: 1247–51.

McMurran, M. (1994) *The Psychology of Addiction*. London: Taylor & Francis.

Magni, G., Moreschi, C., Rigatti-Luchini, S. and Merskey, H. (1994) 'Prospective study on the relationship between depressive symptoms and chronic musculoskeletal pain', *Pain, 56*: 289–97.

Maguire, P. (1984) 'Communication skills and patient care', in A. Steptoe and A. Mathews (eds), *Health Care and Human Behaviour*. London: Academic Press. pp. 153–73.

Maguire, P., Fairbairn, S. and Fletcher, C. (1989) 'Consultation skills of young doctors: benefits of undergraduate feedback training', in M. Stewart and D. Roter (eds), *Communicating with Medical Patients*. London: Sage. pp. 124–37.

Maier, S.F. and Watkins, L.R. (1998) 'Cytokines for psychologists: implications of bi-directional immune-to-brain communication for understanding behaviour, mood and cognition', *Psychological Review, 105*: 83–107.

Makoul, G., Arntson, P. and Schofield, T. (1995) 'Health promotion in primary care: physician–patient communication and decision-making about prescription medications', *Social Science and Medicine, 41*: 1241–54.

Maniadakis, N. and Gray, A. (2000) 'The economic burden of back pain in the UK', *Pain, 84*: 95–103.

Manne, S., Sherman, M., Ross, S., Ostroff, J., Heyman, R.E. and Fox, K. (2004) 'Couples' support-related communication, psychological distress, and relationship satisfaction among women with early stage breast cancer', *Journal of Consulting and Clinical Psychology, 72(4)*: 660–70.

Marcus, B.H., Banspach, S.W., Lefebvre, R.L., Rossi, J.S., Carleton, R.A. and Abrams, D.B. (1992) 'Using the stages of change model to increase the adoption of physical activity among community participants', *American Journal of Health Promotion, 6*: 424–9.

Marcus, D.A. (2000) 'Treatment of non-malignant chronic pain', *American Family Physician, 61*: 1331–1338.

Marcus, D.A. (2000) 'Treatment of non-malignant chronic pain', *American Family Physician, 61*: 1331–8.

Marinker, M. (1997) 'Writing prescriptions is easy', *British Medical Journal, 314*: 747.

Marks, D. (1999a) 'Dimensions of oppression: theorising the embodied subject', *Disability and Society, 14(5)*: 611–26.

Marks, D. (1999b) *Disability: Controversial Debates and Psychosocial Perspectives*. London: Routledge.

Marks, D.F. (1992) 'Smoking cessation as a testbed for psychological theory: a group cognitive therapy programme with high long-term abstinence rates', *Journal of Smoking-Related Disorders, 3*: 69–78.

Marks, D.F. (1993) *The QUIT FOR LIFE Programme: An Easier Way to Stop Smoking and not Start Again*. Leicester: British Psychological Society.

Marks, D.F. (1996) 'Health psychology in context', *Journal of Health Psychology, 1*: 7–21.

Marks, D.F. (1998) 'Addiction, smoking and health: developing policy-based interventions', *Psychology, Health and Medicine, 3*: 97–111.

Marks, D.F. (1999) 'Health psychology as agent of change: reconstructing health psychology', First International Conference on Critical and Qualitative Approaches to Health Psychology. St John's, Newfoundland, Canada.

Marks, D.F. (2002a) *The Health Psychology Reader*. London: Sage.

Marks, D.F. (2002b) 'Freedom, responsibility and power: contrasting approaches to health psychology', *Journal of Health Psychology, 7*: 5–14.

Marks, D.F. (2004) 'Rights to health, freedom from illness: a life and death matter', in M. Murray (ed.), *Critical Health Psychology*. London: Palgrave. pp. 61–82.

Marks, D.F. (2005) *Overcoming Your Smoking Habit*. London: Constable.

Marks, D.F. and Sykes, C.M. (2002a) 'A randomised controlled trial of cognitive behaviour therapy for smokers living in a deprived part of London', *Psychology, Health and Medicine, 7*: 17–24.

Marks, D.F. and Sykes, C.M. (2002b) 'Evaluation of the European Union Programme of Community Action on Health Promotion, Information, Education and Training 1996–2000', *Health Promotion International, 17*: 105–18.

Marks, D.F. and Yardley, L. (2004) *Research Methods for Clinical and Health Psychology*. London: Sage.

Marks, D.F., Baird, J.M. and McKellar, P. (1989) 'Replication of trance logic using a modified experimental design: highly hypnotizable subjects in both real and simulator groups', *International Journal of Clinical and Experimental Hypnosis, 37*: 232–48.

Marks, D.F., Brücher-Albers, C., Donker, F.J.S., Jepsen, Z., Rodriguez-Marin, J., Sodit, S. and Wallin Backinan, B. (1998) 'Health psychology 2000: the development of professional health psychology', *Journal of Health Psychology, 3*: 149–60.

Marlatt, G. and Gordon, J. (eds) (1985) *Relapse Prevention: Maintenance Strategies in the Treatment of Addictive Behavior*. New York: Guilford Press.

Marmot, M. (2001) 'Inequalities in health', *New England Journal of Medicine*, 345: 183–203.

Marmot, M., Shipley, M., Brunner, E. and Hemmingway, H. (2001) 'Relative contribution of early life and adult socio-economic factors in adult morbidity in the whitehall II study', *Journal of Epidemiology and Community Health*, 53: 301–7.

Martens, W.J.M., Niessen, W., Rotmans, J., Jetten, T.H. and McMichael, A.J. (1995) 'Potential impact of global climate change on malaria risk', *Environmental Health Perspectives*, 103: 458–64.

Martin, E. (1994) *Flexible Bodies: The Role of Immunity in American Culture from the Days of Polio to the Age of AIDS*. Boston: Beacon Press.

Martin-Baro, I. (1994) *Writings for a Liberation Psychology*, ed. A. Aron and S. Corne. Cambridge, MA: Harvard University Press.

Maslach, C. and Jackson, S. (1981) 'The measurement of experienced burnout', *Journal of Occupational Behaviour*, 2: 99–113.

Mason, J.W. (1971) 'A re-evaluation of the concept of "non-specificity" in stress theory', *Journal of Psychiatric Research*, 8: 323–33.

Mason, J.W. (1975) 'A historical view of the stress field: Parts 1 & 2', *Journal of Human Stress*, 1: 6–12, 22–36.

Masters, W.H. and Johnson, V. (1966) *Human Sexual Response*. Boston: Little Brown.

Masunaga, R. (1972) *A Primer of Soto Zen: A Translation of Dogen's Shobogenzo Zuimonki*. London: Routledge.

Masur, H. (1981) 'Infection after kidney transplantation', *Archives of Internal Medicine*, 141: 1582–4.

Matarazzo, J.D. (1980) 'Behavioral health and behavioral medicine: frontiers for a new health psychology', *American Psychologist*, 35: 807–17.

Matarazzo, J.D. (1982) 'Behavioral health's challenge to academic, scientific and professional psychology', *American Psychologist*, 37: 1–14.

Mausner-Dorsch, H. and Eaton, W.W. (2000) 'Psychosocial work environment and depression: epidemiologic assessment of the demand-control model', *American Journal of Public Health*, 90: 1765–70.

Maynard Campbell, S. and Maynard Lupton, A. (2000) *Bureaucratic Barriers to Day-to-day Activities*. London: Muscle Power! (On www.leeds.ac.uk/disabilityarchive)

Mead, G.H. (1934) *Mind, Self, and Society*. Chicago: University of Chicago Press.

Meeuwesen, L., Schaap, C. and van der Staak, C. (1991) 'Verbal analysis of doctor–patient communication', *Social Science and Medicine*, 32: 1143–50.

Meichenbaum, D. (1985) *Stress Innoculation Training*. New York: Perganon.

Meichenbaum, D. and Turk, D.C. (1987) *Facilitating Treatment Adherence: A Practitioner's Guidebook*. New York: Plenum Press.

Meijman, T.F., van Dormolen, M., Herber, R.F.M., Rongen, H. and Kuiper, S. (1995) 'Job strain, neuroendocrine activation, and immune status', in S.L. Sauter and L.R. Murphy (eds), *Organizational Risk Factors for Job Stress*. Washington, DC: American Psychological Association. pp. 113–26.

Melzack, R. (1975) 'The McGill Pain Questionnaire: major properties and scoring methods', *Pain*, 1: 277–99.

Melzack, R. (1999) 'From the gate to the neuromatrix', *Pain*, August(Suppl 6): S121–6.

Melzack, R. and Wall, P.D. (1982) *The Challenge of Pain*. New York: Basic Books.

Melzack, R. and Wall, P.D. (1988) *The Challenge of Pain*, 2nd edn. London: Penguin Books.

Mennella, J.A. and Beauchamp, G.K. (1996) 'The early development of human flavor preferences', in E.D. Capaldi (ed.), *Why We Eat What We Eat: The Psychology of Eating*. Washington, DC: American Psychological Association. pp. 83–112.

Merskey, J. (1996) 'Classification of chronic pain: descriptions of chronic pain syndromes and definitions of pain terms', *Pain*, 3(Suppl): S1–225.

Meszaros, J.R., Asch, D.A., Baron, J., Hershey, J.C., Kunreuther, H. and Schwartz-Buzaglo, J. (1996) 'Cognitive processes and the decisions of some parents to forego pertussis vaccination for their children', *Journal of Clinical Epidemiology*, 49: 697–703.

Metts, R.L. (2000) *Disability Issues, Trends and Recommendations for the World Bank*. Washington, DC: World Bank. (www.worldbank.org)

Meyer, T.J. and Mark, M.M. (1995) 'Effects of psychosocial interventions with adult cancer patients: a meta-analysis of randomized experiments', *Health Psychology*, 14: 101–8.

Meyerowitz, B.E., Richardson, J., Hudson, S. and Leedham, B. (1998) 'Ethnicity and cancer outcomes: behavioral and psychosocial considerations', *Psychological Bulletin*, *123*: 47–70.

Mezey, G. and Robbins, I. (2001) 'Usefulness and validity of post-traumatic stress disorder as a psychiatric category', *British Medical Journal*, *323*: 561–3.

Michie, S. and Marteau, T.M. (1996) 'Predictive genetic testing in children: the need for psychological research', *British Journal of Health Psychology*, *1*: 3–14.

Michie, S., McDonald, V. and Marteau, T. (1996a) 'Understanding responses to predictive genetic testing: a grounded theory approach', *Psychology and Health*, *11*: 455–70.

Michie, S., Axworthy, D., Weinman, J. and Marteau, T. (1996b) 'Genetic counselling: predicting patient outcomes', *Psychology and Health*, *11*: 797–809.

Middleton, D. (1996) 'A discursive analysis of psychosocial issues: talk in a "parent group" for families who have children with chronic renal failure', *Psychology and Health*, *11*: 243–60.

Midford, R. and McBride, N. (2001) 'Alcohol education in schools', in N. Heather, T.J. Peters and T. Stockwell (eds), *International Handbook of Alcohol Dependence and Problems*. London: Wiley. pp. 785–804.

Miles, A. (1981) *The Mentally Ill in Contemporary Society*. Oxford: Martin Robertson.

Miller, E.A. (2002) 'Telemedicine and doctor–patient communication: a theoretical framework for evaluation', *Journal of Telemedicine and Telecare*, *8*: 311–18.

Miller, G.E. and Cohen, S. (2001) 'Psychological interventions and the immune system: a meta-analytic review and critique', *Health Psychology*, *20*: 47–63.

Miller, T.Q., Smith, T.W., Turner, C.W., Guijarro, M.L. and Hallet, A.J. (1996) 'A meta-analytic review of research on hostility and physical health', *Psychological Bulletin*, *119*: 322–48.

Miller, W.R. and Brown, S.A. (1997) 'Why psychologists should treat alcohol and drug problems', *American Psychologist*, *52*: 1269–79.

Miller, W.R. and Rollnick, S. (2002) *Motivational Interviewing: Preparing People to Change Addictive Behaviours*, 2nd edn. New York: Guilford Press.

Mintz, S. (1997) 'Sugar and morality', in A.M. Brandt and P. Rozin (eds), *Morality and Health*. New York: Routledge. pp. 173–84.

Mischel, W. (1968) *Personality and Assessment*. New York: Wiley.

Modood, T., Berthoud, R., Lakey, J., Nazroo, J., Smith, P., Virdee, S. and Beishon, S. (1997) *Ethnic Minorities in Britain: Diversity and Disadvantage*. London: Policy Studies Institute.

Mookadam, F. and Arthur, H.M. (2004) 'Social support and its relationship to morbidity and mortality after acute myocardial infarction: systematic overview', *Archives of Internal Medicine*, *164(14)*: 1514–8.

Mooney, C. (2004) *Doubt and About*: http://www.csicop.org/doubtandabout/

Moore, P.J., Sickel, A.E., Malat, J., Williams, D., Jackson, J. and Adler, N.E. (2004) 'Psychosocial factors in medical and psychological treatment avoidance: the role of the doctor–patient relationship', *Journal of Health Psychology*, *9(3)*: 421–33.

Morgan, J.E. (1873) *University Oars*. London: Macmillan.

Morgenstern, J., Langenbucher, J., Labouvie, E. and Miller, K.J. (1997) 'The comorbidity of alcoholism and personality disorders in a clinical population: prevalence rates and relation to alcohol typology variables', *Journal of Abnormal Psychology*, *106*: 74–84.

Morinis, C.A. and Brilliant, G.E. (1981) 'Smallpox in northern India: diversity and order in a regional medical culture', *Medical Anthropology*, *5*: 341–64.

Morris, J. (1991) *Pride Against Prejudice: Transforming Attitudes in Disability*. London: Women's Press.

Morris, J.K., Cook, D.G. and Sharper, A.P. (1994) 'Loss of employment and mortality', *British Medical Journal*, *308*: 1135–9.

Morrison, D.L., Upton, D.M. and Cordery, J. (1999) 'The role of supervisor behaviour in facilitating opportunities for skill development and utilization', *Human Factors and Ergonomics in Manufacturing*, *9*: 46–67.

Moscovici, S. (1973) Foreword, in C. Herzlich, *Health and Illness: A Social Psychological Analysis*. London: Academic Press.

Moscovici, S. (1984) 'The phenomenon of social representations', in R.M. Farr and S. Moscovici (eds), *Social Representations*. Cambridge: Cambridge University Press. pp. 3–70.

Moss-Morris, R., Petrie, K.J. and Weinman, J. (1996) 'Functioning in chronic fatigue syndrome: do illness perceptions play a regulatory role', *British Journal of Health Psychology*, *1*: 15–26.

Moss-Morris, R., Weinman, J., Petrie, K.J., Horne, R., Cameron, L.D. and Buick, D. (2002) 'The Revised Illness Perception Questionnaire (IPQ-R)', *Psychology and Health*, *17*: 1–17.

Moser, D.K. and Dracup, K. (2004) 'Role of spousal anxiety and depression in patients' psychosocial recovery after a cardiac event', *Psychosomatic Medicine, 66(4)*: 527–32.

Mowday, R.T. (1996) 'Equity theory predictions of behaviour in organizations', in R.M. Steers, L.W. Porter and G.A. Bigley (eds), *Motivation and Leadership at Work*, 6th edn. New York: McGraw-Hill. pp. 53–71.

Mulkay, M. (1991) *Sociology of Science: A Sociological Pilgrimage*. Milton Keynes: Open University Press.

Mullen, K. (1992) 'A question of balance: health behaviour and work context among male Glaswegians', *Sociology of Health and Illness, 14*: 73–95.

Muller, J., Hicks, R. and Winocur, S. (1993) 'The effects of employment and unemployment on psychological well-being in Australian clerical workers: gender differences', *Australian Journal of Psychology, 45*: 103–8.

Mulrow, C.D. (1987) 'The medical review article: state of the science', *Annals of Internal Medicine, 106*: 485–8.

Muntaner, C., Lynch, J.W., Hillemeister, M., Lee, J.H., David, R., Benach, J. and Borrell, C. (2002) 'Economic inequality, working class power, social capital, and cause specific mortality in wealthy countries', *International Journal of Health Services, 32*: 629–56.

Murdock, G.P. (1937) 'Comparative data on the division of labour by sex', *Social Forces, 15*: 551–3.

Murdock, G.P. (1980) *Theories of Illness: A World Survey*. Pittsburgh: University of Pittsburgh Press.

Murphy, E.M. (2003) 'Being born female is dangerous for your health', *American Psychologist, 58(3)*: 205–10.

Murray, C.J.L. and Lopez, A.D. (1997) 'Alternative projections of mortality and disability by cause 1990–2020: Global Burden of Disease Study', *Lancet, 349*: 1498–1504.

Murray, M. (1997a) 'A narrative approach to health psychology: background and potential', *Journal of Health Psychology, 2*: 9–20.

Murray, M. (1997b) *Narrative Health Psychology*. Palmerston North, NZ: Massey University.

Murray, M. (2000) 'Levels of narrative analysis in health psychology', *Journal of Health Psychology, 5*: 337–48.

Murray, M. (2003) 'Narrative psychology', in J.A. Smith (ed.), *Qualitative Psychology: A Practical Guide to Research Methods*. London: Sage.

Murray, M. (2004) *Critical Health Psychology*. Basingstoke: Macmillan.

Murray, M. and Campbell, C. (2003) 'Living in a material world: reflecting on some assumptions of health psychology', *Journal of Health Psychology, 8*: 231–6.

Murray, M. and Jarrett, L. (1985) 'Young people's perception of health, illness and smoking', *Health Education Journal, 44*: 18–22.

Murray, M. and McMillan, C. (1988) *Working Class Women's Views of Cancer*. Belfast: Ulster Cancer Foundation.

Murray, M. and McMillan, C. (1993a) 'Gender differences in perceptions of cancer', *Journal of Cancer Education, 8*: 53–62.

Murray, M. and McMillan, C. (1993b) 'Health beliefs, locus of control, emotional control and women's cancer screening behaviour', *British Journal of Clinical Psychology, 32*: 87–100.

Murray, M. and Tilley, N. (2004) 'Developing community health action and research through the arts', in R. Flowers (ed.), *Education and social action conference 2004*. Sydney: University of Technology Sydney. pp. 150–56.

Murray, M., Jarrett, L., Swan, A.V. and Rumun, R. (1988) *Smoking Among Young Adults*. Aldershot: Gower.

Murray, M., Kiryluk, S. and Swan, A.V. (1985) 'Relation between parents' and children's smoking behaviour and attitudes', *Journal of Epidemiology and Community Health, 39*: 169–74.

Murray, M., Pullman, D. and Heath Rodgers, T. (2003) 'Social representations of health and illness among "baby-boomers" in Eastern Canada', *Journal of Health Psychology, 8*: 485–500.

Murray, M., Swan, A.V. and Mattar, N. (1983) 'The task of nursing and risk of smoking', *Journal of Advanced Nursing, 8*: 131–8.

Murray, R.P., Connett, J.E., Tyas, S.L., Bond, R., Ekima, O., Silversides, C.K. and Barnes, G.E. (2002) 'Alcohol volume, drinking pattern and cardiovascular disease morbidity and mortality: is there a U-shaped function?', *American Journal of Epidemiology, 155*: 242–8.

Myrtek, M. (2001) 'Meta-analyses of prospective studies on coronary heart disease, type A personality and hostility', *International Journal of Cardiology, 79*: 245–51.

Mystakidou, K., Parpa, E., Tsilila, E., Katsouda, E., Vlahos, L. (2004) 'Cancer information disclosure in different cultural contexts', *Support Care Cancer, 12(3)*: 147–54.

Nafziger, E.W., Stewart, F. and Vayrynen, R. (eds) (2000) *War, Hunger and Displacement: The Origins of Humanitarian Emergencies*, Vol 1 & 2. New York: Oxford University Press.

National Center for Health Statistics (1994b) *Healthy People 2000 Review, 1993*. Hyattsville, MD: Public Health Service.

National Institutes of Health (1997) 'Acupuncture'. *NIH Consensus Statement, Vol 15 (5)*. Rockville, MD: US Dept. of HHS Public Health Services.

National Statistics (2004) 'MMR immunization of children by their second birthday', *Social Trends, 34*.

Nesbitt, P.D. (1973) 'Smoking, physiological arousal, and emotional response', *Journal of Personality and Social Psychology, 25*: 137–44.

Ness, A.R. and Powles, J.W. (1997) 'Fruit and vegetables, and cardiovascular disease: a review', *International Journal of Epidemiology, 26*: 1–13.

Neuberg, S.L., Smith, D.M. and Asher, T. (2000) 'Why people stigmatize: toward a biocultural framework', in T.F. Heatherton, R.E. Kleck, M.R. Hebl and J.G. Hull (eds), *The Social Psychology of Stigma*. New York: Guilford. pp. 31–61.

New, S.J. and Senior, M. (1991) '"I don't believe in needles": qualitative aspects of study into the update of infant immunisation in two English health authorities', *Social Science and Medicine, 33*: 509–18.

Nichter, M. (2003) 'Smoking: what does culture have to do with it?', *Addiction, 98(suppl 1)*: 139–45.

Niedhammer, I. and Chea, M. (2003) 'Psychosocial factors at work and self reported health: comparative results of cross sectional and prospective analyses of the French GAZEL cohort', *Occupational and Environmental Medicine, 60*: 509–15.

NIH Consensus Development Panel on Physical Activity and Cardiovascular Health (1996) 'Physical activity and cardiovascular health', *Journal of the American Medical Association, 276*: 241–6.

Norman, P. and Bennett, P. (1996) 'Health locus of control', in M. Conner and P. Norman (eds), *Predicting Health Behaviour*. Buckingham: Open University Press. pp. 62–94.

Norman, P., Bennett, P., Smith, C. and Murphy, S. (1998) 'Health locus of control and health behaviour', *Journal of Health Psychology, 3*: 171–80.

Nutbeam, D. (1999) 'Health promotion effectiveness: the questions to be answered', in International Union for Health Promotion and Education, *The Evidence of Health Promotion Effectiveness: Shaping Public Health in a New Europe*. ECSC-EC-EAEC, Brussels–Luxembourg.

Nutton, V. (1995) 'Medicine in the Greek world, 800–50 BC', in L.I. Conrad, M. Neve, V. Nutton, R. Porter and A. Wear (eds), *The Western Medical Tradition 800 BC–1800 AD*. Cambridge: Cambridge University Press. pp. 11–38.

O'Brien, M. and Petrie, K.J. (1996) 'Examining patient participation in medical consultations: a combined quantitative and qualitative approach', *Psychology and Health, 11*: 871–90.

O'Driscoll, M. and Beehr, T. (1994) 'Supervisor behaviours, role stressors and uncertainty as predictors of personal outcomes for subordinates', *Journal of Organizational Behaviour, 15*: 141–55.

O'Driscoll, M.P. and Cooper, C.L. (1996) 'Sources and management of excessive job stress and burnout', in P.B. Warr (ed.), *Psychology at Work*, 4th edn. Harmondsworth: Penguin. pp. 188–223.

Odom, S.L., Peck, C.A., Hanson, H., Beckham, P.J., Kaiser, K.P., Leiber, J., Brown, W.H., Hom, E.M. and Schwartz, I.S. (1996) 'Inclusion at the pre-school level: an ecological systems analysis. Social Policy Report', *Society for Research Child Development, 10, 2*: 18–30.

Oeppen, J. and Vaupel, J.W. (2002) 'Demography: Broken limits to life expectancy', *Science, 296*: 1029–31.

Office of Inspector General (1990) *Medication Regimens: Causes of Non-compliance*. Washington, DC: Government Printing Office. DHHS Publication no. OEI-04–89–89121.

Ogden, J. (1992) *Fat Chance*. London: Routledge.

Ogden, J. (1997) 'The rhetoric and reality of psychosocial theories: a challenge to biomedicine', *Journal of Health Psychology, 2*: 21–9.

Ogden, J. (2003) 'Some problems with social cognition models: a pragmatic and conceptual analysis', *Health Psychology, 22*: 424–28.

O'Leary, A. (1990) 'Stress, emotion and human immune function', *Psychological Bulletin, 108*: 363–82.

O'Leary, A. and Helgeson, V.S. (1997) 'Psychosocial factors and women's health: integrating mind, heart, and body', in S.J. Gallant, G.P. Keita and R. Royat-Schder (eds), *Health Care for Women: Psychological, Social, and Behavioral Influences*. Washington, DC: American Psychological Association. pp. 25–40.

Oliver, M. (1990) *The Politics of Disablement*. Basingstoke: Macmillan.

Oliver, R.L. and Berger, P.K. (1979) 'A path analysis of preventive care decision models', *Journal of Consumer Research, 6*: 113–22.

Ong, L.M.L., de Haes, J.C.J.M., Hoos, A.M. and Lammes, F.B. (1995) 'Doctor–patient communication: a review of the literature', *Social Science and Medicine, 40*: 903–18.

ONS (1999) 'First release: Living in Britain 1998', *General Household Survey*. London: The Stationery Office.

ONS (2001) *Living in Great Britain: Results from the 2000 General Household Survey*. London: The Stationery Office.

Orbell, S. and Sheeran, P. (2002) 'Changing health behaviours: The role of implementation intentions', in D.R. Rutter and L. Quine (eds), *Changing Health Behaviour: Intervention and Research with Social Cognition Models*. Buckingham: Open University Press. pp. 123–37.

Oxman, A.D. and Guyatt, G.H. (1988) 'Guidelines for reading literature reviews', *Canadian Medical Association Journal, 138*: 697–703.

Oygard, L. and Anderssen, N. (1998) 'Social influences and leisure-time physical activity levels in young people: a twelve-year follow-up study', *Journal of Health Psychology, 3*: 59–69.

Ozer, E.J., Best, S.R., Lipsey, T.L. and Weiss (2003) 'Predictors of posttraumatic stress disorder and symptoms in adults: a meta-analysis', *Psychological Bulletin, 129*: 52–73.

Pallonen, U.E., Prochaska, J.O., Velicer, W.F., Prokhorov, A.V. and Smith, N.F. (1998) 'Stages of acquisition and cessation for adolescent smoking: an empirical integration', *Addictive Behaviors, 23*: 303–24.

Paludi, M.A. (1992) *The Psychology of Women*. Dubuque, IA: Brown and Benchmark.

Papadopoulos, L., Bor, R., Walker, C., Flaxman, P. and Legg, C. (2002) 'Different shades of meaning: illness beliefs among vertiligo sufferers', *Psychology, Health and Medicine, 7*: 425–33.

Park, C.L., Folkman, S. and Bostrom, A. (2001) 'Appraisals of controllability and coping in caregivers and HIV+ men: testing the goodness-of-fit hypothesis', *Journal of Consulting and Clinical Psychology, 69*: 481–8.

Parker, I. (1992) *Discourse Dynamics*. London: Routledge.

Parker, I. (1997) 'Discursive psychology', in D. Fox and I. Prilleltensky (eds), *Critical Psychology: An Introduction*. London: Sage.

Parker, I. (ed.) (1998) *Social Constructionism, Discourse and Realism*. London: Sage.

Parliamentary Office of Science and Technology (2002) *Access to Water in Developing Countries* (Postnote, May, No. 178).

Parry, M.L. and Rosenzweig, C. (1999) 'Climate change and world food security: a new assessment', *Global Environmental Change*, S51–S67.

Pate, R.R., Pratt, M., Blair, S.N., Haskell, W.L., Macera, C.A., Bouchard, C., Buchner, D., Caspersen, C.J., Ettinger, W., Heath, G.W., King, A.C. et al. (1995) 'Physical activity and public health: a recommendation from the Centers for Disease Control and Prevention and the American College of Sports Medicine', *Journal of the American Medical Association, 273*: 402–7.

Pavlov, I.P. (1927) *Conditioned Reflexes*. Oxford: Oxford University Press.

Paxton, W. and Dixon, M. (2004) *The State of the Nation: An Audit of Injustice in the UK*. London: Institute for Public Policy Research.

Payne, N., Jones, F. and Harris, P. (2002) 'The impact of working life on health behaviour: The effect of job strain on the cognitive predictors of exercise', *Journal of Occupational Health Psychology, 7*: 342–53.

Payne-Jackson, A. (1999) 'Biomedical and folk medical concepts of adult onset diabetes in Jamaica: implications for treatment', *Health, 3(1)*: 5–46.

Peckham, C., Bedford, H., Senturia, Y. and Ades, A. (1989) *National Immunization Study: Factors Influencing Immunization Uptake in Childhood*. Horsham: Action Research for the Crippled Child.

Peele, S. and Grant, M. (eds) (1999) *Alcohol and Pleasure: A Health Perspective*. Washington, DC: International Center for Alcohol Policies.

Pelosi, A.J. and Appleby, L. (1992) 'Psychological influences on cancer and ischaemic heart disease', *British Medical Journal, 304*: 1295–8.

Pelosi, A.J. and Appleby, L. (1993) 'Personality and fatal diseases', *British Medical Journal, 306*: 1666–7.

Pennebaker, J.W. (1995) *Emotion, Disclosure, and Health*. Washington, DC: American Psychological Association.

Penninx, B.W., Guralnik, J.M., Pahor, M., Ferrucci, L., Cerhan, J.R., Wallace, R.B. and Havlik, R.J. (1998) 'Chronically depressed mood and cancer risk in older persons', *Journal of the National Cancer Institute*, *90*: 1888–93.

Perugini, M. and Bagozzi, R.P. (2001) 'The role of desires and anticipated emotions on goal-directed behaviours: broadening and deepening the theory of planned behaviour', *British Journal of Social Psychology*, *40(1)*: 79–98.

Peters, S. (2000) 'Is there a disability culture? A syncretisation of three possible world views', *Disability and Society*, *15*: 583–601.

Peterson, C., Seligman, M.E.P. and Vaillant, G.E. (1988) 'Pessimistic explanatory style is a risk factor for physical illness: a thirty five year longitudinal study', *Journal of Personality and Social Psychology*, *55*: 23–7.

Petrie, K. and Revenson, T. (2005) 'Editorial for Special Issue on Behavioural Medicine', *Journal of Health Psychology*, *10*: 179–184.

Petrie, K.J., Cameron, L.D., Ellis, C.J., Buick, D. and Weinman, J. (2002) 'Changing illness perceptions after myocardial infarction: an early intervention randomized controlled trial', *Psychosomatic Medicine*, *64*: 580–6.

Petrie, K.J. and Weinman, J. (eds) (1997) *Perceptions of Health and Illness*. Amsterdam: Harwood Academic.

Petrie, K.J., Weinman, J., Sharpe, N. and Buckley, J. (1996) 'Role of patients' view of their illness in predicting return to work and functioning after myocardial infarction: longitudinal study', *British Medical Journal*, *312*: 1191–4.

Petticrew, M., Bell, R. and Hunter, D. (2002) 'Influence of psychological coping on survival and recurrence in people with cancer: systematic review', *British Medical Journal*, *325*: 1066–9.

Petticrew, M., Fraser, J.M. and Regan, M.F. (1999) 'Adverse life events and risk of breast cancer: a meta-analysis', *British Journal of Health Psychology*, *4*: 1–17.

Piaget, J. (1930) *The Child's Conception of Physical Causality*. London: Routledge and Kegan Paul.

Pierce, J.P., Choi, W.S., Gilpin, E.A., Farkas, A.J. and Merritt, R.K. (1996) 'Validation of suscepti-bility as a predictor of which adolescents take up smoking in the United States', *Health Psychology*, *15*: 355–61.

Pincus, T., Griffith, J., Isenberg, D. and Pearce, S. (1997) 'The Well-Being Questionnaire: testing the structure in groups with rheumatoid arthritis', *British Journal of Health Psychology*, *2(3)*: 167–74.

Pinney, E.M., Gerrard, M. and Denney, N.W. (1987) 'The Pinney Sexual Satisfaction Inventory', *Journal of Sex Research*, *23*: 233–51.

Pirozzo, S., Summerbell, C., Cameron, C. and Glasziou, P. (2004) 'Advice on low-fat diets for obesity (Cochrane Review)', in *The Cochrane Library*, Issue 2. Chichester: John Wiley.

Plant, M. (2004) 'Editorial: The alcohol harm reduction strategy for England', *British Medical Journal*, *328*: 905–6.

Plante, T.G. and Rodin, J. (1990) 'Physical fitness and enhanced psychological health', *Current Psychology: Research and Reviews*, *9*: 3–24.

Pleck, J.H., Sonnenstein, F.L. and Ku, L.C. (1990) 'Contraceptive attitudes and intention to use condoms in sexually experienced and inexperienced adolescent males', *Journal of Family Issues*, *11*: 294–312.

Plummer, K. (1996) *Telling Sexual Stories*. London: Routledge.

Pomerlau, D.F. (1979) 'Behavioral factors in the establishment, maintenance, and cessation of smoking', in *Smoking and Health: A Report of the Surgeon General*. Washington, DC: US Department of Health, Education and Welfare. pp. 161–2.

Popay, J., Bennett, S., Thomas, C., Williams, G., Gatrell, A. and Bostock, L. (2003) 'Beyond "beer, fags, egg and chips"? Exploring lay understandings of social inequalities in health', *Sociology of Health and Illness*, *25*: 1–23.

Porter, R. (1997) *The Greatest Benefit to Mankind: A Medical History of Humanity*. New York: Norton.

Potter, J. and Wetherell, M. (1987) *Discourse and Social Psychology*. London: Sage.

Powers, P. (2003) 'Empowerment as treatment and the role of health professionals', *Advances in Nursing Science*, *26*: 227–37.

Powles, J. (1992) 'Changes in disease patterns and related social trends', *Social Science and Medicine*, *35*: 377–87.

Prescott-Clarke, P. and Primatesta, P. (eds) (1998) *Health survey for England '95–97*. London: The Stationery Office.

Prescott-Clarke, P. and Primatesta, P. (eds) (1999) *Health survey for England: The health of young people '95–97*. London: The Stationery Office.

Price, J.M. and Pecjak, V. (2003) 'Obesity and stigma: important issues in women's health', *Psychology Science, 45(Supplement II)*: 6–42.

Probst, T.M. (2002) 'Layoffs and tradeoffs: production, quality and safety demands under the threat of job loss', *Journal of Occupational Health Psychology*, 7: 211–20.

Prochaska, J.O. and DiClemente, C.C. (1983) 'Stages and processes of self-change in smoking: toward an integrative model of change', *Journal of Consulting and Clinical Psychology*, 51: 520–8.

Prochaska, J.O. and DiClemente, C.C. (1992) *The Transtheoretical Approach: Crossing the Traditional Boundaries of Therapy*. Homewood, IL: Dow Jones/Irwin.

Project MATCH Research Group (1997) 'Matching alcoholism treatments to client heterogeneity: Project MATCH post-treatment drinking outcomes', *Journal of Studies on Alcohol*, 58: 7–29.

Ptacek, J.T. and Eberhardt, T.L. (1996) 'Breaking bad news: a review of the literature', *Journal of the American Medical Association, 276*: 496–502.

Putnam, R.D. with Leonarchi, R. and Nanetti, R.Y. (1993) *Making Democracy Work: Civic Traditions in Modern Italy*. Princeton, NJ: Princeton University Press.

Putnam, R. (2000) *Bowling Alone: The Collapse and Revival of American Community*. New York: Simon & Schuster.

Quah, S.-H. and Bishop, G.D. (1996) 'Seeking help for illness: the roles of cultural orientation and illness cognition', *Journal of Health Psychology*, 1: 209–22.

Query, J.L. and Kreps, G.L. (1996) 'Testing a relational model for health communication competence among caregivers for individuals with Alzheimer's disease', *Journal of Health Psychology*, 1: 335–51.

Quick, J. and Quick, J. (1984) *Organizational Stress and Prevention Management*. New York: McGraw-Hill.

Quick, J.C., Nelson, D.L. and Quick, J.D. (2001) 'Occupational stress and self-reliance: development and research issues', in J. Dunham (ed.), *Stress in the Workplace: Past, Present and Future*. London: Whurr Publishers.

Rabinowitz, W., Falkenbach, K., Travers, J., Valentine, C. and Weener, P. (1983) 'Worker motivation: unsolved or untapped resource?', *California Management Review, 25(2)*: 48–53.

Radley, A. (1994) *Making Sense of Illness: The Social Psychology of Health and Illness*. London: Sage.

Radley, A. and Billig, M. (1996) 'Accounts of health and illness: dilemmas and representations', *Sociology of Health and Illness*, 18: 220–40.

Radtke, H.R. and Van Mens-Verhulst, J. (2001) 'Being a mother and living with asthma: an exploratory analysis of discourse', *Journal of Health Psychology*, 6: 379–91.

Raeburn, J. and Rootman, I. (1998) *People-centred Health Promotion*. Chichester: Wiley.

Ragland, D.R. and Brand, R.J. (1988) 'Type A behaviour and mortality from coronary heart disease', *New England Journal of Medicine, 318*: 65–9.

Ramirez, A., Addington-Hall, J., Richards M. (1998) 'ABC of palliative care: the carers', *British Medical Journal, 316*: 208–11.

Ramirez, A.J., Richards, M.A., Gregory, W. and Craig, T.K.J. (1990) 'Psychological correlates of hormone receptor status in breast cancer', *Lancet, 335*: 1408.

Randhawa, G. (1995) 'Organ donation: social and cultural issues, *Nursing Standard*, 9: 25–7.

Rappaport, J. (1981) 'In praise of paradox: A social policy of empowerment over prevention', *American Journal of Community Psychology*, 9: 1–25.

Rappaport, J. (1987) 'Terms of empowerment/examples of prevention: towards a theory for community psychology', *American Journal of Counseling Psychology*, 15: 121–49.

Rappuoli, R., Miller, H.I. and Falkow, S. (2002) 'The intangible value of vaccination', *Science, 297*: 937–9.

Ratzan, S.C. (1996) 'Introduction', *Journal of Health Communication. International Perspectives*, 1: v–vii.

Rawls, J. (1999) *A Theory of Justice*. Cambridge, MA: Belknap Press.

Reed, G.M., Kemeny, M.E., Taylor, S.E., Wang, H.J. and Visscher, B.R. (1994) 'Realistic acceptance as a predictor of decreased survival time in gay men with aids', *Health Psychology*, 13: 299–307.

Rees, K., Bennett, P., West, R., Davey, S.G. and Ebrahim, S. (2004) 'Psychological interventions for coronary heart disease', *Cochrane Database of Systematic Reviews, 2004(2)*: CD002902.

Rehse, B. and Pukrop, R. (2003) 'Effects of psychosocial interventions on quality of life in adult cancer patients: meta analysis of 37 published controlled outcome studies', *Patient Educational Counselling, 50(2)*: 179–86.

Reid, K., Asbury, J., McDonald, R. and Serpell, M. (2003) 'Dear diary: exploring the utility of diaries as a powerful and multi-functional research tool', *Health Psychology Update, 12(2)*: 7–12.

Reiss, I.L. (1991) 'Sexual pluralism: ending America's sexual crisis', *SIECUS Report,* February–March.

Report of the Scientific Committee on Tobacco and Health, Department of Health. London: The Stationery Office, 1998. See also: http://www.archive.official-documents.co.uk/document/doh/tobacco/report.htm

Resnik, D.B. (2001) 'Ethical dilemmas in communicating medical information to the public', *Health Policy, 55*: 129–49.

Rhodes, T. (1994) 'Outreach, community change and community empowerment: contradictions for public health and health promotion', in P. Aggleton, B. Davis and G. Hart (eds), *AIDS: Foundation for the Future*. London: Taylor & Francis. pp. 48–64.

Riesen, W.F., Darioli, R. and Noll, G. (2004) 'Lipid-lowering therapy: strategies for improving compliance', *Current Medical Research and Opinion, 20*: 165–73.

Rimal, R.N. (2001) 'Longitudinal influences of knowledge and self-efficacy on exercise behavior: tests of a mutual reinforcement model', *Journal of Health Psychology, 6*: 31–46.

Riska, E. (2000) 'The rise and fall of Type A man', *Social Science and Medicine, 51*: 1665–74.

Robinson, I. (1990) 'Personal narratives, social careers and medical courses: analysing life trajectories in autobiographies of people with multiple sclerosis', *Social Science and Medicine, 30*: 1173–86.

Robinson, J.I. and Rogers, M.A. (1994) 'Adherence to exercise programmes: recommendations', *Sports Medicine, 17*: 39–52.

Rodgers, G.B. (1979) 'Income and inequality as determinants of mortality: an international cross-section analysis', *Population Studies, 33*: 343–51.

Rogers, R. (1992) 'Living and dying in the USA: sociodemographic determinants of death among blacks and whites', *Demography, 29*: 287–303.

Rose, G. (1992) *The Strategy of Preventive Medicine*. Oxford: Oxford University Press.

Rose, J.E. (1996) 'Nicotine addiction and treatment', *Annual Review of Medicine, 47*: 493–507.

Rosengren, A., Tibblin, G. and Wilhelmsen, L. (1991) 'Self-perceived psychological stress and incidence of coronary artery disease in middle-aged men', *American Journal of Cardiology, 68*: 1171–5.

Rosenstock, I.M. (1996) 'Why people use health services', *Millbank Memorial Fund Quarterly, 44*: 94–124.

Ross, M.W. and Rosser, B.R.S. (1989) 'Education and AIDS risks: a review', *Health Education Research: Theory and Practice, 4*: 273–84.

Ross, N.A., Wolfson, M.C., Dunn, J.-M., Kaplan, G.A. and Lynch, J.W. (2000) 'Relation between income inequality and mortality in Canada and in the United States: cross-sectional assessment using census data and vital statistics', *British Medical Journal, 320*: 898–902.

Rossner, S. (2002) 'Obesity: the disease of the 21st century', *International Journal of Obesity, 26*: S2–S4.

Roter, D.L. (1977) 'Patient-participation in the patient–provider interaction: the effects of patient question-asking on the quality of interaction, satisfaction and compliance', *Health Education Monographs, 5*: 281–330.

Roter, D. (1989) 'Which facets of communication have strong effects on outcome – a meta-analysis', in M. Stewart and D. Roter (eds), *Communicating with Medical Patients*. London: Sage.

Rotter, J.B. (1966) 'Generalised expectancies for internal versus external control of reinforcement', *Psychological Monographs, 80(609)*: 1.

Royal College of Physicians (1962) *Smoking and Health*. London: RCP.

Royal College of Surgeons and Anaesthetists (1990) *Commission on the Provision of Surgical Services: Report of the Working Party on Pain After Surgery*. London: RCSA.

Royal Pharmaceutical Society of Great Britain (1997) *From Compliance to Concordance: Toward Shared Goals in Medicine Taking*. London: RPS.

Rozanski, A., Blumenthal, J.A. and Kaplan, J. (1999) 'Impact of psychological factors on the pathogenesis of cardiovascular disease and implications for therapy', *Circulation, 99*: 2192–217.

Rozin, E. (1982) 'The structure of cuisine', in L.M. Barker (ed.), *The Psychobiology of Human Food Selection*. Westport, CT: AVI. pp. 192–202.

Rozin, P. (1996) 'Sociocultural influences on human food selection', in E.D. Capaldi (ed.), *Why We Eat What We Eat: The Psychology of Eating*. Washington, DC: American Psychological Association. pp. 233–63.

Ruitenberg, A., van Swieten, J.C., Witteman, J.C.M., Mehta, K.M., van Duijn, C.M., Hofman, A. and Breteler, M.M.B. (2002) 'Alcohol consumption and risk of dementia: The Rotterdam Study', *Lancet*, *359*: 281–6.

Russell, K.M., Swenson, M.M., Skelton, A.M. and Shedd-Steele, R. (2003) 'The meaning of health in mammography screening for African American women', *Health Care for Women International*, *24*: 27–39.

Ruusuvuori, J. (2001) 'Looking means listening: coordinating displays of engagement in doctor–patient interaction', *Social Science and Medicine*, *52*: 1093–108.

Sacker, A., Bartley, M.J., Frith, D., Fitzpatrick, R.M. and Marmot, M.G. (2001) 'The relationship between job strain and coronary heart disease: evidence from the English sample of the working male population', *Psychological Medicine*, *31*: 279–90.

Saffer, H. and Dave, D. (2002) 'Alcohol consumption and alcohol advertising bans', *Applied Economics*, *34*: 1325–34.

Sallis, J.F., Bauman, A. and Pratt, M. (1998) 'Environmental and policy interventions to promote physical activity', *American Journal of Preventive Medicine*, *15*: 379–97.

Salmon, J., Bauman, A., Crawford, D., Timperio, A. and Owen, N. (2000) 'The association between television viewing and overweight among Australian adults participating in varying levels of leisure-time physical activity', *International Journal of Obesity and Related Metabolic Disorders*, *24*: 600–6.

Salmon, P. and Hall, G.M. (2003) 'Patient empowerment and control: a psychological discourse in the service of medicine', *Social Science and Medicine*, *57*: 1969–80.

Saunders, B. (1985) 'The case for controlling alcohol consumption', in N. Heather, I. Robertson and P. Davies (eds), *The Misuse of Alcohol: Crucial Issues in Dependence, Treatment and Prevention*. London: Croom Helm. pp. 214–31.

Sayette, M.A. and Hufford, M.R. (1997) 'Alcohol abuse/alcoholism', in A. Baum, S. Newman, J. Weinman, R. West and C. McManus (eds), *Cambridge Handbook of Psychology, Health and Medicine*. Cambridge: Cambridge University Press. pp. 347–50.

Scarpaci, J.L. (1988) 'Help-seeking behaviour and satisfaction among primary care users in Santiago de Chile', *Journal of Health and Social Behaviour*, *29*: 199.

Scarry, E. (1985) *The Body in Pain: The Making and Unmaking of the World*. New York: Oxford University Press.

Schaal, B. and Orgeur, P. (1992) 'Olfaction in utero: can the rodent model be generalized?', *Quarterly Journal of Experimental Psychology*, *44*: 245–78.

Schober, R. (1997) 'Complementary and conventional medicines working together', *Canadian Health Psychologist*, *5*: 14–18.

Schroeder, D.H. and Costa, P.T. Jr. (1984) 'Influence of life event stress on physical illness: substantive effects or methodological flaws?', *Journal of Personality and Social Psychology*, *46*: 853–63.

Schwartz, G.E. and Weiss, S.M. (1978) 'Behavioral medicine revisited: an amended definition', *Journal of Behavioral Medicine*, *1*: 249–51.

Schwartz, L.M., Woloshin, S., Fowler, F.J. and Welch, H.G. (2004) 'Enthusiasm for cancer screening in the United States', *JAMA*, *291*: 71–8.

Schwarzer, R. (1992) 'Self efficacy in the adaptation and maintenance of health behaviours: theoretical approaches and a new model', in R. Schwarzer (ed.), *Self Efficacy: Thought Control of Action*. Washington, DC: Hemisphere. pp. 217–43.

Schwarzer, R. (1999) 'Self-regulatory processes in the adoption and maintenance of health behaviors', *Journal of Health Psychology*, *4*: 115–27.

Segal, L. (1994) *Straight Sex. The Politics of Pleasure*. London: Virago.

Segal, L. (1996) 'Freud and feminism: a century of contradiction', *Feminism and Psychology*, *6*: 290–7.

Segerstrom, S.C. and Miller, G.E. (2004) 'Stress and the human immune system: a meta-analytic review of 30 years of inquiry', *Psychological Bulletin*, *130*: 601–30.

Selye, H. (1976) *Stress in Health and Disease*. Reading, MA: Butterworth.

Shakespeare, T. (1998) 'Choices and rights: eugenics, genetics and disability equality', *Disability and Society*, *13(5)*: 665–81.

Shakow, A. and Irwin, A. (1999) 'Terms reconsidered: decoding development discourse', in J.Y. Kim, J.V. Millen, A. Irwin and J. Gershman (eds), *Dying for Growth: Global Inequality and the Health of the Poor*. Monroe, ME: Common Courage Press.

Shannon, C. (2004) 'Public health programmes will have to prove they are cost effective', *British Medical Journal*, *328*: 1, 222.

Sharpe, K. and Earle, S. (2002) 'Feminism, abortion and disability: irreconcilable differences?', *Disability and Society, 17(2)*: 137–45.

Shaw, S. (1979) 'A critique of the concept of the alcohol dependence syndrome', *British Journal of Addiction, 74*: 339–48.

Shaw, J.S. and Bassi, K.L. (2001) 'Lay attitudes toward genetic testing for susceptibility to inherited diseases', *Journal of Health Psychology, 6*: 405–23.

Sheeran, P. (2002) 'Intention–behaviour relations: a conceptual and empirical review', in W. Strobe and M. Hewstone (eds), *European Review of Social Psychology*, Vol. 12. Chichester: Wiley. pp. 1–30.

Sheeran, P. and Abraham, C. (1995) 'The Health Belief Model', in M. Conner and P. Norman (eds), *Predicting Health Behaviour*. Buckingham: Open University Press. pp. 23–61.

Sheeran, P., Abraham, C. and Orbell, S. (1999) 'Psychosocial correlates of heterosexual condom use: a meta-analysis', *Psychological Bulletin, 125*: 90–132.

Sheeran, P., Milne, S., Webb, T.L. and Gollwitzer, P.M. (in press) 'Implementation intentions and health behaviours', in M. Conner and P. Norman (eds), *Predicting Health Behaviour: Research and Practice with Social Cognition Models*, 2nd edn. Buckingham: Open University Press.

Shickle, D. (2000) '"On a supposed right to lie [to the public] from benevolent motives": communicating health risks to the public', *Medicine, Health Care and Philosophy, 3*: 241–9.

Shorter, E. (1992) *From Paralysis to Fatigue: A History of Psychosomatic Illness in the Modern Era*. New York: Free Press.

Showalter, E. (1997) *Hystories: Hysterical Epidemics and Modern Culture*. London: Picador.

Shweder, R.A., Much, N.C., Mahapatra, M. and Park, L. (1997) 'The "big three" of morality (autonomy, community, divinity) and the "big three" explanations of suffering', in A.M. Brandt and P. Rozin (eds), *Morality and Health*. London: Routledge. pp. 119–72.

Siegal, M., Patty, J. and Eiser, C. (1990) 'A re-examination of children's conceptions of contagion', *Psychology and Health, 4*: 159–65.

Siegel, S. (1975) 'Conditioned insulin effects', *Journal of Comparative Physiology and Psychology, 89*: 189–99.

Siegrist, J. and Marmot, M. (2004) 'Health inequalities and the psychosocial environment – two scientific challenges', *Social Science and Medicine, 58*: 1463–73.

Silverman, D. (1987) *Communication and Medical Practice: Social Relations in the Clinic*. London: Sage.

Silverman, D. (1997) *Discourses of Counselling: HIV Counselling as Social Interaction*. London: Sage.

Singer, P. (1993) *Practical Ethics*. Cambridge: Cambridge University Press.

Sirois, F.M. and Gick, M.L. (2002) 'An investigation of the health beliefs and motivations of complementary medicine clients', *Social Science and Medicine, 55*: 1025–37.

Skelton, J.A. and Croyle, R.T. (eds) (1991) *Mental Representation in Health and Illness*. New York: Springer-Verlag.

Skevington, S.M. (1995) *Psychology of Pain*. Chichester: John Wiley & Sons.

Skinner, B.F. (1938) *The Behaviour of Organisms*. New York: Appleton Century Crofts.

Skrabanek, P. (1985) 'False premises and false promises of breast cancer screening', *Lancet, 2(8450)*: 316–20.

Skytthe, A. Pedersen, N.L., Kaprio, J. Stazi, M.A., Hjelmborg, J.V.B., Iachine, I., Vaupel, J.W. and Christensen, K.L. (2003) 'Longevity studies in GenomEU twin', *Twin Research, 6*: 448–54.

Sleasman, J.W. and Goodenow, M.M. (2003) 'HIV-1 Infection', *Journal of Allergy and Clinical Immunology, 111*: S582–92.

Slovic, P. (2000) 'What does it mean to know a cumulative risk? Adolescents' perceptions of short-term and long-term consequences of smoking', *Journal of Behavioral Decision Making, 13*: 259–66.

Smailbegovic, M.S., Laing, G.J. and Bedford, H. (2003) 'Why do parents decide against immunization? The effect of health beliefs and health professionals', *Child: Care, Health and Development, 29*: 303–11.

Smedslund, G. (2000) 'A pragmatic basis for judging models and theories in health psychology: The axiomatic method', *Journal of Health Psychology, 5*: 133–49.

Smee, C., Parsonage, M., Anderson, R. and Duckworth, S. (1992) Effect of Tobacco Advertising on Tobacco Consumption: A Discussion Document Reviewing the Evidence. London: Economics and Operational Research Division, Department of Health.

Smith, A.P., Wadsworth, E., Johal, S.S., Davey-Smith, G., Peters, T. (2000) *The Scale of Occupational Stress: The Bristol Stress and Health at Work Study*. London: HSE Books.

Smith, J. (2004) *Building a safer NHS for patients: Improving medication safety. A report by the Chief Pharmaceutical Officer.* London: The Stationery Office.

Smith, J.A. (1996) 'Beyond the divide between cognition and discourse: using interpretative phenomenological analysis in health psychology', *Psychology and Health*, 11: 261–71.

Smith, J.A. and Osborn, M. (2003) 'Interpretative phenomenological analysis', in J.A. Smith (ed.), *Qualitative Psychology: A Practical Guide to Research Methods.* London: Sage. pp. 51–80.

Smith, J.A., Jarman, M. and Osborn, M. (1999) 'Doing interpretative phenomenological analysis', in M. Murray and K. Chamberlain (eds), *Qualitative Health Psychology: Theories and Methods.* London: Sage.

Smith, R. (1992) 'Without work all life goes rotten', *British Medical Journal*, 305: 972.

Smith, T.W. (1992) 'Hostility and health: current status of a psychosomatic hypothesis', *Health Psychology*, 11: 139–50.

Smyth, J.M., Stone, A.A., Hurewitz, A. and Kaell, A. (1999) 'Effects of writing about stressful experiences on symptom reduction in patients with asthma and rheumatoid arthritis', *JAMA*, 281: 722–33.

Smyth, M. and Browne, F. (1992) *General Household Survey.* London: HMSO.

Somerfield, M.R. (1997) 'The utility of systems models of stress and coping for applied research: the case of cancer adaptation (with peer criticism and author's response)', *Journal of Health Psychology*, 2: 133–83.

Sontag, S. ([1978] 2002) *Illness as Metaphor.* London: Penguin.

Sontag, S. (1988) *AIDS and its Metaphors.* London: Penguin.

Soucat, A.L.B. and Yazbeck, A.S. (2002) *HNP and the Poor: Inputs into PRSPs and World Bank Operations. (Session 1).* New York: World Bank.

Spector, P. (1998) 'A control theory of the job stress process', in C. Cooper (ed.), *Theories of Organizational Psychology.* New York: Oxford University Press. pp. 153–69.

Spector, R.E. (1991) *Cultural Diversity in Health and Illness*, 4th edn. Stamford, CT: Appleton & Lange.

Spicer, J. and Chamberlain, K. (1996) 'Developing psychosocial theory in health psychology', *Journal of Health Psychology*, 1: 161–71.

Sprecher, S. and McKinney, K. (1993) *Sexuality.* London: Sage.

Stacy, A.W., Bentler, P.M. and Flay, B.R. (1994) 'Attitudes and health behavior in diverse populations: drunk driving, alcohol use, binge eating, marijuana use, and cigarette use', *Health Psychology*, 13: 73–85.

Stainton-Rogers, W. (1991) *Explaining Health and Illness: An Exploration of Diversity.* Hemel Hempstead: Wheatsheaf.

Stainton-Rogers, W. and Stainton-Rogers, R. (2001) *The Psychology of Gender and Sexuality*, Buckingham: Open University Press.

Stam, H.J. (2004) 'A sound body in a sound mind: a critical historical analysis of health psychology', in M. Murray (ed.), *Critical Health Psychology.* London: Palgrave.

Standen, P., Daniels, K. and Lamond, D. (1999) 'The home as a workplace: work–family inter action and psychological well-being in telework', *Journal of Occupational Health Psychology*, 4: 368–81.

Stanley, L. (1995) *Sex Surveyed 1949–1996.* Basingstoke: Taylor & Francis.

Stansfeld, S., Head, J. and Marmot, M. (2000) *Work Related Factors and Ill Health: The Whitehall II Study*, CRR 266/2000. London: HSE Books.

Stanton, A. and Revenson, T.A. (2005) 'Progress and promise in research on adaptation to chronic illness', in H.S. Friedman and R.C. Silver (eds), *The Oxford Handbook of Health Psychology.* New York: Oxford University Press.

Staub, E., Tursky, B. and Schwartz, G. (1971) 'Self-control and predictability: their effects on reactions to aversive stimulation', *Journal of Personality and Social psychology*, 18: 157–62.

Stein, J.A. and Rotheram-Borus, M. (2004) 'Cross-sectional and longitudinal associations in coping strategies and physical health outcomes among HIV-positive youth', *Psychology and Health*, 19(3): 321–36.

Steiner, G. (1978) *Heidegger.* London: Faber and Faber.

Steinitz, V. and Mishler, E.G. (2001) 'Reclaiming SPSSI's radical promise: a critical look at JSI's "Impact of welfare reform" issue', *Analyses of Social Issues and Public Policy*, 1: 163–73.

Stensland, P. and Malterud, K. (1999) 'Approaching the locked dialogues of the body: Communicating illness through diaries', *Journal of Primary Health Care*, 17: 75–80.

Stewart, D.E., Abbey, S.E., Shnek, Z.M., Irvine, J. and Grace, S.L. (2004) 'Gender differences in health information needs and decisional preferences in patients recovering from an acute ischemic coronary event', *Psychosomatic Medicine, 66*: 42–8.

Stewart, F. (2001) 'Horizontal inequalities as a source of conflict', in F. Hampson and D. Malone (eds), *From Reaction to Prevention*. London: Lynne Renner. pp. 105–36.

Stewart, F. (2002) 'Root causes of violent conflict in developing countries', *British Medical Journal, 324*: 342–5.

Stewart, M.A. (1984) 'What is a successful doctor–patient interview? A study of interactions and outcomes', *Social Science and Medicine, 19*: 167–75.

Stewart, M.J., Gillis, A., Brosky, G., Johnston, G., Kirkland, S., Leigh, G., Persaud, V., Rootman, I., Jackson, S. and Pawliw-Fry, B.A. (1996) 'Smoking among disadvantaged women: causes and cessation', *Canadian Journal of Nursing Research, 28*: 41–60.

Stewart, W.F., Lipton, R.B., Simon, D., Liberman, J. and Von Korff, M. (1999) 'Validity of an illness severity measure for headache in a population sample of migraine sufferers', *Pain, 79*: 291–301.

Stiles, W.B. (1996) 'Stability of the verbal exchange structure of medical consultations', *Psychology and Health, 11*: 773–85.

Stiles, W.B., Putnam, S.M., Wolf, M.H. and James, S.A. (1979) 'Verbal response mode profiles of patients and physicians in medical screening interviews', *Journal of Medical Education, 54*: 81–9.

Stokols, D. (1992) 'Establishing and maintaining healthy environments: toward a social ecology of health promotion', *American Psychologist, 47*: 6–22.

Stolerman, I.P. and Jarvis, M.J. (1995) 'The scientific case that nicotine is addictive', *Psychopharmacology, 117*: 2–10.

Stone, G.C., Weiss, S.M., Matarazzo, J.D., Miller, N.E. and Rodin, J. (eds) (1987) *Health Psychology: A Discipline and a Profession*. Chicago: University of Chicago Press.

Stone, S.V. and Costa, P.T. (1990) 'Disease-prone personality or distress-prone personality? The role of neuroticism in coronary heart disease', in H.S. Friedman (ed.), *Personality and Disease*. London: Wiley. pp. 178–200.

Strauss, A.L. (1987) *Qualitative Analysis for Social Scientists*. New York: Cambridge University Press.

Street, R.L. (1991) 'Information-giving in medical consultations: the influence of patients' communicative styles and personal characteristics', *Social Science and Medicine, 32(5)*: 541–8.

Stritzke, W.G., Lang, A.R. and Patrick, C.J. (1996) 'Beyond stress and arousal: a reconceptualisation of alcohol-emotion relations with reference to psychophysiological methods', *Psychological Bulletin, 120*: 376–95.

Stroebe, M.S. and Stroebe, W. (1983) 'Who suffers more? Sex differences in health risks of the widowed', *Psychological Bulletin, 93*: 279–301.

Stroebe, W. and Stroebe, M.S. (1995) *Social Psychology and Health*. Buckingham: Open University Press.

Sulloway, F.J. (1980) *Freud, Biologist of the Mind*. London: Fontana.

Suls, J. and Rittenhouse, J.D. (1990) 'Models of linkages between personality and disease', in H.S. Friedman (ed.), *Personality and Disease*. London: Wiley. pp. 38–64.

Summerbell, C.D., Ashton, V., Campbell, K.J., Edmunds, L., Kelly, S. and Waters, E. (2004) 'Interventions for treating obeisity in children (Cochrane Review)', in *The Cochrane Library*, Issue 4. Chichester: John Wiley.

Summerfield, D. (2001) 'The intervention of post-traumatic stress disorder and the social usefulness of a psychiatric category', *British Medical Journal, 322*: 95–8.

Surtees, P., Wainwright, N., Luben, R., Khaw, K.-T. and Day, N. (2003) 'Sense of coherence and mortality in men and women in the EPIC-Norfolk United Kingdom prospective cohort study', *American Journal of Epidemiology, 158*: 1202–9.

Sutton, S., Bickler, G., Aldridge, J. and Saidi, G. (1994) 'Prospective study of predictors of attendance for breast screening in inner London', *Journal of Epidemiology and Community Health, 48*: 65–73.

Swinburn, B. and Ravussin, E. (1993) 'Energy balance or fat balance?', *American Journal of Clinical Nutrition, 57*: 766S–770S.

Sykes, C.M., Willig, C. and Marks, D.F. (2004) 'Discourses in the European Commission's 1996–2000 Health Promotion Programme', *Journal of Health Psychology, 9*: 131–41.

Tatchell, P. (1996) 'It's just a phase: why homosexuality is doomed', in M. Simpson (ed.), *Anti-gay*. London: Freedom Editions.

Tatzer, E., Schubert, M.T., Timischi, W. and Simbruner, G. (1985) 'Discrimination of taste and preference for sweet in premature babies', *Early Human Development*, 12: 23–30.

Taylor, S.E. (1983) 'Adjustment to threatening events: A theory of cognitive adaption', *American Psychologist*, 38: 1161–73.

Taylor, S.E. and Brown, J.D. (1988) 'Illusion and well-being: a social psychological perspective on mental health', *Psychological Bulletin*, 103: 193–210.

Taylor, S.E., Repetti, R.L. and Seeman, T. (1997) 'Health psychology: what is an unhealthy environment and how does it get under the skin?', *Annual Review of Psychology*, 48: 411–47.

Terry, D.J., Gallois, C. and McCamish, M. (1993) *The Theory of Reasoned Action: Its Application to AIDS-preventive Behaviour*. Oxford: Pergamon.

Thomas, K.J., Nicholl, J.P. and Coleman, P. (2001) 'Use and expenditure on complementary medicine in England: a population based survey', *Complementary Therapies in Medicine*, 9: 2–11.

Thomas, S.H., Glynn-Jones, R., Chait, I. and Marks, D.F. (1997) 'Anxiety in long-term cancer survivors influences the acceptability of planned discharge from follow up', *Psycho-oncology*, 6: 190–6.

Tibben, A., Frets, P.G., van de Kamp, J.J., Niermeijer, M.F., Vegter-van der Vlis, M., Roos, R.A., van Ommen, G.G., Duivenvoorden, H.J. and Verhage, F. (1993) 'Presymptomatic DNA testing for Huntington disease: pre-test attitudes and expectations of applicants and their partners in the Dutch program', *American Journal of Medical Genetics*, 48: 10–16.

Tiefer, L. (1995) *Sex is not a Natural Act and Other Essays*. Oxford: Westview Press.

Todaro, J.F., Shen, B.J., Niaura, R., Spiro, A. and Ward, K.D. (2003) 'Effect of negative emotions on frequency of coronary heart disease', *American Journal of Cardiology*, 92: 901–6.

Todd, K.H., Deaton, C., D'Adamo, A.P. and Goe, L. (2000) 'Ethnicity and analgesic practice', *Annals of Emergency Medicine*, 35: 11–16.

Tolley, K. (1985) *Health Promotion: How to Measure Cost-effectiveness*. London: Health Education Authority.

Tones, K. (1987) 'Devising strategies for preventing drug misuse: the role of the Health Action Model', *Health Education Research: Theory and Practice*, 2: 305–17.

Tostes, M.A., Chalub, M. and Botega, N.J. (2004) 'The quality of life of HIV-infected women is associated with psychiatric morbidity', *AIDS Care*, 16(2): 177–86.

Townsend, P. and Davidson, N. (1982) *Inequalities in Health: The Black Report*. London: Penguin.

Treharne, G.J., Lyons, A.C. and Kitas, G.D. (2004) 'Medication adherence in rheumatoid arthritis: effects of psychosocial factors', *Psychology, Health and Medicine*, 9: 337–49.

Trostle, J.A. (1998) 'Medical compliance as an ideology', *Social Science and Medicine*, 27: 1299–1308.

True, W.R., Heath, A.C., Scherrer, J.F., Waterman, B., Goldberg, J., Lin, N., Eisen, S.A., Lyons, M.J. and Tsuang, M.T. (1997) 'Genetic and environmental contributions to smoking', *Addiction*, 92: 1277–87.

Trumbull, R. and Appley, M.H. (1986) 'A conceptual model for the understanding of stress dynamics', in M.H. Appley and R. Trumbull (eds), *Dynamics of Stress: Physiological, Psychological and Social Perspectives*. New York: Plenum. pp. 21–45.

Turner, B. (1984) *The Body and Society: Explorations in Social Theory*. Oxford: Blackwell.

Turner, S. and Moss, S. (1996) 'The health needs of adults with learning disabilities and the Health of the Nation strategy', *Journal of Intellectual; Disability Research*, 40: 438–50.

Uchino, B.N., Cacioppo, J.T. and Kiecolt-Glaser, J.K. (1996) 'The relationship between social support and physiological processes: a review with emphasis on underlying mechanisms and implications for health', *Psychological Bulletin*, 119: 488–531.

Uitterhoeve, R.J., Vernooy, M., Litjens, M., Potting, K., Bensing, J., De Mulder, P. and Van Achterberg, T. (2004) 'Psychosocial interventions for patients with advanced cancer: a systematic review of the literature', *British Journal of Cancer*, advance online publication 17 August 2004, doi: 10.1038/sj.bjc.6602103.

UNAIDS (2004) *Report on the Global AIDS Epidemic*: 4th Global Report. Geneva: Joint United Nations Programme on HIV/AIDS.

Unden, A.L., Orth-Gomer, K. and Elofsson, S. (1991) 'Cardiovascular effects of social support in the work place: twenty-four-hour ECG monitoring of men and women', *Psychosomatic Medicine*, 53: 50–60.

United Nations Development Programme (1995) *Human Development Report*. New York: Oxford University Press.

Unruh, A.M. (1996) 'Gender variations in clinical pain experience', *Pain*, 65: 123–67.

Upmark, M., Moeller, J. and Romelsjoe, A. (1999) 'Longitudinal, population-based study of self reported alcohol habits, high levels of sickness absence, and disability pensions', *Journal of Epidemiology and Community Health*, *53*: 223–9.

Urban, B.J., France, R.D., Steinberger, E.K., Scott, D.L. and Maltbre, A.A. (1986) 'Long-term use of narcotic/antidepressant medication in the management of phantom limb pain', *Pain*, *24(2)*: 191–6.

US Census Bureau (2005) http://www.census.gov/cgi-bin/ipc/popclockw (1 January 2005).

US Census Bureau of Labor Statistics (2004) 'The employment situation: June 2004', *Household Survey Data*. Available online: www.bls.gov/

US Centers for Disease Control and Prevention (1993) 'Prevalence of sedentary lifestyle – behavioral risk factor surveillance system, United States, 1991', *Morbidity and Mortality Weekly Report*, *42*: 576–9.

US Centers for Disease Control and Prevention (1995) 'Trends in cancer screening – United States 1987 and 1992', *Morbidity and Mortality Weekly Report*, *45*: 57–61.

US Centers for Disease Control and Prevention (2005) http://www.cdc.gov/nccdphp/ (consulted 7 January 2005).

US Department of Health, Education and Welfare (1964) *Smoking and Health. Report of the Advisory Committee to the Surgeon General of the Public Health Service*. Washington, DC. PHS Pub. No. 1103.

US Department of Labor (2005) 'Working in the 21st century' http://www.bls.gov/opub/home.htm

US Public Health Service (1990) *The Health Consequences of Smoking: A Report of the Surgeon General* (COL Report No. 90–8416). Rockville, MD: US Department of Health and Human Services.

US Surgeon General (1989) *Reducing the Health Consequences of Smoking: 25 Years of Progress: A Report of the Surgeon General*. Bethesda, MD: Center for Chronic Disease Prevention and Health Promotion.

Van der Brink-Muinen, A., van Dulmen, S., Messerli-Rohrbach, V. and Bensing, J. (2002) 'Do gender-dyads have different communication patterns? A comparative study in Western-European general practices', *Patient Education and Counseling*, *48*: 253–64.

Van der Velde, F.W. and Van der Pligt, J. (1991) 'AIDS-related health behaviour: coping, protection motivation and previous behaviour', *Journal of Behavioural Medicine*, *14*: 429–51.

Van Haaften, E.H. and Van de Vijver, F.J.R. (1996) 'Psychological consequences of environmental degradation', *Journal of Health Psychology*, *1*: 411–29.

Vance, Y. and Eiser, C. (2004) 'Caring for a child with cancer: a systematic review', *Pediatric Blood and Cancer*, *42(3)*: 249–53.

Verbrugge, L.M. and Jette, A.M. (1994) 'The disablement process', *Social Science and Medicine*, *38*: 1–14.

Vincent, C. and Furnham, A. (1996) 'Why do patients turn to complementary medicine? An empirical study', *British Journal of Clinical Psychology*, *35*: 37–48.

Vinokur, A.D. and Schul, Y. (1997) 'Mastery and inoculation against setbacks as active ingredients in the JOBS intervention for the unemployed', *Journal of Consulting and Clinical Psychology*, *65*: 867–77.

Vlaeyen, J.W.S. and Linton, S.J. (2000) 'Fear-avoidance and its consequences in chronic musculo-skeletal pain: a state of the art', *Pain*, *85*: 317–32.

Von Lengerke, T., Vinck, J., Rutten, A., Reitmeir, P., Abel, T., Kannas, L., Luschen, G., Rodriguez Diaz, J.A. and Van der Zee, J. (2004) 'Health policy perception and health behaviours: a multi-level analysis and implications for public health psychology', *Journal of Health Psychology*, *9*: 157–75.

Wadden, T.A., Brownell, K.D. and Foster, G.D. (2002) 'Obesity: responding to the global epidemic', *Journal of Consulting and Clinical Psychology*, *70*: 510–25.

Waitzkin, H. (1985) 'Information giving in medical care', *Journal of Health and Social Behaviour*, *26*: 81–101.

Waitzkin, H. (1989) 'A critical theory of medical discourse: ideology, social control, and the processing of social context in medical encounters', *Journal of Health and Social Behavior*, *30*: 220–39.

Wald, N., Kiryluk, S., Darby, S., Doll, R., Pike, M. and Peto, R. (1988) *UK Smoking Statistics*. Oxford: Oxford University Press.

Wall, T., Jackson, P., Mullarkey, S. and Parker, S. (1996) 'The demands–control model of job strain: a more specific test', *Journal of Occupational and Organizational Psychology*, *69*: 153–66.

Wallston, K.A., Wallston, B.S. and DeVellis, R. (1978) 'Development of multidimensional health lows of control (MHLC) scales', *Health Education Monographs*, 6: 160–70.

Wang, C., Burris, M. and Xiang, Y.P. (1996) 'Chinese village women as visual anthropologists: a participatory approach to reaching policymakers', *Social Science and Medicine*, 42: 1391–1400.

Warchol, G. (1998) *National Crime Victimisation Survey: Workplace Violence, 1992–1996*. US Department of Justice, Office of Justice Programs, No. NCJ 168634. Washington, DC: US Department of Justice.

Wardle, J. and Pope, R. (1992) 'The psychological costs of screening for cancer', *Journal of Psychosomatic Research*, 36: 609–24.

Wardle, J., McCaffery, K., Nadel, M. and Atkin, W. (2004) 'Socioeconomic differences in cancer screening participation: comparing cognitive and psychosocial explanations', *Social Science and Medicine*, 59: 249–61.

Warr, P. (1987) *Work, Unemployment and Mental Health*. New York: Oxford University Press.

Warr, P.B. (1994) 'A conceptual framework for the study of work and mental health', *Work and Stress*, 8: 84–97.

Warr, P.B. and Downing, J. (2000) 'Learning strategies, learning anxiety and knowledge acquisition', *British Journal of Psychology*, 91: 311–33.

Wassertheil-Smoller, S., Shumaker, S., Ockene, J., Talavera, G.A., Greeland, P., Cochrane, B., Robbins, J., Aragaki, A. and Dubar-Jacob, J. (2004) 'Depression and cardiovascular sequelae in postmenopausal women', *Archives of Internal Medicine*, 164: 289–98.

Watson, M., Davidson-Homewood, J., Haviland, J. and Bliss, J. (2003) 'Study results should not have been dismissed', *British Medical Journal*, 326: 598.

Watson, M., Haviland, J.S., Greer, S., Davidson, J. and Bliss, J.M. (1999) 'Influence of psychological response on survival in breast cancer: a population-based cohort study', *Lancet*, 354: 1331–6.

Wear, A. (1985) 'Puritan perceptions of illness in seventeenth century England', in R. Porter (ed.), *Patients and Practitioners: Lay Perceptions of Medicine in Preindustrial Society*. Cambridge: Cambridge University Press. pp. 55–100.

Webb, G.P. (1995) *Nutrition: A Health Promotion Approach*. London: Arnold.

Webster, R. (1995) *Why Freud was Wrong*. London: HarperCollins.

Weeks, J. (1985) *Sexuality and its Discontents. Meanings, Myths and Modern Sexualities*. London: Routledge.

Weiner, B., Frieze, I., Kukla, A., Reed, L., Rest, S. and Rosenbaum, R.M. (1972) 'Perceiving the causes of success and failure', in E.E. Jones, D.E. Kanouse, H.H. Kelley, R.E. Nesbitt, S. Valins and B. Weiner (eds), *Attribution: Perceiving the Causes of Behaviour*. Hillsdale, NJ: General Learning Press.

Weingart, S.N., Wilson, R., Gibberd, R.W. and Harrison, B. (2000) 'Epidemiology of medical error', *British Medical Journal*, 320: 774–7.

Weinman, J. and Petrie, K.J. (1997) 'Illness perceptions: a new paradigm for psychosomatics?', *Journal of Psychosomatic Medicine*, 42: 113–16.

Weinman, J., Petrie, K.J., Moss-Morriss, R. and Horne, R. (1996) 'The Illness Perception Questionnaire: a new method for assessing the cognitive representation of illness', *Psychology and Health*, 11: 431–46.

Weinstein, N.D. (1988) 'The precaution adoption process', *Health Psychology*, 7: 355–86.

Wertheimer, A.I. and Santella, T.M. (2003) 'Medication compliance research: Still so far to go', *Journal of Applied Research in Clinical and Experimental Therapeutics*, 3: 1–11.

West, C. (1990) 'Not just doctors' orders: directive-response sequences in patients' visits to women and men physicians', *Discourse and Society*, 1: 85–113.

Whitehead, M. (1995) 'Tackling inequalities: a review of policy initiatives', in M. Benzeval, K. Judge and M. Whitehead (eds), *Tackling Inequalities in Health: An Agenda for Action*. London: King's Fund. pp. 22–52.

Whitehead, K. and Williams, J. (2001) 'Medical treatment of women with lupus: the case for sharing knowledge and decision-making', *Disability & Society*, 16: 103–21.

Whiteman, M.C., Fowkes, F.G.R., Deary, I.J. and Lee, A.J. (1997) 'Hostility, cigarette smoking and alcohol consumption in the general population', *Social Science and Medicine*, 44: 1089–96.

Whitmarsh, A., Koutantji, M. and Sidell, K. (2003) 'Illness perceptions, mood and coping in predicting attendance at cardiac rehabilitation', *British Journal of Health Psychology*, 8: 209–21.

Whittaker, K. (2002) 'Lay workers for improving the uptake of childhood immunication', *British Journal of Community Nursing*, 7: 474–79.

Whooley, M.A. and Browner, W.S. (1998) 'Association between depressive symptoms and mortality in older women', *Archives of Internal Medicine, 158*: 2129–35.

Wiggins, S., Potter, J. and Wildsmith, A. (2001) 'Eating your words: discursive psychology and the reconstruction of eating practices', *Journal of Health Psychology, 6*: 5–15.

Wilhelmsen, L., Sanne, H., Elmfeldt, D., Grimby, G., Tibblin, G. and Wedel, H. (1975) 'A controlled trial of physical training after myocardial infarction: effects of risk factors, nonfatal reinfarction, and death', *Preventive Medicine, 4*: 491–508.

Wilkinson, R. (1996) *Unhealthy Societies.* London: Routledge.

Wilkinson, S. (1998) 'Focus groups in health research: exploring the meaning of health and illness', *Journal of Health Psychology, 3*: 329–48.

Wilkinson, S., Joffe, H. and Yardley, L. (2004) 'Qualitative data collection: interviews and focus groups', in D.F. Marks and L. Yardley (eds), *Research Methods for Clinical and Health Psychology.* London: Sage.

Williams, D.C., Golding, J., Phillips, K. and Towell, A. (2004) 'Perceived control, locus of control and preparatory information: effects on the perception of an acute pain stimulus', *Personality and Individual Differences, 36*: 1681–91.

Williams, D.R. and Collins, C. (1995) 'US socioeconomic and racial differences in health: patterns and explanations', *Annual Review of Sociology, 21*: 349–86.

Williams, D.R., Yu, Y., Jackson, J.S. and Anderson, N.B. (1997) 'Racial differences in physical and mental health: socio-economic status, stress and discrimination', *Journal of Health Psychology, 2*: 335–51.

Williams, G. (1984) 'The genesis of chronic illness: narrative reconstruction', *Sociology of Health and Illness, 6*: 175–200.

Williams, G.H. (2003) 'The determinants of health: structure, context and agency', *Sociology of Health and Illness, 25*: 131–54.

Williams, R.J.L.I., Hittinger, R. and Glouzer, G. (1994) 'Resource implications of head injuries on an acute surgical unit', *Journal of the Royal Society of Medicine, 87*: 83–6.

Williams, S.J. and Calnan, M. (1996) 'The "limits" of medicalization?: modern medicine and the lay populace in "late" modernity', *Social Science and Medicine, 42*: 1609–20.

Willig, C. (1994) 'Marital discourse and condom use', in P. Aggleton, P. Davies and G. Hart (eds), *AIDS: Foundations for the Future.* London: Taylor & Francis.

Willig, C. (1995) '"I wouldn't have married the guy if I'd have to do that": heterosexual adults' constructions of condom use and their implications for sexual practice', *Journal of Community and Applied Social Psychology, 5*: 75–87.

Willig, C. (1998) 'Constructions of sexual activity and their implications for sexual practice', *Journal of Health Psychology, 3*: 383–92.

Willig, C. (ed.) (1999) *Applied Discourse Analysis: Social and Psychological Interventions.* Buckingham: Open University Press.

Willig, C. (2000) 'A discourse-dynamic approach to the study of subjectivity in health psychology', *Theory and Psychology, 10*: 547–70.

Willig, C. (2004) 'Discourse analysis and health psychology', in M. Murray (ed.), *Critical Health Psychology.* London: Palgrave.

Willis, P. (1997) *Learning to Labour: How Working Class Kids Get Working Class Jobs.* Westmead: Saxon House.

Wilson, J. and Junger, G. (1968) 'Principles and practice of screening for disease'. Geneva, WHO. World Health Organization Public Health Paper 34.

Winefield, H., Murrell, T., Clifford, J. and Farmer, E. (1996) 'The search for reliable and valid measures of patient-centredness', *Psychology and Health, 11*: 811–24.

Winett, R.A., King, A.C. and Altman, D.G. (1989) *Health Psychology and Public Health.* New York: Pergamon.

World Bank (1993) *World Development Report 1993: Investing in Health.* New York: Oxford University Press.

World Bank (2002) http://www.worldbank.org/poverty/health/data/index.htm

World Bank (2004) http://www.prb.org/template.cfm?template=InterestDisplay.cfm&Interest CategoryID=206

World Development Report (2000/2001) *Attacking Poverty.* New York: Oxford University Press. http://www.cmhealth.org/cmh_papers&reports.htm

World Health Organization (1980) *International Classification of Impairments, Activities and Participation: A Manual of Dimensions of Disablement and Health. Beta-1 draft for field trials.* Geneva: WHO.

World Health Organization (1986) Ottawa Charter for Health Promotion. *Health Promotion, 1*: iii–v.

World Health Organization (1989) *World Health Statistics Annual.* Geneva: WHO.

World Health Organization (1995) *World Health Report.* Geneva: WHO.

World Health Organization (2002) *Investing in Health: A Summary of Findings of the Commission on Macroeconomics and health.* Geneva: WHO.

World Health Organization (2003) *Global Action Against Cancer.* Geneva: WHO.

World Health Organization (2004) *Palliative Care: The Solid Facts.* Copenhagen: WHO.

Wright, E.C. (1993) 'Non-compliance – or how many aunts has Matilda?', *Lancet, 342*: 909–13.

Yardley, L. (ed.) (1997) *Material Discourses of Health and Illness.* London: Routledge.

Yardley, L., Sharples, K., Beech, S. and Lewith, G. (2001) 'Developing a dynamic model of treatment perceptions', *Journal of Health Psychology, 6*: 269–82.

Yaskowich, K.M. and Stam, H.J. (2003) 'Cancer narratives and the cancer support group', *Journal of Health Psychology, 8*: 720–37.

Yeich, S. (1996) 'Grassroots organizing with homeless people: a participatory research approach', *Journal of Social Issues, 52*: 111–21.

Young, A. (1995) *The Harmony of Illusions: Inventing Post-traumatic Stress Disorder.* Princeton, NJ: Princeton University Press.

Yousfi, S., Matthews, G., Amelang, M. and Schmidt-Rathjens, C. (2004) 'Personality and disease: correlations of multiple trait scores with various illnesses', *Journal of Health Psychology, 9*: 623–43.

Zigmond, A.S. and Snaith, R.P. (1983) 'The Hospital Anxiety and Depression Scale', *Acta Psychiatrica Scandinavica, 67(6)*: 361–70.

Zuckerman, M. (1979) *Sensation Seeking: Beyond the Optimal Level of Arousal.* Hillsdale, NJ: Lawrence Erlbaum.

Zuckerman, M. and Antoni, M.H. (1995) 'Social support and its relationship to psychological, physical and immune variables in HIV infection', *Clinical Psychology and Psychotherapy, 2(4)*: 210–19.

Name Index

Subject Index

DATE DUE

MAR 2 6 2007			

GAYLORD   PRINTED IN U.S.A.